Nations and Households
in Economic Growth

Nations and Households in Economic Growth

Essays in Honor of Moses Abramovitz

Edited by *PAUL A. DAVID*
DEPARTMENT OF ECONOMICS
STANFORD UNIVERSITY
STANFORD, CALIFORNIA

MELVIN W. REDER
DEPARTMENT OF ECONOMICS
THE CITY UNIVERSITY OF NEW YORK
NEW YORK, NEW YORK

ACADEMIC PRESS   New York and London   1974
A Subsidiary of Harcourt Brace Jovanovich, Publishers

ACADEMIC PRESS, INC.
111 Fifth Avenue, New York, New York 10003

United Kingdom Edition published by
ACADEMIC PRESS, INC. (LONDON) LTD.
24/28 Oval Road, London NW1

Library of Congress Cataloging in Publication Data
Main entry under title:

Nations and households in economic growth.

Includes bibliographies.
CONTENTS: Microeconomic foundations: Arrow, K. J.
The measurement of real value added.–David, P. A.
Fortune, risk, and the microeconomics of migration.–
Easterlin, R. A. Does economic growth improve the human
lot? [etc.]
1.   Microeconomics–Addresses, essays, lectures.
2.   Macroeconomics–Addresses, essays, lectures.
3.   Economic policy–Addresses, essays, lectures.
I.   Abramovitz, Moses, Date   II.   David, Paul A.,
ed.   III.   Reder, Melvin Warren, Date   ed.
HB34.N36   330.1   73-5308
ISBN 0–12–205050–9

PRINTED IN THE UNITED STATES OF AMERICA

Contents

Are Men Rational or Economists Wrong? 223

TIBOR SCITOVSKY

Part II

MACROECONOMIC PERFORMANCE: GROWTH AND STABILITY

Demand, Structural Change, and the Process of Economic Growth 239

RUSSELL J. CHEETHAM, ALLEN C. KELLEY,
AND JEFFREY G. WILLIAMSON

Monetary Policy in Developing Countries 265

MILTON FRIEDMAN

Government: The Fourth Factor   279

ELI GINZBERG

What Became of the Building Cycle?   291

BERT G. HICKMAN

Instability in Underdeveloped Countries: The Impact of the International Economy   315

DONALD J. MATHIESON AND RONALD I. McKINNON

Economic Indicator Analysis during 1969–1972   333

GEOFFREY H. MOORE

The Dollar Standard and the Level of International Reserves   361

LORIE TARSHIS

Long Swings and the Atlantic Economy: A Reappraisal   383

BRINLEY THOMAS

List of Contributors

Numbers in parentheses indicate the pages on which the authors' contributions begin.

KENNETH J. ARROW (3), Department of Economics, Harvard University, Cambridge, Massachusetts

RUSSELL J. CHEETHAM (239), International Bank for Reconstruction and Development, Washington, D. C.

PAUL A. DAVID (21), Department of Economics, Stanford University, Stanford, California

RICHARD A. EASTERLIN (89), Department of Economics, The Wharton School, University of Pennsylvania, Philadelphia, Pennsylvania

MILTON FRIEDMAN (265), Department of Economics, University of Chicago, Chicago, Illinois

ELI GINZBERG (279), Graduate School of Business, Columbia University, New York, New York

BERT G. HICKMAN (291), Department of Economics, Stanford University, Stanford, California

ALLEN C. KELLEY (239), Department of Economics, Duke University, Durham, North Carolina

SIMON KUZNETS* (127), Department of Economics, Emeritus, Harvard University, Cambridge, Massachusetts

RONALD I. McKINNON (315), Department of Economics, Stanford University, Stanford, California

DONALD J. MATHIESON (315), Department of Economics, Columbia University, New York, New York

* Correspondence should be addressed to 67 Francis Avenue, Cambridge, Massachusetts.

GEOFFREY H. MOORE* (333), Bureau of Labor Statistics, United States Department of Labor, Washington, D.C.

MELVIN W. REDER (147), Department of Economics, Graduate Center, City University of New York, New York, New York

WARREN C. SANDERSON (173), Department of Economics, Stanford University, Stanford, California

TIBOR SCITOVSKY (223), Department of Economics, Stanford University, Stanford, California

LORIE TARSHIS (361), Scarborough College, University of Toronto, West Hill, Ontario, Canada

BRINLEY THOMAS (383), Department of Economics, University College, Cardiff, United Kingdom

JEFFREY G. WILLIAMSON (239), Department of Economics, University of Wisconsin, Madison, Wisconsin

* Present address: National Bureau of Economic Research, Inc., New York, New York.

Preface

The papers which form this book were pledged in celebration of Moses Abramovitz's sixtieth birthday, on January 1, 1972.

By allowing the individual contributors perfect freedom in their choice of subject matter, the editors happily have succeeded in marshalling a collection whose range reflects the broad sweep of Abramovitz's recent interests within the disciplines of economics and economic history. The individual and social welfare significance of quantitative indices of economic growth, the mechanisms of economic–demographic interdependence and their bearing particularly upon "long swings" in the rate of growth, the changing role of international relations in processes generating national economic development and domestic economic instability—all these, and still other topics to which Abramovitz's attention has turned, are treated in the present group of essays.

It is to be hoped that the volume as a whole will be accepted as a fitting expression of appreciation of the exacting standards of scientific inquiry, depth of insight, and modesty of exposition that continue to be the hallmarks of Abramovitz's own scientific contributions.

These papers, however, cannot be expected to convey the warmth of affection, nor the sincerity of admiration felt for an exemplary human being. Yet such sentiments, no less than those of scholarly respect, are shared by all who know Moses Abramovitz as a colleague, as a teacher, and as a friend.

P. A. DAVID
M. W. REDER

Nations and Households
in Economic Growth

Part I

Microeconomic Foundations

The Measurement of Real Value Added

KENNETH J. ARROW

HARVARD UNIVERSITY

1. Introduction

The concept of "value added" has played an essential role in both private and national income accounting, as a device for allocating the origins of income to the various points in the productive sector of the economy at which primary factors are brought to bear on the creation of the total value of final products. It provides an accounting which exactly exhausts total product.

It is, however, a monetary magnitude and as such subject to all the vicissitudes which have made economists engage in the unavailing search for an invariable standard of value. Variations in absolute and relative prices make difficult meaningful comparisons of value added across space and time. Just as we seek real measures of outputs and inputs, either by an index number of quantities or by deflating monetary magnitudes by means of a suitable price index, so it seems to be a reasonable goal to measure real value added in terms of capital and labor or to deflate money value added, which may be thought of as the money value of the *net* output of the industry, by some suitable index number.

3

This search is indeed part of a larger aim, one which is purportedly achieved by government statistical agencies, such as the Department of Commerce—namely, the construction of a complete set of national income accounts in real terms. It has, however, been argued convincingly by Stone and Prais (1952) in an important but neglected paper that such a construction can never be carried through with complete consistency. The inconsistencies are likely to show up with special force in those items which represent differences between well-defined flows—items such as value added or balance of payments. The difficulties in using the "double-deflation" method are pointed up by Stone's analysis. If money value added is the difference between the value of output and the value of raw materials, then presumably real value added ought to be the difference between the quantity of output and the quantity of raw materials. This measurement has been used by Fabricant (1940, pp. 25 ff.) and Greary (1944, p. 255). But as David (1962) has cogently pointed out, it is by no means impossible that the double-deflation measure of real value added can lead to a negative measurement.

To be sure, Sims (1969) has recently pointed out that the double-deflation approach can be given a reasonable foundation if Divisia price indices rather than fixed-base indices are used for the two deflations. In effect, only small changes are considered, so that negative values cannot occur (since the value added was necessarily positive in the base period).

To assess more deeply the relative merits of alternative measures of real value added, it is necessary to ask what its economic meaning is, that is, what we are trying to measure. I will argue first that the most natural meaning, indeed the only one I can think of, arises from the estimation of production functions. The output of any commodity is determined by the inputs of a number of commodities, of which some are primary factors and others are produced goods, which we will refer to as *materials*. The attribution of a special role to primary factors, capital and labor, and the construction of an aggregate for them can be justified only for the usual reasons: that their use in production is *separable* from that of the materials. If Q is output of the commodity, and K, L, and M stand for capital, labor, and materials, respectively, a production function is a relation,

$$Q = Q(K, L, M).$$

Here, K, L, and M appear to play a symmetric role, and there is no apparent reason to aggregate K and L rather than, say, K and M. The notion of real value added has meaning in a production function framework only if this relation can be assumed to take on the special *nested* form,

$$Q = Q[V(K, L), M].$$

As is well known, this is equivalent to requiring that the marginal rate of substitution between K and L in the production of Q is independent of M. Metaphorically, we can imagine capital and labor cooperating to produce an intermediate good, real value added (V), which in turn cooperates with materials to produce the final product. This is an empirical and refutable assumption about the nature of production functions. It would seem to be reasonable for a broad variety of cases where the production process consists of taking a mass of raw materials and transforming them into some finished product, e.g., as in cotton spinning. The transformation may be accomplished by varying combinations of capital and labor. But in other cases capital and materials may seem to be a more natural aggregate, for example, in electric power generating where increased capital expenditures basically serve to economize on fuel. Without the separability assumption, however, it is hard to assign any definite meaning to real value added, and probably the best thing to say is that the concept should not be used when capital and labor are not separable from materials in production.

Note that Q, K, L, and M are *observable* variables, but V is not. In the language sometimes used by statisticians, particularly those working with psychological data, V is a *latent* variable, while the others are *manifest* variables. This remark has important implications. It shows that we can never hope to achieve a *unique* measurement of V. If we determine any measurement of V for which the nested form is valid, we can always find another in which the magnitude of V is multiplied by some factor, and the marginal product of V divided by the same factor.

In principle, it is possible to estimate a production function if one has data on outputs and inputs over a sufficient variety of observations. If constant returns to scale are assumed, something more is true: The equation of any isoquant can be inferred from data on input quantities and input prices alone. Hence, the whole production function can be reconstructed, even if output is not directly measured, except that output is defined not uniquely but only up to an arbitrary, multiplicative constant. Thus data on capital and labor quantities and prices suffice to determine a production function for real value added; this function could be thought of as a quantity index for real value added.

Duality theory for production shows that another method is possible with the same given data; it is possible to derive a price index which is interpreted as the minimum cost of producing one unit of real value added. Then the latter can be obtained by using this price index to deflate nominal value added.

The same general principles can be applied in a somewhat different way to compute real value added in terms of output and materials (rather than in terms of capital and labor). Here the prices of output and raw materials are needed data. The quantity measure of real value added is an "external" average of output and materials, that is, a function homogeneous of degree one but decreasing in the quantity of materials.

For application to time series, it is also necessary to consider the possibility that one or both of the production functions involved (relating gross output to real value added and materials, or relating real value added to capital and labor) have shifts in time. The problems raised here are no different than those involved in estimating production functions when all variables are observable.

Independently of this work, Bruno (1972) has analyzed the concept of value added using duality methods. His analysis is more thorough in some respects, but does not overlap the results found here, its interests being differently focused.

Remark. The discussion in this paper focuses on measuring real value added in some one industry. No attempt is made to construct a complete accounting framework in which real value added is comparable across industries and can be summed to yield some measure of real national income. Actually, this aggregation of real value added is of the same order of difficulty as the aggregation of quantities of final goods. Money national income can be written as the sum of money values of final commodities; then real national income is some aggregate of the quantities of final commodities. Money national income is also the sum of money values added for all industries; then, if it is meaningful to measure real value added for each industry, it is meaningful to construct real national income as an aggregate of real values added, with the same problems of approximation as obtain in the measure of real national income from final commodities.

2. Notation and Assumptions

We use the following notation: p will be a price, q a quantity, and the following symbols are used as subscripts to p and q.

o   output
v   real value added
k   capital
l   labor
m   raw materials

Thus p_k is the price of capital and q_v the quantity of real value added. Finally, let V be value added in money terms. If there is a meaning to real value added, then

$$V = p_v q_v. \tag{1}$$

Under constant returns, we also have

$$V = p_k q_k + p_l q_l = p_o q_o - p_m q_m. \tag{2}$$

Output is a function of inputs, related by a production function:

$$q_o = H(q_k, q_l, q_m). \tag{3}$$

The usual assumptions that H is homogeneous of degree one and concave in its arguments are made. It has been implied that capital, labor, and raw materials are scalar variables, but in fact the subsequent argument would be equally valid were each a vector. Hence, in principle, the method used would be valid for any number of types of capital, labor, or raw materials, provided the data were available.

The basic maintained assumption of this paper is that the input variables q_k, q_l are (weakly) *separable* from q_m [see Leontief (1947), Goldman and Uzawa (1964)]; i.e., the function H has the special form

$$H(q_k, q_l, q_m) = F[G(q_k, q_l), q_m] \tag{4}$$

for some suitably chosen functions F and G. This assumption is equivalent to the statement that the marginal rate of substitution between capital and labor in the production of the output is independent of the quantity of raw materials.

Notice that if the function G is replaced by any monotonic transformation and the function F redefined correspondingly, (4) will remain satisfied. Hence, so far the function G is defined only up to a monotone transformation. It can easily be seen, however, that we can choose G to be homogeneous of degree one.

Since H is homogeneous of degree one, the marginal productivities (the partial derivatives of H with respect to its arguments) are all homogeneous of degree zero (Tintner, 1948). Thus the marginal rate of substitution between q_k and q_l, which is the ratio of their marginal productivities, is also homogeneous of degree zero in q_k, q_l, and q_m, and therefore can be written as a function of the two ratios, q_k/q_l and q_k/q_m. But we already know, from the separability assumption (4), that the marginal rate of substitution between q_k and q_l is independent of q_m; hence it must depend only on the ratio q_k/q_l. But,

$$\partial H/\partial q_k = (\partial F/\partial G)(\partial G/\partial q_k), \qquad \partial H/\partial q_l = (\partial F/\partial G)(\partial G/\partial q_l),$$

so that

$$(\partial H/\partial q_k)/(\partial H/\partial q_l) = (\partial G/\partial q_k)/(\partial G/\partial q_l),$$

and the latter ratio has been shown to depend on q_k and q_l only through their ratio. As is well known, it immediately follows that the function $G(q_k, q_l)$ is *homothetic* in those two variables, i.e., that the isoquants are all similar to each other. But for every homothetic function which is increasing in its argument, there is a monotone transformation which is homogeneous of any given positive degree and, in particular, of degree one.

Hence, without loss of generality, we can assume that G is homogeneous of degree one. *It is this function G which we will identify with real value added.*

Notice that, as remarked in Section 1, this function is still undefined, but only up to an arbitrary positive factor. Then let

$$q_v = G(q_k, q_l) \tag{5}$$

so that

$$q_o = F(q_v, q_m). \tag{6}$$

Note that from (4) and the assumption of constant returns to scale, it follows that F is homogeneous of degree one. For if we multiply q_k, q_l, and q_m by a common multiplier, we multiply q_v, q_m, and $q_o = H(q_k, q_l, q_m)$ by the same multiplier.

It can also be seen that the functions G and F are concave. First, the concavity of G is proved. Let $(q_k{}^0, q_l{}^0)$ and $(q_k{}^1, q_l{}^1)$ be two capital–labor pairs. Let,

$$q_v{}^0 = G(q_k{}^0, q_l{}^0), \qquad q_v{}^1 = G(q_k{}^1, q_l{}^1).$$

Take any α, $0 \leqslant \alpha \leqslant 1$, and define

$$q_v = \alpha q_v{}^0 + (1-\alpha) q_v{}^1, \qquad q_k = \alpha q_k{}^0 + (1-\alpha) q_k{}^1, \qquad q_l = \alpha q_l{}^0 + (1-\alpha) q_l{}^1.$$

Then we seek to prove that

$$G(q_k, q_l) \geqslant q_v.$$

Choose $q_m{}^0$ arbitrarily, and let $q_m{}^1 = (q_v{}^1/q_v{}^0) q_m{}^0$, $q_m = \alpha q_m{}^0 + (1-\alpha) q_m{}^1$. Then the concavity of H implies

$$H(q_k, q_l, q_m) \geqslant \alpha H(q_k{}^0, q_l{}^0, q_m{}^0) + (1-\alpha) H(q_k{}^1, q_l{}^1, q_m{}^1).$$

From (4)–(6) this can be written,

$$F[G(q_k, q_l), q_m] \geqslant \alpha F(q_v{}^0, q_m{}^0) + (1-\alpha) F(q_v{}^1, q_m{}^1).$$

But from the choice of $q_m{}^1$ and the fact that F is homogeneous of degree one,

$$F(q_v{}^1, q_m{}^1) = (q_v{}^1/q_v{}^0) F(q_v{}^0, q_m{}^0),$$

and therefore,

$$\begin{aligned}
\alpha F(q_v{}^0, q_m{}^0) + (1-\alpha) F(q_v{}^1, q_m{}^1) &= [\alpha + (1-\alpha)(q_v{}^1/q_v{}^0)] F(q_v{}^0, q_m{}^0) \\
&= F[\alpha q_v{}^0 + (1-\alpha) q_v{}^1, \alpha q_m{}^0 + (1-\alpha) q_m{}^1] \\
&= F(q_v, q_m).
\end{aligned}$$

Hence, $F[G(q_k, q_l), q_m] \geqslant F(q_v, q_m)$; since F is monotonic increasing in each variable, this is possible only if $G(q_k, q_l) \geqslant q_v$, as was to be proved.

The concavity of F is proved similarly. Let $(q_v{}^0, q_m{}^0)$ and $(q_v{}^1, q_m{}^1)$ be two pairs, $0 \leqslant \alpha \leqslant 1$. Choose $q_k{}^0, q_1{}^0$ so that

$$q_v{}^0 = G(q_k{}^0, q_1{}^0),$$

and then let $q_k{}^1 = (q_v{}^1/q_v{}^0) q_k{}^0$, $q_1{}^1 = (q_v{}^1/q_v{}^0) q_1{}^0$. Finally, let

$$q_v = \alpha q_v{}^0 + (1-\alpha) q_v{}^1, \qquad q_k = \alpha q_k{}^0 + (1-\alpha) q_k{}^1,$$
$$q_1 = \alpha q_1{}^0 + (1-\alpha) q_1{}^1, \qquad q_m = \alpha q_m{}^0 + (1-\alpha) q_m{}^1.$$

Then

$$q_v = \alpha G(q_k{}^0, q_1{}^0) + (1-\alpha) G(q_k{}^1, q_1{}^1) = [\alpha + (1-\alpha)(q_v{}^1/q_v{}^0)] G(q_k{}^0, q_1{}^0)$$
$$= G[\alpha q_k{}^0 + (1-\alpha) q_k{}^1, \alpha q_1{}^0 + (1-\alpha) q_1{}^1] = G(q_k, q_1),$$

so that

$$F(q_v, q_m) = F[G(q_k, q_1), q_m] = H(q_k, q_1, q_m)$$
$$\geqslant \alpha H(q_k{}^0, q_1{}^0, q_m{}^0) + (1-\alpha) H(q_k{}^1, q_1{}^1, q_m{}^1)$$
$$= \alpha F[G(q_k{}^0, q_1{}^0), q_m{}^0] + (1-\alpha) F[G(q_k{}^1, q_1{}^1), q_m{}^1]$$
$$= \alpha F(q_v{}^0, q_m{}^0) + (1-\alpha) F(q_v{}^1, q_m{}^1)],$$

as was to be proved. The homogeneity of degree one of G is used as well as the concavity of F.

The functions F and G, therefore, have all the usual properties of neoclassical production functions. We can think of producing real value added from capital and labor, as described by G, and then producing output from real value added and raw materials, as described by F.

3. Method I: Estimation of the Production Function for Real Value Added

In this section, we consider the problem of inferring the function G from a hypothetically infinite set of observations. We assume that each observation records information on p_k, p_1, q_k, and q_1. We·have no data on the "output" q_v. But under the assumption of constant returns this information is not as important as might appear. For under this hypothesis, and even under the weaker hypothesis of homotheticity, every observation in effect falls on the same isoquant. Hence, the quantity and price ratios suffice, under competitive assumptions, to determine any one isoquant, and therefore all isoquants. Admittedly, the labeling of each isoquant as to its output is not determined; but under constant returns the labeling is unique up to a multiplicative constant.

Formally, the function G must satisfy the condition,

$$(\partial G/\partial q_k)/(\partial G/\partial q_1) = p_k/p_1. \tag{7}$$

The left-hand side is, however, a function of q_k/q_1. Suppose, then, we find a functional relation between p_k/p_1 and q_k/q_1. These magnitudes are all observable. Then if we replace p_k/p_1 by this function on the right-hand side of (7), we have an equation for an isoquant; in technical terms, we have a partial differential equation for G. Because G is assumed increasing and homogeneous of degree one, the solution is unique up to a positive constant. Then G is an index number for real value added.

This approach finds its simplest application in the Cobb–Douglas case,

$$G = A q_k^{\alpha} q_1^{1-\alpha}. \tag{8}$$

Then (7) reduces to the condition,

$$p_1 q_1 / p_k p_k = (1-\alpha)/\alpha. \tag{9}$$

If G is known or assumed to be of Cobb–Douglas form, then the parameter α can be calculated from the (constant) ratio of factor shares. The parameter A cannot be so estimated, and indeed, as repeatedly emphasized, the multiplicative parameter A is unidentified. Hence, having estimated α, we can use $q_k^{\alpha} q_1^{(1-\alpha)}$, or any multiple thereof, as a measure of real value added.

If we assume instead fixed proportions between capital and labor, then

$$G = \min(\alpha q_k, \beta q_1). \tag{10}$$

In this case efficiency requires that $\alpha q_k = \beta q_1$ at every observation; hence, the ratio α/β is simply the observed constant labor–capital ratio, and the measure of real value added is simply (10) with some pair α, β in the ratio prescribed by the observations. The pair is again not identified; the posssible pairs differ only by constant multiples.

The cases so far have been special cases of constant elasticity of substitution (CES) production functions, but it has been assumed that the elasticity of substitution was known—1 in the first case, 0 in the second. Suppose instead it is assumed that G is a CES production function, without, however, any *a priori* knowledge of any of the parameters. It is convenient to formulate the parameters of the production function in a slightly unusual fashion:

$$G(q_k, q_1) = [(\alpha q_k)^{-\rho} + (\beta q_1)^{-\rho}]^{-1/\rho}, \tag{11}$$

where $\sigma = 1/(1+\rho)$ is the elasticity of substitution. As is well known [see Arrow *et al.*, 1961, Eq. (20a)], Eq. (7) is equivalent to

$$\ln(q_k/q_1) = (1-\sigma) \ln(\alpha/\beta) + \sigma \ln(p_1/p_k), \tag{12}$$

where ln denotes natural logarithm. Equation (12) can be fitted from observable data. Thus again the production function or index number for real value added, in this case (11), is determined from the data, except for a positive multiple of α and β; but this is equivalent to defining $q_v = G$ up to a positive multiple.

Thus, we see that if we dispose of a number of observations on capital and labor quantities and prices, we can use an appropriate maintained hypothesis about the structure of the real-valued-added production function to compute an index of real value added from the data.

4. Method I Modified: The Use of Duality Relations

The data used in Section 3 (prices and quantities of capital and labor) can define real value added by a different route. That is, we can seek to define not the production function for real value added but an appropriate price deflator. This deflator, the minimum cost of producing a unit of real value added, is a function of input prices which is, in an appropriate sense, dual to the production function. This approach was developed by Shephard (1970), though it had been used earlier by Hotelling (1932) and Roy (1947). Let

$$C_v(p_k, p_l) = \min_{G(q_k, q_l) = 1} (p_k q_k + p_l q_l). \tag{13}$$

Under constant returns, of course, the minimum cost of producing q_v units of real value added is $q_v C_v(p_k, p_l)$. A fundamental duality relation, known as Shephard's lemma, states that

$$\partial C_v / \partial p_k = q_k / q_v, \qquad \partial C_v / \partial p_l = q_l / q_v,$$

and therefore,

$$(\partial C_v / \partial p_k) / (\partial C_v / \partial p_l) = q_k / q_l. \tag{14}$$

The parallelism between (14) and (7) is obvious. Further, C_v is, by its definition, homogeneous of degree one. It can also be seen that C_v is a concave function, and that C_v is not only uniquely defined by G but uniquely defines it.

The right-hand side of (14) is homogeneous of degree zero in p_k and p_l. Hence, again we find a functional relation between q_k / q_l and p_k / p_l, but now we take the former as a function of the latter, and integrate (14) to find a function $C_v(p_k, p_l)$, homogeneous of degree one. This function can be interpreted as a price of real value added; then real value added can be determined by deflating V, the nominal value added, by this index. We will call this approach Method I'.

Note that the functional relation between q_k / q_l and p_k / p_l is in fact the same whether obtained from (7) or from the dual (14). It is only in the subsequent use of this relation that Methods I and I' differ.

It is easy to calculate that the dual of the Cobb–Douglas production function (8) is

$$C_v(p_k, p_l) = B p_k^\alpha p_l^{1-\alpha}, \tag{15}$$

for some constant B, arbitrary for our purpose. Then the procedure of this section can be described as follows: Estimate α as before from factor shares.

Now substitute this value of α into (15) with some convenient value of B (for example, if we want to measure real value added in terms of prices at one particular observation, let $p_k = p_1 = p_v = 1$ there, so that $B = 1$). Then measure real value added by dividing nominal value added, V, by C_v, which is a geometric mean.

Now consider the case of fixed proportions (13). In this case, the dual is

$$C_v = (p_k/\alpha) + (p_1/\beta). \tag{16}$$

(It is intuitively obvious that when two commodities are used in fixed proportions, the appropriate price index is essentially the cost of the bundle.) Estimate α/β, as before, as the (constant) ratio of labor to capital, and use a pair α, β with this ratio in (16) as the value added deflator. [If it is desired that all prices be one at some base observation, then α and β are chosen so that $(1/\alpha) + (1/\beta) = 1$.]

Finally, the dual of the general CES production function (11) is

$$C_v(p_k, p_1) = [(p_k/\alpha)^{-\rho^*} + (p_1/\beta)^{-\rho^*}]^{-1/\rho^*}; \tag{17}$$

here, $1/(1+\rho^*) = \sigma^* = 1/\sigma$. Now σ and α/β can be found from (12); an alternative form of (12), which makes the connection clearer, is obtained by solving (12) for $\ln(p_1/p_k)$:

$$\ln(p_1/p_k) = (1-\sigma^*)\ln(\alpha/\beta) + \sigma^* \ln(q_k/q_1).$$

(From a statistical viewpoint, where error terms are introduced, of course, it makes a difference which way the regression is estimated; but we are not concerned with such problems here. In any case, the direction of the fitting or the use of more general simultaneous equation methods should be the same whichever way we choose to measure real value added.) With estimates of σ (and therefore σ^*) and of α/β, (17) is determined up to a multiplicative constant and therefore can be used as a nonlinear price deflator.

It may be asked what relation can be expected between the results of Methods I and I'. If all the assumptions hold, that is, the assumptions that the production functions are correctly specified (including separability and homogeneity of degree one) and the markets are competitive, then the two methods should yield exactly the same results. Otherwise, they will yield divergent measures, and the comparison supplies a test of the maintained assumptions (still another test will be supplied by using Method II and its variants, if the data are available).

Still another method, which I will call Method I'', combines the primal and dual approaches. Intuitively, it seems to me more likely to adjust for failure of the assumptions to hold, but I cannot supply any justification for this guess. (In fact, Method I'' was my original solution to this problem, and it was only later that I hit upon the methods just sketched.) It is also more complicated to apply than either of the preceding methods.

If all assumptions hold, $p_v = C_v(p_k, p_l)$, and therefore

$$G(q_k, q_l) C_v(p_k, p_l) = V, \tag{18}$$

for each observation, from (1), while by marginal productivity theory,

$$\partial G/\partial q_k = p_k/C_v, \qquad \partial G/\partial p_l = p_l/C_v. \tag{19}$$

Divide each equation in (19) by (18) and then multiply both sides by C_v:

$$(1/G)(\partial G/\partial q_k) = p_k/V, \qquad (1/G)(\partial G/\partial q_l) = p_l/V;$$

or

$$\partial(\ln G)/\partial q_k = p_k/V, \qquad \partial(\ln G)/\partial q_l = p_l/V. \tag{20}$$

Guess a production function G', and compute its dual C_v. Then (18) holds by construction. Suppose it turns out that the marginal productivity conditions (19) also hold. Then (20) holds, with G replaced by G'. But p_k, p_l, and V are observables; their value is the same whether G or G' is the true production function. Thus,

$$\partial(\ln G)/\partial q_k = \partial(\ln G')/\partial q_k, \qquad \partial(\ln G)/\partial q_l = \partial(\ln G')/\partial q_l,$$

and therefore $\ln G$ differs from $\ln G'$ by a constant. Hence, G' is a constant multiple of the true production function G.

This demonstrates the validity of the following criterion for determining the real-value-added production function and its dual simultaneously.

Choose a cost function, $C_v(p_k, p_l)$, homogeneous of degree one and increasing and concave in its arguments. Compute real value added for any observation as V/C_v. Then fit a production function $G(q_k, q_l)$ by the "indirect" method, i.e., so that the marginal productivity relations are satisfied. If C_v is in fact the dual of G, then $G(q_k, q_l)$ is the (nonlinear) quantity index for real value added and C_v is the correct deflator to money value added. Either of these is defined uniquely up to a multiplicative constant.

In practice, this method will require iterations, with guessed cost functions followed by calculated production functions. I have not investigated convergence properties of the more obvious iterative procedures. Of course, if the assumptions are not satisfied, then there will be no pair G, C_v satisfying the criterion. This suggests as an open question finding a pair minimizing deviations from perfect fit in some appropriate metric.

In the Cobb–Douglas case, Method I'' does not lead to an essentially different procedure from those given previously. Consider now the fixed coefficients case as given by (10) and (16). Assume then that the analyst starts with a guess α^0, β^0 for the parameters α, β. He then calculates a deflator $C_v{}^0$ from (16), with α, β replaced by α^0, β^0, respectively. Then he calculates the corresponding guess at real value added for each observation,

$$q_v{}^0 = V/C_v{}^0.$$

In fact, at each observation, $q_k = (\beta/\alpha) q_1$. If we substitute $p_k q_k + p_1 q_1$ for V and then substitute for q_k as just shown, we find that

$$q_v^0/q_1 = (\alpha^0 \beta/\alpha)[(p_k/p_1) + (\alpha/\beta)]/[(p_k/p_1) + (\alpha^0/\beta^0)]. $$

If the initial guesses had the correct ratio, $\alpha^0/\beta^0 = \alpha/\beta$, then q_v^0/q_1 would be constant. If $\alpha^0/\beta^0 < \alpha/\beta$, then q_v^0/q_1 would decrease as p_k/p_1 increases. Hence, a negative correlation between q_v^0/q_1 (the ratio of guessed real value added to labor) and the rental–wage ratio is a signal that the initial guess at α/β is too low and should be revised upward. Thus, an iterative process is suggested for achieving the correct value.

Let us turn briefly to the general CES production function (11), with its dual (17). Method I″ in this case would appear as follows. Let $\alpha^0, \beta^0, \sigma^0$ be a guess at the parameters of (11). Let $\sigma^{*0} = 1/\sigma^0$, and define $p_v^0 = C_v^0$ by replacing α, β, and σ^* with α^0, β^0, and σ^{*0}, respectively, in (17). Then define, for each observation, $q_v^0 = V/p_v^0$. As shown by Arrow *et al.* (1961, Eq. (25)), the equality of marginal productivity of labor to wage is equivalent to

$$\ln(q_v/q_1) = (1-\sigma) \ln \beta + \sigma \ln(p_1/p_v), \tag{21}$$

and there is a similar equation with labor replaced by capital,

$$\ln(q_v/q_k) = (1-\sigma) \ln \alpha + \sigma \ln(p_k/p_v). \tag{22}$$

Then we can fit (21) and (22), with q_v^0 and p_v^0 replacing q_v and p_v, respectively. If these relations fit and yield the same estimates of σ, α, and β as those guessed (with possibly a multiplicative shift in α and β), we have verified the original guess.

As a final remark to this section, we note that there is a dual method to Method I″: Choose a production function, $G(q_k, q_1)$, and define the value added price deflator for each observation as V/G. Then fit a unit cost function in such a way as to satisfy the dual relations.

$$\partial C_v/\partial p_k = q_k/q_v, \qquad \partial C_v/\partial p_1 = q_1/q_v. $$

If the original G is in fact the dual of the fitted function C_v, then G is again the quantity measure of real value added and C_v the deflator to money value added.

5. Method II: Estimation of the Production Function for Gross Output and Measurement of Real Value Added from Output and Materials

It is noteworthy that Method I and its variants use price and quantity data only about capital and labor. A different method can also be derived from (4), a measure of real value added in terms of output and raw materials. Naturally, real value added will have to be an increasing function of output and a decreasing function of materials.

The simplest case is that in which materials are in a fixed ratio to output in real terms. This is, after all, the most common assumption. That is,

$$q_o = \beta q_m.$$

Then, from (2),

$$V = p_o q_o - p_m q_m = (\beta p_o - p_m) q_m.$$

But q_m is proportional to q_v, under fixed coefficients, and $V = p_v q_v$, so that p_v is proportional to $\beta p_o - p_m$. Hence $q_v = V/p_v$ is defined up to a factor of proportionality; of course, it is defined even more directly as being in proportion to q_m or to q_o.

This method of deflation extends. From (3) and (4),

$$q_o = F(q_v, q_m). \tag{23}$$

If we were to solve for q_v in terms of q_o and q_m, we would have a function which is homogeneous of degree one and concave in its variables. It would differ from a neoclassical production function only in that it is decreasing in q_m, rather than increasing. It follows that Method I and its variants could be applied to this new production function.

This is done, but is not solved explicitly. Instead, the marginal productivity relation for materials derived from (23) states that

$$\partial F/\partial q_m = p_m/p_o. \tag{24}$$

The left-hand side is homogeneous of degree zero in q_o and q_m. If we assume that prices and quantities of output and of materials are observed, then we can fit p_m/p_o to q_o/q_m, and then substitute into (24) to define a partial differential equation characterizing F; the characterization is unique up to a multiplicative constant in the measurement of q_v. We could then solve for q_v in (23) to derive a measurement of real value added. This algorithm is called Method II.

If F is assumed to be Cobb–Douglas,

$$F(q_v, q_m) = A q_v^\alpha q_m^{1-\alpha},$$

then α can be estimated as the (constant) ratio of nominal value added to money value of output. If we assume $A = 1$ (since A is arbitrary),

$$q_v = q_o^{1/\alpha} q_m^{1-(1/\alpha)}.$$

This index is homogeneous of degree one, but it is a *decreasing* function of q_m (since $0 < \alpha < 1$). Hence it is an "external" average; q_v does not lie between q_o and q_m but lies on the other side of q_o from q_m. Thus if q_o has risen by 10% and q_m by 20% from one observation to another, q_v must have risen by less than 10%.

In the dual form of Method II, analogous to Method I′, the estimate of α would be used to compute a price deflator,

$$p_v = p_o^{1/\alpha} p_m^{1-(1/\alpha)},$$

and q_v found equal to V/p_v. This is the Cobb–Douglas parallel to the deflation with which this section began.

Suppose now it assumed that F has a general CES form. Then (24) is the same as (21), with appropriate changes in the names of the variables. If the production function for output in terms of real value added and materials is

$$q_o = F(q_v, q_m) = [(\alpha q_v)^{-\rho} + (\beta q_m)^{-\rho}]^{-1/\rho}, \tag{25}$$

and $\sigma = 1/(1+\rho)$ is now the elasticity of substitution between real value added and materials in the production of output, then we fit

$$\ln(q_o/q_m) = (1-\sigma)\ln\beta + \sigma\ln(p_m/p_o),$$

a relation in observables which can be fitted. No estimate of α can be obtained, but of course this fact is simply the unobservability of real value added up to a multiplicative constant. If σ and β are estimated, we can solve in (25) for q_v:

$$q_v = (1/\alpha)[q_o^{-\rho} - (\beta q_m)^{-\rho}]^{-1/\rho},$$

an unusual-looking but well-defined external average.

I leave to the reader the exercise of stating the analogs of Methods I′ and I″ and of applying them to the CES production function.

6. Time Series Observations

The possibility of measuring real value added by any of the methods discussed thus far seems to depend upon having a number of observations on the same production function; it can, however, be either the function for the production of real value added or the production function for output in terms of real value added and materials. Method I and its variants are valid in the first case, Method II and its variants in the second.

But the assumption that either production function does not shift is not one we wish to maintain. If, in fact, some assumption of regularity in the shifts of the production function with respect to some observed exogenous variable can be made, then the methods given thus far can be applied.

I consider the case where the observations form a time series and the production functions may be shifting in time. If no a priori restrictions are made on the nature of the shifts, then production functions could not be estimated even if all variables were observed [see, in the case of the CES production function, the discussions of Diamond and McFadden (1972) and

Nerlove (1967, pp. 92–98)]. It will therefore be necessary to assume that the production functions,

$$q_o = F(q_v, q_m, t) \tag{26}$$

and

$$q_v = G(q_k, q_l, t), \tag{27}$$

depend on time but are some way restricted *a priori*.

There is, however, one conceptual point that needs to be cleared up. It has been noted repeatedly that real value added, being a latent variable, can be measured only up to an arbitrary factor. When the functions involved shift over time, this principle becomes still weaker: Real value added can be measured only up to a multiplier which is itself a function of time. To see this, if demonstration be needed, define

$$q_v' = A(t)q_v,$$

where $A(t)$ is an arbitrary function of time. Then,

$$q_o = F[q_v'/A(t), q_m, t] = F'(q_v', q_m, t)$$
$$q_v' = A(t)G(q_k, q_l, t) = G'(q_k, q_l, t),$$

so that the specification in terms of the new definition of real value added has the same general form as the old.

To be sure, the arbitrariness can be replaced by imposing conditions on the functions F and G which are convenient. If, for example, either F or G is to be independent of t, then the multiplier $A(t)$ would have to be a constant. Notice, though, that such a condition is basically a convention, not a restriction on the real world. To illustrate, there is *no* operational difference between specifying that shifts in G are Hicks-neutral and specifying that G has no shifts at all; the effects which appear in the first description as Hicks-neutral shifts in the production of real value added from capital and labor appear in the second as real-value-added-augmenting shifts in the production of the final output.

Paul David has remarked to me that if we assume technological change is factor-augmenting but make no further restrictions, there is only one simple convention that we can always enforce: namely, that the technological change in the production of final output is purely materials-augmenting. For if

$$q_o = H[A_k(t)q_k, A_l(t)q_l, A_m(t)q_m],$$

then separability implies,

$$q_o = F\{A_v(t)G[A_k'(t)q_k, A_l'(t)q_l], A_m(t)q_m\},$$

where $A_v(t)A_k'(t) = A_k(t)$ and $A_v(t)A_l'(t) = A_l(t)$. Clearly, $A_v(t)$ can be chosen arbitrarily, provided $A_k'(t)$ and $A_l'(t)$ are chosen correspondingly.

The simplest choice then is to set $A_v(t)$ identically equal to one. In that case,

$$q_v = G[A_k(t)q_k, A_1(t)q_1]$$

can be interpreted as real value added measured in efficiency units.

This ambiguity of description does not, of course, imply any inability to estimate the entire production function [Eqs. (3) and (4)]. If we measure real value added according to some convention, then, if we also have data on output and materials, we can estimate a production function for output in terms of materials and real value added, with a convention as to shifts which exactly offsets the convention used in the determination of the real-value-added production function.

Suppose we assume $G(q_k, q_1, t)$ is Cobb–Douglas with neutral shifts:

$$G(q_k, q_1, t) = A(t)q_k{}^\alpha q_1^{1-\alpha}. \tag{28}$$

Then α is still found to be the constant share of capital in nominal value added. The efficiency $A(t)$ is arbitrary; but for any given specification, we can estimate the production function,

$$q_0 = F(q_v, q_m, t),$$

provided we make specification of the way t enters.

If G is a CES production function and if Method I is used, then the relation (12),

$$\ln(q_k/q_1) = (1-\sigma)\ln(\alpha/\beta) + \sigma \ln(p_1/p_k),$$

can be fitted where the parameters are functions of time of some specified form. If technological change is assumed factor-augmenting, σ is constant, but α and β are specified functions of time, and therefore so is α/β. For example, if α and β are exponential functions of time,

$$\alpha = \alpha_0 e^{\gamma t}, \qquad \beta = \beta_0 e^{\delta t},$$

then

$$\alpha/\beta = (\alpha_0/\beta_0)e^{(\gamma-\delta)t},$$

and (12) becomes

$$\ln(q_k/q_1) = (1-\sigma)\ln(\alpha_0/\beta_0) + (1-\sigma)(\gamma-\delta)t + \sigma \ln(p_1/p_k), \tag{29}$$

from which $\gamma-\delta$ can be found, but not γ or δ separately.

Now assume that $F(q_v, q_m, t)$ is also factor-augmenting in its time shifts:

$$q_0 = F(e^{\mu t}q_v, e^{\nu t}q_1).$$

The determination of q_v by Method I is ambiguous up to an arbitrary exponential function of time, but this arbitrary element is simply incorporated into $e^{\mu t}$, so that the final function, $H(q_k, q_1, q_m, t)$, is uniquely specified. We can, according to David's remark, incorporate $e^{\mu t}$ into the definition of q_v.

Many variations of the above are possible, provided only that sufficiently detailed specification of the time shifts is made. For example, it might also be allowed that σ is varying in time, provided that it varies according to some well-specified law, e.g., linearly. The introduction of time shifts can also be carried out with Method II or any of the variants of Methods I and II.

ACKNOWLEDGMENT

This work was supported by National Science Foundation Grant GS-3269 at the Institute for Mathematical Studies in the Social Sciences at Stanford University, Stanford, California.

REFERENCES

Arrow, K. J., Chenery, H. B., Minhas, B. S., and Solow, R. M. (1961) Capital-labor substitution and economic efficiency. *Review of Economics and Statistics* **43**: 225–250.

Bruno, M. (1972) Duality, intermediate inputs, and value-added. In *An econometric approach to production theory* (D. McFadden, ed.). Amsterdam: North Holland Publ.

David, P. A. (1962). The deflation of value added. *Review of Economics and Statistics* **44**: 148–155.

Diamond, P., and McFadden, D. (1972) Identification of the elasticity of substitution and the bias of technological change: An impossibility theorem. In *An econometric approach to production theory* (D. McFadden, ed.). Amsterdam: North Holland Publ.

Fabricant, S. (1940) *The output of manufacturing industries: 1899–1937.* New York, National Bureau of Economic Research.

Geary, R. C. (1944) The concept of net volume of output, with special reference to Irish data. *Journal of the Royal Statistical Society* [N.S.], **107**: 251–259.

Goldman, S., and Uzawa, H. (1964) A note on separability in demand analysis. *Econometrica* **32**: 387–398.

Hotelling, H. (1932) Edgeworth's taxation paradox and the nature of demand and supply functions. *Journal of Political Economy* **40**: 577–616.

Leontief, W. W. (1947) Introduction to a theory of the internal structure of functional relationships. *Econometrica* **15**: 361–373.

McFadden, D. (Editor) (1972) *An econometric approach to production theory.* Amsterdam: North-Holland Publ.

Nerlove, M. (1967) Recent empirical studies of the CES and related production functions. In *The theory and empirical analysis of production* (M. Brown, ed.), pp. 55–122. New York: National Bureau of Economic Research.

Roy, R. (1947) La distribution du revenu entre des divers biens. *Econometrica* **15**: 205–225.

Shephard, R. W. (1970) *The theory of cost and production functions*, 2nd edition. Princeton, New Jersey, Princeton Univ. Press (1st edition, 1953).

Sims, C. (1969) Theoretical basis of a double-deflated index of value added. *Review of Economics and Statistics* **51**: 470–471.

Stone, J. R. N., and Prais, S. J. (1952) Systems of aggregative index numbers and their incompatibility. *Economic Journal* **62**: 565–583.

Tintner, G. (1948) Homogeneous systems in mathematical economics. *Econometrica* **16**: 273–294.

Fortune, Risk, and the Microeconomics of Migration

PAUL A. DAVID
STANFORD UNIVERSITY

PART I

The germinal idea of this essay is formulated simply enough: Fortune is the opportunity present in Risk. Hence, howsoever men would comport themselves in the company of Risk, their actions must in some part betray Fortune's influence.

Neat, but admittedly a little too cryptic to be immediately edifying. Some brief elaboration is required.[1] By Risk I refer to the casual element of men's experience, the unreasoning and unforetold ways of the world, the irremovable dispersion in the imaginable assortments of events attending actions taken in ignorance. This conforms to the meaning more or less conventional in current economic writings, allowing Risk to stand in the place of Aristotle's *causa per accidens*, most particularly in place of his *Tyche*—the cause *per accidens* of

---

[1] In the following passages, I have drawn upon the discussion of the Aristotelian treatment of Chance and Fortune provided by Cioffari (1935, pp. 23–24), and equally, regarding medieval and Renaissance conceptions of Fortuna, upon Patch (1927), and Cioffari (1940, 1944).

occurrences that proceed from human deliberation, as distinguished from events lying wholly within the domain of nature.

By Fortune, on the other hand, I mean the scope left for human judgment and volition where Fate does not rule and outcomes are not all predetermined. Fortune here represents the element of disorder essential to opportunity, the uncharted paths that afford men the freedom to learn and profit from the mutability of the world. It is Fortune that furnishes occasions for the trials and training which are the substance of the human adventure. This usage reflects a thoroughly Renaissance view of the function of the casual element in the universal design, a merging of the traditions of Boethius, St. Thomas, and Dante. For its testing and corrective value, all Fortune is good, even that which men call bad; it is the impulse that assists one to succeed at the right moment, an impulse seen to operate through the gifts of reason, will power, and free will which have been granted to man. To boast of one's Fortune in this sense may be immodest, but it does not tempt the gods.[2]

By now it will be plain that I am not merely taking Fortune and Risk as symbols of success and failure, of the ascent to wealth and dignity by some, and—with the same turn of the wheel—the tragic fall of others from their exalted stations in life; these two figures are not intended as allusions to the fact that the Goddess Fortuna has two faces, one benign, the other horrible.

Rather, Fortune and Risk are contending conceptions of the role of chance in the universe, and therefore in the lives of men. From Chance, that region veiled from human knowledge, there issues both "hazard" and "opportunity." And to each conception corresponds a suitable mode of behavior: One may either shun or abandon oneself passively to hazard, whereas the fitting response to opportunity is by means of reason, inquiry, and active pursuit. Let Chance be portrayed as a probability distribution over events, then the idea of Risk proceeds from acquiescence (in varying degree, of course) to an existence entirely governed by that distribution. But the conception of Fortune is founded on the possibility of exercising some measure of choice over the outcomes one will accept from Chance, of engaging in some studied and selective adventuring, some essentially exploratory sampling.

From a recognition of the duality of the conceptions of Fortune and Risk as just delineated, there follows the realization that the modes of behavior apposite to each view of the world need not be mutually exclusive, as these conceptions themselves are not. Instead, where circumstances will permit it, both the active and the passive modes of adaptation may be expected to manifest themselves concurrently in the activities of ordinary men—although in varying proportions to be sure.

---

[2] Burckhardt (1929, p. 482), notices that in Italy it was probably the *condottieri* of the fifteenth century who first ventured to boast so loudly of their fortune.

In developing a formal theory of economic action around the kernel of this insight, the baggage of allegorical allusions with which we embarked may be quietly left behind. It will have served well if it has conveyed the idea that there is a place, and perhaps even a need, for a theory representing economic decision making as a balancing of opposing reactions, the attainment of an equilibrium of ambivalent responses to the existence of uncertainties arising from ignorance.

For this occasion I have attempted to cast such a theory in the concrete shape of a normative model of selective information acquisition by individuals who do not assign equal positive and negative weights to success and failure. The element of selectivity is quite crucial and presents itself on two counts, for neither the denseness of the fog of ignorance in which decisions must be made, nor the dimensions of the hazards which that fog is presumed to obscure, need be treated as if they lay entirely beyond men's control. This is explicitly recognized by the model of optimizing behavior articulated here. In it, the problem posed is one of determining how much should be allocated to selecting or controlling the parameters of the stochastic environment within whose confines some activity akin to a search is to be undertaken, and how much in the way of resources should be expended on the actual process of that search.

The resulting formulation is one in which familiar aspects of the work of Tobin (1958), Markowitz (1959), and Arrow (1965) on risk-averting investment strategies can be easily integrated with the recent lines of analysis springing from Stigler's (1961, 1962) papers on market search activity as a rational response to the presence of risk (or should we here say "fortune"?) inherent in the absence of perfect information.[3] One hopes, of course, that the progeny of such a mating will turn out to have interest value other than as a mere intellectual sport. And indeed closer consideration of the general structure of the decision problem posed in the remaining pages of Part I does suggest an array of potential applications—to empirically interesting topics as diverse as the optimal selection among fields of occupational specialization, or the best way to go house-hunting, to prospect for oil, or to allocate resources in basic and applied scientific research.

But rather than casting so wide a net, the balance of the essay (Parts II and III) concentrates on drawing out in more rigorous detail the implications of the general formulation in yet another specific connection: the microeconomics of human migration decisions.

---

[3] Roberts (1971) offers a comprehensive review of the literature dealing with portfolio models. A compact and lucid account of theoretical questions relating to search behavior and the organization of markets with imperfect information is given by Rothschild (1971). I have found both these papers extremely helpful.

As an expository vehicle for the basic analytical framework, a more natural application could hardly suggest itself. Think of Sir William Whittington's third son, Dick, thrust from the bosom of the Gloucestershire gentry to make his way first as a mercer's apprentice in London—the station from which, as the legends accurately relate, he would rise to be thrice Lord Mayor of the city. Or of Thomas Lincoln, moving Nancy and the boy from the western Kentucky wilderness to make a new farm by Pidgeon Creek in Indiana, only to repeat the process 14 years later, so that young Abe reached his manhood splitting rails in the Sangamon River country of Illinois. Or perhaps of Malcolm Little, yet to become Malcolm X, venturing from the comparative haven of Roxbury's south end to try making the scene in "the Big Apple"— Harlem. The quitting of hearth and home, the wrench of emigration to some foreign place is commonly viewed, and probably rightly so, as the classic and essential means by which the mass of men have been able to extend the horizon of their personal quest for Fortune.

1. Some Higher Moments in the Life of Man: A Paradigm

To quickly dispel any lingering sense of mystery or paradox without having immediate recourse to mathematics, it is best to commence with an analogy of the kind calculated to put statisticians at their ease. A man has been presented with a set of labeled urns, each containing many balls. Every ball has a dollar value inscribed upon it, but the value of any ball can only be obtained after it is withdrawn from the urn. Upon the label of each urn appear the parameters of the particular probability distribution to which the values of the balls therein conform. Also written upon every label is the fixed "entry fee" that must be paid just for the right to put one's hand in the urn, and, further, a schedule of "sampling charges" describing the (dollar) costs of withdrawing different numbers of balls therefrom. Were our friend able to inventory the contents of all the urns and choose a single ball on the basis of full knowledge, he would prefer the one with the highest value—although he might decide that the whole game had not been worth the candle. This, however, is not even a practicality. He is, instead, required to choose an action strategy composed of two elements: He must designate (1) the single urn from which (2) a specified number of balls are to be drawn, say, in sequence, replacing each before extracting the next and recording its value. He will then be allowed, without further expense, to retrieve any one ball—and obviously he will want it to be the highest valued—among those comprising the (random) sample. How should he proceed in making this strategy decision? If given a fixed budget, how should he divide it between purchasing "entry" and sampling? And how large a sum should he be willing to spend in this game?

A theory of action in this context must begin with a statement of his subjective valuation of the consequence of drawing n balls from the ith urn. For the moment some complications may be spared by supposing the fellow is risk-neutral: He evaluates the balls at their face values. Therefore, given any sum spent on the entry fee and sampling charges combined, he is concerned to chose an action mix that maximizes the expected value of the highest valued ball in his sample—because that is the one he will ultimately keep.[4]

The second necessary component in his decision process must be the notions he is able to form as to the occurrence of different "states of the world"—describing these simply in terms of the highest value actually found on the balls in a particular sample. For, with such notions (expressed as probability statements) in mind, it is possible to arrive at some belief about the most likely consequence, i.e., the expected highest valued ball, produced by a given action strategy. Here the parameter information conveyed by the labeling of the urns should prove most helpful to him, permitting probability statements conditioned on the stipulation of not only the sample's size but the shape of the distribution from which it is drawn.

Now notice that the relevant way for our subject to describe his beliefs about various actions' "consequences" is by reference to the extreme-value distribution, the set of probabilities defined over the value of the "best" ball drawn. The shape of this last, more relevant distribution obviously must be governed by the underlying population distribution and the number of balls in the sample. Most transparently, in the trivial case where only one draw is made from any urn, the expected maximum values will coincide with the respective expected values, i.e., the population means disclosed on the labels of the respective urns. As the sample size is increased, however, the expected maximum value rises from that initial level, precisely because the probability of having picked balls carrying values successively farther and farther above the population mean will be increased as more of the population is caught within the sample.[5] But in general, for *bounded* continuous probability density functions (which are, of course, of finite variance), the expected maximum

---

[4] As Part II explicitly states, the individual is assumed to maximize utility in the von Neuman–Morgenstern sense, and will thus maximize his expected utility with respect to the available actions. Since we suppose here, if only momentarily, that his utility index is a particular (one-to-one) *linear* transformation of the values of the balls, utility maximization implies maximizing the expected value of the "best" ball. In Part II the maximization of a more general utility index is performed subject to cost function and budget constraints.

[5] On the assumption that the number of balls in the urns remains very large in relation to the feasible sample size (given the sampling charges), or that—as stated here—the game dictates sampling *with replacement*, the so-called "hysteresis effect" is excluded, and the probabilities remain independent of the values previously drawn.

value will be an increasing, *concave*, bounded function of the sample size.[6] And against the (consequently diminishing) marginal gain in the expected maximum value must be set the additional cost entailed by enlarging the sample size. Having made a commitment to sample within any particular urn, it is evident therefore that the information as to the shape of the population of values contained therein, and the schedule of (marginal) sampling costs, provide sufficient grounds for predetermining the "best" size of the sample for our risk-neutral subject to draw. The relevant rule is the one indicated by Stigler (1962): Do not increase the sample beyond the point at which the marginal improvement in the expected maximum becomes less than the incremental sampling cost.

When we next look across the array of urns and abstract from any differences among the population means that might be indicated on their labels, the remaining information concerning higher moments of those distributions will permit some fairly obvious general inferences about the corresponding distributions of the extreme value.[7] Holding constant the size of the sample taken from either a symmetric or a positive skew population distribution, we find the expected maximum value will be bigger, the bigger is the underlying population variance. Similarly, the expected maximum value will be greater where the degree of positive skewness—loosely speaking, the comparative length of the distribution's upper tail—is greater. Against these potential sources of difference among the expected consequences of drawing the same

---

[6] The restriction of this general discussion to nonnegative finite offers x seems not unreasonable. If $f(x) = F'(x)$, $x \in [0, M]$ is a continuous frequency distribution function (f.d.f.), the probability element for x to be the maximum in a sample of n is $h_n(x)\, dx = nf(x)[F(x)]^{n-1}\, dx$. The expected maximum value,

$$g_n = E[x_{\max}(n)] = \int_0^M x h_n(x)\, dx,$$

wherefrom—by substitution and integration by parts—it is found that

$$g_n = x[F(x)]^n \Big|_0^M - \int_0^M [F(x)]^n\, dx.$$

By calculation it is possible to derive the incremental gain from enlarging the sample:

$$g_{n+1} - g_n = \int_0^M [F(x)]^n [1 - F(x)]\, dx.$$

As the cumulative distribution function (c.d.f.) $F(x) \leqslant 1$, the *marginal* gain is obviously a positive, nonincreasing function of n. I am indebted to Michael Rothschild for guiding me through this proof of a proposition that has been asserted more generally, but supported only by casual reference to the special case in which $f(x)$ is a normal f.d.f., as in Stigler (1962, p. 97) or Alchian (1970, p. 29). The Appendix, below, shows that the proposition holds where the variate x is *unbounded* but normally distributed.

[7] On the properties of order statistics, and specifically of extreme value distributions, cf. Gumbel (1958) or the briefer treatment by H. Cramér (1963, Chap. 28).

size sample from the different urns, there must be set any corresponding differences among the indicated "entry fees."

Suppose, however, that the entry fee is everywhere the same and the sampling cost schedules are also uniform, so that those considerations provide no basis on which to choose among actions involving different urns. If, in addition, the mean values of the contents of all urns were identical, the sole grounds for selection among them would consist in the inter-urn variations of the expected extreme value due to differences in the dispersion and skewness characterizing the underlying population distributions. Assume those distributions are symmetric, and it is evident that for every size of sample considered, the expected maximum value, net or gross of (the uniform) cost outlays, will be greatest for the urn where the underlying population variance happens to be greatest absolutely and (by assumption) greatest in relation to its mean. On this account alone the individual utility maximizer should be lured to sample from those urns where it appears the "hazard"—as represented by the relative dispersion in the underlying population—is greatest. Indeed, it is precisely the possibility of sampling prior to making a final selection that has opened a way for the variance, and more generally the higher moments of the distribution of balls, to exert influence upon the choice of an urn and sample size combination. In the simplified case envisaged, the effect of those higher moments on the expected returns, specifically on the expected extreme value, represents the *only* mode through which their influence can be felt. It should be recalled that we began with the stipulation that our subject was risk-neutral as regards his subjective (utility) valuation of the consequences of following a specific action strategy under alternative states of the world.

This is the key proposition. From its embellishment derives whatever element of novelty there is to be found in the theory of behavior under uncertainty set forth here. And fittingly enough, it serves to define operationally what I have hitherto referred to as the element of Fortune, distinguishing its influence from the influence exercised by Risk. Considerations of Fortune may now be seen to impinge on the choice among actions necessarily, through the effect that assessments of the probable occurrence of different states of the world must have upon the expected consequence of each plan of action. Considerations of Risk, on the other hand, may make themselves felt through the effect that assessments of the probable occurrence of different states of the world can have upon the subjective valuation of the uncertain consequence of each plan of action.

Thus, as economists have been given to understand,[8] the element of Risk

---

[8] Cf. Arrow (1965, Chaps. 1, 2) for the classic modern exposition. It should be quite plain that its influence pervades the very terms in which the decision problem has been presented in this section.

enters the choice problem *via* the risk-averse or risk-loving preferences of the economic agent involved. Such nonneutral attitudes regarding risk, however, do not arouse in the utility maximizer any *intrinsic* concern with the higher moments of the underlying population distribution. Rather they create a second basis for a derived, *instrumental* concern—inasmuch as in the present context these population moments will affect the higher moments of the distribution of the extreme value, for which the actor does have an intrinsic regard.

From the preceding illustration it is apparent that where the underlying population distributions are symmetric, a larger variance creates a relative attraction in the form of a "fortune-hunting," or, still more appropriate, a "bargain-hunting" effect, because it raises the mean of the extreme value distribution. Yet by the same token, for any given sample size above one, a comparatively large variance implies there will be greater dispersion around the expected extreme value. Lovers of risk, who value gains in absolute terms more than equal absolute losses, will on that account tend to be drawn toward environments characterized by relatively great underlying dispersion—an effect quite distinct from and additional to that produced by the attractive "bargain-hunting" opportunities contained therein. They might also be disposed to devote less of their resources to the sort of heavy sampling activity that would tend to lower the variance in the distribution of the extreme value. Risk averters, on the other hand, will tend on that account to be repelled by such comparatively hazardous environments, and if tempted to enter them in pursuit of bargains, may do so only when it appears it will be possible to recoup the added expense of drawing a comparatively large sample.[9]

A complete theory of action where sampling strategies are feasible ought thus to acknowledge the dual influence of the higher moments in the life of economic man. Otherwise, were the existence of possibilities for acquiring information by sampling (or kindred modes of coping with ignorance) to be disregarded, and were the attractions of bargain-hunting present in disorderly environments to be therefore neglected, our hypotheses about the predominance of one or another attitude toward risk would be forced to perform double duty in accounting for many economic phenomena.

Of course, this has been for some time the prevailing state of affairs. Indeed, in the development of economic thought on behavior under uncertainty, the neglect of considerations of Fortune deserves to be accorded the status of an original oversight, that is to say, one that must be charged against Adam

---

[9] The comparison here is with the sample size that a risk-neutral or risk-loving individual would draw from the same urn. *Ceteris paribus*, the "bargains" effect would operate to elicit more intensive sampling of environments characterized by greater underlying dispersion—quite independent of preferences regarding risk. The model presented in Part II develops these points more explicitly.

Smith. The famous disquisition in *The Wealth of Nations*[10] on the way men choose among "certain and uncertain occupations" begins by observing that in the instance of the law the average compensation was comparatively low considering the substantially uniform expenses incurred and the wide dispersion of the incomes received by the members of the profession. The law appeared to Smith then as a distinctly unfair lottery, into which the slight chance of great success drew mortals blind enough or conceited enough to show "contempt for risk" and "absurd presumption in their own good fortune."

By long-standing tradition, therefore, mere ignorance or a ruling passion for gambling have been cited as the operative causes wherever it appears that a more hazardous occupation or environment has been entered without there being some compensating observed difference in average returns. But with these two diagnoses the modern economist is patently ill at ease. The first of them (miscalculation) is destructive of any effort to explain observed behavior by reference to normative models; whereas, in the instance of the second, there are simply too many other circumstances in which it seems necessary to make a conflicting appeal to the *predominance* of risk aversion among economic agents.

A new, alternative line of interpretation for the behavior of those eighteenth-century lawyers, one that already will have been suggested by the analogy of the urns and the balls, consequently ought to be welcomed with some sense of relief. Adam Smith's characterization of the legal profession simply as a lottery was amusing but fundamentally misleading, if only because the counselor at law is peculiarly free to sample the universe of prospective clients prior to accepting one. On this latter reconstruction, the existence of an underlying population of potential clients whose respective stakes in litigation vary as widely as do the merits of their individual cases would create in the "urn" of the law (vis-à-vis other occupations) the attraction of a potent bargain-hunting effect. It is then quite conceivable that against such an attraction, the countervailing effects of risk-averse attitudes—held by fledgling lawyers no less than by other men—might prove insufficient to restrain new entrants from depressing the average compensation of the profession to the level that occasioned Adam Smith's initial perplexity.

Beyond clarifying this classic problem of an occupational choice, numerous uses may be found for our paradigm of urns and balls, and by now its applicability to the other "prospecting" or literal bargain-hunting situations mentioned earlier should have become reasonably transparent. In the slightly less obvious case of optimal allocation strategies for organized science, it would seem intriguing to ask the same questions when basic science in

---

[10] Cannan ed., 1937, pp. 106–108 (see References).

specified fields is likened to the building of urns whose respective population parameters are in some measure known, and applied research endeavors are construed as the drawing of balls from urns already thus constructed.[11]

Yet, other applications notwithstanding, the strong parallelism between the theories of occupational and *spatial* mobility—both having been jointly advanced by Adam Smith as applications of his theory of "net advantages"— should leave one well-disposed toward the notion that this paradigm might prove especially illuminating with regard to the behavior of the rational worker contemplating migration.

2. Eppur Si Muovono!

In place of "urns" we should then quickly substitute local labor markets: rural districts, towns, cities, or even different countries. And instead of "balls," read job offers. For simplicity's sake a traditional Japanese arrangement may be imagined to prevail—permanent job tenure; the value of a job offer thus becomes the present value of an annual wage annuity received over the remainder of the worker's earning life. To what does "sampling" correspond here? Obviously to local job search, an activity which is presumed to be distinct from employment (job tenure) and can be conducted only at some (scheduled) expense to the individual concerned. Since the contemplated search is to be carried on within the local confines of a single local market, we must suppose that migration thither is a prerequisite for its conduct. Hence the fixed "entry fee" that appeared (along with the schedule of sampling charges) on each urn's label now represents the pure pecuniary and psychic costs of the migration activity necessary to effect entry into the respective local labor markets from some standard-origin place in the system—the "null urn" initially inhabited by the prospective migrant.

If the analogy is accepted as apt, a question to which I shall have to return, it is possible immediately to discern a number of respects in which the resulting theory will depart rather strikingly from the familiar classical analysis of migration behavior. Imagine a world in which the expected value of a job offer was identical everywhere, and, further, in which a worker born into the dull uniformity of "the countryside" (the null urn) found the costs of moving to one or another of several distant towns to be all the same. Were a man in that position indifferent to risk, or willing to make his calculations on the basis of certainty equivalents, it is now more than conceivable that he should find it attractive to emigrate to seek his fortune in the town where the relative variance of the prevailing distribution of job offers was *greatest*. Here, then,

---

[11] Having made some preliminary trials in the latter vein, my attention was directed to the interesting, quite independent, and still unpublished work of Evenson and Kislev (1972). They have tackled the question in a similar but empirically more appropriate dynamic framework, using optimal control theory.

is a context in which the existence of differences between the levels of average real earnings prevailing in geographically separated markets ceases to figure as a necessary condition for the occurrence of work-related net migration. It is a world where the mere elimination of pure spatial differentials in average real wage rates and job vacancy rates will not suffice to halt the voluntary spatial redistribution of the population!

The theory toward which this leads remains very much rooted in the normative economic analysis of individual migration decisions, but, as a corollary of the preceding observations, it should be seen to offer a natural and consistent way of admitting the influence of interregional and international differences in political, legal, and cultural conditions *on the supply side* of spatial population movements, For such conditions, no less than narrowly economic factors, are bound to affect the degree of dispersion directly, and perhaps also the skewedness of the distributions of earnings opportunities which characterize different societies.

But thus far we have only arrived at a new conception of the migrant's decision problem, and not at a full theory of his action. It remains to work out the characteristics of an optimal migration–job search strategy for a von Neumann–Morgenstern utility maximizer who is constrained to spend no more than a fixed budget for those purposes. Indeed, conditions of the game have yet to be established under which there will exist a unique maximum solution to that problem. These tasks, however, are best carried out in the context of the more precise and detailed statement of the model provided by the following Part (II)—which is devoted to completing the theory of optimal migration–search behavior for individuals constrained by capital market imperfections, and to exploring its empirical implications.

Having laid that foundation, it is not difficult to extend the analysis into a portfolio choice theory of the optimal amount of investment for the household to make in migration and search activities. But as this development would considerably lengthen an already lengthy essay, it must be left for presentation on another occasion. Instead, the final Part (III) redirects attention to several fundamental issues, touching on the aptness of the correspondence I have drawn between the game of urns and balls and a worker's choice among alternative strategies involving migration and local job hunting.

PART II

3. Movers and Searchers with Limited Means: A Formal Model

The model I shall now set out describes the choice of an optimal single-period strategy of wealth accumulation for a von Neumann–Morgenstern utility-maximizing household which may allocate as much as a fixed proportion $\bar{s}$ of its initial wealth Y_0 to investments in migration and local job search. To keep the affair simple, the kth household is reduced to a monolithic decision entity which, effectively, has only one breadwinner. Any nonlabor sources of pecuniary income at its disposal are assumed to be perfectly transportable and therefore will not be affected by a change in place of residence. Although the household may be enjoying some element of psychic rent from residing at the jth location, satisfactions that would have to be sacrificed in moving elsewhere, the present value of this stream of pure spatial rents P'_{jk} is assumed to be immediately commensurate with pecuniary wealth; pure locational preferences thus do not enter the household's utility function separately from considerations of "wealth." Such preferences are taken into account, however, because they are assumed to be reducible to statements about Y_{ijk}, the terminal (pecuniary and psychic) wealth following a move from the jth to the ith locale.

a. Terminal Wealth Relationships

The balance sheet of the household's total "wealth" position after such a move therefore reflects the following set of accounting relationships:

$$Y_{ijk} = Y_{0k}(1 - s_k) - P_{ijk} + y_{ijk}; \tag{1}$$

$$y_{ijk} = R_k[{}_i w_{max} - \mu_i] + R_k[\mu_i - \mu_j]; \tag{2}$$

$$P_{ijk} = P'_{ijk} + R_k[w^0_{jk} - \mu_j]. \tag{3}$$

The first equation says that terminal wealth is initial wealth *less* the out-of-pocket expenditures on migration and search activities, and *less* the pecuniary and/or net psychic costs P_{ijk} incurred in quitting the jth locale to look for work, *plus* the gross pecuniary increment in wealth y_{ijk} obtained by virtue of shifting the locus of job search from j to i. In Eq. (2), y_{ijk} has been decomposed into the gain which this relocation affords to the recipient of μ_i or μ_j, the average annual wage offer in each place, and the present value of the fruits of an actual search of the destination market. This latter is represented as the difference between the capitalized values of the income streams ${}_i w_{max}$ and μ_i, respectively, the maximum wage offer secured from a search involving the collection of $n > 1$ offers, and the (average) wage offer which an individual who planned to take the first job offered him upon his arrival would expect to receive. R_k represents the present value of a dollar of wage-annuity income and thus reflects r, the rate of time discount, and $a_{max} - a_k$, the length of the kth breadwinner's remaining working life.[12]

---

[12] Actually employing the annuity formulation, if w_k is the annuity wage, $w_k = w_k(a)$, for $a \in [a_k, a_{max}]$, we have

$$R_k = V_k/w_k = \int_{a_k}^{a_{max}} \exp[-ra]\, da = (1/r)\{1 - \exp[-r(a_{max} - a_k)]\}.$$

It is obvious that r can be suitably interpreted as the discount rate *net* of the *exponential* age gradient of the wage over the earnings life-span. Hence the assumption of permanent tenure of a *constant*-wage job may be relaxed somewhat.

The definition of P_{ijk} acknowledges that irrespective of the choice of destination, the act of emigrating not only may mean losing the value of the stream of psychic location rents P'_{ijk}, but may require surrendering an "above-average job" paying w^0_{jk} in the jth locale.[13] Another possible interpretation for the term $R_k(w^0_{jk} - \mu_j)$ is that it represents the present value of accumulated seniority or pension rights which would be lost by quitting an average-offer job (paying μ_j) and winding up with another just like it—as far as the wage rate was concerned.

b. Utility Function and Expected Utility

We may suppose the household's preference structure conforms with the axioms giving rise to a von Neumann–Morgenstern utility index whose only argument is terminal wealth: $U(Y_{ijk})$. Since the component y_{ijk} in Eq. (1) will be given a stochastic specification in Section 3c below, Y_{ijk} has a random distribution and utility maximization becomes equivalent to maximizing the expected utility: $E[U(Y_{ijk})]$.

Now let $U(Y_{ijk})$ be replaced by its Taylor series expansion around $E[(Y_{ijk})] = \bar{Y}_{ijk}$, and (momentarily dropping the subscripts) take the expectation

$$E[U(Y)] = U(\bar{Y}) + E[(Y-\bar{Y})]\,U'(Y) + \tfrac{1}{2}E[(Y-\bar{Y})^2]\,U''(Y) + \cdots.$$

(4a)

Noting that the random distribution of Y implies

$$E[(Y-\bar{Y})] = 0 \quad \text{and} \quad E[(Y-\bar{Y})^2] = \sigma_Y{}^2,$$

(4b)

and that if the variance of Y, $\sigma_Y{}^2$, is relatively small it is admissible to neglect the higher order terms above those made explicit by Eq. (4), we arrive at the approximation

$$E[U(Y)] = U(\bar{Y}) + \tfrac{1}{2}\sigma_Y{}^2 U''(\bar{Y}).$$

(4c)

As shall be seen, this approximation is of considerable heuristic convenience, in that it affords access to graphical methods of exposition of the sort made familiar by the literature of portfolio models based on mean-variance analysis, while at the same time avoiding reliance on the assumption of a quadratic form for the utility function and all the unacceptable implications that specific form entail.[14]

---

[13] Alternatively, $R_k[w^0_{jk} - \mu_i] < 0$ would imply that the individual had already accepted a below-average offer and might on that account expect some *gross* gain from surrendering it to solicit just one offer in the same location.

[14] I am indebted to my colleague Hayne Leland for suggesting the gambit of replacing $U(Y)$ by a suitable Taylor series. After working out the approximation with the power function specification of $U(Y)$ [cf. Eq. (5)], I came upon the recently published work of

A concrete form may now be postulated for the utility index

$$U(Y_{ijk}) = Y_{ijk}^v, \qquad 0 < v \leqslant 1, \tag{5}$$

leading to the specific expected utility approximation

$$E[U(Y_{ijk})] = \overline{Y}_{ijk}^v \{1 - v\rho_Y\}, \tag{6a}$$

where the "rel-variance" of Y is defined as

$$\rho_Y \equiv \sigma_Y^2 / \overline{Y}_{ijk} \tag{6b}$$

and the constant v is related to the exponent v by

$$v \equiv [v(1-v)]/2. \tag{6c}$$

With this usefully flexible form, by setting $v = 1$, $v \to 0$, we can in a stroke render the household risk-neutral and therefore adherent to the certainty equivalents rule: it makes calculations under uncertainty by replacing stochastic variables with their expected values. More interestingly, for $0 < v < 1$ risk aversion is implied. The Pratt–Arrow measures of absolute and relative risk aversion derived for the function in Eq. (5) are

$$R_A = -U''(Y)/U'(Y) = (1-v)/Y > 0$$
$$\qquad\qquad\qquad\qquad\qquad\qquad\qquad \text{when } 0 < v < 1, \tag{7}$$
$$R_R = -Y\{U''(Y)/U'(Y)\} = (1-v) > 0$$

respectively; they decrease and remain invariant with increasing wealth.

The family of iso-expected utility contours to which Eq. (6a) gives rise may be conveniently mapped in $(\overline{Y}, \rho_Y)$-space.[15] As Fig. 1 indicates, for the case of risk aversion the typical contour $E(U)_0$ is upward sloping and concave to the $\overline{Y}$-axis. Successively higher expected utility contours intercept the

---

Tsiang (1972), showing that neglecting terms involving moments higher than the variance is justified when the *relative* variance is small. On the unsatisfactory implications of appealing to a quadratic utility function, namely, that $U(Y)$ declines absolutely after some Y and that the absolute and relative degree of risk aversion *increases* with Y, cf. Arrow (1965, Chap. 3) and the amplification provided by Roberts (1971, pp. 14–20).

[15] The mapping in Fig. 1 follows immediately from total differentiation of Eq. (6a), for $0 < v < 1$. From this we obtain:

(a) $$\left.\frac{d\rho}{d\overline{Y}}\right|_{E(U)_0} = 2/(1-v)\, E(U)_0\, [\overline{Y}]^{-(1+v)} > 0.$$

(b) $$\left.\frac{d^2\rho}{d\overline{Y}^2}\right|_{E(U)_0} = -2E(U)_0\, [\overline{Y}]^{v+2} < 0.$$

(c) $$\lim \left.\frac{d\rho}{d\overline{Y}}\right|_{\rho_Y = 0} \to 0 \quad \text{since} \quad \left.\frac{d\rho}{d\overline{Y}}\right|_{\rho_Y = 0} = 2/(1-v)[\overline{Y}]^{-1}.$$

(d) Setting the expression in (a) equal for different $E(U)_1 > E(U)_0 \Rightarrow \overline{Y}_1 > \overline{Y}_0$, which indicates the contours are not parallel w.r.t. the $\overline{Y}$-axis.

abscissa at successively larger values of $\overline{Y}$, exhibiting smaller and smaller slopes at those interceptions—and indeed at any given level of $\rho_Y < 1/v$. Another notable feature exhibited by Fig. 1 is that these contours are not

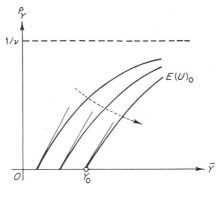

FIG. 1

parallel with reference to the $\overline{Y}$-axis: in the limit they all have a common upper bound at $1/v$, and the absolute vertical gap between any pair diminishes as $\overline{Y} \to \infty$. Of course, in the case of risk neutrality, the relevant iso-expected utility contours become a system of (parallel) lines perpendicular to the $\overline{Y}$ axis.

c. Payoff Functions for the Search Process

When Y_0 and P are known with certainty, and the household cannot spend more on migration and search than its prespecified budget limit $\bar{s}Y_0$, the expected gross increment in wealth bears the following relationship to expected terminal wealth $\overline{Y}$, as may be seen from Eq. (1):

$$E[y_{ijk}] = \overline{Y}_{ijk} - Y_{0k}(1 - \bar{s}_k) - P_{ijk}. \tag{8}$$

As has been previously shown, for continuous distributions of non-negative finite wage offers, the component of $E[y]$ relating to the expected gain from actually searching the ith market—the difference between the prevailing average offer, $\mu_i = E[w_i]$, and the expected maximum offer obtained—turns out to be a positive, concave function of n, the number of offers collected. For any given level of $n > 1$, this expected "pure gain from search" increases with σ_i^2, the variance of the underlying offer distribution. These properties also hold when the stochastic variate w_i is unbounded but follows a Gaussian distribution; consideration of the expression for the first moment of the extreme value distribution of a normal variate (cf. the Appendix) suggests specifying a function in which there is a positive interaction between the effects of n and σ_i^2 upon the expected maximum wage offer:

$$E[_iw_{max}] = \mu_i + B\sigma_i n^\beta, \qquad 0 < \beta < 1. \tag{9a}$$

Taking the expectation of y_{ijk} in Eq. (2) and making the appropriate substitution, we have

$$E[y_{ijk}] = R_k[\mu_i - \mu_j] + R_k[B\sigma_i n^\beta]. \tag{9b}$$

Next, consider the variance of Y_{ijk}, σ_Y^2. Since Y_{ijk} is distributed as y_{ijk}, making use of Eq. (2) again yields

$$\sigma_Y^2 = var[y_{ijk}] = var[R_k\{_iw_{max} - \mu_j\}] = R_k^2\, var[_iw_{max}]. \tag{10}$$

Clearly the variance of the extreme value should decrease as the size of the sample increases, and should be larger, the larger the variance of the underlying distribution. Reference once more to the extreme value distribution of a normal variate (in the Appendix) suggests a multiplicative specification analogous to that in Eq. (9a):

$$var[_iw_{max}] = A\sigma_i^2 n^{-\alpha}, \qquad \alpha > 0. \tag{11}$$

d. The "Dispersion–Opportunities Boundary"

For a potential migrant situated in the jth locale, the highest $\hat\sigma_i$ characterizing any of the local labor markets that he can reach by moving a distance of D_{ij} may be denoted by $\hat\sigma_i$. The boundary of *maximum* dispersion within his reach is thus delimited by the function $\hat\sigma_{ij} = f_j(D_{ij})$.

Now suppose $f_j(\cdot)$ is itself bounded from above at σ_{max} (there being some finite limit to the real or imagined level of disorder in local labor markets), as well as being necessarily bounded from below at σ_j. Then if the optimal strategy always called for a migrant to be on the $f_j(\cdot)$ boundary if he moved at all, we could represent $\sigma_{ij} = \hat\sigma_{ij}$ in any migration–search plan as a *quasi-concave* function of D_{ij}.[16] Yet, in order to assure that any optimum solution to the migrant's problem will be a *global* optimum, and to facilitate recourse to the differential calculus in locating such optima, rather stronger assumptions are required. The boundary function $f_j(D_{ij})$ is taken here to be continuous, twice-differentiable, and strictly concave in D_{ij}.[17]

---

[16] $f(x)$ is quasi-concave if $f(x) \geqslant f(x^0)$ implies $f[\xi x + (1-\xi)x^0] \geqslant f(x^0)$, $0 \leqslant \xi \leqslant 1$. Thus, the solution to the migrant's problem is more naturally tackled as an exercise in quasi-concave programming [cf. Arrow and Enthoven (1961)], rather than as an application (here) of the standard Kuhn–Tucker–Lagrange conditions.

[17] Cf. Part III. The interpretation suggested is that (σ_{ij}/μ_i) is an increasing function of city size, and the size of the largest city that can be reached from any fixed point increases with the distance moved, up to a maximum level. The specification of the spatial uniformity of $\mu_i = \mu$, in (18), makes this interpretation consistent with writing σ_i as a function of D_{ij}.

A convenient specification satisfying these and also the aforementioned boundedness requirements is given by the following expression:

$$\hat{\sigma}_{ij} = \sigma_{\max}[1 - \gamma_j\, e^{-\theta D}ij], \qquad \theta > 0, \tag{12}$$

where

$$\gamma_j = [1 - \{\sigma_j/\sigma_{\max}\}] \geqslant 0.$$

This function, it should be noted, actually generates an entire family of consistent $f_j(\cdot)$ boundaries, one for every $\sigma_j \in [0, \sigma_{\max}]$. Although such consistency is highly artificial, it thereby facilitates discussion of the optimal migration–search strategy applicable to a household situated initially at any jth place within a spatial system.[18] The essential purpose this specification fulfills in the model is to ensure that for a migrant constrained by the boundary function, i.e., when $\sigma_{ij} = \hat{\sigma}_{ij}$, the marginal cost of access to "wage-offer dispersion" (measured by σ_i) is continuously increasing in every direction, from any arbitrarily chosen point of departure within the system. Denoting this marginal cost by $mc_{\sigma ij}$, and the marginal pecuniary cost of migration travel by $C_2'(D_{ij})$—as in Subsection e, below—it is clear from the following definitional relationship that plausibly assuming constancy (or even decline) in the latter will not be inconsistent with requiring increases in the former:

$$mc_{\sigma ij} \equiv \frac{C_2'(D_{ij})}{F'(D_{ij})} = \frac{C_2'(D_{ij})}{\theta \sigma_{\max}\gamma_j} \exp(\theta D_{ij})$$

$$= \{C_2'(D_{ij})\}/\{\theta(\sigma_{\max} - \hat{\sigma}_{ij})\}. \tag{13}$$

e. Budget Constraint and Cost Functions

The investment budget restriction pertains only to the pecuniary outlays on migration and job-search activities, although these embrace both out-of-pocket expenses and forgone earnings:[19]

$$\bar{s}Y_0 \geqslant C_1{}^i(n) + C_2{}^j(D_{ij}). \tag{14}$$

$C_1{}^i(n)$ represents the total variable cost of the search activity required to elicit n job offers—at some positive wage rate—in the ith (destination) labor market. $C_2{}^j(D)$ represents the total variable cost of the migration activity required to relocate at a distance D from the jth (origin) market.

---

[18] The spatial system that affords such consistency is rather extraordinary. One must first imagine a population distributed in places that are arranged, by ascending place size, in successive rings surrounding a single, central city. The routes leading toward the largest city are like the spokes of a wheel and pass through larger and larger cities, but city size rises less and less as the distance from the rim is lengthened. Upon this configuration one may then impose the stipulation that place size and the degree of dispersion, σ_i are linearly related (positively).

[19] Capital losses sustained in quitting a job or leaving a residence are thereby excluded from the scope of the budget limitation.

Now in order to collect n positive offers, it will in general be necessary to anticipate visiting N prospective employers, where $n/N = \Phi(V_i) \in [0, 1]$, is simply the average probability of there being at least one job vacancy at a place of employment visited. We shall assume that $\Phi(V_i)$ is regarded as a parameter by the kth household; its level varies positively with the positive or negative overall vacancy rate, V_i, prevailing in the ith market on a typical search day; i.e., $\Phi'(V_i) > 0$.[20] If each visit in the ith market may be supposed to require from all individuals a standard amount of time, $t_{ik} = t_i$, the anticipated time forgone per job offer secured is merely a transform of $\Phi(\cdot)$: $\phi_i = t_i[\Phi(V_i)]^{-1}$. For simplicity it will be assumed that the value of the searcher's time constitutes the only element of cost incurred in hunting for work, and that the potential migrant planning his strategy for the ith market will value his fixed commitment of search time at the unit opportunity cost equal to the expected wage rate he would earn were he simply to accept the first proposition put to him and not bother conducting any real search at all. In the ith destination the relevant unit opportunity cost obviously would be μ_i. Hence we can represent $C_1{}^i(n)$ as the linear function,

$$C_1{}^i(n) = \omega_i n, \qquad (15)$$

where

$$\omega_i = (\mu_i/\Phi_i)t_i, \qquad \Phi_i'(V_i) > 0. \qquad (16)$$

The corresponding (linear) specification of $C_2{}^j(D)$ is

$$C_2{}^j(D_{ij}) = \tau_j D_{ij}, \qquad (17)$$

where τ_j, the marginal cost of moving from j to some destination i, a total distance of D_{ij}, is taken to be constant.[21]

For the sake of generality it would be entirely possible to allow different locales to be more or less advantageous as embarkation points; Eq. (17) thus indexes the (constant) marginal cost of distance according to the ith place of origin. This is analogous to the "place effects" which may be exerted upon $C_1'(n)$—the marginal cost of search, or, more strictly the marginal cost of

[20] The vacancy rate may be defined for these purposes as the number of job openings (at positive wage rates) per searcher. Obviously the *equilibrium* level of V_i will be affected by the number of migrants searching the ith market, but the focus here is upon the individual (supply) response and not the general equilibrium of the system.

[21] The unit (marginal) cost of distance moved from j, τ_j includes (1) expenditures for transportation net of consumption satisfactions derived from travel, and (2) forgone earnings during the time spent in transit. For many historical migrations, and especially for long-distance movements these cost elements are not inconsequential. Note that the co-existence of fast and slow transport modes for journeys of equal distance suggests that the *sum* of forgone earnings and transportation expenses per mile τ is rather more uniform with distance than consideration of travel fare schedules alone would imply.

eliciting nonzero wage offers—by particular levels of the average offer and the vacancy rate that prevail in the ith destination market. For heuristic reasons, however, it is desirable to thoroughly suppress all such "place effects" on the cost side of migration and search activity, thereby throwing into clearer relief the impact of "place effects" (due to varying degrees of dispersion in the distribution of offers) upon the gains to be expected from such investments and the variance therein. *Throughout the ensuing discussion, therefore, the following sweeping set of spatial price-uniformity conditions will be maintained:*

$$\left.\begin{array}{l} \mu_i = \mu_j = \mu \\ t_i = t \\ \Phi(V_i) = \Phi(V) \\ \tau_j = \tau \end{array}\right\} \left.\begin{array}{c} \phi_i = \phi \end{array}\right\} \left.\begin{array}{c} \omega_i = \omega \end{array}\right\} \quad \Omega_{ij} \equiv \omega_i / \tau_j = \Omega \qquad (18)$$

The novel aspects of the model should become evident from the fact that a full analysis of migration behavior will be carried out here, suggesting explanations of many observed phenomena entirely in terms of the (partial equilibrium) responses by the representative household, all under the assumption that there exist no actual or perceived differences whatsoever among the expected wage offers and vacancy rates prevailing in local labor markets.

f. The Maximand and a Necessary Condition for Voluntary Migration

It is now a straightforward matter to depict the household's objective as the maximization of $E[U(Y)]$ with respect to its choice of a migration–search strategy, subject to the financial limitations of its budget and the topographical constraints imposed by its initial location and the shape of the "dispersion–opportunities" frontier. Thus, we have the problem

$$\max_{(n,\, D_{ij})} F,$$

where F is a Lagrangian expression,

$$F = E[U(Y_{ij})] + \lambda_1 [\bar{s}Y_0 - C_1(n) - C_2(D_{ij}) - x_1]$$
$$+ \lambda_2 [\sigma_i - \sigma_{max}\{1 - \gamma_j \exp(-\theta D_{ij})\} + x_2], \qquad (19)$$

in which x_1 and x_2 are implicitly defined "slack variables":

$$x_1 = (\bar{s} - s)Y_0 \geqslant 0, \qquad x_2 = (\hat{\sigma}_{ij} - \sigma_i) \geqslant 0. \qquad (20)$$

If one asks what is required for our rational household to decide to depart to place j for i, it is clear that it must find a solution to this problem involving an optimal strategy: (n^*, D_{ij}^*), $n^* D_{ij}^* > 0$. But that is not enough, for the "best" migration–search plan must also lead to any *interior* maximum in the sense of improving upon the household's original welfare position. If, as we have assumed, the initial wealth of the household is "sure," this necessary condition for voluntary emigration takes the form:

$$E[U(Y_{ijk}^*)] - U(Y_{0k}) > 0. \tag{21}$$

Substituting into Eq. (21) from Eqs. (5) and (6a), we see plausibly enough that it is equivalent to

$$\overline{Y}_{ijk}^*(1 - v\rho_Y^*)^{1/v} > Y_{0k}, \tag{21a}$$

i.e., the expected terminal wealth of the emigrant household, appropriately discounted for the associated rel-variance (ρ_Y^*) when $v < 1$, should at very least exceed its initial wealth.

By this point it will have become apparent that as conceived here the household's problem of selecting an optimal migration–search strategy is isomorphic with a class of constrained maximization problems encountered in the theory of the firm. There are, in effect, two outputs, $\overline{Y}$ and ρ_Y—or the latter's complement $(1 - \rho_Y)$—which might loosely be called "security." Each of the outputs is generated as a joint product, in accord with production constraints specified in Sections 3a, c, and d, using a combination of the two inputs: distance moved (D) and search intensity (n). Together the outputs will yield a "revenue," in accord with the implicit pricing rules indicated by a "joint revenue function"—the direct analog of which is the function $E[U(Y)]$ specified in Section 3b.[22] Given a linear budget constraint (see Section 3f) the enterprise is to maximize short run profits by choosing an optimal, i.e., revenue maximizing combination of n^* and D^*. Since we assume the firm has the option to produce nothing at all and to thereby avoid incurring any costs, the only revenue-maximizing solutions of interest as a prescription for action are those which yield a positive surplus. Reference to this isomorphism proves useful in locating significant landmarks in a *seemingly* new terrain; to find one's way, it will be sufficient to follow some rather well-known maps.

Most immediately, it indicates two likely lines that may be pursued in analyzing the optimal allocation of investment between migration and search activities. One is to focus on the least-cost combinations of the inputs n and D, and to identify the point in (n, D)-space at which the budget ("isocost outlay") line intersects the "least-cost input expansion path." Along the latter locus one expects there should obtain conditions analogous to those encountered in the theory of production: Equate the ratio of marginal costs of the inputs to the ratio of their respective marginal revenue products. The

---

[22] A more direct parallel is furnished by regarding ρ_Y as a noxious by-product of $\overline{Y}$. ρ_Y carries a negative shadow price, since the enterprise will be obliged to use some marketable output ($\overline{Y}$) to either dispose of ρ_Y itself or compensate for its presence.

groundwork for this analysis is laid in Section 3g, which develops the first-order conditions for max F.

An alternative tack exists, however. Given the budget constraint, the $f(D)$-boundary, and the functions describing the payoffs from the stochastic search process, one may consider the analog of the output transformation frontier in $(\overline{Y}, \rho_Y)$-space. This locus, which describes the maximum level of security (or minimum ρ_Y) that can be obtained with any given $\overline{Y}$ by allocating a fixed budget between purchases of n and D, is conveniently referred to as the household's "migration–search opportunities frontier" (MSOF). An optimal solution, viewed from this vantage point, would correspond to a production situation in which the marginal rate of transformation (i.e., the $\overline{Y} - \rho_Y$ "tradeoff" dictated by production conditions) was equated with the inverse of the ratio of marginal revenues generated by the outputs. This would render the marginal rates of revenue transformation equal: the incremental revenue gained by shifting the mix of inputs to obtain more of one output (say, expected wealth) is just counterbalanced by the loss occasioned by the reduction of the other positively valued output (security). But it is equally possible to present the same story in the framework of a model of portfolio choice, each efficient migration–search strategy being described by a point in mean $(\overline{Y})$, rel-variance ρ_Y space. This heuristically attractive approach, which has the virtue of emphasizing that the migrant's decision problem is one involving investment under uncertainty, is developed in Section 3h, where it will be seen to lead quite naturally to the identification of necessary and sufficient conditions for the existence of a unique interior optimum solution.

g. First-Order Conditions for max F

The Kuhn–Tucker–Lagrange conditions for a solution to the optimization problem stated in Eq. (19) take the general form:

$$n^*[\partial F/\partial n] = 0; \tag{22a}$$

$$\sigma_i{}^*[\partial F/\partial \sigma_i] = 0; \tag{22b}$$

$$D_{ij}^*[\partial F/\partial D_{ij}] = 0; \tag{22c}$$

$$\partial F/\partial \lambda_1 = 0; \tag{22d}$$

$$\partial F/\partial \lambda_2 = 0; \tag{22e}$$

$$x_1{}^*[\partial F/\partial x_1] = 0; \tag{22f}$$

$$x_2{}^*[\partial F/\partial x_2] = 0. \tag{22g}$$

Evaluating (22a, b, and c), the explicit conditions obtained may be stated in terms of n^* and σ_i^* as follows:

$$\frac{n^*}{\overline{Y}} \frac{\partial \overline{Y}}{\partial n} H_1 = \lambda_1 \omega n^* - \alpha H_2, \tag{23}$$

$$\frac{\sigma_i^*}{\overline{Y}} \frac{\partial \overline{Y}}{\partial \sigma_i} H_1 = \lambda_1 \sigma_i^* \{mc_\sigma\} + 2H_2, \tag{24}$$

where we define

$$H_1 \equiv vE[U(Y)] + 2v\rho_Y; \qquad H_2 \equiv v\rho_Y, \tag{25}$$

$$\text{s.t.: } H_1 = v\{1 - H_2\}\overline{Y}^v + 2H_2.$$

Note, from Eqs. (13) and (17), that

$$mc_\sigma = \tau \{\exp[\theta D_{ij}]\}/\{\theta\gamma_j \sigma_{\max}\}; \tag{26}$$

and, further, that from Eqs. (6a), (8), and (9b), by partial differentiation we obtain the relationship

$$n^* \frac{\partial E[U]}{\partial n} = \frac{n^*}{\overline{Y}} \frac{\partial \overline{Y}}{\partial n} H_1 + \alpha H_2, \tag{27}$$

whereas, from Eqs. (6a), (10), and (11) by similar substitutions and partial differentiation, we have

$$\sigma_i^* \frac{E[U]}{\partial \sigma_i} = \frac{\sigma_i^*}{\overline{Y}} \frac{\partial \overline{Y}}{\partial \sigma_i} H_1 - 2H_2. \tag{28}$$

A straightforward economic interpretation of Eq. (23) is therefore available. First, making use of Eq. (27), we immediately obtain the condition $\partial E[U]/\partial n^* = \lambda_1 \omega$. But the Lagrangian multiplier λ_1 is in effect the "shadow price" of the budget constraint, and thus equals the marginal utility of wealth in the neighborhood of the "certain" endowment Y_0:

$$\lambda_1 = U'(Y_0) = \left.\frac{\partial E[U]}{\partial \overline{Y}}\right|_{\overline{Y}=Y_0} \tag{29}$$

Thus, Eq. (23) says that for an optimum solution, the expected utility gain from incrementally increasing n should be equated to the marginal cost of search evaluated in utility space, i.e., the expected utility represented by the certain expenditure of wealth required in order to collect an additional non-zero offer. Equations (28) and (29) give us a comparably transparent reading of the second necessary condition for an optimum, as stated by Eq. (24): the change in expected utility from access to marginally greater intramarket wage dispersion should be set equal to the entailed marginal intramarket migration costs (mc_σ)—evaluating the latter as "sure" expenditures.

The evaluation of Eqs. (22d) and (22e) simply recovers the equality formulation, respectively, of the budget constraint

$$\bar{s}Y_0 = \omega n^* + \tau D^*_{ij} + x_1{}^*$$ (30)

and of the dispersion–opportunities boundary

$$\sigma_i{}^* = \sigma_{max}[1 - \gamma_j \exp\{-\theta D^*_{ij}\}] + x_2{}^*.$$ (31)

Finally, from Equations (22f) and (22g) we obtain the conditions on the optimal values of the slack variables $x_1{}^*$ and $x_2{}^*$ when both the constraints in the Lagrangian expression are binding:

$$\left.\begin{array}{r} -x_1{}^*\lambda_1 = 0, \\ x_2{}^*\lambda_2 = 0, \end{array}\right\} \quad x_1{}^* = x_2{}^* = 0, \quad \text{when} \quad \left\{\begin{array}{l} \lambda_1 \neq 0, \\ \lambda_2 \neq 0. \end{array}\right.$$ (32)

The argument that was advanced in Section 3d regarding the quasi-concavity of σ_i in D_{ij} turned on the proposition that σ_i would be set equal to $\hat{\sigma}_i$ where the latter necessarily was a quasi-concave boundary, namely, the maximum σ_i attainable for any given D_{ij}. Hence more than usual interest attaches to showing that the optimum requires $x_2{}^* = 0$ without assuming that $\lambda_2 \neq 0$. This point is readily proved by contradiction: Suppose that $\lambda_2 = 0$. Then, as evaluating condition (22) alone leads to

$$-\lambda_1 = \{mc_\sigma\}^{-1}\lambda_2,$$ (33)

and as $mc_\sigma > 0$ everywhere, $\lambda_2 = 0$ implies $\lambda_1 = 0$. Now, imposing the latter in Eqs. (23) and (24) and solving the resulting expressions, gives rise to the statement,

$$\frac{\partial \bar{Y}}{\partial n} = -\left\{\frac{\sigma_i{}^*}{2n}\right\}\frac{\partial \bar{Y}}{\partial \sigma_i}.$$

Yet, from Eqs. (8) and (9b), by partial differentiation, it is found that

$$\frac{\partial \bar{Y}}{\partial n} = \left\{\beta\frac{\sigma_i{}^*}{n}\right\}\frac{\partial \bar{Y}}{\partial \sigma_i}.$$ (34)

Hence, allowing solutions where $\lambda_2 = 0$ would force us to accept the implication that $\alpha = -2\beta$, in clear contradition of the specification (Section 3c) that α and β both are nonnegative. The preceding first-order conditions for an optimum yield meaningful results only when the Lagrangian multipliers λ_1 and λ_2 are positive, and the slack variables in the constraints are set at zero.

Plausibly enough, in the set of efficient strategies, choices of n^* and $\sigma_i{}^*$ turn out to be positively related. And, since σ_i is an increasing, concave function of D_{ij}, this means that in any pair of strategies the one calling for the longer distance move will also call for the more intensive search upon arrival. The first of these propositions is immediately seen upon dividing Eq. (24) by (23) and solving the quotient with Eq. (33) to obtain

$$\omega n^* = \beta [\{mc_{\sigma_i}\} \sigma_i^*] + (2\beta + \alpha)\left\{\frac{v}{\lambda_1}\right\} \rho_Y. \tag{35}$$

The term involving σ_i may then be written as an increasing, convex function of D_{ij}:

$$\{mc_{\sigma_i}\} \sigma_i = Z(D_{ij}) = \frac{\tau}{\theta}\left\{\frac{\exp(\theta D_{ij})}{\gamma_j} - 1\right\}, \tag{36}$$

where

$$Z'(D_{ij}) = \theta Z(D_{ij}) + \tau > 0$$
$$Z''(D_{ij}) = \{Z'(D_{ij})\}/\theta > 0 \qquad \text{because} \quad \theta > 0.$$

Application of the inverse function rule tells us that a mapping—in (n, D)-space—of the "input expansion path" implied by (35) and (36) will exhibit D_{ij}^* as a positively sloped concave function of n^*. (See Fig. 3a for the general picture.)

Turning now to consider the special case of risk-neutrality, it should be apparent that the first-order conditions stated as Eqs. (30), (31), and (32) continue to apply generally, but those given by Eqs. (27) and (28) will assume a simpler form. Recalling that for the risk-neutral individual $v = 1$ in Eq. (5), and therefore $v = 0$, in the definitional equations (25) we now find $H_1 = \bar{Y}$ and $H_2 = 0$. Consequently, Eqs. (23) and (24) are reduced, respectively, to

$$\{\partial \bar{Y}/\partial n\}_N = \lambda_1 \omega, \tag{37}$$

and

$$\{\partial \bar{Y}/\partial \sigma_i\}_N = \lambda_1 \{mc_{\sigma_i}\}. \tag{38}$$

Since the multiplier λ_1 represents the marginal utility of the investment constraint and is equivalent to $U'(Y)|_{Y_0}$, for $v = 1$ (the case of risk neutrality), we have $\lambda_1 = 1$. Equation (37) thus says that for an optimum the marginal effect of local search upon expected wealth should be equated to ω, the (constant) marginal cost of search—the first-order condition for the choice of an optimal fixed sample size, made familiar by the work of Stigler (1962). Analogously, Eq. (38) tells us that the risk-neutral migrant should move to the point in the system at which the marginal effect upon his expected terminal wealth of access to greater wage-offer dispersion (σ_i) just equals the marginal cost of σ_i.

Evaluating the partial derivatives in these conditions, we have $\partial \bar{Y}/\partial n = \{\beta \bar{y}\}/n$ and $\partial \bar{Y}/\partial \sigma_i = \bar{y}/\sigma_i$. Equation (37) thus becomes equivalent to the rule that the optimal outlay (ωn^*) for local job search should equal the fraction β of the gross increment in expected wealth ($\bar{y}$); correspondingly, the shadow valuation of the degree of dispersion attained at the global maximum, i.e., $\sigma_i^* \{mc_{\sigma_i}\}$—evaluating σ_i at the (increasing) marginal cost of reaching the market so characterized—should be set equal to the entire gross increment in expected wealth, or the multiple $1/\beta$ of the outlay on local job search. These relationships hold along the least-cost input expansion path defined by the following risk-neutral counterpart to Eqs. (35) and (36):[23]

$$\omega n_N^* = \beta \{mc_{\sigma_i}\} \sigma_i^* = \beta \{Z(D_{ijN}^*)\}. \tag{39}$$

Mapped in (n, D)-space, this describes a path with the same general features that appear in the case of the risk-averse household: it is positively sloped and concave to the n axis.[24] But as we shall see, the two paths are not the same.

h. A Portfolio Choice Representation and Some Immediate Implications

Every migration–search plan, as we have seen, gives rise to a probability distribution of the migrant's terminal wealth, of which the mean ($\bar{Y}$) and rel-variance (ρ_Y) are of the most immediate concern in the choice of an optimal plan—given the approximation proposed for the household's expected utility function. The subset of *efficient* (or expected utility dominant) migration–search plans is comprised of those which, for a fixed outlay $\bar{s}Y_0$, minimize the level of ρ_Y that accompanies each attainable level of $\bar{Y}$: the locus of such points in ($\bar{Y}, \rho_Y$)-space describes the MSOF.

In Fig. 2a such a frontier, labeled OF, has been drawn (a) positively sloped, (b) convex to the $\bar{Y}$-axis, and (c) intercepting the latter at the positive point $Y_0(1 - \bar{s}) - P$. It represents the efficient alternatives available to a household initially situated in a region where there is no underlying dispersion of wage offers, i.e., where $\sigma_j = 0$. Were the entire migration–search budget $\bar{s}Y_0$ to be devoted exclusively to local job search, leaving nothing to be spent on purchasing access to dispersion (i.e., on migration), the outcome would be that represented by the point of the intersection of OF with the $\bar{Y}$-axis; all the pecuniary and psychic costs ($Y_0\bar{s} + P$) would be incurred without deriving any offsetting benefits in terms of gross additions to wealth. Starting from this point and allocating some expenditures to migration activity (therefore

---

[23] This is obtained by dividing Eq. (37) into (38) and solving the quotient with Eq. (34).

[24] Implicit differentiation of (39), using the sign conditions on the $Z'(D)$ and $Z''(D)$ from Eq. (36) gives us the immediate results

$$dn^*/dD^* > 0 \quad \text{and} \quad d^2n^*/dD^{*2} > 0.$$

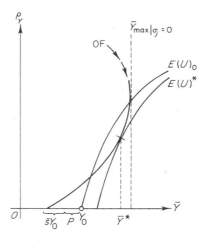

FIG. 2a

reducing n), $\bar{Y}$ may be raised, but so too will ρ_Y.[25] But because the marginal cost of σ_i is rising and further increases in underlying offer dispersion are thus bought only at the expense of more and more marked reductions in the intensity of local search, it will come to pass eventually, at $\bar{Y}_{max}$ corresponding to $(\hat{n}, \hat{D}_{ij})$, that expected terminal wealth ceases to rise; thereafter $\bar{Y}$ would actually be reduced by further increases in D_{ij}.

For any $\sigma_j < \sigma_{max}$, when no more than the total initial wealth of the household is committed to emigration and job search [i.e., when $(1 - \bar{s})Y_0 > P$], the convexity of the MSOF to the $\bar{Y}$-axis throughout its positively sloped range is guaranteed if the parameters α and β satisfy two restrictions: $0 < \beta < 1$, and $2\beta < \alpha$. The Appendix proves that this second limitation—requiring the elasticity with respect to n of the second moment of the extreme value distribution to be more than twice the magnitude of the elasticity with respect to n of the first moment—is sufficient for the convexity of the MSOF under the stated conditions. In the same place it is also pointed out that the extreme value distribution generated by random sampling from a normal population would satisfy the indicated restrictions.

From Fig. 2a it is plain that the existence of a positively sloped, convex opportunity frontier, coupled with the concavity of the typical iso-$E[U]$ contour previously introduced, is enough to ensure that if there is a point of

[25] The rise in ρ_Y proceeds from the combined effect of raising σ_i (while necessarily reducing n) upon σ_Y^2, causing the latter to increase more rapidly than the denominator of the rel-variance, $\bar{Y}^2$. [Cf. the Appendix, where the same mapping is performed (Fig. 7) using n as the mapping variable.]

tangency between these two it will be unique and will define the solution at which max $E[U] = E[U^*]$ is attained. The restrictions on α and β ensuring the convexity of MSOF thus guarantees that a solution in terms of positive values of n^* and D_{ij}^* satisfying the first-order conditions in Section 3g will automatically represent the *global maximum* point. This is not to say that there must always exist a tangency solution such as $(\overline{Y}^*, \rho_Y^*)$ in Fig. 2a, for the slope of MSOF could conceivably be everywhere greater than the slope of the iso-expected utility contours. Nor does it mean that any tangency point that exists must constitute an *interior* maximum, in the sense of implying an improvement over the initial welfare of the household can be achieved by expenditures on migration and job search. The graphical analog of the necessary condition for an interior maximum stated by Eq. (21a) is that the $E[U_0]$ contour—the one passing through the initial, "sure" wealth position described by $(Y_0, 0)$—must be intersected from below by the MSOF;[26] although this is the case in Fig. 2a, we should not expect it to be so as a general rule. Indeed, as students of migration behavior, what we want to establish is precisely how various personal and general economic circumstances dictate whether it will or will not be possible for the household to effect some improvement in its welfare by moving rather than remaining put.

Of course, one such conclusion—some intimation of which has already been given—may now be read directly from Fig. 2a: Risk aversion, although not militating absolutely against emigration, must be less conducive to such decisions than is an attitude of neutrality toward risk. For a risk-neutral individual, the necessary condition for an interior maximum involving migration is comparatively easier to meet: It would be satisfied if the MSOF simply intersected a line perpendicular to the $\overline{Y}$-axis at Y_0. Further, in the case of the risk-neutral migrant, the global optimum would evidently be attained (within the limits of the standard budget $\bar{s}Y_0$) at $\overline{Y}_{max} > \overline{Y}^*$. This implies an optimal strategy that, by comparison with the risk averter's, entails a longer move and therefore a rather less-intensive search of the destination market; but the implication is not utterly obvious and the subject of the effect of the degree of risk aversion on the mix of n^* and D^* will be taken up more explicitly in the following section.

The special case of potential migrants located where $\sigma_j = 0$ is convenient for purposes of graphical exposition because the representation of the limiting

---

[26] If we imagine individuals as holding "certain" jobs, no matter what their initial location, and if Y_0 is their initial wealth, it cannot be worthwhile forgoing their initial situation in favor of some other local market unless the MSOF cuts $E[U_0]$ from below. In the case displayed in Fig. 2a, the absence of any dispersion in wage offers available at the initial location makes it unnecessary to distinguish between potential migrants who initially hold sure jobs and those who do not.

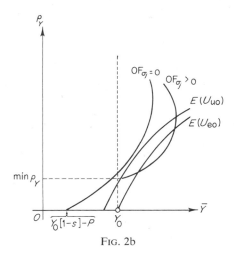

FIG. 2b

strategy $(n^*, D_{ij}^*) = (\bar{s}Y_0/\omega, 0)$ as the point $\{Y_0(1-\bar{s})-P\}$ on the $\bar{Y}$-axis is clear-cut. When a higher minimal $\sigma_j > 0$ is available without any movement from the origin market, the relevant MSOF is displaced upward and to the right, as shown in Fig. 2b.[27] In addition, it may be seen that the opportunity frontier for $\sigma_j = 0$ is dominated by MSOF $(\sigma_j > 0)$ over its entire domain. Given identical investment budgets, the households at the location where there is some underlying dispersion of wage offers are, *ex hypothesis*, within closer reach of the σ_{max}-labor market; for them any given level of n will imply a higher $\bar{Y}$ than that obtaining in the case of potential migrants situated where σ_j lies closer to zero.

The implication is that, *ceteris paribus*, initial location in lower dispersion markets tends to discourage movement—considering the latter without regard to the actual distances moved. For risk averters who do not hold a "sure job," there is obviously some loss of welfare attached to starting out in, say, an urban market where (by assumption) the expected wage offer is no greater than elsewhere, but where the rel-variance of the distribution of offers exceeds that prevailing in the rural districts. But by the same token, since the urban dweller with the same means at his disposal can afford a more intensive local search for every level of wage-offer dispersion he might attain, migration toward markets characterized by higher σ_i will be comparatively more attractive for him than for his country cousin. As Fig. 2b shows, the worker with an initial endowment of Y_0 would find it advantageous to emigrate from the market where $\sigma_j > 0$, but to stay where $\sigma_j = 0$. *On this argument alone* it

---

[27] The position of the point of minimal $\rho_Y > 0$ shown for $OF\,(\sigma_j > 0)$ reflects the fact that with $\bar{s}Y_0$ allocated entirely to n, both σ_Y^2 and $E[y]$ are *positive*; whereas in the case $\sigma_j = 0$ both are zero.

seems we should expect higher frequencies of migration to appear in the more thoroughly urbanized socieities, at least by comparison with settled, predominantly rural societies where the mass of the working population was hired in markets characterized by a relatively low dispersion of wage offers.[28]

4. Determinants of the Effective Demand for Investment in Migration and Search

How are the decision whether or not to emigrate and the choice a migrant makes along alternative available relocation–search strategies affected by various personal characteristics such as the degree of risk aversion, the level of initial wealth and the limit set on investment outlays for such purposes, the length of the individual's remaining working life, and his employment status? How will these same decisions be influenced by alterations in global, economy-wide conditions (contrasted with personal or local circumstances) such as will manifest themselves in the prevailing levels of job vacancy rates and of the real marginal costs of search throughout the whole array of local labor markets?

We shall confine ourselves to considering populations of potential migrants who are individually constrained by fixed investment budgets—the budgets either being taken to be identical for all, or assumed to vary within the population according to a predetermined distribution, as suits the convenience of the argument. It is then a reasonably straightforward matter to review the ways in which the existence of an interior maximum, and the optimal mix of n and D are governed by the foregoing "personal" and "market" variables. One should bear in mind, however, that the conclusions reached in this analysis form only a part of the picture that is relevant to the empirical study of migration phenomena. For, these very same factors also exercise an influence upon the total amount of resources that given households would desire to invest in migration and search activities if they were afforded access to perfect capital markets. Such (long-run) effects via the determination of the optimal investment level may in some instances even be qualitatively different from those exhibited (in the short run) when the household's investment budget has been more or less arbitrarily predetermined.

a. Effects of Risk Aversion

Risk aversion patently renders migration toward markets characterized by higher wage-offer dispersions a less attractive, less welfare-enhancing prospect than it would otherwise be. This much already has been indicated

---

[28] Remember that among the items impounded in the *ceteris paribus* statement we have the maintained hypothesis that no spatial differences exist in either of these "societies" as far as average wage offers or expected vacancy rates are concerned.

as an immediate conclusion from the analysis represented in Figs. 2a and b. But what of the effects upon the allocation of resources by those who do find migration worthwhile?

The risk averter will have a set of dominant migration–search strategies $\Psi(n^*, D^*)$, which is unambiguously more search-intensive than the corresponding set $\Psi_N(n^*, D^*)$ defined for the risk-neutral migrant. The sets Ψ and Ψ_N are, of course, the input expansion paths described by Eqs. (35, 36, and 39), respectively. And from these it follows that there must exist a positive difference $\Delta n^* \equiv n^* - n_N^*$ between the amounts of search activity that would be combined with a move of a given distance by a risk averter on the one hand, and a risk-neutral individual on the other. Concretely, subtracting Eq. (39) from (35) yields

$$\Delta n^* = \frac{\beta}{\omega}[Z(D_{ij}^*) - Z(D_{ij}^*)_N] + \left\{ \frac{2\beta + \alpha}{\omega} \right\} \left\{ \frac{v}{\lambda_1} \right\} \rho_Y^*, \qquad (40)$$

implying that where $D_{ij}^* = D_{ijN}^*$, $\Delta n^* > 0$, if and only if $v > 0$.

The paths traced by Ψ and Ψ_N are depicted in Fig. 3a, from which it is seen that along any single budget line the risk averter's constrained maximum solution entails a shorter move, and a more intensive search than does the constrained maximum appropriate for a risk-neutral migrant. A corollary proposition can be proved immediately from the same figure, by construction: The investment budget which is just large enough to cover the risk-neutral individual's minimal efficient plan of migration and search,[29] will be in-

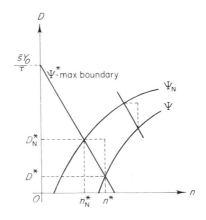

FIG. 3a

---

[29] By the "minimal efficient plan" I refer to the point on the Ψ-path just above its intercept on the n-axis in Fig. 3a, i.e., where D_{ij}^* is just positive.

sufficient, *ceteris paribus*, to cover the cost of the corresponding minimal plan for a risk averter.

In the foregoing paragraphs risk aversion has been treated as if it were an undifferentiated attitude, and the contrast has been drawn between the optimal behavior of risk-averse and risk-neutral individuals. Distinguishing now between different degrees of concern with risk, the same qualitative effects can be shown to hold: Given the budget $\bar{s}Y_0$, the greater the individual's relative risk aversion, the more pronounced will be the attendant intensification of his search.

First, recall from Eq. (7) that the Arrow–Pratt measure of relative risk aversion in the present model is simply $R_R = 1 - v$. Next, following the interpretation in Eq. (29), note that $\lambda_1 \simeq v Y_0^{v-1}$. Consequently, the substitution

$$v/\lambda_1 = 1/2 R_R (Y_0)^{R_R} \qquad (41)$$

can be made on the right-hand side of Eq. (40). Upon differentiating the resulting expression partially with respect to R_R, the sign condition stated above is immediately obtained, since

$$\frac{\partial \Delta n^*}{\partial R_R} = \left\{ \frac{2\beta + \alpha}{2\omega} \right\} \rho_Y^* [1 + \log Y_0](Y_0)^{R_R} > 0, \qquad (42)$$

and sign $\{\partial n^*/\partial R_R\}$ = sign $\{\partial \Delta n^*/\partial R_R\}$. From the existence of a stable linear budget constraint we know (by writing down the coordinates of its intersection with Ψ and Ψ_N) that

$$\Delta D^* \equiv D^* - D_N^* = -\{\omega/\tau\} \Delta n^*, \qquad (43)$$

whence it follows that greater relative risk aversion must lower the optimal distance moved as it increases the (corresponding) level of local job search.

Let us think then of a population comprising individuals who differ only in their attitudes toward risk: having a common budget constraint, those for whom migration was attractive would be distributed along the Ψ_{max}^*-boundary in Fig. 3a. It is a long-standing empirical observation that frequency distributions of residence changes by distance moved are positive skew distributions, there being many more short moves (say of length D^* in Fig. 3a) than there are long ones (of length D_N^* and greater).[30] Although many explanations for

---

[30] This relationship between distance and frequency of moves was systematically discussed first by Ravenstein (1885, 1889). Celestial mechanics subsequently continued to figure prominently as the paradigm underlying attempts to explain the phenomenon, in terms of the so-called "gravity" models of migration. [cf., e.g., Zipf (1949) and Stewart (1947).] Lowry (1966) reports recent econometric research in this genre, whereas Morrill and Pitts (1967) discuss geographers' recent efforts to interpret distance–frequency relationships as reflections of the spatial characteristics of the typical individual's information field.

this phenomenon have been proposed, could it not be viewed as a reflection of the existence of the prevailing negative skewedness of the distribution of relative risk aversion (R_R) in the populations under consideration? If there is anything in this simple suggestion, one should look for indications that the duration (or intensity) of local-market job search also exhibits a characteristic negatively skewed distribution—more protracted (voluntary) search being the most typical experience of immigrant workers.[31]

b. The Investment Constraint, "Blocked" Emigration, and Initial Wealth Effects

It has been seen (Section 3h, Fig. 2a) that situations in which migration *cum* search barely constituted an interior maximum solution for a risk-neutral worker would represent an unattractive option for an identically placed risk averter. But does this mean that in the present model it is only the risk averse who may choose not to move; that risk-neutral (and *a fortiori* risk-loving) individuals always can be tempted into trying their fortunes in a higher rel-variance market so long as the expected wage offer and the marginal cost of search is essentially the same everywhere? The answer is "no," at least not when the size of the investment budget $\bar{s}Y_0$ has been set arbitrarily, and thus independently of P, the fixed pecuniary and psychic costs the worker incurs as a consequence of any relocation. This is surely not difficult to see: one may always imagine the extreme case in which emigration is ruled out simply because an individual having only finite resources to devote to migration and search (and therefore having only hopes for finite gains) happens to attach an infinitely large cost to any move. The problem here is not one of financing the fixed "costs," since these take the form of forgone wealth, but rather of making gross gains large enough to recoup those losses.

What may be less obvious is that under reasonable restrictions as to the shape of the distribution of wage offers, the emigration of a risk-neutral individual can never be foreclosed or "blocked" if he is able to allocate to the total project an amount $\bar{s}Y_0 \geqslant P$.

Consider, therefore, the necessary condition for an interior maximum given by Eq. (21a): in the case of risk-neutrality, as $v = 1$ and $v = 0$, it collapses to the self-evident restriction,

$$\bar{y} - \bar{s}Y_0 - P > 0. \tag{44}$$

---

[31] In economically backward regions where average wages are low relative to the price of transportation, compared with the situation expected to prevail in a high-wage country such as the United States, the slope of the Ψ^*_{max}-boundary is comparatively flat, and the observed range of variations in n^* would be comparatively wide—particularly in relation to the range of variation observed for D^*.

Differentiating (8) and (9) partially with respect to n, we obtain

$$\bar{y} = \{\partial\bar{Y}/\partial n\}\,(n/\beta), \tag{45a}$$

and solving this with the first-order condition given in Eq. (37), noting that $\lambda_1 = U'(Y) = 1$ for the risk-neutral case, we arrive at

$$\bar{y} = (\omega n^*)(1/\beta). \tag{45b}$$

Substituting this last in (44), and using the budget constraint from Eqs. (30) and (32) to replace $\bar{s}Y_0$, we now have a linear restriction ($\Psi^*_{\min}$) in the (n, D)-plane; the solutions of interest are those which satisfy

$$D^* > D_{\min} = P/\tau - \Omega\left\{\frac{1-\beta}{\beta}\right\}n^*. \tag{46}$$

In Fig. 3b the segment of any $\Psi_N(n^*, D^*)$-path which represents the set of

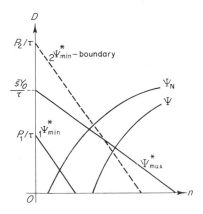

FIG. 3b

potentially attainable *interior* maxima for a risk-neutral individual is the portion lying above the relevant $\Psi^*_{\min}$-boundary. If the budget line prohibits entry into the region above $\Psi^*_{\min}$, then all strategies involving emigration will be effectively "blocked." To rule out the possibility of such blockage, it obviously will be sufficient for the $\Psi^*_{\min}$-boundary to lie everywhere within the $\Psi^*_{\max}$-boundary defined by the budget constraint,

$$D^*_{\max} = \{\bar{s}Y_0\}/\tau - \Omega n^*. \tag{47}$$

It is readily seen that the slope of the $\Psi^*_{\min}$-boundary will be steeper than that of the $\Psi^*_{\max}$-boundary—which Fig. 3b shows it to be—whenever $\beta < 1/2$.

The latter is a quite plausible condition and would be satisfied by the extreme-value distributions generated by sampling a normal distribution of wage offers, as is pointed out in the Appendix. Given this further restriction on the function (Eq. 9a) describing the expected payoffs from local job search at different levels of intensity, inspection of Eqs. (41) and (47) discloses that whatever $\bar{s}Y_0 \geqslant P$, the Ψ^*_{max}-boundary constitutes the sole effective constraint on the risk-neutral migrant's selection of n^* and D^*.

Another way of stating the proposition just established is to observe that for risk-neutral workers who attach finite costs to relocation, it should always be possible under the stipulated conditions to find a level of investment $(\bar{s}Y_0)$ at which moving becomes the superior alternative to staying put. Now, if the proportion $\bar{s}$ is taken to be much the same across all households, and P is distributed in the population independently of Y_0, the foregoing is tantamount to the suggestive conclusion that in a uniformly risk-neutral population the fraction of households for whom emigration is blocked should turn out to be a decreasing function of the initial level of household wealth. At very least it prompts a closer look at evidence regarding the migration experience of members of different occupations, taking gross occupational differences (e.g., "farm laborers" versus "craftsmen," or versus "farmers and farm managers") as a proxy for wealth differences between individuals of specified ages. Quite strikingly, there does appear to be some positive association between annual migration frequencies and the "socioeconomic" (occupational-wealth) status of males at the beginning of their working lives, when investment considerations of the sort considered here are most likely to dominate.[32]

On the strength of the preceding inference, the distribution of wealth among migrants (of given age, from equivalent points of origin) ought to turn out to be less skewed than the distribution of wealth among the (age-specific) population groups from which they came. But so long as some

---

[32] From Wilber (1963, Table 6), one may compute the average annual frequency of residence changes for employed civilian males age 18–24 in the United States in 1958, by gross occupational categories, as follows:

Nonfarm occupations		Farm occupations	
Managers, officials, and proprietors	0.576	Farmers and farm	
Professionals (young)	0.458	managers	0.374
Operatives and craftsmen	0.481	Farm laborers	0.325
Laborers, clerical, and sales workers	0.418		

This evidence is somewhat surprising, inasmuch as there is a more widely remarked upon *negative* association between "socioeconomic status" (occupational class) and *lifetime* migration frequencies inferred from age cross sections and from aggregated observations on occupations.

skewedness remains in the distribution of wealth among the subpopulation deciding to emigrate from a specific locale, one should expect to observe a corresponding positive skew in the distribution of the distances they move. For, among those risk-neutral individuals who do move at all in this model, as has been shown, the only thing stopping them from moving all the way to the highest rel-variance labor market will be the budget constraint related (by assumption) to the level of their respective initial wealth.

The observed frequency of long-distance moves is indeed much lower than that of short distance changes in residence location, and if the evidence of age stratified cross-sectional data is to be admitted, it appears this hold true throughout individuals' working lives.[33] But the explanatory nexus of budget constraint effects of wealth differences seems rather inadequate here; at best it may be regarded as one among the many possible economic causes adduced for this phenomenon. Moreover, once we reintroduce the existence of risk-averse attitudes—which in themselves could directly give rise to a skewed distribution of distances moved, as we have already seen—the direction of the impact of wealth differences on the lengths of moves becomes less clear-cut.

For individuals whose utility functions are linear transforms of their wealth, the only thing that matters is the *increment* in terminal wealth to be expected from a given strategy. Consequently, for them initial wealth exercises no effects independent of those that may operate via the influence of the investment constraint. For the risk averse, on the other hand, the form of the utility function specified here dictates that "security" is to be treated as a superior good, and hence the "pure" effect of greater initial wealth (holding $\bar{s}Y_0$ constant) is to further enlarge the risk averter's compensatory increase in search activity. This proposition follows from consideration of the effect of Y_0 on Δn^*, since for a given level of $\bar{s}Y_0$, Ψ_N and hence the constrained optimum n_N^* remain independent of variations in Y_0. From Eqs. (40) and (42) we obtain, by partial differentiation,

$$\frac{\partial \Delta n^*}{\partial Y_0} = \left\{ \frac{2\beta + \alpha}{2\omega} \right\} \rho_Y^* (R_R)^2 Y_0^{-v} > 0. \tag{48}$$

Correspondingly, Eq. (43) tells us $\partial \Delta D^* / \partial Y_0 < 0$.

Thus, although the combined effects of increasing wealth on the optimal intensity of local market search, n^*, must be positive, the direction of the net effects of wealth variations on the distance moved *by risk-averse migrants* remains ambiguous in this analysis. The indirect wealth effect via $\bar{s}Y_0$ would

---

[33] Cf. Wilber (1963, Table 3) for computions of the expected numbers of moves to a different house with the same county, outside of the county but within the same state, and to contiguous and noncontiguous states, on an age- and sex-specific basis for the United States in 1958.

tend to increase D^*, whereas (holding the investment allocation unchanged) the intensified preference for more "security" which accompanies greater wealth tends to decrease D^*.

c. Age Effects, Spurious and Pure

Horace Greeley's advice to "Go West" was not addressed to all and sundry, and subsequent empirical generalizations about the behavior of large populations confirms casual personal observation in the view that migration remains primarily a *young* man's game. In the United States, for example, the frequency of interstate changes of residence is highest among adults in the age group 20–24; it traces a monotonically falling curve as older groups are considered, reaching barely one-sixth the peak level in the case of the 45–64 age group.[34] The shape of this profile of age-specific migration rates may be treated statistically (as in covariance studies) by regarding it as the consequence of differential "age effects." For analytical clarity, however, we should avoid needlessly confounding what merely may be *age-correlated* influences with the pure effect that considerations of age per se will exert upon migration decisions.

The indirect, correlative influences of age are manifold. At least so one might conjecture from even brief contemplation of the way age interacts with the handful of variables considered thus far. It seems quite conceivable that systematic alterations of attitudes toward risk occur over the course of a person's life, in which case perhaps the simplest interpretation of statistical age effects is that these reflect a rise in the relative risk-aversion parameter (R_R) accompanying the passage from youth to middle age. No less plausible, and no less far beyond the line of demarcation between economics and psychology, is the notion that, with the advance of age, "place attachments" grow stronger, reflecting themselves in the rise of the psychic rent component (P') of the fixed costs of moving. Leaving aside risk aversion, to the extent that this enlarges the proportion of the older population for whom the condition $sY_0 \geqslant P$ is not fulfilled, the analysis of Section 4b already will have served to show that the frequency of "blocked migration" can be expected to be greater among the older members of the population.

Not all the correlatives of age resemble the degree of relative risk aversion and the psychic cost of relocation in eluding direct observation. Nor do they always operate so as to depress the migration rate as age rises. Wealth generally

[34] For the period 1953–1964 annual rates of gross interstate migration by civilians averaged 88 per thousand among those age 20–24, 61 per thousand among those age 25–29, and so on down to 14 per thousand among those age 45–64. [Cf. CPR Series P-20, as compiled by Lowry (1966, p. 28.] Eldridge (1964) finds a similarly placed peak rate from a cohort analysis of decadal net interstate migration in the United States in the long period 1870–1950 covered by Everett Lee's estimates.

increases over the course of an individual's working life, and it has already been seen that the investment constraint effect of greater wealth would in effect tend to favor higher migration frequency among older population groups. On the other hand, for the risk averse the pure wealth effect—and hence the indirect age effect—would have the opposite, depressant influence on the frequency of migration. Further pressure in the same direction could arise from the fact that seniority rights (reduced exposure to the risk of layoffs) and nontransferable pension benefits figure among the specific assets that accumulate with age. These typically must be sacrificed in relocating and seeking new employment. If it is true that a greater portion of the "wealth" of older workers takes the form of precisely those elements which turn up among the pecuniary fixed costs of migration, this certainly should tend to reduce the frequency with which fulfillment of the condition $sY_0 \geqslant P$ prevents emigration by older workers from becoming totally blocked.

One feature common to all the foregoing indirect—shall we say "spurious" —age effects is that each would be accompanied by some predictable age-related variations in the relationship of search intensity and distance moved. The pure effect of increased age, by contrast, leaves the mix of n^* and D^* in the optimal strategy entirely unaltered; in reducing the length of an individual's remaining working life, aging per se unambiguously lowers the contingent likelihood of his finding emigration attractive as an investment proposition.

To establish the first part of the antecedant statement is a trivial matter: expressions (35), (36), and (39), describing the unconstrained sets of solutions $\Psi(n^*, D^*)$ and $\Psi_N(n^*, D^*)$ simply do not contain the age-dependent capitalization factor $R(a_k)$, $\partial R/\partial a < 0$. Proving the second part of the proposition is scarcely harder, although it will take a few more lines.

Following Appendix equation (A1), we may begin by forming the explicit expression for $\overline{Y}(n)$:

$$\overline{Y} = Y_0(1 - \bar{s}) + \{R(a)\} B\sigma_{max} n^\beta [1 - \gamma_j \exp\{\theta(n\Omega - \bar{s}Y_0)\}]. \qquad (49)$$

This may be shown—as in Appendix equations (A4) and (A5)—to attain a maximum at $\overline{Y}(\hat{n})$, where $n = \hat{n}$, a value which Eq. (A4a) shows to be invariant with respect to $R(a)$. Making the explicit substitution in (49) yields

$$\overline{Y}_{max} = Y_0(1 - \bar{s}) + \{R(a)\} B\sigma_{max} \hat{n}^\beta [1 - (\gamma_j/\beta)\{\beta + \theta\Omega\hat{n}\}]. \qquad (50)$$

From this it is immediately clear that $\{\partial \overline{Y}_{max}/\partial a\} < 0$.

Now consider the other coordinate of the $\overline{Y}_{max}$ point of the OF locus in Fig. 2a: $\rho_Y(\hat{n})$. From Appendix equation (A6) we see this can be represented as

$$\rho_Y(\hat{n}) = A\{R(a)\}^2 [\overline{Y}_{max}]^{-2} [G(\hat{n})]^2 J(\hat{n}). \qquad (51)$$

Here A is a constant and $G(n)$ and $J(n)$ are functions, defined in the Appendix, which do not involve $R(a)$. We have already seen from (50) that $\overline{Y}_{max}$ increases with $R(a)$, but wherever $Y_0(1 - \bar{s}) > 0$, $[Y_{max}]^2$ must increase less rapidly than $[R(a)]^2$ itself. Consequently, we can infer directly from (51) that $\rho_Y(n)$ increases with $R(a)$, and thus conclude that $(\partial \rho_Y(\hat{n})/\partial a) < 0$.

The foregoing means that an increase in a_K, *ceteris paribus*, will displace the coordinates of the relevant OF in a southwesterly direction. Since the conditions for the convexity of OF will be fulfilled for all positive finite values of $R(a)$, if for any, the pure "aging effect" must produce an inward curling of the individual's OF such as Fig. 4 depicts.

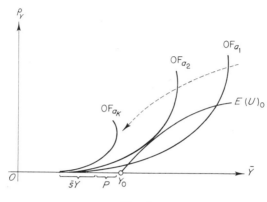

FIG. 4

Common sense is thus confirmed. For risk averters and risk-neutral people alike, with the approaching end of the working span, the fall in the present value of a permanent addition to annual earnings inexorably transforms situations where the costs of migration–search investment can be more than recouped into ones in which there is no advantage to be gained from emigration. Just how potent an impact this may have upon the age-specific frequency of migration is another question, the answer to which depends (even under the simplest version of the model imaginable) on at least two considerations. The first is the strength of the effect of a on $R(a)$, which will be much diminished when rates of discount are applied to future earnings. The second is represented in the shape of the distribution of attitudes toward risk, even if we supposed that the relative risk-aversion parameter $(1 - v)$ were distributed independently of age in the population under examination.

Figure 4 makes it apparent that the mere progression from youth, in the near neighborhood of age a_1, to middle age immediately beyond a_2, should not alter the migration frequency observed when the population is homogeneous and all its members are *risk-neutral*. The frequency would remain unchanged at 1. On the other hand, for a homogeneous population having thc identical initial wealth endowment (Y_0) but a uniform degree of relative risk aversion $(1-v) > 0$, Fig. 4 shows that aging beyond a_2 will reduce the migration frequency to zero if the iso-expected utility contours happen to have the shape indicated by $E(U)_0$. For a population within which both degrees of risk aversion (0 and $1-v$) were represented, the extent of the decline observed in the migration rate between the age groups younger than a_2 and those older than a_2 would obviously reflect the relative sizes of the contingents holding each of these attitudes toward risk.

Through such aggregation effects even the pure influence of age would become entangled with other factors in the determination of cross-sectional migration rates. This alone—quite apart from confusions with spurious, age-collinear effects—makes their identification from aggregated data a more intricate econometric exercise than current empirical studies seem to recognize.[35]

d. Employment Status

A proposition recurring throughout the economic and sociological literature on internal migration is that "unemployed persons are more migratory" than employed persons. Curiously, for want of information on employment status at the point in time preceding migration, an ostensible empirical basis for the assertion in the case of the United States has been found largely in data which relate employment status at the *end* of a specific interval (typically a year) to migration experience during the interval. Among persons recorded in Census Bureau surveys as (nominally) unemployed, in recent years the proportion who were migrants within the year preceding the survey is approximately twice as large as it is among employed persons.[36]

Patently such statistics have no direct bearing on the common presumption that it is the condition of being unemployed which precipitates migration, rather than the obverse. Indeed, there is evidence from a special survey for the United States which lends strength to the latter interpretation: among male migrants aged 18–64 who were found to be *subsequently* "unemployed," almost 50% reported having been employed prior to their move.[37] This is to

---

[35] Cf., e.g., Sjaastad's (1962) comments on the difficulty of getting pure age effects (via capitalization of differential earnings streams of varying lengths) to account for the profile in age-specific migration rates. The recent empirical literature on migration, some of which is cited in the footnotes in Part III, deals with "age effects" in the grossest form imaginable when it deals with them at all; it entertains none of the analytical distinctions developed here.

[36] Cf. United States Bureau of the Census (1966), and Masnick (1968, p. 79).

[37] In addition, some of the postmigration unemployed reported themselves as not having entered the civilian labor force prior to the migration period. [Cf. Masnick (1968) for analysis of the special inquiry described in United States Bureau of Census (1966)].

say nothing of the appearance of exceptionally heavy, open unemployment among rural immigrants in the major urban centers of less-developed countries.

Getting around such findings presents a bit of a challenge for the classical theory of migration, and some interesting contributions have been thereby elicited.[38] Within the framework of the present model, however, nothing could be easier to explain: the complementarity of investment in migration to reach "high-dispersion" labor markets and investment upon arrival in local job search—an activity that we have supposed to be competitive with regular employment—lies at the core of the entire analysis.[39]

All that is not to deny involuntary disruption of job tenure (equally signified by the transition to the state of "unemployment" recorded by labor market surveys) an important place among the conditions precipitating migration by individual workers. There is even some microeconomic evidence on employment status prior to migration which is consistent with this more conventional view, although by no means is it conclusive on the question of the existence of a *pure* employment status effect.[40] The present model, moreover, suggests that an adverse change in employment status per se would tend to induce the emigration of risk-averse workers—when they are thereby thrust into markets characterized by some dispersion in the distribution of wage offers.

This last may be inferred directly from Fig. 2b. The worker who is turned out of a sure job yielding him an earnings stream worth Y_0, by devoting $\bar{s}Y_0$ exclusively to searching his present (jth) locale might expect to retrieve the same job—but only with a real-variance of $\min \rho_Y$ around that expectation

---

[38] Todaro (1969), for example, works through an equilibrium model in which it is assumed that there are large rural–urban real wage rate differentials which persist in the face of variations on the supply side of the labor market. Despite a lower probability of finding any work at the higher wage rate, the expected earning differential in favor of the urban sector continues to induce migration until the rate of unemployment therein rises and the migrant's probability of finding work falls to the equilibrium level.

[39] The present model thus can account for migration flows toward destinations where vacancy rates are low (even negative) without assuming spatial differences in expected real wage offers. This contrasts sharply with Todaro's (1969) extension of the classical approach.

[40] Masnick (1968, pp. 82–83), for example. Among males 18–64 recorded as unemployed in March 1962, the proportion who migrated during the following 12 months was almost twice as large as the proportion of the employed who migrated. But the sample populations of employed and unemployed were not stratified by age. Reynolds (1951, pp. 241–242) also concludes that involuntary job terminations are an important cause of migrations by blue-collar workers, without effectively standardizing for other personal characteristics—such as age and wealth—which may be correlated with the probability of job termination. Suppose "the unemployed" show higher migration propensities simply because, as a class, they tend to be younger and (being less wealthy) less concerned with the relative variance of their terminal wealth.

of terminal wealth Y_0. Obviously he is the worse off for having been fired; his former position corresponded to the expected utility level $E[U_{e0}]$ in Fig. 2b, whereas now he is reduced to $E[U_{u0}]$. Supposing that other things remain unaltered—particularly his wealth and the resources he has committed to migration and search; the pure effect of the shift in employment status will be to raise the likelihood of his emigrating. It is now more likely that for a worker of any given age the relevant migration–search opportunity frontier will afford an interior maximum solution involving movement toward a still higher dispersion distribution of wage offers. Observe that the explanation thereby furnished for the appearance of higher migration rates among those (previously) reported as "unemployed" does not require one to suppose that such workers had been laid off in local markets where finding a job vacancy was particularly difficult, or where real wages were depressed by comparison with other places. The employment status effect isolated here is conceived of as being strictly of a partial equilibrium character.

e. Labor Market Conditions: Vacancy Rate and Marginal Cost of Search

The preceding remarks bring us, finally, to the effects of changes in prevailing conditions in the market for labor. Unlike the "effects" so far considered, these must be treated as deriving from a uniform shift in the parameters of the "game" confronting all potential migrants. The nominative singular "market" in the first sentence is used advisedly: for simplicity's sake the analysis will continue to assume that there is but one kind of labor, and we will suppose that the relevant market parameters for all locations in the spatial system undergo simultaneous *pari passus* alterations. This preserves the spirit of the spatial uniformity assumptions in Eq. (18); and it permits us to work with scalar variates rather than changes in vectors of local market parameters.

There are two basic parameters to be considered: the uniform expected real wage offer μ, and the uniform job vacancy rate V—which governs the average search time needed to find a single nonzero wage offer. Together they determine the real marginal cost of search ω, defined in Section 3e. But as the marginal cost of "transportation" τ can be made to serve as a numéraire, $\Omega \equiv \omega/\tau$, the relative "price" of local search activity, provides a convenient summary variable to employ in analyzing the main effects that are of interest. For interpretive purposes the following partial relationships should be borne in mind:

$$\partial\Omega/\partial\mu > 0$$

because the valuation placed on search time is increased relative to the uniform distance tariff τ, and

$$\partial\Omega/\partial V < 0$$

because a higher global vacancy rate raises the probability of there being at least one vacancy at each potential place of employment visited within any specified market, thereby lowering the cost of obtaining an additional nonzero offer.

Regarding $d\Omega$ as a relative price change, we may begin by inquiring into its effect upon the allocation of migrants' resources between geographical relocation and local job hunting. From Eqs. (35) and (36) it is immediately seen that increasing Ω must displace the $\Psi(n^*, D^*)$-path to the left as is shown in Fig. 5.[41] *There is consequently a "substitution effect" of $d\Omega$:* On this count

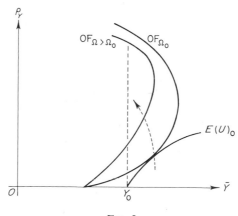

Fɪɢ. 5

the relative price rise unambiguously lowers the relative search intensity (n^*/D^*) of the optimal strategy.

An "income effect" from $d\Omega$ is also to be expected, since the slope of the Ψ_{max}-budget line will be altered. In the case of risk-neutrality—the instance illustrated by Fig. 5—the adverse income effect of the increase in Ω always perfectly offsets the substitution effect's impact upon D^{**}; the absolute distance moved in the constrained solution remains unchanged, and the adjustment is therefore confined to the reduction of n^{**}. This result is most readily obtained by solving Eqs. (39) and (48); observe that Ω is thereby eliminated along with n^{**} from the resulting expression for the constrained optimum level of D^{**}:

$$\beta \exp[\theta D^{**}] + \gamma_j \theta D^{**} - \{1 - (\bar{s} Y_0/\tau)\} = 0. \tag{52}$$

Under conditions of risk aversion, however, it is quite possible for the income effect of $d\Omega > 0$ to be still more potent in relation to the substitution

---

[41] Comparison with Eq. (39) shows that the $\Psi(\cdot)$- and $\Psi_N(\cdot)$-paths are shifted in the same direction by $d\Omega$.

effect, so that the absolute level of D^{**} as well as n^{**} will be *lowered*. The optimum strategy *may* thus be made comparatively more search-intensive—in the sense that the ratio (n^{**}/D^{**}) is actually raised. The economic nub of this proposition is that the rise of the relative marginal cost of search $(d\Omega > 0)$ carries an additional adverse real income effect for risk averters, because the latter attach particular weight to "security" (the inverse of ρ_Y). Greater local market search constitutes specific means by which ρ_Y may be reduced.[42] With a fixed budget to be spent, such reductions in ρ_Y are to be purchased only at the expense of the level of $\overline{Y}$ because—as the Appendix demonstrates—utility maximizers will always be making choices in the range where the necessary curtailment of expenditures on (migration) access to greater underlying dispersion of offers exerts a negative effect not offset by the positive effect on $\overline{Y}$ of additional local search. But when the utility tradeoff especially favors additional "security"—as it would among the comparatively well-to-do and all those having a peculiarly high degree of relative risk aversion—moving a shorter distance, to a market with less relative dispersion in the distribution of offers, is likely to be the most satisfactory form of adjustment to a rise in the relative "price" of local search activity.

It is an interesting implication of the peverse price effect just discussed that a rise in the marginal cost of search everywhere—resulting from secular or cyclical forces raising real wages or the cost of finding a job—would operate to discourage *long*-distance migration on the part of the comparatively well-to-do members of society before it curtailed the distances moved by the poor. This differential impact at different initial wealth levels runs directly counter to the possible wealth-correlated effects on distance moved which differences in $\bar{s}Y_0$ can create; it derives from our specification of a utility function that depicts "security" (vis-à-vis expected terminal wealth) as a superior good for all households having a positive, constant degree of relative risk aversion.

Bear in mind that the exclusive concern here has been with a *partial* price effect. The results considered so far take $\{\bar{s}Y_0/\tau\}$ to remain fixed, even though the contemplated alteration of Ω may be thought to have derived from a change

[42] The following derivation underlies the text discussion:

Solve Eqs. (35) and (36) with (47), and substitute for λ_1 from Eq. (41). This eliminates n, leaving an expression containing functions in D^*—including among them $\rho_Y(D)$—and in Y_0. Concretely,

$$[Z(D^*)/Y_0^{R_R}] - K_1(D^*/Y_0^{R_R}) - K_2\rho_Y(D^*) + K_3Y_0^{1-R_R} = 0,$$

where K_1, K_2, K_3 are positive constants not containing Ω, and $Z(D)$ is the function defined by (36). From the Appendix we know that $\rho_Y(n)$ is a decreasing convex function. Since the linear budget relation in (47) has been used to replace n by D, $\rho_Y(D)$ must be an *increasing* convex function which is *shifted positively* by $d\Omega > 0$. On inspection of the above expression, it is seen that as Y_0 becomes large, there will be a more pronounced negative effect of $d\Omega > 0$ on the (positive) root(s), D^{**}.

in the general level of real wage offers or in the global vacancy rate. To be sure, even under conditions of risk neutrality, if $d\Omega > 0$ *is* accompanied by an *adverse* change in the amount of resources the typical household can devote to migration and search activities, the latter concomitant would tend to reduce D^{**}. Indeed, it can be shown[43] for the risk-neutral case that, when no capital market imperfections are constraining $\bar{s}Y_0$, $d\Omega > 0$ decreases the amount it is *optimal* to allocate on migration and search. Via this direct effect upon investment, if not through the perverse price effect just examined, a relative rise in marginal search costs may be expected to cause those who still opt to emigrate to plan on moving a shorter distance and conducting a more limited job search at their place of destination.

That leads naturally to the question whether when Ω increases the "price effect" by itself will render emigration totally unattractive as an investment proposition for households subject to a budget constraint. The answer is that $d\Omega > 0$ certainly works in the direction of lowering the frequency of migration. An easy proof of this proposition is afforded by considering the way $d\Omega > 0$ alters the shape and position of the MSOF, as shown in Fig. 6. First,

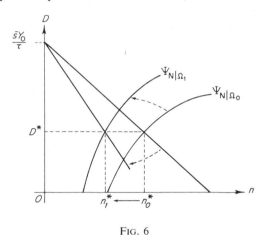

FIG. 6

differentiating $\overline{Y}_{\max}(\hat{n})$ in Eq. (49) with respect to $\hat{n}$, and noting that application of the implicit function rule to the solution of Appendix equations (A4b,c) yields

$$d\hat{n}/d\Omega = -\hat{n}/\Omega < 0, \tag{53}$$

we obtain

$$d\overline{Y}_{\max}/d\Omega = -(\beta/\Omega)[\overline{Y}_{\max} - Y_0(1-\bar{s})] < 0. \tag{54}$$

[43] This proof has been omitted. Although the analysis is quite straightforward, some considerable development is required before obtaining the result cited in the text.

Second, Appendix Eqs. (A2), (A3), and (A12) establish that $\rho_Y'(n) < 0$. Hence, upon evaluating the function at $\hat{n}$ and making use of Eq. (53), it is found immediately that

$$d\rho_Y/d\Omega = \rho_Y'(\hat{n}) \cdot (d\hat{n}/d\Omega) > 0. \tag{55}$$

The point $\overline{Y}_{\max}$ of OF corresponding to $\Omega_1 > \Omega_0$ therefore must be displaced in a northwesterly direction, while the OF's intercept on the $\overline{Y}$-axis (in the convenient case $\sigma_j = 0$) remains undisturbed. Now, as both loci are convex in $\overline{Y}$, considering only the displacement just described it appears conceivable for the frontier $OF|_{\Omega_0}$ to intersect $OF|_{\Omega_1}$ from below. But the latter readily can be shown on other grounds to be an impossibility,[44] thus completing the proof that opportunity set represented by $OF|_{\Omega_0}$ dominates $OF|_{\Omega_1 > \Omega_0}$ in expected utility space.

f. Beyond Partial Equilibrium Analysis

Does the present model therefore provide an aspatial explanation of the well-known procyclical behavior of gross migration rates—on the argument that the relative marginal cost of search would be temporarily raised by the general, economy-wide fall of job-vacancy rates during business recessions, blocking some emigration plans and converting others from long-distance to shorter movements? As one reaches for interpretations in such macroeconomic contexts, the partial equilibrium character of the present analysis rapidly becomes unsatisfactory. Were the vacancy rate to fall precipitously, for example, it would be strange if none of the other market "parameters" facing the individual worker underwent a concurrent or near-term change. At the aggregate level the vacancy rate, which compares the number of job openings with the number of searchers (both those who quit work and those who lose jobs), cannot be parameterically varied; in a general equilibrium formulation V will appear as jointly determined with μ and other variables.

About as far as it is useful to go within the limits of the present partial analysis will be to give some brief indication of plausible joint variations in market conditions that would induce—via the microeconomic responses already examined on the supply side of the labor market—a positive association between the rate of gross and net migration and the intensity of resource utilization in the economy.

The first point to note is that even some positive covariation of V and μ can be admitted as consistent with maintenance of the condition: $\text{sign}\{d\Omega/dV\} = \text{sign}\{\partial\Omega/\partial V\}$. For this all that is needed is that the effect of a

---

[44] Consider the expression for ρ_Y in Appendix Eq. (A6) and set $\rho_Y(n|\Omega_1) = \rho_Y(n|\Omega_0)$, holding $\overline{Y}(n|\Omega_1) = \overline{Y}(n|\Omega_0)$. Such an intersection is thereby seen to imply an impossibility: $G(n|\Omega_1) = G(n|\Omega_0)$, where $G(\ )$ is defined by Eq. (A2) as $F[(\tilde{s}Y_0/\tau) - \Omega n]$. [Note that neither $J(n)$, nor the other terms on the right-hand side of Eq. (A6) contain Ω.]

fall in the vacancy rate on search time per job offer obtained (Φ^{-1}) be greater than the effect on the general level of expected real wage offers, i.e., $\Phi'(V) > (\partial\mu/\partial V)(\Phi/\mu) > 0$.

On the extreme hypothesis that structural conditions (discussed in Part III) determine the rel-variance of local market wage offer distributions in a fashion that leaves the vector $\{\sigma_i/\mu_i\}$ unaffected by the state of excess demand throughout the economy, the V-correlated variation of $\mu = \mu_i$ just contemplated would be reflected in a proportionate change of all the elements of the vector $\{\sigma_i\}$. This can be represented simply by supposing the scaling parameter σ_{max} to vary positively with V: $\partial\sigma_{max}/\partial V > 0$.

We must therefore take account of the effect on the individual worker's opportunity frontier of covariation in the parameter σ_{max}. From Eq. (50) it is seen that σ_{max} is symmetrical with $R(a)$ in the expression for $\overline{Y}_{max}$. And from Eq. (51) it is seen that $(\sigma_{max})^2$, which is a separable argument of $[G(\hat{n})]^2$, is likewise symmetrical with $[R(a)]^2$ in the expression for $\rho_Y(\hat{n})$. Hence the results obtained in Section 4c tell us immediately that

$$\partial\overline{Y}_{max}/\partial\sigma_{max} > 0 \quad \text{and} \quad \partial\rho_Y(\hat{n})/\partial\sigma_{max} > 0.$$

Now, forming the differential expressions

$$d\overline{Y}_{max} = \left\{ \frac{\partial\overline{Y}_{max}}{\partial\sigma_{max}} \cdot \frac{d\sigma_{max}}{dV} + \frac{\partial\overline{Y}_{max}}{\partial\Omega} \cdot \frac{d\Omega}{dV} \right\} dV,$$

$$d\rho_Y(\hat{n}) = \left\{ \frac{\partial\rho_Y(\hat{n})}{\partial\sigma_{max}} \cdot \frac{d\sigma_{max}}{dV} + \frac{\partial\rho_Y(\hat{n})}{\partial\Omega} \cdot \frac{d\Omega}{dV} \right\} dV,$$

(56)

and making use of the sign conditions already established on the elements of the right-hand side, we are led to a somewhat ambiguous result: $(d\overline{Y}_{max}/dV) > 0$ whereas $(d\rho_Y(\hat{n})/dV) \gtrless 0$. Because there is nothing precluding an intersection of the locus $[OF|\Omega_2, (\sigma_{max})_2]$ with $[OF|\Omega_1, (\sigma_{max})_1]$ when $(d\sigma_{max}/d\Omega) < 0$, it is only possible to be analytically unequivocal about the likely impact of trade cycle movements on the frequency of migration to be observed in a population comprised entirely of *risk-neutral* workers. For such a population $(d\overline{Y}_{max}/dV) > 0$ alone implies a tendency for the proportion who find migration and search attractive to vary procyclically, with the vacancy rate.[45]

As far as the behavior of risk averters is concerned, the foregoing remains disappointingly jejune. Everything depends upon the shape of individuals' respective iso-expected utility maps and the particular way that joint shifts in market parameters alter the configuration of the migration-search opportunity set. So long as one remains disposed to regard risk-neutrality as the

---

[45] For risk-neutral individuals the pure employment states effect discussed in Section 4d is not relevant, so it will not matter that V falls because of mass layoffs.

exception rather than the norm, the persistence of clear procyclical variations in internal migration rates must serve to forcibly direct attention to the possibility that an important cause of this phenomenon may lie in the very circumstances from which the preceding discussion has been abstracted.

Recall in the first place that we have neglected all spatial differences in the level of average real wage offers. Yet there is good reason to think not only that these exist, but that they undergo regular variations over the course of the business cycle. On this count it is to be expected that net movements of population form the cyclically volatile component of gross internal migration flows.

In the second place, it is necessary to advert to the very real possibility that the rel-variance of the typical distribution of wage offers is in fact systematically altered as the labor market passes back and forth between states of excess demand and excess supply. Clearly, in a general equilibrium treatment of migration it would be inappropriate to assume that the structural features of local labor markets to be discussed in Part III not only create chronic spatial differences in the relative dispersion of wage offers, but determine the shapes of offer distributions uniquely and quite independently of what is happening in the local markets as a consequence of the migration flows thereby set in motion. Quite apart from the way that employers' offers will be influenced by their evolving perceptions of the local availability of labor, i.e., through the length of time advertised offers remain unaccepted, it is only to be expected that the information transmission characteristics of local labor markets will be altered by pronounced changes in the density of job searchers moving through them.

Yet it remains an open question whether the tendency envisioned in the present model for labor to be drawn into local markets where a higher relative dispersion of offers prevails will or will not induce an equilibrating transformation of the shape of the offer distributions therein. Of course, if no such transformation were to take place, a spatial equilibrium might nonetheless be established through the rise of Ω_i—entailed by a comparative reduction of the local vacancy rate, any associated fall in the average real wage offer notwithstanding—in those locales where the influx of migrants was not being readily absorbed. And if that did not suffice, the eventual emergence of such places among the class of "comparatively low expected real wage offer markets" would bring to a halt their population growth via immigration. Thus, the gross observation that the spatial distribution of the labor force does not seem so very unstable in no way implies that conditions in which vacancy rates become negative must witness the emergence of strong pressures making the offer distribution more compact and skewing it in a fashion inimical to continued migration. But the materialization of such pressures is certainly plausible and may be a major reason why rates of internal migration fluctuate in conformity with business cycles.

Part III

To rigorously test the foregoing statement of the model against observations drawn from the real world could hardly be instructive, considering the sweeping spatial uniformity assumptions (Section 3e) under which the whole analysis has been conducted. And yet, as this exercise has been advanced with transparent pretensions to empirical relevance and not merely as a contribution to the "pure" (i.e., normative) theory of migration, it really will not do for me to duck the fundamental empirical issue: How apt is the correspondence drawn here between the game of urns and balls, and the potential migrant's choice among alternative strategies involving movement and local search activities?

Two distinct questions deserve closer examination than they hitherto have been afforded. The first, and the more complex, has to do with the characterization of the process of job search. The second, and the more essential in some respects, concerns the conception of local labor markets as distinguishable search environments, structurally differentiated from one another by the shapes of the job-offer distributions prevailing therein, and particularly by the degree of dispersion relative to the average offer.

5. The Limits of Analogy

Probably the most general and natural way to model migration behavior is to conceive of spatial relocation as an integral part of the finding or accepting of employment situations located through a continuous, lifetime program of search. Instead, the analogy suggests a static separation between (1) a phase of migration activity, (2) a phase of (localized) random job search at the migrant's destination, and (3) acceptance of the permanent tenure of a job. Artificiality is the price paid for the reduction of complexity, and these distinctions have long been allowed by students of migration. The usual approach of migration theory, however, is to treat the search phase as a period of involuntary unemployment that imposes an exogenously determined —albeit uncertain—cost upon the immigrant; in this way the distinctness and interdependence of decisions involving phases (1) and (2) is effectively suppressed by the migration literature built upon classical foundations.[46] In recent writings on the microeconomics of employment and inflation theory, the same suppression is accomplished by the opposite absorption of phase (1)

---

[46] Cf. Sjaastad (1962, p. 84), for a well-known exposition in which the opportunity costs *of migration* are taken to include "the earnings forgone while traveling, searching for, and learning a new job." Kelley (1965), Todaro (1969), and more recently Gallaway and Vedder (1971), Vanderkamp (1971), and Laber and Chase (1971), all continue in this vein.

into phase (2), job search more broadly defined being made the focus of attention. But here insistence on the distinction between phases (2) and (3) in the life of a worker is even more critical, inasmuch as the main claim of this work to empirical relevance turns on its identification of job search with frictional or voluntary unemployment, and in some accounts with all observable unemployment.[47]

Critics of the latter literature, like Tobin (1972), have been quick to pounce on the key assertion that search is significantly more efficient when the searcher is not already holding a job.[48] Any Dean of Faculty will tell you how successful economists have been in soliciting job offers from other, far-removed places, while remaining on his payroll. And in truth, it is evident in many professions that the labor market is organized in a way that affords frequent job-seeking contacts—visiting lectures, consultations, conferences—to members of the pool of jobholders, and relatively few such occasions to those out of work. But as peripatetic as the members of the professoriate may appear to be, the essential point is that the market for academic economists is not an interesting paradigm for the study of mass behavior, much less mass migrations. Among the blue-collar workers studied by Reynolds (1951), for example, only one-quarter of those who quit work had jobs lined up in advance, and it was Reynolds' conclusion that the overwhelming proportion of job changes recorded represented shifts between positions whose availability and terms were not known beforehand.[49]

Quite clearly, then, no universal validity can be claimed for the specification that workers must quit their jobs and move in order to search for employment

---

[47] Stigler's (1962) seminal paper assumed that forgone earnings were among the costs of job search, but for analyses built on this specification, the *locus classicus* is now Phelps *et al.* (1970). Alchain (1970), in that collection, argues the extreme position. The absence of any recognition of a spatial dimension in the process of job search on the part of the contributors to this more recent literature is perhaps understandable in view of the macroeconomic motivation underlying it. As a first approximation it is not unreasonable to assume a point economy when asking whether or not there exists an equilibrium or "natural" rate of voluntary unemployment associated with job search, an unemployment rate that is independent of expectations regarding the future course of wages and prices.

[48] Whether it is more efficient, in the social sense of "technical" efficiency, rather than in the private sense, will not be a question of moment here. Tobin (1972, pp. 6–7) alludes to the finding that employer collusion—antipirating agreements—may render it impossible to receive a job offer while employed elsewhere, although there is no technical reason for quitting work to look for such an offer. It will of course matter a good deal to any welfare valuation of time spent unemployed whether this yields a positive social return (for technical reasons) or simply a positive private return. But we are interested here only in the latter.

[49] Reynolds (1951, pp. 214–215, 240). Parnes (1954, p. 166) makes the same point. Tobin's (1972, pp. 6–7) references to this evidence curiously extract the opposite interpretation.

elsewhere. It does seem plausible, however, to maintain its relevance to market situations in which (1) there are many, rather than a few identifiable potential employers; (2) the conditions of employment will not permit workers to be absent with any frequency; (3) the criteria for hiring workers make many eligible and dispenses with the need to evaluate references, records, or other evidence of qualification extrinsic to the individual; (4) cheap and effective channels of communication, such as telephones or reliable mail service, are either nonexistent or not appropriate media for transmitting the information exchanged in the process of search. In all but the late stages of industrialization, unskilled, semiskilled, and even craft manual labor is probably hired in technical and organizational contexts that render it considerably less efficient to look for work while remaining employed and residing at a distance from the geographical locus of that search. And for members of those groups it is more likely that the random compoment in the rewards of the search will predominate over such systematic effects as may derive from "learning" or the acquistion of job-hunting experience.

But here one runs into a difficulty with the supposition that the immigrant will find it possible to collect a number of job offers and, after comparing them, retrieve the best. This second specification, which keeps options open at zero marginal cost of deferral and endows the search process with a memory in which a nondepreciating, nonobsolescent stock of information may be accumulated for use in the future, was also implicit in Stigler's (1962) original formulation of an optimal search strategy decision as involving the choice of the best *fixed* sample size. The trouble is that for precisely the class of job seekers who fit the analogy on the first count considered, the collection and costless storage of offers will not generally be practical. After all, the sorts of workers who must visit the shop door, or the factory gate, or put in an appearance at the hiring hall are infrequently afforded the luxury of contemplation—the euphoria of being twice or thrice chosen by prospective employers. Typically there will be many workers at least outwardly like themselves, all seeking work at the same time; in the presence of close substitutes for jobs with broadly defined qualifications, vacancies cannot be expected remain unfilled while shopping is continued.[50] Offers, when they come, come on a basis of "Take it or leave it. You can start this afternoon."

Where offers cannot be deferred without decaying, a model of sequential job search—rather than predetermined sampling—would seem most appro-

[50] There is a real organizational asymmetry—which remains obscured in the development of optimal stopping rules for sequential search, shortly to be discussed—between visiting market stalls to collect price quotations and presenting oneself for an employment interview. The merchant does not screen his potential customers, whereas the potential employer makes such an investment and thus tends to discourage pure "shopping" by applicants, especially whenever there is a cost to leaving vacancies unfilled.

priate.[51] Indeed, there are circumstances in which a sequential procedure may be shown to dominate adherence to the fixed sample design strategy suggested by Stigler—even if the information obtained (offers received) can be stored indefinitely without cost. *When considerations of risk aversion are put aside*, it is not difficult to see why this should be so: from a known probability distribution of offers, one may determine the increase—above the value of some specific offer in hand—which is to be expected as a result of further extending the search, and, so long as this marginal expected gain exceeds the marginal search costs (sampling charges), it will pay to go on looking. But at any point in the sequence, and hence quite conceivably before all the "balls" in the best predetermined sample are drawn, an offer may be obtained such that the expected gain from continuing would just equal the marginal cost. That offer, upon the receipt of which it is optimal to terminate the search, in effect should be made the worker's "reservation wage" for accepting a job.[52]

When the marginal cost of search and the frequency distribution of offers are stable, they define a unique optimal reservation wage; adherence to this as a rule for the termination of search enables the worker to dispense with the need to store offers, inasmuch as it ensures that he would never fail to accept an offer whose rejection he would subsequently come to regret. Of course, the dual of the optimal reservation wage—also defined by reference to the shape of the underlying offer distribution—is the *expected* optimal duration of the search, the number of trials before receiving an offer matching or exceeding the reservation wage. Corresponding to that duration, there will be an *expected* cost of the optimal search, against which may be reckoned the expected value of the offer that will serve to terminate the process. It is therefore evident that, in place of the fixed sample size strategy, the formulation of a stationary reservation price rule for sequential search could be integrated into our analogy without any essential change in the structure of the problem facing the potential migrant searcher.

But the gain of realism in this is dubious.[53] The guarantee that a sequential search will never terminate with the acceptance of an offer inferior to one previously spurned, which makes the storage of offers superfluous for risk-neutral searchers, requires the "stationarity" of the optimal reservation price.

---

[51] In the following I have been guided by the survey discussion by Rothschild (1971) and McCall (1971).

[52] Cf. McCall (1970) and Mortensen (1970). An analogous formulation of a reservation price rule for buyers is developed by Nelson (1970). Neither of these papers demonstrates the optimality of the stopping rule under conditions of risk aversion.

[53] It seems that the only notable conceptual change is that the cost of job search upon arrival is no longer treated as predetermined by the migrant when he fixes an (optimal) sample size; it now appears, more realistically, among the stochastic variables about which the migrant may form some expectation based on his knowledge of the offer distribution prevailing in the destination labor market(s).

And that, in turn, requires the stipulation that the marginal cost of search be stationary. Realism would suggest otherwise. Inasmuch as learning effects can raise an individual's personal efficiency in search activities, there may well exist an initial range of decreases in marginal costs. Eventually, however, the latter increase, due to any one or all of several other factors. Variations in the spatial density of prospective employers within a local market could raise the unit "carfare" costs of soliciting additional offers; the approaching exhaustion of financial resources could imply that each decision to continue looking raised the expectation of winding up "broke, without a job, or the means of finding one"; and (on more subjective grounds) the marginal disutility of not finding offers that meet one's aspirations may mount as the search wears on.[54]

It should be no less apparent that the invariance of the reservation price rule obtaining throughout a sequential search must derive equally from the assumed stationarity of the expected marginal benefits. Yet, where employers are relatively few in number and unchanging in their offers, the search will not progress far before a hysteresis effect materializes: the distribution of remaining, unknown offers shifts upward as a consequence of sampling, in effect, without replacement.[55] Alternatively, if workers are approaching the end of a finite earnings span, it is evident that the distribution of the marginal returns must be adversely altered by prolonging the search and consequently shortening the prospective period of employment in the job eventually accepted.[56]

Rising marginal costs or declining marginal benefit distributions can readily be taken into account in the optimal fixed sample size strategy, but if workers are forced to proceed sequentially under such conditions, which alas do not lack for realism, they *will* accept disappointing offers and regret

[54] Holt (1970) identifies the reservation price as the worker's "wage aspiration level," and *hypothesizes* that it will fall with the prolongation of search for essentially the reasons stated here. Holt does not, however, derive a falling optimal reservation wage path. Kasper (1967) entertains the hypothesis that the marginal utility of "leisure" declines as the period of unemployment is (voluntarily) prolonged—but the simple leisure-work dichotomy does not readily accommodate models in which search, like work, is a productive activity. Gronau (1971) mentions some conditions creating nonstationary marginal costs of search, but develops a model in which the optimal reservation wage fails for other reasons—to be noted momentarily.

[55] By hypothesis, the search has been continued because the preceding, unreplaced offers fell below the searcher's reservation wage. His previous disappointments thus induce him to expect more from the future. In large—albeit finite—populations of offers, this will not be a significant effect.

[56] Cf. Gronau (1971) for a search model in which the reservation wage is shown to decline due to the latter effect. It is not unreasonable to think of this as an important consideration for young workers if their labor services are in effect perishable, i.e., their trade has a marked seasonal pattern in any specific locale. The behavior of migratory farm laborers, for example, or of specialized workers in the canning industry, therefore could not be usefully treated within the framework of a *stationary* reservation wage theory.

previous refusals. And as there will be some driven to "corner solutions" by the prospective exhaustion of their resources (pecuniary or psychic), or the deterioration of offer prospects, it is only to be anticipated that after a period of recuperative employment thay may quit in "dissatisfaction" to resume their search.

Moreover, even under the most favorable stationarity conditions, it turns out that adopting a particular stopping rule (reservation price) would not be the best strategy to pursue when one cannot completely trust the available information about the parameters of the underlying distribution of offers. Small mistakes with regard to that distribution's shape can spectacularly, and unexpectedly, extend the duration of the search, thereby compounding the problem which sequential sampling presents for risk averters worried by the possible dispersion around the expected marginal benefit from each successive drawing. To circumscribe such wild-goose chases, the optimal class of search rules may be of a mixed form, combining both the reservation price and fixed sample size properties: e.g., continue searching until either the fixed limit of n offers is reached and selection is made from among them, or after taking m anterior observations, an offer is obtained that exceeds some prespecified reservation level.[57] But this brings us full circle, back to the supposition that some storage of offers is possible and the contention that our analysis of a model which admits solution in terms of an optimal sample size is not devoid of empirical interest—even if considerations of realism suggest that the latter would best be interpreted as a limit on the duration of the search carried out in the chosen local job market.[58]

6. Why Are the Shapes of Offer Distributions Different?

Turning then to the second issue, there are two possible grounds for the assumption that potential migrants can distinguish among alternative local environments for job search on the basis of the relative dispersion of the offers

---

[57] At the mth offer, an obvious minimum for the reservation wage would be x^* in $E[x_{m+1}] - x^* \geqslant c_{m+1}$, the cost of securing the $m+1$th offer; but a more pertinent lower bound might be the maximum offer expected among the remaining $n-m$ trials. For other formulations of mixed search rules, cf. Rothschild's (1971, pp. 8, 9) discussion of the work of Gastwirth (1971).

[58] True subservience to realism would seem to dictate casting the problem in an explicitly Bayesian framework, where information actually acquired can be used to revise the reservation price and the optimal limit set on the duration of the search—in accord with the changing costs of deferring acceptance of offers already received. Such cost changes occur due to "decay," and nonstationarity of the marginal costs and benefits of the process of search itself. This points toward simulation experiments and numerical analysis; in a Bayesian framework with nonstationary marginal search costs, it is not even possible to solve analytically for *the* expected path of the reservation price.

to be found therein. The first of these grounds involves an appeal to purely subjective considerations. We may suppose a worker situated, say, in the countryside will not really know anything definite about the frequency distributions of offers awaiting him in each of several more or less remote places and, further, credit him with an awareness that casual observation will do him little good—finding out about the distribution of *actual* wages paid will merely inform him of the (extreme-value) selections made by other workers within the limits of the samples they *actually* drew from the underlying offer distribution.[59] On the Principle of Insufficient Reason he might then assume the expected (average) value of an offer was the same everywhere. But he might also reflect his greater uncertainty about prevailing conditions in environments remote from, and possibly dissimilar to his own, by assigning such locales a higher relative variance in making his calculations. Thus, a rural dweller might imagine the greatest relative dispersion characterized the job offer distribution of the distant metropolis—either because it was most remote and distance attenuates the volume and quality of information flows, or simply because by comparison with village life the ways of the biggest city seemed most mysterious of all.[60]

But, this last being a possible exception, it is not very persuasive to depict ignorant men making fine distinctions among the states about which they admit to being uninformed. More plausibly, we might think of people ordering their perceptions of the world with simple, binary codes, and thereby assigning a uniformly higher subjective variance to all but their familiar environments. That, unfortunately, does not correspond with the conception of a game involving an array of *differentiated* urns, much less the specification (see Section 3d) of a continuous function making the rel-variance of the offer distribution increase with the cost of reaching the destination in question.[61]

---

[59] This should make it clear that observed wage distributions in any specific market cannot be viewed as the relevant, *ex ante* distribution of offers. Neither can it be taken as an unbiased estimate of the extreme value distribution, because every observation should be normalized to remove the effects of variations in the size of the samples from which these were culled. On its face, the latter does not seem to present an insuperable obstacle to econometric implementation.

[60] According to the latter reasoning, the city dweller would have to regard the country as offering a greater relative dispersion of earning opportunities, which admittedly seems rather less intuitively appealing. The association of *a priori* variance with distance, implied by the hypothesis that distance impedes information flows in a systematic fashion, is (similarly) neutral with respect to the direction of movements. Nelson (1959) emphasizes the distance–information nexus, but elsewhere in the literature of migration it is recognized that information flows are not uniformly attenuated by geographical distance [cf. e.g., Orsagh and Mooney (1970), and Tomaske (1971) on the role of "friends and relatives"].

[61] Although it furnishes an economic rationale for emigration even by risk averters among the uninformed, the model of migration built on this base contributes nothing new to explaining their choices among alternative destinations. It says that with a spatially

There are, however, objective, structural conditions that could equally well give rise to a migrant's perceptions of differences among the relative degrees of dispersion in the distributions of job offers characteristic of alternative destinations. Local labor markets vary in extent, and associated with such size variations come differences (1) in the industrial diversity, and (2) in the modal scale of enterprises found bidding for workers in each place, as well as (3) in the ethnic homogeneity (in formal sociological terms, the "completeness") of the resident population's social structure. As a rule large cities are industrially more diversified than small towns, and within any branch of production—by stark contrast to the company town—they boast an aggregation of many smaller firms, reckoning size here in terms of the modal number of employees per plant.[62] Further, the metropolis is cosmopolitan, an agglomeration of distinct neighborhoods (some would say "urban villages"); its social structure is fractured, or compartmentalized, in comparison to the complete, homogeneous continuum of the country town.

Each of these correlates to city size lends some plausibility to the notion that (mainly as a consequence of structural conditions on the demand side) the relative variance of the distribution of offers tends to be greater in the larger urban labor markets. The variety of industries and the myriad of firms exposed to differing exogenous influences creates more opportunities for the wage rate structure of a major industrial center to be continually disturbed by random events impinging on different employers. Further, as there are likely to be scale economies in labor recruitment and hiring, the smaller number of employees and smaller volume of employee turnover in the modal establishment would tend to militate against the resulting wider dispersion of offers in metropolitan areas being reduced by any correspondingly heavier investments in search activities by those on the buyer's side of the labor market.[63] Larger numbers of employers, comparative anonymity, and the ethnic balkanization of the community of entrepreneurs may also make citywide collusive agreements on wage scales more difficult to arrive at, and more difficult to police

---

dispersed, homogeneneous population one should expect to observe much gross movement between places at which the expected real wage was the same, without any actual spatial r edistribution (net movement) emerging from all "the to-ing and fro-ing."

[62] A cursory glance at the average (not, as desired, the modal) number of manufacturing employees per establishment reported for United States cities by the Census of 1890 and the Census of 1930 will confirm that employer size tends to decline with increasing city size, for places with populations above 30,000. In the case of establishments in the distribution sector, however, the presence of a relatively small number of large department stores and wholesale houses in the major urban centers appears to prevent the same relationship from reflecting itself in the *average* establishment size observations derived from the Census of 1930.

[63] This argument I owe to a suggestion by Michael Rothschild, although he may not approve of the use to which he will find it put here.

from the buying side of the market. More generally, the diffusion of (market) information through random contacts (probabilistic "contagion") can be shown to proceed substantially less rapidly and less uniformly in an incomplete social structure, where members of the population of workers—as well as the population of employers—all do not have equal probability of coming into communicative contacts with all their fellow residents.[64] The foregoing may constitute some of the structural conditions that have drawn employment agencies into existence in the larger cities, especially in more recent times when the costs of local (telephone) communications have been much reduced. But it does not follow that the profitability of the brokerage activities in which such agencies engage must have actually reduced, rather than simply placed an upper bound upon, the rising relative variance encountered as one approaches the top of the urban size hierarchy.

On the strength of the foregoing it would be natural to interpret the postulated "dispersion-opportunities boundary" [Part II, Eq. (12)] as an idealization of the relationship created by structural rather than ephemeral conditions. Any single migrant may, by traveling progressively longer distances (D_{ij}), reach larger cities and thus obtain entry to labor markets in which the distributions of wage offers are characterized by higher and higher relative variance—up to (σ_{max}/μ) the level prevailing in the largest metropolis.[65]

Would that this hypothesis could be put to the test immediately. Alas it cannot, so long as direct information is lacking regarding wage offers; the offer distribution confronting a searcher with specific personal "qualifications" must be something quite different than the distribution of wage offers which have already been accepted and thus recorded as market transactions.[66] The latter represents, we might say, the commingled distributions of maximum wage offers received in searches of different prespecified durations. Quite possibly, in the context of a suitably explicit model of the (optimal) search proceedure, it may be feasible to infer the parameters of the underlying offer distribution from the distribution of wages paid. Until that trick is managed,

[64] Cf. Coleman (1964, Chap. 17), for mathematical modeling of diffusion in incomplete social structures.

[65] While this much is not terribly limiting, it is quite another matter to attempt a full justification along these lines for the mathematically convenient specification of $\sigma_1 = \mu f_j(D)$ as continuously differentiable and concave in D, as is pointed out in footnote 18 (p. 37). (The specification $\mu_i = \mu$ should be recalled in making this interpretation.)

[66] It should be clear that this is an econometric hurdle in the path of direct behavioral tests of most recent work on the economics of market information acquisition via stochastic "search" activities, rather than a difficulty peculiar to the present contribution to this body of literature. Stigler's (1962) presentation of empirical material did not come to grips with this problem, and it remains a challenge to ingenuity.

however, it will remain a virtue of the foregoing hypothesis that it advances empirical application of the model: measures of comparative city size might be used as a proxy for the unknown rel-variances of the wage-offer distributions prevailing in different local labor markets.

Bearing in mind this interpretive frame of reference, as well as the limits on the applicability of the caricature of the process of local job search, the analogy I have drawn with the game of urns and balls would certainly appear reasonably apt in studying the microeconomics of rural–urban migration choices by all but highly skilled manual workers, and perhaps the general run of nonprofessional service workers. If this restricts us to a special theory of labor migration, rather than affording a perfectly general treatment, then for economic historians, as for contemporary urban planners in developing and industrially advanced societies, at least the special case is not one without interest.

APPENDIX

On Sufficient Conditions for the Existence of a Unique Maximum Solution

a. Objective

The purpose of this Appendix is to show that by placing a set of simple and reasonable restrictions on the functions governing the payoffs from the random local job-search process modeled in this essay, one may guarantee that a risk-averse von Neumann–Morgenstern utility maximizer will be led to an optimal migration–search plan (D^*, n^*) which is unique. The optimal solution in question need not be an interior maximum, in the sense of achieving an improvement of the individual's welfare via the allocation of resources to positive levels of migration and search activity. There is no reason to insist that as a general rule there should exist such an *interior* position; quite the contrary, for the grass is not *always* greener in some other pasture. At the same time, it does prove convenient to identify a class of stochastic "payoff functions" which insures the existence of a unique optimum at whatever point in (D, n)-space happens to satisfy the *first-order* conditions for the constrained maximization of expected utility. By confining the exposition in the text to consideration of specific payoff functions of that class, it has been possible to spare the reader an explicit statement and analysis of the rather messy second-order conditions for maximization of the Lagrangian in Eq. (19).

b. Strategy

A direct line of access to the objective stated above is afforded by considering the determinants of the shape of the migration-search opportunity frontier (MSOF), which traces the minimum ρ_Y corresponding to every level of $\overline{Y}$ attainable for a given total outlay on D and n. For our purposes it is clearly sufficient that this boundary be *positively sloped and convex to the $\overline{Y}$-axis*, as depicted in Fig. 2a of the text. If there then exists any point $(\overline{Y}^*, \rho_Y^*)$ in the positive $\rho_Y - \overline{Y}$ plane at which MSOF is tangent to one of the family of positively sloped, concave iso-expected utility curves, the solution (D^*, n^*) corresponding to $(\overline{Y}^*, \rho_Y^*)$ will be unique and will yield the highest expected utility attainable within the constraints.

The one-to-one correspondence of $(\overline{Y}^*, \rho_Y^*)$ with (D^*, n^*) is readily established; explicit substitution of the constraints, i.e., Eqs. (12) and (14), into the specifications provided by Eqs. (9a, b) and (11) for the first- and second-moment payoff functions, permits n to be employed as a mapping variable in generating a nonintersecting locus in $\rho_Y - \overline{Y}$ space. It is the dominant segment of this locus, where for any given level of $\overline{Y}$, ρ_Y is lowest, that defines the MSOF and thereby establishes the latter boundary as a continuous function of n. It then remains to show that, for the function MSOF to exhibit the required slope and convexity, a sufficient condition is that two key structural parameters in the payoff functions obey the following restrictions:

$$0 < \beta < 1 \quad \text{and} \quad 2\beta < \alpha.$$

The proportionate effects of changes in the intensity of local job search upon the migrant's expected terminal wealth, and upon the variance around that expected value, are described by the parameters β and α, respectively. Or, to put the matter in other, equivalent terms, these two magnitudes represent the elasticities with respect to n of the first and second moments of the distributions of "best job offers" that will confront a migrant engaged in searching any particular local labor market. For heuristic purposes, it should be recalled, we postulate that these elasticities are (1) identical in all local markets, i.e., at all potential destinations, and (2) remain strictly constant as the number of wage offers elicited in any specified market is increased, i.e., over the entire range of n considered.

By way of indicating that the above-cited restrictions on the absolute and relative magnitudes of β and α are not empirically implausible and irrelevant, it should be noticed that the first of our two expositional simplifications would be entirely warranted where the distributions of wage offers $(_iw)$ in each local market was generated by processes giving rise to Gaussian frequency density functions having uniform means $(_i\mu = \mu)$ but different variances (σ_i^2).

The second postulate—requiring constancy of the elasticities—will not, on the other hand, be strictly obeyed by the extreme-value distributions of a normal variate; instead, for the variate $(_iz)$ which follows the distribution $N(\mu, \sigma_i)$, it is found that (cf. Cramér, 1963, Sec. 28.6.5)

$$E[_iz_{max}]$$

$$= \mu + \sigma_i\left[2\{\log(n)\}^{1/2} - \frac{\{\log^2(n) + \log 4\pi + 2(1-k)\}}{2\{2\log(n)\}^{1/2}} + \Theta\left\{\frac{1}{\log(n)}\right\}\right]$$

and

$$\text{var}[_iz_{max}] = \frac{\sigma_i'^2}{2\log(n)}\left[\frac{\pi^2}{6} - 1\right] + \Theta\left\{\frac{1}{\log^2(n)}\right\},$$

where k represents Euler's constant, i.e., $0 < k < 1$, and $\Theta\{f(n)\}$ signifies the remainder is at most of the order $f(n)$. Although the elasticity of neither expression with respect to n is strictly constant, a reasonable approximation to $\{E[_iz_{max}] - \mu\}$ is given by a constant elasticity function of the form indicated by Eq. (9a, b) when $\hat{\beta} \simeq 0.37$. This Stigler (1962, p. 97) points out by way of justification of his (and our) assumption of the diminishing marginal productivity of search within a market characterized by imperfect information.[67] Analogously, it is found that for values of n in the range from 2 to 40 the constant elasticity function of the form indicated in Eq. (11) approximates $\text{var}[_iz_{max}]$ when the (fitted) value of $\hat{\alpha}$ exceeds unity, and hence when $\hat{\alpha} > 2\hat{\beta}$.

This is as much as to say that extreme-value distributions approximating those generated by normal distributions of wage offers will satisfy the restrictions on β and α which are shown by this Appendix to be sufficient for the existence of a convex, positively sloped labor market opportunity frontier. Indeed, among the multitude of restrictions that might with the same effect be imposed on the relationship between the magnitudes of β and α, the particular inequality developed here is the one most immediately suggested by the foregoing expressions for the first two moments of the extreme-value distribution of a normal variate. Notice that if only the first of the terms involving n in $E[_iz_{max}]$ were to be replaced by the constant elasticity approximation

$$Bn^{\beta'} \sim \{2\log(n)\}^{1/2},$$

and if only the first of the terms involving n in $\text{var}[_iz_{max}]$ were to be similarly replaced by

$$An^{-\alpha'} \sim \{2\log(n)\}^{-1},$$

[67] But note the more general justification provided in Section 1, p. 26 above.

then consistency would require that $\alpha' = 2\beta'$. Of course, since the second of the terms of $E[_i z_{max}]$ involving n is negative, and $\Theta\{\log^2(n)\} < \Theta\{\log(n)\}$, it is easy to see why constant-elasticity approximations to the complete expressions for the first two moments of the extreme-value distribution must, in the case of a normal variate, conform with the indicated inequality conditions on β and α.

c. Tactics

We begin by considering the general form of the expected wealth function defined by Eqs. (8) and (9a, b). When the job seeker has allocated his resources up to the limits imposed by the investment-budget constraint, $Y_0 s$, and the dispersion-opportunities boundary, $\sigma = F(D)$ concretely specified in Eq. (12), his expected terminal wealth can be written as a function of the variable n alone:

$$\overline{Y}(n) = \{Y_0(1-s) - P\} + R\{G(n)\}\{H(n)\}. \tag{A1}$$

The terms $Y_0(1-s)$ and P are both constants for the individual, as is the capitalization factor R; $G(n)$ represents σ as a *concave* decreasing function of n:

$$\sigma = G(n), \qquad G'(n) < 0, \qquad \text{and} \qquad G''(n) < 0. \tag{A2}$$

This last makes use of the budget constraint and costs functions—Eqs. (14), (15), and (17)—to first express D as a linear decreasing function of n, and then substitute for D in $F(D)$; since $F(D)$ is, according to Eq. (12), increasing and concave in D, we are led immediately to the general form for $G(n)$ indicated above. The remaining term appearing in Eq. (A1) is simply the concave, increasing power function

$$Bn^\beta = H(n), \qquad H'(n) > 0, \qquad \text{and} \qquad H''(n) < 0, \tag{A3}$$

whose general form follows from the stipulation that $0 < \beta < 1$, given $B > 0$.

From this general representation it becomes evident that $\overline{Y}(n)$ must be a strictly concave function of n; it has a unique maximum at $\hat{n}$, where $\overline{Y}'(\hat{n}) = 0$ and hence where

$$G(\hat{n})/H(\hat{n}) = -G'(\hat{n})/H'(\hat{n}) > 0. \tag{A4}$$

Wherever the foregoing, first-order condition for max $\overline{Y}$ is fulfilled, the second-order condition $\overline{Y}''(n) < 0$ will also be satisfied: twice differentiating (A1) yields the expression,

$$\overline{Y}''(n) = R[2\{G'(n)H'(n)\} + \{G(n)H''(n)\} + \{H(n)G''(n)\}]. \tag{A5}$$

But since $H''(n) < 0$, $G''(n) < 0$ and $\{G(n)H'(n)\} < 0$, it appears that $\overline{Y}''(n) < 0$ for *all* n, including $\hat{n}$.

From the general expression for the first-order condition in (A4), it is seen that the level of search intensity $\hat{n}$ at which $\max \overline{Y}$ is reached is independent of R—although that is not true of the value of $\max \overline{Y}$ itself. Upon specific evaluation of the functions represented in (A4) it is found that the solution for $\hat{n}$ depends upon the budget allocation sY_0, the relative shadow price of local-market search activity $\Omega \equiv \omega/\tau$, and the structural parameters β, θ, and γ_j. Concretely,

$$\beta \exp\{\theta[sY_0 - \Omega\hat{n}]\} - \gamma_j\{\beta + \Omega\theta\hat{n}\} = 0 \qquad \text{(A4a)}$$

or

$$Z(\hat{n}) = \theta Y_0 s - \log\{\gamma_j/\beta\}, \qquad \text{(A4b)}$$

where $Z(\hat{n})$ is the increasing, concave function of $\hat{n}$:

$$Z(\hat{n}) \equiv \theta\Omega\hat{n} + \log\{\beta + \theta\Omega n\}. \qquad \text{(A4c)}$$

Consider next the corresponding general representation of ρ_Y as a function of the variable n, where ρ_Y is defined by Eqs. (6b), (10), and (11):

$$\rho_Y(n) = a\{[G(n)]^2\}\{J(n)\}\{X(n)\}. \qquad \text{(A6)}$$

Here $a = R^2 A$, a positive constant. $G(n)$ has already been defined by (A2), and the two functions newly introduced denote the decreasing, convex power function,

$$J(n) = n^{-\alpha}, \qquad J'(n) < 0, \qquad J''(n) > 0, \qquad \text{(A7)}$$

given that $\alpha > 0$, and the transformation of $\overline{Y}(n)$,

$$X(n) = \{\overline{Y}(n)\}^{-2}. \qquad \text{(A8)}$$

From the form of $\overline{Y}(n)$ it is evident that $X(n)$ must be strictly convex and have a unique minimum at $\hat{n}$, i.e., $x'(n) \lessgtr 0$ as $n \lessgtr \hat{n}$, and $x''(n) > 0$ for all n.

It is thus a comparatively straightforward matter to show that in the relevant range of cases, with the foregoing restrictions on $G(n)$, $H(n)$, $J(n)$, and $X(n)$, ρ_Y must be a monotone decreasing function of n. First, by differentiating (A6) and rearranging the results we obtain

$$\rho_Y'(n) = 2a\{G(n)\}^2 J(n) X(n) G'(n)\left[1 + \frac{1}{2}\frac{G(n)}{G'(n)}\frac{J'(n)}{J(n)} - \frac{G(n)}{G'(n)}\frac{\overline{Y}'(n)}{\overline{Y}(n)}\right]. \qquad \text{(A9)}$$

Note the factor multiplying the bracketed terms contains only positive elements, excepting $G'(n) < 0$. Hence when the sum within the brackets is positive, $\rho_Y'(n) < 0$. From (A1), however, it is found that

$$\frac{\overline{Y}'(n)}{\overline{Y}(n)} = \frac{RG(n)\,H(n)}{\overline{Y}(n)}\left[\frac{H'(n)}{H(n)} + \frac{G'(n)}{G(n)}\right], \qquad (A10)$$

which leads us to rewrite the bracketed expression of Eq. (A9) as follows:

$$\left\{1 - \frac{RG(n)\,H(n)}{\overline{Y}(n)}\right\} + \frac{1}{2}\frac{G(n)}{G'(n)}\frac{J'(n)}{J(n)} - \frac{H'(n)}{H(n)}\frac{G(n)}{G'(n)}\left\{\frac{RG(n)\,H(n)}{\overline{Y}(n)}\right\}.$$

$$(A11)$$

Now the only cases of any empirical interest will be those in which the first term within these brackets is nonnegative; otherwise we should be considering individuals who either committed pecuniary resources in migration and search in amounts exceeding their *ex ante* human and nonhuman *wealth* Y_0, or for whom the fixed monetary and psychic costs of leaving their original location exceeded the portion of their total initial wealth not devoted to variable migration–search outlays. Hence restricting the discussion to situations satisfying the "relevancy condition," stated as

$$\{Y_0(1-s) - P\} \geqslant 0, \qquad (A12)$$

suffices to guarantee that the entire expression in (A11) will be positive. This is the case inasmuch as $[G'(n)]^{-1}J'(n) > 0$, and $-H(n)\{G'(n)\}^{-1} > 0$, making each of the two other terms positive. *Hence (A2), (A3), and (A12) form a set of conditions sufficient for* $\rho_Y'(n) < 0$.[68]

From the mapping of the "payoffs" from alternative allocations in Fig. 7,

---

[68] A more general condition for $\rho_Y' < 0$ may, of course, be provided. The bracketed expression on the right-hand side of Eq. (A9) will be positive when

$$\frac{G'}{G} + \frac{1}{2}\frac{J'}{J} - \frac{\overline{Y}'}{Y} < 0, \qquad (A9')$$

as may be seen by multiplying through by the negative quantity $\{G'/G\}$. Then, defining

$$\psi \equiv RG(n)\,H(n)/\overline{Y}(n), \qquad (A10')$$

(A10') can be used to substitute for $\overline{Y}'/\overline{Y}$ in (A9'), yielding

$$\psi\frac{H'}{H} - \frac{1}{2}\frac{J'}{J} > (\psi - 1)\left\{-\frac{G'}{G}\right\}. \qquad (A11')$$

The condition given in the text as (A12) implies that $(\psi - 1) < 0$, which suffices to guarantee that (A11') will be satisfied. Evaluating (A11) by referring to (A3), (A7) and (A14a), below, furnishes us with the more general condition which will ensure that $\rho_Y' < 0$ even when $(\psi - 1) > 0$:

$$\frac{2\beta + \alpha}{2n\theta\Omega[(\sigma_{\max}/\sigma) - 1]} > (\psi - 1). \qquad (A12')$$

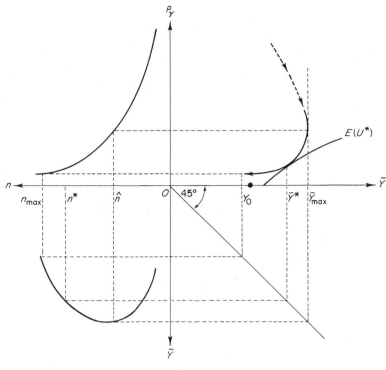

FIG. 7

it is seen that $\rho_Y'(n) < 0$ implies that all migration–search plans involving $n < \hat{n}$ are dominated by solutions involving $n \geqslant \hat{n}$. As $n \to \hat{n}$, it is possible simultaneously to raise $\overline{Y}(n)$ while reducing ρ_Y. Beyond $\hat{n}$, $\overline{Y}'(n)$ becomes negative, and therefore further increases of n within the domain

$$\hat{n} < n < n_{\max} \equiv \{sY_0/\omega\}$$

cause $\rho_Y(n)$ and $\overline{Y}(n)$ to decline concomitantly. The lower wing of the "pay-off-locus" thereby generated slopes downward to the left as $\overline{Y}(n)$ recedes from $\overline{Y}_{\max} = \overline{Y}(\hat{n})$. It is this dominant portion of the locus which is referred to as the migration–search opportunity frontier (MSOF).

   Figure 7 makes it evident that for MSOF to be convex, as well as positively sloped with reference to the $\overline{Y}$-axis, it is sufficient that the function $\rho_Y(n)$ be decreasing and convex in n. Thus, *subject to condition* (A12), $\rho_Y''(n) \geqslant 0$ *is a sufficient condition for the existence of a unique optimum solution. Obviously it is not a necessary one.* We have thus reduced the problem of insuring the existence of a unique maximum to that of finding a sufficient condition for $\rho_Y''(n) \geqslant 0$.

Differentiation of Eq. (A9) with respect to n, and some slight manipulation of the result, provides us with the expression,

$$\frac{\rho''(n)}{2a\{G(n)\}^2 J(n) X(n)} = \left\{\frac{G'(n)}{G(n)}\right\}^2 + \frac{G''(n)}{G(n)} + 2\frac{G'(n)}{G(n)}\left\{\frac{J'(n)}{J(n)} - 4\frac{\overline{Y}'(n)}{\overline{Y}(n)}\right\}$$
$$+ \left\{\frac{Y'(n)}{Y(n)}\right\}^2 \left\{2 - \frac{1}{\overline{Y}'(n)}\right\} - 2\frac{J'(n)}{J(n)}\frac{\overline{Y}'(n)}{\overline{Y}(n)} + \frac{J''(n)}{J(n)}\frac{Y''(n)}{Y(n)},$$

$$(A13)$$

from whence it may be seen that $\rho_Y''(n) \geqslant 0$ requires

$$S_1 \geqslant S_2, \tag{A14}$$

where S_1 is the summation of elements

$$|\{G'(n)/G(n)\}^2| = |\{x\}^2|,$$
$$|2\{G'(n)/G(n)\}\{J'(n)/J(n)\}| = |2\{x\}\alpha n^{-1}|,$$
$$|2\{\overline{Y}'(n)/\overline{Y}(n)\}^2| = |2q[\{x\} + \beta n^{-1}]|,$$
$$|\{\overline{Y}'(n)/\overline{Y}(n)\}^2 \{\overline{Y}'(n)\}^{-1}| = |q[\{x\} + \beta n^{-2}]\{\overline{Y}(n)\}^{-1}|,$$
$$|\{J''(n)/J(n)\}| = |\alpha(\alpha+1)n^{-2}|,$$
$$|\{\overline{Y}''(n)/\overline{Y}(n)\}| = |q[\theta\Omega n^{-\beta} + 2\beta n^{-1}\{x\} + \beta(\beta-1)n^{-2}]|;$$

S_2 is the summation of elements

$$|4\{G'(n)/G(n)\}\{\overline{Y}'(n)/\overline{Y}(n)\}| = |4\{x\}q[\{x\} + \beta n^{-1}]|,$$
$$|2\{J'(n)/J(n)\}\{\overline{Y}'(n)/\overline{Y}(n)\}| = |2\alpha n^{-1}q[\{x\} + \beta n^{-1}]|,$$
$$|\{G''(n)/G(n)\}| = |\theta\Omega\{x\}|.$$

In the right-hand side evaluation of the elements of S_1 and S_2, $\{x\}$ denotes the function of n,

$$\{x\} \equiv G'(n)/G(n) = \frac{-\{\theta\Omega[\sigma_{max}\gamma_j \exp\{-\theta\Omega(n_{max}-n)\}]\}}{\sigma_{max}[1 - \gamma_j \exp\{-\theta\Omega(n_{max}-n)\}]} \tag{A14a}$$
$$= \theta\Omega[1 - \{\sigma_{max}/\sigma\}] < 0;$$

and $\{q\}$ denotes the variable

$$\{q\} = 1 - \frac{\{Y_0(1-s) - P\}}{\overline{Y}(n)}, \qquad 0 < q < 1 \tag{A14b}$$

whose relevant range is delimited by (A12).

By resort to algebraic brute force, the condition stated as (A13) can be reduced to the more compact specific expression

$$0 < [(1/4q)-1] - \{x\}^{-1} ([\{(\theta\Omega/q)-(1/\overline{Y}(n))\}/4] - [\{1-(\alpha/n)\}/2])$$
$$+ \{x\}^{-2} [(\beta n^{-1})/2 + (\theta\Omega n^{-\beta})/4 + \{\beta n^{-2}/4\}\{\alpha(\alpha+1)/\beta q\}]$$
$$+ \{x\}^{-2} [\{\overline{Y}(n)\}^{-1} - \{1-\beta+2\alpha\}]. \tag{A15}$$

And from this it emerges readily enough that for (A14a, b) to be satisfied the following conditions (jointly) are sufficient:

$$\left[\left(\frac{1}{4q}\right)-1\right] \geqslant \{x\}^{-1}\left[\left[\frac{1}{4}\left\{\frac{\theta\Omega}{q} - \frac{1}{\overline{Y}(n)}\right\}\right] - \frac{1}{2}\left[1 - \frac{\alpha}{n}\right]\right] \tag{A16a}$$

and

$$\{\overline{Y}(n)\}^{-1} \geqslant \left\{1 - \beta + 2\alpha - \frac{\alpha(\alpha+1)}{\beta q} - 2n\right\}. \tag{A16b}$$

Eliminating $\overline{Y}(n)$ by solving (A16a) and (A16b), we obtain the combined condition sufficient to enforce the inequality in (A15):

$$\frac{1}{q}\left[\frac{1}{4} - \{x\}\left\{\frac{1}{4}\theta\Omega + \frac{\alpha(\alpha+1)}{\beta}\right\}\right] + x\left[\frac{1}{2} - \frac{\alpha}{2n} + (1-\beta) - 2n + 2\alpha\right] \geqslant 1. \tag{A17}$$

Recalling condition (A12)—or (A14b)—we can assert that over the relevant range $Y_0 \leqslant \overline{Y}(n) \leqslant Y_{\max}(\hat{n})$, $(1/q) > 1$, so that (A.17) must hold whenever

$$2n + \frac{\theta\Omega}{4} + \left\{\frac{\alpha(\alpha+1)}{\beta} + \frac{\alpha}{2n}\right\} - \{2\alpha+\beta\} \geqslant 2\frac{1}{2}. \tag{A18}$$

Since $\theta > 0$ by assumption, and $\Omega > 0$ by the requirement that the shadow prices of the migration and search activities be positive, it is now a trivial matter to establish that (A18) must, in turn, hold whenever we have $0 < \beta < 1$ *and* the additional restriction

$$\alpha > 2\beta. \tag{A19}$$

First, observe that the inequality in (A19) implies the further inequalities

$$\alpha(\alpha+1)/\beta > 4\beta + 2; \qquad 2\alpha + \beta > 5\beta; \qquad \alpha/2n > \beta/n.$$

Hence the addition of (A19) reduces condition (A18) to the weak restriction

$$2n + \frac{\theta\Omega}{4} > \beta\left\{1 - \frac{1}{n}\right\} + \frac{1}{2},$$

which can be satisfied by all n in the range: $1 < n \leqslant \infty$.

$$Q.E.D.$$

ACKNOWLEDGMENTS

I have had many conversations with Moe Abramovitz about migrants and their economic behavior, and by now my general thinking on the subject is thoroughly permeated with his views. He cannot be implicated, however, in the faults or peculiarities of the present formulation.

An economic historian does not stray from his proper *metier* so far as I have in these pages without heavily taxing the patience and generosity of colleagues and friends. Beyond the specific debts on technical matters that are noticed in the paper itself, an embarrassingly large number of people deserve some expression of my gratitude for their help. Takeshi Anemiya, Theodore Anderson, Yoram Ben-Porath, Zvi Griliches, Robert Hall, Hayne Leland, Walter Oi, John Pencavel, Sherwin Rosen, Warren Sanderson, Michael Spence, and Richard Zeckhauser have given me useful comments on earlier drafts and seminar presentations of this material, or simply allowed me to pick their brains. Three further debts of a somewhat special nature must be acknowledged. Melvin Reder encouraged me to start working on the formal theory of migration in the summer of 1971, and has continued to supply an unremitting stream of tough, skeptical questions—as only he can. Michael Rothschild freely gave much time to helping me understand recent work by himself and others on the organization of markets with imperfect information and the behavior of individuals participating in them. And Ronald Rebholz, incredulously but unerringly, guided me to the literature of Fortuna.

Financial support for this research was received under OEO Grant CG-9027; and through the Stanford Economics Faculty Research Seminar on the Household (Summer Session, 1972).

REFERENCES

Alchian, A. A. (1970)   Information costs, pricing and resource unemployment. In *The microeconomic foundations of employment and inflation theory* (E. Phelps *et al.*, eds.). New York: Norton.

Arrow, K. J. (1965)   *Aspects of the theory of risk-bearing*, Yrjo Jahnsson Lectures. Helsinki: The Academic Bookstore.

Arrow, K. J. and Enthoven, A. C. (1961).   Quasi-concave programming. *Econometrica* **29**: 779–800.

Burckhardt, J. (1929)   *The civilization of the renaissance in Italy.* New York: Harper.

Cioffari, V. (1935)   *Fortune and fate from Democritus to St. Thomas Aquinas.* New York: Privately printed.

Cioffari, V. (1940)   *The conception of fortune and fate in the works of Dante.* Cambridge, Massachusetts: Harvard Univ. Press for the Dante Society.

Cioffari, V. (1944)   *Fortune in Dante's fourteenth century commentators.* Cambridge, Massachusetts: Harvard Univ. Press for the Dante Society.

Coleman, J. S. (1964)   *Introduction to mathematical sociology.* New York: Free Press.

Cramér, H. (1963)   *Mathematical methods of statistics.* Princeton, New Jersey: Princeton Univ. Press.

Eldridge, H. T. (1964).   A cohort approach to the analysis of migration differentials. *Demography* **1**: 212–219.

Evenson, R. E., and Kislev, Y. (1972)   A model of technological research. Unpublished working paper. New Haven, Connecticut: Economic Growth Center, Yale Univ.

Gallaway, L. E., and Vedder, R. K. (1971)   Emigration from the United Kingdom to the United States: 1860–1913. *Journal of Economic History* **31**: 885–897.

Gastwirth, J. L. (1971). On probabilistic models of consumer search for information, Preliminary version. Unpublished paper. Johns Hopkins Univ. and the National Science Foundation.

Gronau, R. (1971) Information and frictional unemployment. *American Economic Review* **61**: Pt. 1, 290–301.

Gumbel, E. J. (1958). *Statistics of extremes.* New York: Columbia Univ. Press.

Holt, C. C. (1970) Job search, Phillips' wage relations, and union influence: Theory and evidence. In *The microeconomic foundations of employment and inflation theory* (E. Phelps, *et al.*, eds.). New York: Norton.

Kasper, H. (1967) The asking price of labor and the duration of unemployment. *Review of Economics and Statistics* **49**: 165–172.

Kelley, A. C. (1965) International migration and economic growth, Australia: 1865–1935. *Journal of Economic History* **25**: 333–354.

Laber, G., and Chase, R. X. (1971) Interprovincial migration in Canada as a human capital decision. *Journal of Political Economy* **79**: 795–804.

Lowry, I. S. (1966) *Migration and metropolitan growth: Two analytical models.* San Francisco, California: Chandler.

McCall, J. J. (1970) Economics of information and job search. *Quarterly Journal of Economics* **84**: 113–126.

McCall, J. J. (1971) Probabilistic microeconomics. *Bell Journal of Economics and Management Science* **2**.

Markowitz, H. (1959) *Portfolio selection.* New York.

Masnick, G. (1968) Employment status and retrospective and prospective migration in the United States. *Demography* **5**: 79–85.

Morrill, R. L., and Pitts, F. R. (1967) Marriage, migration, and the mean information field: A study in uniqueness and generality. *Annals of the Association of American Geographers* **57**: 401–422.

Mortensen, D. T. (1970) Job search, the duration of unemployment, and the Phillips curve. *American Economic Review* **60**: 847–862.

Nelson, P. (1959) Migration, real income, and information. *Journal of Regional Science* **1**: 43–74.

Nelson, P. (1970) Information and consumer behavior. *Journal of Political Economy* **78**: 311–329.

Orsagh, T. J., and Mooney, P. J. (1970) A model for the dispersion of the migrant labor force and some results for the United States, 1880–1920. *Review of Economics and Statistics* **52**: 306–312.

Parnes, H. S. (1954) *Research on Labor Mobility*, Bull. 65. New York: Social Science Research Council.

Patch, H. R. (1927) *The Goddess Fortuna in medieval literature.* Cambridge, Massachusetts: Harvard Univ. Press.

Phelps, E. *et al.* (eds.) (1970) *The microeconomic foundations of employment and inflation theory*, New York: Norton.

Ravenstein, E. G. (1885) The laws of migration. *Journal of the Royal Statistical Society* **48**: 167–227.

Ravenstein, E. G. (1889) The laws of Migration. *Journal of the Royal Statistical Society* **52**: 241–301.

Reynolds, L. G. (1951) *The structure of labor markets, wage and labor mobility in theory and practice.* New York: Harper.

Roberts, M. J. (1971) Portfolio models and the impact of taxation on investment: A reconsideration. Unpublished Discussion Paper 213. Cambridge, Massachusetts: Institute of Economic Research, Harvard Univ.

Rothschild, M. (1971)   Models of market organization with imperfect information: A survey. Unpublished paper. Cambridge, Massachusetts: Harvard Univ. Presented at *Econometric Society Meeting, December 1971.*

Sjaastad, L. A. (1962)   The cost and returns of human migration. *Journal of Political Economy Supplement* **70**: 80–93.

Smith, A. (1937)   *An inquiry into the nature and causes of the wealth of nations* (E. Cannan, ed.). New York: The Modern Library.

Stewart, J. Q. (1947)   Empirical mathematical rules concerning the distribution and equilibrium of population. *Geographical Review* **37**: 467–485.

Stigler, G. (1961)   The economics of information. *Journal of Political Economy* **69**: 213–225.

Stigler, G. (1962)   Information in the labor market. *Journal of Political Economy Supplement* **70**: 94–105.

Tobin, J. (1958)   Liquidity preference as behavior toward risk. *Review of Economic Studies* **25**: 65–86.

Tobin, J. (1972)   Inflation and employment. *American Economic Review* **62**: 1–18.

Todaro, M. P. (1969)   A model of labor migration and urban unemployment in less developed countries. *American Economic Review* **59**: 138–148.

Tomaske, J. A. (1971)   The determinants of intercountry differences in European migration: 1881–1900. *Journal of Economic History* **31**: 840–853.

Tsiang, S. C. (1972)   The rationale of the mean-standard deviation analysis, skewness preference, and the demand for money. *American Economic Review* **62**: 354–371.

United States Bureau of Census (1966)   Mobility of the population of the United States. *Current population reports*, Series P-20.

United States Bureau of Census (1966)   Reasons for moving: March 1962 to March 1963. *Current population reports*, Series P-20, No. 154.

Vanderkamp, J. (1971)   Migration flows, their determinants and the effects of return migration. *Journal of Political Economy* **79**: 1012–1031.

Wilber, G. L. (1963)   Migration expectancy in the United States. *Journal of the American Statistical Association* **58**: 444–453.

Zipf, G. K. (1949)   *Human behavior and the principle of least effort.* Reading, Massachusetts: Addison-Wesley.

Does Economic Growth Improve the Human Lot ? Some Empirical Evidence

RICHARD A. EASTERLIN

UNIVERSITY OF PENNSYLVANIA

Over a decade ago, Moses Ambramovitz published an essay, "The Welfare Interpretation of National Income and Product," in a predecessor volume to this one, honoring another distinguished Stanford economist (Abramovitz, 1959). Abramovitz concluded that "we must be highly skeptical of the view that long term changes in the rate of growth of welfare can be gauged even roughly from changes in the rate of growth of output,"[1] and called for "further thought about the meaning of secular changes in the rate of growth of national income and empirical studies that can fortify and lend substance to analysis [pp. 21, 22]."[*]

This paper is offered in the spirit of this little-heeded call. It brings together the results of surveys of human happiness that have been conducted in

[1] A differing conclusion, perhaps more representative of the profession at large, is reached by Nordhaus and Tobin (1972): "Is growth obsolete? We think not. Although GNP and other national income aggregates are imperfect measures of welfare, the broad picture of secular progress which they convey remains after correction of their most obvious deficiencies [p. 24]."

[*] M. Abramovitz, "The welfare interpretation of secular trends in national income and product." In *The Allocation of Economic Resources: Essays in Honor of Bernard Francis Haley* (M. Abramovitz *et al.* eds.), Stanford, California: Stanford Univ. Press, 1959.

nineteen countries, developed and less-developed, during the period since World War II, to see what evidence there is of an association between income and happiness. Are the wealthy members of society usually happier than the poor? What of rich versus poor countries—are the more developed nations typically happier? As a country's income grows during the course of economic development, does human happiness advance—does economic growth improve the human lot?

Happiness is not confined, of course, to economic well-being. Abramovitz noted that "since Pigou ... economists have generally distinguished between social welfare, or welfare at large, and the narrower concept of economic welfare," with "national product ... taken to be the objective, measurable counterpart of economic welfare [p. 3]." Happiness corresponds to the broader of these two concepts, that of social welfare, or welfare at large. However, as Abramovitz points out, economists have normally disregarded possible divergences between the two welfare concepts, and operated on Pigou's dictum "that there is a clear presumption that changes in economic welfare indicate changes in social welfare in the same direction, if not in the same degree [p. 3]." It is this dictum, as applied to the study of economic growth, that is the central concern of this paper. Is there evidence that economic growth is positively associated with social welfare, i.e., human happiness?

The term "happiness" is used intermittently, albeit loosely, in the literature of economics.[2] To my knowledge, however, this is the first attempt to look at the actual evidence. The initial section of this paper is devoted to a somewhat lengthy discussion of the concept and measurement of happiness, as the term is used in this study. The second section presents the results of the empirical analysis, and the third, an interpretation of the findings. The conclusions, in brief, are that the evidence supports Abramovitz's skepticism of a positive correlation between output and welfare, and for a good reason. The increase in output itself makes for an escalation in human aspirations, and thus negates the expected positive impact on welfare.

1. The Concept and Measurement of Happiness

a. Concept

The basic data used here are statements by individuals on their subjective happiness. These self-reports are sometimes designated "avowed" or "reported" happiness to underscore the possibility that they may not accurately

---

[2] It is used, for example, in welfare economics by Mishan (1968): "If, for instance, welfare is used as a synonym for happiness ... [p. 504]." Similarly, Little (1950) comments: "And, according to our present definition of 'welfare' (= 'happiness') ... [p. 30]." In a recent economics text, Eckaus (1972) writes: "What is the economic system supposed to do? The answer that it should contribute to human happiness is as good a start as any [p. 7]."

reflect the true state of the respondents' feelings. This possibility will be examined shortly.

The data are of two types. The first consists of the responses to a Gallup-poll-type survey in which a direct question of the following sort was asked: "In general, how happy would you say that you are—*very* happy, *fairly* happy, or *not very* happy?" Sometimes this was preceded by a question asking the respondent to state "in your own words, what the word 'happiness" means to you."

The other set of data comes from a more sophisticated procedure, devised by Cantril (1965) in a pioneering study of the hopes, fears, and happiness of persons in 14 countries of the world. Since Cantril's study figures prominently in the following analysis, it is worth quoting him at some length. He starts with a general description of the technique he calls the "Self-Anchoring Striving Scale":

> A person is asked to define on the basis of *his own* assumptions, perceptions, goals, and values the two extremes or anchoring points of the spectrum on which some scale measurement is desired—for example, he may be asked to define the "top" and "bottom," the "good" and "bad," the "best" and the "worst." This self-defined continuum is then used as our measuring device.
>
> While the Self-Anchoring Striving Scale technique can be used on a wide variety of problems, it was utilized in this study as a means of discovering the spectrum of values a person is preoccupied or concerned with and by means of which he evaluates his own life. He describes as the top anchoring point his wishes and hopes as he personally conceives them and the realization of which would constitute for him the best possible life. At the other extreme, he describes the worries and fears, the preoccupations and frustrations, embodied in his conception of the worst possible life he could imagine. Then, utilizing a nonverbal ladder device [showing a scale from 0 to 10], symbolic of "the ladder of life," he is asked where he thinks he stands on the ladder today, with the top being the best life *as he has defined it*, the bottom the worst life *as he has defined it*.

· ·

The actual questions, together with the parenthetical instructions to interviewers, are given below:

> 1. (A) All of us want certain things out of life. When you think about what really matters in your own life, what are your wishes and hopes for the future? In other words, if you imagine your future in the *best* possible light, what would your life look like then, if you are to be happy? Take your time in answering; such things aren't easy to put into words.
>
>   PERMISSIBLE PROBES: What are your hopes for the future? What would your life have to be like for you to be completely happy? What is missing for you to be happy? [Use also, if necessary, the words "dreams" and "desires."]
>
>   OBLIGATORY PROBE: Anything else?
>
>   (B) Now, taking the other side of the picture, what are your fears and worries about the future? In other words, if you imagine your future in the *worst* possible light, what would your life look like then? Again, take your time in answering.

PERMISSIBLE PROBE: What would make you unhappy? [Stress the words "fears" and "worries."]

OBLIGATORY PROBE: Anything else?

Here is a picture of a ladder. Suppose we say that the top of the ladder (POINT-ING) represents the best possible life for you and the bottom (POINTING) represents the worst possible life for you.

(C) Where on the ladder (MOVING FINGER RAPIDLY UP AND DOWN LAD-DER) do you feel you personally stand at the *present* time? Step number_____ [pp. 22–23, italics in original].*

This technique thus yields a rating by each individual of his personal standing on a scale from 0 (the worst possible life) to 10 (the best possible life), where "worst" and "best" are defined by each person for himself. The survey also asked for current evaluations of past and prospective personal standings, plus a similar set of evaluations by each individual of the situation of the nation as a whole. In the present analysis, use will be made only of the rating by each individual of his personal happiness at the time of the survey, since this is relevant to subjective well-being, and reports on one's feelings at the moment are likely to be more accurate than those on how one might feel or did feel in other situations.

Although the procedures differ in the Gallup poll and Cantril approaches, the concept of happiness underlying them is essentially the same. Reliance is placed on the subjective evaluation of the respondent—in effect, each individual is considered to be the best judge of his own feelings. He is seen as having a frame of reference that defines for him the range from unhappy to happy states of mind. His summary response—whether in terms of broad categories of happiness, as in the Gallup poll, or in terms of a numerical rating from 0 to 10, as in Cantril's approach—is a statement of his present position within that frame of reference.

The approach has a certain amount of appeal. If one is interested in how happy people are—in their subjective satisfaction—why not let each person set his own standard and decide how closely he approaches it? The alternatives of obtaining evaluations by outside observers or seeking to use objective indicators of happiness inevitably run into the problem of what observers or what indicators one should rely on. Moreover, despite the use of ratings based on a scale that varies from one individual to the next, it is possible to make meaningful comparisons. For example, consider two population groups. These might be two segments of a national population at a given time, say rich and poor, or the populations of an entire country at two different times, or the populations of two different countries at a given time. Whatever the

---

* *Patterns of Human Concerns* by Hadley Cantril. Rutgers University Press, New Brunswick, New Jersey (1965).

case, it is of interest to ask whether on the average individuals in the first population differ significantly from those in the second in how high they rate themselves in terms of personal happiness, even though the scale being applied differs within each population and between the two. After all, in opinion surveys on the relative merit, say, of presidential aspirants, the criteria used by respondents in forming their evaluations doubtless differ. Indeed, it is of interest to ask whether there are systematic differences in the criteria used for the evaluations (a point we shall look into later). It may be argued, of course, that political opinion polls are of value because of their implications for prospective behavior of the respondents. But perhaps the same may be said of opinions on personal happiness—might not individuals with a low personal happiness rating be expected to behave differently from those with a high personal rating?

At the same time, a number of reservations on the meaningfulness of the data come to mind. There is first the question of the relevance of the happiness concept to populations differing widely in cultural characteristics. It is true that the present approach allows each individual to define his own standard of happiness. But is the idea itself present in all cultures? One indication that it is is the observation by Inkeles (1960) that happiness, in contrast to certain other concepts relating to emotional states, "may be translated fairly well from one language to another ... [p. 15]." Cantril (1965) devoted considerable effort to this translation issue:

> One of the problems that had to be overcome was translating the original questions from English into the various languages used. In some cases this was by no means an easy task, and considerable time was spent with experts to be sure the translation contained the precise nuances wanted. One of the methods often utilized in this translation process was to have someone who knew the native language, as a native, for example, an Arab, and who also was completely fluent in English translate our questions into Arabic. Then someone whose native language was English but who had a perfect command of Arabic would translate the Arabic back into English so a comparison could be made with the original question and, through discussion and further comparisons, difficulties could be ironed out.
>
> Translations from English had to be made into the following twenty-six other languages which we list here alphabetically: Arabic, Bengali, Cebuano, German, Gujarati, Hausa, Hebrew, Hindi, Ibo, Ilocano, Ilongo, Malayalam, Marathi, Oriya, Polish, Portuguese, Serbo-Croatian, Slovenian, Spanish, Tagalog, Tamil, Telugu, Urdu, Waray, Yiddish, and Yoruba [p. 26].*

Apparently the effort paid off, for the nonresponse rate was generally low. To judge from this experience, happiness is an idea that transcends individual cultures.

* *Patterns of Human Concerns* by Hadley Cantril. Rutgers University Press, New Brunswick, New Jersey (1965).

Moreover, the considerations affecting personal happiness in different cultures turn out to be quite similar. In his survey, Cantril found that typically certain hopes and fears were more frequently expressed than others. Here, for example, is a tabulation he prepared of the things mentioned most frequently by Americans in discussing their hopes, and the proportion of the sample mentioning each item (Cantril, 1965, p. 35):*

Own health	40%
Decent standard of living	33
Children	29
Housing	24
Happy family	18
Family health	16
Leisure time	11
Keep status quo	11
Old age	10
Peace	9
Resolution of religious problems	8
Working conditions	7
Family responsibility	7
To be accepted	6
An improved standard of living	5
Employment	5
Attain emotional maturity	5
Modern conveniences	5

To facilitate handling such data, Cantril (1965, p. 36) further classified the items listed above into nine "general" categories of personal hopes:

Economic	65%
Health	48
Family	47
Personal values	20
Status quo	11
Job or work situation	10
International situation, world	10
Social values	5
Political	2

Hopes relating to economic matters appear to be foremost in the minds of Americans, but clearly do not exhaust the content of happiness.

Similar classification of the replies for other countries enabled Cantril to compare the personal hopes of people in widely differing national and cultural circumstances (Table 1). What stands out is that hopes regarding economic,

* *Patterns of Human Concerns* by Hadley Cantril. Rutgers University Press, New Brunswick, New Jersey (1965).

TABLE 1

PERSONAL HOPES BY COUNTRY, CA. 1960[a,b]

Country	Economic	Family	Health	Values and character	Job/work	Social	International	Political	Status quo	Total
					Personal hopes					
Brazil	68	28	34	14	8	1	1	—	1	155
Cuba	73	52	47	30	14	4	3	15	1	239
Dominican Republic	95	39	17	15	25	2	—	9	—	202
Egypt	70	53	24	39	42	9	2	4	—	243
India	70	39	4	14	22	8	—	—	2	159
Israel	80	76	47	29	35	10	12	2	4	295
Nigeria	90	76	45	42	19	14	—	—	—	286
Panama	90	53	43	26	26	3	—	1	1	243
Philippines	60	52	6	9	11	5	—	—	—	143
United States	65	47	48	20	10	5	10	2	11	218
West Germany	85	27	46	11	10	3	15	1	4	202
Yugoslavia	83	60	41	18	20	4	8	—	2	236

[a] From *Patterns of Human Concerns* by Hadley Cantril, Rutgers University Press, New Brunswick, New Jersey (1965).
[b] Percentage of population mentioning hopes that fall in indicated category. Sum of percentages exceeds 100 percent because some respondents mention hopes falling in more than one category.

family, and health matters repeatedly dominate the perceptions of happiness by individuals in the various countries, with economic concerns typically the most frequently mentioned. Needless to say, the specific nature of these concerns often differs (some evidence on this regarding economic aspirations is presented toward the end of this essay), and there are undoubtedly variations among people within countries as well. If one looks at a like tabulation for personal fears rather than hopes, a similarity among countries again appears, though the relative importance of the categories changes somewhat (e.g., typically health increases in relative importance). On reflection, the similarity in the results for different countries is plausible. In all cultures the way in which the bulk of the people spend most of their time is similar—in working and trying to provide for and raise a family. Hence the concerns that they express when asked about happiness are similar.

b. Measurement Problems

Let us turn to some technical issues regarding the data. For one thing, there is the question of the stability of the replies. Are emotional states so highly variable that the replies to questions about personal happiness tend to fluctuate widely over short periods of time, with the ups and downs of daily life? This problem has been studied by comparing the results of surveys of the same population run at short intervals. The conclusion, reported by Robinson and Shaver (1969, p. 17), is that "[o]ne of the most impressive features of the questions ... is the stable test–retest reliabilities they exhibit." This result is confirmed by the data used here. Two surveys by the American Institute of Public Opinion (AIPO) containing a happiness question were taken within two weeks of each other in September 1956. The results were virtually identical. A third poll taken six months later still showed very little change (see Table 8 below).

Another important issue is the validity of self-reports on happiness. Are people capable of assessing their own emotional states? One test, though hardly a definitive one, is to examine the consistency of self-reports with evaluations by outside judges—peers, professional psychologists, and so on. The results of such tests are summarized as follows by Wilson (1967):

> Data from these several studies suggest that judges agree poorly among themselves, that judges vary in the extent to which they agree with self-ratings, and that few judges agree closely with self-ratings. At the same time, the data show that most judges agree with self-ratings to some extent and that the pooling of judges' estimates increases the agreement with self-ratings. These facts would seem, if anything, to support the validity of self-ratings [p. 295].*

* From W. Wilson, "Correlates of avowed happiness," *Psychological Bulletin* **67**, 1967, 294–306. Copyright 1967 by the American Psychological Association and reproduced by permission.

Comparisons have also been made between self-reports on happiness and measures presumed to be indicative of happiness, e.g., indicators of physical health, and between self-reports on happiness and measures of other psychological states such as depression and self-esteem (Bradburn, 1969, p. 39; Robinson and Shaver, 1969, pp. 26–31). In both cases the self-reports show significant correlations with the other measures of the type expected. In all of these comparisons, there is inevitably the question of what is to be taken as the ultimate arbiter of "happiness." Perhaps the most that can be said is that the general consistency of self-reports with the other bases of evaluation bolsters one's confidence in the ability of people to assess with some validity their own feelings.

The result bears also on another issue—whether a person is likely to report his true feelings to an anonymous interviewer. The fact that the self-reports check out fairly well with other bases of evaluation suggests that the replies are reasonably honest. Indeed, in view of the considerable success in obtaining reports on such matters of intimate concern as personal income and sex, it might be felt that there would be no serious problem in getting people to state how happy they are. However, one possibly important source of bias exists. In formulating replies to survey questions, respondents are influenced by considerations of what they believe to be the proper or socially desirable response (Davis, 1965).[3] Thus, if the social norm is that happiness is a good thing, there might be a tendency toward an upward bias in the replies due to considerations of social desirability.

Again, there have been attempts to test for this factor. Comparisons have been made between replies given to an interviewer and the responses on a self-administered questionnaire, the presumption being that one is likely to be more honest in the latter situation. Also, correlations have been run between people's statements of their happiness and their tendencies toward social conformity, as measured by standard psychological tests. Sometimes the tests suggest some influence of social desirability in the replies; sometimes they do not (Bradburn, 1969, p. 38; Wilson, 1967, p. 295).

Of course, if all responses were similarly biased, there would be no real problem for the present study. The concern here is with the relation of happiness to income, and the real question is whether there may be differential bias in the replies by income level. Is it likely, for example, that rich people would feel that they were expected to reply that they are "very happy," and conversely for poor people? On reflection it is not wholly certain what reply people might think was expected of them. While most respondents might feel that the social norm is that "money makes one happy," there is the

---

[3] Cf. Edwards (1957). Recent work by Block (1965) and Rorer (1965) suggests that the importance of this factor in biasing survey results has been exaggerated.

possibility that others would be influenced by the notion of the "carefree, happy poor." The expected bias in the replies would clearly be different depending on which is perceived as the social norm. Beyond this there is the question of the universality of the norm. Has "the" norm been the same in the United States since 1946, or has it perhaps been altered by public attention in the 1960s to the "poverty problem"? Is the norm the same in 19 different countries ranging over the various continents of the world?

It is also pertinent to consider the context in which the happiness question is asked. If one were asked his income and then, immediately following, how happy he was, the respondent might link the two questions, and his awareness of a social norm might bias his reply. In the Gallup poll surveys used here, however, the happiness question is intermixed with 50 or more survey questions, most of which deal with current events, usually political. The question on economic status comes at the end of these surveys along with other inquiries as to personal characteristics. Under these circumstances, the respondent, in formulating his reply to the happiness question, is not likely to feel the interviewer is regarding him as a "rich person" or as "a poor person" and to answer the way he thinks such a person "ought" to answer. The Cantril survey is specifically focused on people's feelings—their hopes, fears, and how happy they are. Even in this case, however, the question on economic status comes at the end of the survey. It is far from clear that in considering questions a respondent would feel himself especially cast in the role, say, of a poor person, as distinct from that of one who is young or married or has any one of a number of other personal characteristics.

Finally, it is instructive to note the effect of variations in the wording of the happiness question. The National Opinion Research Center (NORC) has asked a question similar to that in the AIPO surveys, but the happiness categories differ as follows:

	(1)	(2)	(3)
AIPO	Very happy	Fairly happy	Not very happy
NORC	Very happy	Pretty happy	Not too happy

The first and third categories are virtually alike. It seems reasonable to suppose, however, that many individuals would consider the NORC's rating (2), "pretty happy," closer to (1) and farther from (3) than the AIPO's rating "fairly happy." Hence, one might expect that some respondents who chose category (1) in the AIPO poll would have chosen (2) in the NORC poll, and some who chose (2) in the AIPO poll would have chosen (3) in the NORC poll. The results of polls taken at similar dates confirm this expectation— the percentage in group (1) tends to run lower and the percentage in group (3) runs higher in the NORC polls (see Table 8, panels A and B). Moreover, a shift of this type is common to all income classes, with no systematic difference in magnitude.[4] The direction of the shift and the consistency by income level suggest that respondents throughout the population are placing similar interpretations on the question asked and are answering, at least to some extent, in terms of their real feelings.

However, when all is said and done, the possibility of differential bias in the replies by income level cannot be ruled out, though the magnitude remains uncertain, and this qualification must be borne in mind in interpreting the findings presented here. My own feeling is that while such bias may exist, it is not significant enough to invalidate the conclusions on the association between income and happiness. Perhaps the most important basis for this judgment is the impressive consistency of the results in a variety of times and places with widely differing cultural and socioeconomic circumstances.

2. The Evidence

a. Within-Country Comparisons

Does greater happiness go with higher income? Let us look first at the comparative status of income groups within a country at a given time.

Table 2 presents the data from the most recent survey of the American population, conducted in December 1970. Of those in the lowest income group, not much more than a fourth report that they are "very happy." In the highest income group the proportion very happy is almost twice as great. In successive income groups from low to high the proportion very happy rises steadily. There is a clear indication here that income and happiness are positively associated.

How typical is this result? Tables 3–5 summarize the results of 29 additional surveys. Sixteen of these surveys are of the Gallup-poll type; 13, of the Cantril type. Ten of the surveys relate to the United States between 1946 and 1966; 19 to other countries, including 11 in Asia, Africa, and Latin America. The classifications by socioeconomic status tend to differ among the surveys and are typically broad and nonnumerical, consisting of designations such as

---

[4] This statement is based on a comparison of the 1963 AIPO data, shown here in part in Table 10, with the NORC data (from a somewhat more restricted population) in the work of Bradburn (1969, p. 45). I am grateful to William H. Kruskal for suggesting this comparison.

"poor," "wealthy," "lower class," and "upper class." But the results are clear and unequivocal. In every single survey, those in the highest status group were happier, on the average, than those in the lowest status group.

TABLE 2

PERCENTAGE DISTRIBUTION OF POPULATION BY HAPPINESS, BY SIZE OF INCOME, UNITED STATES, 1970[a, b]

Income (in $1000)	(1) Very happy	(2) Fairly happy	(3) Not very happy	(4) No answer
All classes	43	48	6	3
15+	56	37	4	3
10–15	49	46	3	2
7–10	47	46	5	2
5–7	38	52	7	3
3–5	33	54	7	6
Under 3	29	55	13	3

[a] Data from AIPO Poll of December 1970.
[b] $N = 1517$.

TABLE 3

PERCENTAGE NOT VERY HAPPY IN LOWEST AND HIGHEST STATUS GROUPS, UNITED STATES, 1946–1970[a]

Date	Number of groups	Lowest status group Designation	N.V.H. (%)	Highest status group Designation	N.V.H. (%)	N
Apr. 1946	4	Poor	11	Wealthy	3	3151
June 1947	4	Poor	9	Wealthy	0	3088
Dec. 1947	4	Poor	12	Wealthy	3	1434
May 1948	4	Poor	10	Wealthy	0	1800
Aug. 1948	4	Poor	15	Wealthy	4	1596
Nov. 1952	3	Poor	12	Average +	8	3003
Jan. 1960	3	Low income	6	Upper income	2	2582
July 1963	6	Income < $3000	10	Income = $15,000 +	0	3668
Oct. 1966	6	Income < $3000	6	Income = $15,000 +	0.3	3531
Dec. 1970	6	Income < $3000	13	Income = $15,000 +	4	1517

[a] Data from Table 2 and AIPO polls 369, 399, 410, 418, 425, 508, 623, 675, and 735. In No. 623 (Jan. 60), the responses were on a scale ranging from −5 to +5. For the present purpose, all negative values were classified as "not very happy (N.V.H.)." Comparisons among surveys are of uncertain reliability because of variations in the specific question asked and in the group designations.

TABLE 4

Percentage Not Very Happy in Lowest and Highest Status Groups, Seven Countries, 1965[a]

Country	Number of groups	Lowest status group Designation	N.V.H.[b] (%)	Highest status group Designation	N.V.H.[b] (%)	N
Great Britain	3	Very poor	19	Upper, upper middle, middle	4	1179
West Germany	3	Lower middle, lower	19	Upper, upper middle	7	1255
Thailand	2	Lower/middle	15	Middle/upper	6	500
Philippines	2	Lower middle, lower	15	Upper, upper middle	5	500
Malaysia	2	Lower/middle	20	Middle/upper	10	502
France	3	Lower	27	Upper	6	1228
Italy	3	Lower middle, lower	42	Upper, upper middle	10	1166

[a] Data from World Survey III, 1965.
[b] Not very happy.

TABLE 5

PERSONAL HAPPINESS RATING IN LOWEST AND HIGHEST STATUS GROUPS, THIRTEEN COUNTRIES, CA. 1960[a,b]

(1)		(2)	(3)	(4)	(5)	(6)	(7)	(8)
		Number of groups	Lowest status group		Highest status group		Difference, high minus low	
Country	Date		Designation	Rating	Designation	Rating	[(6)−(4)]	N
United States	Aug. 1959	5	Lower economic	6.0	Upper economic	7.1	1.1	1549
Cuba	Apr.–May 1960	3	Lower socioeconomic	6.2	High, upper middle socioeconomic	6.7	0.5	992
Israel	Nov. 1961–June 1962	3	Lower income	4.0	Upper income	6.5	2.5	1170
West Germany	Sept. 1957	3	Lower economic	4.9	Upper economic	6.2	1.3	480
Japan	Fall 1962	3	Lower, middle lower socioeconomic	4.3	Upper, upper middle socioeconomic	5.8	1.5	972
Yugoslavia	Spring 1962	4	Lower, farmer	4.3	Upper, nonfarmer	6.0	1.7	1523
Philippines	Spring 1959	4	Lower economic	4.1	Upper economic	6.2	2.1	500
Panama	Jan.–Mar. 1962	2	Lower socioeconomic	4.3	Upper socioeconomic	6.0	1.7	642
Nigeria	Sept. 1962–spring 1963	2	Lower socioeconomic	4.7	Upper socioeconomic	5.8	1.1	1200
Brazil	Late 1960–early 1961	5	Lower socioeconomic	3.9	Upper socioeconomic	7.3	3.4	2168
Poland	Spring 1962	5	Unskilled	3.7	White-collar	4.9	1.2	1464
India	Summer 1962	4	Income < R75	3.0	Income > R301	4.9	1.9	2366
Dominican Republic	Apr. 1962	2	Lower socioeconomic	1.4	Upper socioeconomic	4.3	2.9	814
Average				4.2		6.0	1.8	

[a] Data from Cantril, 1965, pp. 365–377.
[b] Minimum: 0; maximum: 10.

This finding is corroborated by the results of other studies of happiness and related emotional states. In an article published 10 years ago, Inkeles (1960) concluded:

> Those who are economically well off, those with more education or whose jobs require more training and skill, more often report themselves happy, joyous, laughing, free of sorrow, satisfied with life's progress. Even though the pattern is weak or ambiguous in some cases, there has not been a single case of a *reversal* of the pattern, that is, a case where measures of happiness are inversely related to measures of status, in studies involving fifteen different countries—at least six of which were studied on two different occasions, through the use of somewhat different questions. There is, then, good reason to challenge the image of the "carefree but happy poor" [p. 17, italics in original].*

Similar conclusions are reached by Bradburn (1969), Robinson and Shaver (1969), Wilson (1967), and Gurin et al. (1960). In a comprehensive study surveying the literature on mental health, Davis (1965, p. 68) reported that "study after study shows that mental health is positively related to socio-economic status in a variety of measures of mental health and SES."

In addition to classification by income level, data on happiness are sometimes available by characteristics such as sex, age, race, education, and marital status. While the association of happiness with income is the most pervasive, some other patterns are apparent, though not without exception. Perhaps the firmest is a positive association between happiness and years of schooling. There is also some suggestion that the young are happier than the old, married persons than unmarried, and whites than blacks. Where the data permitted multivariate analysis, the independent association of income and happiness has been confirmed (Bradburn, 1969, p. 294; Gurin et al., 1960, p. 221; Robinson and Shaver, 1969, pp. 19–23). Also, the available evidence indicates low happiness levels among the unemployed and those on relief.

Inevitably, a question arises as to the direction of causality. Does higher income make people happier? Or are happier people more likely to be success-ful, i.e., receive higher income? It would be naïve to suppose that the issue is an either/or one. But emotional states are noticeably absent among the many factors usually cited by economists in explaining income differences. Factors such as education, training, experience, innate ability, health, and inheritance are among those principally mentioned. It might be felt that emotional well-being is implicit in the ability factor, or perhaps in that of health, though health is usually taken to refer to physical well-being. But it is doubtful that one would expect the influence of emotional well-being on earnings to stand out as clearly as in the simple bivariate comparisons shown

* A. Inkeles, "Industrial man: The relation of status to experience, perception and value," *American Journal of Sociology* **66**: 1960, 1–31. Published by the University of Chicago Press; Copyright 1960, 1961 by the University of Chicago.

here. Moreover, for some countries, some of the status designations, such as "upper class," are essentially hereditary. To argue that happiness causes such class differences is akin to arguing that, where happiness is correlated with age, happiness causes the age differences. Finally, as we have seen, when people are asked about the things that make them happy or unhappy, personal economic concerns are typically foremost [Table 1; cf. also Gurin *et al.* (1960, pp. 22–28)]. The worries of less-happy respondents differ most from those who are more happy in their emphasis on financial security [(Gurin *et al.*, 1960, p. 29; Wessman, 1956, pp. 213, 216); cf. also Table 11 below]. On the whole, therefore, I am inclined to interpret the data as primarily showing a causal connection running from income to happiness.[5]

b. International Comparisons

What happens when one looks at cross-sectional differences among countries? Are richer countries happier countries? Let us examine the Cantril data first, since that study made the greatest effort to assure comparability of approach among the various countries.

Table 6 presents the average personal happiness ratings for each of fourteen countries, along with figures on real GNP per capita. Cantril's own reading of these data is that they show a positive association between income and happiness and he presents correlation results to this effect (Cantril, 1965, p. 194).[6] He generalizes this into a five-stage scheme, reminiscent of Rostow's stages of growth, to describe the phases of emotional well-being through which a country passes in the course of economic development (Rostow, 1960; Cantril, 1965, Chapter XV). However, as with Rostow's classification, countries do not fall neatly into one or another stage. One's confidence in the generality of the scheme is further undermined by the following passage, which concludes the presentation of the stage scheme:

> It should be noted in passing, however, that people in some cultures or subcultures may seem to qualify for placement in this fifth [highest] stage of "satisfaction and gratification" who have not gone through earlier stages of development but appear to outside observers to be stuck at relatively primitive levels. The Masai of Kenya and Tanganyika might be regarded as such a pocket of contentment within their microcosm. There is, of course, every likelihood that once the boundaries of such a microcosm are penetrated by "advanced" cultures with the aspirations they intrude into people's minds, then the people within such a microcosm will alter the standards by means of which they judge satisfaction *and revert to an earlier stage of development* [*ibid.*, p. 310, italics added].*

[5] In interpreting the association between mental health and socioeconomic status, Davis (1965, pp. 74–77) leans in this direction also.

The point that for some countries some of the status designations are essentially hereditary also indicates that we are dealing here in substantial part with "permanent income" differences, and that the results cannot be dismissed on the grounds that they are dominated by transitory influences.

TABLE 6

PERSONAL HAPPINESS RATING AND REAL GNP PER HEAD,
FOURTEEN COUNTRIES, CA. 1960[a, b]

Country	Period of survey	(1) Rating of personal happiness (min: 0; max: 10)	(2) Real GNP per head 1961 ($U.S.)
United States	Aug. 1959	6.6	2790
Cuba	Apr.–May 1960	6.4	516
Egypt	Fall 1960	5.5	225
Israel	Nov. 1961–June 1962	5.3	1027
West Germany	Sept. 1957	5.3	1860
Japan	Fall 1962	5.2	613
Yugoslavia	Spring 1962	5.0	489
Philippines	Spring 1959	4.9	282
Panama	Jan. –Mar. 1962	4.8	371
Nigeria	Sept. 1962–spring 1963	4.8	134
Brazil	Late 1960–early 1961	4.6	375
Poland	Spring 1962	4.4	702
India	Summer 1962	3.7	140
Dominican Republic	Apr. 1962	1.6	313
Average		5.0	

[a] Data in column (1) from Cantril, 1965, p. 184; data in column (2), except for West Germany, from Rosenstein-Rodan, 1961, pp. 118, 126, 127; data in column (2) for West Germany from Table 7.

[b] For sample sizes see Table 5.

To judge from this paragraph, some cultures or subcultures may "have it made" before they are touched by, or as long as they can remain free from, economic development.

Actually the association between wealth and happiness indicated by Cantril's international data is not so clear-cut. This is shown by a scatter diagram of the data (Fig. 1). The inference about a positive association relies heavily on the observations for India and the United States. [According to Cantril (1965, pp. 130–131), the values for Cuba and the Dominican Republic reflect unusual political circumstances—the immediate aftermath of a successful revolution in Cuba and prolonged political turmoil in the Dominican

---

[6] Actually Cantril (1965, pp. 193–194) uses a somewhat different measure of socioeconomic development, of which the GNP data shown here are one component.

* *Patterns of Human Concerns* by Hadley Cantril. Rutgers University Press, New Brunswick, New Jersey (1965).

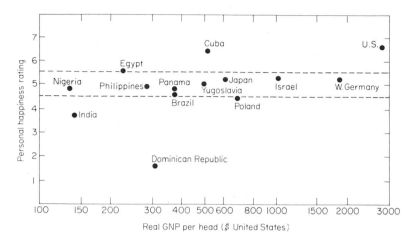

FIG. 1.   Personal happiness rating and GNP per head, 14 countries, ca. 1960. (Source: Table 6.)

Republic].[7] What is perhaps most striking is that the personal happiness ratings for 10 of the 14 countries lie virtually within half a point of the midpoint rating of 5, as is brought out by the broken horizontal lines in the diagram. While a difference of rating of only 0.2 is significant at the 0.05 level, nevertheless there is not much evidence, for these 10 countries, of a systematic association between income and happiness. The closeness of the happiness ratings implies also that a similar lack of association would be found between happiness and other economic magnitudes such as income inequality or the rate of change of income.

Of course, picking and choosing among points is a dubious practice. What one can perhaps safely say is this: In the within-country data shown in Table 5, the difference in happiness rating between low- and high-status groups averages almost 2 points, and for only 1 of the 13 countries is the difference less than 1 point. In contrast, in the comparison of national averages shown in Table 6, the ratings for 10 of 14 countries lie within a range of 1.1 points. The tenfold range in per-capita income covered by these countries almost surely exceeds the typical income range between low- and high-status groups covered in the within-country data. The happiness differences between rich and poor countries that one might expect on the basis of the within-

---

[7] The comparability of the Cuban data is further qualified by the fact that the survey was confined to the urban population. For Egypt, the coverage of the rural population was quite limited, and the survey is labeled by Cantril (1965, pp. 346–347) as a "preliminary pilot investigation".

country differences by economic status are not borne out by the international data.

The other principal sources of international data are of the Gallup-poll type. In this case, the effort to secure comparability in asking the happiness question, which was only one of many questions, was less than in Cantril's study. In 1965, however, a survey obtained responses to a uniform inquiry in seven different countries. The results of this, plus that of a 1958 survey in Japan and a 1966 survey in the United States, are reported in Table 6.

There are four countries represented in both Tables 6 and 7—the United States, West Germany, Japan, and the Philippines. One's confidence in the data is bolstered by the striking similarity in the results. In both cases the United States appears much happier than West Germany, and West Germany slightly happier than the Philippines. The Japanese data in Table 7 are least

TABLE 7

PERCENT DISTRIBUTION OF POPULATION BY HAPPINESS,
NINE COUNTRIES, 1965[a]

Country	Very happy	Fairly happy	Not very happy	Other	N	Real GNP per head 1961
Great Britain	53	42	4	1	1179	$1777
United States[b]	49	46	4	2	3531	2790
West Germany	20	66	11	3	1255	1860
Thailand	13	74	12	1	500	202
Japan[c]	— 81	—	13	5	920	613
Philippines	13.5	73	13.5	0	500	282
Malaysia	17	64	15	4	502	552
France	12	64	18	5	1228	1663
Italy	11	52	33	4	1166	1077

[a] Happiness data are from World Survey III, 1965, except those for the United States and Japan, which are from Table 8 and the 1958 survey of Japanese national character, respectively. GNP data are from Rosenstein-Rodan, 1961, except those for Great Britain, France, West Germany, and Italy. For these countries GNP was estimated to bear the same proportion to the United States figure as that shown by the geometric mean estimates by Gilbert *et al.*, 1958, p. 36, extrapolated from 1955 to 1961 by the per-capita volume indexes in OECD, 1970, p. 11.

[b] 1966.

[c] 1958. (Question read "not happy" rather than "not very happy.")

comparable with those of the other countries, but even the relative position of Japan vis-à-vis the other three is not much different in Table 7 from that in Table 6.

What association between happiness and income is indicated by the Table 7 data for all nine countries? The results are ambiguous. The four lowest income countries are neither at the top nor at the bottom of the Table, but are clustered in the middle. This result cannot be attributed to the younger age of the populations in these countries, for it shows up in comparisons for individual age classes. (This is true also of the data in Table 6.) If there is a positive association between income and happiness, it is certainly not a strong one. In contrast, in the within-country comparisons by economic status, shown in Tables 3 and 4, the happiness differences are clear and consistent. The conclusion indicated by the Gallup-poll data is thus consistent with that shown by the Cantril data.

International happiness comparisons for 1946 and 1949 are given by Cantril (1951, p. 281), Wessman (1956, p. 166), and Inkeles (1960, p. 13). These are confined to a few Western European countries and their overseas descendants. The comparability of the questions is uncertain, but for what it is worth, the results are similar to those shown above—if there is a positive association among countries between income and happiness it is not very clear.

The international data are intriguing in various respects. For example, notice the high position of Great Britain compared with the United States in Table 7. This result is a persistent one, to judge from the polls mentioned in the preceding paragraph. Also, in those polls Canada and Australia show levels of happiness comparable in magnitude to Great Britain and the United States. There is also a noteworthy closeness in the results for the four Asian countries shown in Table 7. Perhaps there are cultural influences in the international happiness data, though one should hesitate before lumping together Thailand, Malaysia, the Philippines, and Japan as having a common culture. Of course, even if there are cultural influences, they would not necessarily systematically bias the relation of happiness to income indicated by the international data. Suppose, for example, one were to argue that cultural biases are obscuring a strong positive relation between income and happiness among countries. This implies that, *ceteris paribus*, in poorer countries cultural influences operate systematically to elevate happiness as compared to richer countries, an implication which seems doubtful in view of the cultural heterogenity among countries within both the rich and poor categories.

c. National Time Series

What one would like most, of course, is historical series on happiness as countries develop. The crucial question is: "Will raising the incomes of all increase the happiness of all ...?" (Inkeles, 1960, p. 18). Unfortunately, as is too often the case, time series data are in short supply. In addition, comparability over time is impaired by variations in the wording of the happiness question. It was possible, however, to put together a series for one country, the United States, covering intermittent dates from 1946 through 1970. (Three of these dates, in 1956–1957, are only six months apart, and demonstrate the point made earlier regarding the short-run stability of the survey results.) In the first seven surveys the happiness classification was the same— "very happy," "fairly happy," or "not very happy." In the last three, "not happy" was used instead of "not very happy." This more negative designation of the lowest happiness category resulted, for the lowest happiness class, in a downward bias compared with the earlier data, and for the middle "fairly happy" category, in a corresponding upward bias. However, the "very happy" class seems comparable over all 10 surveys and reliance is therefore placed on the trend shown by this category. Fortunately, it is possible to utilize as a check happiness data obtained by NORC and Cantril, which overlap the AIPO data in the period when the change in AIPO question wording occurred.

TABLE 8

PERCENT DISTRIBUTION OF POPULATION BY HAPPINESS,
UNITED STATES, 1946–1970[a]

	A. AIPO Polls				
Date	Very happy	Fairly happy	Not very happy	Other	N
Apr. 1946	39	50	10	1	3151
Dec. 1947	42	47	10	1	1434
Aug. 1948	43	43	11	2	1596
Nov. 1952	47	43	9	1	3003
Sept. 1956	53	41	5	1	1979
Sept. 1956	52	42	5	1	2207
Mar. 1957	53	43	3	1	1627
July 1963	47	48	5[b]	1	3668
Oct. 1966	49	46	4[b]	2	3531
Dec. 1970	43	48	6[b]	3	1517

	B. NORC Polls			
Date	Very happy	Pretty happy	Not too happy	N
Spring 1957	35	54	11	2460
Dec. 1963	32	51	16	1501
June 1965	30	53	17	1469

[a] Data from Table 2 and AIPO Polls 369, 410, 425, 508, 570, 571, 580, 675, and 735. NORC data from Bradburn, 1969, p. 40.
[b] Question read "not happy" rather than "not very happy."

The upper panel of Table 8 presents the results of the 10 AIPO surveys covering 1946–1970. From 1946 through 1956–1957, the proportion "very happy" drifts slowly but steadily upward. There is then a noticeable decline between 1957 and 1963, and a second one from 1966 to 1970. By 1970 the proportion "very happy" is just about the same as in 1947. If one views the period as a whole, there is a noticeable swing, but little indication of any net trend up or down.[8]

The finding of a downturn between 1957 and 1963 runs into the difficulty that the question wording changed between these two dates, though as indicated this should not have affected the "very happy" replies. However, three NORC polls were taken independently around this time. As noted earlier, the happiness categories in the NORC polls differ from those in the AIPO polls. Our interest, however, is in the change over time shown by the NORC polls (Table 8, panel B). The results confirm those shown by the AIPO polls— a decline in happiness between the late 1950s and mid-1960s. (The exact timing is obviously open to question because of the intermittent nature of both sets of survey data.) Further support is provided by two United States surveys reported by Cantril (1965, p. 43) which show a decline in the national average personal happiness rating between 1959 and 1963 from 6.6 to 6.2.

To a limited extent, it is possible to follow the trends for individual income groups. Table 9 presents the data for the first four surveys, which appear to

TABLE 9

PERCENT VERY HAPPY BY SIZE OF INCOME,
UNITED STATES, 1946–1952[a]

Date	All classes	Average + and wealthy	Average	Poor
Apr. 1946	39	47	43	34
Dec. 1947	42	52	46	37
Aug. 1948	43	54	50	37
Aug. 1948	43	51	51	37
Nov. 1952	47	51	51	42

[a] Data from AIPO Polls 369, 410, 425, and 508.

have had roughly consistent income classifications. (Unfortunately, no subdivision by income is available for the three 1956–1957 surveys.) To judge from the data in Table 9, there was a common advance in happiness in all major income groups through 1952.

[8] The Gallup article on the 1970 survey reported that there was an upward trend over the last quarter century, apparently because a comparison was made only between the first and last surveys shown in Table 8 above.

The surveys relating to the period of declining happiness show a rather interesting difference from this pattern (Table 10). Whereas the national average shows a slight rise between 1963 and 1966, the data by income class show a decline for the poorest groups. Thus the slight rise shown by the

TABLE 10

PERCENTAGE VERY HAPPY BY SIZE OF INCOME,
UNITED STATES, 1963–1970[a]

Date	All classes	$15,000+	$10,000–14,999	$5000–9999	$3000–4999	Under $3000
July 1963	47	59	50	50	46	40
Sept. 1966	49	67	62	50	42	34
Dec. 1970	38	56	49	43	33	29

[a] Data from Table 2 and AIPO Polls 675 and 735.

national average reflects an upward movement for the higher income groups which more than offsets the decline among the lower. (Could this be partly due to the national prominence given to the poverty problem at this time?) Between 1966 and 1970, however, all income classes show a noticeable decline, and in 1970 there is no class which is higher than it was in 1963.

Certainly, one must be cautious about drawing any strong conclusions from the limited United States time series studied here. As in the case of the international cross sections, however, it seems safe to say that if income and happiness go together, it is not as obvious as in the within-country cross-sectional comparisons.

3. Interpretation

a. Theory

Why do national comparisons among countries and over time show an association between income and happiness which is so much weaker than, if not inconsistent with, that shown by within-country comparisons? To economists, long accustomed to dealing with anomalies such as these, the possible relevance of Duesenberry's "relative income" explanation of the celebrated United States income–savings paradox will immediately spring to mind [(Duesenberry, 1952), cf. also Brady and Friedman (1947)]. The basic idea was stated quite simply by Karl Marx over a century ago: "A house may be large or small; as long as the surrounding houses are equally small it satisfies all social demands for a dwelling. But if a palace rises beside the little house, the little house shrinks into a hut."[9]

Suppose one assumes, following Duesenberry, that the utility a person obtains from his consumption expenditure is a function, not of the absolute level of his expenditure, but of the ratio of his current expenditure to that of other people, that is,

$$U_i = f\left[\frac{C_i}{\sum a_{ij} C_j}\right],$$

where U_i and C_i are the utility index and consumption expenditures, respectively, of the ith individual, C_j is consumption of the jth individual and a_{ij} is the weight applied by the ith consumer to the expenditure of the jth (Duesenberry, 1952, p. 32). In the simplest case, in which the expenditures of every other person are given equal weight, the utility obtained by a given individual depends on the ratio of his expenditure to the national per-capita average. The farther he is above the average, the happer he is; the farther below, the sadder. Moreover, if the frame of reference is always the current national situation, then an increase in the level of income in which all share proportionately would not alter the national level of happiness. A classical example of the fallacy of composition would apply: An increase in the income of any one individual would increase his happiness, but increasing the income of everyone would leave happiness unchanged. Similarly, among countries, a richer country would not necessarily be a happier country.

The data are presently too limited to warrant pushing this line of explanation very far, and the illustration above is certainly too simple. An intriguing research issue, for example, is the appropriate values of the a_{ij}'s [which can be viewed as a variant of the sociologist's problem of "reference groups" (Merton, 1968, Chaps. X and XI)]. Any given individual in the population does not give equal weight to all others in forming his reference standard; among other things, "peer group" influences play a part. Thus, the reference standard of a rich man probably gives disproportionate weight to the consumption of his well-to-do associates vis-à-vis persons living in poverty, and conversely for the reference standard of the poor man.

Nevertheless, the general form of the argument remains valid. Despite peer group influences, there is a "consumption norm" which exists in a given society at a given time, and which enters into the reference standard of virtually everyone. This provides a common point of reference in self-appraisals of well-being, leading those below the norm to feel less happy and those above the norm, more happy. Over time, this norm tends to rise with the

---

[9] As quoted by Lipset (1960, p. 63). I am grateful to Leonard Berkowitz for bringing this to my attention.

general level of consumption, though the two are not necessarily on a one-to-one basis.

Other possible interpretations of these data come to mind. For example, emphasis might be placed on external diseconomies of production. At a given time, it might be argued, the rich are better able to avoid these sources of "ill-fare" and hence are happier. But over time and across societies increases in income are largely or wholly offset by a corresponding growth in pollution, congestion, and so forth.

A radical interpretation of the data might emphasize power as the key factor in happiness. At any given time those who have more power (the rich) are happier. But over time and across societies, increases in income have not been accompanied by a wider diffusion of power among the various socio-economic strata (the Establishment persists), and hence happiness has not grown.

b. Evidence for a "Relative Income" Interpretation

There are a number of reasons why an interpretation based chiefly on "relativity" notions seems more plausible. First, a certain amount of empirical support has been developed for the relative income concept in other economic applications, such as savings behavior and, more recently, fertility behavior and labor force participation (Duesenberry, 1952; Easterlin, 1973, 1969; Freedman, 1963; Wachter, 1971a,b). Second, similar notions, such as "relative deprivation," have gained growing theoretical acceptance and empirical support in sociology, political science, and social psychology over the past several decades (Berkowitz, 1971; Davies, 1962; Gurr, 1970; Homans, 1961; Merton, 1968; Pettigrew, 1967; Smelser, 1962; Stouffer et al., 1949). Indeed, to scholars vitally concerned with professional reputation in a competitive field of learning, it should hardly come as a surprise that relative status is an important ingredient of happiness. Third, historical changes in the definition of poverty attest to the importance of relative position in society's thinking on this matter. For example, Smolensky (1965, p. 40) has pointed out that estimates of "minimum comfort" budgets for New York City workers throughout the course of this century "have generally been about one-half of real gross national product per capita." [cf. also Fuchs (1967), Rainwater (unpublished paper), Tabbarah (1972).]

By no means least important are the statements in the surveys of the respondents themselves on what they take to comprise happiness. These statements overwhelmingly emphasize immediate personal concerns, such as adequacy of income, family matters, or health, rather than broader national or social issues such as pollution, political power, or even threat of war. Furthermore, economic worries appear to be especially important among lower income persons. Table 11, for example, reports on the "one thing"

TABLE 11

RELATION OF ECONOMIC STATUS AND MAJOR WORRIES,
UNITED STATES, 1946[a, b]

| | Economic status (percent) | | |
Major worry	Upper	Middle	Lower
My family and children	20	20	24
Health (personal and family)	19	21	18
Financial worries, money	6	12	22
Security, job, future	13	17	12
World and national conditions	7	6	4
Work conditions	7	5	3
Personal traits	3	2	2
Housing	2	1	1
Miscellaneous	9	7	5
Nothing	13	10	10
No answer	5	7	5
	104	108	106
Sample size	195	637	1506

[a] From A. E. Wessman, A psychological inquiry into satisfactions and happiness. Ph.D. dissertation in psychology, Princeton Univ. Princeton, New Jersey, 1956.

[b] The question asked was "What one thing do you worry about most?" Percentages add to more than 100 because some respondents gave more than one answer.

worried about most by Americans of upper, middle, and lower economic status in a 1946 survey. For all three groups worries about economic, family, and health matters predominate. However, the item on which the three groups most markedly differ is that labeled "financial worries, money." Such concerns increase significantly as economic status declines.

Finally, there is evidence that consumption norms vary directly with the level of economic development. Here, from Cantril's survey (1965, pp. 205, 206, 222), are some statements by Indians on their material aspirations, and, for comparison, those of Americans:

INDIA: I want a son and a piece of land since I am now working on land owned by other people. I would like to construct a house of my own and have a cow for milk and ghee. I would also like to buy some better clothing for my wife. If I could do this then I would be happy. (thirty-five-year-old man, illiterate, agricultural laborer, income about $10 a month)

INDIA: I wish for an increase in my wages because with my meager salary I cannot afford to buy decent food for my family. If the food and clothing problems were solved, then I would feel at home and be satisfied. Also if my wife were able to work the two of us could then feed the family and I am sure would have a happy life and our worries would be over. (thirty-year-old sweeper, monthly income around $13)

INDIA: I should like to have a water tap and a water supply in my house. It would also be nice to have electricity. My husband's wages must be increased if our children are to get an education and our daughter is to be married. (forty-five-year-old housewife, family income about $80 a month)

INDIA: I hope in the future I will not get any disease. Now I am coughing. I also hope I can purchase a bicycle. I hope my children will study well and that I can provide them with an education. I also would sometime like to own a fan and maybe a radio. (forty-year-old skilled worker earning $30 a month)

UNITED STATES: If I could earn more money I would then be able to buy our own home and have more luxury around us, like better furniture, a new car, and more vacations. (twenty-seven-year-old skilled worker)

UNITED STATES: I would like a reasonable enough income to maintain a house, have a new car, have a boat, and send my four children to private schools. (thirty-four-year-old laboratory technician)

UNITED STATES: I would like a new car. I wish all my bills were paid and I had more money for myself. I would like to play more golf and to hunt more than I do. I would like to have more time to do the things I want to and to entertain my friends. (Negro bus driver, twenty-four-years old)

UNITED STATES: Materially speaking, I would like to provide my family with an income to allow them to live well—to have the proper recreation, to go camping, to have music and dancing lessons for the children, and to have family trips. I wish we could belong to a country club and do more entertaining. We just bought a new home and expect to be perfectly satisfied with it for a number of years. (twenty-eight-year-old lawyer)*

It is a well-accepted dictum among social scientists other than economists that attitudes or "tastes" are a product of the socialization experience of the individual. What more eloquent testimony could be provided than the foregoing statements? Cantril (1965) puts it this way:

> People in highly developed nations have obviously acquired a wide range of aspirations, sophisticated and expensive from the point of view of people in less-developed areas, who have not yet learned all that is potentially available to people in more advanced societies and whose aspirations concerning the social and material aspects of life are modest indeed by comparison [p. 202].*

In a comprehensive survey of long-term trends in American consumption, Brady has pointed out that "today, the great majority of American families

* *Patterns of Human Concerns* by Hadley Cantril. Rutgers University Press, New Brunswick, New Jersey (1965).

live on a scale that compares well with the way *wealthy* families lived 200 years ago" [cf. Davis *et al.*, 1972, p. 84, italics added]. But, as the above statements show, the typical American today does not consider himself wealthy. His consumption standards are not those of his colonial predecessors; rather they are formed by his personal experience with the human condition as evidenced in contemporary America. The same is true of the typical Indian living in modern India. Material aspirations or tastes vary positively with the level of economic development. Moreover, these changes in tastes are caused by the process of income growth itself (though the cause–effect relation may run both ways). As a result of secular income growth, the socialization experience of each generation embodies a higher level of living and correspondingly generates a higher level of consumption standards. Even within the life cycle of a given generation, the progressive accretion of household goods due to economic growth causes a continuous upward pressure on consumption norms. This upward shift in standards (tastes) tends to offset the positive effect of income growth on well-being that one would expect on the basis of economic theory. Dramatic supporting evidence is provided by the results of a survey of recent experience in Taiwan, analyzed by Freedman (unpublished paper):

> While economic growth has increased income levels, it has, at the same time, expanded consumption possibilities with the result that present incomes seem no more adequate relative to needs. Only 20 percent of the respondents said their financial position had improved during the last five years, although real per capita income increased about 40 percent during that period [p. 38].

It would be premature to assert that "everything is relative," but it is hard to resist the inference that relative considerations play an important part in explaining the evidence presented here.

c. An Analogy[10]

The present interpretation may be clarified by an analogy with comparisons of height. Americans today are taller than their forebears and than their contemporaries in present-day India. Suppose, however, that representative samples of Americans and Indians in 1970 were asked the following question: "In general, how tall would you say that you are—*very* tall, *fairly* tall, or *not very* tall?" It seems reasonable to suppose that this question would elicit a similar distribution of responses in the two countries, even though on an objective scale most Americans are, in fact, taller than most Indians. The reason for the similar distributions would be that, in answering, individuals

---

[10] My colleagues, Stefano Fenoaltea and John C. Lambelet, have contributed importantly to the development of the argument in this section.

in each country would apply a subjective norm of "tallness" derived from their personal experience. The reference standard in terms of which Americans would evaluate "tallness" would be larger than that applied by Indians, because Americans have grown up in and live in a society in which persons are generally taller. An American male 5 ft 9 in. in height living in the United States, though tall on an international scale, is not likely to feel tall. By the same token, Americans today are not likely to feel taller than their forebears, because today's standard of reference is higher.

What, then, are the "facts" of tallness? By an objective scale, current-day Americans are, indeed, taller. If, however, one is interested in *feelings* about height, the truth is quite possibly different. Today's Americans may not, on the average, feel any taller than do contemporary Indians or than their ancestors did. The reconciliation between the "objective facts" and "subjective states of mind" lies in the mediating role of the social norm for height, which enters together with one's actual height in determining feelings of tallness. This norm varies among societies both in time and space, and is a direct function of the heights typical of these societies.

The situation with regard to happiness is like that for height, but with one critical difference. It is similar in that each individual, in evaluating his happiness, compares his actual experience with a norm derived from his personal social experience. It is different in that there is no objective scale of measurement for happiness, independent of the individual. On the contrary, the concern is precisely with subjective states of mind. One may attempt to use "objective" indexes such as consumption, nutrition, or life expectancy to infer happiness. Or one may seek to gauge well-being from various behavioral indicators, for example, measures of the prevalence of social disorganization (delinquency, suicide, and so forth). Ultimately, however, the relevance of such measures rests on an assumed connection between external manifestations and internal states of mind—in effect, on a model of human psychology. And if it is feelings that count, there is a real possibility that subjective reports may contradict the "objective" evidence. To social scientists, and especially economists, this can be frustrating. As Mishan (1969) observes,

> [t]here is a temptation . . . to lose patience with human cussedness and to insist that if both the Smith family and the Jones family receive a 10 percent increase in their "real" income they are better off, even if they both sulk at the other's good luck. But while this may be salutary morals, if welfare is what people experience there is no escape for us in honest indignation [p. 82].*

On the contrary, there are good psychological reasons why people may not feel better off, even though they "should." This is because the standard with

* E. J. Mishan, *Welfare Economics: Ten Introductory Essays*, 2nd ed. New York: Random House, 1969. Copyright 1969 by Random House, Inc.

reference to which evaluations of well-being are formed is itself a function of social conditions. As these conditions "improve," the norm tends to advance along with people's actual experience. Economic analysis has been able, for a long time, to resist the uncomfortable implications of this mechanism, by assuming that tastes are given and/or are unmeasurable. For many of the short-term problems with which economists have traditionally been concerned, this may not be seriously damaging. But with the growth in concern about long-term economic growth, on the one hand, and in evidence on people's feelings and aspirations, and the factors governing them, on the other, one can only wonder whether this view will be much longer defensible.

4. Summary and Concluding Observations

The concern of this paper has been with the association of income and happiness. The basic data consist of statements by individuals on their subjective happiness, as reported in thirty surveys from 1946 through 1970, covering nineteen countries, including eleven in Asia, Africa, and Latin America. Within countries there is a noticeable positive association between income and happiness—in every single survey, those in the highest status group were happier, on the average, than those in the lowest status group. However, whether any such positive association exists among countries at a given time is uncertain. Certainly, the happiness differences between rich and poor countries that one might expect on the basis of the within-country differences by economic status are not borne out by the international data. Similarly, in the one national time series studied, that for the United States since 1946, higher income was not systematically accompanied by greater happiness.

As for why national comparisons among countries and over time show an association between income and happiness which is so much weaker than, if not inconsistent with, that shown by within-country comparisons, a Duesenberry-type model, involving relative status considerations as an important determinant of happiness, was suggested. Every survey that has looked into the meaning of happiness shows that economic considerations are very important to people, though by no means the only matters of concern. In judging their happiness, people tend to compare their actual situation with a reference standard or norm, derived from their prior and ongoing social experience. While norms vary among individuals within a given society, they also contain similar features because of the common experiences people share as members of the same society and culture. Thus, while the goods aspirations of higher status people probably exceed those of lower status people, the dispersion in reference norms is less than in the actual incomes of rich and poor. Because of this, those at the bottom of the income distribution tend to feel less well off than those at the top. Over time, however, as economic conditions advance, so too does the social norm, since this is formed by the changing economic socialization experience of people. For the same reason, among different societies at a given time, there tends to be a rough correspondence between living levels and the social norm. As a result, the positive correlation between income and happiness that shows up in within-country comparisons appears only weakly, if at all, in comparisons among societies in time or space. Various pieces of evidence were noted in support of this interpretation.

In a sense, these results are a testimony to the adaptability of mankind. Income and aspirations in time and space tend to go together, and people seemingly can make something out of what appears, in some absolute sense, to be a sorry lot. At the same time, the conclusions raise serious questions about the goals and prospective efficacy of much social policy. As sociologist George C. Homans remarks (1961, p. 276) regarding similar findings on another subject, "[t]hings like this have persuaded some people who would prefer to believe otherwise that any effort to satisfy mankind is bound to be self-defeating. Any satisfied desire creates an unsatisfied one."

The present results do not necessarily imply that a redirection of attention is needed from economic growth to income redistribution as a vehicle for improving welfare. The data themselves give no indication that international differences in happiness are systematically related to inequality. And the theoretical relationship is uncertain—if relative positions were unchanged and income differences halved, would happiness be greater? It is at least plausible that sensitivity to income differences might be heightened, so that lower income people might suffer as much in the new situation from an income spread of 50% as they previously had from a spread of 100%. If this were so, then subjective welfare would be unchanged.

The only sure conclusion is that we need much more research on the nature and causes of human welfare. Bradburn (1969, p. 233) makes the point simply and effectively: "Insofar as we have greater understanding of how people arrive at their judgments of their own happiness and how social forces are related to those judgments, we shall be in a better position to formulate and execute effective social policies."

The present analysis also points to a clear need for research on the formation of preferences or tastes. Economists have generally insisted that the determination of tastes is not their business. But on this matter there are hopeful signs of change in economists' tastes themselves. Katona (1951, 1971), Morgan (1968), Strumpel (1973), and their associates at the Survey Research Center in Michigan have been doing pioneering studies on this subject [cf. also Pfaff (1973)]. In the 1950s, Siegel (1964) did some little-noticed work modeling the formation of aspirations. A central tenet of Galbraith's (1958, 1967) assault on economic theory has been the "dependence effect," that tastes are subject to substantial manipulation by the business system.[11] Recently, Houthakker and Pollak (to be published, Chapter 2) have initiated a formal inquiry into habit formation.

In the area of growth economics, the present findings raise doubt about the importance of the "international demonstration effect." If those in rich and poor countries shared a common scale of material aspirations, then countries higher on the scale of actual income should show a higher level of happiness. At the same time, the within-country cross-sectional findings, indicating a similarity in the aspirations of members of the same society, lend support to the concept of an internal demonstration effect.[12]

Economists' models of economic growth tend uniformly to exclude tastes as a variable.[13] But it is possible that not only are tastes affected by economic growth, but that taste changes serve as a spur to growth, in the manner suggested by Mack some years ago (1956). Thus one might conceive of a mutually reinforcing interaction between changes in tastes and changes in per capita income, which, *ceteris paribus*, drives the economy ever onward and per capita income ever upward.

Another interesting analytical possibility opened up by recognition of taste changes is in the relation of economic changes to political behavior. Recent work on the causes of political agitation and revolution has stressed the importance of disparities between the aspirations of the population and their fulfillment (Davies, 1962; Gurr, 1970). Since economic goods form such an important part of human concerns, a growth model which included material aspirations as a variable might incorporate also the political consequences of unfulfilled expectations, and possible feedback effects of any resultant political activity on the growth process itself.

Finally, with regard to growth economics, there is the view that the most developed economies, notably the United States, have entered an era of satiation. Economic growth, it is said, tends to eventuate in the "mass con-

---

[11] The present view of taste formation, while not precluding the mechanism stressed by Galbraith, is different and broader. This is shown clearly by the height analogy, where the norm is seen to change as a function simply of the social experience of individuals, without any overt attempt at manipulation by persons or organizations in the society.

[12] In a five-country study of attitudes toward ways of life, Morris found much greater differences among countries than among economic classes within countries. The study, however, was confined to college students, and economic status referred to the income group of parents (Morris, 1956, Chap. 4).

[13] An exception is Hagen's work (1962), based on McClelland's n-achievement motive (McClelland, 1961). It should be noted that achievement motivation, which relates to goal-striving, differs from level of aspiration, the concern here, which refers to goal-setting.

sumption society" (Rostow, 1960), the "affluent society" (Galbraith, 1958), the "opulent society" (Johnson, 1967), or the "post-industrial society" (Bell, 1970). The present analysis raises serious doubts whether the United States is in such an era, or, indeed, whether such a terminal stage exists. Long-term fluctuations aside, the present generation is not noticeably more advanced over its predecessor than has been the case for over a century—the long-run growth rate of per-capita income has been remarkably steady since at least the first half of the nineteenth century (Davis *et al.*, 1972, Chap. 2). The view that the United States is now in a new era is based in part on ignorance of the rapidity of growth in the past. Consider the following statement: "The advancement of the arts, from year to year, taxes our credulity, and seems to presage the arrival of that period when human improvement must end" [as quoted by Davis *et al.* (1972, p. 177)]. This was made by Henry L. Ellsworth, Commissioner of Patents, in 1843! Similarly, a writer in the Democratic Review of 1853 predicted that electricity and machinery would so transform life that fifty years thereafter: "Men and women will then have no harassing cares, or laborious duties to fulfill. Machinery will perform all work—automata will direct them. The only task of the human race will be to make love, study and be happy."[14] Brady's recent work catalogs in great detail the myriad advances in food, clothing, housing, transportation, and style of life in general that followed one upon the other throughout the nineteenth century (Davis *et al.*, 1972, Chap. 2). Is there any reason to suppose that the present generation has reached a unique culminating stage in this evolution, and the next will not have its own catalog of wonders, which, if only attained, would make it happy? An antimaterialistic cultural revolution may be in the making, but it seems dubious that a major cause is an unprecedented affluence which American society has recently attained. If the view suggested here has merit, economic growth does not raise a society to some ultimate state of plenty. Rather, the growth process itself engenders ever-growing wants that lead it ever onward.

ACKNOWLEDGMENTS

This paper was made possible by the opportunities and facilities offered by the Center for Advanced Study in the Behavioral Sciences, Stanford, California, where I was a Fellow in 1970–1971. It is not possible to acknowledge all those from whom I benefitted while at the Center, but special appreciation must be expressed to Elliot Aronson, Leonard Berkowitz, David Krantz, William H. Kruskal, Amos Tversky, and Stanton Wheeler. I am also grateful to Jack Meyer for statistical assistance. This research was partially supported by NSF grant GS-1563.

[14] As quoted by Ekirch (1944, p. 120). I am grateful to Joseph S. Davis for bringing this to my attention.

A first draft of this paper was circulated during the academic year 1971–1972, and elicited many valuable and instructive reactions. It has been possible to take account of only a few comments in this revision, and for these I am especially grateful to Paul A. David, Stefano Fenoaltea, Henry A. Gemery, J. Robert Hanson, Alex Inkeles, John C. Lambelet, and Melvin W. Reder.

REFERENCES

Abramovitz, M. (1959)   The welfare interpretation of secular trends in national income and product. In *The Allocation of economic resources: Essays in honor of Bernard Francis Haley* (M. Abramovitz *et al.*). Stanford, California: Stanford Univ. Press.

AIPO Poll (December 1970)   Reported in *San Francisco Chronicle*, January 14, 1971.

Bell, D. (1970)   Unstable America. *Encounter* **34**: 11–26.

Berkowitz, L. (1971)   *Frustrations, comparisons, and other sources of emotion arousal as contributors to social unrest.* Multilith.

Block, J. (1965)   *The challenge of response sets.* New York: Appleton.

Bradburn, N. M. (1969)   *The structure of psychological well-being.* Chicago, Illinois: Aldine.

Brady, D. S., and Friedman, R. (1947)   Savings and the income distribution. *Studies in income and wealth*, Vol. 10, pp. 247–265. New York: National Bureau of Economic Research.

Cantril, H. (1951)   *Public opinion, 1935–1946.* Princeton, New Jersey: Princeton Univ. Press.

Cantril, H. (1965)   *The pattern of human concerns.* New Brunswick, New Jersey: Rutgers Univ. Press.

Davies, J. C. (1962)   Toward a theory of revolution. *American Sociological Review* **37**: 5–18.

Davis, J. A. (1965)   *Education for positive mental health.* Chicago, Illinois: Aldine.

Davis, L. E., Easterlin, R. A., and Parker, W. N., (eds.) (1972)   *American economic growth: An economist's history of the United States.* New York: Harper.

Duesenberry, J. S. (1952)   *Income, saving and the theory of consumer behavior.* Cambridge, Massachusetts: Harvard Univ. Press.

Easterlin, R. A. (1969)   Towards a socio-economic theory of fertility. *In Fertility and family planning: A world view* (S. J. Behrman, L. Corsa, Jr., and R. Freedman, eds.), pp. 127–156. Ann Arbor: Univ. of Michigan Press.

Easterlin, R. A. (1973)   Relative economic status and the American fertility swing. In *Social structure, family life styles, and economic behavior* (E. B. Sheldon, ed.). Philadelphia, Pennsylvania: Lippincott for Institute of Life Insurance.

Eckaus, R. S. (1972)   *Basic economics.* Boston, Massachusetts: Little, Brown.

Edwards, A. L. (1957)   *The social desirability variable in personality assessment and research.* New York: Holt.

Ekirch, A. A. (1944)   *The idea of progress in America, 1815–1860.* New York: Columbia Univ. Press.

Freedman, D. S.   Consumption of modern goods and services and their relation to fertility: A study in Taiwan. Unpublished paper.

Freedman, D. S. (1963)   The relation of economic status to fertility. *American Economic Review* **53**: 414–426.

Fuchs, V. R. (1967)   Redefining poverty and redistributing income. *The Public Interest* **8**: 88–95.

Galbraith, J. K. (1958)   *The affluent society.* Boston, Massachusetts: Houghton.

Galbraith, J. K. (1967)   Review of a review. *The Public Interest* **9**: 109–118.

Gilbert, M. *et al.* (1958)   *Comparative national products and price levels.* Paris: OECC.

Gurin, G., Veroff, J., and Feld, S. (1960)   *Americans view their mental health.* New York: Basic Books.

Gurr, T. R. (1970)   *Why men rebel.* Princeton, New Jersey: Princeton Univ. Press.

Hagen, E. E. (1962)   *On the theory of social change: How economic growth begins.* Homewood, Illinois: Dorsey Press.

Homans, G. C. (1961)   *Social behavior: Its elementary forms.* New York: Harcourt.

Houthakker, H. S., and Pollak, R. A. (to be published)   *The theory of consumer's choice.* San Francisco, California: Holden-Day.

Inkeles, A. (1960)   Industrial man: The relation of status to experience, perception, and value. *American Journal of Sociology* **66**: 1–31.

Johnson, H. G. (1967)   *Money, trade, and economic growth.* Cambridge, Massachusetts: Harvard Univ. Press.

Katona, G. (1951)   *Psychological analysis of economic behavior.* New York: McGraw-Hill.

Katona, G., Strumpel, B., and Zahn, E. (1971)   *Aspirations and affluence.* New York: McGraw-Hill.

Lipset, S. M. (1960)   *Political man: The social bases of politics.* Garden City, New York: Doubleday.

Little, I. M. D. (1950)   *A critique of welfare economics.* London and New York: Oxford Univ. Press.

McClelland, D. C. (1961)   *The achieving society.* Princeton, New Jersey: Van Nostrand-Reinhold.

Mack, R. P. (1956)   Trends in American consumption and the aspiration to consume. *American Economic Review* **46**: 55–68.

Merton, R. K. (1968)   *Social theory and social structure,* 1968 ed. New York: Free Press.

Mishan, E. J. (1968)   Welfare economics. *International encyclopedia of the social sciences,* Vol. 16, pp. 504–512. New York: Macmillan.

Mishan, E. J. (1969)   *Welfare economics: Ten introductory essays,* 2nd ed. New York: Random House.

Morgan, J. N. (1968)   The supply of effort, the measurement of well-being, and the dynamics of improvement. *American Economic Review* **58**: 31–39.

Morris, C. (1956)   *Varieties of human value.* Chicago, Illinois: Univ. of Chicago Press.

Nordhaus, W., and Tobin, J. (1972)   Is growth obsolete? In *Economic growth,* 5th Anniversary Series, National Bureau of Economic Research, pp. 1–80. New York: Columbia Univ. Press.

OECD (1970)   *National accounts statistics: 1950–1968.* Paris: Organisation for Economic Cooperation and Development.

Pettigrew, T. F. (1967)   Social evaluation theory: Convergences and applications. *Nebraska Symposium on Motivation* (D. Levine, ed.). Lincoln: Nebraska Univ. Press.

Pfaff, M. (1973)   Economic life styles, values, and subjective welfare: A comment. *In Social structure, family life styles, and economic behavior* (E. B. Sheldon, ed.). Philadelphia, Pennsylvania: Institute of Life Insurance.

Rainwater, L.   A decent standard of living: Subsistence vs. membership. Unpublished paper.

Robinson, J. P., and Shaver, P. R. (1969)   *Measures of social psychological attitudes* (Appendix B to *Measures of political attitudes*). Ann Arbor, Michigan: Survey Research Center, Institute for Social Research.

Rorer, L. G. (1965)   The great response-style myth. *Psychological Bulletin* **63**: 129–156.

Rosenstein-Rodan, P. N. (1961)   International aid for underdeveloped countries. *Review of Economics and Statistics* **43**: 107–138.

Rostow, W. W. (1960)   *The stages of economic growth*. London and New York: Cambridge Univ. Press.

Siegel, S. (1964)   Level of aspiration and decision making. In *Decision and choice: Contributions of Sidney Siegel* (A. H. Brayfield and S. Messick, eds.). New York: McGraw-Hill.

Smelser, N. J. (1962)   *Theory of collective behavior*. New York: Free Press.

Smolensky, E. (1965)   The past and present poor. *The concept of poverty* (First Report of the Task Force on Economic Growth and Opportunity), pp. 35–67. Washington, D. C.: Chamber of Commerce of the United States.

Stouffer, S. A., *et al.* (1949)   *The American soldier: Adjustment during wartime life*, Vol. I. Princeton, New Jersey: Princeton Univ. Press.

Strumpel, B. (1973)   Economic life styles, values, and subjective welfare—An empirical approach. In *Social structure, family life styles, and economic behavior* (E. B. Sheldon, ed.). Philadelphia, Pennsylvania: Lippincott for Institute of Life Insurance.

Tabbarah, R. B. (1972)   The adequacy of income: A social view of economic development. *Journal of Development Studies*. **8**: 57–76.

Wachter, M. L. (1971a)   A labor supply model for secondary workers. Discussion Paper No. 194, Revised.Wharton School of Finance and Commerce, Univ. of Pennsylvania.

Wachter, M. L. (1971b)   A new approach to the equilibrium labor force. Discussion Paper No. 226. Wharton School of Finance and Commerce, Univ. of Pennsylvania.

Wessman, A. E. (1956)   A psychological inquiry into satisfactions and happiness. Ph.D. dissertation in psychology, Princeton Univ. Princeton, New Jersey.

Wilson, W. (1967)   Correlates of avowed happiness. *Psychological Bulletin* **67**: 294–306.

World Survey III (1965)   International Data Library and Reference Service, Survey Research Center, Univ. of California, Berkeley.

ADDITIONAL BIBLIOGRAPHY

Arrow, K. J., and Scitovsky, T. (eds.) (1969)   *Readings in welfare economics*. Homewood, Illinois: Irwin.

Baumol, W. J. (1952)   *Welfare economics and the theory of the state*. Cambridge, Massachusetts: Harvard Univ. Press.

Bradburn, N. M., and Caplovitz, D. (1965)   *Reports on happiness*. Chicago, Illinois: Aldine.

Brenner, B. (1971)   Mental well-being: Conceptual framework. *Annual meeting of the American Sociological Association, 66th, Denver, Colorado, August 1971*, revised paper.

Dalkey, N. C., and Rourke, D. L. (1971)   Experimental assessment of delphi procedures with group value judgments. R-612-ARPA. Santa Monica, California: The Rand Corporation.

Dalkey, N. C., Lewis, R., and Snyder, D. (1970)   Measurement and analysis of the quality of life: With exploratory illustrations of applications to career and transportation choices. RM-6228-DOT. Santa Monica, California: The Rand Corporation.

Easterlin, R. A. (1968)   Economic growth: An overview. *International encyclopedia of the social sciences*, Vol. 4, pp. 395–408. New York: Macmillan.

Freedman, D. S. Consumption aspirations as economic incentives in a developing economy—Taiwan. Unpublished paper.

Graff, J. deV. (1957)   *Theoretical welfare economics*. London and New York: Cambridge Univ. Press.

Harsanyi, J. C. (1953–1954)   Welfare economics of variable states. *Review of Economic Studies* **21**: 204–213.

Inkeles, A. (1969)   Making men modern: On the causes and consequences of individual change in six developing countries. *American Journal of Sociology* **75**: 208–225.

Lewin, K., *et al.* (1944)   Level of aspiration. In *Personality and the behavior disorders* (J. McV. Hunt, ed.). New York: Ronald Press.

Linder, S. B. (1970)   *The harried leisure class.* New York: Columbia Univ. Press.

Lingoes, J. C., and Pfaff, M.   Measurement of subjective welfare and satisfaction. Unpublished paper.

Mishan, E. J. (1967)   *The costs of economic growth.* New York: Praeger.

Schnore, L. F., and Cowhig, J. D. (1959–1960)   Some correlates of reported health in metropolitan centers. *Social Problems* **7**: 218–226.

Veblen, T. (1934)   *Theory of the leisure class.* New York: The Modern Library.

Weisskopf, W. A. (1964)   Economic growth and human well-being. *Quarterly Review of Economics and Business* **4**: 17–29.

Wessman, A. E., and Ricks, D. F. (1966)   *Mood and personality.* New York: Holt.

Income-Related Differences in Natural Increase : Bearing on Growth and Distribution of Income

SIMON KUZNETS
HARVARD UNIVERSITY

1. Differences in Natural Increase among Income Classes

The operating hypothesis here is as follows. If among the population in its reproductive ages (say women 18 to mid-40s and their husbands), groups are distinguished by long-term levels of family income (allowing for family size), the rate of natural increase will be found higher among the low than among the upper income groups. This hypothesis appears to hold for many developed countries during the long transition, in the course of industrialization and economic growth, from high to low birth- and death rates. The basic shift began at the upper income levels, and spread only gradually downward. The same hypothesis may have become relevant to many less-developed countries, as they entered recently the phase of urbanization and modernization. Subordinate hypotheses would specify the negative association between income and fertility; and while admitting that the death rate is also associated negatively with income, would recognize that the income-related mortality differentials are, and were, much narrower than the fertility differentials—

thus assuring a negative association between income and the rate of natural increase.

These statements may sound familiar, and are apparently amply confirmed by the findings in the demographic literature on the subject.[1] Yet the evidence to support the main hypothesis, as formulated with precise relevance to the implications for growth and distribution of income, is difficult to come by. Long-term family income levels would have to be established for population groups at ages when most of the reproduction takes place—insofar as effects on fertility are concerned; and the income levels would have to be undisturbed by annual fluctuations, and with proper allowance for the phase of the long lifetime cycle of earnings and income (so that low incomes of physicians in their late 20s or early 30s are not mistaken for their long-term income levels). Furthermore, family income would have to be related to size of family. Data that would yield such information are quite different from the commonly available sample data on money family income, for a given year, and shown for family units of differing size (e.g., the data used in the two substantive tables below). While observations on fertility would have to be concentrated on the major reproductive ages (i.e., roughly from 18 to the mid-30s for the wife), data on mortality would have to extend over the long span over which a given generation in its prime reproductive ages is replaced by its direct descendants entering their income earning and family formation careers; and such mortality data would have to be given with different death rates (or life tables) for the several long-term income levels. A full test of the quantitative dimensions of the main hypothesis here is probably impossible with the present data, and would certainly be out of place here.

Yet it is possible to accept the hypothesis as plausible, not only because of the direct evidence on the negative correlation between income (although annual) and fertility and hence implicitly the rate of natural increase, but also because of much more numerous findings on differential fertility (and natural increase) by degree of rurality (rural versus urban, and small cities versus large cities), by occupation (manual unskilled versus white-collar professional), and by industry of attachment (agriculture and mining versus manufacturing and services)—all of which are fairly closely and negatively correlated with implicit income differentials.[2] Under the circumstances we can assume

---

[1] See, for example, the discussion of differences in fertility by economic status in United Nations (1953) which begins with the sentence: "That the poor have more children than the rich is a well established fact"—and then proceeds to summarize the findings, with proper qualifications. Other sources that summarize the evidence are the three papers by Johnson (1960), Kiser (1960), and Ruggles and Ruggles (1960) on differential fertility in the European countries and in the United States; United Nations (1965); and Roberts (1965).

[2] Discussion of these differentials can be found in the references cited in footnote 1 above. See also Blau and Duncan (1967).

that the hypothesis is sufficiently plausible to warrant exploration of its implications and use the available data only to illustrate and convey the sense of the magnitudes involved.

The data selected for this illustrative presentation relate to the United States, a country for which relevant statistics are available, and one that, despite the high level of economic development, still shows substantial income-related differentials in fertility (and implicitly in rates of natural increase).[3] The data in Table 1 relate to 1960, the last census year for which a wide coverage of the detailed statistics on fertility by income class is available and one that comes close to a high level of the post-World War II birthrate in this country. The summary measures in Table 1 suggest several findings.

1. The ratio of children under 5 to married women, which reflects fertility over the last quinquennium reduced by death rates over that period, is consistently, at every age level of the wife, higher at the low family income levels than at the high (lines 1–18). The cumulative effects of this are confirmed by the ratios of children ever born (not reduced by deaths) to wives aged 35–39 and 45–49 in lines 19–24.

2. This negative association between family income and fertility (and implicitly rate of natural increase) is more conspicuous for the nonwhites, with their higher general level of fertility and lower median income levels, than for the whites. With the rise in income levels, fertility for the nonwhites declines much more sharply than for the whites; and for some high-income levels, the rates for the two groups become about the same, or that for nonwhites is lower (lines 4 and 5, columns 5–7; lines 7 and 8, columns 6 and 7; lines 10 and 11, column 7; lines 19 and 20, columns 6 and 7).

3. Comparing the cumulative ratios of children ever born in lines 19–21 with those in lines 22–24, we find that, with the overall higher birthrates in 1945–1959 dominating lines 19–21 than those in 1935–1949 dominating lines 22–24, the spread in birthrates between the lower and upper income groups, absolute and *relative*, is also wider in lines 19–21. Thus, for whites the range between the top and lowest income groups (columns 7 and 3) is 26.4% of the higher fertility ratios in line 19 and 23.5% in line 22; for the nonwhites, the range (in percentage of the top fertility level) is 47.2% in line 20 and 23% in line

---

[3] It would have been of interest to use data on rates of natural increase, or at least fertility, by family income classes for a less-developed country. But no such data are available. The evidence would have to be derived from sample data on family income for families of differing size, a task complicated by the importance of the extended family in some less-developed countries (so that large size does not necessarily mean large numbers of children). Such exploration was not feasible here. The whole field of economic determinants of differential rates of natural increase within the less-developed countries requires systematic study yet to be undertaken.

TABLE 1

CHILDREN UNDER 5 AND CHILDREN EVER BORN, PER 1000 MARRIED WOMEN,
BY AGE OF WOMAN AND 1959 FAMILY MONEY INCOME
(UNITED STATES, MARCH 1960)[a]

	Number of wives[b]	Median family money income ($)	Children per 1000 wives Family income classes ($)[b]					Total
			Less than 2	2 to 3.99	4.0 to 6.99	7.0 to 9.99	10.0 and over	
	(1)	(2)	(3)	(4)	(5)	(6)	(7)	(8)
			A. Children under 5					
Wives aged 20–24								
1. White	3028	5158	1300	1306	1260	887	819	1124
2. Nonwhite	292	3265	1674	1596	1408	1000	1000	1511
3. Total	3321	4983	1397	1346	1267	891	825	1218
Wives aged 25–29								
4. White	3967	6012	1342	1325	1304	1113	1030	1237
5. Nonwhite	414	3851	1595	1445	1264	924	915	1339
6. Total	4381	5855	1417	1349	1301	1105	1028	1247
Wives aged 30–34								
7. White	4585	6504	932	867	845	760	771	817
8. Nonwhite	459	4102	1261	1060	872	707	646	966
9. Total	5044	6330	1031	908	847	758	767	830
Wives aged 35–39								
10. White	4880	6880	582	538	504	418	410	468
11. Nonwhite	451	4337	870	690	589	441	383	633
12. Total	5331	6698	667	568	511	419	409	482
Wives aged 40–44								
13. White	4382	7223	270	249	223	178	158	200
14. Nonwhite	388	4205	462	345	280	220	192	320
15. Total	4771	6868	321	267	228	180	158	209
Wives aged 45–49								
16. White	3972	7095	63	62	52	42	38	48
17. Nonwhite	343	3864	137	139	106	83	74	118
18. Total	4315	6836	82	80	56	43	39	53
			B. Number of children ever born					
Wives aged 35–39								
19. White	4880	6880	3316	3053	2737	2515	2440	2672
20. Nonwhite	451	4337	4432	3537	3081	2527	2340	4059
21. Total	5331	6698	3625	3148	2765	2516	2448	2727
Wives aged 45–49								
22. White	3972	7095	2935	2729	2364	2228	2244	2383
23. Nonwhite	343	3864	3579	3023	2637	2573	2757	2969
24. Total	4315	6836	3091	2779	2385	2260	2257	2430

[a] Lines 1–18: Taken or calculated from United States Bureau of the Census (1960). The median income was calculated from the more detailed income distribution given in the source.
Lines 19–24, columns 3–8: Taken or calculated from United States Bureau of the Census (1964).
[b] Numbers in thousands.

23; for total population the two ranges are 32.4% in line 21 and 27.0% in line 24. Apparently, when birthrates are kept down by adverse circumstances, the reduction is proportionately greater at the high-fertility, low-income levels, than at the upper income, low-fertility levels; and the relative income-related differences in fertility are narrower.

4. Although the point is not covered in Table 1, one may add that the ratios, either of children under 5 or of children ever born, to wives at different age levels, reveal the same consistent negative association with family income when we distinguish urban and rural groups, or subgroups among the nonfarm population by degree of urbanization.

While the summary measures in Table 1 illustrate the prevalence of the negative association whose implications are explored below, they tend to understate, by a substantial margin, the differences in rate of natural increase associated with long-term family income per person (or per consuming unit). There are several sources of such understatement. First, the grouping in Table 1 is based on income for the current year. High secular incomes, associated with low fertility and rate of natural increase, if reduced for the year by a transient factor, would therefore be grouped with low incomes and tend to reduce the birthrates or rates of natural increase shown; and the same effect would be produced by low, long-term incomes raised temporarily to high levels during the single year. Second, the income classification makes no allowance for low life-cycle phases of long-term high incomes (e.g., for the early years already cited of medical practitioners or lawyers); yet clearly the birthrate and natural increase patterns of these groups are set by their high lifetime incomes. Third, even assuming mortality rates somewhat higher for the low than for the high-income groups, the effect of differences in fertility on those in rate of natural increase tend to be greatly magnified with the subtraction of attrition by mortality. Thus, assume that the entries in line 19 refer to the income levels of a cohort all through the childbearing period, and relate the cohort at the end of the period when the parental generation has practically moved out of the labor force and of full-time earning. If so, the 2000 husbands and wives in line 19, column 7, would have produced 2440 children and, allowing for an attrition of 10%, would yield 2196 survivors, a net rise of 9.8%. The 2000 husbands and wives in line 19, column 3, would have produced 3316 children and, allowing for an attrition of 20%, would yield 2653 survivors, or a rate of natural increase of 32.6%.[4] Finally, the family income used for the classifi-

---

[4] The illustration is clearly crude and exaggerated. The survival rate to the age of say 70 (from the age of 30) is from 94.4% of the original cohort to 53.8 for white males, and from 90.3 to 39.9 for nonwhite males an attrition rate of about 43% for white males and 56% for nonwhite males [see United States National Center for Health Statistics, (1964)]. If we use these as proxies for the top and bottom income levels in line 19, and also allow for an

cation in Table 1 is *not* adjusted for the number of persons or consuming units in the family. Yet the low-income family that tends to produce more children in the early years of the reproduction period increases in size, as compared with the upper income family with its smaller number of children born somewhat later; and even if the two families start, in our analysis, with husband and wife, by the time the wife is in her late 20s or early 30s, the low-income family will be larger than the high-income family; yet it is the former that will continue to have more children. A reclassification of families by per-person or per-consuming-unit income would shift many large, multichildren families to the lower income levels, and many small, no-children families (including un-married adults, not covered in Table 1) to higher income levels than they are now in Table 1. The contrast between a greater number of children per wife in the lower income brackets than in the higher income brackets would thus be substantially accentuated.

This latter comment is of importance because it points to the fact that a greater proportion of children than of adults is found in families at low-income levels; and this implication bears on the assumptions that we can make concerning growth in per-capita product of the descendants of low- and high-income groups. Table 2 is included here because it illustrates the association between number of children and income per person or per consuming unit in the family, but most important because the number of children in the family, rather than family income (as in Table 1), is the basis of classification.[5]

---

attrition of children ever born of 7.6% for the top income group and 14.3% for the lowest income group (corresponding to survival rates from age 0 to age 40 for white and nonwhite males, respectively), the survivors would be $(2000 \times 0.44) + (3316 \times 0.857) = 3722$ for line 19, column 3, and $(2000 \times 0.57) + (2440 \times 0.924) = 3395$ for line 19, column 7. Even here the rate of natural increase for the low-income group, of 86%, is distinctly higher than for the high-income group, 70%. But the major relevant difference is in the *second* of the two brackets in the two equations above—in the number of descendants who at the end of the period account for all of the working force (with the parental generation 70 years of age or older). And it is the rise in the economically active members of the population, in the second generation relative to the first, that is important. It was potentially 2000 each in the illustration for the first generation; it grew to 2842 and 2255, respectively, a rise of 42% for the low-income group and about 13% for the high-income group.

[5] For the association studied here, it is most important that families be classified either by the number of children, with the average family income reduced to a per-person (or per-consuming-unit) basis; or by per-person at per-consuming-unit income, with the average number of children then calculated for the resulting groups. Classifying families by income per family regardless of family size obscures or completely conceals the association: small families, with no children, will tend to rank low on a per-family income scale, although their per-person income would be much higher relatively; and large families, with children, would tend to rank high on a per-family income scale although their per-person or per-consuming-unit rate would be relatively low.

Thus for the white families in Table 2, ranked by per-family income, the lowest number

TABLE 2

AVERAGE FAMILY MONEY INCOME PER PERSON OR PER CONSUMING UNIT,
FAMILIES GROUPED BY NUMBER OF RELATED CHILDREN UNDER 18
(MARCH 1971; INCOME FOR 1970)[a]

	Groups of families by number of related children under 18						
	0	1	2	3	4	5 and over	Total
	(1)	(2)	(3)	(4)	(5)	(6)	(7)
	A. White families						
1. Number of families[b]	20.30	8.86	8.34	4.91	2.36	1.76	46.53
2. Persons per family	2.3	3.3	4.2	5.2	6.2	8.2	3.52
3. Consuming units per family	2.3	2.8	3.2	3.7	4.2	5.2	2.89
4. Average money income per family[c]	10.91	11.59	12.08	12.49	12.05	11.49	11.50
5. Income per person[c]	4.74	3.51	2.88	2.40	1.94	1.40	3.27 A–3.68 C–2.45
6. Income per consuming unit[c]	4.74	4.14	3.77	3.38	2.87	2.21	3.98 A–4.13 C–3.32
	B. Negro families						
7. Number of families[b]	1.50	1.03	0.82	0.59	0.41	0.58	4.93
8. Persons per family	2.3	3.1	4.1	5.2	6.3	8.3	4.26
9. Consuming units per family	2.3	2.6	3.1	3.7	4.3	5.3	3.26
10. Money income per family[c]	7.58	7.59	7.74	7.30	7.26	5.74	7.44
11. Income per person	3.29	2.45	1.89	1.40	1.15	0.69	1.75 A–2.19 C–1.34
12. Income per consuming unit	3.29	2.92	2.49	1.97	1.69	1.08	2.28 A–2.53 C–1.79

[a] Lines 1, 2, 4, 7, 8, 10: Taken or calculated from United States Bureau of the Census (1971).

Lines 3 and 9: Calculated from the other lines and the source on the assumption that a child under 18 is equivalent to 0.5 consuming units, that for an adult being 1.0. This is a rough approximation, and probably understates the consuming unit equivalent per child.

Lines 5, 6, 11, 12: All entries except those marked A and C in column 7, were obtained by division of arithmetic mean income per family in lines 4 and 10 by the number of persons or consuming units per family in lines 2 and 3, and 8 and 9.

Lines 5, 6, 11, 12, column 7: The entries marked A and C are weighted arithmetic mean incomes, using the income per person or per consuming unit, and the numbers derived from lines 1–2, 1–3, or 7–8 and 7–9, as weights. A stands for adults (weights derived from total number of persons minus numbers of children); C stands for children (weights are the numbers of children in the successive groups in columns 1–6).

[b] Numbers in millions.

[c] Thousands of dollars.

The findings in Table 2 reveal even more sharply the associations suggested in Table 1. First, for both white and Negro families income per person or per consuming unit declines sharply as we move from families with no children under 18 to those with increasing number of children—the per-person differentials between the extreme being in the range of $3\frac{1}{2}$ or $4\frac{1}{2}$ to 1; and the per-consuming-unit differentials in the range of 2 or 3 to 1. Second, the negative association between *per-unit* family income and number of children is more conspicuous for the Negro family group, with their much larger average number of children, than for the white family group. Thus, on a per-person basis the ratio of the income of the no-children group to that of the group with 5 or more children is 3.4 for the white families (line 5, columns 1 and 6), and 4.7 for the Negro families (line 11, columns 1 and 6). On a per-consuming-unit basis, the analogous ratios are 2.1 for the white families, 3.0 for the Negro families.

It follows that a large proportion of children is in families with rather low per-unit income, a much larger proportion than among adults. The two sets of arithmetic means in column 7, lines 5 and 6 and 11 and 12, are intended to summarize this difference in average economic status of children as compared with adults. On a per-person basis, the average family income of the universe of children is about a third lower than the average family income of the universe of adults for white families (line 5, column 7); and about four-tenths lower for the comparison within Negro families (line 11, column 7). On a per-consuming-unit basis, the shortfall is about a fifth for white children, compared with white adults, and about a third for Negro children, compared with Negro adults (lines 6 and 12, column 7). But the distributions are more important than the summary arithmetic means: A substantial proportion of children is found in families whose per-person or per-consuming-unit income is much below the average for the relevant universe, whether it be in all-white or all-Negro families; and the conclusion would only be strengthened were the two groups combined.

The statistical evidence of the type summarized in Tables 1 and 2, particularly in Table 2, could be extended to other years in this country, and perhaps to other developed countries. But its value is necessarily only illustrative; and we can rest with the presumptions that the negative association

---

of children per family, 0.84 and 0.89, is found in the two low-income groups, those with incomes less than $2500 and from $2500 to $5000; the highest number of children per family, at 1.46 and 1.45, are in the $10,000–$12,000 and $12,000–$15,000 income classes (and then decline to 1.22 per family in the top family-income class of $25,000 and over). But when the grouping is by number of children, and the family income is reduced to a per-person or per-consuming-unit basis, as is done in Table 2, the association is clearly negative (lines 5 and 6)—not positive, as suggested in the grouping by family income with no allowance for family size.

between the rates of natural increase and levels of family income per relevant unit is persistent and significant—even if the income differences represent differences in rurality, occupation, industry attachment, and the like—and that this association will be found, with differing and changing amplitudes, in both economically developed and in the less-developed countries, in current years and probably in the future. We can now turn to exploring the implications, the possible bearing on growth and distribution of income.

2. Implications for Growth and Distribution of Income

In considering the effects of the higher rates of natural increase among lower income groups on growth and distribution of income, we deal with notional quantities and illustrative examples. Indeed, in view of the lack of data specifically relevant to the properly formulated variables in the negative association, any substantive research would have to focus for a long while on samples of limited scope and of too narrow a base to yield broad findings. The purpose here is mainly to suggest the directions in which significant implications may lie, to raise the questions rather than to provide the answers.

Table 3 begins with a set of realistic figures relating to an initial distribution of income among quintiles (lines 1–3)—realistic in that such shares are found in the statistically recorded distributions of income among families, although usually for annual income. (Indeed, distributions in several less-developed countries show even wider inequalities.) It then introduces various differentials in rate of natural increase among given income groups (Cases 1–3); and with the help of one major assumption calculates the effect of these differentials on total and per-unit income at the end of the period of increase in numbers. The major assumption is that, over the period, the per-unit income grows at the *same percentage rate* for the groups and their descendants in the several initial quintiles. Thus, the assumption specifies that the original relative inequalities in per-unit income among the quintiles remain unchanged with the increased numbers of surviving units and their descendants.

The significance of this assumption, which is retained throughout this illustrative exercise, is discussed below, and will become clearer as we note the various effects that the calculations in Table 3 suggest. They may be listed briefly:

1. If the rate of growth of per-unit income is set at g, the inverse association between initial income level and the rate of increase in numbers yields an *aggregate* per-unit growth that falls short of g. The source of this shortfall is the rise in the share of the survivors and descendants of the lower income brackets, which means an increase in relative weight in the terminal

TABLE 3

EFFECT ON GROWTH OF INCOME PER UNIT OF DIFFERENTIALS IN RATE OF
INCREASE OF THE DIFFERENT INCOME GROUPS (WITH A GIVEN
INEQUALITY IN SIZE DISTRIBUTION OF INCOME)

	Quintiles					
	First	Second	Middle	Fourth	Top	Total
	(1)	(2)	(3)	(4)	(5)	(6)
Initial shares						
1. Number	20	20	20	20	20	100
2. Total income	4	8	16	24	48	100
3. Income per unit	0.2	0.4	0.8	1.2	2.4	1.0
Case 1						
4. Assumed % increase in numbers	100	75	50	25	0	
5. Terminal numbers	40	35	30	25	20	150
6. % shares, line 5	26.7	23.3	20.0	16.7	13.3	100.0
7. Assumed terminal income per unit:						
a. line 3 × 2.0	0.4	0.8	1.6	2.4	4.8	
b. line 3 × 1.5	0.3	0.6	1.2	1.8	3.6	
c. line 3 × 1.25	0.25	0.5	1.0	1.5	3.0	
d. line 3 × 1.0	0.2	0.4	0.8	1.2	2.4	
8. Total terminal income; line 6 times:						
a. line 7a	10.68	18.64	32.00	40.08	63.84	165.24
b. line 7b	8.01	13.98	24.00	30.06	47.88	123.93
c. line 7c	6.675	11.65	20.0	25.05	39.90	103.275
d. line 7d	5.34	9.32	16.00	20.04	31.92	82.62
9. First component of shortfall (change in share in numbers)	6.7	3.3	0	−3.3	−6.7	
10. Second component of shortfall (deviations in per unit income):						
a. line 7a	−1.6	−1.2	−0.4	0.4	2.8	
b. line 7b	−1.2	−0.9	−0.3	0.3	2.1	
c. line 7c	−1.0	−0.75	−0.25	0.25	1.75	
d. line 7d	−0.8	−0.6	−0.2	0.2	1.4	
11. Total shortfall (line 9 times lines 10a–10d)						
a. for line 8a	−10.72	−3.96	0	−1.32	−18.76	−34.76
b. for line 8b	−8.04	−2.97	0	−0.99	−14.07	−26.07
c. for line 8c	−6.70	−2.475	0	−0.825	−11.725	−21.725
d. for line 8d	−5.36	−1.98	0	−0.66	−10.04	−17.38

TABLE 3 (*continued*)

	First	Second	Middle	Fourth	Top	Total
	(1)	(2)	(3)	(4)	(5)	(6)
Case 2						
12. Assumed % increase in numbers	50	37.5	25	12.5	0	
13. Terminal numbers	30	27.5	25.0	22.5	20	125.0
14. %, line 13	24.0	22.0	20.0	18.0	16.0	100.0
15a. Total terminal income (line 14 times line 7a)	9.6	17.6	32.0	43.2	76.8	179.2
16a. Sources of shortfall of total in line 15a from 200	(4.0) ×(−1.6) =−6.4	(2.0) ×(−1.2) =−2.4	(0) ×(−0.4) =0	(−2.0) ×(0.4) =−0.8	(−4.0) ×(2.8) =−11.2	−20.8
Case 3						
17. Assumed % increase in numbers	70	60	50	40	30	
18. Terminal numbers	34.0	32.0	30.0	28.0	26.0	150.0
19. %, line 18	22.7	21.3	20.0	18.7	17.3	100.00
20a. Total terminal income, line 19 times line 7a	9.08	17.04	32.00	44.88	83.04	186.04
21a. Sources of shortfall of total in line 20a from 200	(2.7) ×(−1.6) =−4.32	(1.3) ×(−1.2) =−1.56	(0) ×(−0.4) =0	(−1.3) ×(0.4) =−0.52	(−2.7) ×(2.8) =−7.56	−13.9

distribution of groups with per-unit income below the expected countrywide average (i.e., initial income times $1+g$).

2. The proportional shortfall is the greater, the larger g, the assumed growth rate of per-unit income (compare lines a–d, under line 11, column 6). With g assumed to be 100, 50, and 25%, the shortfall is 34.8, 26.1, and 21.7 percentage points, respectively. But the effect in reducing total rate of growth *per unit* is the more striking, the lower the assumed g. Thus, the 100% growth rate of income per unit is reduced, in the aggregate, to 65%, i.e., to two-thirds; the 50% growth rate is reduced to 24%, i.e., to less than half; and the 25% growth rate was cut to 3.3%, i.e., almost completely offset (all of this for Case 1—see lines 8a–8c, column 6).

3. This shortfall in the aggregate growth rate per unit is partly a function of the magnitude of the differences assumed in the rate of natural increase (i.e., of numbers) among the initial quintiles. It is the *absolute* differences among the rates of increase in numbers, rather than the relative differences

in these rates, that are important. Thus, in Case 2 the *relative* disparities in rate of increase in numbers among the quintiles are the same as in Case 1, with that for the first quintile being double the increase rate in total population; that for the second quintile being one and a half times the aggregate rate of population increase; and so on (compare lines 4 and 12). But in Case 1 the aggregate rate of population increase is 50%, double that of Case 2, and the *absolute* differences in rates of increase among the quintiles are double those of Case 2. In consequence, for the same g, of 100%, the shortfall in Case 2, of 21 percentage points is only somewhat over half that for Case 1, of 34.8 percentage points. And the reduction in the shortfall is further marked in Case 3, in which the rate of increase in numbers among quintiles differs much less than in Case 1, both on an absolute and relative basis.

4. It is clear that with the rate of increase in per-unit income being the same for all initial quintiles, the negative association between rate of increase in numbers and initial income level *must* result in an aggregate rate of growth of income per unit short of g. If it is desired that the aggregate growth rate in per-unit income reach g, either the growth rate (the same) assigned to each initial quintile must be above g, or the assumption of equality of growth rates of income among the initial quintiles must be abandoned.

If it is abandoned, the modification, involving raising growth rates for some quintiles more than for others will necessarily change the size distribution of income from that assumed originally. If the growth rates of the lower quintiles are to be raised, thus making for lesser inequality, it is important to note that the shortfall represents a large magnitude relative to the shares of the lowest two quintiles as derived before the modification. Thus, in Case 1a the total income of the lower two quintiles, the only ones that show large deviations below the countrywide average, was $10.68 + 18.64$ or 29.32 (line 8a, columns 1 and 2); whereas the shortfall that had to be offset amounted to 34.76. Even for Case 3a, the shortfall to be offset was 13.96, compared with the total income of the lower two quintiles of 26.12 (line 20a, columns 1 and 2). Adding the shortfall, for the purpose of reaching g, to the income for the lower two quintiles would raise the growth rates of their per-unit income strikingly, compared with the growth rates initially assumed and retained for the higher quintiles.

Before we discuss the significance of the assumptions and the relevance of the implications suggested in Table 3, it would be well to round out the illustration and consider the effect of variations in the range of income inequality among the initial quintiles—given a fixed set of differentials in rates of increase of numbers among low- and high-income levels. The relevant illustrations are in Table 4.

5. The extent of initial income inequality is clearly of effect on the magnitude of the shortfall, once we assume a given differential in rates of increase in

TABLE 4

EFFECT ON GROWTH OF INCOME PER UNIT OF DIFFERING INITIAL INEQUALITIES
IN THE SIZE DISTRIBUTION OF INCOME (WITH GIVEN DIFFERENTIALS IN RATE
OF INCREASE OF NUMBERS AMONG THE SEVERAL INCOME GROUPS)

	Quintiles					
	First	Second	Middle	Fourth	Top	Total
	(1)	(2)	(3)	(4)	(5)	(6)
Assumed differences in rate of increase of numbers						
1. Initial share in numbers	20	20	20	20	20	100
2. Assumed % increase	100	75	50	25	0	
3. Terminal numbers	40	35	30	25	20	150
4. %, line 3	26.7	23.3	20.0	16.7	13.3	100.0
Case 1						
5. Initial shares in income	4	8	16	24	48	100
6. Initial income per unit	0.2	0.4	0.8	1.2	2.4	1.0

(Here proceed with lines 7–11 of Case 1 of Table 3, which is identical with Case 1 here.)

	First	Second	Middle	Fourth	Top	Total
Case 2						
7. Initial shares in income	7	9	12	30	42	
8. Initial income per unit	0.35	0.45	0.60	1.50	2.10	1.00
9a. Assumed terminal income per unit (line 8 times 2)	0.7	0.9	1.2	3.0	4.2	
10a. Total terminal income (line 9a times line 4)	18.69	20.97	24.00	50.10	55.86	169.62
11a. Sources of shortfall in line 10a from 200	$6.7 \times (-1.3) = -8.71$	$3.3 \times (-1.1) = -3.63$	$0 \times (-0.8) = 0$	$-3.3 \times (1.0) = -3.30$	$-6.7 \times (2.2) = -14.74$	-30.38
Case 3						
12. Initial shares in income	11	15	18	23	33	100
13. Initial income per unit	0.55	0.75	0.90	1.15	1.65	1.00
14a. Assumed terminal income per unit (line 13 times 2)	1.10	1.50	1.80	2.30	3.30	
15a. Total terminal income (line 14a times line 4)	29.37	34.95	36.00	38.41	43.89	182.62
16a. Sources of shortfall in line 15a from 200	$6.7 \times (-0.9) = -6.03$	$3.3 \times (-0.5) = -1.65$	$0 \times (-0.2) = 0$	$-3.3 \times (0.3) = -0.99$	$-6.7 \times (1.3) = -8.7$	-17.38

139

numbers negatively associated with income levels, and the same growth rate in per unit income for all initial income levels. The greater the initial income inequality, the greater the shortfall. Thus, Cases 2 and 3, which begin with income inequality somewhat narrower than that in Case 1, show more moderate shortfalls than the latter.

6. The major effect is associated with *total* deviations of quintile shares from equality, rather than with the *range* between the top and bottom. Thus, in Case 2, line 7, initial inequality is characterized by a range of 6.0, half that of Case 1, line 5. Yet the reduction in the shortfall, from 34.8 to 30.4, is relatively minor (the sum of deviations from equality for Cases 1 and 2 is the same, at 64.0). It is only in Case 3, where the sum of deviations from equality, in line 12, is halved, that the reduction in the shortfall (to 17.4) becomes significant, the latter being half of that in Case 1. The reason, of course, is that the second component in the product forming the shortfall (lines 11a and 16a) is a direct reflection of the deviation of the quintile share from equality.

Given that the shortfall is a function of initial income inequality, of the assumed differentials in rate of increase in numbers, and is likely to be most reductive of aggregative rate of increase in per-unit income when the assumed rate of growth in that income is moderate, what is the realism of the basic assumption and what is the meaning of the implied shortfall? (a) Is it realistic to assume the same rate of increase of per-unit income for the low and the high ordinal groups in the initial size distribution of income? (b) What is the significance of the shortfall of the actual aggregate growth rate of per-unit income, relative to some imaginary aggregate growth rate that would be attained with no natural increase differentials negatively associated with income?

(a) Beginning with the first question, let us consider it over a fairly long period, so that we shall be dealing largely with the per-unit income of the descendants, the second generation, compared with the per-unit income of the parents, the first generation, within the initial quintiles. Let us also view the units here as workers rather than as families or persons, implying that the rate of natural increase of workers is also inversely related to their incomes. Are there grounds for assuming that the increases in per-worker income or product are a function of the initial level, so that relative or percentage increases tend to be similar among the various per-worker income groups?

Examining this question with reference to long-term income levels, not those affected by transient changes or by a phase in a long life-span of incomes (for which the question can be answered more easily), one may note factors that would yield different answers. On the one hand, the low-income levels (and the high-fertility and natural-increase rates) are associated with attachment to traditional sectors (such as agriculture, handicrafts, etc.) which provide diminishing opportunities for employment and force the members and descendants of a low-income quintile to migrate to other sectors and areas—toward modern industry and urban communities. This prevalence of migration toward greater employment and higher income opportunities among the members and descendants of the lower income quintiles would, all other conditions being equal, make for a *higher* rate of growth of per-worker income and product than would be true of the upper quintiles, which are already attached to the more urbanized and advanced sectors of the economy and for whose members and descendants the possibilities of such upward migration may be more restricted. On the other hand, growth in per-worker product partly depends on the investment made in the human being, in the way of education, formal and informal, and in the way of raising his capacity to face increasingly complicated problems of adequate participation in the economy and society. Here the low-income level of the parents in the lower quintiles and the associated low educational levels would make for a much lower per-capita investment in the descendants, in absolute and even in relative terms (relative to income of parents), than would be true of higher quintiles. (One should bear in mind particularly the contribution of the parental household to informal training and education of descendants.) To the extent that this is so, the growth in per-worker incomes among the lower quintiles may be at a lower percentage rate than among the upper quintiles and their descendants.

The two groups of factors just noted, closely associated with the differences in rate of natural increase among the lower and higher income brackets, may be qualified by other factors—among them government intervention to assist by providing real services in the way of education and health largely to the low-income groups; and tendencies toward monopolization and restriction of high-level economic opportunities, combined with economic discrimination against some groups within the population. The relative weights of the two major, and the subordinate factors, making for narrowing and widening inequality in the distribution of income, have probably changed in successive phases of economic growth in the presently developed countries and may differ widely in the several less-developed countries. To attempt a general appraisal, and thus to test the realism of assuming unchanging relative inequality, would require much more organized knowledge than is presently available.

We used the assumption as a simplifying step; but this is little more than an excuse, and should not be interpreted so as to neglect the major problems that lurk behind the negative association whose implications we are considering. For given the association and the higher rates of increase in numbers among the low-income groups, the ameliorative mechanisms—be they migration to better employment and economic opportunities, or provision of government assistance to offset the negative effects of low income on investment in children, or others—carry costs of their own, and may not be sufficiently effective to avoid even long-term shortfalls and widening of income inequalities. In the process of internal migration that accompanied economic growth, the migrant, from the high-fertility families, had to go through a process of adjustment and assimilation that kept him for a long while at the lower income levels. And in recent decades the sharp accentuation of income-related differences in rates of natural increase in the less-developed countries, due to a rapid decline in death rates probably more marked among the low- than among the high-income groups, must have contributed to the accelerated internal migration, increased unemployment and underemployment, and apparently a widening of inequality in the size distribution of income.

The purpose of these comments is to stress that if reduction or limitation of relative income inequality is an important desideratum—so long as it does not seriously curb the growth rate of total income per capita—the negative association between rate of natural increase and income levels represents a continuous threat and problem; and that we need to know much more how this problem was resolved in the past growth of presently developed countries, and the magnitudes that it is assuming in many less-developed countries today. Our use of the same growth rates in per-unit income of the several ordinal groups in the initial size distribution of income is a simplification which, in disregarding the persistent threat of widening inequality, may be on the optimistic side and should be replaced by more realistic assumptions as soon as more specific knowledge accumulates on this aspect of economic growth.[6]

(b) Given the result that a negative correlation between rates of natural increase and initial income levels, combined with an identical growth rate of per-unit income in the several quintiles, will necessarily yield an aggregate

[6] The Blau–Duncan study (1967) appears to suggest, for the experience of the United States, a less pessimistic picture. The members of the labor force of lower social origin (i.e., with lower level occupations, and presumably lower income levels, of parents) show greater upward mobility than sons of parents of higher occupational and presumably higher income levels [see Blau and Duncan (1967, footnote 1, p. 402)]. But there is a question as to whether these results would be confirmed for a more sensitive variable like per-unit family income; for differential movements on the income scale, relative to the changing absolute per unit income; and particularly for the less-developed countries, in which the impact of differences in rates of natural increase (given higher population growth rates) and lower growth rates in per-capita income (as compared with the developed countries) may be so much greater. At any rate, there is no basis for arguing that a long-term income level, if low, automatically guarantees a higher rate of increase in per unit income than an initial middle- or high-income level (stochastic and phase elements having been removed by definition); there is nothing that would prevent an initially low secular income level from rising not more (or less) than the rest, and thus remaining relatively as low or lower than at the start.

growth rate per capita or per worker *short* of that assumed for the initial income groups, what is the significance of the shortfall? Should we be concerned about it, as if it were a loss of some possible real attainment, or is it just an arithmetic artifact, without real significance? This question may seem particularly appropriate, because in a recent paper I argued that for many types of analysis an aggregate rate of growth of income per capita should be derived by weighting by numbers the percentage growth rates of per-capita income of the various income groups within the population (which procedure would, in the illustrations in Tables 3 and 4, remove any shortfall).[7]

The answer to the question depends upon whether we can assume significant constraints to the rate of growth of per-unit income—for say a given growth rate of total population (or total labor force). If we can argue that, for an overall growth rate in numbers over the period of, say, 50%, the top level of *attainable* growth in income per unit is, say, 50%—and that it is roughly the same for per-unit income in the lower and in the upper quintiles—then the shortfall resulting from the negative association under discussion is significant. For it means that, *without* this negative association, the country, while still achieving a 50% rise in income per unit for each quintile and its descendants, could also attain a growth rate of total income per unit of 50%—and not a rate reduced by a shortfall; and thus attain a growth of total income of 125%, not the significantly lower figure attainable under conditions in which the second generation, stemming from the low-income levels, would be proportionately more numerous. And regardless of any distributional considerations, that attainment of higher aggregate per unit and total income is significant.

It does seem more realistic to assume fairly close constraints on the percentage growth rates of per-unit income, given an assumed rate of increase in total numbers, than to argue for absence of such constraints. After all, the investments in improvement of quality of labor must be limited to a moderate proportion of initial income or product; and proportional gains from migration to the more productive sectors are restricted by limitations on the volume of migration and by the ties between the post- and premigration income levels. And, with some straining, we may accept the notion that the limits on the percentage growth rate of per-unit income or product are roughly the same for the several initial quintiles and their descendants. If so, it would seem that the negative association between rates of natural increase and initial income spells real losses in yielding a growth rate of total and per-unit income that falls significantly short of that attainable without such negative association.

And yet this conclusion must be seriously qualified. For doing away with

[7] See Kuznets (1972), particularly in the present connection pages 197 and 199.

the negative association between rates of natural increase and initial income levels means, implicitly and particularly under the conditions of the *same* aggregate rate of increase in numbers, a more equal size distribution of income per consuming unit than would exist with the negative association; and this may reduce the flow of savings for investment in material capital. This might, in turn, reduce the feasible rate of growth in per-unit income below that attainable otherwise. Hence, what would be gained by removing the shortfall between the actual aggregate growth in per-unit income and one otherwise feasible would be lost because of the possible reduction in the limits of the feasible. We are thus back to the old problem of choice between the returns from the more equal size distribution of income in the way of greater productivity rise among the lower income group due to greater investment in human beings, and the returns from a more unequal size distribution of income in the way of greater contributions to savings and material capital formation.

3. Summary

The paper began with the recognition of a feature of demographic growth, widely observed in both developed and less-developed countries—the marked differences between the higher rate of natural increase in the lower income groups and the lower rate in the upper income groups. In attempting to explore the implications of this association, abstracting from differences or changes in the aggregate rate of natural increase, we proceeded to illustrate changes in an initial cohort of income groups (quintiles) as they were transformed into the next generation groups of different *relative* size. While the discussion was in terms of a single cohort, it could be applied to a succession of cohorts— yielding a succession of generations of descendants. The results would be either a repetition or a cumulation, depending upon whether the initial series was of identical cohorts just moving in time, or a series that reflected cumulative changes of earlier differences in rates of natural increase among the several ordinal groups within the income distribution.

The negative association between rates of natural increase and initial secular income levels clearly poses a major problem, if wider inequality in the size distribution of income is to be avoided—since lower income levels of parents mean proportionately lower investment in quality of the descendants and hence possibly lower growth rates in the per-capita income of the lower income groups and their descendants. The magnitude of the problem and of the necessary compensating offsets is clearly a function of the differential spread in the rates of natural increase and of the initial differences in income levels of parents. If no offsets are provided, all other conditions being equal, the negative association between rates of natural increase and initial income levels would result both in the widening of income inequality and the probable keeping down of the growth rate of aggregate income per unit (per person or per worker). The conditions being equal involves the same aggregate growth rate in population or labor force; the "probable" keeping down of growth rate refers to the likely negative balance of the opportunity losses in higher human quality at the lower income end over the possible gain from greater savings at the lower fertility, upper income end.

This conclusion, particularly with respect to widening income inequality, has not been explored here and is only stressed as a possible qualification on the realism of the basic assumption used in the illustrative analysis, viz., that the growth rate in per-unit income or product is the same for the several ordinal groups in the initial income distribution (i.e., quintiles or deciles), while their numbers would be increasing at different rates.

Given this assumption, which assures rough constancy in *relative* inequality in the income distribution, we have considered the influence of the negative association between natural increase and income on growth of aggregate product or income per unit (person or worker). The illustrative analysis shows that the combination of an assumed growth rate in per-unit income, the same for all ordinal groups, with the greater growth in numbers among the lower income brackets, yields a growth rate in *total* income per unit that is *lower* than the basic growth rate assumed for per-unit income within each ordinal group. This shortfall is relatively greater, the larger the differential in rates of natural increase, the wider the income inequality among the original ordinal groups, and the lower the assumed growth rate identical for all ordinal groups.

It has proved difficult to establish the significance of this shortfall unequivocally. Even if we assume realistic limits to percentage growth of per-unit income or product, and roughly equal limits for the several ordinal groups in the initial income distribution, it is not clear that, for a given growth rate of total population or labor force, reduction in the negative association between rate of natural increase and initial income level would raise the growth of total income per unit (by reducing the shortfall). For the implied reduction in the association would also imply a less unequal income distribution, which in the process of movement from the parental cohort to that of descendants might mean a lesser *relative* volume of savings and hence of investment in material capital. To arrive at determinate conclusions, we need empirical evidence on the weights of various factors or offsets, which tend to narrow or widen income inequality, and which, in so doing, may affect investment in human, relative to investment in material, capital.

Given the substantial differences in rates of natural increase negatively correlated with income, the implications for growth of income per capita or per worker, and for the size distribution of income in the process of growth, must clearly be important. But since the operating factors are of conflicting effect, it is not possible to derive firm conclusions as to these implications, without empirical findings on the magnitude of these factors in different phases of economic growth and at different levels of economic development. There is obvious need for such empirical findings, both for the developed and the less-developed countries; and only few of the available data on size distribution of income and on demographic patterns are effectively relevant to this need.

REFERENCES

Blau, P. M., and Duncan, O. D. (1967) *The American occupational structure*, particularly Chap. 11, pp. 361–400. New York: Wiley.

Johnson, G. Z. (1960) In *Demographic and economic change in developed countries* (A. J. Coale, ed.), pp. 36–72, for NBER Conference. Princeton, New Jersey: Princeton Univ. Press.

Kiser, C. V. (1960) In *Demographic and economic change in developed countries* (A. J. Coale, ed.), pp. 77–113, for NBER Conference. Princeton, New Jersey: Princeton Univ. Press.

Kuznets, S. (1972) Problems in comparing recent growth rates for developed and less developed countries. *Economic Development and Cultural Change* **20**: 185–209.

Roberts, G. W. (1965) Background paper on fertility. Prepared on behalf of the United Nations. *World Population Conference, 1965, Belgrade*, mimeographed.

Ruggles, R., and Ruggles, M. (1960) In *Demographic and economic change in developed countries* (A. J. Coale, ed.), pp. 155–208, for NBER Conference. Princeton, New Jersey: Princeton Univ. Press.

United Nations (1953) *The determinants and consequences of population trends*, pp. 86–87. New York: United Nations.

United Nations (1965) *Population Bulletin No. 7, 1963* (with special reference to conditions and trends of fertility in the world) particularly Chaps. VIII and IX, pp. 122–151. New York: United Nations.

United States Bureau of the Census (1964) *United States census of population: 1960. Subject reports. Women by number of children ever born.* Final Report PC (2)-3A, Table 38, pp. 187–198. Washington, D. C.: United States Bureau of Census.

United States Bureau of the Census (1968) *United States census of population: 1960. Subject reports. Women by children under 5 years old.* Final Report PC (2)-3C, Tables 56 and 57, pp. 114–117. Washington, D. C.: United States Bureau of the Census.

United States Bureau of the Census (1971) Income in 1970 of families and persons in the United States. *Current Population Reports.* Series P-60, No. 80, Table 19, pp. 41–46, October 4, 1971. Washington, D. C.: United States Bureau of the Census.

United States National Center for Health Statistics (1964) *United States Life Tables: 1959–61*, Tables 5 and 8, pp. 16–17, 22–23. Washington, D. C.: United States National Center for Health.

An Economic Theory of Imperialism

MELVIN W. REDER
CITY UNIVERSITY OF NEW YORK
AND NATIONAL BUREAU OF ECONOMIC RESEARCH

My title is a *double entendre*. I am presenting an economic theory in the sense that the model used attempts to explain a behavior as the result of decisions of individuals maximizing utility subject to limited resources and market prices. It is also an economic theory in the sense that it stresses the pecuniary gain of individuals—loosely, private profit—as the driving force behind the behavior that will be characterized as imperialist.

In Section 1, I outline a theory of the exchange of political favors for wealth as ordinarily defined. (Imperialism is treated as the result of a subclass of such transactions.) Section 2 presents a number of examples of imperialist behavior and shows how they relate to the theory of Section 1. Section 3 relates the theory presented in this paper to other discussions of imperialism. In Section 4 I indicate some of the empirical implications of the theory. The final section attempts to explain the politico-economic basis of resistance to imperialism and to indicate the issues of international economic policy created by such resistance.

1. Political Favor as a Commodity

It will not be disputed that holders of public office have the power in varying degree to raise the utility of particular households and/or the pecuniary income (profits) of particular business firms. Let us suppose that in any one year a given official possesses a limited stock of *political favors* that he can grant. Some of these favors consist of jobs that pay more than the market rate of compensation for the services of the individuals chosen to fill them. The *value* of one of these jobs when dispensed as a political favor is the *pecuniary value* of the difference between the utility of holding the job (nonpecuniary satisfaction plus stipend) and the utility derived from working at a nonpolitical job. (Where the job entails no duties upon its incumbent, it is called a sinecure). The number of (political) jobs at the disposal of a given official is sometimes called his "patronage."

Patronage is only one component of the stock of favors an official has to bestow. For example, if an individual or a firm is involved or financially interested in a regulated industry, his pecuniary income may be a function of the manner in which the regulatory body sets the rates that may be charged customers.[1] An analogous statement holds where effective tariff rates may be raised by administrative regulations; where an effective tax rate can be varied by negotiation with the collector; where the severity of a criminal charge and/or the vigor with which it is prosecuted is subject to the discretion of the prosecutor; where the terms of government contracts are negotiable; and where the outcome of litigation may be subject to intervention extraneous to the logic of the judicial process. Obviously, the votes and the administrative influence of legislators may also be of value to private parties.

The implication of the above remarks is that those who possess political power may use it to increase their personal wealth. This is hardly news; allegations to this effect are and have been a staple of political discussion for hundreds of years, but only recently has this rather commonplace observation begun to be exploited to develop a systematic theory of political behavior. Such a development is needed to provide theoretical underpinning for the argument of this paper, and for many other politico-economic analyses as well. However, to do this properly would require a paper much longer than the present one. Accordingly, I eschew any pretense of theoretical elaboration and offer only a rough and incomplete sketch of a model, but sufficient to indicate what it implies about Imperialism.

For the immediate purpose it suffices to posit the following (drastically simplified) model: All acts of a government consist of transfers of wealth from one individual (or firm) to another. Explicitly, I abstract from those (important) aspects of gevernmental activity that are associated with the production of public or quasi-public goods. Transfers are called "political favors" to the beneficiary.[2]

[1] Stigler (1971) has advanced the theory that regulatory bodies function, and are usually established, for the purpose of furthering the economic interest of the producer groups regulated. His argument is in much the same spirit as that offered here.

Political favors are sold (exchanged) by a (monolithic) government for cash, services rendered, or other "valuable consideration." Favors are "produced" by transferring wealth from others to those favored. The transfers may be accomplished in a number of ways: (1) direct physical conveyance of a fief from one vassal to another by royal decree; (2) disproportionate taxation of the unfavored and/or highly favorable purchase or sale arrangements with the favored; (3) direct or indirect farming out of the tax power to favored individuals, as in an officially protected monopoly; etc. Transfers may also be made from the public or a quasi-public domain to particular individuals.

The sale of favors may be either open or secret. Normally the government possesses some degree of monopoly power and often is able to discriminate (charge different prices for identical favors) among buyers. However, favors that are capable of resale and have a wide market will be priced competitively. Such favors are worth their market price (less a transactions cost) to anyone and therefore will not be sold (by a profit maximizing seller) for less to one buyer than to another. (Favors of this kind are exemplified by franchises, contracts to buy from or sell to the government on specified terms, sinecures, etc.)[3]

The government's monopoly on favor granting gives it some latitude in setting prices. However, it is always subject to some potential competition from rivals whose chance for success depends (partly) on support from actual and potential buyers.[4] Consequently, a government's monopoly power is limited by its need to avoid driving customers for favors to alternative suppliers.[5]

In nuce, a government's monopoly power over the price of a given favor is limited by the ability of potential customers to wait till a rival can replace it, and by the probability that by some given date it will be (somehow) replaced.[6]

---

[2] The existence of government is posited but not explained. It is further assumed that the government has a natural monopoly in the production and sale of favors.

[3] N.B.: Marketable favors may be "given" as a reward for past or expected services. However, we interpret this as amortization of an obligation under an unwritten contract; and the theory implies that the (discounted) value of the favor is equal to the value of the services for which it is compensation.

[4] Political rivals include revolutionary antagonists as well as (and sometimes in place of) electoral competitors.

[5] An "unreasonably honest" government, by selling too small a number of favors and/or by demanding an excessive price for these it does sell, encourages its dissatisfied customers to seek alternative suppliers; i.e., it alienates its potential supporters.

[6] So far as our argument is concerned, replacement of a government may occur by election, revolution, or any other process that relates performance (including distribution of favors) to length of incumbency.

Mathematically, the imaginary demand function for a specific class of government favors i by individual j at moment t is given by

$$p_{ij}(t_0) = \sum_{j=1}^{m} \sum_{i=1}^{n} \int_{t_0}^{t_1} e^{-\rho t} [P(t) l_{ij}(t) - Q(t) v_{ij}(t)] \, dt$$

That is, a government behaves like a (typical) patent holder; it has a temporary grasp on a product or process whose immediate exploitation has an appreciable market value. However, the grasp is uncertain and known to be temporary; the higher the royalty rate is set, the greater the effort to break the patent.

The objective of the government may be taken as some combination of pecuniary gain and tenure in office (power). That is, the government prefers a larger number of years in power over (say) the next decade to a smaller number, and it also prefers a larger to a smaller pecuniary gain to "its organization".[7] Assume also that there is a positive and finite rate of substitution between pecuniary gain and years in power and that the indifference curve between the two variables is convex to the origin.

The elasticity of substitution between pecuniary gain and years in power is not only (or even mainly) a matter of organizational taste, but rather of the technology of transforming economic resources into political power. Most money raised by political organizations is "plowed back" into extending or refurbishing its organizational base. In this respect, political organizations do not differ greatly from profit-seeking corporations that strive to accumulate capital to make more profits to accumulate more capital, etc. The tension between "dividend seekers" and organizational statesmen (those concerned only with organizational well-being) exists within political as well as business organizations.[8]

---

where p_{ij} is the (maximum) price that the government can charge the jth individual for a favor of the ith kind at moment t_0 (for simplicity assume no individual desires more than one unit of any class of favor, both government and favor seekers have an horizon from t_0 to t_1); $l_{ij}(t)$ is the loss to j at moment t for lack of a favor of the ith class; $P(t)$ is the probability that the government will be in power at moment t (i.e., not displaced before t); e is the discount term where p is the rate of discount; $Q(t) = 1 - P(t)$; and $v_{ij}(t)$ is the presumed price at which the favor would be offered by the government's most probable successor. $l_{ij} - v_{ij} > 0$.

Total revenue increases with i and with j. Total *profit* increases (with i and j) only if $p_{ij} > c_{ij}$ is the marginal cost of bestowing the favor to the individual in question.

[7] The pecuniary gain must be suitably discounted for risk and futurity.

[8] A significant difference between business corporations and political organizations is the availability of a share (stock) market to dissatisfied participants in a business organization.

Our model of the "government" belongs to the same genus as Downs's theory of the political party as vote maximizer (Downs, 1957). In the case where all proceeds from the sale of favors are used to enhance the prospects for remaining in power, our model and Downs's become virtually identical. However, personal income for members of the government organization is an important matter that often compels a government to risk election-losing scandals in order to achieve a minimum cash payoff to organization wheelhorses. In effect, the political entity may choose to strive for a smaller number of expected years in power than the maximum possible in order to obtain some "dividends" for its members.

As constructed, our model refers only to a government that has no ideological commitments and simply maximizes a combination of persistence in office and pecuniary gain, indifferent to the policies it follows. The spirit of the model is well conveyed by the power–wealth-seeking behavior of the Mafia families described in Mario Puzo's novel *The Godfather*. Indeed, this might be termed a "Godfather Model" of the state.

However, it would not be difficult to extend the scope of the model by introducing particular policies as arguments into the government's utility function. If this were done, the prices of favors might be related to the effect of such favors on policy objectives, and might even vary with the ideology of the buyer. However, such a generalization would not be useful in the present context.

Even in organizations dominated by wealthy and public-spirited men, free from any temptation to tap the public till, the need for resources is such as to compel the sale of favors. To see why this is so, note that a major use of cash contributions is to hire workers. Generating volunteer campaign work, by promising or conferring benefits, is *de facto* an exchange of benefits for contributions in kind (campaign labor).

The power of a government to confer—or withhold—benefits is such that promises to use power in behalf of one cause or another are very effective in prompting offers of contributions in cash or kind (volunteer campaign services). A party that ignored the problem of obtaining support would be at a serious disadvantage in competing with those that (implicitly or explicitly) bartered favors for support. Hence, if only to cope with competitors, a party would be forced to mold its program (at least partially) to attract support.

It should be noted that the term "favor" is not intended pejoratively. "Favors" include benefits to large and "aid-worthy" groups as well as to small and undeserving "special interests."[9] All that is required for the present purpose is that governments, current or aspiring, should optimize by selling (exchanging) promises of benefits for contributions in cash or kind.

The quantity of favors of each type that a government will sell depends not only upon the marginal revenue from sale but also upon the marginal cost of producing favors. Since we have defined a favor as a transfer to a favored individual or firm, the cost of producing it is the least of (1) the marginal cost of fully compensating those injured,[10] (2) the resource cost necessary to offset the effect of the (hostile) political activity upon the

---

[9] By definition, favors are granted to individuals or firms not to groups or collectivities. Hence, for our purpose, the value of a favor to a group is the sum of the values to the individuals constituting the group.

[10] The cost of compensating an injured party is the amount of money required to leave him indifferent as between (1) the transfer plus the compensation and (2) neither the transfer nor the compensation.

(uncompensated) injured, or (3) the least cost combination (to the government) of partially compensating the injured and braving their residual displeasure. For our purpose it is usually (2) or (3) that is relevant.

The cost to a government of leaving individuals partially uncompensated for an adverse transfer varies with their ability to improve their situation by seeking redress through some political process. For example, the greater is (a) the number of voters injured by a given transfer (favor)—either personally or through their sympathies, (b) the expected number of votes lost because of (a), and (c) the probability that the loss of votes will be decisive in the next election, the greater is the cost of granting the favor.[11]

Similarly, in a situation where political assent is not measured by an electoral process, the cost of granting a favor will vary with the resulting increment in the probability of a revolution. In an electoral situation, where the parties injured have a low propensity to vote, but are able to exert political pressure by rioting, etc., the cost of the favor will be measured by the effect of the increment in "civil disturbance" on the outcome of the next election.

The number and value of the favors a government will find it profitable to sell will vary (*inter alia*) with the number and per-capita wealth of the victims of the transfer process who are "helpless."[12] While a general discussion of this topic might prove interesting, it will suffice to note that where displeased victims cannot affect the officeholding prospects of a government, either through the electoral process or by rebellion, the cost of offending them is negligible. Accordingly, the government will tend to grant favors (to others) at their expense, until the marginal valuation of additional favors equals the marginal cost of further transferring wealth away from them. In general, the marginal cost of transferring wealth is likely to increase with the quantity transferred as greater impoverishment drives people to acts of desperation. *Ceteris paribus*, the larger the number of potential victims of transfers who are politically helpless, the greater will be the volume of favors (at their expense) that will be sold.[13]

---

[11] Where voters are very strongly attached to a government (or party, faction, etc.), up to a point, they may be injured without fear of inducing desertion. The reverse applies where voters are irreconcilably opposed to a government.

[12] Helplessness is of course a matter of degree. An individual is completely helpless, vis-à-vis a given government, if the latter will pay him no compensation no matter how great the injury it inflicts upon him. Such an individual would have no property and zero life expectancy as a free man; i.e., he could withstand the government only if he found someone with political influence to serve as his "protector." The completely helpless individual would have no effective rights of any kind.

The polar opposite of the completely helpless individual is the "oriental despot," most real-life cases lying between the two extremes. The degree of power a given individual possesses vis-à-vis a given government varies with the issue involved, the legal system, etc. For my immediate objective it is not necessary to provide a general purpose measure of power and I shall not attempt one.

The helpless victim, par excellence, is an individual or firm located beyond the territorial limits of the political entity that victimizes him through sale of a favor. For example, in the seventeenth century, it cost European sovereigns very little to make huge grants of land in the New World to favored subjects. The displeasure of the aboriginal owners of the land had little effect on the utility of the European potentates. Similarly, in the nineteenth century it cost "Western" governments little to obtain for their nationals economic and political concessions in Asia and Africa. Again, to the present day, it has rarely cost any branch of government very much to extend monopoloid advantages to its own (favored) nationals in making transactions in occupied territories or countries where grants (or loans on better than market terms) make the politically potent natives acquiescent. In a nutshell, imperialism is domestic politics extended to other areas.

Clearly, economic favors may be "cross-hauled." That is, set a individuals in area A can purchase favors at the expense of set b individuals in area B at the same time as set c individuals in A are victimized for the benefit of set d in B.[14] On our definition, economic imperialism arises where the balance of payments for favors clearly shows a chronic surplus to one area; i.e., if area A, on balance, is an exporter of favors to area B, B is an imperialist with respect to A. On this definition, imperialism is a matter of degree. However, it is only where the imbalance of payments for favors is quite marked that the term "Economic Imperialism" becomes appropriate.

An individual in A may buy a favor at the expense of one or more individuals in B in at least two ways: (1) He may purchase it from the government in B directly or (2) he may purchase the influence of the A government in negotiating with the B government. Method (1) may involve lending support to a revolutionary movement in B, and method (2) may involve invasion by A and/or support of a revolution. The technique, or combination of techniques used will vary with relative costs, and we shall assume that favor buyers seek, in a conventional manner, to minimize the cost of acquiring whatever favors are purchased. As will be seen below, (areas) A and B need not be in separate countries, though geographical discreteness of beneficiaries and victims is an essential ingredient of imperialism.[15]

---

[13] Greater per-capita wealth of the "almost helpless" also induces a greater volume of sales of favors. However, where victims are really helpless they are not likely to possess (retain) much wealth.

[14] Nothing in our argument requires that either a and c or b and d be disjoint; i.e., both a and d and b and c may have as many common members as the argument requires.

[15] In the absence of geographical discreteness of beneficiaries and victims, the operation of the government favor market simply divides the populace into the under and overprivileged—i.e., a class division. In short, imperialism exists where a favored class is locationally distinct from an unfavored one.

Assume an initial distribution of wealth between "favor obtainers" *a*, and others *b*. Favors consist of wealth transfers by the government to *a*. These favors may be at the expense of *b*, though this is not logically necessary (see below). Given the initial wealth distribution, the marginal utility to the government from transferring various quantities of wealth to *a* is given by the ordinates of the marginal gain (MG) curve in Fig. 1. The gain to the government from transferring a dollar to *a* may be derived in any combination of

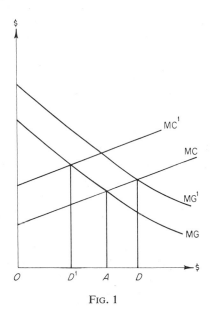

FIG. 1

direct support (e.g., additional votes at the next election because of approval of the transfer) and instrumental support (e.g., pecuniary contributions and/or labor time for electioneering).[16] Analogously, the ordinates of the marginal cost (MC) curve reflect the disutility to the government from transferring a dollar to *a*. This disutility arises from increased opposition from *b* elements of the population, and is assumed to be manifested by the opposite of *a*'s supportive activities. Given that the relevant curves are MG and MC, with the indicated slopes, the government optimizes by transferring *OA* wealth to *a*.

As reflected in Fig. 1, the sale of favors to *a* reduces the wealth of *b*. This is because there is a positive marginal cost to the government, and this cost

[16] As with other aspects of the government's utility function, I do not attempt to analyze the relative values attached to cash, electioneering activity, and direct support or their respective impacts upon political behavior.

may reasonably be considered as positively associated with the change in *b* wealth. The condition that the marginal cost of transferring wealth to *a* is positive must hold in the vicinity of an optimal position for the government.

As we shall see, however, this conditon will not always be satisfied; there are cases where transferring wealth to *a* will also add to that of *b*. These are represented in Fig. 2 by the negative range of MC. Obviously, only ignorance

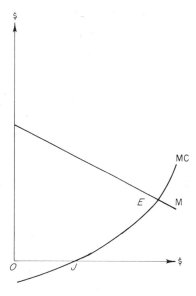

FIG. 2

or strong ideological commitment could lead a government to operate to the left of *OJ* (in Fig. 2). Should, for some reason, a government find itself operating to the left of *J*, it would be faced with demands to grant favors to *a* coming not only from *a* but also from *b*. (Examples of this type of situation are given below, pp. 161–162.) In such cases the government would optimize by moving to a point whose abscissa lies to the right of *J*, e.g., *E*.

In Figs. 1 and 2, the abscissa measures the amount of wealth transferred to *a* by one or more specific government acts. The origin, point of zero transfer, is arbitrary and may correspond to any desired initial level of *a*'s wealth, including that due to government transfers other than those under analysis. Also, Figs. 1 and 2 may be interpreted as referring to rates of wealth transfer per time period, instead of level of wealth transfer.

Consider Fig. 1; if MG should shift upward to MG^1 (given MC) because changes in tastes or productive techniques make a unit of *b*'s wealth more valuable to a than previously, then the government will increase a's wealth to OD, expropriating b to the extent required. Similarly, if the cost of expropriating b's wealth increases, causing an upward shift of MC to MC^1 (given MG), then the equilibrium volume of transfers to a would decrease from OD to OD^1.

The conquest of the "rest of the world" by the countries of Europe and their North American offshoot during the 400 + years from (say) 1500 to 1914 may be interpreted as one or more episodes in which an MG curve was shifted upward relative to an MC curve by one or more of the following: a decline in the cost of overseas transport of goods and persons; an increased value of land and raw materials to European colonizers because of increasing population, or because of the aforementioned improvement of the means of transport and/or the discovery of new crop and mineral resources.

The discovery or initial "opening" of a new territory had the effect of shifting MG upward (in Fig. 1) to MG^1 causing a transfer of wealth from natives to Europeans. (In addition to overt or disguised expropriation of natives, there may also have been voluntary trades between natives and Europeans, but I shall confine attention to the former.)[17] The rise of national or anticolonialist sentiment in the twentieth century, combined with the spread of competence in the use of modern weaponry, is reflected in Fig. 1 by the shift of MC to MC^1 (MG given), causing a decline of "European" wealth in "colonial" areas from OA to OD^1, where OA represents the "preliberation" stock of such European–American wealth as of (say) 1943.

At any given moment, the distribution of wealth in a given area reflects the past history of transfers from dominated to dominators, more or less legitimized by long acquiescence of the descendants of the dominated. Consequently any particular wealth distribution we might designate as initial (or zero transfer) is arbitrary. In practice, a history of fairly recent imperialism will be reflected in a heavy concentration of ownership in the hands of foreigners who are often absentee owners. Where the process of domination is more remote in time, the erstwhile conquerors will often have been converted into an indigenous upper class, through intermarriage or assimilation.

---

[17] When trade occurs between parties with (initially) different technologies an interesting problem of valuation arises. For example, when Peter Minuit bought Manhattan Island from the Indians for trinkets worth $24, presumably he made a good deal. But it is not clear that the Indians made a bad one. Given tastes, techniques, and (especially) transportation costs, one might well ask what better could the Indians have done with Manhattan?

I do not propose to speculate about the relative shares of the gain from Minuit's deal, but merely to point out that their sizes will vary the numéraire used. In Fig. 1, and subsequently, I shall value whatever is transferred in the prices relevant to the beneficiary. The justification for this decision is that the behavior I seek to explain is that of favor buyers and not that of victims.

2. Some Examples of Imperialist Behavior

The purpose of this section is to indicate the empirical content of the theory by means of examples. While the examples given are believed to be descriptively accurate, they have not been independently verified and I would treat evidence (or proof) of historical inaccuracy as implying need for other examples, and not as indicating deficiency of the theory. (Possible tests of the theory are considered in Section 4.)

(a) One notorious type of imperialist behavior arises where the armed forces of one sovereign power conquer an alien territory and transfer title to pieces of land in the conquered area to soldiers, court favorites, or other persons favored by the victorious sovereign. Examples of this are furnished by the English conquest of Ireland; the conquest of North and South America by the powers of Western Europe; the occupation of the interior of North America by white settlers; the occupation of Australia by British colonists; the annexation of Texas, California, Hawaii, etc., by the United States; the "purchase" of Alaska in 1867; etc.[18]

The common denominator of all these examples is the scant or nonexistent concern of the conquering sovereign with the property rights of the conquered population. In the case of hunting tribes, hunting rights in tribal lands were simply ignored, and attempts at asserting them were violently repressed. The rights of an unconquered sovereign (e.g., the czar of Russia in Alaska) and his subjects were respected (i.e., purchased), but those of the Indians and Eskimos were not. Put in terms of Fig. 1, the argument states that where the MC curve was relatively low, given MG, much wealth was transferred to the conquerors; but where the reverse was the case (MC high and MG low), little wealth was transferred.

The theory expounded in Section 1 explains the conqueror's behavior as an optimizing response to internal pressure for plunder where the victim was incapable of effective resistance. Traditional historical methodology would resist such cavalier treatment of a rich variety of specific historical episodes and would suggest case by case study of the particular incidents adduced. But this would be inappropriate in the context of the present discussion.

I am not suggesting that the decision process that led to a particular act of conquest involved a *conscious* balancing of costs and benefits to the sovereign. Indeed, the theory offered is quite compatible with the (extreme) assumption that imperialistic behavior is engaged in only by governments for

[18] Zevin (1972, especially pp. 321–333), gives a good brief survey of relevant episodes in American history.

whom war is sport. Such governments, when successful in war, have power to redistribute the wealth of the vanquished and may use it as an instrument of utility maximization. Moreover, governments with a proclivity for success in war and attendant plundering will attract plunder seekers—if they are not there at the outset—and sooner or later the freebooters' importunities will become the political exigencies of the sovereign.

All that our model assumes is (1) that governments have the capacity to redistribute wealth at increasing marginal cost per dollar transferred; (2) that some individuals desire to receive transferred wealth sufficiently to be willing to invest resources (including time) in support of a government that promises such transfers; and (3) that the probability of a government's remaining in office (or coming to power within any given time interval) increases with the value of the resources committed to its support.

Given these assumptions, governments willing and able to redistribute wealth will tend to accumulate support relative to those lacking an equal degree of will or capacity. Given that the marginal cost of expropriating a given volume of noncitizen wealth is lower than that of expropriating an equal amount of citizen wealth, it follows that a rational government will tend to reward its supporters by helping them expropriate noncitizen wealth. (This does not preclude the possibility of simultaneous attempts at expropriating some wealth from nonsupporting citizens.)

(b) A second species of imperialist behavior occurs when the returns from colonization are insufficient to attract enough settlers to make it either feasible or desirable for the dominant country directly to govern the area. In this case, native rulers are allowed to retain some share of authority and the transfer of native wealth to foreigners occurs via "sale" of monopoly trading privileges; conveyance of mineral rights and/or title to land on better than competitive terms; etc.[19] Protection and utilization of the property rights conveyed to foreigners frequently involved, *de facto* or *de jure*, special legal status for appropriate foreigners in the dominated area.[20] Examples of this type of imperialism are afforded by British rule in India; the operations of Western powers in China and in the oil-producing areas of the Middle East; American activity in Latin America; etc.

---

[19] The concept of "competitive terms," in this context, is quite tricky. Roughly what is intended is the following: competitive terms would approximate those that would prevail if each of the various rights and/or privileges were sold at a (widely advertised) auction and there was complete confidence in the validity (enforceability) of the property rights purchased. The thrust of the argument is that the various rights and privileges under discussion were obtained on terms considerably more favorable to the (European) purchasers than competitive terms would have been, and that part of the difference was paid to local governmental functionaries.

[20] This is a species of insurance against future adverse (though possibly justified) exercise of sovereign authority by the dominated government.

In many examples of this type of imperialism, the military presence of the investors' home country was at least part of the background. But an almost universal characteristic was a supply of local capital inadequate for funding investment projects contemplated. Whether the inadequacy reflected insufficient domestic savings, or inability to mobilize these savings in sufficiently large units to finance the projects characteristic of the building of a country's economic infrastructure is unimportant.[21] In either case, funds had to be raised in one advanced country or another, and political favors were part of the supply price.

It was not inevitable that political favors (beyond those available to domestic investors) should have been accorded foreign investors as part of the return on their investment. Political favors—characteristic of imperialism—were extended because they were part of the utility-maximizing barter package available to the *local* government. That is, from their own point of view, the local rulers made a good deal with the foreign investors. However, much of the cost of the favors granted the foreigners was borne by politically impotent natives.

Foreign investment, per se, does not require the granting of extensive political favors to the investors. For example, the private investments made by citizens of one advanced capitalist country in another advanced country do not usually involve such favors. There are a number of reasons why this should be the case; probably the most important is that political activity among the domestic population of an advanced country is sufficiently widespread to make the marginal cost of granting special favors to foreigners prohibitively high. This activity is reflected in demands by politically potent native capitalists that they be treated as well or better than foreign investors, as well as in the demands of labor and agricultural interests for protection against "exploitation" by foreign capitalists. Recognition of this leads foreign investors to seek the participation of native capitalists in their projects as protective coloration.

In short, in an *advanced* country foreign investors must take the political environment substantially as given, and make the best of it—or not invest.[22] To be sure, like domestic investors, foreign capitalists may demand various tax, tariff, and other political favors as part of their supply price. And negotiation between the government and prospective investors over these terms may well involve the purchase of favors. But because of the availability of domestic

[21] That is, the imperfections of the local capital market inhibit flotation and sale of securities of native firms to native wealth owners.

[22] They can lobby (attempt to buy favors) like natives though there is usually a greater prejudice against selling political favors to foreigners than to natives. An example of a foreign lobby becoming quite influential in the United States is the case of the (Nationalist) China lobby [see Adler (1957)].

supplies of capital as well as of alternative foreign sources, no consortium of foreign investors can exercise major political influence over the government.

In a more complete analysis it would be necessary to explain why the MC curve (in Fig. 1) for favors to foreign investors is generally higher in a developed than in an underdeveloped country. While a serious discussion of this matter is beyond the scope of this paper, let me speculate briefly. Economic development requires, *inter alia*, an increase in average years of schooling of the population. Schooling and its concomitants increase awareness both of the importance of governmental action and of citizen capacity to engage in political activity. Economic development further leads to the accumulation of funds in the hands of local capitalists who can finance political action, and to the growth of labor unions, agricultural cooperatives, and like institutions that are capable of articulating their interest, which often are antithetical to those of foreign investors. As a result of this, granting more than normal favor to a foreign investor in Switzerland, Sweden, Belgium, etc. would be politically suicidal for a local government; i.e., the MC curve for foreign investors would lie above that for domestic, creating a bias toward domestic investment.

But prior to 1945, in underdeveloped areas, a low level of schooling and of political consciousness made it easy to sell favors to foreign investors. Since then, the rise of nationalism (aided by international revolutionary propaganda emanating from the U.S.S.R., China, and Cuba) has increased local resistance to extending favors (real or imaginary) to foreign investors. This has had the effect of inhibiting private international investment throughout the underdeveloped world.

However, in underdeveloped countries domestic savings are not yet an adequate substitute for foreign investment. As a result there is continuing internal conflict within native governments that need foreign capital, but find great political difficulty in granting terms adequate to attracting it. The terms necessary to attract private foreign capital to a newly developing area include political favors, now more than ever. This is because of the growing tendency for governments in newly developing countries to nationalize foreign-owned plant and equipment or to interfere with the repatriation both of principal and earnings.

Potential investors obviously seek either guarantees against such uses of local sovereignty and/or demand high-risk premiums to compensate for the inevitable inadequacy of such guarantees as can be given. Nor would it be surprising if foreign investors attempted to influence the course of political events so as to protect their property claims and their international convertibility. In short, the threat of expropriation in a newly developing country increases the importance of political influence to a profit-seeking investor.

(c) A third type of imperialist behavior arises from the movement of capital from one part of a given country to another. The imperialist aspect of such transactions stems from the influence over local governments that investors seek and acquire. Examples of such influence may be found in the relation of the state and local governments of Rocky Mountain mining states to the eastern mining investors during the late nineteenth and the twentieth century,[23] and in the relation of state governments in the Middle West to eastern railroad builders during the nineteenth century.[24] Populist sentiment, with its battle cry of opposition to Wall Street and eastern capitalist interests, was partly an expression of local (i.e., native) opposition to investor influence over political institutions.

The political influence of regionally alien investors over a local government springs from much the same sources regardless of the nationality of the investors. Local savings are inadequate in total and/or are incapable of mobilization in units appropriate to the financing of relatively large projects. Concentration of funds on large projects makes certain types of political favors (those beneficial to big enterprises) valuable to absentee investors but to few others. As a result, the political activity of "foreign" investors encompassed by the term "imperialism," arises in connection with a small number of big projects and not with a large number of small ones. Moreover, concentration of absentee wealth in a relatively few hands makes it cheaper to collect sizable sums for political purposes from the few absentee investors than from the many local citizens of small wealth.[25]

Competition for political favors among absentee investors may improve the terms on which a local government can sell (some) political favors. However, since in this context all absentee interests are, *ex hypothesi* those of large enterprise, they will all tend to seek similar favors (e.g., nonassertive labor unions, or none at all; favorable tax treatment; good transportation facilities at minimal cost to the enterprise) which encourages joint lobbying and creates the impression of a monolithic absentee political interest.

(d) Yet another species of imperialism arises when an enterprise located in one area negotiates with a local government over the terms on which it will locate a facility (e.g., a plant or franchise). It is not essential that the enterprise possess monopoly or monopsony power vis-à-vis the local government, though it may. However, it is necessary that the facility be sufficiently large for its purchases and sales to have favorable (external) effects upon the costs and recipts of other local enterprise.

---

[23] For example see the work of Jensen (1950) and Dubofsky (1969), and the references there cited.

[24] A lurid, but suggestive, picture of these relations is given by Josephson (1934).

[25] This is both because cost of collection per dollar falls with average size of contribution, and because the temptation to take a "free ride" on the contributions of others is weaker when the number of potential contributors is small.

To obtain these favorable effects, local enterprises importune the (local) government to solicit "outsider industry" to make investments in the community, and press the government to grant favors such as tax concessions, sale of real estate at less than market prices, etc. To attract and hold such alien enterprises, local businesses have been known to engage in union busting, to cause alteration of zoning requirements, to redraft political boundaries (for tax reasons), etc.

Examples of this sort of behavior are found most frequently where local governments try to entice a large company to establish a branch plant in the area; or where (say) a professional sport league is considering establishing a team in one of a number of cities or where (in the nineteenth century) a railroad was considering through which town, among several competing alternatives, it should route itself. A vivid (though fictionalized) illustration of the power of a rich alien over a local community is memorably presented in Duerenmatt's play *The Visit*.

In situations such as the above, political favors granted an alien benefit not only him, but also local business and possibly local labor. In these situations the government's initial position lies to the left of J in Fig. 2. To the left of J, a demands favors as a condition of coming to the locality, while b demands that the government grant the favors in order to attract a. In effect, the local government serves as negotiating agent for local business interests.

Of course, the government may be more than a mere agent. One important reason why local interests should want to act through a public instrumentality (rather than offer side payments directly to the alien) is the desire to shift part of the cost of granting the favors (via the tax system) to parties other than those who directly benefit. However, it is not necessary for our immediate purpose to enter into an analysis of the distribution of the costs and benefits of attracting an alien investor to a given community. It suffices to indicate that the concern of the government in attracting an alien investor creates a situation in which the (potential) investor can successfully bargain for political favors.

(e) Sometimes governments manipulate subsidies, trade privileges (such as tariff exemptions), and the like to induce a foreign government to modify its course of behavior.[26] This may be considered as a manifestation of a species of imperialism. In general, the power to give or withhold something of value can be used to influence behavior—individual or collective—and its use may be (properly) viewed as economic coercion. Thus foreign aid or personal gifts, if offered subject to any condition whatever, may be viewed as purchase of the behavior satisfying the condition.

---

[26] For example, the United States quota on imports of sugarcane, and the exemptions in favor of Cuba and the Philippines.

Obviously if a (rational) government extends aid to a foreign government, it will simultaneously sell favors to its own citizens to be paid by the recipient country; i.e., it will sell favors and direct the recipient country to grant them on pain of being denied aid. Such favors will often be at the expense of some residents of the recipient country, who may but need not be identical with those who benefit from the aid.

This theory implies that (some) citizens of a country that is potentially able to grant aid will press for an aid program as a means of obtaining favors (from a foreign government) on more advantageous terms than would otherwise be possible.[27] This could explain a domestic demand, in wealthy countries, for granting foreign aid. However, it does not preclude the relevance of other explanations of such policies, e.g., desire to attain military advantage.[28]

If two distinct groups of people desire the same program, obviously they may find it mutually advantageous to join political forces. In such cases, the assessment of relative causal importance in explaining the generation of a program for granting economic aid (as between military and "economic" objectives) becomes akin to a problem in deciding, in a situation of joint production, on the relative importance of the various outputs (see below, pp. 169–170).[29] In any case, the existence of a program of foreign benefaction whatever its origin, generates a strong tendency for the sale of favors to citizens of the granting country, to be paid by the government (or residents) of the recipient.

3. Alternative Theories of Imperialism

The theory of imperialism offered here obviously differs from any theory that depends upon a "need for markets," e.g., a theory such as that espoused by Hobson (1902) or Luxemburg (1913). I reject such theories on two grounds: (1) the chronic shortage of effective demand view of capitalism is wrong and (2) there is no satisfactory explanation of the political process by which a

---

[27] It further implies that they will bid up the price of such favors until the rate of return on investment in the prospect of obtaining them is equal to the going rate of return. Obviously the risk in such investments is substantial and must be treated as a cost to would-be favor purchasers.

[28] For example, to grant that businessmen seek to profit from foreign-aid programs does not imply denying that big powers are engaged in a game of "King of the Mountain" in which being number one is an important objective in itself.

[29] Because we treat all governmental acts as transfers, we cannot (in this context) consider the government as a producer of anything and therefore are barred from considering defense as a public good.

systemic need for increased demand for output is translated into political pressure upon the government to engage in imperialist behavior.[30]

To dismiss the political importance of demand for improved export markets *in general* is not to deny that *some* businessmen and labor unions have (rationally) pressed their government to promote (*inter alia*) foreign sales of the *particular products* with which they are concerned.[31] Given the fact that one's own government has influence over a foreign government, the theory implies that some businessmen will press for said influence to be used in behalf of their various objectives, including enhanced sales volume. Our theory also implies that those whose operations make them most concerned with obtaining political favors abroad are most likely to press their own government both to expand its influence abroad, and to use it in their behalf.[32]

These implications of the theory are quite compatible with Lenin's view of imperialism (1917) as a manifestation of monopoly or finance capitalism.[33] Indeed, the theory would suggest that one large organization would find it easier (i.e., cheaper) to buy a given favor than would a group of small ones because of economies of scale in raising funds and in negotiating with a government.[34] Hence the growth of large organizations would tend to promote the purchase of favors from government, both at home and abroad.[35]

The theory has nothing to say as to whether there is a tendency for economic growth secularly to reduce the rate of return to investment in developed relative to underdeveloped areas. Like Lüxemburg and Hobson, Lenin assumed the existence of such a secular tendency. Such an assumption gives neo-Marxian theories a historical dimension that this one lacks. However, this is a weakness of neo-Marxism: (1) it is doubtful that the historical trends in the rate of return posited by the theory have occurred[36] and (2) regardless

[30] The bluntness of this statement does not reflect dogmatism, but lack of space.

[31] Put differently, what is asserted is that the marginal private return to political pressure for a particular policy toward *aggregate demand* is too small to induce private political activity.

[32] Businessmen not having a particular project in hand, or at least in mind, in a particular area are not likely to spend much time or money urging their government to enhance its influence in that area; search cost for totally new ventures is too high. It is where outlay for political favors is a part of investment in an on-going project that such outlay is most likely to occur.

[33] I interpret Baran and Sweezy (1966) as presenting essentially a Leninist view.

[34] This is both an application of the "free rider" argument, noted above, and a recognition that it is easier (i.e., less costly) to negotiate with one party than with many.

[35] Large organizations do not, per se, imply monopoly. For example, a large firm may be a pure competitor in a large number of markets. However, despite its verbiage the logic of the Leninist argument refers to large business firms rather than to monopolies, *sensus stricto*.

[36] For example see the work of Fieldhouse (1972), Blaug (1972), and Zevin (1972, pp. 33–48).

of trends in relative rates of return in developed and underdeveloped countries, imperialist behavior will persist so long as it is profitable for a government to sell political favors to foreigners. In my view, disparity of political power is the essence of imperialist behavior. The similarity between the discussion in (a) of Section 2 and Karl Marx's observations on primitive accumulation should not escape notice.[37]

Schumpeter's view (1951) of imperialism as "objectless expansion" stemming from precapitalist modes of thought is obviously different from that advanced here. However, this theory and his do not conflict: If Schumpeter was right, the utility functions of governments engaging in imperialistic behavior have contained arguments reflecting a desire for expansion per se. Schumpeter's view of imperialism is obviously complementary to that of Landes who argues that "imperialism is a multifarious response to a common opportunity that consists simply in disparity of power. Whenever and wherever such disparity has existed, people and groups have been ready to take advantage of it."[38] Obviously "objectless expansion" is encouraged by disparity of power.

"Disparity of power" does not appear explicitly in the argument of Section 1. However, it would be reflected in low ordinates of an MC curve (in Fig. 1) for granting favors to citizens of an imperialist country at the expense of natives of a dominated area. In short, the political power of natives to resist transfers of wealth to citizens of the imperialist country is reflected in the height of the MC ordinate at any specified volume of transfers.

4. Empirical Tests

Useful theories explain known facts (observations) and suggest relations to be found among others yet to be gathered. The theory developed here is a particular application of a theory of government behavior. Consequently, evidence for the more general theory is also evidence for this particular application, i.e., for the theory of imperialism. To deny the relevance of a theory of domestic political behavior by a government to its international behavior is to suggest that governments experience a special disutility in permitting actions that affect the wealth of foreigners to reflect the same considerations as those affecting the wealth of their own citizens. While it is conceivable that this might be the case, I shall assume the contrary. Nevertheless, if the theory advanced is to gain credence, direct evidence bearing upon the theory of imperialism must be provided.

[37] "*Capital*," Vol. I; Part VIII; Chapter XXXI.
[38] Landes (1972) and Zevin (1972) explain American imperialist behavior in terms similar to the view expressed here.

Essentially the theory offered in this paper states that the government of a given country will cause the transfer of wealth to particular individuals or groups (favor buyers) from others so long as the *marginal gain to the government* from the increased support of beneficiaries exceeds the marginal loss attributable to the increased opposition of the victims. This proposition is expressed in Fig. 1, where the government transfers OA wealth to a if the relevant marginal gain and marginal cost curves are represented by MG and MC, respectively.

The *hypothesis* that the government maximizes its utility (i.e., makes MG equal to MC) should be considered as "maintained"; i.e., it is not subject to direct test. What should be tested are such implications of the hypothesis as (1) if the MG curve is fixed, shifts in the parameters of MC will lead to increases or decreases—as the case may be—in the quantity of wealth transferred and (2) if the MC curve is fixed, shifts in the parameters of MG will lead to increases or decreases in transfers. The (important) practical problems of disentangling the effects of contemporaneous shifts in both MC and MG are similar to those encountered in most situations where econometric techniques are to be applied.

To see how this theory bears upon the phenomenon of imperialism, consider the following hypothesis: the greater the political influence of the government of a given country, X, in determining the behavior of the government of a second country, Y, the greater will be the volume of wealth transferred to (designated) nationals of X. The inference from the theory is that having greater political influence lowers the *marginal cost to the government of X* of inducing the government of Y to grant favors to its (X's) nationals.

Measuring the degree of political influence that the government of X exercises over (relevant aspects of) the behavior of the government of Y is always a difficult problem. For simplicity, let us indicate degree of influence by the (weighted) sum of the number of man-hours of contact between employees of the governments of the two countries concerning relevant matters; the weights might reflect the organizational status of the individuals involved (e.g., annual salaries). For this purpose, it does not matter—at least as a first approximation—how many of the contact hours are furnished by (employees of) either country. In this context, the question of whether X influences Y, or vice versa, can usually be determined by cursory inspection; i.e. if it is stipulated that there is a relation of imperialism, there is no doubt as to which is the dominant country.

Favoring the nationals of the dominant country implies transferring wealth to them. The manifestations of such wealth transfer would include (1) the share of Y's total (private) trade with X *after adjusting* for any "natural

---

[39] That is, after adjusting for differences in freight charges or costs of production (as usually defined) in X and in other possible trading partners of Y. Interpreting "natural

advantages" of X as a trading partner;[39] (2) the share of total private investment made in Y that is made by nationals of X after adjusting for X's natural advantages as an investor; and (3) the value of special concessions—licenses, tariff and/or exchange discrimination and the like—extended to X nationals relative to those extended to other foreigners.

A few brief comments follow:

(a) the mere fact of a large volume of trade does not imply anything concerning wealth transfers. However, if the volume of trade, commodity by commodity, is disproportionately large relative to that with third parties, and if this cannot be explained by differences in (unsubsidized) transport costs[40] and/or if there have been shifts in the relative shares of trade parallel to shifts in the political influence of X, then one might reasonably infer that the incentive to trade (with the influenced country) was greater for nationals of the influencing country than for those of third countries.[41] This inference could be further tested by studying the behavior of the firms engaging in the trade; e.g., do they aggressively seek to expand volume (at present prices) or the reverse; do other firms seek to get into the trade? Of course, where available, study of profits from the trade would be very appropriate; where imperialism is present, such profits should be higher than "normal," before allowing for the cost of buying political influence.

(b) The remarks of the preceding paragraph apply also to the pattern of investment. The one additional point to be stressed is the role of the X government in assuring the security of the investor's property. Usually, one can buy protection of his foreign property more cheaply from his own than from a foreign government.[42] Establishment (or increase) of influence in Y will increase the degree of protection the X government can afford to any foreign investor in Y, but it will usually sell such protection cheaper to its own nationals, which gives them a differential advantage in making such investments.[43] Therefore, if the theory is correct, an increase in the

---

advantage" must be done ad hoc, and with care. In general, it refers to differences in wage rates corrected for efficiency differences, in raw material prices, in transport costs (both of raw materials and finished goods), and in scale factors. While not easy, estimating "natural advantages" would not constitute an unusual econometric task.

[40] Subsidies must be explained by the theory.

[41] N.B.: It does not necessarily follow that special advantages to nationals of X are financed by additional burdens to nationals of Y.

[42] This is because one is more likely to know how to purchase such favors at home (i.e., search cost is lower) than abroad. Also favors are more easily (i.e., cheaply) bought in large blocks (by establishing a long-term relationship) than piecemeal. This creates economies of scale which usually—though not always—encourage buying favors at home rather than abroad.

[43] One reason for this (in addition to those adduced in footnote 41) is that payment for favors by "own nationals" can be made by labor services as well as cash, while payment

influence of X in Y will lead to an increase in the private investment of the nationals of X in Y relative to the private investment in Y by the nationals of any third country, Z, after adjusting for any natural advantage of X nationals relative to Z nationals.

This implication might be tested by comparing the volume of private investment in Y by nationals of X and Z. Evidence might also be furnished by the manner of private investment in Y by nationals of X and of various other countries; i.e., if the hypothesis is true, investors from other countries will tend to invest in Y (if at all) by buying into (or lending to) projects started by investors from X, rather than by starting projects on their own.[44]

(c) The hypothesis under discussion refers to the *association* of trade and/or investment with political influence, and is taken to imply a *parallelism* of (various aspects of) economic intercourse and political influence; e.g., the shares of X nationals in the private international investment made in various other countries vary in the same direction as the relative degree of political influence of X in these countries, after adjusting for differences in relative natural advantages of X investors.[45]

It is to be emphasized that the hypothesis speaks of parallelism; it says nothing of direction of causality. The theory of political behavior from which

---

by foreigners must usually be made in cash. The advantage of payment in labor services is that much of it may appear voluntary, and use of a great deal of paid labor in the political process often arouses voter hostility.

[44] The importance of X government influence in Y in stimulating the economic activity of X nationals in Y can be more readily appreciated if we bear in mind the difficulty (i.e., search cost) for an underdeveloped country of locating acceptable suppliers, and the importance of technical complementarity among sets of suppliers. The influence of the X government in directly fostering dealings by the Y government with a few firms owned by nationals of X starts a "transaction chain" in which one X firm operating in Y introduces another X firm, which lowers the relative search cost of dealing with the (second) X firm.

This introduction need not reflect national favoritism, but simply the fact that spatial contiguity and a common language make the probability that an X firm will know another X firm (favorably) greater than the probability that it will know a Z firm. Moreover, a common nationality is likely to promote a common technology through common technical–educational background, common technical–legal requirements, etc. This, in turn, is likely to lead to technological complementarity between products made in the same country, which further extends the "chain of transactors."

The nature, strength, and extent of these chains of transactors (reflecting economies of search and communication in addition to technological complementarity) requires extensive analysis and study which lie well beyond the purview of this essay. However, I conjecture that these chains are an important part of the "special relations," often regarded as part of imperialism, which persist long after the initial political influence has disappeared.

[45] A suggestion for measuring degree of political influence would proceed in this same spirit. Clearly, spelling out details will be a sizeable task.

the hypothesis is deduced does not permit an inference of causality. To make such an inference it would be necessary to specify all the considerations that bear upon the policy of the X government toward Y. Clearly among the important considerations will be factors of geography and military strategy. Another relevant factor will be the "political maturity" of Y; the greater the maturity, the greater the marginal cost to X of acquiring a given degree of influence in Y.

The theory of political behavior discussed in Section 1 implies that a national government will treat political influence in Y as an input in producing favors for sale. This means (*ceteris paribus*) that the lower the marginal cost of acquiring it, the more influence the X government will acquire; also, the greater the marginal product of such influence—the greater the price for which a favor resulting from it can be sold—the more influence the X government will attempt to acquire.

Thus, if the military-strategic considerations and the marginal costs of acquiring influence are equal as between two foreign countries, Y and Z, our theory implies that the government of X will focus its efforts to acquire political influence in the place where they will make the greater increment in the value of the marginal product of salable favors. In circumstances where the value of the salable favors reflects only the contribution to producing a salable output (e.g., the value of a raw-material deposit or of an import license), our theory becomes much like that of Lenin, Baran-Sweezy or, loosely, neo-Marxian. That is, in such cases, political influence is sought only to the extent that it adds to business profits.

However, the neo-Marxian theory is not universally applicable: (1) Military-strategic considerations often have greater power than business profits in explaining the allocation of governmental resources in acquiring political influence, and (2) the sale value of political favors to "households" may be greater than to business firms and would lead to a different pattern of government behavior than would obtain if the reverse were true.

At least as a possibility, (1) is sufficiently obvious to obviate the need for elaboration. However, an illustration may help the reader appreciate (2): United States concern with the political fate of Israel obviously is related to the political influence of American Jewry. It will not be disputed that this concern arises from the personal (household) concerns of Jews and other Americans with the well-being of the people of Israel, and from the United States military strategy in the Middle East, and not (appreciably) from the desire of United States business firms to profit from trade or investments in Israel. If the interests of American business firms dominated American foreign policy in this area, the large investments in Arab-controlled oil fields would prompt more aid and assistance to Arab countries with the object of obtaining better transaction terms and greater security of property rights for the oil companies. By the same token, less help would go to Israel, since this angers the Arabs and thwarts their anti-Israeli aspirations If these assertions are correct, they tell against a neo-Marxian interpretation of the theory.

5. Policy Implications

So far, nothing has been said about the distributional effects of imperialism, or the distributional effects of selling political favors generally. This is no accident. What is offered here is a positive (i.e., predictive) theory of governmental behavior, not a theory of the incidence of the activities of governments.

Since the theory says nothing about the distributional effects of imperialism, obviously it can offer no assistance in judging them. However, it does point to one important consequence of imperialism—the sensitization of the political affairs of the influenced country to the political and/or economic exigencies of the imperialist. Although the opposition to imperialism is always a mélange of emotional outburst and intellectual analysis, one detectable and reasonably coherent ingredient is a demand for *political* autarchy.

By definition, where imperialism is present political independence cannot exist. Conceivably, imperialism could coexist with two-sided political interaction between dominated and dominator, but this must be very rare.[46] Effectively, imperialism involves situations in which shifts in the MC and/or MG curves (in Fig. 1) in the imperialist country affect both political and economic conditions in the dominated country.

Unfortunately for clarity, both of policy and discussion, the anti-imperialist defenders of the political independence of Third World countries, are rarely able to accept the essential condition of such independence, i.e., refusal to accept aid or investment by wealthy countries. In principle, aid and/or investment (at least that funded from governmental sources) could be unconditional. Relatives can make unconditional gifts. However, conditions do tend to get attached, especially if the gifts recur frequently, and the hate–dependence syndrome is very hard to avoid.

Worse still, for those prizing political autarchy, is the fact that economically big countries, especially the United States, cannot avoid having major impact upon the economies of other countries, regardless of intention. To ignore this impact and allow economic policies to be determined solely by the internal sale of political favors is hardly what any other country would want us to do. But consciously to consider the impact of our actions upon

---

[46] Two examples where "dominated" areas exercised political influence within the government of the imperialist area are the Irish bloc in the British parliament during the latter part of the nineteenth century and the case of the "China Lobby" of the government and friends of Nationalist China, already mentioned.

other economies is to invite negotiation by their governments about our economic policies. Since the negotiation would necessarily be two-sided it would involve precisely the type of American "pressure" upon the policy of other countries that is the subject of recurrent protest at international economic conferences. In fine, economic imperialism is a matter of situation, not of disposition.

ACKNOWLEDGMENTS

This study has been supported by a grant for the study of law and economics from the National Science Foundation to the National Bureau of Economic Research. I would like to thank my colleague, William M. Landes, for helpful comments. I also benefited from comments made in a seminar at the Industrial Relations Section at Princeton University. This is not an official National Bureau publication since the findings reported herein have not yet undergone the full critical review accorded the National Bureau's studies, including approval by the Board of Directors.

REFERENCES

Adler, S. (1957) *The isolationist impulse*, pp. 375 et seq. Glencoe, Illinois: Free Press.

Baran, P. A., and Sweezy, P. M. (1966) *Monopoly capital: and essay on the American economic and social order*. New York: Monthly Review Press.

Blaug, M. (1972) Economic imperialism revisited. In *Economic imperialism* (K. E. Boulding and T. Mukerjee, eds.), pp. 142–155. Ann Arbor: Univ. of Michigan Press.

Downs, A. (1957) *An economic theory of democracy*. New York: Harper.

Dubofsky, M. (1969) *We shall be all*, Chap. 3. Chicago, Illinois: Quadrangle Books.

Fieldhouse, D. K. (1972) Imperialism: An historiographical revision. In *Economic imperialism* (K. E. Boulding and T. Mukerjee, eds.), pp. 95–123. Ann Arbor: Univ. of Michigan Press.

Hobson, J. A. (1902) *Imperialism: A study*. Reprinted, 1967. Ann Arbor: Univ. of Michigan Press.

Jensen, V. H. (1950) *Heritage of conflict*. Ithaca, New York: Cornell Univ. Press.

Josephson, M. (1934) *The robber barons*. New York: Harcourt.

Landes, D. S. (1972) The nature of economic imperialism. In *Economic imperialism* (K. E. Boulding and T. Mukerjee, eds.), pp. 124–141. Ann Arbor: Univ. of Michigan Press.

Lenin, V. I. (1917) *Imperialism, the highest stage of capitalism*. Moscow: Foreign Languages Publishing House, 1947.

Luxemburg, R. (1913) *The accumulation of capital*. English translation, 1951. London: Routledge & Kegan.

Marx, K. (1867) *Capital*, Vol. I, Part VIII, Chap. XXI.

Schumpeter, J. A. (1951) *Imperialism and social classes*, especially Chap. 1, pp. 3–8, reprinted. Oxford: Blackwell.

Stigler, G. J. (1971) The theory of economic regulation. *Bell Journal of Economics and Management Science* **2**: 3–21.

Zevin, R. B. (1972) An interpretation of American imperialism. *Journal of Economic History* **32**: 316–360.

Does the Theory of Demand Need the Maximum Principle?

WARREN C. SANDERSON
STANFORD UNIVERSITY
AND NATIONAL BUREAU OF ECONOMIC RESEARCH

Many writers have held the utility analysis to be an integral and important part of economic theory. Some have even sought to employ its applicability as a test criterion by which economics might be separated from the other social sciences. Nevertheless, I wonder how much economic theory would be changed if either of the two conditions above [which are the essence of the theory of revealed preference] *were found to be empirically untrue. I suspect very little.*

　　　　　　　　　　　　　—*Paul A. Samuelson* [Foundations of Economic Analysis, *1947*]

Précis

This paper consists of six parts. In the first section, the Introduction, it is suggested that, since many economists are interested in market phenomena, it is appropriate to consider a theory of demand whose implications are consistent with this interest. In this paper, we present a theory of demand in terms of aggregates and demonstrate that it is possible to derive many important economic theorems without making any assumptions concerning utility functions or preference orderings.

In the second section, the role of constraints in the theory of demand is discussed. There it is shown that certain familiar economic propositions such

173

as, "the weighted sum of income elasticities of demand is unity," and "demand functions are homogeneous of degree zero in money income and prices," are easily derived for aggregates and follow from the nature of constraints faced by households rather than any specification of their decision-making processes. In this section, the notion of household constraints is broadened through the introduction of the concept of household production pioneered by Becker (1965), Lancaster (1966), and Muth (1966). Thus throughout the remainder of the paper, constraints facing households appear in the form of production possibilities frontiers.

At the heart of the theory of market demand are testable assumptions concerning relationships between variations in constraints and variations in the distributions of amounts of household commodities consumed. These relationships are discussed in the third section of the paper. There, we limit the class of constraint differences which we consider and discuss two possible relationships between distributions of quantities of household commodities consumed. We call these relationships between distributions superiority and weak bimajorization and relating these to the admissible class of constraint differences results in what we call the Strong Normality Assumption and the Weak Normality Assumption, respectively. The assumptions are so named because they are used, in the fourth section of the paper, to demonstrate the conditions under which inputs into household production processes are normal goods.

In the fourth section, the implications for market demands of the relationships discussed above are drawn. The statements in this section include propositions concerning the signs of income, own-price, and cross-price elasticities of demand where these elasticities are measured using either arithmetic or geometric means of quantities purchased of some market good. Of particular interest are the use of certain classes of nonhomothetic household production functions and an aggregate relation similar to the Hicks–Slutsky equation. In Statement 9 (the proposition akin the Hicks–Slutsky equation) and the discussion following it, it is shown that, in the aggregate and for discrete changes in the price of a market good, the own-price elasticity of demand for that market good may be written as the sum of two terms, a term representing the substitution effect which is never positive and a term representing the income effect which may either be positive or negative. Thus, the familiar economic notion that own-price elasticities of demand may be decomposed into income and substitution effects holds in the aggregate, under certain conditions, even though no assumptions are made concerning utility functions or preference orderings. Also of interest in the fourth section are propositions concerning the stability of orderings of elasticities derived from aggregate data.

In the fifth section of the paper some immediate extensions of the theory of market demand are suggested. The sixth section contains a brief conclusion.

1. Introduction

Unlike the concepts of comparative advantage, competition, monopoly, rent, economies of scale, specialization, diminishing returns, and downward sloping aggregate demand curves, the notion of the utility (or indifferently, preference) maximizing consumer cannot be found in the writings of Adam Smith or David Ricardo. Rather, its introduction into the family of familiar economic constructs came in the 1870s through the contributions of Jevons, Menger, and Walras. It fell into a rather moribund condition in the 1930s when logical positivism led people to question the meaningfulness of the concept of utility itself, but having been resuscitated by Hicks and Allen before the decade had ended, it lives on in spectacular good health surrounded by its many offspring. Today, one can find maximizing consumers with lexographic preferences, random preferences, separable preferences, and even whole parameterized families of maximizing consumers.[1] Indeed, the paradigm of the maximizing consumer[2] quite nearly monopolizes the thinking of economists on matters relating to household behavior.

Economic theory would suggest that the result of such a monopoly is likely to have been a reduction in the production of testable hypotheses concerning household behavior to a level below what it would have been had there existed competing modes of analysis. The same line of thought also leads us to ponder the persistence of the monopoly and to ask why competing hypotheses concerning household behavior did not arise? After all, barriers to entry were quite minimal. The answer seems to be that this analysis had a great technological superiority over other modes of explanation. Not only did it produce a product which was pleasing to the eyes of many economists, it appeared to elucidate a wider range of phenomena than could be elucidated using any other technique. But this is not to say that there are no alternative modes of analysis in sight. Nor should we agree to shrug off the obviously awkward fact that whereas many of the phenomena "illuminated" by the paradigm of the maximizing individual consumer are actually collective phenomena, the result of aggregation of many separate market actions, the standard *modus operandi* is to ignore the aggregation problem by hypothesizing a representative household which consumes at the average rates indicated by aggregated market-transactions data.

---

[1] Chipman *et al.* (1971) contains an excellent bibliography in which the reader will find numerous references to lexographic preferences, random preferences, and separable preferences. The reference to parameterized families of maximizing consumers is to the work of Lancaster (1971, Chap. 5).

[2] By the paradigm of the maximizing consumer we mean those representations in which a consumer is assumed to maximize a utility function or in which he is assumed to choose from a set of feasible alternatives that alternative which he prefers the most.

It is the purpose of this paper to present another paradigm for the study of household behavior. The main differentiating feature of this theory is that it analyzes group behavior rather than the behavior of a single household. The theory presented here substitutes postulates on aggregate behavior for the axioms on a single household's preference orderings or utility function, which characterize the theory of individual choice. Thus, rigorously the two theories are not equally broad. The theory of individual households may in principle be aggregated into a theory of group behavior, but the theory of aggregate choice, which is immediately suited to the study of market phenomena, is not naturally disaggregated into an explanation of each household's behavior. Another differentiating feature of our theory is that all the results can be stated in terms of finite rather than infinitesimal changes. The main conclusion of the paper, like the conclusion of Becker's (1962) pioneering work on demand theory without maximization, is that some of the most important economic theorems on household behavior are quite robust and may be inferred from plausible characterizations of groups without the application of the Maximum Principle.

2. The Role of Constraints in the Theory of Demand

We begin by considering the following situation. Let there be m households each with money income V for some period, and let us say that this income is used to purchase n market goods (including savings), called X_1 through X_n, whose market prices, denoted by $p_1, ..., p_n$, are assumed to be fixed exogenously. We say that X_{ik} is the quantity of Good i purchased by household k and that $\overline{X}_i$ is the arithmetic mean of the quantities of Good i purchased by the m households. The two-good case is depicted in Fig. 1. The line segment AB represents the equation of the budget constraint which, in general, is written

$$V \equiv p_1 X_{1k} + p_2 X_{2k} + \cdots + p_n X_{nk} \qquad \text{for} \quad k = 1, ..., m.$$

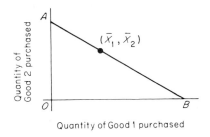

Quantity of Good 1 purchased

FIG. 1

Here we define the budget constraint as the accounting identity which relates income in a given period to expenditures and savings during that period.[3] Because of the definition of the budget constraint, the point representing the quantities of the market goods purchased by each household must lie on the constraint. Because of the linearity of the budget constraint, the point representing the arithmetic mean of the quantities of each good purchased must lie on the constraint.[4]

We can immediately establish two important economic statements.

Statement 1.

$$\sum_{i=1}^{n} \alpha_i E_i = 1$$

where E_i is the income elasticity of demand for X_i, computed from arithmetic means of the quantities of X_i purchased, and $\alpha_i \ (= p_i \sum_{k=1}^{m} X_{ik}/mV)$ is the share of aggregate expenditure spent on Good i.[5]

Statement 2.

$$\sum_{i=1}^{n} \alpha_i e_{ih} = -\alpha_h, \qquad h = 1, \ldots, n$$

where α_i is the share of aggregate expenditures spent on Good i, e_{ih} is the price elasticity of demand for X_i with respect to a change in the price of Good h, and where the elasticities are computed from arithmetic means of quantities of goods purchased.[6]

It is interesting to note that Statements 1 and 2 depend only on the nature of the budget constraint and are completely independent of the distribution of the points $(X_{1k}, X_{2k}, \ldots, X_{nk})$ along the budget constraint.

Generally, we would not expect all households having the same money income and facing the same market prices to choose the same combinations of goods. Rather, we would expect to find variations in the quantities of goods consumed by different households. For any good, say Good i, we can order families so that $X_{i1} \geqslant X_{i2} \geqslant \cdots \geqslant X_{im}$. We denote this ordered set of quantities consumed as $\{X_i\}$ and call it the distribution of X_i. Now we would

---

[3] There is an alternative view of the budget constraint which considers it as being defined only over those goods which yield utility. However, we know of no way of operationally implementing this definition of the budget constraint.

[4] For any given household, say household k, we know that $V \equiv p_1 X_{1k} + p_2 X_{2k} + \cdots + p_n X_{nk}$. Summing the budget constraints of the m households and dividing by m, we obtain $V \equiv p_1 \bar{X}_1 + p_2 \bar{X}_2 + \cdots + p_n \bar{X}_n$. Therefore, the arithmetic means of the quantities of each good consumed must lie on the budget constraint.

[5] See Appendix C, Technical Note 5.

[6] See Appendix C, Technical Note 6.

like to formalize the notion that the distribution of each of the X_i depends on some economic and some noneconomic factors. In order to do this, we define D_i as the distribution function of X_i and write $D_i[C; a_1, ..., a_r] = \{X_i\}$, where C is the constraint and a_1 through a_r are a set of auxiliary variables, which we assume do not include prices and income. As we have written it, the distribution of X_i depends on the constraint facing the households and the auxiliary variables which are outside the scope of the present inquiry. Since prices and income are assumed not to be auxiliary variables, their variation affects the distribution of X_i only through their effects on the constraint. This allows us to make Statements 3 and 4.

Statement 3. The demand functions for the average quantities of X_i purchased $(i = 1, ..., n)$ are homogeneous of degree zero in income and prices.

Proof of Statement 3. Since multiplying income and prices by any nonzero constant leaves the constraint unaffected, it does not affect the distribution nor any average of the X_i.

Statement 4.

$$\sum_{h=1}^{n} e_{ih} = -E_i, \qquad i = 1, ..., n$$

where E_i is the income elasticity of demand for X_i, e_{ih} is the price elasticity of demand for X_i with respect to a change in the price of Good h, and where the elasticities are computed from arithmetic means of quantities purchased.[7]

Unlike Statements 1 and 2, Statements 3 and 4 do not depend on the linearity of the budget constraint.

Within the last decade, Becker (1965), Lancaster (1966), and Muth (1966) developed a powerful new tool for the study of household decision-making, the theory of household production. In essence, this approach treats households as units which purchase market goods and services as inputs into household production-consumption processes. The power of this technique is derived from the observation that interesting inferences concerning a wide variety of economic behavior may be obtained from plausible *a priori* specifications of household production structures.[8] In the remainder of this paper, we use this representation of households.

---

[7] See Appendix C, Technical Note 7.

[8] A few interesting applications of household production functions are listed: the production of human capital, Ben-Porath (1967, 1970); the demand for leisure, Owen (1971); fertility and female labor force participation rates, Willis (1973); education and the commodity composition of consumption, Michael (1972); the demand for medical care, Grossman (1972); the choice of mode of transport, Gronau (1970).

Let us consider a household which produces q household commodities and let us denote the ith household commodity Z_i. We write

$$Z_{ik} = \phi_i(X_{ijk}, \ldots, X_{in_ik})$$

where ϕ_i is the production function whose output is Z_i, Z_{ik} is the quantity of output of Z_i produced by the kth household, X_{ijk} is the quantity of the jth input into the production of Z_i used by household k, and n_i is the number of inputs in the production function ϕ_i. If ϕ_i is homothetic, we can write the derived functions as follows:

$$X_{ijk} = f_{ij}(p_{i1}, \ldots, p_{in_i}) F_i(Z_{ik}), \qquad j = 1, \ldots, n_i,\ i = 1, \ldots, q,\ \text{and}\ \ k = 1, \ldots, m$$

where the f_{ij} are functions which are homogeneous of degree zero, the F_i are strictly monotonically increasing functions, and the p_{ij} are the market prices of the X_{ij}.[9] We also know that if $\lambda > 1$, then

$$f_{ij}(p_{i1}, \ldots, \lambda p_{ij}, \ldots, p_{in_i}) \leqslant f_{ij}(p_{i1}, \ldots, p_{ij}, \ldots, p_{in_i}).[10]$$

The constraint facing any household, say household k, can now be written

$$V \equiv \sum_{i=1}^{q} \left[F_i(Z_{ik}) \sum_{j=1}^{n_i} p_{ij} f_{ij}(p_{i1}, \ldots, p_{in_i}) \right].$$

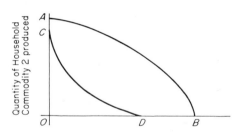

Quantity of Household Commodity 1 produced

Fig. 2

Unless all the F_i are identity functions, the constraint is not linear in the Z_{ik}'s although it is still linear in the inputs, and Statements 1–4 still apply to them. When we write the budget constraint in terms of the household commodities, we refer to the constraint as the household's production possibilities frontier, and two of these production possibilities frontiers, AB and CD, are shown in Fig. 2. Given a constraint, say AB, the distribution function D_1, for example, now tells us how the quantities of Z_1 produced by the

[9] See Appendix C, Technical Note 9.
[10] See Appendix C, Technical Note 10.

m households are distributed over the line segment OB. In passing we note that, generally, the point representing the arithmetic mean of the quantities of the household commodities consumed will not lie on the production possibilities frontier. Therefore, if the "representative" household is assumed to choose a bundle of household commodities on the production possibilities frontier, this bundle will not, in general, coincide with the arithmetic means of the quantities of household commodities consumed.

3. The Relationships between Changes in Constraints and Changes in Distributions

At the heart of any theory of aggregate behavior are the restrictions that are placed on the distribution functions so that certain changes in constraints produce known changes in the distributions of the quantities of household commodities produced. In this section, we shall first define a limited class of constraint changes, and then proceed to relate this class of constraint changes to two ways in which distributions may change. Let us define the production possibilities frontier with respect to Household Commodity i as

$$
Z_{ik}^{(l)} = \begin{cases} H_i^{(l)}(Z_{1k}, ..., Z_{(i-1)k}, Z_{(i+1)k}, ..., Z_{qk}) & \text{if it is feasible to produce} \\ \quad (Z_{1k}, ..., Z_{(i-1)k}, 0, Z_{(i+1)k}, ..., Z_{qk}) \quad \text{with the resources} \\ \quad \text{available in situation}^{11} \quad l \\ \\ 0 \qquad \text{if} \quad (Z_{1k}, ..., Z_{(i-1)k}, 0, Z_{(i+1)k}, ..., Z_{qk}) \quad \text{is infeasible in} \\ \quad \text{situation} \quad l \end{cases}
$$

where $H_i^{(l)}(Z_{1k}, ..., Z_{(i-1)k}, Z_{(i+1)k}, ..., Z_{qk})$ is the maximum amount of Household Commodity i which can be produced with the resources available in situation l, given that the household also produced the quantities of the other household commodities specified as arguments in the function. Let us define $\Delta = Z_{ik}^{(2)} - Z_{ik}^{(1)}$ over all points $(Z_{1k}, ..., Z_{(i-1)k}, Z_{(i+1)k}, ..., Z_{qk})$, such that $Z_{ik}^{(2)}$ and $Z_{ik}^{(1)}$ are not both zero.

Definition. We say that *the opportunity to consume Household Commodity i is greater (smaller) in situation 2 than in situation 1* if Δ is always positive (negative) for any point $(Z_{1k}, ..., Z_{(i-1)k}, Z_{(i+1)k}, ..., Z_{qk})$, such that both $Z_{ik}^{(2)}$ and $Z_{ik}^{(1)}$ are not zero.

---

[11] By situation l we simply mean a period of time in which there is some given configuration of money income and market prices. The methodology used in this paper is the familiar comparative statics approach. The interested reader can easily extend the results presented here by considering a multiplicity of groups of people and a number of income–price situations.

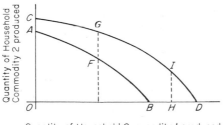

Quantity of Household Commodity 1 produced

FIG. 3

Now let us return to the two-commodity case, and see what happens to the opportunity to consume Household Commodities 1 and 2 when income increases. Figure 3 shows a production possibilities frontier before and after an income increase. The curve AB represents the *ex ante* constraint and the curve CD the *ex post* constraint. The opportunity to consume Household Commodity 2 increases if given any point in the interval $[0, D)$ more of Household Commodity 2 can be produced after the income increase than before it. It is clear from Fig. 3 that point G must always be higher than point F and point I must be above point H. Similarly it can be seen that the opportunity to consume Household Commodity 1 also increases.

Let us now decrease the price of an input used in the production of Household Commodity 1 but not Household Commodity 2. In this case the production possibilities frontier shifts as is shown in Fig. 4, with AB being the *ex ante* constraint and AC being the *ex post* constraint. The opportunity to consume Household Commodity 1 increases since, given any point in the interval $[O, A)$, more of Good 1 can be produced after the constraint change than before it. The opportunity to consume Household Commodity 2, however, has not increased, since at zero production of Household Commodity 1, the maximum quantity of Household Commodity 2 that can be produced does not increase.

It would be plausible to assume that when the opportunity to consume

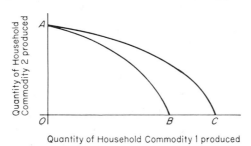

Quantity of Household Commodity 1 produced

FIG. 4

Household Commodity i increases (decreases), the mean amount of Household Commodity i produced increases (decreases). However, in the case of a homothetic production structure this assumption is insufficient to obtain the implication that the inputs into the production of Household Commodity i are normal goods. Let us consider an input into the production of Household Commodity i which is not used in the production of any other household commodity. Then $\bar{X}_{ij} = f_{ij}(p_{i1}, ..., p_{in_i})\bar{F}_i(Z_i)$, where $\bar{X}_{ij}$ is the arithmetic mean of X_{ij} and $\bar{F}_i(Z_i)$ is the arithmetic mean of $F_i(Z_i)$. It is not generally true that an increase in $\bar{Z}_i$ implies an increase in $\bar{F}_i(Z_i)$ for any strictly increasing monotonic function F_i. Therefore we are confronted with the following question: Under what conditions is it true that $\bar{F}_i(Z_i)$ increases whenever $\bar{Z}_i$ increases for any strictly monotonically increasing function F_i?

Fortunately, the answer to this question is known. Suppose $\{Z_i^{(2)}\} = (Z_{i1}^{(2)}, Z_{i2}^{(2)}, ..., Z_{im}^{(2)})$ is the distribution of Household Commodity i in situation 2 (i.e., the *ex post* distribution) and $\{Z_i^{(1)}\} = (Z_{i1}^{(1)}, Z_{i2}^{(1)}, ..., Z_{im}^{(1)})$ is the distribution in situation 1 (i.e., the *ex ante* distribution); then a necessary and sufficient condition for $\bar{F}_i(Z_i^{(2)})$ to be greater than $\bar{F}_i(Z_i^{(1)})$ whenever $\bar{Z}_i^{(2)}$ is greater than $\bar{Z}_i^{(1)}$ is that[12]

$$Z_{ik}^{(2)} \geqslant Z_{ik}^{(1)} \qquad \text{for} \quad k = 1, ..., m.$$

Since $\bar{Z}_i^{(2)} > \bar{Z}_i^{(1)}$, the inequality must hold for at least one value of k. We now use this information in the following definition.

Definition.[13] We say that the distribution $\{Z_i^{(2)}\}$ is *superior* to the distribution $\{Z_i^{(1)}\}$ and write $\{Z_i^{(2)}\} \gg \{Z_i^{(1)}\}$ if $Z_{ik}^{(2)} > Z_{ik}^{(1)}$ for $k = 1, ..., m$. A simple six-household example may help to clarify the notion of superiority (Table 1). It is clear that $\{Z_i^{(2)}\}$ is superior to $\{Z_i^{(1)}\}$ since, after ordering the observations, the jth largest observation from $\{Z_i^{(2)}\}$ is always larger than the jth largest observation from $\{Z_i^{(1)}\}$. This does not imply that any particular household's consumption must increase. Indeed, in this example, five households' consumption of Z_i decreased, while the Z_i consumption of only one household increased.

Below, we shall discuss superiority in greater detail and show its plausibility and its relation to more traditional economic analysis, but we should not lose sight of our primary objective of placing plausible restrictions on the distribution function. We now have enough information to make such a restriction.

[12] A proof of this assertion can be found in the work of Hardy *et al.* (1952, p. 89).

[13] In this definition of superiority, we used a slightly stronger assumption than is, strictly speaking, necessary. In the definition of superiority we assumed that $Z_{ik}^{(2)} > Z_{ik}^{(1)}$ (for $k = 1, ..., m$), while we could have assumed that $Z_{ik}^{(2)} \geqslant Z_{ik}^{(1)}$ (for $k = 1, ..., m$) as long as the strict inequality held for at least one value of k. We believe the definition of superiority given in the text makes for a clearer development below than its alternative would have.

TABLE 1

An Example of Superiority Where $\{Z_i^{(2)}\} \gg \{Z_i^{(1)}\}$

Name	$Z_{ik}^{(1)}$	Name	$Z_{ik}^{(2)}$
Tinbergen	500	Hicks	525
Frisch	450	Tinbergen	475
Samuelson	400	Frisch	425
Kuznets	350	Samuelson	375
Arrow	300	Kuznets	325
Hicks	250	Arrow	275

a. The Strong Normality Assumption

We assume that if the constraints in situations 1 and 2 are such that the opportunity to consume Z_i is greater (smaller) in situation 2 than in situation 1, then $\{Z_i^{(2)}\} \gg \{Z_i^{(1)}\}$ ($\{Z_i^{(1)}\} \gg \{Z_i^{(2)}\}$).

We call this the Strong Normality Assumption because later we shall discuss a considerably weaker assumption which suffices to ensure that the inputs, X_{ij}, exhibit the properties of normal goods.

Superiority lends itself to a simple graphical representation. If $\{Z_i^{(2)}\} \gg \{Z_i^{(1)}\}$, then the cumulative density function of purchases of Household Commodity i in situation 2 lies to the right of the cumulative density function of purchases of Household Commodity i in situation 1. This is shown in Fig. 5.[14] The reason that OB must always lie to the left of OA is that the

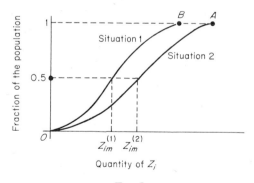

Fig. 5

[14] Although the algebraic argument in the text assumes discrete distributions, it is convenient to make the graphical argument in terms of continuous density functions and cumulative density functions. Nothing essential is changed by doing this and it considerably simplifies the presentation. The interested reader may easily develop parallel graphs and arguments in terms of discrete density and cumulative density functions.

cumulative density function in situation 1 must go through the points $(Z_{ik}^{(1)}, k/m)$ and in situation 2 through the points $(Z_{ik}^{(2)}, k/m)$. Thus given any value of k/m on the ordinate, the value on the abscissa must be higher in situation 2 than in situation 1.

We can now put the Strong Normality Assumption in somewhat different terms. The Strong Normality Assumption asserts that when the constraint shifts to the right (left), the cumulative density function also shifts to the right (left). An example of this is shown in Fig. 6, where the production possibilities curve AB is associated with the cumulative density function OE and the production possibilities curve CD is associated with the cumulative density function, OF. In this case, the shift in the cumulative density function of Z_1 to the right (left) must be consistent with a rightward (leftward) shift in the cumulative density function of Z_2.

The main question concerning the Strong Normality Assumption is whether it is an empirical regularity of sufficient consistency to justify its use in a model of household behavior. The assumption is clearly testable and the theory which is developed below suggests that it may be of interest to test it.

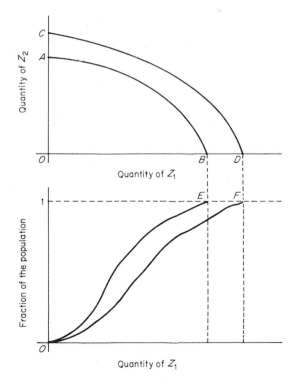

FIG. 6

For the moment, we shall be content to demonstrate its plausibility. We cannot observe the distributions of the Z_i directly, but we can observe the distributions of the inputs. If Z_i is produced by a homothetic production function and $\{Z_i^{(2)}\} \gg \{Z_i^{(1)}\}$, then, if X_{ij} is used only in the production of Z_i, $\{X_{ij}^{(2)}\} \gg \{X_{ij}^{(1)}\}$, where $\{X_{ij}^{(l)}\}$ is the distribution of the jth input into the production of Z_i in situation l. Therefore, in discussing the plausibility of superiority, we are speaking of the plausibility of superiority in the observed distributions of the inputs. If $\{X_{ij}^{(2)}\} \gg \{X_{ij}^{(1)}\}$, then not only is $\overline{X}_{ij}^{(2)} > \overline{X}_{ij}^{(1)}$, but the median of the distribution of X_{ij} in situation 2 is greater than the median of the distribution of X_{ij} in situation 1, and it is true that all of the fractiles of the distribution of X_{ij} are larger in situation 2 than in situation 1.[15] One argument in favor of the plausibility of superiority is that it is not unlikely that the median and all the fractiles of a distribution increase as the mean increases.

The second argument is that superiority is implied by quite plausible relationships between density functions. Let us consider two continuous density functions, $\phi_1'(X_{ij})$ and $\phi_2'(X_{ij})$, where ϕ_l' represents the density function is situation l, and let us denote the cumulative density function of ϕ_l' by ϕ_l. If ϕ_1' and ϕ_2' are such that they meet the following four conditions, then the distribution of X_{ij} in situation 2 is superior to its distribution in situation 1.

(1) $\int_0^{M_1} \phi_1'(X_{ij}) \, d(X_{ij}) = 1$.

(2) $\int_0^{M_1} \phi_2'(X_{ij}) \, d(X_{ij}) < 1$.

(3) ϕ_1' and ϕ_2' intersect only once in the open interval $(0, M_1)$, say at X_{ij}^*.

(4)   For X_{ij} in the open interval $(0, M_1)$, $X_{ij} < X_{ij}^*$ implies $\phi_1'(X_{ij}) > \phi_2'(X_{ij})$ and $X_{ij} > X_{ij}^*$ implies $\phi_1'(X_{ij}) < \phi_2'(X_{ij})$.

Figure 7 graphically represents the four conditions written above. The proof that the distribution in situation 2 is superior to the distribution in situation 1 is straightforward. It is sufficient to show that for any point in the open interval $(0, M_1)$, say X_{ij}^{**}, that

$$\int_0^{X_{ij}^{**}} \phi_2'(X_{ij}) \, d(X_{ij}) < \int_0^{X_{ij}^{**}} \phi_1'(X_{ij}) \, d(X_{ij})$$

or, in other notation, that $\phi_2(X_{ij}^{**}) < \phi_1(X_{ij}^{**})$.

---

[15] If we look at Fig. 5, it is clear why superiority implies that all the fractiles of a distribution must increase. Suppose we associate cumulative density function OA with situation 2 and cumulative density function OB with situation 1, then the median of the distribution in situation l is $Z_{im}^{(l)}$. Any other fractile of the distributions may be similarly determined.

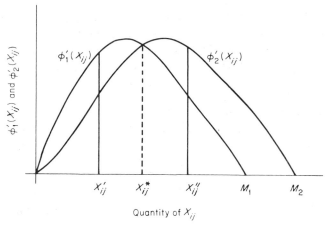

FIG. 7

Let us consider any point to the left of X_{ij}^*, say, X_{ij}'. From condition 4, we must have

$$\int_0^{X_{ij}'} \phi_1'(X_{ij}) \, d(X_{ij}) > \int_0^{X_{ij}'} \phi_2'(X_{ij}) \, d(X_{ij}).$$

Let us consider any point to the right of X_{ij}^* say X_{ij}''. We know from conditions 2 and 4 that

$$\int_{X_{ij}''}^{M_1} \phi_1'(X_{ij}) \, d(X_{ij}) < \int_{X_{ij}''}^{M_1} \phi_2'(X_{ij}) \, d(X_{ij}) < \int_{X_{ij}''}^{M_2} \phi_2'(X_{ij}) \, d(X_{ij}).$$

Hence

$$1 - \int_{X_{ij}''}^{M_1} \phi_1'(X_{ij}) \, d(X_{ij}) > 1 - \int_{X_{ij}''}^{M_2} \phi_2'(X_{ij}) \, d(X_{ij})$$

and

$$\int_0^{X_{ij}''} \phi_1'(X_{ij}) \, d(X_{ij}) > \int_0^{X_{ij}''} \phi_2'(X_{ij}) \, d(X_{ij}).$$

This completes our demonstration that if two density functions, ϕ_1' and ϕ_2', meet conditions (1)–(4) above, the distribution of X_{ij} in situation 2 will be superior to its distribution in situation 1. Since the situation shown in Fig. 7 seems reasonable enough, the observation of superiority in the real world seems to be plausible.

Economists, for a long time, have been making use of the notion of superiority. Let us consider a group of people with different tastes, but with identical money incomes and observing identical market prices, all of whom consume some of a market good, say X_{ij}. The interaction of their preferences and the budget constraint will yield a distribution of X_{ij}, which we write $\{X_{ij}^{(1)}\}$. Now if money income increases or the price of the good decreases and X_{ij} is a normal good with respect to all the households, then a new distribution, $\{X_{ij}^{(2)}\}$ will be generated which is superior to the initial distribution.[16] Thus the common assumption that a good is normal for all households implies superiority with respect to income increases and own-price decreases. However, superiority does not imply that X_{ij} is a normal good for each individual household as was shown in Table 1. In terms of its implications for market goods, the Strong Normality Assumption is weaker than the assumption that a good is normal for each household.

Although the Strong Normality Assumption seems plausible, we would like to know whether it is possible to obtain interesting economic implications from a model which allows cumulative density functions to cross one another. To put the matter somewhat differently, we would like to know whether we can deal with the case where the mean of the distribution increases and some of the fractiles of the distribution decrease.

Since a *necessary* condition for $\bar{F}_i(Z_i)$ to increase with $\bar{Z}_i$ for any strictly monotonically increasing function F_i is for $Z_{ik}^{(2)} \geqslant Z_{ik}^{(1)}$ ($k = 1, ..., m$), if we restrict ourselves to the consideration of strictly monotonically increasing functions and require that $\bar{Z}_i^{(2)} \geqslant \bar{Z}_i^{(1)}$ implies $\bar{F}_i(Z_i^{(2)}) \geqslant \bar{F}_i(Z_i^{(1)})$, then the cumulative density functions may intersect but never cross.[17] This suggests that in order to maintain the statement that $\bar{Z}_i^{(2)} > \bar{Z}_i^{(1)}$ implies $\bar{F}_i(Z_i^{(2)}) > \bar{F}_i(Z_i^{(1)})$ under weaker conditions on the change in the distribution, we must impose stronger conditions on class of functions F_i and hence restrict the generality of production functions we are considering. We shall demonstrate that it is possible to obtain a considerably less restrictive specification of the relationship between distributions at the price of only slightly more restrictive production functions. Further, we shall show that the added restriction put on the production functions has an interesting economic implication.

---

[16] In order to show that the assumption that a good is a normal good for all households implies that the distribution of the purchases of the good after an income increase or a decrease in its price is superior to the *ex ante* purchase distribution, let us consider the kth largest quantity purchased in the *ex ante* distribution. The *ex post* distribution is superior if it can be shown that given the kth largest quantity purchased in the *ex ante* distribution, there are always at least k quantities purchased in the *ex post* distribution which are larger than it. Since the assumption that a good is normal for each household means that each household's consumption of that good increases as income increases or the price of the good decreases, there must always be at least k observations in the *ex post* distribution greater than the kth observation in the *ex ante* distribution.

[17] If $\bar{Z}_i^{(2)} \geqslant \bar{Z}_i^{(1)}$ implies $\bar{F}(Z_i^{(2)}) \geqslant \bar{F}(Z_i^{(1)})$, then $Z_{ik}^{(2)} \geqslant Z_{ik}^{(1)}$ for $k = 1, ..., m$ [see Hardy *et al.* (1952, p. 89)]. If the cumulative density functions crossed, then there would have to be some k, say k^*, such that $Z_{ik^*}^{(1)} > Z_{ik^*}^{(2)}$. Clearly under the above assumption no such k^* can exist.

The weaker restriction on changes in distributions is described in the following definition.

Definition. We say that a distribution $\{Z_i^{(2)}\} = (Z_{i1}^{(2)}, Z_{i2}^{(2)}, ..., Z_{im}^{(2)})$ *weakly bimajorizes* the distribution $\{Z_i^{(1)}\} = (Z_{i1}^{(1)}, Z_{i2}^{(1)}, ..., Z_{im}^{(1)})$, and we write $\{Z_i^{(2)}\} > \{Z_i^{(1)}\}$ if $\{Z_i^{(2)}\}$ and $\{Z_i^{(1)}\}$ meet the following three conditions:[18]

(1)
$$\sum_{k=1}^{h} Z_{ik}^{(2)} \geqslant \sum_{k=1}^{h} Z_{ik}^{(1)}, \qquad h = 1, ..., m-1;$$

(2)
$$\sum_{k=h}^{m} Z_{ik}^{(2)} \geqslant \sum_{k=h}^{m} Z_{ik}^{(1)}, \qquad h = 2, ..., m;$$

(3)
$$\sum_{k=1}^{m} Z_{ik}^{(2)} > \sum_{k=1}^{m} Z_{ik}^{(1)}.$$

This definition of the relationship between distributions is considerably weaker than superiority and includes superiority as a special case. Weak bimajorization allows the cumulative density functions to cross an even number of times, as is shown in Fig. 8, where the distribution associated with

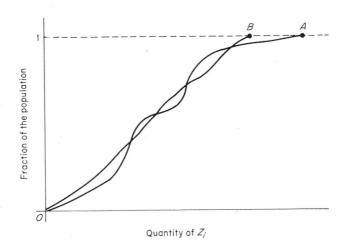

Fig. 8

[18] If conditions 1 and 3 are met we say that $\{Z_i^{(2)}\}$ weakly majorizes $\{Z_i^{(1)}\}$. If condition 1 is met and if in condition 3 the inequality is replaced by an equality, then we say that $\{Z_i^{(2)}\}$ majorizes $\{Z_i^{(1)}\}$. This definition of majorization is presented by Hardy *et al.* (1952, p. 45). I am grateful to Hayne Leland for pointing out the similarity between the concepts of superiority and weak bimajorization as used in this paper and the concepts of first- and second-degree stochastic dominance defined by Hadar and Russell (1971).

the cumulative density function OA weakly bimajorizes the distribution associated with cumulative density function OB. We conjecture that weak bimajorization is sufficiently general that further investigation will prove it to be an important empirical regularity. This leads us to the Weak Normality Assumption.

b. Weak Normality Assumption

If the production possibilities frontiers are such that the opportunity to consume Z_i is greater (smaller) in situation 2 than in situation 1, then $\{Z_i^{(2)}\}$ weakly bimajorizes (is weakly bimajorized by) $\{Z_i^{(1)}\}$.

A simple six-household example may be helpful in clarifying the concept of weak bimajorization (Table 2).

TABLE 2

EXAMPLE OF WEAK BIMAJORIZATION WHERE
$$\{Z_i^{(2)}\} > \{Z_i^{(1)}\}$$

Name	$Z_{ik}^{(1)}$	Name	$Z_{ik}^{(2)}$
Tinbergen	600	Frisch	675
Frisch	500	Tinbergen	475
Samuelson	400	Kuznets	375
Kuznets	300	Samuelson	275
Arrow	200	Hicks	200
Hicks	100	Arrow	175

It is clear that $\{Z_i^{(2)}\}$ is not superior to $\{Z_i^{(1)}\}$, since after reordering, all $Z_{ik}^{(2)}$ are not larger than their corresponding $Z_{ik}^{(1)}$. Indeed, in this case, the median of $\{Z_i^{(2)}\}$ is less than the median of $\{Z_i^{(1)}\}$. However, the reader may easily show that all the conditions for weak bimajorization are met.

Now that we have defined a relationship between distributions that is weaker than superiority, let us consider the price that we have to pay in terms of more restrictive production functions. In order to do this we need another definition.

Definition. We call a function, $F(X)$, a strictly monotonically increasing *concex* function, if it falls into any of the following three categories:

(1) It is a strictly monotonically increasing convex[19] function.
(2) It is a strictly monotonically increasing concave[19] function.

[19] In this paper we deal only with continuous functions whose first and second derivatives are defined. In this case a convex function is one whose second derivative is always positive or zero and a concave function one whose second derivative is always negative in the region with which we are concerned.

(3) It can be written as $r_1 G_1(X) + r_2 G_2(X) + \cdots + r_n G_n(X)$, where each G_i is in either category 1 or 2, where each $r_i > 0$, and where n is any positive integer.

We now define a concave homothetic production function.

Definition. We call a production function θ_i [where $Z_{ik} = \theta_i(X_{i1k}, X_{i2k}, \ldots, X_{in_ik})$] a *concave homothetic production function*, if its derived demand functions can be written

$$X_{ijk} = f_{ij}(p_{i1}, \ldots, p_{in_i}) F_i(Z_{ik}), \qquad j = 1, \ldots, n_i$$

where all the f_{ij} are homogeneous of degree zero and where $F_i(Z_i)$ is a strictly monotonically increasing concave function.

Proposition 1. Any production function which is homogeneous of degree α, where $\alpha > 0$, is a concave homothetic production function.

Proof of Proposition 1. If a production function, say θ_i [where $Z_{ik} = \theta_i(X_{i1k}, X_{i2k}, \ldots, X_{in_ik})$] is homogeneous of degree α, then its derived demand functions can be written

$$X_{ijk} = f_{ij}(p_{i1}, p_{i2}, \ldots, p_{in_i}) Z_{ik}^{1/\alpha}, \qquad j = 1, \ldots, n_i$$

where all the f_{ij} are homogeneous of degree zero.[20] If $\alpha \leqslant 1$, then $F_i(Z_{ik}) = Z_{ik}^{1/\alpha}$ is a convex function. If $\alpha > 1$, then $F_i(Z_{ik}) = Z_{ik}^{1/\alpha}$ is a concave function. Hence $F_i(Z_{ik}) = Z_{ik}^{1/\alpha}$ is a strictly monotonically increasing concave function, which proves Proposition 1.

An important theorem connects concavity and weak bimajorization.

Proposition 2. If $\{Z_i^{(2)}\} > \{Z_i^{(1)}\}$ and if $F_i(Z_{ik})$ is a strictly monotonically increasing concave function, then $\sum_{k=1}^m F_i(Z_{ik}^{(2)}) > \sum_{k=1}^m F_i(Z_{ik}^{(1)})$.

Proof of Proposition 2. We begin the proof by stating the following theorem, which was proved by Polya (1950).

Proposition 3. Given two sequences $\{Z_i^{(2)}\}$ and $\{Z_i^{(1)}\}$ conforming with conditions 1 and 3 of our definition of weak bimajorization, i.e., such that $\{Z_i^{(2)}\}$ weakly majorizes $\{Z_i^{(1)}\}$, then $\sum_{k=1}^m F_i(Z_{ik}^{(2)}) > \sum_{k=1}^m F_i(Z_{ik}^{(1)})$ for all strictly monotonically increasing convex functions F_i.[21]

We shall now show that given conditions 2 and 3 of our definition of weak bimajorization that $\sum_{k=1}^m F_i(Z_{ik}^{(2)}) > \sum_{k=1}^m F_i(Z_{ik}^{(1)})$ for any strictly monotonically increasing concave function F_i.

---

[20] We know that if a production function is homogeneous of degree α then multiplying all inputs by some constant, say λ, greater than zero implies that output will increase by λ^α. The reader can easily confirm that this condition is met by these derived demand functions.

[21] See Appendix C, Technical Note 21.

We can write conditions 2 and 3 as follows:

$$Z_{im}^{(2)} \geqslant Z_{im}^{(1)}$$

$$Z_{i(m-1)}^{(2)} + Z_{im}^{(2)} \geqslant Z_{i(m-1)}^{(1)} + Z_{im}^{(1)}$$

$$\vdots$$

$$Z_{i1}^{(2)} + \cdots + Z_{im}^{(2)} > Z_{i1}^{(1)} + \cdots + Z_{im}^{(1)}.$$

Multiplying both sides of all these equations by -1, we obtain:

$$(-Z_{im}^{(1)}) \geqslant (-Z_{im}^{(2)})$$

$$(-Z_{i(m-1)}^{(1)}) + (-Z_{im}^{(1)}) \geqslant (-Z_{i(m-1)}^{(2)}) + (-Z_{im}^{(2)})$$

$$\vdots$$

$$(-Z_{i1}^{(1)}) + \cdots + (-Z_{im}^{(1)}) > (-Z_{i1}^{(2)}) + \cdots + (-Z_{im}^{(2)}).$$

We can see from the equations immediately above that $\{-Z_i^{(1)}\}$ weakly majorizes $\{-Z_i^{(2)}\}$. From Proposition 3, we know that

$$\sum_{k=1}^{m} \theta(-Z_{ik}^{(1)}) > \sum_{k=1}^{m} \theta(-Z_{ik}^{(2)})$$

for any strictly monotonically increasing convex function θ. If θ is a continuous function with defined first and second derivatives, $d\theta/d(-Z_i) > 0$ and $d^2\theta/d(-Z_i)^2 \geqslant 0$. We shall show that $\theta(-Z_i) = -\phi(Z_i)$ is a strictly monotonically increasing convex function of the variable $-Z_i$, whenever $\phi(Z_i)$ is a strictly monotonically increasing concave function of the variable Z_i. Now

$$\frac{d\theta}{d(-Z_i)} = -\frac{d\phi}{d(Z_i)}\frac{d(Z_i)}{d(-Z_i)} = -\frac{d\phi}{d(Z_i)}(-1) = \frac{d\phi}{dZ_i}.$$

Since $d\phi/dZ_i > 0$, by definition, $d\theta/d(-Z_i) > 0$. Now we determine the sign of the second derivative

$$\frac{d^2\theta}{d(-Z_i)^2} = \frac{d}{d(-Z_i)}\left(\frac{d\phi}{dZ_i}\right) = -\frac{d^2\phi}{dZ_i^2}.$$

Since $d^2\phi/dZ_i^2$ is negative by the definition of a concave function, $d^2\theta/d(-Z_i)^2$ is positive. Thus far we have shown that $-\phi(Z_i)$ is a strictly monotonically increasing convex function of the argument $(-Z_i)$ if ϕ is a strictly monotonically increasing concave function of the argument Z_i. Therefore we can define $\theta(-Z_{ik}^{(l)}) = -\phi(Z_{ik}^{(l)})$, where $l = 1$ or 2. Now we obtain

$$\sum_{k=1}^{m} -\phi(Z_{ik}^{(1)}) > \sum_{k=1}^{m} -\phi(Z_{ik}^{(2)})$$

and, multiplying both sides by -1,

$$\sum_{k=1}^{m} \phi(Z_{ik}^{(2)}) > \sum_{k=1}^{m} \phi(Z_{ik}^{(1)})$$

for any strictly monotonically increasing concave function ϕ.

Now that we have shown that weak bimajorization implies

$$\sum_{k=1}^{m} F_i(Z_{ik}^{(2)}) > \sum_{k=1}^{m} F_i(Z_{ik}^{(1)})$$

for any strictly monotonically increasing concave or convex function F_i, it is straightforward to show that it must be true for any function $F_i(Z_{ik})$ where $F_i(Z_{ik}) = r_1 G_1(Z_{ik}) + \cdots + r_n G_n(Z_{ik})$, where all the r_i are positive and where all the G_i are strictly monotonically increasing and either concave or convex. This ends the proof of Proposition 2.

Thus the added restriction, which must be put on a homothetic production function in order to ensure that its inputs are normal goods under the Weak Normality Assumption, is that its derived demand functions may be written

$$X_{ijk} = f_{ij}(p_{i1}, \ldots, p_{in_i}) F_i(Z_{ik}), \qquad j = 1, \ldots, n_i,$$

where all the f_{ij} are homogeneous of degree zero and the F_i is a strictly monotonically increasing concex function of Z_{ik}.[22] Since we have shown that $F_i(Z_{ik}) = Z_{ik}^{\alpha}$ ($\alpha > 0$) is a strictly monotonically increasing concex function of Z_{ik}, production functions which are homogeneous of any positive degree are included in the above specification.

One is naturally curious about the intuitive meaning of concexity. Since strictly monotonically increasing concex functions include all strictly monotonically increasing concave and convex functions, and any function which can be written as a positive sum of those two types, what functions are left out? What functions are strictly monotonically increasing, but not concex? While it is difficult to characterize that whole class of functions, there is one type of function which is strictly monotonically increasing, but not concex, and which has an interesting economic interpretation. Strictly increasing monotonic functions which closely approximate discontinuous changes are not concex.[23] An example of such a function is shown in Fig. 9.

---

[22] The signs of elasticities are discussed in greater detail beginning with Statement 5 below.

[23] See Hardy et al. (1952, p. 89). Although it is not shown there that continuous functions which approximate discontinuous changes are not concex, it is shown there that for these functions Proposition 3 does not hold. It is a small step from there to show that Proposition 2 does not hold for these functions and that therefore they are not concex.

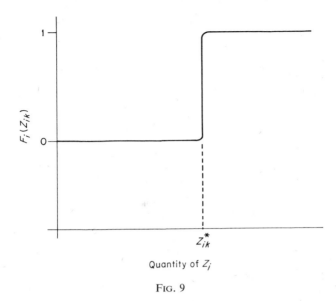

Fɪɢ. 9

The graph in Fig. 9 is supposed to be of a strictly monotonically increasing function, so that it is not precisely zero when Z_i is between zero and Z_{ik}^*, but imperceptably rising. Similarly if $Z_i > Z_{ik}^*$, $F_i(Z_i)$ is rising, but so slowly as to make no practical difference. Since functions of the sort shown in Fig. 9 are not concex, concex homothetic production functions require a certain amount of smoothness in the relationship between inputs and output which is not required, in general, by homothetic production functions. Concex homothetic production functions are well within the spirit as well as the letter of a neoclassical production theory which assumes no indivisibilities.

The concepts of superiority and weak bimajorization would not be very useful if they were limited to comparing distributions over equal numbers of households. It is very common for cross-sectional studies to examine aspects of household behavior across groups whose numbers differ. Superiority and weak bimajorization can be readily extended so as to be applicable in those cases.

Given $\{Z_i^{(2)}\}$ and $\{Z_i^{(1)}\}$, where $\{Z_i^{(2)}\} = (Z_{i1}^{(2)}, Z_{i2}^{(2)}, ..., Z_{is}^{(2)})$ and $\{Z_i^{(1)}\} = (Z_{i1}^{(1)}, Z_{i2}^{(1)}, ..., Z_{ir}^{(1)})$, let us consider the extended sequences $\{Z_i^{(3)}\}$ and $\{Z_i^{(4)}\}$, where $\{Z_i^{(3)}\}$ is obtained from $\{Z_i^{(1)}\}$ by repeating each of its elements s times and $\{Z_i^{(4)}\}$ is obtained from $\{Z_i^{(2)}\}$ by repeating each of its elements r times.[24] The sequences $\{Z_i^{(3)}\}$ and $\{Z_i^{(4)}\}$ each have $r \times s$

---

[24] Let $\{Z_i^{(2)}\} = (4, 3, 2)$ and $\{Z_i^{(1)}\} = (2, 1)$ then the extended series $\{Z_i^{(4)}\} = (4, 4, 3, 3, 2, 2)$ and the extended series $\{Z_i^{(3)}\} = (2, 2, 2, 1, 1, 1)$.

elements. We are now ready for a broader definition of superiority and weak bimajorization.

Definition. We say that $\{Z_i^{(2)}\} = (Z_{i1}^{(2)}, ..., Z_{is}^{(2)})$ is superior to (weakly bimajorizes) $\{Z_i^{(1)}\} = (Z_{i1}^{(1)}, ..., Z_{ir}^{(1)})$ if the extended sequence $\{Z_i^{(4)}\}$ is superior to (weakly bimajorizes) the extended sequence $\{Z_i^{(3)}\}$.

Proposition 4 follows immediately from this definition.

Proposition 4. Consider two sequences,

$$\{Z_i^{(2)}\} = (Z_{i1}^{(2)}, ..., Z_{is}^{(2)}) \quad \text{and} \quad \{Z_i^{(1)}\} = (Z_{i1}^{(1)}, ..., Z_{ir}^{(1)}).$$

1. If $\{Z_i^{(2)}\}$ is superior to $\{Z_i^{(1)}\}$, then

$$\frac{\sum_{k=1}^{s} F_i(Z_{ik}^{(2)})}{s} > \frac{\sum_{k=1}^{r} F_i(Z_{ik}^{(1)})}{r}$$

for any strictly monotonically increasing function F_i. For simplicity we just write $\bar{F}_i(Z_i^{(2)}) > \bar{F}_i(Z_i^{(1)})$.

2. If $\{Z_i^{(2)}\}$ weakly bimajorizes $\{Z_i^{(1)}\}$, then

$$\frac{\sum_{k=1}^{s} F_i(Z_{ik}^{(2)})}{s} > \frac{\sum_{k=1}^{r} F_i(Z_{ik}^{(1)})}{r}$$

for any strictly monotonically increasing concave function F_i. For simplicity we just write $\bar{F}_i(Z_i^{(2)}) > \bar{F}_i(Z_i^{(1)})$.

4. Implications for Market Phenomena

Now let us see what inferences can be drawn from the normality assumptions. For ease of exposition, we will posit the following background information.

1. Now observe r households in situation 1 and s households in situation 2.
2. In each situation, households produce q household commodities, $Z_1, ..., Z_q$, with production functions $\theta_1, ..., \theta_q$, respectively.
3. The Z_i's are so defined that their input sets are disjoint. In other words, if some market good is used in the production of Z_i it is not used in the production of any other household commodity.[25]

---

[25] The assumption of the disjointness of the input sets is a considerable analytic convenience. It is not necessary for the statements concerning the signs of elasticities which follow, but is necessary for the statements concerning the orderings of elasticities which are proved below. Whether it would be wise to make this assumption in the context of a given problem is something which has to be decided on a case-by-case basis.

4. The Z_i's are defined so that they are not close substitutes for one another.[26]

If, in addition to this, we specify that household production functions are homothetic, we encounter a problem first noticed by Muth (1966). The assumption that the input sets are disjoint and the assumption that household production functions are homothetic imply that the income elasticities of demand for all inputs used in the production of the same output are identical. Thus, using this representation, if beef and pork are both inputs into the same production function, their income elasticities must be the same. This may be shown simply in the present framework. Let E_{ij} be the income elasticity of demand for X_{ij} measured in terms of arithmetic means:

$$E_{ij} = \frac{\Delta \log \overline{X}_{ij}}{\Delta \log V} \quad \text{and} \quad E_{ij} = \frac{\log \overline{X}_{ij}^{(2)} - \log \overline{X}_{ij}^{(1)}}{\log V^{(2)} - \log V^{(1)}}$$

where $V^{(l)}$ is money income in situation l and $\overline{X}_{ij}^{(l)}$ is the arithmetic mean of the quantities of X_{ij} purchased in situation l. Since

$$\overline{X}_{ij}^{(l)} = f_{ij}(p_{i1}, ..., p_{in_i}) \overline{F}_i(Z_i^{(l)}) \quad \text{for} \quad l = 1, 2,$$

$$E_{ij} = \frac{\log \overline{F}_i(Z_i^{(2)}) - \log \overline{F}_i(Z_i^{(1)})}{\log V^{(2)} - \log V^{(1)}} \quad \text{for} \quad j = 1, ..., n_i.$$

Since the index j does not appear on the right-hand side of the equation, the income elasticity is independent of j and therefore must be identical for all X_{ij}.

This is a sad state of affairs and it suggests that something is awry with our representation of reality. We would like a representation of the household production structure, which allows the income elasticities of inputs into the same output to be different. One interesting way to accomplish this is to drop the assumption that household production functions must be homothetic. In order to do this, and still maintain some restrictions on the production structure, we make the following three definitions.

Definition. We say that a production function θ_i [where $Z_{ik} = \theta_i(X_{i1k}, ..., X_{in_ik})$] is *heterogeneous*, if its derived demand functions can be written

$$X_{ijk} = f_{ij}(p_{i1}, ..., p_{in_i}) Z_{ik}^{\alpha_j}$$

where $\alpha_j > 0$, and f_{ij} is homogeneous of degree zero for $j = 1, ..., n_i$.

---

[26] The Z_i are conceived to be reasonably broad products like food, clothing, shelter, transport services, and the like, which are not good substitutes for one another. In practice we take this to mean that if the price of an input into the production of, say, Z_i increases, not only will $\{Z_i^{(1)}\} > \{Z_i^{(2)}\}$, but $\{Z_h^{(1)}\} > \{Z_h^{(2)}\}$ ($h = 1, ..., n_i$). An analogous statement holds for price decreases. This is not a very important assumption and only a small portion of the argument presented below depends on it.

Definition. We say a production function θ_i [where $Z_{ik} = \theta_i(X_{i1k}, ..., X_{in_ik})$] is *heterothetic*, if its derived demand functions can be written

$$X_{ijk} = f_{ij}(p_{i1}, ..., p_{in_i}) F_{ij}(Z_{ik}) \qquad \text{for} \quad j = 1, ..., n_i$$

where all f_{ij} are homogeneous of degree zero.[27]

Definition. We say a production function θ_i [where $Z_{ik} = \theta_i(X_{i1k}, ..., X_{in_ik})$] is a *concex heterothetic production function* if its derived demand functions can be written

$$X_{ijk} = f_{ij}(p_{i1}, ..., p_{in_i}) F_{ij}(Z_{ik}) \qquad \text{for} \quad j = 1, ..., n_i$$

where all the f_{ij} are homogeneous of degree zero and where all F_{ij} are strictly monotonically increasing concave functions.

A few points are evident from the definitions. Homogeneity is a special case of heterogeneity which occurs when all the α_j's are identical. Homotheticity is a special case of heterotheticity which occurs when all the F_{ij}'s are identical. Finally just as we noted that homogeneous production functions were concave homothetic production functions, we now note that heterogeneous production functions are concave heterothetic production functions.

We are now ready to state some implications of the theory of aggregate behavior. In Statements 5 through 14, we show how familiar economic propositions concerning the purchases of individual consuming units may be derived for aggregates without the use of the Maximum Principle. In all these statements, we consider one of q household production functions, θ_i [where $Z_{ik} = \theta(X_{i1k}, ..., X_{in_ik})$], posit the Weak Normality Assumption, and pay particular attention to those cases in which signs of elasticities are invariant to whether they are measured using arithmetic or geometric means.

Notation. Throughout the remainder of the paper the notation "$^{-}$" indicates an arithmetic mean or an elasticity measured in terms of an arithmetic mean. The notation "$^{\wedge}$" indicates a geometric mean or an elasticity measured in terms of a geometric mean. The number of observations over which either mean is taken can vary from situation to situation.

Statement 5. Given a concave heterothetic production function θ_i and the Weak Normality Assumption, if the income elasticities of demand for the X_{ij} are measured using arithmetic means, then they are all positive. Further, if all the $\log[F_{ij}(Z_i)]$ are strictly monotonically increasing concave functions for $(j = 1, ..., n_i)$, then the income elasticities of demand for the X_{ij} measured in terms of geometric means are also positive.

---

[27] Since we are dealing with the derived demand functions which are associated with the production function θ_i, there are other restrictions on the f_{ij} and the F_{ij}.

Proof of Statement 5. First, let us consider income elasticities derived from arithmetic means.

$$E_{ij} = \frac{\Delta \log \overline{X}_{ij}}{\Delta \log V} = \frac{\log \overline{X}_{ij}^{(2)} - \log \overline{X}_{ij}^{(1)}}{\log V^{(2)} - \log V^{(1)}}$$

$$= \frac{\log f_{ij}^{(2)} + \log \overline{F}_{ij}(Z_i^{(2)}) - \log f_{ij}^{(1)} - \log \overline{F}_{ij}(Z_i^{(2)})}{\log V^{(2)} - \log V^{(1)}},$$

where $f_{ij}^{(l)} = f_{ij}(p_{i1}^{(l)}, p_{i2}^{(l)}, \ldots, p_{in_i}^{(l)})$ (for $l = 1, 2$). Since prices do not change, $f_{ij}^{(2)} = f_{ij}^{(1)}$ and we have

$$E_{ij} = \frac{\log \overline{F}_{ij}(Z_i^{(2)}) - \log \overline{F}_{ij}(Z_i^{(1)})}{\log V^{(2)} - \log V^{(1)}}.$$

It is now sufficient to show that the numerator is always positive when the denominator is positive and vice versa. If income increases, the opportunity to consume Z_i increases, and by the Weak Normality Assumption $\{Z_i^{(2)}\} > \{Z_i^{(1)}\}$. By Proposition 4 we then know that $\overline{F}_{ij}(Z_i^{(2)}) > \overline{F}_{ij}(Z_i^{(1)})$. Since a similar argument holds for decreases in income, this concludes the portion of the proof concerning income elasticities computed from arithmetic means.

Let $\hat{E}_{ij}$ be the income elasticity of demand for X_{ij} measured using geometric means. Then

$$\hat{E}_{ij} = \frac{\Delta \log \hat{X}_{ij}}{\Delta \log V} = \frac{\log \hat{X}_{ij}^{(2)} - \log \hat{X}_{ij}^{(1)}}{\log V^{(2)} - \log V^{(1)}}$$

$$= \frac{\overline{\log[F_{ij}(Z_i^{(2)})]} - \overline{\log[F_{ij}(Z_i^{(1)})]}}{\log V^{(2)} - \log V^{(1)}}.$$

If $\log[F_{ij}(Z_i)]$ is a strictly monotonically increasing concave function of Z_i, then by an argument parallel to that made in terms of elasticities computed from arithmetic means, $\hat{E}_{ij}$ must be positive.

Statement 6. Given a heterogeneous production function θ_i and the Weak Normality Assumption, the income elasticities of demand for the X_{ij} ($j = 1, \ldots, n_i$) are positive regardless of whether the elasticities are measured in terms of arithmetic or geometric means.

Proof of Statement 6. Since a heterogeneous production function is a concave heterothetic production function, we need only show that $\log(Z_i^{\alpha_j})$ is concave. This follows immediately since $\log(Z_i^{\alpha_j}) = \alpha_j \log(Z_i)$ and $\log(Z_i)$ is a concave function.

Statement 7. Given a concave heterothetic production function θ_i and the Weak Normality Assumption, if the own-price elasticity of demand for X_{ij}

is computed from arithmetic means, then the own-price elasticity is negative. Further, if $\log [F_{ij}(Z_i)]$ is a strictly monotonically increasing concave function, then the own-price elasticity of demand, computed from geometric means, is also negative.

Proof of Statement 7. Let us first consider the portion of the statement concerning own-price elasticities derived from arithmetic means, and let e_{ij} be this own-price elasticity.

$$e_{ij} = \frac{\Delta \log \overline{X}_{ij}}{\Delta \log p_{ij}} = \frac{\log \overline{X}_{ij}^{(2)} - \log \overline{X}_{ij}^{(1)}}{\log p_{ij}^{(2)} - \log p_{ij}^{(1)}}$$

$$= \frac{[\log f_{ij}^{(2)} - \log f_{ij}^{(1)}] + [\log \overline{F}_{ij}(Z_i^{(2)}) - \log \overline{F}_{ij}(Z_i^{(1)})]}{\log p_{ij}^{(2)} - \log p_{ij}^{(1)}},$$

where $f_{ij}^{(l)} = f_{ij}(p_{i1}^{(l)}, p_{i2}^{(l)}, \ldots, p_{in_i}^{(l)})$ (for $l = 1, 2$) and where $p_{ik}^{(2)} = p_{ik}^{(1)}$ for $k = 1, \ldots, n_i$ and $k \neq j$. By the definition of a derived demand function, we know that[28]

$$\frac{\log f_{ij}^{(2)} - \log f_{ij}^{(1)}}{\log p_{ij}^{(2)} - \log p_{ij}^{(1)}} \leqslant 0.$$

Now we must show that

$$\frac{\overline{F}_{ij}(Z_i^{(2)}) - \overline{F}_{ij}(Z_i^{(1)})}{\log p_{ij}^{(2)} - \log p_{ij}^{(1)}}$$

is always negative. We know that increasing p_{ij} causes the opportunity to consume Z_i to decrease, and hence from the Weak Normality Assumption that $\{Z_i^{(1)}\} > \{Z_i^{(2)}\}$. Therefore, for any strictly monotonically increasing concave function, $\overline{F}_{ij}$, $\overline{F}_{ij}(Z_i^{(1)}) > \overline{F}_{ij}(Z_i^{(2)})$ (by Proposition 4), whenever $p_{ij}^{(2)} > p_{ij}^{(1)}$. Since a similar argument can be made for the case $p_{ij}^{(2)} < p_{ij}^{(1)}$, the portion of the proof concerning own-price elasticities based on arithmetic means is complete.

Now let us consider own-price elasticities derived from geometric means.

$$\hat{e}_{ij} = \frac{\Delta \log \hat{X}_{ij}}{\Delta \log p_{ij}} = \frac{(\log f_{ij}^{(2)} - \log f_{ij}^{(1)}) + \{\overline{\log}[F_{ij}(Z_i^{(2)})] - \overline{\log}[F_{ij}(Z_i^{(1)})]\}}{\log p_{ij}^{(2)} - \log p_{ij}^{(1)}}.$$

If $\log[F_{ij}(Z_i)]$ is concave, then by an argument similar to the one above for own-price elasticities computed from arithmetic means,

$$\frac{\overline{\log}[F_{ij}(Z_i^{(2)})] - \overline{\log}[F_{ij}(Z_i^{(1)})]}{\log p_{ij}^{(2)} - \log p_{ij}^{(1)}}$$

must be negative, as must $\hat{e}_{ij}$.

[28] See Appendix C, Technical Note 10.

Statement 8. Given a heterogeneous production function θ_i and the Weak Normality Assumption, the own-price elasticities of demand for X_{ij} ($j = 1, ..., n_i$) are negative regardless of whether the elasticities are computed from arithmetic or geometric means.

Proof of Statement 8. Since a heterogeneous production function is a concave heterothetic production function, Statement 7 is true in this case. The proof is completed by noting that $\log(Z_i^{q_j})$ is a strictly monotonically increasing concave function of Z_i.

In Statements 5–8 we dealt with the signs of income and own-price elasticities under the Weak Normality Assumption and used either a concave heterothetic or heterogeneous production function. Now we turn our attention to another familiar economic concept, the income-compensated own-price elasticity of demand and show that an equation similar to the Hicks–Slutsky equation can be derived in the aggregate without the application of the Maximum Principle.

Definition. Let us consider any heterothetic production function θ_i. We define d_{ij} as the *income-compensated own-price elasticity* of demand for X_{ij}:

$$d_{ij} \equiv \frac{\Delta \log f_{ij}}{\Delta \log p_{ij}} = \frac{\log f_{ij}^{(2)} - \log f_{ij}^{(1)}}{\log p_{ij}^{(2)} - \log p_{ij}^{(1)}}.$$

The observation that the income-compensated own-price elasticity of demand is never positive follows immediately from its definition and the definition of a derived demand function.[29] The amount of income compensation, however, varies depending on whether income elasticities are measured in terms of arithmetic or geometric means. In particular, for any heterothetic production function θ_i, we know that

$$e_{ij} = d_{ij} + \frac{\log[\bar{F}_{ij}(Z_i^{(2)})] - \log[\bar{F}_{ij}(Z_i^{(1)})]}{\log p_{ij}^{(2)} - \log p_{ij}^{(1)}}$$

and

$$\hat{e}_{ij} = d_{ij} + \frac{\log[\hat{F}_{ij}(Z_i^{(2)})] - \log[\hat{F}_{ij}(Z_i^{(1)})]}{\log p_{ij}^{(2)} - \log p_{ij}^{(1)}}.$$

Thus, income compensation in the context of elasticities measured in terms of arithmetic means refers to an income change of sufficient magnitude such that, given this income change and the own-price change, $\bar{F}_{ij}(Z_i^{(2)}) = \bar{F}_{ij}(Z_i^{(1)})$. If we measured elasticities in terms of geometric means, then the income change in concert with the own-price change would have to be such that $\hat{F}_{ij}(Z_i^{(2)}) = \hat{F}_{ij}(Z_i^{(1)})$.

---

[29] See Appendix C, Technical Note 10.

Now, we shall demonstrate how the definition of the income-compensated own-price elasticity of demand given above enables us to obtain a result quite similar to the Hicks–Slutsky equation.

Statement 9. Given a concex heterothetic production function θ_i and the Weak Normality Assumption, then for any change in p_{ij} there exists a K such that $0 < K < 1$ and such that $e_{ij} + K \cdot E_{ij} = d_{ij}$, where E_{ij} is the income elasticity obtained from changing income in identical proportion to the change in p_{ij}, given the prices in situation 2. If $\log[F_{ij}(Z_i)]$ is a strictly monotonically increasing concex function of Z_i, then the statement is also true for elasticities measured in terms of geometric means.

Proof of Statement 9. Let us first consider the case in which elasticities are measured in terms of arithmetic means. We know that

$$e_{ij} = d_{ij} + \frac{\log[\bar{F}_{ij}(Z_i^{(2)})] - \log[\bar{F}_{ij}(Z_i^{(1)})]}{\log p_{ij}^{(2)} - \log p_{ij}^{(1)}}.$$

Hence

$$e_{ij} = d_{ij} + \left\{ \frac{\log[\bar{F}_{ij}(Z_i^{(2)})] - \log[\bar{F}_{ij}(Z_i^{(1)})]}{\log p_{ij}^{(2)} - \log p_{ij}^{(1)}} \right\} \cdot \left\{ \frac{\log V^{(3)} - \log V^{(1)}}{\log[\bar{F}_{ij}(Z_i^{(3)})] - \log[\bar{F}_{ij}(Z_i^{(2)})]} \right\}$$

$$\times \left\{ \frac{\log[\bar{F}_{ij}(Z_i^{(3)})] - \log[\bar{F}_{ij}(Z_i^{(2)})]}{\log V^{(3)} - \log V^{(1)}} \right\}$$

where we specify $V^{(3)}$ so that $\log V^{(3)} - \log V^{(1)} = \log p_{ij}^{(2)} - \log p_{ij}^{(1)}$. Now,

$$e_{ij} = d_{ij} + \frac{\log[\bar{F}_{ij}(Z_i^{(2)})] - \log[\bar{F}_{ij}(Z_i^{(1)})]}{\log[\bar{F}_{ij}(Z_i^{(3)})] - \log[\bar{F}_{ij}(Z_i^{(2)})]} \cdot E_{ij}$$

and

$$e_{ij} + K \cdot E_{ij} = d_{ij}$$

where

$$K = \frac{\log[\bar{F}_{ij}(Z_i^{(1)})] - \log[\bar{F}_{ij}(Z_i^{(2)})]}{\log[\bar{F}_{ij}(Z_i^{(3)})] - \log[\bar{F}_{ij}(Z_i^{(2)})]}.$$

A word of explanation is in order concerning the meanings of $V^{(3)}$ and $\bar{F}_{ij}(Z_i^{(3)})$. The analysis may be represented as starting in situation 1 with a given money income and a given vector of prices. Situation 2 differs from situation 1 in that a single price, p_{ij}, is altered and situation 3 differs from situation 2 in that income is changed in precisely the same proportion that p_{ij} was originally varied. The three situations are depicted in Fig. 10, where we have assumed that $p_{1j}^{(2)} > p_{1j}^{(1)}$. In the figure the arc AB represents the

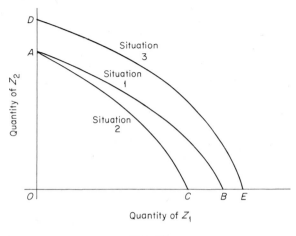

FIG. 10

constraint in situation 1, the arc AC represents the constraint in situation 2 (after the price increase), and the arc DE represents the constraint in situation 3 (after both the price and income increases). If Z_i is produced with more than one input, equiproportional increases in V and p_{ij} will cause the opportunity to consume Z_i to be greater in situation 3 than in situation 1.[30] In that case $\bar{F}_{ij}(Z_i^{(3)}) > \bar{F}_{ij}(Z_i^{(1)})$ (by Proposition 4), and since $\bar{F}_{ij}(Z_i^{(3)})$ and $\bar{F}_{ij}(Z_i^{(1)})$ are both greater than $\bar{F}_{ij}(Z_i^{(2)})$ (by Statements 5 and 7), K must lie between zero and unity. If Z_i is produced with more than one input then equiproportional decreases in V and the price of p_{ij} will cause the opportunity to consume Z_i to be greater in situation 1 than in situation 3. In that case $\bar{F}_{ij}(Z_i^{(1)}) > \bar{F}_{ij}(Z_i^{(3)})$ (by Proposition 4), and since both $\bar{F}_{ij}(Z_i^{(3)})$ and $\bar{F}_{ij}(Z_i^{(1)})$ are less than $\bar{F}_{ij}(Z_i^{(2)})$ (by Statements 5 and 7), again K must lie between zero and unity. If Z_i is produced using a single input, then equiproportional increases (decreases) in income and the price of that input cause the constraint to shift as if all prices except the price of the single input into the production of Z_i were reduced (increased). In Fig. 10, if Z_1 were produced with a single input, points B and E would coincide, but point D would still be above point A. This situation is covered in point 4 on page 195 and in footnote 26. Given the assumption made there, the argument above for the multi-input case is also true in the single-input case.

---

[30] If Z_i is produced by more than one input then a $W\%$ increase in the price of X_{ij} must increase the cost of producing any given quantity of Z_i by less than $W\%$. Since income increases by $W\%$, for any given production of the other household commodities it is always possible to produce more Z_i after the equiproportional increases in the price of X_{ij} and in income than before the changes.

In terms of elasticities computed from geometric means we know that

$$\hat{e}_{ij} + K\hat{E}_{ij} = d_{ij}$$

where

$$K = \frac{\overline{\log[F_{ij}(Z_i^{(1)})]} - \overline{\log[F_{ij}(Z_i^{(2)})]}}{\overline{\log[F_{ij}(Z_i^{(3)})]} - \overline{\log[F_{ij}(Z_i^{(2)})]}}.$$

If $\log[F_{ij}(Z_i)]$ is a strictly monotonically increasing concex function of Z_i, then the proof of the portion of the statement concerning elasticities derived from arithmetic means may be applied to show that, in the case where elasticities are computed from geometric means, K must lie between zero and unity. This completes the proof of Statement 9.

We can see from Statement 9 that own-price elasticities of demand, measured either in terms of arithmetic means or geometric means, can be written as the sum of a substitution effect and an income effect. For example, we have shown that

$$e_{ij} = d_{ij} - KE_{ij}$$

where d_{ij}, the income-compensated own-price elasticity of demand, is the substitution effect and KE_{ij} is the income effect. The substitution effect is always negative or zero, and the income effect may be either positive or negative.[31] Thus we have shown that the decomposition of own-price elasticities of demand into a substitution effect and an income effect may be derived in the aggregate without any assumptions about utility functions or preference orderings.

The relationship proved in Statement 9 bears an obvious resemblance to the Hicks–Slutsky equation, since the latter states that for a single utility-maximizing household $e_{ij} + \pi_{ij}E_{ij} = d_{ij}$, where π_{ij} is the proportion of money income spent on X_{ij}, and where d_{ij}, the income-compensated own-price elasticity of demand, is defined such that the initial ordinal level of utility is maintained. In the case of a single utility-maximizing household, d_{ij} is not observed, but is known to be negative. Thus, for a single household we have the following relationship between observable quantities:

$$e_{ij} + \pi_{ij}E_{ij} < 0.$$

We have shown that even without invoking the Maximum Principle the following relationships hold in terms of aggregates:

$$e_{ij} + K_1 E_{ij} \leqslant 0, \qquad \hat{e}_{ij} + K_2 \hat{E}_{ij} \leqslant 0, \qquad \text{where} \quad 0 < K_1, K_2 < 1.$$

[31] Under the conditions of Statement 9, the income effect $K \cdot E_{ij}$ was positive. However, $K \cdot E_{ij}$ may also be negative. This happens when a market good is inferior. See Statements 12–14.

Indeed, we conjecture that only a few additional (plausible) assumptions would suffice to render the equations

$$e_{ij} + \pi_{ij} E_{ij} < 0, \qquad \hat{e}_{ij} + \pi_{ij} \hat{E}_{ij} < 0$$

true in the aggregate.[32] But not having attempted the demonstration, we remain content to leave it to the interested reader. Clearly, attempts to verify the above two equations with market observations must not be construed as "tests" which can distinguish between formulations of demand theory which are or are not based on the preference structures of individuals.

In Statement 9 we demonstrated that an equation similar to the Hicks–Slutsky equation holds in the aggregate under the assumptions we have made. Now we shall consider inferences which can be drawn from the theory of aggregate behavior concerning the signs of uncompensated cross-price elasticities of demand. Let us denote the cross-price elasticities of demand for X_{ij} with respect to a change in p_{ik} by C_{ijk} and $\hat{C}_{ijk}$ according to whether the cross-price elasticities are computed using arithmetic or geometric means, respectively.

Statement 10. Given a concave heterothetic production function θ_i, the Weak Normality Assumption, and that $\log[F_{ij}(Z_i)]$ is a strictly monotonically increasing concave function of Z_i (for $j = 1, ..., n_i$), then without further information, the signs of C_{ijk} and $\hat{C}_{ijk}$ $(k \neq j)$ cannot be determined.

Proof of Statement 10. First, we consider the case of cross-price elasticities derived from arithmetic means:

$$
\begin{aligned}
C_{ijk} &= \frac{\Delta \log \overline{X}_{ij}}{\Delta \log p_{ik}} = \frac{\log \overline{X}_{ij}^{(2)} - \log \overline{X}_{ij}^{(1)}}{\log p_{ik}^{(2)} - \log p_{ik}^{(1)}} \\
&= \frac{[\log f_{ij}^{(2)} - \log f_{ij}^{(1)}]}{\log p_{ik}^{(2)} - \log p_{ik}^{(1)}} + \frac{[\log \overline{F}_{ij}(Z_i^{(2)}) - \log \overline{F}_{ij}(Z_i^{(1)})]}{\log p_{ik}^{(2)} - \log p_{ik}^{(1)}}
\end{aligned}
$$

where $f_{ij}^{(l)} = f_{ij}(p_{i1}^{(l)}, p_{i2}^{(l)}, ..., p_{in_i}^{(l)})$ (for $l = 1, 2$) and where $p_{ij}^{(2)} = p_{ij}^{(1)}$ for $j = 1, ..., n_i$ and $j \neq k$. The ambiguity arises because neither the sign of the first term to the right of equality sign is known in general nor its magnitude relative to the second term (the income effect). The source of ambiguity in the case of $\hat{C}_{ijk}$ is essentially the same as with C_{ijk}, which completes the proof.

Let us denote the cross-price elasticities of demand for X_{ij} with respect to a change in the price of X_{tu} by b_{ij}^{tu} and $\hat{b}_{ij}^{tu}$, according to whether the elasticities are computed using arithmetic or geometric means.

[32] See Appendix C, Technical Note 32.

Statement 11. Given a concave heterothetic production function θ_i and the Weak Normality Assumption, all cross-price elasticities of demand for X_{ij} $(j = 1, \ldots, n_i)$ with respect to changes in the price of a good X_{tu} $(i \neq t)$ are negative if the elasticities are computed from arithmetic means. This is also true in the case of the cross-price elasticities of demand derived from geometric means if $\log[F_{ij}(Z_i)]$ is a strictly monotonically increasing concave function of Z_i $(j = 1, \ldots, n_i)$.

Proof of Statement 11. Here we use the notion that Z_i and Z_t are not close substitutes. The restriction is discussed in greater detail in footnote 26. First, let us deal with the case where the elasticities are measured in terms of arithmetic means.

$$b_{ij}^{tu} = \frac{\Delta \log \overline{X}_{ij}}{\Delta \log p_{tu}} = \frac{\log \overline{X}_{ij}^{(2)} - \log \overline{X}_{ij}^{(1)}}{\log p_{tu}^{(2)} - \log p_{tu}^{(1)}}$$

$$= \frac{\log \overline{F}_{ij}(Z_i^{(2)}) - \log \overline{F}_{ij}(Z_i^{(1)})}{\log p_{tu}^{(2)} - \log p_{tu}^{(1)}}.$$

Since we have assumed that changing p_{tu} causes $\{Z_i^{(1)}\} \gtrless \{Z_i^{(2)}\}$ as $p_{tu}^{(2)} \gtrless p_{tu}^{(1)}$, Proposition 4 informs us that the numerator and denominator of the fraction are always of opposite sign. This completes the proof for elasticities measured in terms of arithmetic means. In the case of elasticities measured in terms of geometric means, we have

$$\hat{b}_{ij}^{tu} = \frac{\Delta \log \hat{X}_{ij}}{\Delta \log p_{tu}} = \frac{\log \hat{X}_{ij}^{(2)} - \log \hat{X}_{ij}^{(1)}}{\log p_{tu}^{(2)} - \log p_{tu}^{(1)}}$$

$$= \frac{\overline{\log[F_{ij}(Z_i^{(2)})]} - \overline{\log[F_{ij}(Z_i^{(1)})]}}{\log p_{tu}^{(2)} - \log p_{tu}^{(1)}}.$$

If $\log[F_{ij}(Z_i)]$ is a strictly monotonically increasing concave function, using Proposition 4 we readily obtain the implication that $\hat{b}_{ij}^{tu}$ is negative, which ends the proof of Statement 11.

In Statements 5 through 11, we have considered the case of "normal" goods (since the Weak Normality Assumption combined with a concave heterothetic production function implies positive income elasticities of demand) and have shown how familiar economic statements concerning the signs of income and price elasticities may be derived in the aggregate. Now we shall treat the cases of inferior and Giffen goods.

Definition. Let us consider a heterothetic production function θ_i, whose derived demand functions may be written

$$X_{ijk} = f_{ij}(p_{i1}, \ldots, p_{in_i}) F_{ij}(Z_{ik}) \qquad \text{for} \quad j = 1, \ldots, n_i,$$

where all the f_{ij} are homogeneous of degree zero. In the case of general hetero-thetic production functions all the F_{ij} need not be increasing functions over all ranges of Z_i. We say that X_{ij} is *arithmetically inferior* if $\bar{F}_{ij}(Z_i^{(2)}) > \bar{F}_{ij}(Z_i^{(1)})$ $[\bar{F}_{ij}(Z_i^{(2)}) < \bar{F}_{ij}(Z_i^{(1)})]$ when the opportunity to consume Z_i is smaller [greater] in situation 2 than in situation 1. We say that X_{ij} is *geo-metrically inferior* if $\hat{F}_{ij}(Z_i^{(2)}) > \hat{F}_{ij}(Z_i^{(1)})$ $[\hat{F}_{ij}(Z_i^{(2)}) < \hat{F}_{ij}(Z_i^{(1)})]$ when the opportunity to consume Z_i is smaller [greater] in situation 2 than in situation 1.

Statement 12. Given a heterothetic production function θ_i and that X_{ij} is arithmetically and geometrically inferior, then both E_{ij} and $\hat{E}_{ij}$ (the income elasticities of demand for X_{ij} derived from arithmetic and geometric means, respectively) are negative.

Proof of Statement 12. From the proof of Statement 5, we know that

$$E_{ij} = \frac{\log[\bar{F}_{ij}(Z_i^{(2)})] - \log[\bar{F}_{ij}(Z_i^{(1)})]}{\log V^{(2)} - \log V^{(1)}}.$$

When the denominator is positive, the opportunity to consume Z_i is greater in situation 2 than in situation 1. From the definition of arithmetic inferiority, we know that in this case $\bar{F}_{ij}(Z_i^{(2)}) < \bar{F}_{ij}(Z_i^{(1)})$ and hence the numerator is negative whenever the denominator is positive and vice versa. This suffices to show that E_{ij} is negative. From the proof of Statement 5, we also know that

$$\hat{E}_{ij} = \frac{\overline{\log[F_{ij}(Z_i^{(2)})]} - \overline{\log[F_{ij}(Z_i^{(1)})]}}{\log V^{(2)} - \log V^{(1)}}.$$

Similarly it follows immediately from the definition of geometric inferiority that $\hat{E}_{ij}$ is negative.

Statement 13. Given a heterothetic production function, θ_i, and that X_{ij} is arithmetically and geometrically inferior, then both e_{ij} and $\hat{e}_{ij}$ (the own-price elasticities of demand for X_{ij} measured in terms of arithmetic and geo-metric means, respectively) may be either positive or negative.

Proof of Statement 13.

$$e_{ij} = d_{ij} + \frac{\log[\bar{F}_{ij}(Z_i^{(2)})] - \log[\bar{F}_{ij}(Z_i^{(1)})]}{\log p_{ij}^{(2)} - \log p_{ij}^{(1)}},$$

where $d_{ij} \leqslant 0$. Thus e_{ij} is the sum of two terms the first of which cannot be positive and the second of which is always positive by the definition of arith-metic inferiority. Since we do not know the relative magnitudes of the two terms, e_{ij} may be either positive or negative. A similar argument will suffice to establish this about $\hat{e}_{ij}$.

Statement 14. Given a heterothetic production function, θ_i, if any input is a Giffen good then it must be inferior. More precisely, if the own-price elasticity of demand for X_{ij}, computed from arithmetic means, is positive, then X_{ij} must be arithmetically inferior, and if the own-price elasticity of X_{ij}, computed from geometric means, is positive, then X_{ij} must be geometrically inferior.

Proof of Statement 14. If $e_{ij} > 0$, we must have

$$\frac{\log[\bar{F}_{ij}(Z_i^{(2)})] - \log[\bar{F}_{ij}(Z_i^{(1)})]}{\log p_{ij}^{(2)} - \log p_{ij}^{(1)}} = e_{ij} - d_{ij} > 0.$$

The observation that the term on the left-hand side of the equality must be positive immediately implies the arithmetic inferiority of X_{ij}. A similar argument can be made in the case where $\hat{e}_{ij} > 0$.

Thus far we have considered the derivation of propositions concerning the signs of income and price elasticities. Next, let us consider the conditions under which stable orderings of these elasticities exist. In other words, we would like to know the conditions under which we can make statements of the form, "The income elasticity of demand for good A is always greater than the income elasticity of demand for good B," or analogous statements with respect to price elasticities. Let us use income elasticities to illustrate the difficulties which can arise in an attempt to make unconditional statements concerning the ordering of elasticities. First, income elasticities may depend on the size in the change in income. Therefore, it is possible that the income elasticity of demand for good A is larger than the income elasticity of demand for good B for some income changes, but not for others. Second, the ordering of income elasticities may depend on the prices of market goods. Thus, it is possible that the income elasticity of demand for good A is larger than the income elasticity of demand for good B under some set of market prices, but not under others. Finally, it is possible that the income elasticity of demand for good A is larger than that for good B when we measure the elasticities in terms of arithmetic means, but that the reverse is true when we measure the elasticities in terms of geometric means. In Statements 15–20, we are concerned with situations in which orderings of elasticities are invariant with respect to the magnitude of a change in income or price, the initial configuration of prices, or whether elasticities are measured using geometric or arithmetic means. In these Statements we deal only with a single heterogeneous production function θ_i, where $Z_{ih} = \theta_i(X_{i1h}, \ldots, X_{in_ih})$.

Statement 15. Given a heterogeneous production function θ_i, the ratio of income elasticities of demand for X_{ij} and X_{ik} (measured in terms of geometric means) is a constant (i.e., it is independent of prices and the size of the income change) and is equal to α_j/α_k. Symbolically, $\hat{E}_{ij}/\hat{E}_{ik} = \alpha_j/\alpha_k$.

Proof of Statement 15.

$$\hat{E}_{ij} = \frac{\alpha_j[\overline{\log}(Z_i^{(2)}) - \overline{\log}(Z_i^{(1)})]}{\Delta \log V}$$

and

$$\hat{E}_{ik} = \frac{\alpha_k[\overline{\log}(Z_i^{(2)}) - \overline{\log}(Z_i^{(1)})]}{\Delta \log V}.$$

Hence, $\hat{E}_{ij}/\hat{E}_{ik} = \alpha_j/\alpha_k$, which concludes the proof of Statement 15.

Statement 16. Given a heterogeneous production function θ_i, a specified income change, and the Weak Normality Assumption, the income elasticities of demand for the X_{ij} derived from geometric means $(j = 1, \ldots, n_i)$ are ordered identically to the α_j. In symbols, if

$$\alpha_j \geqslant \alpha_k \geqslant \alpha_l \quad \text{then} \quad \hat{E}_{ij} \geqslant \hat{E}_{ik} \geqslant \hat{E}_{il}$$

and $\hat{E}_{ij} = \hat{E}_{ik}$ if and only if $\alpha_j = \alpha_k$.

Proof of Statement 16. Since (from Statement 15) $\alpha_j/\alpha_k = \hat{E}_{ij}/\hat{E}_{ik}$, if $\alpha_j = \alpha_k$, then $\hat{E}_{ij} = \hat{E}_{ik}$, and if $\hat{E}_{ij} = \hat{E}_{ik}$, then $\alpha_j = \alpha_k$. Since all the income elasticities are positive (from Statement 6), then $\hat{E}_{ij} \gtrless \hat{E}_{ik}$ as $\alpha_j \gtrless \alpha_k$.

Statement 17. Given a heterogeneous production function, θ_i, and the Weak Normality Assumption, if the cross-price elasticities of demand for the X_{ij} $(j = 1, \ldots, n_i)$ with respect to a change in p_{tu} $(i \neq t)$ are computed from geometric means, then their ratios are constants and equal to the ratios of the corresponding income elasticities (computed from geometric means).

$$\frac{\hat{b}_{ij}^{tu}}{\hat{b}_{ik}^{tu}} = \frac{\alpha_j}{\alpha_k} = \frac{\hat{E}_{ij}}{\hat{E}_{ik}} \quad (i \neq t).$$

Proof of Statement 17.

$$\hat{b}_{ij}^{tu} = \frac{\alpha_j[\overline{\log}(Z_i^{(2)}) - \overline{\log}(Z_i^{(1)})]}{\Delta \log p_{tu}}$$

and

$$\hat{b}_{ik}^{tu} = \frac{\alpha_k[\overline{\log}(Z_i^{(2)}) - \overline{\log}(Z_i^{(1)})]}{\Delta \log p_{tu}}.$$

Therefore,

$$\frac{\hat{b}_{ij}^{tu}}{\hat{b}_{ik}^{tu}} = \frac{\alpha_j}{\alpha_k} = \frac{\hat{E}_{ij}}{\hat{E}_{ik}}$$

where the second equality is from Statement 15. This completes the proof of Statement 17.

Statement 18. Given a heterogeneous production function θ_i and the Weak Normality Assumption, if cross-price elasticities of demand for the X_{ij} $(j = 1, \ldots, n_i)$ with respect to a change in p_{tu} $(i \neq t)$ are derived from geometric means, then the ordering of the cross-price elasticities is the reverse of the ordering of the $\hat{E}_{ij}$. To put this another way, if

$$\hat{E}_{ij} \geqslant \hat{E}_{ik} \geqslant \hat{E}_{il}, \qquad \text{then} \qquad \hat{b}_{ij}^{tu} \leqslant \hat{b}_{ik}^{tu} \leqslant \hat{b}_{il}^{tu} \quad \text{and} \quad \hat{b}_{ij}^{tu} = \hat{b}_{ik}^{tu}$$

if and only if $\hat{E}_{ij} = \hat{E}_{ik}$.

Proof of Statement 18. Statement 18 follows directly from Statement 17 and the demonstration in Statement 11 that all the $\hat{b}_{ij}^{tu}$ are negative.

Statement 16 showed that given a heterogeneous production function, if elasticities are measured with respect to the geometric means of quantities purchased, then the income elasticities of the aggregated quantities of market goods used as inputs into that production process have a stable ordering in the sense that the ordering is independent of the size of the income change and the market prices of the inputs. In Statement 18 we showed that under similar conditions, there was a stable ordering of cross-price elasticities of goods used in the production of a household commodity, if it was the price of a market good used in the production of some other household commodity which varied. This line of thought naturally leads to the questions concerning the stability of orderings of own-price elasticities and the cross-price elasticities, $\hat{C}_{ijl}$.

Unfortunately, given the conditions of Statements 16 and 18, it is impossible to infer the stability of orderings of either own-price elasticities or the $\hat{C}_{ijl}$-type cross-price elasticities. The difficulty in inferring the stability of orderings of these two types of elasticities stems from the fact that they both are written as the sum of two terms, an income effect and a substitution effect. For example, from Statement 9 we know that under certain conditions

$$\hat{e}_{ij} = d_{ij} - K \cdot \hat{E}_{ij}$$

where $0 < K < 1$.

Now it is quite possible that both the income and the substitution effects have stable orderings, but that their sums do not. Thus, under the assumptions specified in Statements 16 and 18, the theory advises us to exercise caution in the interpretation of orderings of own-price elasticities and $\hat{C}_{ijl}$-type cross-price elasticities.

Statements 15 through 18 give us information concerning relationships between elasticities when we can measure the geometric means of quantities of market goods purchased. However, it is more common to observe data on sums or arithmetic means than on geometric means, so it is useful to ask whether stable orderings of elasticities, derived from arithmetic means may be inferred from the theory.

Under certain conditions it is possible to show that the orderings of income elasticities and b_{ij}^{tu}-type cross-price elasticities are invariant whether the elasticities are computed in terms of arithmetic or geometric means. In Statement 19 we show that although for small changes in income the orderings of income elasticities derived from arithmetic and geometric means need not be identical, there always exist sufficiently large changes in income such that the orderings of the income elasticities must be the same regardless of whether arithmetic or geometric means were used in their computation.

Statement 19. Given a heterogeneous production function, θ_i, and the Weak Normality Assumption, if $\hat{Z}_i$ is not bounded from above (with respect to increases in the opportunity to consume Z_i), then there exist income changes, $\Delta V^* > 0$ and $\Delta V^{**} < 0$ such that, for any $\Delta V > \Delta V^*$ or $\Delta V < \Delta V^{**}$ (V remaining positive), we may conclude that if $\hat{E}_{ij} \geqslant \hat{E}_{ik} \geqslant \hat{E}_{il}$, then $E_{ij} \geqslant E_{ik} \geqslant E_{il}$ and $\hat{E}_{ij} = \hat{E}_{ik}$ if and only if $E_{ij} = E_{ik}$.

Proof of Statement 19. The proof of Statement 19 is given in Appendix A.

If in practice, the income changes, ΔV^* and ΔV^{**}, mentioned in Statement 19 are not large relative to empirically observed income variations, then Statement 19 may be of some practical value to those interested in ranking income elasticities because it justifies the use of income elasticities derived from arithmetic means. It is also possible to state a set of sufficient conditions which ensure that the orderings of income and b_{ij}^{tu}-type cross-price elasticities of demand are invariant with respect to whether they were derived from arithmetic or geometric means regardless of the size of the income change. This is done in Statement 20.

Statement 20. Given a heterogeneous production function θ_i and the Weak Normality Assumption, let $\{Z_i^{(2)}\} = (Z_{i1}^{(2)}, ..., Z_{is}^{(2)})$ and $\{Z_i^{(1)}\} = (Z_{i1}^{(1)}, ..., Z_{ir}^{(1)})$, where the opportunity to consume Z_i is greater in situation 2 than in situation 1, and let $\{Z_i^{(3)}\}$ and $\{Z_i^{(4)}\}$ be the augmented distributions discussed on page 193. If $\{Z_i^{(3)}\}$ and $\{Z_i^{(4)}\}$ are such that

$$\frac{Z_{i1}^{(4)}}{Z_{i1}^{(3)}} \geqslant \frac{Z_{i2}^{(4)}}{Z_{i2}^{(3)}} \geqslant \cdots \geqslant \frac{Z_{i(r \times s)}^{(4)}}{Z_{i(r \times s)}^{(3)}},$$

then the ordering of the E_{ij} ($j = 1, ..., n_i$) is identical to the ordering of the $\hat{E}_{ij}$ ($j = 1, ..., n_i$) and is identical to the ordering of the α_j ($j = 1, ..., n_i$). Also the ordering of the b_{ij}^{tu} ($i \neq t$) is identical to the ordering of the $\hat{b}_{ij}^{tu}$ ($j = 1, ..., n_i$).

Proof of Statement 20. The proof of Statement 20 is given in Appendix B.

The condition in Statement 20 that

$$\frac{Z_{i1}^{(4)}}{Z_{i1}^{(3)}} \geqslant \frac{Z_{i2}^{(4)}}{Z_{i2}^{(3)}} \geqslant \cdots \geqslant \frac{Z_{i(r \times s)}^{(4)}}{Z_{i(r \times s)}^{(3)}}$$

whenever the opportunity to consume Z_i is greater in situation 2 than in situation 1, together with the weak bimajorization of the Weak Normality Assumption, imply the Strong Normality Assumption. Indeed, the restriction on possible distribution changes in Statement 20 seems extremely stringent when compared with weak bimajorization. Nonetheless, it is not implausible. One of the purposes of presenting Statement 20, is to suggest that it may be of interest to investigate whether observed distributions of purchases change in a manner consistent with their representation in that Statement.

Under the conditions of Statement 9, own-price elasticities of demand measured in terms of arithmetic and geometric means may be written, respectively, as

$$e_{ij} = d_{ij} - K_1 E_{ij} \quad \text{and} \quad \hat{e}_{ij} = d_{ij} - K_2 \hat{E}_{ij}$$

where $0 < K_1, K_2 < 1$. If K_1 and K_2 are small, say on the order of 0.01, and the magnitude of the difference between income elasticities measured using arithmetic and geometric means does not vary much across the market goods in question, then the orderings of the e_{ij} and $\hat{e}_{ij}$ will be dominated by the ordering of the d_{ij}. Since for identical price changes the d_{ij} are the same regardless of whether the own-price and income elasticities are derived from arithmetic and geometric means, then considering a price change in a given situation, the orderings of own-price elasticities of demand are plausibly but not necessarily quite similar regardless of which sort of mean was used in their computation.

5. Extensions

The theory of aggregate behavior developed above is a framework within which many phenomena may be portrayed. It is impossible to present an exhaustive list of the possible applications of this paradigm, but certain developments seem sufficiently immediate and sufficiently interesting to warrant their mention. One interesting extension would result from following Michael's (1972) suggestion that there may be systematic differences in the household technologies used by different groups of people. Michael proposed that differences in the amounts of formal education possessed by households may be associated with Hicks-neutral differences in household production functions. The analysis there was carried on in terms of a single utility maximizing consumer using homogeneous production functions. Within the framework of the model developed above, Michael's main results can be shown to hold in the aggregate under the less-restrictive assumption of concex heterothetic production functions. Indeed, there may be systematic technological differences between household groups which are associated with household characteristics other than formal education. Certainly the theoretical and empirical development of this area is far from complete.

Another extension is suggested by the observation that economists often encounter situations in which they would like to make *a priori* statements about the consequences of differences in the average incomes of groups of households where within each group there is a dispersion of incomes. We conjecture that in this case the notion that the income distribution in one situation weakly bimajorizes the income distribution in the other may be helpful. The application of weak bimajorization or perhaps some other form of majorization to income distributions seems to be a potentially promising line of development.

One of the most intriguing extensions of the theory of aggregate choice is to follow Becker (1965) and consider time as an input into household production functions. Preliminary work on a model similar to Willis' (1973) suggests neat statements can be derived for wives' labor force participation rates, wives' hours of labor-market work, and their average number of children. Within the model of aggregate choice there is a natural way to represent groups whose tastes differ. Thus it is possible to represent two groups, such as Catholics and non-Catholics, in such a manner that familiar fertility and wives' labor force participation rate differentials are predicted. Models of aggregate behavior which consider the allocation of time as well as goods seem likely to be a productive avenue of future research.

6. Conclusions

In this paper we have shown that it is possible to derive most of the important theorems of demand theory from a plausible specification of aggregate behavior. Thus we have shown that the representation which posits a single individual whose choices are guided by his preferences, is not the only theory from which important economic theorems may be derived nor is it the only theory which may be useful in organizing our observations of empirical phenomena. This is not to say that there is anything wrong with the theory of individual choice. Indeed, most would agree that it is an elegant and powerful theory and the theory of aggregate behavior presented here includes it as a special case. However, the theory of individual choice and the theory of aggregate behavior do provide two *different* approaches to the study of economic phenomena. For example, the theory of individual choice has led people to be concerned about the transitivity of preference orderings. The theory of aggregate behavior does not make any assumptions about any individual's preference orderings, but rather leads to a concern about such things as the empirical relationships between constraint changes and changes in the distribution of purchases.

Whereas the theory of individual choice derives its implications in part from a specification of individual preference orderings which is difficult to test in any meaningful way for groups of people, the theory of aggregate behavior presented here is based on the falsifiable premise that distributions of purchases differ in a certain predictable manner from one situation to the next as incomes and market prices differ. We have not presented any empirical data to test this premise, but the theory developed here suggests that such an investigation might find a previously unrecognized empirical regularity. After all, it is an important function of any economic theory to make such suggestions.

Appendix A. Proof of Statement 19

Statement 19. Given a heterogeneous production function θ_i [$Z_{ih} = \theta_i(X_{i1h}, ..., X_{in_ih})$], the Weak Normality Assumption, and that $\hat{Z}_i$ is not bounded from above with respect to increases in the opportunity to consume Z_i, then there exist income changes $\Delta V^* > 0$ and $\Delta V^{**} < 0$ such that, for any $\Delta V > \Delta V^*$ or $\Delta V < \Delta V^{**}$ $(V + \Delta V > 0)$ if $\hat{E}_{ij} \geqslant \hat{E}_{ik} \geqslant \hat{E}_{il}$, then $E_{ij} \geqslant E_{ik} \geqslant E_{il}$ and $\hat{E}_{ij} = \hat{E}_{ik}$ if and only if $E_{ij} = E_{ik}$, where E_{ij} and $\hat{E}_{ij}$ are the income elasticities of demand for X_{ij} measured using arithmetic or geometric means, respectively.

Proof of Statement 19. First, we shall demonstrate the existence of a ΔV^* such that the statement is true for any $\Delta V > \Delta V^*$. Let us consider the following ratio, which we denote by R:

$$R \equiv [\overline{(Z_i^{(1)})^{\alpha_G}}/\overline{(Z_i^{(1)})^{\alpha_H}}]^{1/(\alpha_G - \alpha_H)}$$

where $\alpha_G > \alpha_H$ and where α_G and α_H are chosen so that

$$R \equiv \max[\overline{(Z_i^{(1)})^{\alpha_j}}/\overline{(Z_i^{(1)})^{\alpha_k}}]^{1/(\alpha_j - \alpha_k)}$$

for all $j = 1, ..., n_i$, and for all k such that $\alpha_j > \alpha_k$.

It is important to notice that $R \geqslant \hat{Z}_i^{(1)}$.[33] If $\hat{Z}_i$ is not bounded from above, there exists some increase in income such that $\hat{Z}_i > R$. We call this increase in income ΔV^*. For any $\Delta V \geqslant \Delta V^*$ we have

$$\hat{Z}_i^{(2)} > R.$$

Taking the logarithm of both sides of this inequality we have

$$\frac{1}{S} \sum_{h=1}^{S} \log(Z_{ih}^{(2)}) > \frac{1}{\alpha_G - \alpha_H} \log \left[\frac{\overline{(Z_i^{(1)})^{\alpha_G}}}{\overline{(Z_i^{(1)})^{\alpha_H}}} \right],$$

---

[33] See Appendix C, Technical Note 33.

where S is the number of households in situation 2, and

$$\frac{1}{S} \sum_{h=1}^{S} \log(Z_{ih}^{(2)}) > \frac{1}{\alpha_j - \alpha_k} \log \left[\frac{\overline{(Z_i^{(1)})^{\alpha_j}}}{\overline{(Z_i^{(1)})^{\alpha_k}}} \right],$$

where $\alpha_j > \alpha_k$. This last inequality follows because R was chosen as a maximum. We shall demonstrate that the last inequality implies that the sequence

$$\{\alpha_j \log Z_i^{(2)} - \log [\overline{(Z_i^{(1)})^{\alpha_j}}/\overline{(Z_i^{(1)})^{\alpha_k}}]\}$$

weakly majorizes[34] $\{\alpha_k \log Z_i^{(2)}\}$. To prove weak majorization we must demonstrate two conditions:

(1)

$$\alpha_j \sum_{h=1}^{\gamma} \log Z_{ih}^{(2)} - \gamma \log \left[\frac{\overline{(Z_i^{(1)})^{\alpha_j}}}{\overline{(Z_i^{(1)})^{\alpha_k}}} \right] \geq \alpha_k \sum_{h=1}^{\gamma} \log Z_{ih}^{(2)} \qquad \text{for} \quad \gamma = 1, ..., S-1,$$

and that

(2) $$\alpha_j \sum_{h=1}^{S} \log Z_{ih}^{(2)} - S \log \left[\frac{\overline{(Z_i^{(1)})^{\alpha_j}}}{\overline{(Z_i^{(1)})^{\alpha_k}}} \right] > \alpha_k \sum_{h=1}^{S} \log Z_{ih}^{(2)}.$$

This last inequality may be rewritten

$$\frac{1}{S} \sum_{h=1}^{S} \log Z_{ih}^{(2)} > \frac{1}{\alpha_j - \alpha_k} \log \left[\frac{\overline{(Z_i^{(1)})^{\alpha_j}}}{\overline{(Z_i^{(1)})^{\alpha_k}}} \right],$$

and we have seen above that a $\{Z_i^{(2)}\}$ always exists such that this inequality holds. Now let us consider the inequalities in condition (1). Rearranging the terms it can easily be seen that we must demonstrate that

$$\frac{1}{\gamma} \sum_{h=1}^{\gamma} \log Z_{ih}^{(2)} \geq \frac{1}{\alpha_j - \alpha_k} \log \left[\frac{\overline{(Z_i^{(1)})^{\alpha_j}}}{\overline{(Z_i^{(1)})^{\alpha_k}}} \right], \qquad \gamma = 1, ..., S-1.$$

Since the $Z_{ih}^{(2)}$ are ordered from highest to lowest, $1/\gamma \sum_{h=1}^{\gamma} \log Z_{ih}^{(2)}$ can never increase as γ increases. Suppose now that there exists some γ, say γ^* $(1 \leq \gamma^* \leq S-1)$ such that

$$\frac{1}{\gamma^*} \sum_{h=1}^{\gamma^*} \log Z_{ih}^{(2)} < \frac{1}{\alpha_j - \alpha_k} \log \left[\frac{\overline{(Z_i^{(1)})^{\alpha_j}}}{\overline{(Z_i^{(1)})^{\alpha_k}}} \right].$$

---

[34] See footnote 18 for a definition of weak majorization and Proposition 3 on page 190 for a statement relating it to strictly monotonically increasing convex functions.

Since $1/\gamma \sum_{h=1}^{\lambda} \log Z_{ih}^{(2)}$ can never increase as γ increases, we must have

$$\frac{1}{S} \sum_{h=1}^{S} \log Z_{ih}^{(2)} < \frac{1}{\alpha_j - \alpha_k} \log \left[\frac{(Z_i^{(1)})^{\alpha_j}}{(Z_i^{(1)})^{\alpha_k}} \right].$$

But this last inequality contradicts condition 2 which we have demonstrated to be true. Thus, we have proved by contradiction that, given the assumptions made, condition (1) obtains.

Since we have demonstrated both conditions (1) and (2) hold, we have proved that

$$\{\alpha_j \log Z_i^{(2)} - \log [\overline{(Z_i^{(1)})^{\alpha_j}/(Z_i^{(1)})^{\alpha_k}}]\}$$

weakly majorizes $\{\alpha_k \log Z_i^{(2)}\}$. Since e^x is a strictly monotonically increasing convex function of x, from Proposition 2 we know that

$$\sum_{h=1}^{S} \exp \left\{ \alpha_j \log Z_{ih}^{(2)} - \log \left[\frac{(Z_i^{(1)})^{\alpha_j}}{(Z_i^{(1)})^{\alpha_k}} \right] \right\} > \sum_{h=1}^{S} \exp (\alpha_k \log Z_{ih}^{(2)})$$

and therefore that

$$\frac{\sum_{h=1}^{S} (Z_{ih}^{(2)})^{\alpha_j}}{(Z_i^{(1)})^{\alpha_j}/(Z_i^{(1)})^{\alpha_k}} > \sum_{h=1}^{S} (Z_{ih}^{(2)})^{\alpha_k} \quad \text{and} \quad \frac{\overline{(Z_i^{(2)})^{\alpha_j}}}{\overline{(Z_i^{(1)})^{\alpha_j}}} > \frac{\overline{(Z_i^{(2)})^{\alpha_k}}}{\overline{(Z_i^{(1)})^{\alpha_k}}}.$$

This last inequality is sufficient to establish that if $\alpha_j > \alpha_k$, then for sufficiently large increases in income $E_{ij} > E_{ik}$, since

$$\frac{E_{ij}}{E_{ik}} = \frac{\log [\overline{(Z_i^{(2)})^{\alpha_j}}] - \log [\overline{(Z_i^{(1)})^{\alpha_j}}]}{\log [\overline{(Z_i^{(2)})^{\alpha_k}}] - \log [\overline{(Z_i^{(1)})^{\alpha_k}}]}.$$

If $\hat{E}_{ij} > \hat{E}_{ik}$, then $\alpha_j > \alpha_k$ (by Statement 16), and for sufficiently large increases in income, $\alpha_j > \alpha_k$ implies that $E_{ij} > E_{ik}$. If $\hat{E}_{ij} = \hat{E}_{ik}$, then $\alpha_j = \alpha_k$ (by Statement 16) and $E_{ij} = E_{ik}$. E_{ij} and E_{ik} cannot be equal, given the assumption of this statement, unless $\alpha_j = \alpha_k$ since if $\alpha_j > \alpha_k$, we have shown above that $E_{ij} > E_{ik}$, and similarly if $\alpha_j < \alpha_k$, we would have $E_{ij} < E_{ik}$. Therefore, $E_{ij} = E_{ik}$ implies $\alpha_j = \alpha_k$ and (by Statement 16) that $E_{ij} = E_{ik}$. This concludes the portion of the proof concerning income increases.

Now we shall prove the portion of the statement concerning income reductions. Let us define the ratio R' as follows:

$$R' \equiv [\overline{(Z_i^{(2)})^{\alpha_G}/(Z_i^{(2)})^{\alpha_H}}]^{1/(\alpha_G - \alpha_H)}$$

where α_G and α_H are chosen so that

$$R' \equiv \max [\overline{(Z_i^{(2)})^{\alpha_j}/(Z_i^{(2)})^{\alpha_k}}]^{1/(\alpha_j - \alpha_k)}$$

for all $\alpha_j = 1, ..., n_i$ and for all k such that $\alpha_j > \alpha_k$.

Given $\hat{Z}_i^{(1)}$, we shall show that it is always possible to find some income reduction and hence some $\{Z_i^{(2)}\}$ such that $\hat{Z}_i^{(1)} > R'$. We know that $R' \leqslant Z_{i1}^{(2)}$.[35] Hence if $\hat{Z}_i^{(1)} > Z_{i1}^{(2)}$, then $\hat{Z}_i^{(1)} > R'$. However, the condition $\hat{Z}_i^{(1)} > Z_{i1}^{(2)}$ simply means that the largest element of $\{Z_i^{(2)}\}$ is smaller than the geometric mean of $\{Z_i^{(1)}\}$. It is obvious that income can be reduced to the point where the maximum possible quantity of Z_i produced must be lower than $\hat{Z}_i^{(1)}$. However, the income decrease necessary for $\hat{Z}_i^{(1)} > R'$ may not be so drastic. Let ΔV^{**} be such an income reduction. For any reduction in income such that $\Delta V < \Delta V^{**}$ and income remains positive, we must have

$$\hat{Z}_i^{(1)} > [\overline{(Z_i^{(2)})^{\alpha_G}}/\overline{(Z_i^{(2)})^{\alpha_H}}]^{1/(\alpha_G - \alpha_H)}.$$

Following the same line of argument as we used above in the case of income increases, we can show that

$$\{\alpha_j \log Z_i^{(1)} - \log[\overline{(Z_i^{(2)})^{\alpha_j}}/\overline{(Z_i^{(2)})^{\alpha_k}}]\}$$

weakly majorizes $\{\alpha_k \log Z_i^{(1)}\}$, and that

$$\overline{(Z_i^{(1)})^{\alpha_j}}/\overline{(Z_i^{(2)})^{\alpha_j}} > \overline{(Z_i^{(1)})^{\alpha_k}}/\overline{(Z_i^{(2)})^{\alpha_k}}.$$

The above equation is sufficient to imply that given sufficiently large decreases in income, $\alpha_j > \alpha_k$ implies $E_{ij} > E_{ik}$. The remainder of the proof is identical to the case of an increase in income.

Appendix B. Proof of Statement 20

Statement 20. Given a heterogeneous production function θ_i [$Z_{ih} = \theta_i(X_{i1h}, \ldots, X_{in_ih})$], and the Weak Normality Assumption, let the oppotunity to consume Z_i be greater in situation 2 than in situation 1; let $\{Z_i^{(2)}\} = \{Z_{i1}^{(2)}, \ldots, Z_{is}^{(2)}\}$ and $\{Z_i^{(1)}\} = \{Z_{i1}^{(1)}, \ldots, Z_{ir}^{(1)}\}$ be the distributions of Z_i in these situations, respectively; and let $\{Z_i^{(4)}\}$ and $\{Z_i^{(3)}\}$ be augmented distributions based on $\{Z_i^{(2)}\}$ and $\{Z_i^{(1)}\}$, respectively.[36] If $\{Z_i^{(3)}\}$ and $\{Z_i^{(4)}\}$ are such that

$$\frac{Z_{i1}^{(4)}}{Z_{i1}^{(3)}} \geqslant \frac{Z_{i2}^{(4)}}{Z_{i2}^{(3)}} \geqslant \cdots \geqslant \frac{Z_{im}^{(4)}}{Z_{im}^{(3)}} \qquad \text{where} \quad m = r \cdot s,$$

then the orderings of the income elasticities of demand for the X_{ij} ($j = 1, \ldots, n_i$) will be identical regardless of whether the elasticities are computed using arithmetic or geometric means. Also the orderings of cross-price elasticities of demand for the X_{ij} ($j = 1, \ldots, n_i$), with respect to a change in the price of a good not used in the production of Z_i, will be identical regardless

[35] See Appendix C, Technical Note 35.
[36] See page 193 for a discussion of augmented distributions.

of whether the elasticities are derived from arithmetic or geometric means. The orderings of these cross-price elasticities will be the reverse of the orderings of the income elasticities. In symbols, if $\hat{E}_{ij} \geqslant \hat{E}_{ik} \geqslant \hat{E}_{il}$ (or $\hat{b}_{ij}^{tu} \leqslant \hat{b}_{ik}^{tu} \leqslant \hat{b}_{il}^{tu}$), then

(1) $$E_{ij} \geqslant E_{ik} \geqslant E_{il},$$

(2) $$b_{ij}^{tu} \leqslant b_{ik}^{tu} \leqslant b_{il}^{tu}.$$

Further $\hat{E}_{ij} = \hat{E}_{ik}$ if and only if $E_{ij} = E_{ik}$; $\hat{b}_{ij}^{tu} = \hat{b}_{ik}^{tu}$ if and only if $b_{ij}^{tu} = b_{ik}^{tu}$. Here E_{ij} and $\hat{E}_{ij}$ refer to income elasticities of demand for X_{ij} measured in terms of arithmetic and geometric means, respectively, and b_{ij}^{tu} and $\hat{b}_{ij}^{tu}$ refer to cross-price elasticities of demand for X_{ij} with respect to a change in the price of X_{tu} ($i \neq t$) where these elasticities are derived from arithmetic and geometric means, respectively.

In order to prove this statement, we first state the following proposition.

Proposition 5. If

$$Z_{i1}^{(4)} > 0, ..., Z_{im}^{(4)} > 0, \qquad Z_{i1}^{(3)} \geqslant Z_{i2}^{(3)} \geqslant \cdots \geqslant Z_{im}^{(3)} > 0,$$

and

$$\frac{Z_{i1}^{(4)}}{Z_{i1}^{(3)}} \geqslant \frac{Z_{i2}^{(4)}}{Z_{i2}^{(3)}} \geqslant \cdots \geqslant \frac{Z_{im}^{(4)}}{Z_{im}^{(3)}},$$

then the function $f(\lambda)$ defined as

$$f(\lambda) \equiv \left(\frac{(Z_{i1}^{(4)})^\lambda + (Z_{i2}^{(4)})^\lambda + \cdots + (Z_{im}^{(4)})^\lambda}{(Z_{i1}^{(3)})^\lambda + (Z_{i2}^{(3)})^\lambda + \cdots + (Z_{im}^{(3)})^\lambda} \right)^{1/\lambda}$$

is an increasing function of λ.[37]

Proof of Statement 20. From Proposition 5, we immediately have that if $\alpha_j > \alpha_k$

$$[(Z_i^{(4)})^{\alpha_j}/(Z_i^{(3)})^{\alpha_j}]^{1/\alpha_j} \geqslant [(Z_i^{(4)})^{\alpha_k}/(Z_i^{(3)})^{\alpha_k}]^{1/\alpha_k}$$

and

$$[\overline{(Z_i^{(4)})^{\alpha_j}/(Z_i^{(3)})^{\alpha_j}}] > [\overline{(Z_i^{(4)})^{\alpha_k}/(Z_i^{(3)})^{\alpha_k}}].$$

Because of the definition of $\{Z_i^{(3)}\}$ and $\{Z_i^{(4)}\}$, we also have

$$[\overline{(Z_i^{(2)})^{\alpha_j}/(Z_i^{(1)})^{\alpha_j}}] > [\overline{(Z_i^{(2)})^{\alpha_k}/(Z_i^{(1)})^{\alpha_k}}].$$

---

[37] For a proof of this statement see the work of Marshall *et al.* (1967, p. 179).

Taking the logarithm of both sides of this inequality, we obtain

$$\log[\overline{(Z_i^{(2)})^{\alpha_j}}] - \log[\overline{(Z_i^{(1)})^{\alpha_j}}] > \log[\overline{(Z_i^{(2)})^{\alpha_k}}] - \log[\overline{(Z_i^{(1)})^{\alpha_k}}].$$

If $\hat{E}_{ij} > \hat{E}_{ik}$, then $\alpha_j > \alpha_k$ (by Statement 16). Similarly, if $\hat{b}_{ij}^{tu} < \hat{b}_{ik}^{tu}$, then $\alpha_j > \alpha_k$ (by Statement 18). Now

$$\frac{b_{ij}^{tu}}{b_{ik}^{tu}} = \frac{E_{ij}}{E_{ik}} = \frac{\log[\overline{(Z_i^{(2)})^{\alpha_j}}] - \log[\overline{(Z_i^{(1)})^{\alpha_j}}]}{\log[\overline{(Z_i^{(2)})^{\alpha_k}}] - \log[\overline{(Z_i^{(1)})^{\alpha_k}}]},$$

and therefore, if $\hat{E}_{ij} > \hat{E}_{ik}$ or $\hat{b}_{ij}^{tu} < \hat{b}_{ik}^{tu}$,

$$b_{ij}^{tu}/b_{ik}^{tu} = E_{ij}/E_{ik} > 1.$$

Since the income elasticities are positive (by Statement 6), $\hat{E}_{ij} > \hat{E}_{ik}$ implies $E_{ij} > E_{ik}$, and since the cross-price elasticities are negative (by Statement 11), $\hat{b}_{ij}^{tu} < \hat{b}_{ik}^{tu}$ implies $b_{ij}^{tu} < b_{ik}^{tu}$.

It remains to show that $\hat{E}_{ij} = \hat{E}_{ik}$ if and only if $E_{ij} = E_{ik}$, and $\hat{b}_{ij}^{tu} = \hat{b}_{ik}^{tu}$ if and only if $b_{ij}^{tu} = b_{ik}^{tu}$. If $\hat{E}_{ij} = \hat{E}_{ik}$ or $\hat{b}_{ij}^{tu} = \hat{b}_{ik}^{tu}$, then (from Statements 16 and 18) we know that $\alpha_j = \alpha_k$, and it follows immediately that $E_{ij} = E_{ik}$ and $b_{ij}^{tu} = b_{ik}^{tu}$. $E_{ij} = E_{ik}$ and $b_{ij}^{tu} = b_{ik}^{tu}$ are true if $\alpha_j = \alpha_k$, from which it follows that $\hat{E}_{ij} = \hat{E}_{ik}$ and $\hat{b}_{ij}^{tu} = \hat{b}_{ik}^{tu}$. Since we demonstrated above that $\alpha_j > \alpha_k$ implies $E_{ij} > E_{ik}$, and $b_{ij}^{tu} < b_{ik}^{tu}$, it is impossible for $E_{ij} = E_{ik}$ or $b_{ij}^{tu} = b_{ik}^{tu}$ and to have $\alpha_j \neq \alpha_k$. This completes the proof of Statement 20.

Appendix C. Technical Notes

5. Statements 1, 2, and 4 are the only statements in this paper in which elasticities are not computed for discrete but rather for infinitesimal changes in exogenous variables. The reader can easily enough provide the discrete analogs. Statements 1, 2, and 4 are familiar to economists in the form they are stated in the text and since we have nothing new to say about their derivation, we thought that the presentation of a familiar idea in an unfamiliar package would be misleading. To prove Statement 1, first differentiate the averaged budget constraint discussed in footnote 4 with respect to V. This yields

$$p_1 \frac{\partial \overline{X}_1}{\partial V} + p_2 \frac{\partial \overline{X}_2}{\partial V} + \cdots + p_n \frac{\partial \overline{X}_n}{\partial V} = 1$$

and

$$\frac{p_1 \overline{X}_1}{V} \left[\frac{\partial \overline{X}_1}{\partial V} \cdot \frac{V}{\overline{X}_1} \right] + \frac{p_2 \overline{X}_2}{V} \cdot \left[\frac{\partial \overline{X}_2}{\partial V} \cdot \frac{V}{\overline{X}_2} \right] + \cdots + \frac{p_n \overline{X}_n}{V} \cdot \left[\frac{\partial \overline{X}_n}{\partial V} \cdot \frac{V}{\overline{X}_n} \right] = 1.$$

Since $E_i = \partial \overline{X}_i/\partial V \cdot V/\overline{X}_i$ and $\alpha_i = p_i \overline{X}_i/V$, we have $\sum_{i=1}^{n} \alpha_i E_i = 1$.

6. To prove Statement 2, first differentiate the averaged budget constraint discussed in footnote 4 with respect to p_h. This yields

$$p_1 \frac{\partial \overline{X}_1}{\partial p_h} + p_2 \frac{\partial \overline{X}_2}{\partial p_h} + \cdots + p_h \frac{\partial \overline{X}_h}{\partial p_h} + \overline{X}_h + \cdots + p_n \frac{\partial \overline{X}_n}{\partial p_h} = 0$$

and

$$\frac{p_1 \overline{X}_1}{V} \cdot \left[\frac{\partial \overline{X}_1}{\partial p_h} \cdot \frac{p_h}{\overline{X}_1} \right] + \frac{p_2 \overline{X}_2}{V} \left[\frac{\partial \overline{X}_2}{\partial p_h} \cdot \frac{p_h}{\overline{X}_2} \right] + \cdots + \frac{p_n \overline{X}_n}{V} \left[\frac{\partial \overline{X}_n}{\partial p_h} \cdot \frac{p_h}{\overline{X}_n} \right] = -\frac{\overline{X}_h p_h}{V}.$$

Since $e_{ih} = (\partial \overline{X}_i / \partial p_h)(p_h / \overline{X}_i)$ and $\alpha_i = p_i \overline{X}_i / V$, this equation may be rewritten

$$\sum_{i=1}^{n} \alpha_i e_{ih} = -\alpha_h.$$

7. From Statement 3, we know that demand functions written in terms of arithmetic means of the quantities of market goods purchased are homogeneous of degree zero in income and market prices. We can write the demand function for $\overline{X}_i$ as $\overline{X}_i = \phi(p_1, \ldots, p_n, V)$ where ϕ is homogeneous of degree zero. From Euler's theorem we know

$$p_1 \frac{\partial \overline{X}_i}{\partial p_1} + p_2 \frac{\partial \overline{X}_i}{\partial p_2} + \cdots + p_n \frac{\partial \overline{X}_i}{\partial p_n} + V \frac{\partial \overline{X}_i}{\partial V} = 0.$$

From this equation we easily obtain

$$\frac{p_1}{\overline{X}_i} \frac{\partial \overline{X}_i}{\partial p_1} + \frac{p_2}{\overline{X}_i} \frac{\partial \overline{X}_i}{\partial p_2} + \cdots + \frac{p_n}{\overline{X}_i} \frac{\partial \overline{X}_i}{\partial p_n} = -\frac{\partial \overline{X}_i}{\partial V} \cdot \frac{V}{\overline{X}_i}.$$

In other notation, this equation says $\sum_{h=1}^{n} e_{ih} = -E_i$.

9. In this Technical Note we shall answer two questions: (1) How do we know that the derived demand functions corresponding to homothetic production functions are multiplicative in the manner indicated above? (2) How do we know that all the f_{ij} are homogeneous of degree zero? To answer the first question, let us note that we always may define the output so that $F_i(1) = 1$. Therefore, the f_{ij}'s tell us the demands for inputs along the unit isoquant. We know that for homothetic production functions any other isoquant can be derived from the unit isoquant by the multiplicative translation of the unit isoquant. This answers question (1). Question (2) is answered by noting that doubling all prices and keeping output constant can never affect the quantities of inputs demanded regardless of the type of production function considered. The derived demand function tells us the minimum cost input configuration needed to produce a given output. Suppose, given some set of prices and some level of output, the derived demand equations instruct us to purchase a certain quantity of X_{ij}. If that quantity of X_{ij} changes when all input prices double, for example, then the original level of X_{ij} could not have been the cost minimizing level, which is a contradiction. Therefore, all the f_{ij} must be homogeneous of degree zero.

10. From Technical Note 9, we know that the f_{ij} may be considered as representing the demand functions for inputs along the unit isoquant. In the commonly considered case of a production function $y = f(X_i, ..., X_n)$ where $\partial f/\partial X_i > 0$ and $\partial^2 f/\partial X_i^2 < 0$ (for $i = 1, ..., n$), it has been demonstrated that holding y and all other prices constant, $\partial X_i/\partial p_i < 0$ where p_i is the price of X_i [see Samuelson (1947, p. 65)]. However, above we also allow a change in, say p_i, to have no effect on the demand for X_i along the unit isoquant. Such a situation could occur if the production technology we were considering represented a number of fixed-coefficients production functions.

21. The theorem stated in Polya (1950) and Proposition 2 differ slightly in an assumption and in their conclusions. Polya's theorem assumed $\sum_{k=1}^{m} Z_{ik}^{(2)} \geqslant \sum_{k=1}^{m} Z_{ik}^{(1)}$, whereas we have assumed $\sum_{k=1}^{m} Z_{ik}^{(2)} > \sum_{k=1}^{m} Z_{ik}^{(1)}$. Polya concluded that $\sum_{k=1}^{m} \phi(Z_{ik}^{(2)}) \geqslant \sum_{k=1}^{m} \phi(Z_{ik}^{(1)})$, for any increasing convex function ϕ, whereas we have concluded $\sum_{k=1}^{m} \phi(Z_{ik}^{(2)}) > \sum_{=1}^{k} \phi(Z_{ik}^{(1)})$ for any strictly monotonically increasing convex function ϕ. Given that ϕ is continuous and its second derivative always exists (within the relevant interval) and is positive (assumptions that we make about all convex functions in this paper), Proposition 2 may be simply derived from Hardy et al. (1952, p. 89, Theorem 108) using an argument identical to the one stated by Polya (1950).

32. As a practical matter, it seems highly unlikely that an aggregated income-compensated own-price elasticity of demand, defined as

$$d_{ij}^* \equiv e_{ij} + \pi_{ij} E_{ij}$$

would ever be positive. Let us suppose that for some market good $\pi_{ij} = 0.05$. We know from Statement 9 that

$$0 \geqslant e_{ij} + K E_{ij}, \qquad 0 < K < 1.$$

If $K > 0.05$ and the income elasticity is positive, then d_{ij}^* must be negative. A positive d_{ij}^* could only occur if $0 < K \leqslant 0.05$. Let us suppose, for example, that $K = 0.03$. Even in this case, it is hardly likely that d_{ij}^* would be positive, since this would require

$$0.03 \leqslant |e_{ij}|/E_{ij} < 0.05$$

—a highly unusual circumstance. The same argument holds for elasticities computed from geometric means.

33. Here we shall just briefly sketch why $R \geqslant Z_i^{(1)}$. Let us denote $\Delta \equiv \alpha_G - \alpha_H$. Then R may be written as

$$\left[\sum_{h=1}^{r} \delta_h (Z_{ih}^{(1)})^\Delta \right]^{1/\Delta} \qquad \text{where} \qquad \delta_h = \frac{(Z_{ih}^{(1)})^{\alpha_H}}{\sum_{h=1}^{r} (Z_{ih}^{(1)})^{\alpha_H}}.$$

Clearly $\sum_{h=1}^{r} \delta_h = 1$. Applying l'Hospital's rule, we obtain

$$\lim_{\Delta \to 0} \left[\sum_{h=1}^{r} \delta_H (Z_{ih}^{(1)})^\Delta \right]^{1/\Delta} = \prod_{h=1}^{r} (Z_{ih}^{(1)})^{\delta_H}.$$

Since $\delta_1 \geqslant \delta_2 \geqslant \cdots \geqslant \delta_r$ and $Z_{i1}^{(1)} \geqslant Z_{i2}^{(1)} \geqslant \cdots \geqslant Z_{ir}^{(1)}$, we have that

$$\prod_{h=1}^{r} (Z_{ih}^{(1)})^{\delta_H} \geqslant \prod_{h=1}^{r} (Z_{ih}^{(1)})^{1/r} = \hat{Z}_i^{(1)}.$$

Hence $\lim_{\alpha_G \to \alpha_H} R \geqslant \hat{Z}_i^{(1)}$. We conclude the demonstration that $R \geqslant \hat{Z}_i^{(1)}$ (given $\alpha_G > \alpha_H$) by noting that $\partial R / \partial \Delta \geqslant 0$. See Beckenbach and Bellman (1965, p. 16–18) for a proof of this last inequality.

35. We can write

$$R' = \left[\sum_{h=1}^{s} \delta_h (Z_{ih}^{(2)})^\Delta \right]^{1/\Delta}$$

where

$$\Delta = \alpha_G - \alpha_H \quad \text{and} \quad \delta_h = \frac{(Z_{ih}^{(2)})^{\alpha_H}}{\sum_{h=1}^{s} (Z_{ih}^{(2)})^{\alpha_H}}.$$

Clearly all the δ_h are positive and $\sum_{h=1}^{s} \delta_h = 1$. Since $Z_{i1}^{(2)} = \max(Z_{ih}^{(2)})$ for $h = 1, \ldots, s$, we must have that $R' \leqslant [\sum_{h=1}^{s} \delta_h (Z_{i1}^{(2)})^\Delta]^{1/\Delta} = Z_{i1}^{(2)}$. Hence $R' \leqslant Z_{i1}^{(2)}$.

ACKNOWLEDGMENTS

The author is grateful to his colleagues in the Workshop on the Economics of the Household at Stanford University for their comments and criticisms on this paper as it evolved, and particularly to Paul David, whose perceptive remarks were as usual very helpful. This study was in part financed by a grant from the Ford Foundation to the National Bureau of Economic Research. However, this paper has not been submitted to the Board of Directors of the National Bureau of Economic Research for review and therefore is not an official publication of that organization.

REFERENCES

Allen, R. G. D. (1963) *Mathematical Economics*, 2nd ed. New York: Macmillan.

Beckenbach, E. F., and Bellman, R. (1965) *Inequalities*. Berlin and New York: Springer-Verlag.

Becker, G. S. (1962) Irrational behavior and economic theory. *Journal of Political Economy* **70**: 1–13.

Becker, G. S. (1965) A theory of the allocation of time. *The Economic Journal* **75**: 493–517.

Ben-Porath, Y. (1967) The production of human capital and the life cycle of earnings. *Journal of Political Economy* **75**: 352–365.

Ben-Porath, Y. (1970) The production of human capital over time. *Educational Income and Human Capital*, Studies in Income and Wealth (W. L. Hanson, ed.), Vol. 35. New York: National Bureau of Economic Research.

Chipman, J. S., Hurwicz, L., Richter, M. K., and Sonnenschein, H. F. (eds.) (1971) *Preferences, utility and demand: A Minnesota symposium*. New York: Harcourt.

Gronau, R. (1970) *The Value of Time in Passenger Transportation: The Demand for Air Travel*, National Bureau of Economic Research, Occasional Paper 109, New York, National Bureau of Economic Research, 1970.

Grossman, M. (1972) *The Demand for Health: A Theoretical and Empirical Investigation*, National Bureau of Economic Research, Occasional Paper 119, New York: National Bureau of Economic Research.

Hadar, J., and Russell, W. R. (1971) Stochastic dominance and diversification, *Journal of Economic Theory*. 3: 288–305.

Hardy, G. H., Littlewood, J. E., and Pólya, G. (1952) *Inequalities*, 2nd ed. London and New York: Cambridge Univ. Press.

Lancaster, K. (1966) A new approach to consumer theory. *Journal of Political Economy* 74: 132–157.

Lancaster, K. (1971) *Consumer Demand: A New Approach*. New York: Columbia Univ. Press.

Marshall, A. W., Olkin, I., and Proschan, F. (1967) Monotonicity of ratios of means and other applications of majorization. In *Inequalities* (O. Shisha, ed.). New York: Academic Press.

Michael, R. T. (1972) *The Effect of Education on Efficiency in Consumption*, National Bureau of Economic Research, Occasional Paper 116. New York: National Bureau of Economic Research.

Mitrinovíc, D. S. (1970) *Analytic Inequalities*. Berlin and New York: Springer-Verlag.

Muth, R. F. (1966) Household production and consumer demand functions. *Econometrica* 34: 699–708.

Owen, J. D. (1971) The demand for leisure. *Journal of Political Economy* 79: 56–76.

Polya, G. (1950) Remark on Weyl's note "Inequalities between the two kinds of eigenvalues of a linear transformation." *Proceedings of the National Academy of Science, U.S.A.* 36: 49–51.

Samuelson, P. A. (1947) *Foundations of economic analysis*. Cambridge, Massachusetts: Harvard Univ. Press.

Willis, R. (1973) A new approach to the economic theory of fertility behavior. *Journal of Political Economy Supplement* 81: S14–S64.

Are Men Rational or Economists Wrong?

TIBOR SCITOVSKY
STANFORD UNIVERSITY

Economics, having originated in the age of reason, has adopted the rationality of man as one of its basic postulates. Today, in the age of unreason, psychologists and psychoanalysts have gained a lot of understanding of the dark, irrational forces that motivate men; but while the general public has readily accepted their interpretation of human motivation, the economist—perhaps alone among social scientists—still clings to the assumption of human rationality. His reasons for this are understandable enough. The assumption of human rationality is a powerful simplification of the economist's model of reality; and this is not the first, nor the last time that economists sacrifice realism for simplicity. Moreover, economists can proudly point to seeming confirmations of their rationality hypothesis. Many implications of several of the economist's theories of individual behavior are based on this hypothesis; and every time empirical data fail to contradict it, the economist's belief in human rationality is understandably strengthened, whatever psychoanalysts may say to the contrary.

Yet there is a flaw in this logic, if it is true, as it seems to be, that man is neither wholly rational nor wholly irrational. From the proven rationality of a

223

limited aspect of his behavior one cannot deduce that he is rational in everything—just as one cannot generalize from the manifest irrationality of some
of his behavior characteristics either. The insane are so regarded, because a
part of their behavior is irrational to the degree of creating a serious conflict
between what they need or want and what they seem to seek or be asking
for—yet, the mad behavior and reasoning of a madman is often impeccably
logical and maddeningly rational, almost as if to compensate for the irrationality of the one fatal flaw in his mental makeup. This alone should be a warning
against regarding man's rational behavior in one respect as proof of anything
beyond his rational behavior in that particular respect.

Having sounded a warning against a too easy assumption of man's rationality, one may well ask if economists have ever come across proof of man's
irrationality. Not surprisingly, perhaps, economists are human. They sometimes do and sometimes do not find what they are looking for; but very seldom
do they find what they are *not* looking for.[1] Their faith in man's rationality
is almost absolute: Perhaps the only generally accepted exception to it is a
minor one, known as the money illusion.[2]

1. Money Illusion

A person is said to be suffering from money illusion if his market behavior
remains unaffected when rising prices reduce the real purchasing power of
his unchanged money income and money wealth, or if, seeking more income,
he is content with more *money* income although a simultaneous rise in prices
keeps his *real* income unchanged. Economists consider such behavior
irrational—and it is (or would be) irrational in people who acquire money
solely for the purpose of spending it and value it solely for what it will buy.
These are indeed the people who inhabit the economist's world; but what
about those whose attitude toward money is different? Money is sought and
valued, not only for its purchasing power but also as a symbol of achievement,
of success, of society's appreciation of one's services; and this other function of
money does not quite fit into the economist's model of rationality.[3] Economists define man's preference function broadly enough to accommodate

[1] Sparked by Arrow's work (1951) on the social preference function, there were experiments to test the transitivity of individual preferences, which yielded some unexpected results;
these were, however, quickly forgotten.

[2] Professor Peter Temin reminded me that, however minor, this one exception to the
assumption of consumer rationality had become one of the cornerstones of the microfoundations of macroeconomics.

[3] Marx was well aware of this and made it an integral part of his theory of accumulation,
but it never found its way into bourgeois economics; my own attempt (Scitovsky, 1943) to
introduce it into the theory of the firm was a failure.

plenty of variety and aberrations in taste in everything except matters of money. As far as money is concerned, the budgetary constraint in the theory of the consumer's behavior seems to imply that the desire to hold money as anything other than a medium of exchange and a store of value is irrational—just as irrational as money illusion seems to be in those who hold money for these purposes only. Accordingly, we propose to extend the concept of money illusion to embrace all attitudes to money that must be considered irrational in the sense of being excluded from the economist's narrow definition of money rationality.

Unfortunately, the conflict between man's actual behavior and the economist's theory of his behavior, and with it the dividing line between rational and irrational behavior by the economist's standard, are often hard to find, because the economist's theory of rational behavior is far from complete. In this particular instance, the theory of consumer's choice and the theory of choice between work and leisure (and hence also between income and leisure) have been long and well established; but missing, until quite recently, was any connecting link between them, leaving unexplained the interdependence of the threefold choice that determines earning, spending, and saving. Modigliani was the first to fill the gap and provide the missing link with his theory of the consumption function based on the life-cycle hypothesis.[4] Not only was this the first theory of rational choice between spending and saving; but it extended the economist's theory of human rationality and so rendered explicit and empirically testable the implications of the assumption of rationality in a crucially important area.

Modigliani's theory visualizes people as making a deliberate choice between spending and saving, wishing to save just enough to provide for contingencies and their old age, and to some extent also to leave something to their surviving children and relatives. His model assumes away this last, to him lesser, motive; and its failure to fit the statistical facts better than it does he attributes to the desire of many also to leave an inheritance. It is not irrational, of course, to accumulate a fortune to leave behind, provided one has someone to leave it to and wishes to leave it to him or her. Unfortunately, Modigliani had no interest in ascertaining the extent to which this condition of rationality is fulfilled—after all, he was concerned with establishing the microfoundations of the aggregate consumption function and could, for this purpose, concentrate on central tendencies and neglect minor eccentricities and deviant behavior. The question is whether these really are negligible.

It seems plausible that there should be other reasons for saving beyond the rational ones advanced by Modigliani. For one thing, some people have a desire to accumulate a fortune for its own sake, with never a thought, or even

[4] The best published statement perhaps is by Ando and Modigliani (1963).

a horrified rejection of the thought, of ever spending it. The miser has been much discussed in literature, from Plautus to Molière and beyond, and his behavior was usually regarded as a mild (though far from innocuous) form of insanity until the Protestant ethic and the rise of capitalism placed the stamp of respectability on saving for its own sake. Today, to make money just for the heck of it and greatly in excess of one's spending habits has become not only respectable but respected, and society has fully adjusted its notions of normal psychology and rational man to accommodate such behavior. It is something of a paradox that, of all people, the economist alone should have failed to make room in his world for the likes of Anselm Rothschild and John D. Rockefeller.

For another thing, saving is often the unintended result of separate and uncoordinated decisions to earn money and to spend it. When a person is better at spending than at earning money, the tightness of the market for consumer credit soon forces upon him a more rational division of his energies between the two occupations; the reverse disparity between the two, however, though no more rational, generates no inducement to make one mend one's ways. On the contrary, our society puts strong pressures on the individual to make him concentrate on production to the neglect of consumption; this often gives rise to savings in excess of what Modigliani's rational motives would account for. Money is power over so many things that most of us unquestioningly assume its general usefulness while we are busy making it, without ever pausing to ask if an increment of earnings will really be useful to us or our families. This may well be the main reason if savings are, indeed, beyond what is rational.

Modigliani's life-cycle hypothesis makes no allowance for people's inability to predict their day of death and consequent tendency to play safe by overestimating their life expectancy; this explains why many people leave more inheritance than they wish to bequeath to their loved ones. This would account for at least part of the $1.5 billion philanthropic bequests, the $0.5 billion bequests left to federal, state, and municipal governments; and those unknown amounts left by people who die intestate without known relatives.[5] It does not explain, however, philanthropic contributions individuals make during their lifetime, which in 1970 amounted to $14.3 billion, more than a quarter as large as personal savings at $50.2 billion. There is nothing irrational, of course, in philanthropy, but the public is not likely to have deliberately decided to make the extra effort to earn the extra $14.3 billion just in order to make them available to philanthropy—except perhaps for the $2–$2.5 billion they contribute to church collections, United Fund campaigns (which grossed

---

[5] The firms that specialize in tracking down their unknown and long-forgotten relatives for a share (usually a third) of the spoils form quite a large industry.

$800 million), and the like. As concerns the remaining $12 billion, it is likely that people made their earning decisions first; and only afterward, on finding themselves with more accumulated savings than they needed and wanted for their own and their families' use, did they decide to contribute to philanthropy.[6] To propose this argument is not to deprecate the generosity of the American public; although it is to deny that economic rationality, as commonly interpreted in the marginalist neoclassical tradition, is the governing principle of what may be the most important area of economic choice. The part of income given away to charity is far too large, both absolutely and in relation to personal saving, to be dismissed as exceptional or deviant behavior. At the same time, it is by no means the only sign of our tendency to make more money than we know how to spend or what to save for. Money can be squandered as well as given away; and this, while difficult to quantify, is easy enough to illustrate. The billboards and daily press announcements in which Mr. O. L. Nelms thanks people in and around Dallas for having helped him make another million are as good an illustration as any, and not too extreme by Texas standards.[7] Nor is it necessary to go to Texas for examples. The rich are generally believed to spend more carelessly than the poor, and the lesser attention they devote to minimizing the money cost of their desired level of consumption is considered an integral part of their high standard of living. Not having to pinch pennies is a good in itself. Economists rationalize this by saying that the rich are better off in terms of money than in terms of time, so that it is rational for them to spend money on saving time. This is what carefree spending accomplishes. The crucial question is whether they really are short of time and in need of saving it. We shall argue that this is not so.

2. Time Illusion

A close parallel to the desire for money for its own sake and without reference to how and when it will be spent is the desire for leisure time, without reference to how it will be enjoyed. Just as money is general purchasing power over whatever one wants to possess, so leisure is general command over time to spend in whatever way one wishes. Just as the many possible ways of spending money make it seem worth having before one has decided how to spend it, so the many uses of time make leisure seem desirable before one knows what

---

[6] All the data in this paragraph refer to 1970 and come from the 1971 *Statistical Abstract of the United States*, except for the estimate of bequests to government, which comes from publications of the Internal Revenue Service.

[7] These announcements, continued over the past 20 years, are not advertisements, because they do not state Mr. Nelms's form of business. (In any case, this is real estate speculation.)

to do with it. The important difference between money and time is that, while money not spent today can be saved up for tomorrow, time saved today on one thing must be spent today on another thing or be lost forever. One can postpone the spending of money day after day and continue until death to believe that there is yet time to make use of it; no such self-deception is possible with the budgeting of time. If one saves more time than one knows how to spend agreeably or usefully, one is bound to be reminded daily of one's irrationality. One would expect therefore less illusion to prevail in the budgeting of time than in the budgeting of money.

Here again, the implications of economic rationality in the allocation of time have only recently been made explicit in a formal and rigorous theory of the subject.[8] It appears that the higher the productivity and hence the value of a person's labor, the higher his income and the higher the price to him of leisure; and since the former will raise, and the latter lower, his demand for leisure, this may, on balance, move either way. Most people seem, with rising incomes, to free more of their time for leisure, but the proportionate increase in their leisure is usually less than the proportionate increase in their spendable income. It would be rational, therefore, for them to change their consumption activities so as to make them less time-intensive and more goods-intensive. In other words, faced with a rising cost of time relatively to the cost of goods, the rational person ought to consume more goods per hour of consumption, just as he produces more goods per hour of work. This is the economist's expectation, based on his faith in human rationality; how does it compare to man's actual behavior?

The 1934 and 1965–1966 questionnaire surveys of household time budgets are not fully comparable, but one's confidence in the trend they show is strengthened by its similarity to the difference the 1965–1966 international comparison shows between the high-income United States and the low-income European countries.[9] There has been a great reduction in the time spent in preparing and consuming meals, a reduction in time spent on public entertainment, active sports, in reading, club activity, walking for pleasure, and listening to the radio; and most of the time so saved was spent on watching television, shopping, and running errands. All of these changes are matched by a corresponding and very similar difference between the time budgets of Europeans and Americans.

There need be nothing irrational, of course, about such an allocation (or reallocation) of time; still there are other, independent indications that there is. For one thing, the increase in the time spent in shopping probably has much to do with the introduction of the supermarket and other self-

[8] Cf. Becker (1965), and Linder (1970).
[9] Cf. Lundberg *et al.* (1934, 1966).

service-type retail distributors. The rising price of labor has prompted retailers to save on costs by making the customer perform much of the work clerks used to do and making him wait in line at the check-out desk rather than having more clerks wait on him. Part of the resulting savings are passed on to the customer, who—to judge by the popularity of these stores—seems quite willing to spend the additional time if he can thereby save money. Indeed, the thing is so popular that even manufacturers can save on the cost of final assembly by letting the customer do the assembling of certain toys, furniture, hi-fi equipment, etc. Closely related to this is the great success and large sales of do-it-yourself equipment and materials. Time budget studies are not detailed enough to show, as a separate category, the time spent on do-it-yourself activities; if they were, they would almost certainly show an increase.

There is something of a paradox here. We know that the rise in labor productivity, or rather the technical and economic progress which results in a rise in labor productivity, causes earnings to rise faster than prices, and the price of time to rise faster than the purchasing power of income and the price of goods. This was the reason why it seemed rational for people to become (and for the rich to be) more careless in shopping, thereby spending money to save time. How can there be a simultaneous tendency of spending time to save money? Also, can sellers respond to rising wages by shifting onto customers' shoulders some of the work previously done by their employees if, as seems likely, the cost of customers' time is also rising, and presumably rising just as fast as their employees' wages?

There would be no paradox if the people who spent money to save time and those who spent time to save money belonged to different income groups, and if the average customer's earnings rose more slowly than the average employee's, owing to the rise in the standard of living causing the customers for each commodity to be recruited from an ever-larger segment of the population, thus including an ever-increasing proportion of the lower income groups. But this explanation, however logical, is at best a partial one. The serve-yourself and do-it-yourself movement cuts across all income groups— one of its more absurd and inefficient manifestations, mothers (instead of the school bus) driving children to and from school, is concentrated in upper-middle-class suburbs. Also, the argument concerning the lesser rise in customers' than in employees' valuation of time hardly applies to necessities, whose market already includes the bulk of the population; yet it is precisely in the realm of necessities, such as the basic foods and the more essential articles of clothing, that self-service distribution is making the greatest headway.

It seems therefore that the paradox must be accepted and explained by irrationality in the way people budget their time—the more so, because this is not the only paradox that needs explaining. It is not unreasonable that time spent in shopping or painting one's own house or apartment should seem less burdensome than the same amount of time spent in the routine of factory or office work; surprising is only that such a difference in people's evaluation of the two activities should be increasing at the very time when the workweek is getting shorter, presumably rendering the tedium of work lesser too. A tentative explanation is that higher earnings create a feeling that time is getting more precious, and that this feeling in turn causes people to save more time than they know how to spend. If this is so, it will manifest itself in people's hurrying through some activities only to be left with more than enough time to waste on others. The question is where and how the dividing line between the two kinds of activities is drawn. One would expect deliberate decisions, structured and planned activities to economize time, residual activities to squander it; the conscious valuation of time to be high, its unconscious or implied valuation to be low; and one would also expect a lavish expenditure of time on activities that provide a tradeoff. There is evidence to confirm all these expectations.

The 2.1 hours the average adult American watches television on an average day[10] is the obvious and main example of such a residual activity—and not only because it comes at the end of the day. People might, of course, value the one hundred and twenty-sixth minute of the day's TV viewing as highly as they value the sixty-sixth minute spent over meals or the eighteenth minute of public entertainment; but this supposition, implied by the rationality hypothesis, is hard to reconcile with the public's rejection of pay television. If people's enjoyment of television were really great enough to make them cut down for its sake on income earned by work and time spent over meals, at sports, and a variety of other amusements, then they ought, one should think, be equally anxious to reduce or eliminate the many interruptions of television programs, which now take up 10 minutes of each hour of television. Some people grow eloquent in complaining how these interruptions not only waste time but break up the thread of the program's story or argument; yet the general public has clearly revealed the very low nuisance value it attributes to them.

The Hartford experiment with subscription television clearly shows this. The programs, while no more highbrow than commercial television, with movies constituting 86.5 and sports another 4.5% of the total, were better in the sense that the films were newer and the sports events more important. Their average hourly cost was $0.59, so that even if one valued the advantage of better programs at zero, the cost of avoiding interruptions would still be only $0.6 per minute or $3.50 per hour and below the average subscriber's

---

[10] Averaged over weekdays *and* weekends, and including TV watching engaged in simultaneously with other activities.

rate of earnings and marginal valuation of time.[11] Yet, a 2-year promotional drive persuaded less than 1% of all viewers to subscribe, and those who did watched subscription programs only 5.5% of their viewing time, mostly for the sake of especially attractive programs and seldom if ever to avoid interruptions.[12] The fact that the proportion (and absolute number) of high-income subscribers declined and of low-income subscribers rose substantially throughout the experiment is another indication that to utilize television time better was *not* an important aim of subscribers.[13]

These findings are confirmed by various sociological questionnaire studies of television viewers. According to one of these, of the people watching television, 24% "occasionally feel like doing something else," another 12.5% "often" feel that way, and a further 6.5% "almost always" have that feeling. Yet, all of them continue watching![14] Other studies, while phrasing their questions differently, found much the same attitude [cf. Steiner (1963)].

All this is hard to fit into a theory of rational time allocation, which would have people respond to the ever-rising value of time by its more effective use through crowding more goods or more action into each hour of consumption time. American television habits look much more like the relaxed, lazy attitude of people with plenty of time on their hands, or their attitude to residual time, left over when the day's hustle and bustle is done, to be spent or wasted, wisely or foolishly, but without the deliberate planning, choosing, and decision-making economists associate with rational behavior.

Differences in people's valuation of different bits of their time point in much the same direction. Econometric studies of passenger transportation show that commuters value the time they spend in commuting at something between one-fifth and one-half of their wage rate, typically around one-quarter [cf. Beesley (1965), Lisco (1967), Quarmby (1967), Stopher (1969), Traffic Research Corporation (1965)]. This is surprising, because one would not expect people to regard commuting as significantly more pleasant (or less unpleasant) than work, except conceivably on the margin, as a result of a steep rise in the marginal disutility of work at the end of a long workday. However, we have statistical evidence that our present 40- to 42-hour workweek is well within the range of constant marginal productivity, which is *prima facie* evidence that it is also within the range where the marginal disutility of work is also fairly constant [cf. Owen (1970)]. In addition, the wage rate is a good measure of the average worker's valuation of the marginal

[11] Cf. United States Congress. House of Representatives (1967).

[12] This is evident from audience ratings.

[13] Time being more precious to high-income earners, one would expect them to be more willing to spend money on avoiding interruptions.

[14] These data have been obtained for, but not published, in this form by Wilensky (1964). I am indebted to Professor Wilensky for making available these percentages.

disutility of his work if the length of the working week is, as most labor economists believe it to be, just about as long as he wants it.[15] Hence, with the
wage rate a faithful reflection of the average person's valuation of the marginal
disutility of labor, and the latter's marginal disutility not very different from
its average disutility, the so much lower value people attribute to time spent
in commuting is very hard to explain in terms of the narrow rationality the
economist attributes to man.

Becker (1965, p. 510, footnote 5), one of those to estimate empirically
people's implied valuation of their commuting time and the first to formulate a
rigorous theory of rational time allocation, was clearly puzzled by his finding
that people value commuting time at a mere 40% of their wage rate; and he
hesitated whether to attribute this to errors in assumptions or "to severe
kinks in supply and demand functions for hours of work." Now that at least
five other estimates, derived by different people from different data and in
different ways, show much the same result, it is much harder to escape the
conclusion that perhaps the assumption of human rationality is at fault.

For the data fit in very well with our tentative explanation that people
overdo the saving of time under the social pressures of a society that puts a
high premium on minimizing costs and saving resources irrespective of
whether alternative uses for the resources so saved are available. Is it not
plausible that these pressures should have the greatest impact on plans and
decisions that involve an explicit valuation of time, and a much lesser one on
those in which such valuation is merely implied by a choice between one
mode of transportation and another? A further and even more striking
confirmation is the finding of an air-travel study, according to which the
implied valuation of time spent by people in personal (as distinguished from
business) air travel was not significantly different from zero [cf. Gronau
(1970)]. Since long-distance air travel for personal reasons (e.g., vacations) is
bound mostly to occur in what we called residual time, this is very much what
we would expect. However, this being the only study of long-distance travel
so far in which personal and business trips were separated, too much significance should not be attached to its finding.[16]

Coming now to time lavishly spent on activities with a tradeoff, we are
back at the paradox we started with on p. 229 above. If it is true that the public
is caught between its desire to save time and its inability to make good use of
the time so saved, then any activity that can save money must appear as a

---

[15] According to labor economists, there would be much greater disparity between rates
of absenteeism and rates of moonlighting if the representative worker were not fairly well
satisfied with the length of the workweek.

[16] In another study, Institute of Defense Analyses (1966), it was assumed but not tested
that there is no difference between business and personal travelers with respect to their
valuation of travel time.

resolution of the dilemma. If a person has more than he can rationally spend of both money and time, then devoting each to an activity that saves the other becomes an excuse for a more relaxed budgeting of both than he would dare to engage in without excuse. Moreover, the saving of time or money is not the only excuse for spending the other; to save effort may be yet another reason for spending time, or money, or both—a legitimate reason if effort were in short supply, merely another excuse if the budgeting of effort turns out to be at all similar to the budgeting of time.

3. Effort Illusion

To economize human skill and physical effort is the principal aim of all technical and economic progress. Most innovations of methods of production reduce the skill and effort needed in work; invention and improvement of the final products themselves diminish the skill and effort required in house-holding and living in general. These being known as the main aims and achievements of economic development, most people gladly and unquestioningly accept and use whatever private and public amenities, vehicles, appliances, and goods become available for easing and simplifying their lives. This is only natural in a world at whose creation man was condemned to gain his bread by the sweat of his brow. The question arises, however, whether to ease the effort and skill requirements of life remains desirable indefinitely, however much they have been eased already; and, should the answer be no, whether the critical point of optimal effort reduction has not been reached and passed already.

Every organism has innate energies and capacities, the exercise of which seems to give it satisfaction. Experiments with animals have shown that even in captivity they try, if at all possible, to engage in about the same amount of physical activity as they would in their natural habitat: smaller animals by running in activity wheels; larger ones by pacing or moving around in their cages. Children also manifest a spontaneous desire to expend muscular energy and develop and exercise their bodily and mental skills. In adult man, these natural tastes seem, in some societies, to be suppressed by cultural influences—presumably his belief or the belief of society around him in ease and comfort as the supreme aim in life.

Where this is so—and there is plenty of evidence that in the United States it is so[17]—the question arises whether to accept these acquired tastes as rational or whether to regard them as a subversion of man's natural tastes, which impedes rational choice. The basis for the latter view is the well-established fact that the exercise of one's senses, faculties, and muscles is

[17] Cf. Scitovsky (1972) for a small sample of the evidence.

essential for the health of one's limbs and organs, and that the prevalence of obesity and premature heart disease in the United States population has mainly to do with lack of physical exercise. This is why millions of middle-aged, middle-class Americans, following doctors' orders, ride exercycles in their bathrooms or jog around the block in the evenings trying to spend the muscular energy they so carefully saved during the rest of the day. Such uneven budgeting of effort is strongly reminiscent of the uneven budgeting of time discussed earlier; and we question its rationality, because people seem to take exercycle rides as bitter medicine, and not for fun.[18] It is true that people choose this behavior pattern out of their own free will; but to accept this as proof of rational behavior is to ignore its genesis. We first learn to appreciate the saving of effort, the wonderful technology that makes it possible, and the social status it imparts; only many years later, when we are fully addicted to it as a way of life, do we realize its drawbacks; and by then, remedial therapy is often the only recourse left.

The static nature of the economist's theory of human rationality explains its inability to deal with this particular problem, the problem of habit formation and its implications; yet this is not its only shortcoming.[19] We tried to point up some others as well, hoping to hasten the infusion of a little empirical content into the economic theory of man and his behavior.

REFERENCES

Ando, A., and Modigliani, F. (1963)   The life-cycle hypothesis of saving: Aggregate implications and tests. *American Economic Review* **53**: 55–84.

Arrow, K. (1951)   *Social choice and individual values.* New York: Wiley.

Becker, G. S. (1965)   A theory of the allocation of time. *Economic Journal* **75**: 493–517.

Beesley, M. E. (1965)   The value of time spent in travelling. *Economica* **32**: 174–185.

Gronau, R. (1970)   The value of time in passenger transportation. Occasional Paper No. 109, pp. 52–53. New York: National Bureau of Economic Research.

Institute of Defense Analyses (1966)   Demand analysis for air travel by supersonic transport, Washington, D. C., 7 ff.

Linder, S. B. (1970)   *The harried leisure class.* New York: Columbia Univ. Press.

Lisco, T. E. (1967)   The value of commuters' travel time: A study in urban transportation. Ph.D. dissertation, Chicago, unpublished.

Lundberg, G., Komarovski, M., and McInerny, M. (1934)   *Leisure: A suburban study.* New York: Columbia Univ. Press.

Lundberg, G., Komarovski, M., and McInerny, M. (1966)   Recherche comparative internationale sur les budgets temps. *I.N.S.E.E. Etudes et Conjonctures* Sept. 1966: 103–188.

[18] Note the development of motorized exercycles. What once was a wishdream—the effortless exerciser—has become a marketable and widely marketed product. Has it ceased to be a wishdream?

[19] Cf. von Weizsäcker (1971) for an interesting theoretical attempt at a dynamic theory of consumers' preferences.

Owen, J. D. (1970) *The price of leisure, an economic analysis of the demand for leisure time,* pp. 32–33. Montreal: McGill Univ. Press.

Quarmby, D. A. (1967) Choice of travel mode for the journey to work: Some findings. *Journal of Transportation Economics and Policy* **1**: 273–314.

Scitovsky, T. (1943) A note on profit maximization and its implications. *Review of Economic Studies* **11**: 57–60.

Scitovsky, T. (1972) What's wrong with the arts is what's wrong with society. *American Economic Review* **62**. Papers and Proceedings.

Steiner, E. A. (1963) *The people look at television,* Chap. 3.

Stopher, R. R. (1969) A probability model of travel mode choice for the work journey. *Highway Research Record* No. 283, pp. 57–65.

Traffic Research Corporation (1965) Model split analysis: Metropolitan Toronto and region transportation study. Toronto: Traffic Research Corporation.

United States Congress, House of Representatives (1967) Subscription television—especially Joint comments of Zenith Radio Corporation, and Teco, Inc. *Hearing before Committee on Interstate and Foreign Commerce, Subcommittee on Communications and Power, 90th Congress, 1st Session, 1967.* Washington, D. C.

von Weizsäcker, C. C. (1971) Notes on endogenous change of tastes. *Journal of Economic Theory* **3**: 345–372.

Wilensky, H. L. (1964) Mass society and mass culture: Interdependence or independence? *American Sociological Review* **29**: 173–197.

Part II

Macroeconomic Performance: Growth and Stability

Demand, Structural Change, and the Process of Economic Growth

RUSSELL J. CHEETHAM
INTERNATIONAL BANK FOR RECONSTRUCTION AND DEVELOPMENT

ALLEN C. KELLEY
DUKE UNIVERSITY

JEFFREY G. WILLIAMSON
UNIVERSITY OF WISCONSIN

1. Introduction

Economists have long emphasized the role of consumption demand in industrial revolutions and its importance to growth and structural change, but theoretical analysis of this role has been limited. There appear to be two conflicting views concerning the nature and extent of its influence. Challenges to the prime role of demand have developed on two fronts. First, empirical studies have concluded that supply factors occupy the central role in explaining industrial patterns, since changes in relative factor supplies associated with growth cause systematic shifts in comparative advantage as per-capita income rises (Chenery, 1960). Second, many of the theoretical formulations of the growth process have suppressed or omitted a consideration of the role of consumption demand, focusing almost exclusively on supply conditions. In the literature dealing with two-sector growth models, for example, the approaches range from those which are not designed to confront issues of demand, since only one consumption goods sector is postulated (Uzawa, 1961, 1963), to those in which demand influences are suppressed through simplifying assumptions (Jorgenson, 1961).

Support for the view that consumption demand plays an important role in the process of growth and structural change has come mainly from empirical studies establishing the existence of different expenditure and income elasticities for food and nonfood goods. It has been argued that Engel effects not only cause a shift in the industrial origin of production, but also induce high levels of productivity and output (Houthakker, 1960a, b; Kuznets, 1966; Kelley, 1969). There have, however, been few attempts to explore in a theoretical way the influence of Engel effects within a model designed to investigate the relationship between growth and structural change over extended periods of time. The role of consumption demand and the existence of different income elasticities has, of course, been explicitly recognized in those models constructed within an input–output framework. However, with few exceptions, these applications have been confined to problems relating to relatively short-run analyses. The role of consumption demand has also been recognized explicitly in the neo-Keynesian literature, but in these models the focus of the inquiry has centered on growth and stability in the short run rather than on the long-run effects of changes in consumption behavior. Moreover, the level of aggregation in these models frequently is such that there is little scope for changes in the composition of consumption to influence the pattern of growth and structural change. Not only has the theoretical literature given comparatively little attention to the role of Engel effects, but also there has been almost no attention given to the role of consumer tastes, despite a growing amount of empirical evidence suggesting that secular changes in consumer tastes have been a part of the process of structural change in many of the present-day higher income economies.

The role of demand as well as supply factors in explaining growth and structural change can only be successfully appraised in a model in which both elements possess meaningful specifications. Moreover, the complexity of the interaction between supply and demand forces in both factor and commodity markets is such that an appraisal can only be effectively undertaken within a general equilibrium framework in which prices are determined endogenously. In the present paper we construct a simple two-sector model within such a framework, and using both comparative static and dynamic analysis, we explore the influence of demand on growth and structural change. Because of the difficulty in obtaining unambiguous results from the qualitative analysis of the dynamic system, we employ numerical analysis (drawing upon the experience of Southeast Asian countries to establish parameter values and initial conditions) in order to expand our insights into the role of demand in the process of change. Our interest in structural change is confined to changes in the level and rate of industrialization and urbanization and in the composition of consumption expenditures.

Given its neoclassical framework, our model is within the mainstream of the growth and development literature. By recognizing the presence of dualism in the production, consumption, and demographic characteristics of a growing economy, we simultaneously generalize and extend Dale Jorgenson's pioneering work on the notion of a dual economy (Jorgenson, 1961). The most important generalizations are (1) to remove Jorgenson's assumption of zero income and price elasticities of demand for food by developing consumer demand functions based upon the Stone–Geary linear expenditure system; (2) to allow for different consumer tastes and rates of population growth between rural and urban sectors; and (3) to allow for different elasticities of factor substitution in agriculture and manufacturing and thus for biases in rates of technical change. An important extension of Jorgenson's framework is to incorporate capital in the agricultural production function, thereby permitting farmers to utilize modern forms of capital in production and reintroducing a key policy decision in development: investment in industry or agriculture?

Three major conclusions are forthcoming from our study. First, we find that the existence of Engel effects is neither a necessary nor a sufficient condition for industrialization to occur in our simple model. Engel effects, together with the tendency for demand elasticities to converge toward one as development takes place, will *always* be forthcoming from the simple model for *any* theoretically possible set of demand parameters. Second, we find that when we modify the simple model to allow consumption from both wage and rental income, the existence of Engel effects is a sufficient condition to ensure an increase in the level of industrialization when the efficiency capital–labor ratio is rising. This result leads us to conclude that at least in the context of dualistic two-sector models, the extreme assumption of consumption only from wage income can result in a rather misleading interpretation of the role of demand elasticities. Finally, demand *does* play a pervasive and important role in the model through changes in consumer tastes. Indeed, in a simulation experiment we find that the sensitivity of the economy to shifts in tastes toward urban goods may be as stimulatory to structural change in the long run as alterations in savings parameters, the variable of traditional focus in the development literature. Thus the "demonstration effect," commonly a villain in descriptive analyses of growth and development, may turn out to be as much a hero as the touted puritan ethic regarding high savings and spending prudence.

2. A Formal Model of Dualistic Development

a. The Concept of Dualism

The literature on dualism can be divided into two streams. The first utilizes partial equilibrium analysis to explore the implications of sectoral differences in social, political, and economic behavior. The second formalizes specific dualistic properties in a general equilibrium framework and focuses on sectoral production conditions. These models typically obtain well-defined predictions about the course of growth and structural change (Jorgenson, 1961; Fei and Ranis, 1964). Our approach, while in the latter tradition, makes three major departures from the usual formal treatment of dualism.

First, we view dualism as being multidimensional; different sectoral characteristics are found in production, in consumption, and in demographic behavior. Even though the traditional treatment, which emphasized dualistic production conditions, represents a significant advance in theorizing about economic development, the specification of additional empirically relevant features of economic dualism logically constitutes the next theoretical advance. Second, in our model land is not incorporated as an input to the production process, while capital and labor are arguments in both sectoral production functions. This is in contrast to the approach of Fei–Ranis and Jorgenson where dualism in production is introduced solely by varying the arguments of the sectoral production functions. Like other models, ours is not comprehensive but rather highlights certain aspects of development. However, we believe our treatment of agricultural production possesses several advantages. It introduces a key allocation decision in the development process: the choice between industrial and agricultural investment. It also recognizes the increasing importance of purchased inputs to the agricultural sector as development proceeds. Third, by assuming that the sectoral production conditions are geographic-specific (urban and rural), a spatial dimension is added to the concept of dualism. Alterations of the economy's structure thus hinge critically on differences in rural–urban behavior (demand and family size preferences), parameters in production, and on the intersectoral movements of both labor and capital.

b. Production Conditions

We consider a closed economy consisting of an agricultural and an industrial sector. The output of the agricultural sector can be used only as a consumption good, whereas industrial output may be consumed, invested, or both. The latter assumption distinguishes our model from those developed by Uzawa and others where it is assumed that the economy consists of a capital-goods and a consumption-goods sector. The production process in each sector is described by a continuous, twice-differentiable, single-valued function, subject to constant returns to scale and diminishing marginal rates of substitution. Factor-augmenting technical change applies to both capital and labor. Denoting "sector 1" as industry and "sector 2" as agriculture, we specify

$$Q_i(t) = F^i[x(t)K_i(t), y(t)L_i(t)] \qquad (i = 1, 2), \qquad (1)$$

where $Q_i(t)$ is the quantity of the ith good currently produced; $K_i(t) > 0$ and $L_i(t) > 0$ are, respectively, the amounts of capital and labor currently employed in the ith sector; and $x(t) > 0$ and $y(t) > 0$ are the technical progress variables. We further assume that $x(t)$ and $y(t)$ grow at exogenously given rates, λ_K and λ_L, and that the factor-specific rate of augmentation is the same in each sector.

$$x(t) = x(0) \exp(\lambda_K t), \qquad (2)$$

$$y(t) = y(0) \exp(\lambda_L t). \qquad (3)$$

Hereafter, we refer to $x(t)K_i(t)$ as "efficiency capital" and $y(t)L_i(t)$ as "efficiency labor." Full employment is assumed throughout the analysis.

The choice of continuous production functions eliminates the possibility of "technological dualism" as defined by Eckaus (1955). However, we impose an alternative restriction consistent with his view: *Dualism in production* is captured by substitution possibilities being more limited in industry. In particular, $0 < \sigma_1 < 1 \leqslant \sigma_2 < \infty$ where σ_i is the elasticity of factor substitution in the ith sector.

Given the assumption of factor-augmenting technical progress, it is necessary to specify more precisely the nature of changes in factor efficiency. Following Fei and Ranis (1964), the output-raising effect or intensity of technical change, $R_i(t)$, is measured holding inputs constant. The factor-saving bias, $B_i(t)$, traces the output-raising effect to specific inputs. For any given capital–labor ratio, technical progress is laborsaving in the Hicksian sense if $B_i(t) > 0$, Hicks-neutral if $B_i(t) = 0$, and capital-saving if $B_i(t) < 0$. It is well known that the nature of the bias in the ith sector depends on the difference between rates of factor augmentation and on the magnitude of σ_i:

$$B_i(t) = \frac{(\lambda_L - \lambda_K)(1 - \sigma_i)}{\sigma_i}.$$

Assuming that technical progress in industry is laborsaving while in agriculture it is capital-cum-land-saving, and given the restrictions already imposed on σ_i, it follows that $(\lambda_K - \lambda_L) < 0$. This specification is consistent with the theoretical formulations of Leibenstein (1960) and the evidence on the Philippines supplied by Williamson (1969). It also implies that the *intensity* of technical progress, $R_i(t)$, is greater in agriculture, a result perhaps consistent with contemporary qualitative evidence regarding the "Green

Revolution" now taking place throughout Asia. That is, the intensity of technological change measures the output-raising effects given a fixed factor input mix:

$$R_i(t) = \frac{F_K^i x(t) K_i(t)}{Q_i(t)} \frac{\dot{x}(t)}{x(t)} + \frac{F_L^i y(t) L_i(t)}{Q_i(t)} \frac{\dot{y}(t)}{y(t)}.$$

Amano (1964), and Fei and Ranis (1964) have shown that

$$R_i(t) = \lambda_K \alpha_i(t) + \lambda_L [1 - \alpha_i(t)]$$

where $\alpha_i(t)$ is the current elasticity of output with respect to capital. If the output elasticity of capital is greater in industry, then it follows that the intensity of technical progress is greater in agriculture.

Models stressing the source of income as the determinant of savings are common to development theory and consistent with the results of empirical and historical analysis (Kelley and Williamson, 1968; Williamson, 1968). Accordingly, we assume *initially* that the only source of savings is property income and that all property income is saved, so that investment demand is given by

$$I(t) = [x(t)/P(t)] [r_1(t) K_1(t) + r_2(t) K_2(t)], \tag{4}$$

where $P(t)$ is the price of industrial goods relative to agricultural goods, and $r_i(t)$ are the sectoral rental rates on efficiency capital. Current net investment is given by

$$\dot{K}(t) = I(t) - \delta K(t), \tag{5}$$

where δ is the fixed rate of replacement of capital goods.

Dualism in demographic behavior is introduced into the model by assuming that exogeneously given labor force growth is specific to the sector of residence. Based on widely documented empirical evidence, we assume that the rate of rural population growth exceeds that in urban areas. Defining $u(t) = L_1(t)/L(t)$ to be the current proportion of the total labor force resident in the urban sector, it follows that

$$\dot{L}(t) = \{n_1 u(t) + n_2 [1 - u(t)]\} L(t). \tag{6}$$

Urbanization therefore produces a decline in the total population growth rate.

We follow Jorgenson and invoke the neoclassical hypothesis that efficiency factors are paid their marginal value products. If $w_i(t)$ is defined as the current wage per unit of efficiency labor, factor demand can be stated as

$$w_1(t) = P(t) F_L^1, \tag{7}$$

$$w_2(t) = F_L^2, \tag{8}$$

$$r_1(t) = P(t) F_K^1, \tag{9}$$

$$r_2(t) = F_K^2. \tag{10}$$

We assume that there is perfect factor mobility in the economy so that wage and rental rates are always equated at $w(t)$ and $r(t)$, respectively.

c. The Linear-Expenditure Demand System

The prime purpose of this paper is to explore the impact of consumption demand on growth and structural change. This requires the introduction of a meaningful demand system into the above economy. Most recently, demand theory has focused on systems of equations which explain a complete set of commodities, and thus satisfy the "adding-up criterion." Three models have attained considerable popularity: Houthakker's (1960a, b) indirect addilog system, Stone's linear expenditure system, and a modified "Rotterdam" version of the double logarithmic system developed by Theil and Barten. We shall utilize the Stone–Geary system. There is considerable empirical support for this choice (Parks, 1969; Yoshihara, 1969). Building upon earlier work by Stone (1954), Parks introduces greater flexibility into the expenditure system by allowing the demand parameters to vary systematically with variables exogenous to the system: for example, the demand parameters are given a linear time trend. In his empirical analysis of Swedish consumption patterns (1861–1955), Parks found the linear-expenditure system superior to the competing models for the two commodity groups of special interest to the present study: agricultural and manufactured goods. The superiority of the linear-expenditure system is also revealed by Yoshihara when Japanese consumption behavior (1902–1960) is explored.

We assume that each laborer possesses a utility function of the Stone–Geary form (Stone, 1954; Stone and Brown, 1965). As Goldberger (1967) has pointed out, the Stone–Geary expenditure system aggregates perfectly over individuals in a group, given that each group member has the same utility function. The utility function for laborers in the jth sector is given by

$$U_j(t) = \sum_{i=1}^{2} \beta_{ij} \log\left[\frac{D_{ij}(t)}{L_j(t)} - \gamma_{ij}\right] \quad (j = 1, 2),$$

where $U_j(t)$ is the utility derived from the consumption by a member of the labor force in the jth sector and $D_{ij}(t)$ is the amount of the ith good consumed by the labor force in the jth sector. This formulation requires that $0 < \beta_{ij} < 1$ and $\sum_{i=1}^{2} \beta_{ij} = 1$ $(j = 1, 2)$. The parameters β_{ij} and γ_{ij} are, for the present, fixed over time. We adopt an interpretation provided by Goldberger (1967) for the parameters of this system. Given the sectoral wage income per capita and the price ratio, each member of the labor force first purchases the minimum required quantity of output, γ_i. This may be termed "subsistence income." He is left with $[y(t)w_j(t) - \gamma_{ij}]$, which may be called "supernumerary income"; this he distributes among the goods in the proportions

β_{ij}. Interpreting industrial output as being a nonessential consumer good, we assume $\gamma_{1j} = 0$ and $\gamma_{2j} = \gamma > 0$. The utility function makes no prediction about the behavior of a consumer for whom subsistence requirements exceed current income.[1]

Dualism in demand is captured by assuming that there is a difference in consumption behavior in the two sectors. Recent work by Kelley and Williamson [reported by Kelley *et al.* (1972b)] suggests that in the Philippine case consumption behavior in rural and urban areas is significantly different. Their study suggests a greater preference for urban goods among urban than among rural households; that is, $\beta_{11} - \beta_{21} > \beta_{12} - \beta_{22} > 0$. As with demographic and production dualism, we do not insist that demand dualism persist into very high states of industrialization and urbanization. On the contrary, Kaneda's (1948) research on Japan over the period 1878–1964 shows a gradual elimination of dualism in demand; nevertheless, sectoral differences in demand parameters persist during most of the first half-century of modern Japanese development. It turns out that the presence of dualism in demand is not crucial to any of the qualitative analysis which follows, but it does sharpen the relevance of the experiments with demand parameters performed below because its presence may be the *sine qua non* for changes in tastes.

Under the simplifying assumptions $\gamma_1 = 0$, $\gamma_2 = \gamma$, $P_2(t) = 1$, and $P_1(t) = P(t)$, the *demand* system in our two sector model becomes

$$D_{1j}(t)/L_j(t) = [\beta_{1j}/P(t)]\{y(t)w_j(t) - \gamma\} \qquad (i = 1, 2), \qquad (11)$$

$$D_{2j}(t)/L_j(t) = \beta_{2j}[y(t)w_j(t)] + [1 - \beta_{2j}]\gamma \qquad (i = 1, 2). \qquad (12)$$

d. A Formal Restatement of the Model

The static model is composed of 14 endogenous variables: $Q_i(t)$, $K_i(t)$, $L_i(t)$, $w(t)$, $r(t)$, $P(t)$, $D_{ij}(t)$, and $I(t)$, $(i, j = 1, 2)$; and 4 exogenous variables: $K(t) = \overline{K}$, $L(t) = \overline{L}$, $x(t) = \overline{x}$, and $y(t) = \overline{y}$. In addition to (1), (4), (7)–(12), we have the following market equilibrium equations:

$$\overline{K} = K_1(t) + K_2(t), \qquad (13)$$

$$\overline{L} = L_1(t) + L_2(t), \qquad (14)$$

$$Q_1(t) = D_{11}(t) + D_{12}(t) + I(t), \qquad (15)$$

$$Q_2(t) = D_{21}(t) + D_{22}(t). \qquad (16)$$

---

[1] Because of this restriction the model is not defined when the marginal productivity of labor is less than γ; that is, we require that $y(t)w(t) \geqslant \gamma$ for all t. For an analysis of the behavior of the model when the marginal productivity is not sufficient to satisfy the minimum consumption requirements, see Cheetham (1969).

Assuming that there is at least one positive equilibrium price that will satisfy the equilibrium conditions, then one of the two commodity market equations can be shown to be redundant (and thus ignored); we therefore have a static system of 14 equations and variables. Given the solution values to the static model, the time paths of $K(t)$, $L(t)$, $x(t)$, and $y(t)$ are described by (2), (3), (5), and (6).

For purposes of analyzing the properties of the economy, the system can be transformed into per-capita terms as follows:

$$q_i(t) \equiv Q_i(t)/y(t)L_i(t), \qquad u(t) \equiv L_1(t)/L(t),$$

$$\omega_i(t) \equiv w_i(t)/r_i(t), \qquad k_i(t) \equiv x(t)K_i(t)/y(t)L_i(t),$$

$$z_{ij}(t) \equiv D_{ij}(t)/L_i(t) \qquad \phi(t) \equiv I(t)/K(t).$$

A restatement of the static and dynamic models using these definitions is found in Appendix A. It will be convenient to denote the transformed version of the static model as a system of equations described by $\psi[X;k] = 0$, where X is the vector of endogenous variables whose values are to be determined for any given value of $k = \bar{k}$.[2]

3. The Role of Demand in the Dualistic Economy

a. Comparative Statics: Industrialization, Urbanization, and Changes in Consumer Tastes

We now explore the role of demand in influencing structural changes in the model presented above, where "structural change" refers to shifts in the observed sectoral distribution of output and inputs. At this point it is convenient to introduce several more definitions: The value of current output per laborer is given by $g(t) = G(t)/L(t)$, where $G(t) = P(t)Q_1(t) + Q_2(t)$.

---

[2] A detailed analysis of existence, uniqueness, and stability of the solution to the model has been reported elsewhere (Cheetham, 1969; Kelley et al., 1972b). It is sufficient here to point out that it is possible to define numbers a and b such that at least one solution to $\psi[X;k] = 0$ exists for all $k \in \{a, b\}$. Furthermore, it can be shown that the requirements $\sigma_2 \geqslant 1$ and $k_1 - k_2 > 0$ are sufficient to ensure that the solution to $\psi[X;k] = 0$ is uniquely determined and that the static equilibrium is stable.

Uzawa (1961) found that a sufficient condition for uniqueness and stability is that the consumption-goods (agricultural) sector be more capital-intensive than the capital-goods (industrial) sector. This assumption is somewhat artificial, at least when applied to low income economies. Drandakis (1963) has shown that a sufficient condition is that the elasticity of substitution of either of the production functions is equal to or greater than one. In our model, uniqueness is ensured when $k_1 - k_2 > 0$ and $\sigma_2 \geqslant 1$. Uniqueness is not necessarily ensured by either $k_2 - k_1 > 0$ or $\sigma_2 \geqslant 1$ individually.

Industry's share in national output is thus given by

$$v(t) = P(t)Q_1(t)/G(t).$$

Consider the question of changes in tastes (that is, changes in β_{ij} and γ). As already noted, recent empirical evidence reveals that the assumption of fixed tastes may be particularly inappropriate in a study of growth and structural change in which the time horizon of analysis may span decades. Moreover, it is well known that there is considerable pressure in developing nations to increase the minimum wage. In view of our interpretation of γ as a behaviorally determined minimum bundle of wage goods, upward pressure on the minimum wage can be reasonably translated into systematic increases in the demand parameter γ.

The impact of taste changes can be explored by considering the consequences of an increase in γ or β_{ij}. Since the subsequent analysis is invariant to the consumer's sector of residence, only the results for urban consumers are presented (β_{i1}). Moreover, the effects of changes in tastes for agricultural commodities (β_{2j}) are merely opposite in sign to those for urban goods (because $\beta_{1j} + \beta_{2j} = 1$). Thus, our analysis will focus primarily on changes in demand for urban goods.

TABLE 1

Results of Comparative Static Analysis

Demand changes	Key endogenous variables					Structural change variables						
	$d\omega$	dk_1	dk_2	dP	$d\phi$	dz_{11}	dz_{12}	dz_{21}	dz_{22}	dv	du	dg
$d\beta_{11} = -d\beta_{21}$	−	−	−	+	+	?	?	−	−	+	+	+
$d\gamma$	+	+	+	−	−	?	?	+	+	−	−	−

The results of the comparative static analysis are summarized in Table 1.[3] An increase in β_{1j} leads to a fall in the wage–rental ratio as a result of the adjustment to the excess demand for industrial goods in which capital is utilized more extensively than labor. Moreover, because of the increase in the relative cost of capital services, the relative price of industrial goods will be higher than previously. This result can be obtained by noting that while a decline in the wage–rental ratio will reduce the sectoral capital–labor ratios,

[3] The mathematical analysis supporting these results is found in the work of Kelley *et al.* (1972b, Chap. 3).

this reduction will be less in industry given the relative difficulty of factor substitution in this sector. Since the terms of trade depend on the marginal productivity of capital in industry relative to agriculture, the price of industrial goods will increase as a result of the increase in the demand parameter β_{1j}.

The effect of an increase in β_{1j} on the per-capita consumption of agricultural goods may be decomposed into two major influences: One is a decrease in the amount demanded through the "quantity" effect that results from the increase in β_{1j} and hence the allocation of a larger share of any given "supernumerary" income ($\bar{y}\omega f_2' - \gamma$) to industrial goods; the other is the "income" effect that occurs because wage income is lower in the new equilibrium position, and hence a smaller amount of agricultural output is consumed. This "income" effect reinforces the "quantity" effect of an increase in β_{1j} to yield an unambiguous decline in per-capita consumption of agricultural goods. However, the shift in consumer tastes toward urban goods results in an ambiguous change in per-capita *consumption* of industrial goods. The "quantity" effect through supernumerary income is, of course, positive; moreover, in the new equilibrium position the price of industrial goods relative to agricultural goods is higher, but it is not clear whether the combined influence of the "quantity" and "price" effects is sufficient to offset the above-mentioned "income" effect. Should this negative "income" effect be powerful enough, consumption of industrial goods may decline![4] The total demand for industrial goods is our focus, however. With the rise in the nonwage income share, the demand for investment goods rises as well ($d\phi/d\beta_{1j} > 0$). In fact, the capitalists' income elasticity of demand for investment goods in this simple model is assumed to be one while for agricultural goods the elasticity is assumed to be zero. What is the net effect on the value of industrial *output*?

It can be shown that for any given k, an increase in β_{1j} will always result in a higher value of aggregate output per capita in the economy.[5] An increase in the value of per-capita aggregate output, together with the decrease in the per-capita consumption of agricultural goods, therefore implies that the level of industrialization $v(t)$ is given a positive stimulus. Similarly, an increase in

[4] By differentiating z_{1j} with respect to β_{1j} and rearranging, we have

$$\frac{dz_{1j}}{d\beta_{1j}} = \frac{z_{1j}}{\beta_{1j}}\left[1 - \frac{\beta_{1j}}{P}\frac{\partial P}{\partial \beta_{1j}}\right] + \beta_{1j}\bar{y}\alpha_2\frac{f_2'(k_2)}{P}\frac{\partial \omega}{\partial \beta_{1j}}.$$

Now $\partial P/\partial \beta_{1j} > 0$, so when $(\partial P/\partial \beta_{1j})(\beta_{1j}/P) \leqslant 1$, it follows that $dz_{1j}/d\beta_{1j} > 0$.

[5] By differentiating g with respect to β_{1j} and rearranging, we obtain

$$\frac{dg}{d\beta_{1j}} = \frac{-\bar{y}\alpha_2 f_2'(k_2)[\bar{k}-k_2]}{k_2}\frac{\partial \omega}{\partial \beta_{1j}},$$

where α_2 is the elasticity of output with respect to changes in efficiency capital. When $[k_1 - k_2] > 0$, then $[\bar{k} - k_2] > 0$ and given $\partial \omega/\partial \beta_{1j} < 0$, it follows that $dg/d\beta_{1j} > 0$.

food subsistence requirements tends to raise per-capita consumption of agricultural goods and lower the value of aggregate output per capita.

Urbanization levels increase given the additional labor required to produce the newly demanded industrial goods. Even though the decrease in the wage–rental ratio will stimulate the substitution of labor for capital in both sectors, this substitution effect will never offset the initial positive impact on urban in-migration.

b. Dynamics: Changes in Tastes, "Engel Effects," and Growth in the Dualistic Economy

Thus far we have been successful in isolating the effect of changes in tastes on the levels of income per capita, urbanization, and industrialization in the static equilibrium case. The dynamic course of urbanization and industrialization, and the effects of changes in tastes on these time paths, is far more difficult to analyze.

Consider first the impact of shifts in tastes on the long-run behavior of urbanization. This relationship can be explored by combining the comparative static results in Table 1 with a dynamic specification of the long-run behavior of the capital–labor ratio in

$$\dot{k}(t)/k(t) = \phi(t) + [n_2 - n_1]u(t) - [\delta + n_2 + \lambda_L - \lambda_K]. \tag{17}$$

For example, an increase in the subsistence parameter γ results in an initial reduction both in $\phi(t)$ and the level of urbanization (see Table 1). Since the remaining elements in (17) are fixed, then the rate of change in the efficiency capital–labor ratio is initially reduced. Since the rate of change in the urbanization level decreases when the rate of change in the efficiency capital–labor ratio decreases (Kelley et al., 1972b, Chap. 3), it follows that the rate of urbanization, initially at least, would be retarded by the increase in γ. Similarly, a shift in tastes favoring urban goods will initially stimulate the rate of change in urbanization levels. The *ultimate* impact of a once-over change in γ or β_{ij} on the level of urbanization cannot be determined with certainty using qualitative analysis since, in general, $k(t)$ itself is capable of any one of a variety of time paths.[6]

Consider next the response of industrialization over time to shifts in demand. The rate of industrialization can generally be decomposed into price and quantity effects:

$$\frac{\dot{v}(t)}{v(t)} = [1 - v(t)] \left[\frac{\dot{P}(t)}{P(t)} + \frac{\dot{Q}_1(t)}{Q_1(t)} - \frac{\dot{Q}_2(t)}{Q_2(t)} \right].$$

[6] For a more detailed discussion of the dynamic behavior of $k(t)$, see Kelley et al. (1972b, Chap. 3).

The rate of change in the terms of trade is given by

$$\dot{P}(t)/P(t) = [\alpha_2(t) - \alpha_1(t)]\,\dot{\omega}(t)/\omega(t)].$$

Since industry is more capital-intensive, it follows that $\alpha_1(t) > \alpha_2(t)$, and, with rising wage–rental ratios, the relative price of industrial products *always* declines, contrary to the Singer–Prebisch thesis popular in the 1950s. As a result, even if industrial output growth exceeds that of agriculture, the decline in industrial prices may offset this quantity effect. Furthermore, it is not unambiguously the case that with increases in $k(t)$ the rate of industrial output growth will exceed that of agriculture. Sectoral output growth can be written as

$$\frac{\dot{Q}_i(t)}{Q_i(t)} = \lambda_L + \alpha_i(t)\frac{\dot{k}_i(t)}{k_i(t)} + \frac{\dot{L}_i(t)}{L_i(t)},$$

and thus

$$\frac{\dot{Q}_1(t)}{Q_1(t)} - \frac{\dot{Q}_2(t)}{Q_2(t)} = [\alpha_1(t)\sigma_1 - \alpha_2(t)\sigma_2]\frac{\dot{\omega}(t)}{\omega(t)} + \frac{\dot{L}_1(t)}{L_1(t)} - \frac{\dot{L}_2(t)}{L_2(t)}$$

since $\dot{\omega}(t)/\omega(t) = [1/\sigma_i(t)][\dot{k}_i(t)/k_i(t)]$. As already noted, increases in $k(t)$ and hence $\omega(t)$ always produce a redistribution of labor to industry so that the last two terms in the relative output growth equation sum to some positive number. But the expression $[\alpha_1(t)\sigma_1 - \alpha_2(t)\sigma_2]$ *can* assume negative values given our assumption that $\sigma_1 < \sigma_2$. Thus, even the behavior of relative output growth is ambiguous. It can easily be deduced from this result that the temporal relationship between $v(t)$ and $k(t)$ is ambiguous, so without further restrictions we are unable to determine the initial effect of a once-over change in β_{ij} or γ on the level of industrialization through its effect on $k(t)$.

The ambiguity between $v(t)$ and $k(t)$ may at first seem inconsistent with trade theory and the so-called "Rybczynski effect." The Rybczynski theorem states that increases in $k(t)$ should generate a relative expansion in the sector which utilizes capital most intensively. In our model, increases in $k(t)$ do not *necessarily* produce a relative expansion of the industrial sector. The apparent conflict can be easily resolved. The Rybczynski theorem is derived assuming "small-country" assumptions or where relative commodity prices are exogenously fixed rather than endogenously variable as in our model. The small-country assumption is very strong indeed. With it ω is also constant: the latter result is commonly known as the "factor price equalization theorem." This strong assumption yields

$$\frac{\dot{v}(t)}{v(t)} = [1 - v(t)]\left\{\frac{\dot{Q}_1(t)}{Q_1(t)} - \frac{\dot{Q}_2(t)}{Q_2(t)}\right\} > 0,$$

since

$$\frac{\dot{Q}_1(t)}{Q_1(t)} - \frac{\dot{Q}_2(t)}{Q_2(t)} = \frac{\dot{L}_1(t)}{L_1(t)} - \frac{\dot{L}_2(t)}{L_2(t)} > 0, \qquad \text{when} \quad \omega(t) = \bar{\omega}.$$

As long as commodity prices are determined endogenously, industrialization is *not* necessarily assured by increases in $k(t)$.

Not only are we unable to determine the nature of the relationship between $k(t)$ and $v(t)$, but for essentially the same reasons we cannot determine the relationship between $k(t)$ and aggregate output per capita $g(t)$. Paradoxically, *even though increases in $k(t)$ do not necessarily ensure an increase in aggregate income per capita on industrialization, the economy still yields a pattern of consumer expenditure wholly consistent with Engel's hypothesis;* that is, the elasticity of food (nonfood) expenditures with respect to wage income would be observed to be less (greater) than unity. Denote the elasticity of demand for the ith good with respect to per-capita wage income in the jth sector as $\eta_{ij}(t)$. It follows from (11) and (12) that

$$\eta_{1j}(t) = \frac{y(t) w_j(t)}{y(t) w_j(t) - \gamma}, \qquad \eta_{2j}(t) = \frac{\beta_{2j} y(t) w_j(t)}{\beta_{2j} y(t) w_j(t) + [1 - \beta_{2j}] \gamma}.$$

It should first be noted that these elasticities are endogenous variables and not parameters in the model: Indeed, the value for each elasticity is uniquely determined for any given efficiency capital–labor ratio. Since these elasticities are determined endogenously, we cannot say that Engel effects are a cause of industrialization because in any given period the values for $\eta_{ij}(t)$ and $v(t)$ are determined simultaneously. However, if we were able to find plausible restrictions on the values of these elasticities such that we could determine the nature of the relationship between growth and industrialization, then in this sense we could say that income elasticities play an important role in the process of development.

However, it is clear from the above definitions of the income elasticities that for any efficiency capital–labor ratio, and thus $y(t) w(t)$, $0 < \eta_{2j}(t) < 1 < \eta_{1j}(t) < \infty$. This result requires only that $0 < \beta_{2j} < 1$ and $0 < \gamma < \infty$. The implication is that the income elasticity of demand for food is *always* less than one and for industrial goods it is *always* greater than one.[7] But as

---

[7] Furthermore, these elasticities tend toward one as growth takes place. By differentiating η_{ij} with respect to ω, we obtain

$$\frac{d\eta_{1j}}{d\omega} = \frac{\bar{y}(1 - \eta_{1j}) \alpha_2 f_2'(k_2)}{\bar{y} \omega f_2'(k_2) - \gamma} < 0, \qquad \frac{d\eta_{2j}}{d\omega} = \frac{\beta_{2j} \bar{y}(1 - \eta_{2j}) \alpha_2 f_2'(k_2)}{\beta_{2j} \bar{y} \omega f_2' + (1 - \beta_{2j}) \gamma} > 0.$$

Recall that ω and k move together and that $f'(k_j) < 0$. Therefore, as k increases without limit, η_{1j} and η_{2j} approach unity.

we demonstrated above, when the efficiency capital–labor ratio is rising, and hence $y(t)w(t)$ is rising, we are unable to determine whether the level of industrialization rises without more restrictive assumptions about production relationships. The foregoing analysis suggests that while we may empirically observe income elasticities consistent with Engel effects, they are neither necessary nor sufficient for industrialization to occur in our simple dualistic model. On this basis, then, we can conclude that in the simple model Engel effects do not play a role in determining the level of industrialization in our economy.

In a sense, the apparent unimportance of Engel effects in providing sufficient conditions for industrialization is of our own making. By this we mean that we have, to date at least, regarded wage income per laborer, $y(t)w(t)$, as the relevant measure of income in defining income elasticities. This has been done because of our assumption that there is no consumption out of rental income—it is all invested. If consumption out of rental income is allowed, as it is below, then aggregate income per capita would be the relevant measure of income for the purposes of defining income elasticities. We shall then find that the income elasticity of demand for agricultural goods, when constrained within quite plausible limits, provides sufficient conditions for $g(t)$ and $v(t)$ to increase when $k(t)$ increases.

Although more explicit mathematical results relating to demand and industrialization could be obtained by a drastic simplification of the theoretical structure, to do so would involve a major departure from the dualistic characteristics of growth which our model highlights. We could, for example, assume that $\sigma_1(t) = 1 = \sigma_2(t)$, in which case $v(t)$ and $g(t)$ would increase when $k(t)$ increased and vice versa. However, such a restriction would suppress a widely documented feature of the production technology of many low-income economies as well as eliminating the bias in technological progress. Alternatively, following Jorgenson, Fei and Ranis, and others, we could eliminate capital as an argument in the agricultural production function. To do so would rob our model of a key allocation decision relevant to the developing economies: investment in agriculture or industry? It seems more appropriate for an analysis of industrialization and structural change to maintain our existing theoretical structure and instead initiate a more complete exploration of these relationships with the aid of a different technique—simulation analysis. In addition to permitting a more intensive analysis of the model's structure, simulation analysis will provide a preliminary appraisal of the quantitative *importance* of demand in development, an issue which cannot be successfully explored with qualitative analysis alone.

The derivation and justification of the initial conditions and parameter values assumed in the simulation is reported in detail elsewhere (Kelley *et al.*, 1972a, b). They are generally typical of Asian economies, and in many cases are estimated directly from Philippine data (see Appendix A).[8] The model used in the simulation differs from the one discussed above in that we now allow for consumption by capitalists. Capitalists' taste parameters are assumed to be the same as those of urban laborers. The model developed in Section 2d can thus be restated by replacing Eqs. (4), (15), and (16) with Eqs. (4a), (15a), and (16a).

$$I(t) = [s\bar{x}/P(t)]\, r(t)\, \bar{K}, \qquad 0 < s < 1, \tag{4a}$$

$$Q_1(t) = D_{11}(t) + D_{12}(t) + C_1(t) + I(t), \tag{15a}$$

$$Q_2(t) = D_{21}(t) + D_{22}(t) + C_2(t); \tag{16a}$$

and by adding two more demand equations explaining capitalists' consumption demand $C_i(t)$:

$$C_1(t) = \frac{\beta_{11}}{P(t)} \left\{ [1-s]\frac{r(t)\,\overline{xK}}{\phi L(t)} - \gamma \right\} \phi L(t), \tag{18}$$

$$C_2(t) = \beta_{12}[1-s]\, r(t)\,\overline{xK} + (1-\beta_{12})\gamma\phi L(t). \tag{19}$$

That is, we assume that the number of capitalists (property income recipients) is a fixed proportion Φ of the total labor force.

When we expand the model to allow a fixed share of rental income to be consumed, our interpretation of the role of demand elasticities changes. It is still true that when wage income rises a proportionately larger share will be allocated for consumption of industrial goods; similarly, when rental income rises a similar response is observed. However, wage and rental income do not necessarily rise together when the aggregate capital–labor ratio is rising. Thus, it is no longer appropriate to conduct the analysis of the role of income elasticities in terms of wage income and rental income. For an analysis of the aggregate behavior of consumers the relevant measure is aggregate income per capita, which we can now redefine as $g(t) = G(t)/(1+\Phi)L(t)$. On the other hand, if the analysis was in terms of expenditure elasticities, the relevant variable would be

$$e(t) = \frac{y(t)\,w(t)}{1+\Phi} + \frac{(1-s)\,x(t)\,r(t)\,K(t)}{(1+\Phi)L(t)}$$

where $e(t)$ is the total current consumption expenditure outlay per capita in the economy. We have chosen to conduct our analysis in terms of income elasticities rather than expenditure elasticities, although the same results are forthcoming using the latter concept.

---

[8] This model has also been applied to Meiji Japan in order to account for her unusual industrialization experience up to 1915 [see Kelley and Williamson (1974, Chap. 9)].

We define $\eta_i^*(t)$ to be the elasticity of demand for the ith good with respect to changes in aggregate income per capita, that is,

$$\eta_i^*(t) = \frac{\partial d_i(t)}{\partial g(t)} \frac{g(t)}{d_i(t)},$$

where

$$d_i(t) = \sum_{j=1}^{2} \frac{D_{ij}(t) + C_i(t)}{(1+\phi)L(t)}.$$

We find that the behavior of the elasticity variables in response to changes in the efficiency capital–labor ratio is ambiguous: The sign of

$$\frac{\partial d_i(t)}{\partial g(t)} = \frac{\partial d_i(t)}{\partial \omega(t)} \frac{\partial \omega(t)}{\partial k(t)} \frac{\partial k(t)}{\partial g(t)}$$

cannot be determined because of the ambiguity in the sign of $\partial k(t)/\partial g(t)$. But on the other hand, if we require that $\eta_2^*(t) > 0$, then it follows that $\partial g(t)/\partial k(t) > 0$ because $\partial d_2(t)/\partial \omega(t)$ and $\partial \omega(t)/\partial k(t)$ are both positive when $\sigma_2(t) \geqslant 1$ and $k_1(t) - k_2(t) > 0$ [see Kelley et al. (1972b, Chap. 3)]. Moreover, we can show that when $\eta_2^*(t)$ is positive but less than one, then $v(t)$ necessarily increases when $k(t)$ increases. By definition we know that

$$v(t) = 1 - [d_2(t)/g(t)],$$

from which we find that

$$\frac{dv}{dk} = -\frac{\partial g}{\partial k} \frac{d_2}{g^2} \left(\frac{\partial d_2}{\partial k} \frac{\partial k}{\partial g} \frac{g}{d_2} - 1 \right) = -\frac{\partial g}{\partial k} \frac{d_2}{g^2} (\eta_2^* - 1).$$

Clearly if $0 < \eta_2^* < 1$, then $dv/dk > 0$ in view of the fact that $\eta_2^* > 0$ is sufficient to ensure that $\partial g/\partial k > 0$. Thus, in our revised dualistic model, when $k(t)$ is increasing, a sufficient condition for growth and increases in the level of industrialization is that the income elasticity of demand for agricultural goods is positive but less than one. The requirement $0 < \eta_2^*(t) < 1$ does not necessarily imply the existence or absence of Engel effects in the sense as $\eta_1^*(t) > \eta_2^*(t)$. Nevertheless, we can conclude that the existence of Engel effects in the sense that $0 < \eta_2^*(t) < 1 < \eta_1^*(t) < \infty$ is sufficient to ensure growth and industrialization when $k(t)$ is rising, although we have just seen the restriction on $\eta_1^*(t)$ is unnecessary.

This result highlights an important difference between the two models with respect to the role of income of expenditure elasticities. In the simpler model Engel effects are present for any choice of parameter values and for any efficiency capital–labor ratio. *When we admit the possibility of consumption from rental income, restrictions on the value of income or expenditure elasticities are sufficient to provide an unambiguous interpretation of the relation-ship between growth and industrialization when the efficiency capital–labor ratio is rising. Moreover, it suggests that at least in the context of dualistic models, the extreme assumption of consumption only from wage income can result in a rather misleading interpretation of the role of demand.*

An examination of the trajectory of the economy as revealed in the simu-lation is peripheral to the main objectives of this paper and it has been de-scribed elsewhere in some detail [see Kelley *et al.* (1972b, Chap. 4)]. Suffice it to say that the simulation results appear to yield reasonable growth paths of key variables as judged by the quantitative historical record: Labor's share declines throughout, although in industry it turns around at later stages in development; the rate of overall technical change is relatively constant; industrialization and urbanization, rapid in early phases of growth, approach an asymptote; production becomes more capital-intensive overall, although in early development agriculture experiences a period of increasing labor intensity; and output growth, while rising throughout, grows more slowly as time passes.

The key step in the numerical analysis, given our present objectives, is to perform sensitivity analysis on the demand parameters. This is accomplished by computing the elasticities of the model's simulated variables with respect to changes in given parameters (for example, γ, β_{ij}). These are termed "struc-tural elasticities." They measure the elasticity response of a given variable over time to a once-and-for-all change in a given parameter.

A word of caution should be raised in interpreting the structural elas-ticities. While they permit an evaluation of the quantitative significance of changes in various parameters on the economic performance of the economy, they do not necessarily measure the "importance" of changes in demand parameters on growth. The total impact of a parameter depends on the rate at which the parameter changes through time and not just the effect of a once-over change that we analyze here.

Table 2 presents the key sensitivity results relevant to appraising the impact of demand on structural change and aggregate economic growth. Structural elasticities are available for every period, but only those for years 10 and 50 are presented so that the relatively short-run and long-run effects of demand parameter changes may be compared. Elasticities are also pre-sented for the savings parameter to permit a comparison of the demand parameter elasticities not only with another key feature in the consumer's budget allocation, but also with an aspect of development which is frequently highlighted as central to economic progress. Thus, a comparison of the demand elasticities with those of the savings parameter will allow a pre-liminary appraisal of the "importance" of demand in economic growth.

We will focus on the long-run behavior of the industrialization rate in

TABLE 2

The Impact of Changes in Several Demand Parameters
on GNP Per Capita, Urbanization, and the
Industrial-Output Share[a]

Variable	Value of elasticity in year	
	10	50
Per capita GNP growth rate		
Urban demand (β_{i1})	1.306	0.707
Rural demand (β_{i2})	0.905	0.522
Subsistence demand (γ)	−0.815	−0.492
Savings propensity (s)	3.022	0.472
Level of urbanization		
Urban demand (β_{i1})	0.127	0.565
Rural demand (β_{i2})	0.088	0.175
Subsistence demand (γ)	−0.052	−0.019
Savings propensity (s)	0.409	1.216
Industrial-output share		
Urban demand (β_{i1})	0.083	0.314
Rural demand (β_{i2})	0.077	0.121
Subsistence demand (γ)	−0.006	0.143
Savings propensity (s)	0.191	0.373

[a] Since $\beta_{1j} + \beta_{2j} = 1$, in the experiments reported here $d\beta_{1j} = -d\beta_{2j}$.

Table 2. This variable has not only attracted the most attention in the literature on structural change, but in terms of our qualitative analysis above of the dynamic model, the temporal behavior of $v(t)$ was found to be ambiguous. The structural elasticities show that the shift in tastes in favor of urban goods has a positive initial impact on $v(t)$ in early growth phases, and since the rate of growth in the capital–labor ratio is also raised, *the industrial-output share receives an increasingly positive stimulus over time*. In early stages of growth, then, a shift in tastes toward urban goods stimulates industrialization far above the first-order impact which is stressed in the development literature. This conclusion is the opposite of that reached by development theorists in the 1950s who stressed the inhibiting impact of the "demonstration effect" on growth. Although Nurkse (1957) and others typically focus only on savings behavior, their conclusion was that the demonstration effect inhibited growth. We find the contrary. To the extent that the demonstration effect implies a shift out of Z-goods (Hymer and Resnick, 1969) and agricultural goods into Western industrial goods, the effect is to stimulate significantly per-capita income growth in the dual economy. Furthermore, industrialization is fostered beyond the first-order effects and both urbanization and labor absorption rates in industry are increased.

All of these generalizations are reversed for the case of an increase in γ. It has long been recognized that increases in subsistence requirements, however defined, have a depressing influence on growth in the dual economy. Normally that analytical result is forthcoming from quite a different model in which wages are institutionally set equal to some subsistence bundle (Fei and Ranis, 1964). In the labor surplus models, the key analytical focus is the impact of wage setting on available surplus for accumulation. We assume marginal product pricing in our system and, as a result, γ enters only into the expenditure composition decision. A rise in γ causes a reduction in the rate of growth of $k(t)$, in per-capita output growth and in urbanization. These conclusions rest on a limiting assumption; γ is composed entirely of agricultural goods. If, as development proceeds, minimum consumption increasingly involves "necessary" expenditure on nonagricultural commodities—a hypothesis presently in vogue in the development literature and confirmed by Parks (1969), Stone and Brown (1965), and Yoshihara (1969) on Swedish, English, and Japanese historical data, respectively—then our conclusions would require appropriate modification.

Finally, we include in Table 2 an evaluation of the sensitivity of growth to variation in the saving parameter. The economy is generally more sensitive to the savings than to the demand parameters. This result is hardly surprising, but we should emphasize again that the experiments in this section only consider once and for all parameter changes. Judging from the research of Parks and Stone, we can reasonably expect *continued* decreases in β_{2j} over time. As a result, the historical impact of changes in consumer tastes on industrialization and growth are far greater than these sensitivity experiments reveal, based, as they are, on once-and-for-all changes in demand parameters. Note, however, that the relative importance of demand parameter changes *increases* over time compared with the savings parameter. Indeed, the long-run sensitivity of the industrialization rate to changes in urban demand is about the *same* as that for alterations in the savings propensity (0.314 versus 0.373). Given our qualifications above, in the long run the "importance" of shifts in demand behavior may be as significant as that of savings, although the latter has certainly attracted more attention in the literature.

4. Conclusions and Agenda for Future Research

Our special interest in the role of demand is in part a reaction to the development and growth literature which either ignores final demand parameters entirely while focusing on supply conditions, or makes model specifications which leave little room for consumer expenditure decisions to assume an interesting role. Our approach has been to develop a dualistic model of development which includes a more comprehensive treatment of consumer demand. Utilizing the linear expenditure system, we find strong support for the economic historians' emphasis on the importance of demand factors in influencing the pattern of growth and structural change; however, these demand effects are of a form quite different from those emphasized in both the theoretical and empirical literature, for it is changes in tastes rather than the influence of Engel effects that lead us to this conclusion. The results justify far greater empirical research on the determinants of household consumption behavior in developing economies, and in particular, greater historical research on *shifts* in consumption behavior during the growth process.

Appendix A. Restatement of the Model in Per-Capita Terms

Static Model

From (1):[9]

$$q_i(t) = f_i(k_i) \qquad (i = 1, 2) \tag{A1}$$

From (13) and (14):

$$\bar{k} = uk_1 + [1-u]k_2 \tag{A2}$$

From (7) and (9):

$$\omega = \frac{f_1(k_1)}{f_1'(k_1)} - k_1 \tag{A3}$$

From (8) and (10):

$$\omega = \frac{f_2(k_2)}{f_2'(k_2)} - k_2 \tag{A4}$$

From (11), (7), and (8):

$$z_{1j} = \frac{\beta_{1j}}{P} \left[y\omega f_2'(k_2) - \gamma \right] \tag{A5}$$

From (12), (7), and (8):

$$z_{2j} = \beta_{2j} \bar{y}\omega f_2'(k_2) + [1-\beta_{2j}]\gamma \tag{A6}$$

[9] Since the function $F^i(i = 1, 2)$ is linearly homogeneous, it follows that $F^i[\bar{x}K_i, \bar{y}L_i] \equiv \bar{y}L_i F^i[k_i, 1] \equiv \bar{y}L_i f_i(k_i)$, whence we have $q_i = f_i(k_i)$. In view of the restrictions already imposed on the production system, it follows that for $0 < k_i < \infty$ we have $f_i'(k_i) > 0$ and $f_i''(k_i) < 0$. Note also that $F_1^i = f_i'(k_i)$ and $F_2^i = f_i(k_i) - k_i f_i'(k_i)$.

From (4), (9), and (10):

$$\phi = \bar{x} f_1{}'(k_1) \qquad (A7)$$

From (11), (4), and (15):

$$\bar{y} u q_1 = u z_{11} + [1-u] z_{12} + \frac{\overline{y k \phi}}{\bar{x}} \qquad (A8)$$

From (12) and (16):

$$\bar{y}[1-u] q_2 = u z_{21} + [1-u] z_{22} \qquad (A9)$$

From (9) and (10):

$$P = \frac{f_2{}'(k_2)}{f_1{}'(k_1)} \qquad (A10)$$

Dynamic Model

$$\dot{k}(t)/k(t) = x(t) f_1{}'[k_1(t)] + [n_2-n_1] u(t) - [\delta+n_2+\lambda_L-\lambda_K] \qquad (A11)$$

$$\dot{x}(t)/x(t) = \lambda_K \qquad (A12)$$

$$\dot{y}(t)/y(t) = \lambda_L. \qquad (A13)$$

Appendix B. Parameters and Initial Conditions for the Simulation Model

Parameter Values

Production Functions (CES):

$$A_1 = 0.640 \qquad A_2 = 0.350 \qquad \sigma_1 = 0.500 \qquad \sigma_2 = 1.500$$

Technical Change:

$$\lambda_K = 0.003 \qquad \lambda_L = 0.010$$

Labor Supply:

$$n_1 = 0.020 \qquad n_2 = 0.030$$

Capital Depreciation:

$$\delta = 0.050$$

Laborers' Commodity Demand:

$$\beta_{11} = 0.800 \qquad \beta_{12} = 0.500 \qquad \beta_{21} = 0.200$$

$$\beta_{22} = 0.500 \qquad \gamma = 0.648$$

Capitalists' Commodity Demand:

$$s = 0.312 \qquad \beta_{11} = 0.800 \qquad \beta_{21} = 0.200$$

Initial Conditions

Factor Efficiency Units:

$$x(0) = y(0) = 1.000$$

Factor Stocks:

$$K(0) = 30.174 \qquad K_1(0) = 17.135$$
$$K_2(0) = 13.039 \qquad L(0) = 100.000$$

Factor Stocks:

$$L_1(0) = 30.008 \qquad L_2(0) = 69.992$$

Output:

$$P(0)Q_1(0) = 73.307 \qquad Q_2(0) = 93.003$$

Initial Conditions on Key Ratios

Urbanization Level:

$$u(0) = 0.300$$

Industrialization Level:

$$v(0) = 0.429$$

Gross Savings Rate:

$$s^*(0) = 0.150$$

Factor Shares:

$$\alpha_1(0) = 0.636 \qquad \alpha_2(0) = 0.364 \qquad \alpha(0) = 0.481$$

Capital–Labor Ratios:

$$\hat{k}_1(0) = 0.571 \qquad \hat{k}_2(0) = 0.186 \qquad \hat{k}(0) = 0.302$$

Capital–Output Ratios:

$$K_1(0)/Q_1(0) = 2.397 \qquad P(0)K_2(0)/Q_2(0) = 1.398$$
$$P(0)K(0)/G(0) = 1.820$$

Population Growth:

$$n(0) = 0.270$$

ACKNOWLEDGMENTS

Mr. Cheetham is presently a member of the staff of the World Bank, although the work on which this paper is based was undertaken while he was in residence at the University of Wisconsin. The World Bank does not necessarily concur with the contents or conclusions of this paper. Financial support for this study was provided by the National Science Foundation.

REFERENCES

Amano, A. (1964)   Neoclassical biased technological progress and a neoclassical theory of economic growth. *Quarterly Journal of Economics* **70**: 129–138.

Baldwin, R. E. (1966)   *Economic development and export growth: A study of Northern Rhodesia, 1920–1960.* Berkeley, California: Univ. of California Press.

Barten, A. (1964)   Consumer demand functions under conditions of almost additive preferences. *Econometrica* **32**: 1–38.

Cheetham, R. (1969)   Growth and structural change in a two-sector economy. Ph.D. Thesis. Madison: Univ. of Wisconsin.

Chenery, H. (1960)   Patterns of industrial growth. *American Economic Review* **50**: 624–654.

Drandakis, E. M. (1963)   Factor substitution in the two-sector growth model. *Review of Economic Studies* **30**: 217–222.

Eckaus, R. (1955)   The factor proportions problem in underdeveloped areas. *American Economic Review* **45**: 539–565.

Fei, J., and Ranis, G. (1964)   *Development of the labor surplus economy: Theory and policy.* Homewood, Illinois: Richard D. Irwin.

Goldberger, A. (1967)   *Functional form and utility: A review of consumer demand theory.* Paper No. SFM 6703. Madison: Social Systems Research Institute, Univ. of Wisconsin.

Houthakker, H. (1960a)   The influence of prices and income on household expenditures. *Bulletin de l'Institute International de Statistique* **37**: 9–22.

Houthakker, H. (1960b)   Additive preferences. *Econometrica* **28**: 244–257.

Hymer, S., and Resnick, S. (1969)   A model of an agrarian economy with non-agricultural activities. *American Economic Review* **59**: 493–506.

Jorgenson, D. (1961)   The development of a dual economy. *Economic Journal* **71**: 309–334.

Kaneda, H. (1968)   Long-term changes in food consumption patterns in Japan, 1878–1964. *Food Research Institute Studies* **8**: 3–32.

Kelley, A. (1969)   Demand patterns, demographic change, and economic growth. *Quarterly Journal of Economics* **83**: 110–126.

Kelley, A. C., and Williamson, J. G. (1968)   Household saving behavior in the developing economies: The Indonesian case. *Economic Development and Cultural Change* **16**: 385–403.

Kelley, A. C., and Williamson, J. G. (1974)   *Lessons from Japanese development: An analytical economic history.* Chicago, Illinois: Univ. of Chicago Press, to be published.

Kelley, A. C., Williamson, J., and Cheetham, R. (1972a)   Biased technological progress and labor force growth in a dualistic economy. *Quarterly Journal of Economics*, to be published.

Kelley, A. C., Williamson, J. G., and Cheetham, R. J. (1972b)   *Dualistic economic development: Theory and history.* Chicago, Illinois: Univ. of Chicago Press.

Kuznets, S. (1966)   *Modern economic growth: Rate, structure and spread.* New Haven, Connecticut: Yale Univ. Press.

Leibenstein, H. (1960)   Technical progress, the production function and dualism. *Banca Nazionale del Lavoro Quarterly Review* **55**: 13–15.

Nurske, R. (1957)   *Problems of capital formation in underdeveloped countries.* London and New York: Oxford Univ. Press.

Parks, R. (1969)   Systems of demand equations: An empirical comparison of alternative functional forms. *Econometrica* **37**: 629–650.

Stone, R. (1954)   Linear expenditure systems and demand analysis: An application to the pattern of British demand. *Economic Journal* **64**: 511–527.

Stone, R., and Brown, A. (1965)   Behavioral and technical change in economic models. *Problems in Economic Development* (E. Robinson, ed.), pp. 428–439.: London: Macmillan.

Stone, R., Brown, A., and Rowe, D. (1964)   Demand analysis and projections for Britain, 1900–1970. *Europe's Future Consumption* (J. Sandee, ed.). Amsterdam: North Holland Publ.

Uzawa, H. (1961)   On a two-sector model of economic growth, I. *Review of Economic Studies* **29**:40–47.

Uzawa, H. (1963)   On a two-sector model of economic growth, II. *Review of Economic Studies* **30**:105–118.

Williamson, J. G. (1968)   Personal savings in developing nations: An intertemporal cross-section from Asia. *Economic Record* **44**: 194–210.

Williamson, J. G. (1969)   Capital accumulation, labor saving, and labor absorption, a new look at some contemporary Asian evidence. Madison, Wisconsin: University of Wisconsin Social Systems Research Institute.

Williamson, J. G. (1971)   Capital accumulation, labor-saving and labor absorption once more. *Quarterly Journal of Economics* **85**: 40–65.

Yoshihara, K. (1969)   Demand functions: An application to the Japanese expenditure pattern. *Econometrica* **37**: 257–274.

Monetary Policy in Developing Countries

MILTON FRIEDMAN
UNIVERSITY OF CHICAGO AND UNIVERSITY OF HAWAII

1. Cyclical versus Secular Policy

In the developed countries, most discussion of monetary policy is concerned with the problem of business fluctuations—cyclical expansions and recessions—and hence with the effect of monetary policy on stability. Even for such countries, some of us have concluded that monetary policy is a poor instrument for this purpose thanks to the length and variability of the lag in the effects of monetary policy, the limitations of our knowledge about the factors responsible for such lags and about other short-term effects of monetary policy, the conflicting objectives pursued by monetary authorities, and the pressures of politics. These factors, we believe, have made discretionary monetary policy a major independent source of economic instability rather than an offset to instability arising from other sources. We have concluded that the wisest policy, at least for the present, would be to shape monetary policy in the light of longer run objectives and to aim, in the short run, for steady monetary growth in order to provide a favorable climate for stability without either actively promoting stability or unintentionally introducing instability.

265

For developing countries, the case against using monetary policy primarily as an instrument for short-run stabilization is far stronger than for developed countries. The crucial problem for developing countries is to achieve sustained growth not to smooth short-run fluctuations. In addition, such countries seldom have financial markets and banking institutions sufficiently developed and sufficiently sophisticated to permit what has come (most inaccurately) to be called "fine-tuning" of monetary policy.

These policy and institutional considerations reinforce a scientific consideration: We know much more about the long-run effects of monetary changes than we do about their short-term effects. Over short periods, the monetary effects may be swamped by transitory forces that will average out over longer periods. As a result, for developing countries even more than for developed ones, it seems wise to determine monetary policy from long-term considerations. Parenthetically, this conclusion holds equally for fiscal policy, and for the same reasons, regardless of the relative importance attached to fiscal and monetary effects as determinants of economic change.

Accordingly, in the rest of this paper, I shall deal primarily with long-run considerations.

2. Monetary Policy and Inflation

From the long-run point of view, the problem of desirable monetary policy reduces primarily to the desirable rate and form of inflation. Two intermediate steps lead to this identification: the recognition first, that monetary policy is concerned primarily with the quantity of money, not with the terms and availability of credit; second, that inflation is always and everywhere a result of a rapid rate of increase in the quantity of money. I shall comment briefly on these two intermediate steps before turning to the relation between inflation and development.

a. What Is Monetary Policy?

Central banks grew out of commercial banks, and most central bankers have been drawn from the banking community. Even when they have not, most of their dealings have been with the commercial banks. The individual commercial banker rightly regards himself as an intermediary in the credit market, borrowing from some (his depositors) and lending to others. He does not regard himself as in any way "creating" money. The central banker tends to accept this view and thus he tends to regard himself as concerned primarily with the "money market" in the sense of the "credit market" and with the "price of money" in the sense of interest rates.

Yet, as students of fractional reserve banking have recognized for over a century, what is true for the individual bank is not true for the banking system. The system as a whole "creates" most of its deposits. Any one bank that makes a loan from excess funds indirectly adds to deposits in other banks. These banks in turn can make further loans, so producing a "multiple" expansion.

This process means that deposit money is mostly the counterpart of credit. But much money is not the counterpart of credit: gold or silver under specie standards, paper money issued by government. More important, "bank credit" is only a minor part of total credit. Credit and money are related but they are not synonymous. A country's monetary authorities can play a dominant role in determining the amount of money; they are a minor factor in the "credit" market.

The confusion between money and credit has been paralleled and fostered by a confusion between nominal and real magnitudes. In the process of adding to the quantity of money, the banking system can create credit in nominal terms—that is, in terms of the monetary unit: dollars, or pesos, or pounds. But the effect may be to leave unchanged or even to reduce the real amount of credit, if the monetary creation leads to inflation in ways that discourage saving.

Similarly, the monetary authorities may affect the nominal interest rate but, over any long period, they have little effect on the real interest rate. A nominal interest rate of 10% when prices are rising at 4% per year is a real return of 6%, since the rest of the nominal return goes only to make good the loss in the buying power of the principal. Over short periods, by adding to the quantity of money, the monetary authorities may lower both the nominal and real rate, but over longer periods, the result will be inflation that will raise the nominal rate above its earlier level while having little effect on the real rate. Ultimately, the real rate depends far more on the real forces of thriftiness and productivity than on the activities of the monetary authorities.

b. Importance of Quantity of Money

Given that monetary policy is concerned primarily with the quantity of money, why is it important how the quantity of money is controlled or what happens to it?

The answer is that changes in the nominal quantity of money are always *a* and often *the* major determinant of changes in nominal income or nominal spending. In the short run, a change in the rate of growth of nominal income produced by a change in the rate of monetary growth will be divided between prices and output in proportions that will vary from time to time. That is why short-run fluctuations in the rate of monetary growth produce short-run fluctuations in economic activity, varying in timing and intensity in ways that may bear no very precise relation to the monetary impulse. However, over the long run, the rate of output growth is largely determined by other forces, so that the long-run rate of monetary growth determines primarily the rate of inflation.

In this sense, inflation is always a monetary phenomenon, always a result of a more rapid increase in the quantity of money than in output. But in another sense, there are many different sources of inflation because there may be many different reasons for the increase in the quantity of money. The quantity of money increased in the United States, and produced inflation in the 1850s because of gold discoveries; in the 1860s and from 1916 to 1918 because of government deficits to finance wars; in 1919–1920 because of bank credit expansion to finance private investment.

3. Inflation and Development

It is widely believed that there is a close relation between inflation and development. The relation is sometimes supposed to be that economic development is a cause of inflation; sometimes, that inflation fosters economic development. In my opinion, neither is consistently true.

Some striking examples of *development without inflation* are the development of Great Britain in the eighteenth and nineteenth century, of the United States in the nineteenth century, of Japan from the Meiji restoration in 1867 to World War I; of Hong Kong, Malaysia, and Singapore in the past 30 years, of Greece in the late 1950s and early 1960s.

Examples of *inflation without development* include India in recent decades, many South American countries, Indonesia until perhaps recent years, all the hyperinflations after World Wars I and II.

Examples of *no inflation and no development* include Venezuela, many European countries and India in the interwar period, and numerous examples from earlier times.

So all four possible combinations can be found in experience.

What underlies the belief that inflation promotes development? I believe there are two systematic effects that might work in this direction.

First, if inflation is not anticipated, it may for a time transfer resources to active businessmen, innovators, or entrepreneurs, and in this way add to investment. Apparently, this is what happened in Europe in the sixteenth and seventeenth century as a consequence of Spanish imports of specie from the New World. These imports raised the quantity of money, which produced inflation, the inflation was not anticipated so prices of final products went up more rapidly than wages, interest rates failed to reflect inflation fully so that the real interest rate fell, and this process transferred wealth from landowners and landworkers to entrepreneurs. Professor Earl Hamilton's studies of the price revolution are by now classic documentations of this process (Hamilton, 1934, 1936, 1947).

This effect operates only so long as inflation is not anticipated. Once inflation is widely anticipated, wages will escalate as rapidly as prices and interest rates will rise to offset the expected inflation. In the modern era, when inflation comes from the actions of legislatures and central banks rather than from such acts of God as specie discoveries, when the press, radio, and television rapidly transmit information to the ends of the world, inflation is not likely to proceed very long without being anticipated, and perhaps, over-anticipated. So this effect can hardly be counted on as a matter of deliberate development policy.

Second, inflation is, or can be, a method of taxation that yields revenue to the government. This revenue can be used to finance development. I believe that this link between inflation and development has been mainly responsible for the widespread belief that the two go together. In most developing countries in the modern era, governments have—wisely or unwisely—tried to play a large role. This has led to a demand for government revenue that could not be readily met by traditional sources of government revenue, and neither the bureaucratic apparatus nor private attitudes and institutions permitted the large-scale use of such new sources as income and corporation tax. Accordingly, governments have been strongly tempted to resort to the printing press to finance their activities.

Inflation produced in this way has been a mixed blessing as a means of development for several reasons. First, the amount of revenue that can be raised by inflation is not very large in underdeveloped countries, because cash balances are typically rather small relative to total income. This is concealed initially because, when governments first start inflating, they benefit from the fact that the inflation has not been anticipated. For a time, people expect it to be temporary, and so add to rather than reduce their cash balances in real terms. But as soon as people come to expect the inflation to continue, they reduce their cash balances in real terms, and the yield from inflation declines sharply (see also the discussion below).

Second, governments have many demands for funds, so there is no assurance that the revenue will go to promote development.

Third, even if the revenue does go to promote development, it is development as viewed by the government, which means that the revenue may well go for the standard development monuments—international airlines, luxury hotels, steel mills—rather than for productive investment.

Fourth, and probably most important in practice, the inflation is almost always accompanied by governmental controls and intervention which offset much of the possible benefit from governmental development assistance. These controls and interventions discourage private investment, can often lead to a flight of private capital, and produce economic waste and inefficiency.

4. Development without Inflation

These considerations make it worth contemplating the possibility of refraining from using inflation as a method of taxation. I realize that, for most underdeveloped countries, this is a purely hypothetical possibility, since they are already deeply committed to using the printing press as a source of revenue. However, contemplating this possibility serves a useful intellectual purpose by providing a standard with which to compare current practice and thereby a greater degree of perspective.

The surest way to avoid using inflation as a deliberate method of taxation is to unify the country's currency with the currency of some other country or countries. In this case, the country would not have any monetary policy of its own. It would, as it were, tie its monetary policy to the kite of the monetary policy of another country—preferably a more developed, larger, and relatively stable country.

Hong Kong is an obvious example. It has no central bank, no independent monetary policy. It has a currency closely linked to the British pound sterling. Through a currency board, printing of paper currency requires the deposit of British currency in a stated ratio. The quantity of deposits is then indirectly controlled by the need for banks to keep deposits convertible into currency.

Essentially, this is also what the United States did in the nineteenth century, after the return to gold in 1879. Though technically the currency was linked to gold, it could equally well be described as unified with the British pound sterling. The United States in effect had no independent monetary policy. The quantity of money in the United States had to be whatever sum was necessary to keep United States prices in line with world prices. Similarly, this was the policy followed by Japan from the Meiji restoration to World War I.

Such a unified currency must be sharply distinguished from a system that superficially looks very much the same but is basically very different, namely, a national currency subject to national control but linked to other countries by fixed exchange rates.

For example, different states in the United States, like Illinois and New York, have a truly unified currency. Both use exactly the same dollar and there is no central bank in Illinois or New York that can interfere with the flow of funds between them. If Illinois residents buy more from New York residents than New York residents buy from Illinois, and if Illinois residents finance their excess purchases by drawing down their cash balances, then—neglecting all other transactions—the quantity of money in Illinois will go down, in New York it will go up, and the decline in Illinois will be precisely equal in dollars to the rise in New York. Though Hong Kong and the United Kingdom use currencies with different names, essentially the same thing is true. They too have a unified currency with a fixed rate of exchange between them.

Such a unified currency is very different from national currencies linked by a pegged rate, say the United States dollar and the British pound sterling. Until recently there was a fixed rate of exchange—under the short-lived Smithsonian agreement, $2.6057 plus or minus $2\frac{1}{4}\%$. But there were also central banks in the United States and the United Kingdom that could interfere with the flow of funds. If United States residents converted dollars into pounds sterling to finance an excess of purchases in the United Kingdom, the Federal Reserve System could prevent that conversion from leading to a reduction in the United States money stock, and the Bank of England could prevent it from leading to an increase in the United Kingdom money stock—they could "sterilize" the deficit or surplus, in the jargon that developed. As a result, the rate of exchange was a pegged, not a free-market, price and was subject to substantial change from time to time.

Technically speaking, a nation can refrain from using inflation as a method of taxation without going so far as to unify its currency with other currencies. A nation that succeeds in developing and that keeps its prices constant, or in line with the price level in one or more major countries, will require a larger money stock to match its growing output. If it unifies its currency with other currencies, whether through an intermediary like gold, or otherwise, the increase in the quantity of money will have to come through a surplus in the balance of payments (defined to include all interest-bearing loans but not literal money). The country could instead increase a national money (i.e., use the printing press, or the central bank's bookkeeper's pen) by an amount just sufficient to avoid such a surplus without departing greatly from the assumed path of prices. The national money would simply replace the inflow of the foreign currency.

While such a process is technically possible, under present conditions it is highly unlikely to be followed, at least for a long period. The central bank may follow such an austere, self-denying policy for a time, but political pressures are almost sure, sooner or later, to lead to irresistible demands to go further—either for stabilization or to provide the government with funds. Accordingly, I conclude that the only effective way to refrain from using inflation as a method of taxation is to avoid having a central bank. Once a central bank is established, the die is likely to have been cast for inflation.

While the use of a unified currency is today out of fashion, it has many advantages for development, as its successful use in the past and even at present indicates. (Indeed, I suspect that the great bulk, though by no means all, of the success stories of development have occurred with such a monetary policy or absence of monetary policy.)

Perhaps the greatest advantage of a unified currency is that it is the most effective way to maximize the freedom of individuals to engage in whatever transactions they wish. Second, while the major countries are capable of policy that seems unwise to many of their residents and to professional economists, yet they are likely to have far stabler and less erratic policies than the smaller, newer, less-established developing countries. Hence, a unified currency is likely to reduce the possibility of unwise governmental policy. Third, a unified currency assures a maximum degree of integration of the country in question with the greater world.

However great these advantages, the brute fact is that few countries are willing to accept the discipline of a unified currency and to refrain from establishing a central bank. So I turn to the question of the desirable monetary policy, given that money creation is going to be used as a method of government finance.

5. Money Creation as a Source of Government Revenue

The distinctive feature of the inflation tax—the feature that recommends it both to developed and underdeveloped countries—is that it is the one tax that can be levied without explicit legislative enactment or executive announcement. The treasury or the central bank simply prints currency, or does the equivalent by adding to its deposit liabilities; the government uses the additional currency or created deposit liabilities to buy goods or services; the sellers find themselves with larger cash balances than they desire, so they purchase goods or services, make investments, or gifts, which causes the created money balances to spread through the economy—in the process perhaps multiplying through commercial banks; the increased flow of spending raises prices, which reduces the real value of cash balances to the desired level; the holders of cash balances have paid a tax because they have had to use part of their income or noncash wealth to acquire additional pieces of paper or book entries (deposits) to maintain their real balances at the desired level; the additional pieces of paper are the equivalent of certificates from the tax collectors certifying that the tax has been paid.

The tax rate depends on the rate of money issue relative to the existing money stock. The yield of the tax to the government for a given tax rate depends on the size of balances relative to income. Consider a highly simplified ideal case in which the tax is fully anticipated and allowed for. Suppose all money consists of currency notes and suppose the government has been adding to the money stock at the rate of 10% per year and is expected to continue to do so indefinitely. If, when the money stock is increasing at 10% per year, the public chooses to hold money balances equal to one-tenth of a year's income (i.e., income velocity of circulation of money is 10), then the yield to the government will be 1% of a year's income. If the public chooses to hold money balances equal to one-half of a year's income, the yield will be 5% of a year's income.

How rapidly prices will rise under these circumstances depends on (a) how rapidly output is growing and (b) whether the community is seeking to raise or lower the ratio of real balances to income. In the simple example, if output is rising at 5% a year, and velocity is constant, prices will rise 5% a year. If, as is more realistic for underdeveloped countries for moderate and steady rates of inflation, velocity is falling at about the same rate as output is rising (income elasticity of demand for money equals 2), prices would be stable, the 5% growth in money per unit of output being absorbed by higher desired balance per unit of output. This example illustrates that governments may get a yield from issuing money, even if there is no inflation.

The economic effects of the tax depend partly on its rate, but, in my opinion, much more on two other circumstances associated with the tax. Hence, I shall discuss these first before considering what is the right amount of money creation. These other circumstances are (a) whether inflation is open or repressed; (b) whether, as assumed in the example, it is anticipated or, as is often true in practice, unanticipated.

6. Open Inflation versus Repressed Inflation

By open inflation, I mean a situation in which prices are allowed by the government to rise to whatever level is required to clear the market, where "prices" include wages, interest rates, and exchange rates.

By a repressed inflation, I mean a situation in which at least an important class of prices, though not necessarily all prices, are prevented from rising to clear the market by governmental measures fixing maximum legal prices, where "prices" again include wages, interest rates, and exchange rates. Of course, the repression may be more or less extensive and more or less successful.

Open inflation is not desirable, but if the inflation is moderate, it does no great harm to economic efficiency or economic development, though it may do considerable harm to the political fabric of the society. On the other hand, repressed inflation is extremely harmful to efficiency, to development, and to respect for the law. It is an attempted cure that is far worse than the disease.

The most dramatic example of the different effects of open and suppressed inflation is provided by the experience in Germany after the two world wars. After World War I, there was a hyperinflation, in which prices rose at fantastic rates, during some periods doubling or more than doubling every day. The hyperinflation did immense damage to the social coherence and political stability of Germany, but nonetheless, the economy continued to function at a high level until the final months of the hyperinflation. Prices were free to move and hence it continued to be possible to use the price system to organize the economy.

After World War II, Germany again faced an inflation problem, but the problem was of far smaller magnitude. If the inflation had been open, prices after the war would have had roughly to quadruple—a trivial inflation compared to the price rise after World War I. But the inflation was not open. There was price control covering almost all items. Ordinarily, it is impossible to enforce price control when the legal prices are so far away from market-clearing prices; it is impossible to prevent the emergence of extensive black markets. However, it was possible to enforce price control after World War II in Germany because Germany was occupied by the American, French, and British armed forces, and they were willing and able to enforce the controls far more rigidly and ruthlessly than any domestic police or armed forces would have been able to.

The result was that output in Germany was cut to roughly half the prewar level. People were driven to engage in barter. Workers in a factory producing aluminum pots and pans, for example, would work for two or three days, get paid in pots and pans, and then spend the rest of the week scouring the countryside for a farmer who would trade potatoes or other food for the pots and pans. Nobody was willing to buy and sell for official money at prices that were about one-quarter the market-clearing prices. Cigarettes, coffee, and cognac came into wide use as substitute unofficial moneys to reduce the disadvantages of pure barter.

The great German economic miracle of 1948 was produced simply by the elimination of the price controls. Ludwig Erhard, then the economics minister, removed all the price controls one Sunday afternoon. He did it on Sunday, because the offices of the American, British, and French occupation authorities were closed on Sunday, and he was sure that they would have countermanded his order if they had been open.

The elimination of price controls produced a doubling of German output within a fairly brief period, not because of any new capital investment or the discovery of new techniques or the opening of new markets but solely because the price system was permitted to operate freely.

Perhaps the most pernicious and widespread single type of repression of inflation in underdeveloped countries is the attempt to peg the exchange rate. I think of India—an enormous country with extremely poor people that yet has tremendous potential for economic growth. India has many energetic, able, enterprising people; much capital; many well-trained individuals. Yet its record is depressing. I believe that the main reason for failure has been the attempt to repress inflation and particularly to peg the exchange rate. India finally devalued, though not by enough; but then, instead of letting the rupee exchange rate float, it has tried to peg it at a new level. The result has been to force India to ration imports and to subsidize exports and import-competing goods; to waste her resources, not for serving any national purpose but simply to preserve an artificial exchange rate.

In many underdeveloped countries in recent decades, the easiest route to wealth has been special access to import permits and to foreign exchange at pegged rates.

These examples illustrate why I believe that the distinction between open and repressed inflation is more important than the distinction between degrees of inflation.

7. Anticipated versus Unanticipated Inflation

Whether open or suppressed, an inflation that is not anticipated produces both unnecessary economic waste and unnecessary social disruption. The signals given by the price system are distorted. Entrepreneurs, laborers, and other economic actors are led to believe that the prices of their services have gone up relative to the prices of other items when all that is happening is that all prices are destined to rise. Some prices respond more rapidly than others, so production is encouraged that will prove to be a mistake and methods of production are adopted that turn out to be inefficient.

Socially, unanticipated inflation produces an erratic and disruptive redistribution of income and wealth. People who have invested their savings in forms offering a fixed interest return—savings deposits, government bonds, mortgages, life insurance—lose; borrowers gain. Persons whose wages and salary are fixed by custom or long-term contracts lose; people whose incomes adapt quickly gain—and among them always are highly visible classes of the new rich, regarded by the population as profiteers or speculators. The so-called profiteers or speculators are generally performing a valuable social service by speeding up the adjustment of the price system to the inflationary impulse, but that does not prevent them from being the object of public opprobrium and the source of social unrest.

Both the economic and social effects of inflation are far less harmful if inflation is widely anticipated—which is likely to mean, if it has been proceeding fairly steadily for a fairly long time. Under such circumstances, wage arrangements will have escalator clauses, either formal or informal. Interest rates will be high enough to allow for the anticipated inflation—if a rate would be, say 8%, without inflation, it would be 18% if a 10% per year inflation were widely anticipated. Similarly, exchange rates quoted for future dates will allow for the differential inflation anticipated in the interval in the two relevant countries.

An anticipated inflation is inconvenient because it requires changing the numbers written on price tickets; it produces inefficiency because it leads people to waste real resources in order to keep real cash balances low; but an anticipated inflation produces nothing like the amount of harm that an unanticipated inflation does.

Once an inflation has become anticipated, an unanticipated slowing down of inflation will have extremely harmful effects as well. For a time, prices of commodities and wages of labor will continue to rise at the earlier anticipated rates both because of long-term contracts and because the anticipations will affect new prices or wages being set. Many debt contracts will bear high interest rates that allow for the anticipated inflation. Until anticipations change, and until long-term contracts expire, the effect is likely to be a severe setback to business activity, with unemployment of men and machines, and discouragement of new capital investment.

As these comments imply, the distinction between anticipated and unanticipated inflation is largely a distinction between steady and erratic inflation.

8. The Rate of Money Creation

The proper rate of money creation for a developing country depends in the first instance on whether the objective is primarily the health of the economy or the revenue yield to the government.

For the health of the economy, in the most abstract sense which takes minimum account of frictions, the optimum would be a price level declining at a rate that would make the risk-free nominal rate of interest close to zero. A more pragmatic judgment, allowing for some frictions, would regard as best a roughly stable or slowly declining price level of final products, which would mean a moderately rising or roughly stable price of labor (see Friedman, 1969). This latter solution would still mean a rising quantity of money, the rate of rise depending on the rate of economic growth and on the income elasticity of demand for money.

Maximum governmental revenue would generally, though not necessarily, be yielded by a higher rate of monetary growth than is desirable for economic health. This is a technical question that I have considered in detail elsewhere (Friedman, 1971). Here I need only say that the most fascinating conclusion from my detailed analysis is that many developing countries in fact increase the quantity of money at a faster rate than would yield maximum revenue to the government over a long period. One reason seems to be that the initial yield from a high rate of monetary growth is always greater than the ultimate yield from that rate because, until people come to anticipate the higher rate, they do not economize fully on cash balances. Governments, being short-sighted, are led by the short-term gains to accept lower long-term yields.

9. Prescription

Let us bring the threads of this discussion together in the form of a prescription for developing countries.

For most such countries, I believe the best policy would be to eschew the revenue from money creation, to unify their currency with the currency of a large, relatively stable, developed country with which they have close economic relations, and to impose no barriers to the movement of money or of prices, wages, or interest rates. Such a policy requires avoiding a central bank.

The second-best policy, but one which has far greater political feasibility in the present climate of opinion, is to require a central bank to produce a steady and moderate rate of monetary growth, using the new money issued to finance part of government expenditures.

The emphasis on a "moderate" rate of growth is partly to avoid so rapid an inflation that a large amount of real resources are wasted in efforts to hold down cash balances, partly to avoid creating pressures for government intervention to repress the inflation. The emphasis on a "steady" rate of growth is to minimize the economic and social costs of erratic inflation that it is nearly impossible for people to anticipate and adjust to.

But far and away the most important single lesson of experience is that, whatever the rate of monetary growth, the resulting inflation should be permitted to be open. It should not be repressed.

Perhaps the greatest damage is done by trying to repress exchange rates, as in the case of India cited above. Once a country seeks to peg the exchange rate and then inflates, it is led to impose exchange controls, set up multiple exchange rates, give special bonuses to exports, impose quotas on imports and, so on and on, in an effort that always proves vain to defend artificial exchange rates. Fortunately, recent experience among both the developed and underdeveloped countries has done much to demonstrate the undesirability of a pegged exchange rate, so this mistake is perhaps less prevalent today than it was some time back.

A second set of prices that it is particularly desirable to avoid repressing—and yet that are almost always subject to legal maximums—are interest rates. By now, one lesson Irving Fisher tried to spread some 75 years ago has been learned: There is an important difference between nominal and real interest rates. A 25% rate when prices are rising at 15% per year means a 10% real rate of return. As a result, every country that has had substantial inflation also has had high interest rates.

Trying to repress interest rates is a particularly serious mistake for developing countries. In most developing countries, capital is scarce. If the interest rate is pegged at an artificially low level, people who have access to capital at that rate—generally people with political influence—will be encouraged to waste capital by using it in ways that have a low yield. Capital that escapes the controls will command an extremely high rate, much higher than the rate that would prevail in a free market.

An additional cost of trying to repress interest rates is that it leads to intervention into the development of financial institutions as a means of enforcing the legal interest rate ceilings. Yet underdeveloped countries have a great need for active and varied financial institutions, particularly for institutions that can serve small businesses. The best way to foster an effective and diversified financial structure is to let financial institutions develop in response to market forces.

Repressing prices of goods and of labor, while no less frequently attempted than repression of exchange rate and interest rates, generally does less economic harm. The reason is that they tend to be easier to evade. However, they do great social harm. Given price controls, black markets serve a socially useful purpose by preventing the distortions that would otherwise develop. The effect of price controls is therefore to make socially and individually beneficial action which is morally repugnant because it involves breaking the law. The conflict tends to undermine the moral capital of a nation.

Good monetary policy cannot produce development. Economic development fundamentally depends on much more basic forces: the amount of capital, the methods of economic organization, the skills of people, the available knowledge, the willingness to work and to save, the receptivity of the members of the community to change. Given favorable preconditions, good monetary policy can facilitate development. And, perhaps even more important, however favorable the preconditions, bad monetary policy can prevent development.

REFERENCES

Friedman, M. (1969)   The optimum quantity of money. In *The optimum quantity of money and other essays*. Chicago, Illinois: Aldine.
Friedman, M. (1971)   Government revenue from inflation. *Journal of Political Economy* **79**: 846–856.
Hamilton, E. J. (1934)   *American treasure and the price revolution in Spain, 1501–1650*. Cambridge, Massachusetts: Harvard Univ. Press.
Hamilton, E. J. (1936)   *Money, prices and wages in Valencia, Anagon, and Navarre, 1351–1500*. Cambridge, Massachusetts: Harvard Univ. Press.
Hamilton, E. J. (1947)   *War and prices in Spain, 1651–1800*. Cambridge, Massachusetts: Harvard Univ. Press.

Government: The Fourth Factor

ELI GINZBERG
COLUMBIA UNIVERSITY

1. The Title

I owe the title of this essay to a Nigerian student who was in the audience at the University of South Carolina in the early 1960s when I lectured on "The Pluralistic Economy." In light of his knowledge about the Nigerian economy, where government dominates the raising and allocation of capital, the exploitation of natural resources, the control of foreign trade, and the level and distribution of services directed to improving the nation's human resources, he wondered how Anglo-Saxon economists could ignore the dominant role of government in economic development. His surprise and confusion was increased when he heard me say that, according to calculations my colleagues and I had recently completed, the not-for-profit sector (government plus nonprofit institutions) in the United States accounted for between one-third and two-fifths of all employment and between one-fourth and one-third of the GNP. Why then, he asked, did economists, particularly those reared in the Anglo-Saxon tradition, ignore the fact that government was a factor of production? Was it, he continued, because of their political bias? Were they unable to acknowledge the potency of government in economic development because if they did, they would find themselves on the same side as

279

socialists, Marxists, and communists, who look to government as the primary instrument for reforming and improving the operations of the economy?

The student's question intrigued me at the time and it has intrigued me since. I will set down here a more complete answer than I was able to give him at that time. My exposition will deal sequentially with the following facets of the problem: the forces that led the classical economists to ignore or minimize the role of government; the failure of Keynesian macroeconomists to understand the structural changes in the post-World War II American economy; and the need for a dynamic model of societal behavior if the relations between government and economic development are to be seen with clarity. This essay, then, will seek to delineate how economists went so far astray in appraising the role of government; why most American economists have continued to rely on the earlier model of competitive markets; and the new framework that must be put into place if the interactions between government and the economy are to be understood. We will leave to the end whether we agree with the proposition that government should be considered a factor of production.

2. The Neglect of Government: Traditional Economic Thought

The fact that economics as a discipline was born as a counterpoint to the mercantilistic organization of the economy, with its emphasis on centralization, bureaucracy, and regulation, goes a fair distance to explain why Adam Smith's successors fell into the practice of slighting the role of government in their analyses. The author of *The Wealth of Nations* demonstrated to his own satisfaction and that of his enthusiastic followers that governments had a unique capacity to waste scarce resources and to distort the goals of national economic policy. While Smith and his followers, from Ricardo to Pigou, acknowledged that on occasion governments should intervene in the allocation and distribution of resources on grounds of efficiency or equity, most economists believed that a strict limit should be set on these interventions.

Smith saw a role for government in defense, navigation, the development of human resources (education), and in the establishment and maintenance of domestic security and tranquility, all of which are essential conditions for economic development. But his successors, concerned with analyzing the ways in which the competitive market calls forth scarce resources, prices them, and allocates them to different ends, directed their major energies to perfecting the model of the competitive economy.

The economists who dissented, from the early Christian Socialists, through Marx, to Veblen—the purists may prefer to call them political scientists, historians, sociologists—conceived of government as the key institution which affects the ownership of property and the distribution of profits. But, as Veblen demonstrated in his devastating attack on the major tradition, the classical and neoclassical economists refused to consider how government, with the aid of law, police power, and value reinforcement, helps to determine the structure of production and the distribution of rewards. By eliminating government from their analytic schema, the main-line economists had accepted a tradeoff: They were able to elaborate and refine their analyses of the laws of production while neglecting distribution.

If we agree that government is the instrument through which nations modify their institutions to cope with change, we can find a second reason that the economists gave it short shrift. Their models ignored all significant change. They deliberately omitted consideration of changes in population, technology, tastes on the structure and functioning of the economy. They recognized, as evidenced by Ricardo's revision of his chapter on machinery and Marshall's treatment of the Malthusian laws of population, that changes in these parameters could have important consequences for both production and distribution, but they disregarded these forces in order to achieve determinate results.

The concern of economists with analyzing the conditions of equilibrium, departures from equilibrium, and returns to equilibrium within a substantially stable system led them to place government beyond their purview. They would have required an historical, developmental, institutional or, as Veblen phrased it, an evolutionary bias to explore how changes in the governmental structure affect production and distribution.

Influences other than the authority of the founders of the discipline and the limitations of their own methodology deflected economists from a concern with the role of government in economic development. One such influence was their philosophical–psychological orientation. They saw society as a free association of independent human beings, operating under the dictates of rationality, and fixated on the accumulation of wealth. In exploring the dynamics of specialization, the economists used as their prototype not the caste system of India but a Robinson Crusoe setting. They were the direct descendants of the Romantic revolutionists of the eighteenth century, who saw society in terms of a social compact or contract. In their view, the economy was propelled by self-reliant individuals freely entering into contracts with one another to their mutual advantage. They considered the outcomes of competition as natural, inevitable, and desirable. They believed that Marx and his ilk were deluded for considering workers as industrial slaves exploited by capitalists.

Their concepts of the individual as the prime mover in society, social organizations as contractual arrangements among individuals, the maximizing of wealth as the primary goal of human life, and man as a rational being reinforced the economists' decision to exclude government from their system. They saw no need to analyze the political arena which is characterized by groups in conflict, pursuing such nebulous ends as power and prestige, in which the leadership engages in questionable activities to obtain and maintain their positions: deception, trickery, flattery, even fraud. To include government in their model would have sounded the death knell to the economists' efforts to build a new science.

Scholars have always disagreed about the design and improvement of the models with which they work. But there is a consensus that the investigator's intent is less relevant than the strength of his model to illuminate reality. For this reason, British economists were smug and secure: It was clear to them, at least up to World War I, that competition was the mainspring of their economy and it was competition that they had been able to study in depth.

When some continental followers of Karl Marx began to explore the linkages between foreign trade and domestic prosperity in advanced competitive economies and pointed to the marriage of convenience between business and the Foreign Office in determining British policy in India, Southwest Asia, the Middle East, South Africa, and Latin America, most economists pushed the subject aside. They did not want to complicate their increasingly tidy model of competitive markets with the dirty dynamics of imperialism.

The American experience was more equivocal. Most American economists were willing to follow in the footsteps of their British cousins, although a minority early recognized that the economic development of the United States had been and was being substantially affected by governmental decisions involving land distribution, protective tariffs, internal improvements, slavery, free immigration, the financing of higher education, agricultural extension services, and much more.

The recognition of these important arenas of governmental action was not sufficient, however, to wean the majority of American economists away from their preoccupation with the neoclassical model of the competitive market. They remained impressed with the wide latitude for decision-making that enterprises retained and the disinclination of government to interfere with the operation of the marketplace, at least in the hiring of workers and in the output of goods. Resources continued to flow to where the opportunities for profits were greatest. The country grew; individuals prospered. The successful performance of the competitive economy gave economics its internal security and its external strength. No one, not even Karl Marx, had developed a model with greater explicatory power. In the competitive world of thought, the best model, even if flawed, stays ensconced until it is replaced by a better one. But let us remember that the entrenched model had no place for government.

3. The Changing American Economy

We can leave the assessment of the relevance and utility of the Marshallian system for the analysis of British and American capitalism up to World War I, or shortly beyond, to a specialist who has yet to concern himself seriously with this question. For our purposes, it suffices to state that by the late 1930s, when the New Deal sought to rebuild an American economy that had all but collapsed from several years of cumulative shrinkages of output, prices, and employment, there was a crying need for a new model. This, Keynes provided. Within a few years after the publication of the *General Theory*, the Keynesian revolution was victorious. Except for a small minority who were too old or too cranky to go along, the entire economics profession accepted the new system which gave the government a dominant role in assuring an adequate level of investment to keep the economy at full employment. Two decades of chronic underemployment in Great Britain and a decade of severe unemployment in the United States which never fell below a rate of 10% convinced the profession that the free market alone was no longer capable of performing the critical function of utilizing all available resources effectively.

With the passage of the Employment Act in 1946, Keynesian macroeconomics became institutionalized in the United States. At the same time, American economists continued to make use of the competitive model, increasingly in its modern and sophisticated econometric version. However, the structure of the American economy was being transformed in response to the new opportunities on the domestic scene and threats presented by international events.

The old theory, the new theory, and the new reality lived cheek by jowl during the last three decades, and politicians and professors were able to pick and choose among the disparate elements in seeking understanding and guidance. For instance, Clark (1950) found it necessary to write an explanatory note to the United Nations Report on Full Employment in the early fifties which warned his enthusiastic Keynesian colleagues not to expect too much from government spending. Clark insisted that unless cost and price mechanisms perform effectively, no economy would be able to operate continuously at or close to full employment. Clark's reservations were politely noted but disregarded.

The Eisenhower years revealed structural faults in the economy. The President, by instinct and background in attunement with the McKinley economics of his Secretary of the Treasury, Humphrey, followed the advice of his pragmatic Chairman of the Council of Economic Advisors, Arthur F. Burns, who, criticizing Keynes in scholarly journals, borrowed liberally from him in fashioning his policy recommendations.

The Kennedy–Johnson decade revealed a similar dissonance. In his Yale address, President Kennedy insisted that the management of the American economy is not a proper subject for political debate, but is a matter which should be left to the technicians, the economists who know how to use fiscal and monetary policy to establish and maintain the economy at a high level.

At about the same time, James Tobin, a member of Kennedy's Council of Economic Advisors with roots in Yale, sought to allay the fears of American businessmen about the expansion of the federal government into their domain by presenting data that pointed to a *decline* in the role of government in the generation of GNP. He argued that although the federal government was seeking to deploy the instruments of fiscal-monetary policy more effectively, this effort was not, and should not be, considered a threat to the decision-making powers of businessmen.

During the next administration, while his economists sought to fine-tune the economy, President Johnson continued to talk of the strengths of our free-enterprise system in terms not greatly different from his immediate predecessors, Kennedy and Eisenhower, or his successor, Richard Nixon.

Only small differences separate the approach of the Kennedy–Johnson economists, who looked to fiscal-monetary policies to relieve the country of excessive unemployment, and the early game plan of the Nixon administration which sought to bring the mounting inflation under control by resorting to the classic remedies of tight money, reduced governmental expenditures, and rising unemployment. A wide spectrum of academic economists looked to the combination of fiscal-monetary policy and the free market to keep the economy moving upward and onward.

In the 1960s a few dissenters had questioned whether this combination would in fact be powerful enough to overcome the structural impedimenta that appeared to lie back of the excessively high unemployment rates for the disadvantaged. John K. Galbraith, impressed with the growth of private power centers in corporations and trade unions, ridiculed those who continued to look to market mechanisms for salubrious effects. But it was Arthur F. Burns, the consulting architect of the Nixon anti-inflation strategy, who realized early in 1970 that policy was out of phase with reality since, in the face of high and rising unemployment, prices moved upward, imports increased, and improved liquidity failed to stimulate investment. By 1971, he put the matter simply: The economy was not responding as anticipated; new institutions and mechanisms were required.

For three decades, major changes had been taking place in the structure and functioning of the American economy, primarily the steadily expanding role of government, a role that successive Presidents, concerned about public and business confidence, understandably sought to minimize, but which most economists ignored in their infatuation with Keynesian macroeconomics.

The steady expansion of government during these decades can be read in the following summary record: Government's role as a direct employer increased several-fold, and its contribution to GNP, likewise; it set the pace for technological innovation via defense and space expenditures (air transportation, electronics, computers); it helped to keep afloat major industries such as agriculture and shipping which had fallen on hard times; through its expenditures on highways and subsidies for construction, it played a critical part in altering the location of people and industries; through its foreign aid programs, insurance against expropriation, import controls on petroleum, stockpiling of strategic materials, and limitations on foreign investments by domestic corporations, it has increasingly altered the structure of our foreign trade. Moreover, its several regulating commissions exercise leverage over such critically important variables as capital markets, stock exchanges, trade unions, communications and other utilities, and help determine the rate at which new opportunities are opened to minority groups. And government is continuously involved in new arenas, from satellite communications to ecology.

When the Penn Central Railroad collapsed in the late spring of 1970, the Federal Reserve Board acted to prevent a financial panic, and when Lockheed was threatened with bankruptcy in the summer of 1971, Congress helped bail it out. The spokesmen for the banking syndicate, testifying on behalf of a federal bailout for Lockheed, stated that since the government is in every nook and cranny of the economy, there is good reason for it to save a major company whose collapse would have disastrous repercussions. That spokesman was a senior officer of the nation's second largest bank!

In August 1971, President Nixon, in announcing his new economic program—a price–wage freeze, a special import levy of 10%, cutting the dollar loose from gold, new tax concessions for business and the consumer—stated that his proposals represented the most significant departure in national economic policy in 40 years.

Whether his program is successful or not, there is little reason to argue with the President's statement that the introduction of wage, price, and dividend controls in a peacetime economy represents a major break with tradition. An interesting question, however, is why only a few economists understood that the cumulative structural transformations which had taken place would force the President to adopt such a policy, even a President who believed firmly in a free-enterprise economy.

The principal explanation of the economists' failure to foresee this change in policy lies in their continued adherence to an outmoded methodology based on faulty assumptions spiced by a conservative–optimistic tilt.

Competitive price theory, in its simple or sophisticated version, was the professional economist's major inheritance. This is what he had learned and what he knew how to use. Since an operational theory of oligopoly had not been adumbrated, economists made do with what they had, occasionally warning their students to take note of the gap between the assumptions of the theory they used and the realities of the moneymaking world.

The gap between their theory and reality was accentuated as a result of their devotion to mathematical model building and econometrics. Sophisticated theoreticians devote their energies to designing complex models; they pay little attention to the quantity and quality of the data which determine the relevance of their results.

The economists continued to postulate that individualism, voluntarism, and rationality provide a working model of man and society although the overwhelming weight of scholarship denied each in turn. However, these traditional assumptions made it easier for the economists to minimize the growing role of government in charting the direction of the economy, which they saw as responding primarily to the profit-maximizing of entrepreneurs and the utility-maximizing of consumers.

The post-World War II American economic fraternity had felt comfortable with the main thrust of economic and social policy, with its reformist orientation and avoidance of radical reforms. To them, the grafting of Keynes's model to the free market was preferable to experimentation with major institutional changes involving private property, corporate control, income redistribution.

But this rationale about why most American economists did not make room for the vastly expanded role of government in their models has perhaps explained too much. Prior to his retirement from Columbia University, Arthur Burns called attention to the anomaly that, in an era when economics in the real world was political economy, it had become an increasingly esoteric discipline in the halls of academe.

This would be difficult to understand were it not for the fact that once before, in the formative years of Ricardian economics, when England was buffeted by war, inflation, enclosure, blockade, industrialization, urbanization, and other major socioeconomic changes, the classical economists had developed a model that omitted these realities. By ignoring structural changes, the classical economists were able to build a discipline with increasing powers of analysis even at the price of a growing distortion of reality. But the continued neglect of government as a critical decision-making center by contemporary American economists has resulted in the entrenchment of outmoded theory and the establishment of defective policies. Although improved theory is not a guarantee for sound policy, it essential that economists broaden their perspectives with respect to the ever-increasing role of government in shaping the goals and influencing the operations of the contemporary economy.

4. The Functions of the Governmental System

In my forthcoming work on *The Human Economy: A Theory of Manpower Development and Utilization* (Ginzberg, to be published), the process of societal development is analyzed in terms of interaction among four major subsystems—values, government, the economy, and manpower institutions. In the present context we will summarize the principal ways in which the governmental system interacts with the economy in order to make the single point that these interactions are critical for understanding and formulating policy.

In both autocratic and democratic regimes, those in power want to maintain public support. Politicians do not press economic policies that are likely to lead to widespread discontent among the public, which in one instance may take the form of industrial sabotage or noncooperation, and in another, lead to defeat at the polls.

In a democracy elections are the principal instrument for arriving at consensus about the intermediate and long-run goals that the society seeks to achieve and about the preferred ways to accomplish them. When those in power lose the support of the public, the consensus essential for economic growth and development is lacking, which in turn leads to confusion and uncertainty among the decision makers in both government and the economy. Since so much economic activity is geared to the future, a loss of confidence means that consumers and investors are likely to sit and wait and watch, with the result that the economy loses momentum.

Nor is the centrality of government much different in controlled societies. When the leadership is under pressure, riven by conflict, uncertain about its next move, the cues on which the bureaucrats depend to move on the economic front, from investments to price adjustments, will be equivocal, which in turn will lead to slippage, slowdowns, bottlenecks.

The maintenance of public support and confidence, to which might be added the old verities of public security and tranquility, is the first and overriding task of government in nurturing a successful economy. In the absence of competent government whose authority is respected, even if its leaders are not loved, no economy can long prosper.

Among the criteria that a government must meet to pass the test of competence is its strength to raise the substantial sums required to broaden and deepen the infrastructure for sustained economic development. Private savings have a role to play in the process of growth, but unless government and large intermediate bodies (corporations) are able to deflect a substantial proportion of current output from consumption to investment, the economy will drag. The principle of complementarity in public and private investment has not received its due. A single illustration: The dynamism of the automobile industry is predicated on a continuing high level of public investment in highway construction.

A parallel challenge can be subsumed under the term "equity". All governments represent a balancing of conflicting interest groups. Some groups are always in a better position than others to benefit from state action. In a democracy, if those in opposition to government are able to voice their views and to organize to replace those in power, the elected officials must always be on the alert to adjust to the changing views of the public. Although alterations in the societal value structure are made slowly, there are stages in the development of nations which are associated with new value orientations. Momentum builds up only over a period of time, but a severe depression, racial conflicts, or the aftermath of a war often act as precipitants. A major test of political competence is the ability of the leadership to recognize these turning points and to adjust to them. Accommodation to the new can shorten the period of acute conflict situations and mitigate the exacerbation inherent in them. If the government is successful in this task, the economy will suffer less disturbance.

Another arena where governmental action can facilitate or retard economic development relates to its policy affecting the development of human resources. The acquisition of skill depends on, among other things, the access of people to educational and training facilities. These facilities must be provided by government or they will not be broadly available. If the population must rely on the family and job mobility for the acquisition of skills, its competence will be raised quite slowly. Consequently, the ability of government to expand and improve the manpower development institutions so that a steadily increasing proportion of the population will have access to them can accelerate the rate at which the economy grows.

In these several ways—facilitating consensus, building infrastructure, responding to the demands for equity, providing opportunities for skill acquisition—governments engage in functions that are critical to the performance of the economy. The effectiveness with which they operate in these several realms will significantly affect the performance of the economic system.

5. Government as a Factor of Production

Alfred Marshall was not satisfied with the old trilogy of land, labor, and capital as the factors of production; he added management. Josef Schumpeter moved in the opposite direction; he reduced the trilogy to two, arguing that land is a form of capital. Marx had earlier accepted only one factor; he postulated that all surplus value stems only from live labor.

There is no *a priori* method whereby the number of factors of production can be determined. It depends on the model employed by the economist.

We know that the major tradition did not consider government specifically as a factor of production. In our view, that was an error. That error is compounded today when, at least in the United States, government has the following roles:

It is the nation's largest employer.
It is the nation's largest investor.
It is the nation's largest consumer.
It is the nation's largest supporter of science and technology.
It determines in large measure the level at which the economy operates.
It sets the limits within which businessmen cooperate and compete.
It controls the profitability of many large industries.
It provides transfer income for tens of millions of citizens.
It can expand opportunities for the disadvantaged.
It exercises a dominant influence on the changing patterns of consumption.

Since government does all of these things and many more, we must agree with the Nigerian student who saw government as a fourth factor of production. When we do, we should be able to develop a more realistic model and more effective policy.

REFERENCES

Clark, J. M. (1950)   Explanatory note. *United Nations Report on Full Employment*. New York: United Nations.
Ginzberg, E. (to be published)   *The human economy: A theory of manpower development and utilization.*

What Became of the Building Cycle?

BERT G. HICKMAN
STANFORD UNIVERSITY

An inquest into the apparent demise of the building cycle is particularly appropriate for a volume of essays in honor of Moses Abramovitz. During the 1950s and 1960s a notable share of his research activity was devoted to the study of Kuznets cycles, and within that larger frame much of his attention was focused on the great swings in construction activity which were an integral part of the internal dynamics of the Kuznets cycle.[1]

1. Building Cycles, Kuznets Cycles, and Business Cycles

The concept of a long building cycle figures prominently in the pre-World War II literature on economic fluctuations. Between 1933 and 1943, a succession of writers demonstrated the existence and analyzed the possible mechanisms of long cycles in the level of building activity with an average duration of 17 or 18 years (Riggleman, 1933; Burns, 1935; Warren and Pearson, 1937; Long, 1940; Derksen, 1940; Hansen, 1941; Isard, 1942a, b; Silberling, 1943). As Fig. 1 shows, the contraction phases of these long cycles

---

[1] Abramovitz published his principal papers on these subjects in 1959, 1961, 1964, and 1968 (see References).

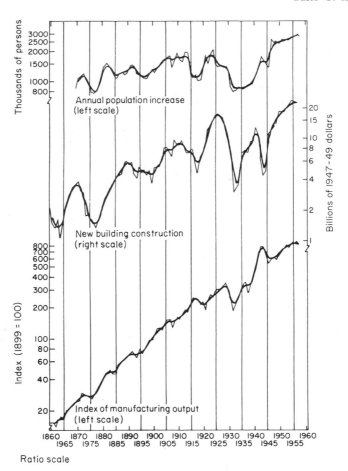

FIG. 1.   Population increases, new building construction, and manufacturing output—annually and three-year moving averages: 1860–1958. [From B. G. Hickman, *Growth and stability of the postwar economy*, Washington, D. C.: Brookings Institution, 1960, p. 307.]

consisted of prolonged and deep declines in the absolute level of new building construction. The long cycles were dominated by residential construction, but other types of building participated as well (Long, 1940; Abramovitz, 1964).

Somewhat earlier, Wardwell (1927) and Kuznets (1930) had established the existence of "secondary secular movements" (as Kuznets called them) in detrended production and price series which had been smoothed to attenuate the influence of business cycles, and Burns (1934) had showed that the existence of such "trend-cycles" (as he called them) was so widespread among individual industries as to strongly suggest the existence of long swings in the growth rate of aggregate economic activity. The national product estimates subsequently developed by Kuznets for the period since 1869 confirmed the existence of long swings in aggregate growth and led to the postwar revival of interest in their nature and significance by such writers as Abramovitz, Easterlin (1966), Thomas (1954), Cairncross (1953), Lewis and O'Leary (1955), Williamson (1964), and Kuznets himself (1952, 1961).

The long swings in building activity and economic growth are closely related historically. The average duration of each is about 17–18 years, they are in one-to-one correspondence, and they bear a similar relationship to ordinary business cycles.

The relationship between Kuznets cycles and business cycles has been stated as follows by Abramovitz (1968):

> When series representing aggregate industrial output are smoothed to eliminate ordinary business cycles, one finds 15 to 20-year waves in the growth rates of the smoothed series. The same is true of GNP growth rates after 1880 when industrial production becomes the dominant sector. There were four such waves from 1840 to 1911; they varied from 16 to 19 years in duration.
>
> These waves in growth rates are the smoothed reflection of the fact that at intervals of 15 to 20 years, the U.S. economy suffered either a severe and protracted depression or else a period of pronounced stagnation in which business-cycle recoveries were disappointing and did not return the economy to full employment. In the intervening years, the economy experienced only mild and short recessions with expansions vigorous enough to make unemployment low at business cycle peaks. One way to state the problem of the Kuznets cycles, therefore, is to ask why it was that America suffered unusually severe depression, or protracted periods of milder recessions with disappointing recoveries, only at these long intervals, while in the interim employment remained at high levels subject to short mild recessions [p. 351].[2]

It was precisely this last question that was responsible for much of the interest in building cycles during the 1930s. Among the writers cited above, Long and Hansen particularly emphasized the historical association between the severe business contractions and long downswings of building, illustrated in Fig. 1. Of the seven major business-cycle contractions usually recognized since the Civil War, three—those of 1873–1878, 1892–1894, and 1929–1932—were superdepressions, and each of them coincided with a long downswing of building construction. In contrast, the major business contractions occurring during building-cycle expansions were either of moderate amplitude (1882–1885) or relatively brief duration (1907–1908, 1920–1921, 1937–1938).

Whether approached from the viewpoint of its relation to the business cycle or the Kuznets cycle, the key question about the building cycle is the

---

[2] M. Abramovitz (1968) "The passing of the Kuznets cycle," *Economica* **35**: 349–367. This conception of the long swings differs from Kuznets' own view. Kuznets (1961, Chap. 7) places no stress on fluctuations of effective demand relative to potential output in his sketch of the long-swing mechanism. For further discussion of this point, see the work of Hickman (1963).

same: Is there (or was there in earlier times) an independent building cycle which sets the basic pattern of mild and severe business cycles or growth swings, or are the building waves themselves part of a larger endogenous mechanism?

If it could be established that the long swings in building were largely independent of feedback from the rest of the economy, the occurrence of severe depressions could be attributed largely to independent weakness in the construction industry. Independent building cycles could occur either because they themselves reflected exogenous driving forces or because of structural factors in the housing sector capable of generating endogenous long cycles. The principal possibility of the first type would be the existence of exogenous cycles in the rate of population growth which impinged directly on housing demand. This hypothesis must be rejected for the period before World War I, however. Although the building swings were associated with long swings in the rate of growth of population (Fig. 1), there is persuasive evidence of a large induced component in the population waves due to the effects of fluctuations of employment opportunities on immigration. Indeed, this feedback is an important component of Abramovitz's conception of the long-swing mechanism in operation prior to 1914 (Abramovitz, 1961).

With regard to the possibility of an endogenous long-cycle mechanism internal to the housing sector, the principal question concerns the supposed existence of sufficiently lengthy lags to produce such prolonged periods of over- and underbuilding in reponse even to powerful disturbances, such as wars. As early as 1940, Derksen (1940) employed an econometric model of the building cycle to show that the period of the implied endogenous cycle after World War I was only 12 years, as contrasted with the actual cycle of 15 or 16 years between 1918 and 1933–1934. Moreover, the endogenous mechanism was so heavily damped as to produce virtually only one cycle in response to a disturbance of the magnitude of World War I. Derksen suggested, however, that the building cycles prior to 1914 might have had a larger endogenous component with longer period and smaller damping owing to longer response lags in the earlier period.

2. Population Growth, Household Formation, and Housing Starts

The historical association between the long swings of population growth and general building activity between the Civil War and World War II was noted in the preceding section. If we concentrate now on the residential construction component of total building, we may make use of the findings of Campbell (1961, 1963) to illuminate the quantitative relationship between housing demand and population. Since there are wide disparities between the propensities of people in different age groups to form independent households, Campbell weighted population changes by "headship rates" (i.e., the ratio of household heads to total population in an age class) to provide a measure of housing demand that varies with the age composition as well as the size of the population. He demonstrated that the long swings in actual household formation (defined as the change in the number of occupied dwelling units) prior to World War I followed the swing in required additions, or population change weighted by headship rates, quite closely, so that changes in headship rates were of minor importance in explaining household formation. Moreover, since immigration was the chief source of population growth and was concentrated in age groups with high headship rates, it was the wave of immigration that was proximately responsible for the wave in household formation. Finally, the number of housing starts closely paralled the swings in household formation in respect both to timing and amplitude. Thus the feedback loop, running from residential construction through aggregate demand to unemployment and immigration and then back to residential construction, was evidently little influenced by speculation or overshooting within the housing market and building industry itself before World War I.

Dramatic changes occurred in the foregoing relationships after World War I had run its course. (1) The restrictive legislation of 1924 greatly reduced the contribution of immigration to population change and at the same time cut the link between employment opportunities and immigration. (2) Household formation no longer conformed closely to population change weighted by headship rates. (3) Housing starts no longer conformed closely to swings in the rate of household formation.

The relationships that prevailed among weighted population change, the rate of household formation, and housing starts after the mid-1920s are pictured in Fig. 2 (see Table 1). The series on standardized households (HHS) is constructed along the lines suggested earlier by Campbell in his concept of required additions, except that it refers to the nonfarm population instead of total population, and is weighted throughout the 1925–1970 period by 1940 headship rates instead of by the moving weights he employed.[3]

Household formations and housing starts display a great deal of short-term or cyclical instability even during the 1920s and after World War II. The longer run movements which are our principal concern in this paper stand out more clearly after the annual series are smoothed by a five-year moving average.

It is apparent that the long swing in the rate of household formation between 1925 and 1940 was much larger than can be explained by weighted population change alone, and that housing starts, in turn, fluctuated widely relative to household formation. If anything, the departures are even more striking following 1945. The rate of household formation far outpaced the growth rate of standardized households, and housing starts greatly exceeded

---

[3] The weights are as follows: Under 15, zero; 15–19, 0.006; 20–24, 0.110; 25–29, 0.281; 30–34, 0.377; 35–39, 0.428; 40–44, 0.465; 45–49, 0.495; 50–54, 0.516; 55–59, 0.531; 60–64, 0.538; 65–69, 0.547; 70–74, 0.549; 75 and over, 0.495.

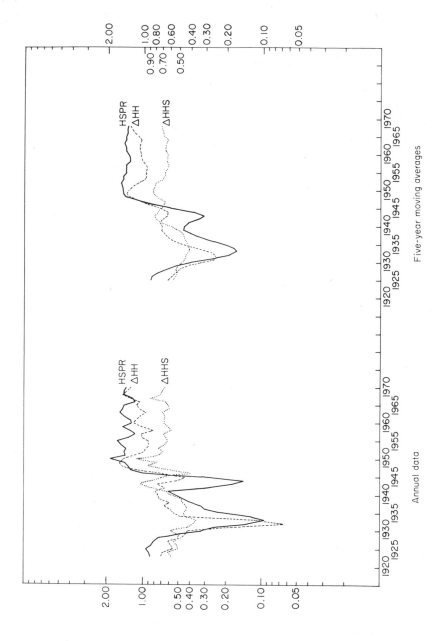

FIG. 2. Relationship among weighted population changes (ΔHHS), rate of household formation (ΔHH), and housing starts (HSPR) after mid-1920s.

TABLE 1
DATA FOR FIG. 2

	Annual data			Five-year moving averages		
	HSPR	ΔHH	ΔHHS	HSPR	ΔHH	ΔHHS
1922						
1923	0.8710	0.712	0.581			
1924	0.8930	0.690	0.609			
1925	0.9370	0.563	0.513	0.8720	0.6322	0.5552
1926	0.8490	0.580	0.522	0.8484	0.5848	0.5406
1927	0.8100	0.616	0.551	0.7716	0.5338	0.5174
1928	0.7530	0.475	0.508	0.6502	0.5046	0.5298
1929	0.5090	0.435	0.493	0.5312	0.4302	0.5098
1930	0.3300	0.417	0.575	0.3960	0.3200	0.4746
1931	0.2540	0.208	0.422	0.2640	0.2474	0.4450
1932	0.1340	0.065	0.375	0.1874	0.2534	0.4366
1933	0.0930	0.112	0.360	0.1645	0.2794	0.4124
1934	0.1260	0.465	0.451	0.1746	0.3554	0.4138
1935	0.2157	0.547	0.454	0.2143	0.4752	0.4266
1936	0.3042	0.588	0.429	0.2755	0.5730	0.4484
1937	0.3324	0.664	0.439	0.3420	0.6262	0.4550
1938	0.3993	0.601	0.469	0.4048	0.6672	0.4822
1939	0.4584	0.731	0.484	0.4678	0.7066	0.5272
1940	0.5296	0.752	0.590	0.4616	0.7032	0.6104
1941	0.6195	0.785	0.654	0.4185	0.7376	0.7292
1942	0.3012	0.647	0.855	0·3545	0.6946	0.7968
1943	0.1837	0.773	1.063	0.3136	0.6314	0.8048
1944	0.1387	0.516	0.822	0.3927	0.6316	0.7540
1945	0.3250	0.436	0.630	0.5855	0.7442	0.7130
1946	1.0150	0.786	0.400	0.8175	0.8868	0.6768
1947	1.2650	1.210	0.650	1.0758	1.0992	0.6676
1948	1.3440	1.486	0.882	1.3924	1.3080	0.7662
1949	1.4300	1.578	0.776	1.4734	1.3914	0.8330
1950	1.9080	1.480	1.123	1.5096	1.3500	0.8380
1951	1.4200	1.203	0.734	1.5212	1.2416	0.8118
1952	1.4460	1.003	0.675	1.5416	1.1048	0.7894
1953	1.4020	0.944	0.751	1.4854	0.9866	0.6884
1954	1.5320	0.894	0.664	1.4664	0.9526	0.6696
1955	1.6270	0.889	0.618	1.4122	0.9582	0.6708
1956	1.3250	1.033	0.640	1.3946	0.9358	0.6356
1957	1.1750	1.031	0.681	1.3871	0.9606	0.6262
1958	1.3140	0.832	0.575	1.3077	1.0252	0.6362
1959	1.4946	1.018	0.617	1.2997	1.0484	0.6418
1960	1.2301	1.212	0.668	1.3525	1.0530	0.6374
1961	1.2848	1.149	0.668	1.4063	1.0768	0.6604
1962	1·4390	1.054	0.659	1.4078	1.0874	0.6574
1963	1.5829	0.951	0.690	1.4519	1.0696	0.6474
1964	1.5023	1.071	0.602	1.4233	1.0534	0.6444
1965	1.4506	1.123	0.618	1.3891	1.1016	0.6806
1966	1.1415	1.068	0.653	1.3693	1.2086	0.6874
1967	1.2684	1.295	0.840	1.3586	1.2698	0.7050
1968	1.4836	1.486	0.724	1.3518	1.3006	0.7128
1969	1.4491	1.377	0.690			
1970	1.4163	1.277	0.657			

household formations until the late 1960s. Thus a startling rise of headship rates after 1940 augmented the postwar demand for dwelling units stemming from population factors, and this development, coupled with the "failure" of housing starts to replicate the pronounced postwar swing in household formation, greatly damped whatever tendency there was toward a long downswing of residential construction during the 1950s. Clearly an adequate explanation of the major fluctuations in residential construction since the mid-1920s needs to account for the newfound independence of household formation from demographic factors and of housing starts from household formation.

In the following pages I will make use of a new econometric model of the housing market and building industry to analyze the fluctuations in housing starts and residential construction expenditures since 1925. The model accounts for economic as well as demographic determinants of household formation and provides an explanation of the marked deviations of housing starts from household formation in both the interwar and postwar periods.

3. Outline of the Housing Model

The model consists of four behavioral equations and five identities. The first two behavioral equations relate to the demand and supply for the total stock of dwelling units in the economy and together determine the level of rent (PYHR) and the number of households or occupied dwelling units (HH). The second pair of behavioral functions is concerned with the construction of new dwelling units. One of them is a builder's production decision equation to determine the number of new private dwelling units started (HSPR), whereas the other predicts the value of construction per new start (HCCA). The various identities serve to relate the number and value of new housing starts to the stock of dwelling units (HU) and its value in constant dollars (HKN).

The housing and construction sectors are intimately related. Landlords and tenants interact in the housing market to determine the level of rent and the proportion of the available stock of dwelling units which is actually occupied (HH/HU_{-1}). In turn, the level of rent and the occupancy ratio (or its complement, the vacancy ratio) serve as market signals to builders concerning the potential demand for new dwelling units. Acting on this and other information affecting prospective demand and construction costs, the builders construct new dwelling units, thereby augmenting the housing stock and affecting rents and occupancies in the next period. Thus there is a stock-adjustment process connecting the housing market and the residential construction industry, but it is a considerably more complicated process than is implicit in the stock-adjustment models usually applied to the investment decision of the business firm bent on augmenting its own capital stock.

The estimated equations are listed in the Appendix. For present purposes, a brief general description of the system will suffice.

a. The Rent and Household Equations

In the absence of lags, the level of rent and the number of households would be jointly determined by the demand and supply of dwelling units and the market clearing equilibrium condition. Since rental units may be withheld from the market, the supply depends positively on the real rental rate

(PYHR/PCE, the rent index deflated by the consumer price index) as well as on the standing stock of dwelling units as inherited from the previous period (HU_{-1}). The number of dwelling units demanded for occupancy (number of households, HH), depends negatively on the real rental rate and positively on the number of standardized households (HHS), and real disposable income per standardized household (YPD/HHS). These equations may be solved for the equilibrium values of rent and households as a function only of predetermined variables. Because rents are sticky, however, owing to market imperfections and leases, it will not do to assume equilibrium in the housing market.

It is assumed instead that rent adjusts toward its equilibrium value each period by a constant proportion of the discrepancy between the actual level in the previous period and the current equilibrium level. (An alternative specification leading to the same estimation form is based on the assumption that rent changes each period by a constant fraction of the excess demand measured at the current rent level.) It is also assumed that landlords are price setters and tenants are price takers. Again because of market imperfections and adjustment lags, however, tenants are not necessarily on the demand curve at all times. Accordingly, it is assumed that the actual number of households adjusts partially each period toward the desired quantity as determined by the structural demand function and the current rent established by landlords.

No distinction is made between tenants and owner-occupants in the model. Owner-occupants are viewed as charging themselves an implicit rent equal to the market rental their unit would command if leased to another household.

b. The Residential Construction Equations

The number of new housing starts depends on the expected profitability of building and selling a new house or apartment building to owner-occupants or landlords. Expected profitability is a function of the ratio of expected selling price to construction cost, where expected sales price is assumed to be estimated by capitalizing current market rents on existing houses (PYHR) by the private long-term interest rate (RL). The cost of building is represented by the price deflator for residential construction (PHGIN).

It is assumed also that expected profitability is affected by the probability of quick sale of finished units to avoid the losses associated with carrying vacant units or reducing price for quick disposal. The probability of quick turnover is assumed to depend positively on the level of the lagged occupancy rate for existing dwelling units $[(HO_{-1}) = (HH/HU)_{-1}]$ and on the level of disposable personal income per household in current dollars (YPD\$/HH).

Finally, except for the 1930s, the volume of housing starts is also a function of credit availability to builders, as represented by the proxy variable (RL/RS), the ratio of the long- and short-term interest rates on private securities.

Housing starts depend positively on (RL/RS), since the ratio falls as credit conditions tighten and builders are prevented from obtaining construction loans.

The rent and occupancy variables appearing in the starts equation provide the links between the housing market and the building industry. The reverse feedback is from housing starts to the stock of dwelling units, as given by the identity

$$HU = HU_{-1} + \tfrac{1}{2}(HSPR + HSPR_{-1}) + HA + HSPU_{-1}. \tag{1}$$

In this relationship, it is assumed that one-half the private units started last year are completed this year, and similarly for this year's starts. Public housing starts (HSPU) are given exogenously and are assumed to be completed with a lag of one year, since they are predominantly multifamily units with longer construction times. Finally, allowance is made for net additions (HA) to the housing stock from other sources than new starts. Net additions may be positive if conversions exceed demolitions and negative otherwise, and are given exogenously.

The rent, household, and starts equations, together with the identity defining the stock of dwelling units, form a closed system to determine the time paths of the housing stocks and flows measured in terms of dwelling units if the other determinants are treated as exogenous. Such a model would be sufficient for some purposes, but it is preferable to augment the system by adding an equation to determine the average value of a new housing start in constant dollars (HCCA). In this way the constant dollar value of new residential construction can be determined endogenously and used as an input to the aggregate demand sector of a macroeconomic model, which in turn allows for feedback to the housing sector via the income and price variables included in the housing and construction equations.

The average value per new start is a function of real personal disposable income per household (YPD/HH), the short-term interest rate (RS), the average size of nonfarm households (NF/HH, where NF is the nonfarm population), and the constant-dollar value of a unit of the existing housing stock $(HKN/HU)_{-1}$. This equation contains two underlying demand factors, real income and household size. In line with the philosophy of the model, these variables are assumed to reflect the builders' views of the potential real value per dwelling unit demanded by consumers. The short-term interest rate reflects the cost and availability of credit to builders and influences their decision about the quality of construction to undertake. Finally, the value per dwelling unit is assumed to be positively related to the value of the existing housing stock, reflecting the long-run trend of real capital per dwelling unit.

The identities to complete the constant-dollar stocks and flows are cited in the Appendix.

4. Some Model Predictions

The housing model was fitted to annual data for 1924–1940 and 1949–1966. Figure 3 (see Table 2) shows the estimated and actual values for several

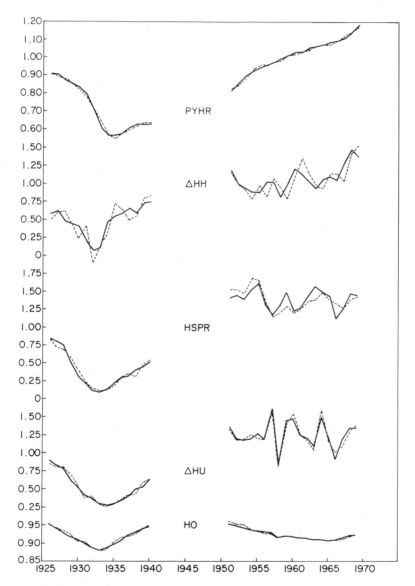

FIG. 3.   Values for important endogenous variables during 1925–1940 and 1950–1969. Solid line (—): actual values; broken line (---): predicted values. See text for definition of variables.

TABLE 2

DATA FOR FIG. 3

	Actual values					Predicted values				
	PYHR	ΔHH	HSPR	ΔHU	HO	PYHR	ΔHH	HSPR	ΔHU	HO
1926	0.9114	0.580	0.8490	0.8940	0.9515	0.9145	0.4882	0.8290	0.8604	0.9517
1927	0.8983	0.616	0.8100	0.8310	0.9414	0.8852	0.5862	7.1034	0.7927	0.9404
1928	0.8745	0.475	0.7530	0.7830	0.9287	0.8768	0.6185	0.6826	0.7961	0.9336
1929	0.8541	0.435	0.5090	0.6320	0.9169	0.8520	0.4405	0.5689	0.6971	0.9220
1930	0.8308	0.417	0.3300	0.5390	0.9106	0.8176	0.2326	0.4000	0.5441	0.9083
1931	0.7856	0.208	0.2540	0.4160	0.8997	0.7773	0.4101	0.2416	0.3748	0.9052
1932	0.7040	0.065	0.1340	0.3810	0.8881	0.7084	0.1013	0.1433	0.3919	0.8872
1933	0.6082	0.112	0.0930	0.3030	0.8797	0.6362	0.1513	0.1125	0.3080	0.8803
1934	0.5673	0.465	0.1260	0.2690	0.8870	0.5664	0.3117	0.1166	0 2546	0.8820
1935	0.5663	0.547	0.2157	0.2960	0.8982	0.5527	0.7251	0.1817	0.2836	0.8997
1936	0.5805	0.588	0.3043	0.3460	0.9098	0.5760	0.6363	0.3034	0.3627	0.9131
1937	0.6095	0.664	0.3324	0.4070	0.9222	0.5987	0.4951	0.3544	0.4184	0.9195
1938	0.6293	0.601	0.3993	0.4900	0.9301	0.6194	0.5637	0.3078	0.4333	0.9261
1939	0.6303	0.731	0.4584	0.5270	0.9396	0.6432	0.7959	0.4652	0.5761	0.7379
1940	0.6297	0.752	0.5296	0.6260	0.9483	0.6363	0.7287	0.5355	0.6255	0.9492
1951	0.8225	1.203	1.4200	1.3590	0.9566	0.8295	1.1903	1.5329	1.3227	0.9587
1952	0.8568	1.003	1.4460	1.2040	0.9496	0.8535	1.0009	1.5282	1.1887	0.9515
1953	0.9020	0.944	1.4020	1.1840	0.9449	0.8915	0.9280	1.4771	1.1804	0.9465
1954	0.9934	0.894	1.5320	1.1950	0.9399	0.9359	0.7942	1.6877	1.2353	0.9392
1955	0.4770	0.889	1.6270	1.2680	0.9347	0.9618	0.9847	1.6610	1.2072	0.9361
1966	0.9631	1.033	1.3250	1.2040	0.9315	0.9648	0.8440	1.3383	1.1936	0.9288
1957	0.9823	1.031	1.1750	1.6230	0.9296	0.9822	1.0928	1.1621	1.6099	0.9283
1958	1.0007	0.832	1.3140	0.8570	0.9160	0.9926	0.9645	1.2105	0.8117	0.9174
1959	1.0152	1.018	1.4946	1.4550	0.9206	1.0220	0.8024	1.3040	1.4115	0.9177
1960	1.0290	1.212	1.2301	1.4680	0.9182	1.0245	1.0999	1.2135	1.5550	0.9132
1960	1.0290	1.212	1.2301	1.4680	0.9182	1.0245	1.0999	1.2135	1.5550	0.9132
1961	1.0432	1.149	1.2848	1.2580	0.9144	1.0361	1.3672	1.2718	1.2597	0.9137
1962	1.0559	1.054	1.4390	1.2030	0.9127	1.0542	1.1518	1.3715	1.1758	0.9137
1963	1.0676	0.951	1.5829	1.0980	0.9101	1.0664	0.9762	1.3897	1.0352	0.9115
1964	1.0762	1.071	1.5023	1.4980	0.9113	1.0820	0.9541	1.5098	1.5983	0.9107
1965	1.0880	1.123	1.4506	1.2150	0.9072	1.0845	1.1509	1.3949	1.1835	0.9071
1966	1.1030	1.068	1.1415	0.8980	0.9066	1.1044	1.1454	1.3330	1.0215	0.9078
1967	1.1226	1.295	1.2684	1.1950	0.9145	1.1277	1.0482	1.2731	1.1016	0.9116
1968	1.1505	1.486	1.4836	1.3460	0.9209	1.1497	1.4296	1.4009	0.3023	0.9171
1969	1.1864	1.377	1.4491	1.3490	0.9231	1.1813	1.5535	1.4414	1.3865	0.9222

important endogenous variables during 1925–1940 and 1950–1969.[4] These are simultaneous, single-period solutions, using actual rather than predicted values for all lagged endogenous variables.[5] The estimates for 1967–1969 are postsample predictions.

It is clear from visual inspection that the model tracks reasonably well in both the prewar and postwar periods. The model was not designed for maximum tracking ability during the minor housing cycles of the postwar period, but it does well enough in that respect to inspire considerable confidence in its lag specification.

5. Explaining Household Formation

An important feature of the model is the incorporation of economic as well as demographic determinants of household formation. As explained above, the basic behavioral hypothesis is that the desire to form independent households, as reflected in the number of dwelling units demanded for occupancy, is a function not only of the size and age distribution of the population, but also of the level of real disposable income per standardized household and the real rental rate per dwelling unit. Since rent is itself determined by the interaction of demand and supply in the housing market, and since the supply of dwelling units changes over time in lagged response to changes in the occupancy ratio and rent level, the ultimate determinants of household formation should properly be interpreted in terms of the (nonlinear) final form solution for the entire housing model. As it turns out, however, the estimated demand function for housing has virtually zero elasticity with respect to rent (see Appendix, Eq. 2). This means that household formation can be treated to a close approximation as if it depended only on changes in standardized households and real disposable personal income, and these are variables which are exogenous to the housing market itself.[6]

Neglecting the rent term, then, and also observing that the estimating

---

[4] Because autoregressive transformations were used in estimating the stochastic equations in the system, one observation is lost at the beginning of each observation period, so that the sample period predictions for HSPR begin in 1925 and 1950. Moreover, since the model predicts the stocks of occupied households and dwelling units, another observation is lost at the beginning of each observation period when the first differences of HH and HU are plotted, as in Fig. 3.

[5] Continuous dynamic solutions have also been made over the sample period. They produce larger errors, of course. For present purposes of structural and historical analysis, the single-period solutions are appropriate.

[6] In the context of a complete macromodel, of course, real disposable income is also an endogenous variable interdependent with the housing market and residential construction industry.

equation is virtually a first difference form in the logarithms,[7] we may set down the following equation for household formation:

$$\ln(HH/HH_{-1}) \approx 0.2744 \ln(HHS/HHS_{-1}) + 0.0606 \ln(YPD/YPD_{-1})$$
$$+ 0.665 \ln(HH_{-1}/HH_{-2}). \tag{2}$$

Thus the short-term elasticity of the relative rate of household formation with respect to a relative increase in standardized households is 0.27, whereas the corresponding elasticity for a relative increase of real disposable personal income is 0.06. Solving for the long-run elasticities, we obtain

$$\ln(HH/HH_{-1}) \approx 0.819 \ln(HHS/HHS_{-1}) + 0.181 \ln(YPD/YPD_{-1})$$
$$\approx \ln(HHS/HHS_{-1}) + 0.181 \ln \frac{(YPD/HHS)}{(YPD/HHS)_{-1}}. \tag{3}$$

That is to say, household formation is unitary elastic in the long run with respect to a change in the growth rate of weighted population, and has an elasticity of 0.18 with respect to the growth rate of real income per standardized household in the long run. The unitary elasticity with respect to population change was assumed *a priori* in the specification of the demand function for housing, but the elasticity for a change in real income per standardized household is estimated from the data.

The principal implication of these findings is that the wide fluctuations of household formation relative to weighted population change in both the interwar and postwar periods are largely traceable to corresponding fluctuations in real income per standardized household. As compared with earlier long swings, after 1924, fluctuations in income and employment opportunities impinged mainly on headship rates instead of inducing concurrent changes in immigration and standardized households. During the 1950s, for example, especially sharp increases occurred in headship rates at the early and late life-cycle stages, leading to a large increase in the number of households headed by primary individuals. As Campbell (1963, p. 515) observes, "In this context, the fact that growing real output could raise per capita real incomes without leading to a burst of immigration may explain why headship rates increased so much more in the fifties than in earlier boom periods."

6. An Endogenous Residential Building Cycle?

In the preceding sections the structure of the new housing model has been described and its ability to track the key endogenous variables during the interwar and postwar periods demonstrated. We turn now to an investigation

---

[7] Assuming first-order autocorrelation in the residual, the estimated value of the autocorrelation coefficient is 0.9655. A value of unity would yield an equation in which all variables were first differences.

of the dynamic properties of the model. In particular, we ask whether an endogenous long cycle is inherent in its structure. As noted above, the same question was asked by Derksen more than 30 years ago—and answered affirmatively. The issue is worth reopening, however, since the present model is sounder structurally and is fitted to a longer historical period with a greater variety of experience.

The theoretical possibility of an endogenous building cycle arises from the existence of long adjustment lags between the development of shortages or surpluses in the available housing stock and the subsequent production of new housing units in greater or lesser numbers. If it is assumed that current starts are always a constant proportion of the gap between the actual and desired or equilibrium housing stock of an earlier year with fixed time lag, the stock-adjustment process may be formalized in a linear difference or differential equation and analyzed by conventional mathematical methods. This was the method pioneered by Tinbergen (1931) in his analysis of the shipbuilding cycle and employed by Derksen (1940) in his study of the American residential building cycle. Now, the present model can be interpreted as a generalized stock-adjustment process, but it is a nonlinear system and must be studied by simulation methods.

It must be stressed that the kind of periodic overshooting of equibilium envisaged in the endogenous long-cycle hypothesis does not depend on a feedback from construction activity to the desired or equilibrium housing stock itself. Neither income nor population growth is assumed to depend on residential construction, so no interaction of the multiplier-accelerator type is included in the hypothesis. Indeed, it was the exclusion of such interactions which gave power to the proposition, noted earlier, that an independent long cycle in building provided at least a partial explanation of the occurrence of severe business depressions with some degree of regularity in United States history.

The first two housing simulations presented in Fig. 4 (see Table 3) for the period 1925–1940 were prepared on the assumption of just such independence from external fluctuations in population or income. The following hypothetical situations are compared with the actual developments in the chart. The series labeled I show what would have happened if all "exogenous" variables had stayed at their 1925 levels throughout the ensuing years, so that neither a change in standardized households nor in real income or consumer prices is permitted to affect demand or supply in the housing market, nor are changes in construction costs or credit availability allowed to influence builders' decisions about housing starts. Real income per standardized household and the consumer and construction price levels are also held constant in simulation II, but now standardized households are assumed to continue to increase steadily at the absolute rate actually observed during 1924–1925.

TABLE 3

DATA FOR FIG. 4

	PYHR				ΔHH				HO			
	Actual	I	II	III	Actual	I	II	III	Actual	I	II	III
1925	0.9216	0.9230	0.9231	0.9230					0.9651	0.9742	0.9696	0.9742
1926	0.9114	0.8959	0.9134	0.9095	0.5800	0.4355	0.6338	0.5791	0.9515	0.9529	0.9572	0.9593
1927	0.8983	0.8511	0.8911	0.8870	0.6160	0.3002	0.6166	0.5501	0.9414	0.9284	0.9456	0.9453
1928	0.8745	0.8011	0.8647	0.8623	0.4750	0.2086	0.6056	0.5180	0.9287	0.9087	0.9389	0.9368
1929	0.8541	0.7537	0.8391	0.8396	0.4350	0.1465	0.5982	0.4914	0.9169	0.8943	0.9355	0.9327
1930	0.8308	0.7117	0.8159	0.8220	0.4170	0.1043	0.5932	0.4946	0.9106	0.8832	0.9339	0.9315
1931	0.7856	0.6754	0.7957	0.8059	0.2080	0.0755	0.5896	0.4540	0.8997	0.8741	0.9332	0.9303
1932	0.7040	0.6446	0.7785	0.7906	0.0650	0.0555	0.5868	0.4131	0.8881	0.8662	0.9330	0.9285
1933	0.6082	0.6183	0.7639	0.7763	0.1120	0.0417	0.5848	0.3807	0.8797	0.8954	0.9330	0.9262
1934	0.5673	0.5961	0.7515	0.7647	0.4650	0.0318	0.5832	0.3832	0.8870	0.8533	0.9332	0.9248
1935	0.5663	0.5771	0.7409	0.7558	0.5470	0.0248	0.5818	0.3850	0.8982	0.8479	0.9334	0.9243
1936	0.5805	0.5607	0.7320	0.7487	0.5880	0.0197	0.5809	0.3786	0.9098	0.8430	0.9337	0.9242
1937	0.6095	0.5466	0.7243	0.7433	0.6640	0.0160	0.5799	0.3766	0.9222	0.8385	0.9339	0.9245
1938	0.6293	0.5344	0.7177	0.7398	0.6010	0.0132	0.5793	0.3825	0.9301	0.8344	0.9342	0.9253
1939	0.6303	0.5236	0.7119	0.7381	0.7310	0.0110	0.5787	0.3900	0.9396	0.8306	0.9344	0.9266
1940	0.6297	0.5141	0.7068	0.7394	0.7520	0.0094	0.5782	0.4227	0.9483	0.8271	0.9346	0.9290

	HSPR				ΔHU			
	Actual	I	II	III	Actual	I	II	III
1925	0.9370	0.9765	0.9843	0.9765	0.8940	0.9142	0.9269	0.9140
1926	0.8490	0.8480	0.8655	0.8473	0.8310	0.7378	0.8129	0.7649
1927	0.8100	0.6237	0.7563	0.6786	0.7830	0.5499	0.7266	0.6337
1928	0.7530	0.4721	0.6928	0.5848	0.6320	0.4274	0.6778	0.5614
1929	0.5090	0.3786	0.6589	0.5341	0.5390	0.3489	0.6513	0.5199
1930	0.3300	0.3152	0.6396	0.5016	0.4160	0.2940	0.6356	0.4949
1931	0.2540	0.2688	0.6278	0.4842	0.3810	0.2802	0.6261	0.4764
1932	0.1340	0.2335	0.6203	0.4646	0.3030	0.2217	0.6200	0.4551
1933	0.0930	0.2059	0.6156	0.4416	0.2690	0.1968	0.6161	0.4319
1934	0.1260	0.1838	0.6127	0.4182	0.2960	0.1769	0.6140	0.4122
1935	0.2157	0.1659	0.6111	0.4021	0.3460	0.1606	0.6126	0.3988
1936	0.3042	0.1512	0.6102	0.3915	0.4070	0.1470	0.6121	0.3892
1937	0.3324	0.1389	0.6099	0.3830	0.4900	0.1357	0.6119	0.3817
1938	0.3993	0.1284	0.6098	0.3764	0.5270	0.1259	0.6118	0.3766
1939	0.4584	0.1195	0.6100	0.3727	0.6260	0.1177	0.6121	0.3741
1940	0.5296	0.1118	0.6102	0.3715				

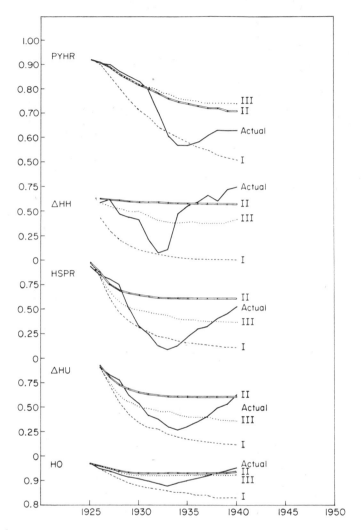

FIG. 4.   Housing simulations: 1925–1940. See text for definition of variables.

Finally, in simulation III, standardized households are entered at their actual values during the simulation period, but all income and price variables are held constant at the 1925 levels. This simulation, unlike the others, attempts to isolate the effect of demographic factors as they actually operated during 1925–1940.

No building cycle is apparent in simulations I and II, as can readily be seen by inspection of Fig. 4. The various endogenous variables approach their equilibrium paths smoothly, with no sign of cyclical fluctuation.[8]

The conditions imposed in simulation I imply a stationary long-run equilibrium in the housing sector. With real income and standardized households held constant, the demand and supply for dwelling units determines equilibrium values for rent and households as a function of the equilibrium number of dwelling units. New starts are needed only for replacement of demolished structures, and this sets the equilibrium value of starts at some level near zero. Since starts are a function of rent and the occupancy ratio, the equilibrium stock of dwelling units is determinate for any given level of replacement starts and the corresponding equilibrium values for households and rent.

To judge from Fig. 4, the simulated stock of households is close to its stationary value by 1940. The decline in household formation is rapid at first, but after eight or nine years it reaches a small value which diminishes very slowly thereafter. The rate of change of the housing stock also decelerates over the period, but even by 1940 the stock is still increasing faster than households, so that the occupancy ratio and rent level are still falling.

The results of this first simulation are a dramatic illustration of the power of the acceleration principle as applied to the demographic determinants of housing demand. The growth rate of standardized households has been assumed to drop abruptly from the 1924–1925 average of about 550 thousand per year to zero thereafter. With real income per standardized household held constant, this implies the abrupt steady-state loss of an equivalent annual demand for new housing units. However, owing to the substantial adjustment lags, the induced decline of housing starts is distributed over many years. Because actual starts were supported by continued population and income growth in the late 1920s, albeit at a diminishing rate, simulated starts fall below the actuals during 1926–1930, and they continue to decline at a decelerating rate through the 1930s.

The second simulation presents a markedly different picture. Since standardized households are assumed to continue to increase at the same annual absolute rate as in 1924–1925, the endogenous variables are approaching their steady-state growth values rather than a stationary equilibrium. Consequently, the equilibrium rate of household formation remains high, and the occupancy ratio, rent level, and volume of housing starts all decline much

[8] Residential construction in constant prices also approaches equilibrium smoothly in these simulations, although the series are not shown on Fig. 4. Since the number of households increases smoothly in the simulations, albeit at a diminishing rate over time, and since the real value of a new housing start varies positively with real income per household and average household size (see Appendix), real expenditures per start decline along with starts.

less than in the stationary case. Again, however, the convergence to equilibrium is monotonic instead of cyclical.

Simulation III incorporates the fluctuation which actually occurred in standardized households during 1925–1940. With immigration no longer an important endogenous variable, the irregular decline in the weighted rate of population increase between 1925 and 1934 (Fig. 2), represents an exogenous depressant to residential construction and GNP during that period, just as its subsequent recovery was an exogenous stimulant. According to simulation III, residential building would have fallen substantially under the demographic depressant, even if the feedback from declining construction to declining income had been neutralized (along with other income determinants in the economy) so that disposable income would have been constant after 1925. The post-1934 upswing in weighted population growth induces a mild response in simulated household formation, but the impact is not large enough to produce any recovery in simulated starts during the last half of the decade.

7. Conclusions

On the basis of the evidence presented in this paper, my answer to the question posed in the title must be: Nothing has become of the *building* cycle, for it never existed as an independent fluctuation. The answer presumes, of course, that the econometric model I have used is correctly specified and that the same model would apply equally to the period prior to World War I.

The contrary finding by Derksen (1940) was based on a faulty specification of the housing sector. The cycle-maker in his model for 1914–1938 was a discrete lag of two years between a change in the occupancy ratio and a change in the rent index, and hence between a change in the occupancy ratio and a change in housing starts. Such a long delay is inherently implausible; some part of the adjustment will surely occur immediately and some in the first year after the occupancy change, as well as in subsequent years. A partial adjustment process which operates continuously and without feedback to a target level which is itself free of substantial lags will not overshoot, and that appears to be the situation in the housing industry. As for the years prior to World War I, Derksen's conjecture that the occupancy ratio–housing starts lag was four years rather than two, and hence capable of explaining an endogenous cycle with a period of 16 or more years, is *a fortiori* even less plausible.

Thus the long swings in building, if cyclical in nature, must be explained by a model incorporating interactions between aggregate economic activity and the housing sector. For the era between the Civil War and 1914, the most plausible mechanism is the one specified by Abramovitz, in his analysis of the Kuznets cycle. In this context, the essential ingredient was the interaction between aggregate demand, unemployment, immigration, and household formation. Because the long waves in population growth were heavily influenced by immigration with its large induced component, they cannot be taken as exogenous, and because actual household formation closely paralleled the swings in required additions due to weighted population change, variations in headship rates attributable to income fluctuations were at most a minor factor.

This essential population link was broken by the Immigration Act of 1924. For the years spanned by the econometric model employed in this paper, the demographic determinants of household formation are exogenous with respect to current or recent .changes in income and unemployment. Household formation is no longer dominated by demographic change, as is evidenced by the marked independence of standardized and actual households during 1925–1970. After 1946, the severe housing disequilibrium resulting from World War II could be gradually eliminated by a stable approach to a moving equilibrium, without the adjustment process itself affecting the equilibrium path as it did before the 1920s. Since the new model is fitted to postwar as well as prewar data, and since it is demonstrably stable when disturbed from equilibrium, it follows that the absence of a pronounced long-swing in building after World War II is due to stabilizing forces outside the housing sector rather than to any change in its internal adjustment mechanism. Perhaps this conclusion should be qualified to allow for the influence of mortgage guarantee programs since the Great Depression, but, in view of the comparatively limited range of income fluctuations since 1946, it is unlikely that they have played a large stabilizing role in the postwar economy.

Appendix

This Appendix contains a listing of the housing model equations in the normalized form in which they were used in the simulation studies reported in the text, together with a list of variable definitions.

a. Housing Model Equations

$$\ln \text{PYHR} = -0.1114 + 0.1336 \ln \text{YPD\$} + 0.6045 \ln \text{HHS}$$
$$+ 0.1337 \ln \text{PCE} - 0.7381 \ln \text{HU}_{-1} + 0.7327 \ln \text{PYHR}_{-1}$$
$$+ 0.8025 \hat{U}_{-1} \tag{A1}$$

$$\ln \text{HH} = -0.0781 + 0.0606 \ln \text{YPD\$} + 0.2744 \ln \text{HHS} - 0.0050 \ln \text{PYHR}$$
$$- 0.0556 \ln \text{PCE} + 0.665 \ln \text{HH}_{-1} + 0.9655 \hat{U}_{-1} \tag{A2}$$

$$\ln \text{HSPR} = -4.1406 + 0.71317(\ln \text{PYHR} - \ln \text{RL} - \ln \text{PHGIN})$$
$$+ 1.69815(\ln \text{YPD\$} - \ln \text{HH}) + 0.12607\text{DHOUS}$$
$$+ 12.7564(\ln \text{HH}_{-1} - \ln \text{HU}_{-1})$$
$$+ 0.46856[\tfrac{1}{2}(\ln \text{RL} - \ln \text{RS}) + \tfrac{1}{2}(\ln \text{RL}_{-1} - \ln \text{RS}_{-1})]$$
$$+ 0.6262\hat{U}_{-1} \tag{A3}$$

$$\ln \text{HCCA} = 2.40505 + 0.63526(\ln \text{YPD\$} - \ln \text{PCE} - \ln \text{HH})$$
$$- 0.05412 \ln \text{RS} + 1.73273(\ln \text{NF} - \ln \text{HH})$$
$$+ 0.63324(\ln \text{HKN}_{-1} - \ln \text{HU}_{-1}) + 0.3139\hat{U}_{-1} \tag{A4}$$

$$\text{HU} = \text{HU}_{-1} + \text{HA} + \text{HSPU}_{-1} + \tfrac{1}{2}(\text{HSPR} + \text{HSPR}_{-1}) \tag{A5}$$

$$\text{HKN} = 0.98\text{HKN}_{-1} + \text{HGIND} + \text{HGP} + \text{HGAA} \tag{A6}$$

$$\text{HGIND} = (\text{WT})(\text{HCCA})(\text{HSPR}) + (1 - \text{WT}_{-1})(\text{HCCA}_{-1})(\text{HSPR}_{-1}) \tag{A7}$$

b. Variable Definitions

DHOUS   Housing dummy for Regulation X. 1950: 1.0; 1951: -1.0; all other years: 0.

HA   Net additions of nonfarm dwelling units, excluding starts. Millions of units.

HCCA   Average value per private housing start, adjusted to make the value of starts series [(HS)(HCCA)] consistent with value put in place (HGIND). Thousands of 1958 dollars.

HGAA   Gross expenditures for additions and alterations on nonfarm housing units. Billions of 1958 dollars.

HGIND   Gross private investment in new, nonfarm housing units. Billions of 1958 dollars.

HGP   Gross public investment in new residential structures. Billions of 1958 dollars.

HH   Total number of nonfarm households. Dated July 1. Millions of households.

HHS   Total number of standardized nonfarm households, weighted by 1940 headship rates. Dated July 1. Millions of standardized households.

HKN   Net stock of nonfarm residential structures, including public units. Dated December 31. Billions of 1958 dollars.

HSPR   Private nonfarm housing starts. Millions of housing units.

HSPU   Public nonfarm housing starts. Millions of housing units.

HU   Number of nonfarm dwelling units. Dated December 31. Millions of units.

NF   Total nonfarm population. Dated July 1. Millions of persons.

PCE   Implicit price deflator for personal consumption expenditures. 1958: 1.0.

PHGIN   Implicit price deflator for investment in nonfarm residential structures. 1958: 1.0.

PYHR   Implicit price deflator for rent of nonfarm dwellings. 1958: 1.0.

RL   Private long-term interest rate: Moody's yield on domestic corporate bonds. Decimal units.

RS   Private short-term interest rate: Four–six months prime commercial paper. Decimal units.

$\hat{U}_{-1}$ Estimated residual from previous period.

WT   Moving weight representing proportion of value of housing starts put into place in year of start. Calculated from $\text{HGIND} = (1 - \text{WT}_{-1})(\text{HCCA}_{-1})$ $(\text{HSPR}_{-1}) + (\text{WT})(\text{HCCA})(\text{HSPR})$ assuming $\text{WT}_{1944} = 0.80$.

YPD$ Disposable personal income. Billions of dollars.

ACKNOWLEDGMENT

The housing model used in this paper was developed as part of a project by the present author and Robert M. Coen to build a medium-term macroeconomic model of the United States economy. The research support of the National Science Foundation under Grant No. GS 2581 is gratefully acknowledged, as is the assistance of Mary Hinz and Robert Willig in the preparation of the simulations and figures used in this paper and in their co-authorship of the housing model itself.

REFERENCES

Abramovitz, M. (1959)   Long swings in the economic growth of the United States. Employment growth and price levels. *Hearings before Joint Committee, 86th Congress, 1st Session, Pt. 2, Washington, D. C., 1959*, pp. 411–466.

Abramovitz, M. (1961)   The nature and significance of Kuznets cycles. *Economic Development and Cultural Change* **9**: 225–248.

Abramovitz, M. (1964)   Evidences of long swings in aggregate construction since the Civil War. Occasional Paper 90. New York: National Bureau of Economic Research, Columbia Univ. Press.

Abramovitz, M. (1968)   The passing of the Kuznets cycle. *Economica* **35**: 349–367.

Burns, A. F. (1934)   *Production trends in the United States since 1870*. New York: National Burea of Economic Research.

Burns, A. F. (1935)   *Long cycles in residential construction. Economic essays in honor of Wesley Clair Mitchell*, pp. 63–104. New York: Columbia Univ. Press.

Cairncross, A. (1953)   *Home and foreign investment, 1870–1914*. London and New York: Cambridge Univ. Press.

Campbell, B. O. (1961)   The housing cycle and long swings. Residential construction: A statistical and theoretical analysis. Ph.D. dissertation, Stanford Univ., Stanford, California.

Campbell, B O. (1963)   Long swings in residential construction: The postwar experience. *American Economic Review* **53**: 508–518.

Derksen, J. B. D. (1940)   Long cycles in residential building: An explanation. *Econometrica* **8**: 97–116.

Easterlin, R. A. (1966)   Economic-demographic interactions and long swings in the rate of growth. *American Economic Review* **56**: 1063–1104.

Hansen, A. H. (1941)   *Fiscal policy and business cycles*. New York: Norton.

Hickman, B. G. (1960)   *Growth and stability of the postwar economy*, p. 307. Washington D. C.: Brookings Institution.

Hickman, B. G. (1963)   The postwar retardation: Another long swing in the rate of growth? *American Economic Review* **53**: 490–507.

Isard, W. (1942a)   A neglected cycle: The transport-building cycle. *Review of Economic Statistics* **24**: 149–158.

Isard, W. (1942b)   Transport development and building cycles. *Quarterly Journal of Economics* **57**: 90–112.

Kuznets, S. (1930)   *Secular movements in production and prices*. New York.

Kuznets, S. (1952)   Long term changes in national income of the United States since 1870. In *Income and wealth* (S. Kuznets, ed.), Series II. London and New York: Cambridge Univ. Press.

Kuznets, S. (1961)   *Capital in the American economy*. Princeton, New Jersey: National Bureau of Economic Research, Princeton Univ. Press.

Lewis, W. A., and O'Leary, P. J. (1955)   Secular swings in production and trade, 1870–1913. *Manchester school of economic and social studies* **13**: 113–152.

Long, C. D., Jr. (1940)   *Building cycles and the theory of industry*. Princeton Univ. Press.

Riggleman, J. R. (1933)   Building cycles in the United States, 1875–1932. *Journal of the American Statistical Association* **28**: 174–183.

Silberling, N. J. (1943)   *The dynamics of business*. Chaps. 9 and 10. New York: McGraw-Hill.

Thomas, B. (1954)   *Migration and economic growth*. London and New York: Cambridge Univ. Press.

Tinbergen, J. (1931)   Ein Schiffbauzyklus? *Weltwirtschaftliches Archiv* **34**: 152–164.

Wardwell, C. A. R. (1927)   *An investigation of economic data for major cycles*. Philadelphia, Pennsylvania:

Warren, G. F., and Pearson, F. A. (1937)   *World prices and the building industry*. New York: Wiley.

Williamson, J. G. (1964)   *American growth and the balance of payments, 1820–1913*. Chapel Hill: Univ. of North Carolina.

Instability in Underdeveloped Countries: The Impact of the International Economy

DONALD J. MATHIESON
COLUMBIA UNIVERSITY

RONALD I. McKINNON
STANFORD UNIVERSITY

Can poor countries ameliorate short-run fluctuations in income and employment by reducing their dependence on foreign trade? Economists have differed sharply over the importance of comparative advantage—the international division of labor—in contributing to long-run growth of less developed countries (LDCs). Until recently, however, it seemed axiomatic that LDCs suffer significant short-run instability transmitted through foreign trade from business cycles experienced by more mature economies.

There were two compelling reasons for this judgment. First, the breakdown and extraordinary instability in international trading relationships in the interwar period seemed to carry over, albeit to a lesser degree, to the early postwar. Price fluctuations in markets for primary commodities of particular interest to LDCs seemed "excessive" to casual observers. Second, the rise of Keynesian macroeconomic theory seemed to provide a conceptual tool kit enabling governments to stabilize their economies better than they had in the past. But exports, imports, and international flows of capital

315

through the foreign exchanges make domestic control over rates of interest or levels of aggregate expenditures (demand) more difficult. Hence, the loss of domestic autonomy in monetary and fiscal policy from outside "shocks" cast the foreign sector as the *bête noire* of economic stability in poor countries.

Our purpose in this paper is to reexamine the basis for the widespread presumption that the international economy, dominated by mature countries, has had a net destabilizing impact on LDCs in the postwar period;[1] and to inquire whether or not more autarkic policies (insulation from foreign trade) have succeeded in achieving greater freedom from short-run variations in real output. Fluctuations in investment expenditures and in the foreign-trade components of aggregate output are compared across developed and less-developed countries. These comparisons are then related to the size, wealth, and "openness"—dependence on foreign trade—of rich and poor countries.

Although instability in poor countries is indeed substantial, we find there is no persuasive evidence that the international economy generally exerted a net destabilizing influence on LDCs from 1950 to 1968; and there is the contrary indication that "outward-looking" trade policies may yield greater stability. Hence, our results throw considerable doubt on the theoretical and empirical grounds for supposing that purely autonomous or insular national economic policies bring greater economic stability.

1. A Bird's-Eye View of Recent Literature

The work of MacBean (1966) in measuring export instability from LDCs marked a major watershed in research on the subject. Using data confined to the 1946–1958 interval, MacBean showed that export instability in poor countries was only marginally greater (30% by his quantitative index) than in mature economies. Moreover, with the exception of a few highly specialized LDCs—e.g., Ghana (in cocoa) and Brazil (in coffee)—proceeds from exports of primary commodities are not more variable than receipts from exports of manufacturers. Insofar as severe export fluctuations did occur, they seemed to be caused by fluctuations in domestic supply arising out of strife, political upheaval, and economic miscalculation rather than due to shifts in international demand. MacBean downgraded the importance of export instabiltiy for fluctuations in Gross Domestic Product (GDP) and domestic investment, because he could not find good short-run statistical correlations among these variables.

Erb and Schiavo-Campo (1969) followed up that portion of MacBean's

---

[1] As assumed, for example, by Rhomberg (1968). Of course, many writers have noted the impact of business cycles transmitted internationally in earlier eras [see Levin (1960) and Prebisch (1950)].

analysis based purely on export instability using data extending up to 1966. To their surprise, they found a significant change had occurred from the 1946–1958 interval used by MacBean to 1954–1966. Export instability in both mature economies and in LDCs declined substantially, but much more in the former than in the latter. From 1954 to 1966, LDCs exhibited twice as much quantitative instability in export receipts as did mature economies[2]—albeit at a reduced level from the earlier period.

Additionally, Erb and Schiavo-Campo gave considerable weight in their conclusions to a rather slight inverse statistical correlation between the size of LDCs (as measured by GDP) and export instability. That is, small LDCs, whatever their per-capita income, tended to have greater export instability from 1954 to 1966—although this relationship was not marked in the earlier period from 1946 to 1958. For some reason they did not perform a similar test for advanced countries. Notwithstanding this, they seem to advance the hypothesis that country size per se is important, and LDCs are less stable simply because their GDPs are smaller.

Massel (1970) did an extensive statistical analysis of the determinants of export instability in 55 countries for the whole 1950–1966 period. For "explanatory" variables, he develops measures of commodity concentration, geographic concentration, dependence on food versus industrial raw materials, the importance of exports in domestic and in foreign markets, per-capita income, the absolute size of the export sector, and a dummy variable indicating whether a country was developed or underdeveloped. Massel found that concentration in exports of a few products generally increases instability, but unusual dependence on food exports reduces it. Export sectors which tend to be large in absolute terms also tend to be more stable. The other variables were not statistically significant. Insofar as large export sectors are positively associated with GDP, this corroborates the results of Erb and Schiavo-Campo regarding the importance of country size.

We accept Massel's results indicating the general benefits of deversification—with some gains in concentrating on food exports—as being plausible in achieving greater export stability. Hence, we do not investigate the diversification issue further. However, the effects of country size and openness have to be interpreted carefully and are investigated more fully below.

2. Instability in LDCs in Comparison to More Mature Economies

In a statistical sense, how important is economic instability in LDCs? There is reason to believe that instability is much more important than aggregate GNP statistics might suggest. Measurement or "smoothing" errors in

---

[2] Although their choice of a quantitative index may make a difference to this result, as pointed out by Leith (1970).

GNP aggregates make them particularly poor indicators of short-term fluctuations in income and employment. Indeed, more accurately measured components of GNP—such as investment and trade flows—appear much less stable than their counterparts in advanced countries. Hence stability itself remains an acute policy issue in poor countries apart from the more "standard" development problems of growth and transformation.

To demonstrate this point, we constructed a rather simple statistical index to measure instability through time in GNP, or in individual components of GNP, for each of 28 developed and underdeveloped countries.[3] Although data availability varies substantially from one country to another, annual observations spanning most of the years from 1950 to 1968 were used. Indices of instability based on a single yardstick—say gross investment—are then compared across mature and less developed countries. Why economic fluctuations so measured differ from one country to the next is then "explained."

First, however, consider how our indices of instability were constructed. Geometric trends were fitted for each country to annual data on five variables: real gross domestic product, real gross investment, real machinery and equipment expenditures, real imports, and real exports. All five variables are denoted by the variable subscript i in Y_i:

$$\log Y_{ti} = a_{0i} + a_i t + e_{ti}, \qquad i = 1, 2, \ldots, 5, \tag{1}$$

where t is an index of time representing annual observations in the ith category. Data were generally not available on all GDP components for all countries, but at least one component and GDP aggregate were available for each country overall for most of the years between 1950 and 1968. Hence, for each country, a maximum of five time-series regressions were run. Our measure of instability through time, then, is simply the standard error of each regression. For the ith component of GNP of each country, we denote this index of instability by S_i, where

$$S_i = \left(\frac{\sum_{t=1}^{n} \bar{e}_{ti}^2}{n-2} \right)^{1/2}. \tag{2}$$

The $\bar{e}_{ti}$ are simply the residuals of the estimated regression equation based on (1) above. It is easy to show that S_i^2 is an unbiased estimator of the variance of GDP, or of its components, around their geometric trends for any given country, and we shall not do so here. Across different countries, moreover,

---

[3] The developed countries considered in the study are the United States, Canada, the United Kingdom, Sweden, Denmark, Norway, France, West Germany, Belgium, Netherlands, Italy, Austria, and Japan. The developing countries include Chile, Brazil, Argentina, Bolivia, Mexico, Uruguay, Colombia, Peru, Pakistan, the Philippines, South Korea, China (Taiwan), Israel, Greece, and Thailand.

the S_i's have the great advantage of being directly comparable within the ith category, say gross investment, because these indices are pure numbers not denominated in pesos, rupees, dollars, etc. Thus, using the logarithmic form spares us from a complicated comparability calculation, which otherwise would have been necessary if the standard error around a linear trend had been used. Fortunately, the specification of proportional rather than linear growth seems to make more intuitive sense in purely economic terms. Hence, S_i can be used directly to compare the instability in one country with that of another.

We computed the S_i's for the gross domestic products of all 28 countries, and the S_i's for gross investment, machinery and equipment expenditures, imports and exports in a slightly smaller number of cases. The underlying "real" or price-deflated data are all taken from fairly new OECD sources so as to be as consistent as possible.[4] The results are listed in Appendix A, where countries are ranked according to the size of their S_i.

What main conclusions can one draw from these rankings as to the relative stability of rich and poor countries? For those S_i based on components of GDP rather than GDP itself, the rankings incidate that LDCs tend to be more unstable. This impression is confirmed when countries are divided into "less" and "more" developed groups, and then an average index of instability is computed for each group as is done in Table 1.

From Table 1, we see that percentage fluctuations in gross investment, machinery and equipment expenditures, and imports all appear about twice as high in LDCs. Export instability is also more marked in the underdeveloped world. Although the differences are fairly clear-cut from casual inspection, a more rigorous nonparametric procedure for testing the null hypothesis that poor countries have the same stability as wealthy ones is provided in Appendix A. From each of our four S_i based on components of GNP, this null hypothesis is decisively rejected. From these four (nonindependent) measures, poor countries seem highly unstable relative to wealthy ones.

But the results in Table 1 are paradoxical. Why does this sharp difference between the two groups fail to show up in measured instability in aggregate GDP itself? The average S_{GDP} is only 0.0280 for poor countries in comparison to 0.0261 for wealthy ones—not a statistically significant difference, as shown in Appendix A. One possible explanation is that LDCs are sufficiently

---

[4] Ideally one would like all quarterly data compiled in a similar manner for all countries. Unfortunately, developing countries seldom publish quarterly data and often the accounts of one country are compiled in a different manner from those in another country. While little has been done about the lack of quarterly data, the OECD has recently attempted to standardize annual national accounts across countries. The data for the developing countries are found in OECD (1968, 1971). The data for the developed countries are taken from OECD (1970).

TABLE 1

MEAN INSTABILITY INDICES
FOR DEVELOPED AND UNDERDEVELOPED COUNTRIES[a]

	Developed countries	Underdeveloped countries
Real gross domestic product	$n = 13$	$n = 15$
	$S_{GDP} = 0.0261$	$S_{GDP} = 0.0280$
Real gross investment	$n = 14$	$n = 13$
	$S_{GI} = 0.0644$	$S_{GI} = 0.1228$
Real machinery and	$n = 13$	$n = 10$
equipment expenditures	$S_{ME} = 0.0886$	$S_{ME} = 0.1949$
Real exports	$n = 13$	$n = 12$
	$S_E = 0.0521$	$S_E = 0.0871$
Real imports	$n = 13$	$n = 12$
	$S_M = 0.061$	$S_M = 0.1221$

[a] n is the number of observations; S_i is an index of instability, where $i =$ GDP, GI, ME, E, M.

fortunate—or clever—to have their relatively greater fluctuations in the major components of GNP offset each other in the aggregate. We reject this explanation as implausible for economic reasons. Instead, the difference seems to arise because of difficulties in measuring gross domestic product.

The OECD's statistics on gross investment, machinery and equipment expenditures, and imports and exports all have the virtue of being *directly* estimated annually for all countries. In LDCs on the other hand, private consumption—which is the most important component of GDP—is *not* estimated directly but is usually calculated as a residual after GDP is projected separately. Sometimes GDP is estimated by the income approach but coverage of agricultural incomes is generally quite poor. In other cases, real GDP is estimated by the use of base-period benchmarks and samples of outputs in various sectors as is illustrated more fully in Appendix B. This type of "smooth" projection from benchmark data *may well eliminate much of the short-term fluctuation we are trying to measure.* Some countries showed no annual declines in real GDP despite substantial variation in its components. For example, Brazil (1954–1966) and Colombia (1954–1966) never showed a year-to-year decline in official measures of real GDP, although it is thought that they went through some severe economic crises.

In summary, indirect estimates of GDP in LDCs may give some idea of long-term growth trends, but they cannot be used to measure short-term fluctuations in economic activity. However, flows of international trade and domestic investment are directly measured annually, and these do indicate that poor countries are significantly less stable than wealthy ones.

3. Openness and Country Size

Can one go further statistically in "explaining" why some countries are less stable than others? Since our indices of instability are comparable pure numbers, S_i can be treated as the dependent variable in cross-country regressions. Real income per capita Y/N should be negatively correlated with S_i in view of the above-noted differences between poor and wealthy countries. From the earlier analysis of Erb and Schiavo-Campo, one might also expect that country size per se is a stabilizing factor, and we shall use Y itself to denote size. Finally, openness to foreign trade has long been considered by many authors as the avenue of externally generated domestic instability. Here we ignore capital flows, and simply use the ratio of exports to GDP—E/Y—as a measure of "openness" in our regressions.

Each of our independent variables Y/N, Y and E/Y is measured at the midpoint of the time period within the 1950–1968 interval over which the corresponding S_i was calculated. Other possibly important determinants of instability—such as an unusual spurt in the rate of growth of output or of exports—are not adequately represented in our regression procedure. Our three independent variables are themselves closely correlated through statistical errors of measurement in real output Y, which enters in all three. But in addition, there also exist strong economic correlations among Y, Y/N, and E/Y because small countries tend to be more open, and because income per capita is related to aggregate income. Hence, alternative cross-country regressions, where these "independent" variables are used together and separately, were run over all countries for which we could compute the relevant S_i. The estimated regression coefficients are reported in Table 2.

Ignoring the regressions run on S_{GDP} for reasons discussed above, the results for the remaining four sets of regressions based on gross investment, machinery, and equipment expenditures, exports and imports all point, remarkably enough, in the same direction(s). Predictably, an increase in income per capita is associated with less instability because most coefficients of Y/N are significantly negative. It is interesting and more surprising, however, to examine the relationship between country size and economic openness. Contrary to the earlier results of Erb and Schiavo-Campo, country size per se does not seem to have any significant effect on instability unless there is a slight (perverse) tendency for small countries to be more stable. What is clear, however, is that the introduction of our measure of openness, E/Y, swamps the effect of country size and points in the *opposite* direction from that called for by the old literature on the international transmission of business cycles. That is, the more open the economy, the more stable each of our four subcategories of GNP appear to be.

This apparently favorable conjunction of openness and stability has to be

TABLE 2

The Effect of Size, Income per Capita, and Openness on Instability for All Countries in the Sample[a]

$S_{\text{GDP}} = 0.0281 + 0.00000002Y - 0.0000018Y/N$	$R^2 = 0.0184$
(8.347) (0.6779) (0.4958)	$n = 28$
$S_{\text{GDP}} = 0.0274 + 0.00000001Y - 0.00000045Y/N - 0.004002E/Y$	$R^2 = 0.0151$
(5.763) (0.3433) (0.0864) (0.1454)	$n = 27$
$S_{\text{GI}} = 0.1289 + 0.00000006Y - 0.0000428Y/N$	$R^2 = 0.3976$
(11.692) (0.6789) (3.473)	$n = 27$
$S_{\text{GI}} = 0.137 - 0.00000003Y - 0.0000283Y/N - 0.09794E/Y$	$R^2 = 0.4019$
(8.994) (0.2495) (1.73) (1.133)	$n = 26$
$S_{\text{ME}} = 0.1897 + 0.0000001716Y - 0.0000563Y/N$	$R^2 = 0.1882$
(6.148) (0.8053) (2.047)	$n = 23$
$S_{\text{ME}} = 0.2251 - 0.00000004Y - 0.0000353Y/N - 0.02777E/Y$	$R^2 = 0.2568$
(5.575) (0.667) (0.8931) (1.325)	$n = 23$
$S_{\text{E}} = 0.0926 - 0.0000001Y - 0.0000305Y/N$	$R^2 = 0.2328$
(8.286) (1.281) (2.546)	$n = 25$
$S_{\text{E}} = 0.1105 - 0.00000003Y - 0.00000991Y/N - 0.1642E/Y$	$R^2 = 0.3786$
(8.45) (0.3216) (0.688) (2.22)	$n = 25$
$S_{\text{M}} = 0.134 + 0.00000013Y - 0.0000534Y/N$	$R^2 = 0.3983$
(9.63) (1.269) (3.585)	$n = 25$
$S_{\text{M}} = 0.1505 + 0.000000004Y - 0.00003448Y/N - 0.1514E/Y$	$R^2 = 0.461$
(8.785) (0.0307) (1.828) (1.562)	$n = 25$

[a] The t ratios are given in parentheses.

interpreted with some care. Only in the export equation is the coefficient of E/Y significant at the 5% level of statistical significance when that equation is considered alone. Nevertheless, in each of the other three equations, the the coefficient of E/Y is also negative (openness reduces instability) and exceeds its standard error; i.e., the t ratio is greater than unity. Hence four separate equations indicate that openness may well reduce instability, although the four are not independent because machinery and equipment expenditures are a component of gross investment, and imports and exports are usually related—even for short-term fluctuations. This lack of independence inhibits any precise probability statement based on all four regressions, but the collective statistical evidence of an association between openness and stability is much stronger than any single equation might indicate. Of course, causality can go in either direction—openness can lead to stability, and stability can lead to openness. They are, however, not antithetical.

One should note that the mere absence of correlation between openness and instability would be sufficient to cast doubt on the old transmission hypothesis. Hence a positive association between openness and stability is more than sufficient.

The coefficients presented in Table 2 are derived from pooling data from diverse sets of countries—developed and underdeveloped. This pooling has the purely statistical advantage of increasing the range of observations on the explanatory variable Y/N—income per capita—and on our index of instability S_i. Over this increased range, significant statistical correlations are easier to establish for a given number of observations. The disadvantage is that we may be dealing with two distinctly different statistical populations—each with its own characteristics which may well differ from those obtained from any pooled regression.

To check out this uncomfortable possibility, we reran the regressions presented in Table 2 first on the developed countries as a group and then separately on the less developed. The results are presented in Appendix C, Table 9. Because of the sharp reduction in the range of observations on dependent and independent variables within each group, as well as substantial reduction in the degrees of freedom, the amount of statistical correlation as measured by the R^2 fell off, so that no coefficients were statistically significant at the 5% level. As one might expect, the amount of "explanation" provided by Y/N fell to almost nothing, and even the sign of its regression coefficient varied from one equation to the next. However, the coefficient of the openness variable E/Y retained its negative sign in seven of the eight regressions involving components of GNP; and, in several cases, this coefficient exceeded its standard error for both developed and developing countries. Certainly, there was no evidence of an unfavorable positive association between openness and instability upon disaggregating into separate groups of rich and poor countries.

4. The Transmission Hypothesis: A Concluding Note

Along with the notion that business cycles originate in mature economies is the idea that those cycles experienced by the "peripheral" countries are transmitted to them from mature ones. Import demand by advanced countries for the primary products of poor ones is cited as the vehicle by which cycles are transmitted. Does this "transmission" hypothesis apply to the postwar period?

From Table 1 it is apparent that individual mature economies are more stable. Thus, for the traditional hypothesis to hold, substantial magnification of fluctuations must somehow take place when they are transmitted to LDCs. One would think that relative openness, or dependence on foreign trade should facilitate this transmission and be positively associated with instability. But our previous cross-country analysis found a *negative* association between trade-dependence and stability. Hence, it is difficult to see how this international magnification effect would operate for all countries in general, and poor ones in particular.

Moreover, focusing attention on the average of fluctuations in individual advanced countries, limited as these fluctuations are, is probably overly favorable to the transmission hypothesis. Although some poor countries may have close economic relationships with particular advanced ones, the more usual situation is for each LDC to trade more widely. Thus, some measure of variation in *aggregate* imports by advanced countries would seem relevant. Using a somewhat different data series[5] from that underlying Tables 1 and 2, we calculated our index of instability for the *sum* of all dollar imports into developed economies—which also represents the overwhelming bulk of world trade. The resulting S_i turned out to be 0.0533 and, unsurprisingly, is significantly less than 0.0725, the average of all the S_i's based on imports for each advanced country. Moreover, 0.0533 is much less than 0.1370, the mean of all the comparable indices of commodity export instability for developing countries.

Apparently, the law of large numbers does operate. Wealthy countries have not experienced the business cycle in unison in the postwar period. Thus, poor countries exporting to several wealthy ones can expect a significant smoothing effect to occur, in comparison to selling to a single buyer. Either way, instability in these overseas markets would seem to be substantially less than that experienced within the underdeveloped world itself.

What are the policy implications of our analysis? Examples of extreme demand fluctuations for some primary products of particular interest to LDCs, such as copper or cocoa, can easily be identified. Overall, however, the evidence suggests that the international economy has had a net stabilizing effect on poor countries in the postwar period. Correspondingly, the autarkic tariff and quota policies of most LDCs, which have led to a sharp decline in their relative share of world trade, probably accentuated the substantial instability they continue to suffer. Hence, authorities might do well to reject the notion that cycles in economic activity are mainly imported, and instead view increased domestic instability as one of the likely costs of restricting foreign trade.

Appendix A

Tables 3–7 in this appendix present the standard errors S_i of the trend regressions for GDP, gross investment, machinery and equipment expenditures, exports, and imports. Each country is ranked according to the size of its S_i. We want to test the following proposition: Are developing or developed countries more unstable?

---

[5] We used pure commodity imports which are different from the "deflated" imports, inclusive of invisibles and net factor incomes, used in Tables 1 and 2. In aggregating, it is convenient to use dollar-commodity data which are directly comparable and additive across countries. The time period 1955–1968 was used for all countries.

TABLE 3

INSTABILITY INDICES FOR REAL GROSS DOMESTIC PRODUCT

Rank	Country	Years	S_{GDP}	Rank	Country	Years	S_{GDP}
1	Chile	1960–1967	0.0095	15	Greece	1950–1968	0.0253
2	France	1950–1968	0.0114[a]	16	Belgium	1953–1968	0.0273
3	Philippines	1959–1967	0.0134	17	Norway	1951–1968	0.0284
4	United Kingdom	1950–1968	0.0141	18	Peru	1950–1968	0.0305
5	Colombia	1950–1967	0.0143	19	Austria	1950–1968	0.0311
6	Italy	1951–1968	0.0153	20	Canada	1950–1968	0.0317
7	Thailand	1957–1966	0.0209	21	Denmark	1950–1968	0.0344
8	Sweden	1950–1968	0.0209	22	Argentina	1950–1968	0.035
9	Mexico	1950–1965	0.0224	23	United States	1950–1968	0.0355
10	Germany	1950–1968	0.0236[b]	24	Pakistan	1950–1966	0.0392
11	Bolivia	1958–1966	0.0242	25	Israel	1959–1968	0.0406
12	Uruguay	1955–1966	0.0248	26	Japan	1952–1968	0.0407
13	Netherlands	1950–1968	0.025	27	South Korea	1959–1968	0.0457
14	Brazil	1950–1967	0.0251	28	China	1952–1968	0.0496

[a] Average of 1950–1958, 1959–1968.
[b] Average of 1950–1959, 1960–1968.

TABLE 4

INSTABILITY INDICES FOR REAL GROSS INVESTMENT

Rank	Country	Years	S_{GI}	Rank	Country	Years	S_{GI}
1	United Kingdom	1950–1968	0.0316	15	Austria	1950–1968	0.0897
2	Sweden	1950–1968	0.0352	16	China	1958–1968	0.0964
3	France	1950–1968	0.0443[a]	17	Italy	1951–1968	0.1091
4	Germany	1950–1968	0.0488[b]	18	Uruguay	1955–1966	0.1168
5	Norway	1951–1968	0.052	19	Argentina	1950–1968	0.1256
6	United States	1950–1968	0.0521	20	Greece	1950–1968	0.1327
7	Chile	1960–1967	0.0564	21	Bolivia	1958–1966	0.1333
8	Belgium	1953–1968	0.0617	22	Brazil	1950–1966	0.1345
9	Philippines	1959–1967	0.067	23	Peru	1950–1968	0.1442
10	Thailand	1957–1966	0.0699	24	Colombia	1950–1967	0.1523
11	Netherlands	1950–1968	0.0715	25	Pakistan	1959–1965	0.155
12	Denmark	1950–1968	0.0775	26	Israel	1959–1968	0.1613
13	Japan	1952–1968	0.0803	27	South Korea	1959–1968	0.1741
14	Canada	1950–1968	0.0836				

[a] Average of 1950–1958, 1959–1968.
[b] Average of 1950–1959, 1960–1968.

TABLE 5

INSTABILITY INDICES FOR REAL MACHINERY AND EQUIPMENT EXPENDITURES

Rank	Country	Years	S_{ME}	Rank	Country	Years	S_{ME}
1	United Kingdom	1950–1968	0.0417	13	Netherlands	1950–1968	0.1111
2	France	1950–1968	0.0555[a]	14	United States	1950–1968	0.1202
3	Sweden	1950–1968	0.0576	15	Italy	1951–1968	0.1328
4	Belgium	1957–1968	0.0647	16	Canada	1950–1968	0.1383
5	Germany	1950–1968	0.0676[b]	17	China	1958–1968	0.1504
6	Denmark	1950–1968	0.0744	18	Peru	1950–1967	0.1600
7	Norway	1951–1968	0.0816	19	Argentina	1950–1968	0.1994
8	Chile	1960–1967	0.0864	20	Bolivia	1958–1966	0.2039
9	Thailand	1957–1966	0.095	21	Colombia	1950–1967	0.2551
10	Japan	1952–1968	0.0957	22	Greece	1950–1968	0.2872
11	Philippines	1959–1967	0.0973	23	Uruguay	1955–1963	0.4138
12	Austria	1950–1968	0.1109				

[a] Average of 1950–1958, 1959–1968.
[b] Average of 1950–1959, 1960–1968.

TABLE 6

INSTABILITY INDICES FOR REAL EXPORTS

Rank	Country	Years	S_E	Rank	Country	Years	S_E
1	Chile	1960–1967	0.0184	14	United States	1950–1968	0.0646
2	Denmark	1950–1968	0.0218	15	Germany	1950–1968	0.0652[b]
3	United Kingdom	1950–1968	0.0313	16	China	1958–1968	0.0772
4	Belgium	1953–1968	0.035	17	Philippines	1959–1967	0.0775
5	Netherlands	1950–1968	0.0352	18	Bolivia	1958–1966	0.08
6	Norway	1951–1968	0.0366	19	Peru	1950–1968	0.0905
7	Sweden	1950–1968	0.0415	20	Canada	1950–1968	0.0905
8	France	1950–1968	0.0423[a]	21	Austria	1950–1968	0.0941
9	Italy	1951–1968	0.0558	22	Brazil	1950–1966	0.112
10	Colombia	1950–1968	0.0567	23	Argentina	1950–1968	0.1257
11	Israel	1959–1968	0.0635	24	Uruguay	1955–1966	0.1267
12	Japan	1952–1968	0.0638	25	South Korea	1959–1968	0.1528
13	Greece	1950–1968	0.0643				

[a] Average of 1950–1958, 1959–1968.
[b] Average of 1950–1959, 1960–1968.

TABLE 7

INSTABILITY INDICES FOR REAL IMPORTS

Rank	Country	Years	S_M	Rank	Country	Years	S_M
1	United Kingdom	1950–1968	0.0311	14	Japan	1952–1968	0.0816
2	France	1950–1968	0.0336[a]	15	Chile	1960–1967	0.0887
3	Belgium	1953–1968	0.0382	16	Israel	1959–1968	0.0896
4	Sweden	1950–1968	0.0423	17	Italy	1951–1968	0.0921
5	Norway	1951–1968	0.0424	18	Austria	1950–1968	0.1062
6	Germany	1950–1968	0.0527[b]	19	Philippines	1959–1967	0.1162
7	United States	1950–1968	0.0613	20	Peru	1950–1968	0.1215
8	Denmark	1950–1968	0.0623	21	Argentina	1950–1968	0.1409
9	Bolivia	1958–1966	0.0624	22	Uruguay	1955–1966	0.1548
10	Greece	1956–1968	0.0661	23	Colombia	1950–1967	0.1570
11	Netherlands	1950–1968	0.0704	24	Brazil	1950–1966	0.1609
12	China	1958–1968	0.0772	25	South Korea	1959–1968	0.2301
13	Canada	1950–1968	0.0797				

[a] Average of 1950–1958, 1959–1968.
[b] Average of 1950–1959, 1960–1968.

Since the estimates of the standard errors of the regression are unbiased, we can utilize the rank–sum test discussed by Hoel (1965), which is a nonparametric test designed to determine whether or not the two sets of data come from the same population. The null hypothesis is that the two sets of data come from the same population (with the same mean), and the alternative hypothesis is that the two samples are drawn from different populations (with different means).

To test the null hypothesis, the rank–sum test requires that we first rank the data in the two samples by size (smallest first). Let n_1 denote the number of developing countries and n_2 the number of developed countries in our sample. Let R be the sum of the ranks of the developing countries. Then under the null hypothesis, we have

$$E(R) = [n_1(n_1+n_2+1)]/2, \qquad \sigma_R^2 = [n_1 n_2(n_1+n_2+1)]/12,$$

$$\rho = [R-E(R)]/\sigma_R.$$

Then, ρ has a standard normal distribution for $n_2 > n_1$ and $n_2 \geqslant 10$.

We calculated the values of ρ as defined above for each of the expenditure categories, and then computed the probabilities of ρ being greater than these calculated values if the null hypothesis holds (see Table 8). These probabilities are minute for gross investment, machinery and equipment expenditures, exports, and imports, being 0.0003, 0.0014, 0.0096, and 0.0001%, respectively.

TABLE 8

CALCULATIONS FOR THE RANK–SUM TEST[a]

Real gross domestic product

$n_{UD} = 15,$ $n_D = 13$
$R_D = 185,$ $E(R) = 188.5,$ $\sigma_R^2 = 471.25,$ $\sigma_R = 21.71$
                        $p = (185 - 188.5)/21.71 = -0.16$

Real gross investment[a]

$n_{UD} = 14,$ $n_D = 13$
$R_D = 111,$ $E(R) = 182,$ $\sigma_R^2 = 424.67,$ $\sigma_R = 20.61$
                        $p = (111 - 182)/20.64 = -3.44$

Real exports

$n_{UD} = 12,$ $n_D = 13$
$R_{UD} = 199,$ $E(R) = 156,$ $\sigma_R^2 = 338,$ $\sigma_R = 18.38$
                        $p = (199 - 156)/18.38 = 2.34$

Real machinery and equipment expenditures

$n_{UD} = 10,$ $n_D = 13$
$R_{UD} = 168,$ $E(R) = 120,$ $\sigma_R^2 = 260,$ $\sigma_R = 16.13$
                        $p = (168 - 120)/16.13 = 2.98$

Real imports

$n_{UD} = 12,$ $n_D = 13$
$R_{UD} = 216,$ $E(R) = 144,$ $\sigma_R^2 = 338,$ $\sigma_R = 18.41$
                        $p = (216 - 144)/18.41 = 3.91$

---

[a] Since the rank–sum test requires the R (the sum of the ranks) to correspond to n_1 (the smallest sample), R in some cases represents the sum of the ranks of the developed countries and in other cases the sum of the developing countries.

For GDP the probability is 0.4364. Thus, for the components of GNP, our tests reject the null hypothesis that the underdeveloped and developed countries are equally stable and accepts the alternative hypothesis of more instability in poor countries. For aggregate GNP itself, however, this test shows no significant difference between these two sets of countries.

Appendix B

As discussed in the text, GDP estimates for many of the developing countries produce misleading indications of stability. This is illustrated in the OECD (1968) discussion of the manner in which GDP is estimated for many of the less-developed countries. One outstanding feature of many of the estimating procedures is the fact that consumption is estimated as a residual. This is true of Bolivia, Brazil, Colombia, Pakistan, and Uruguay. If this is true, how do most of these countries derive estimates of GDP? Let us consider a few examples.

Bolivia combines a 1958 input–output table with volume and price indices as a means of estimating GDP. Colombia estimates GDP by means of "extrapolation of benchmark year data of value added by means of production indices [p. 124]." "Presently available national accounts series of Mexico are calculated by extrapolating by means of various volume and price indices results of the 1950 input–output table [p. 164]." For Peru, "data on value added at constant prices were, on the contrary, calculated by extrapolating the 1963 value added figures—previously adjusted with difficulty to a gross and market prices basis—by various physical production indicators [p. 132]."[6]

Most of the above techniques involve the use of some form of input–output tables and some form of price and volume indices. The production indices are used to extrapolate the base figures derived from the input–output tables. These derived estimates are then multiplied by the price indices to derive current price figures for GDP.

Appendix C. The Determinants of Instability: Separate Regressions for Developed and Developing Countries[7]

a. Real Gross Domestic Product

DEVELOPED

$$S_{\text{GDP}} = 0.0259 + 0.00000002Y - 0.00000073Y/N, \qquad R^2 = 0.0587;$$
$$\quad\quad (3.02) \quad\ (0.639) \quad\quad\quad\ (0.1106)$$

$$S_{\text{GDP}} = 0.0237 + 0.00000003Y - 0.00000159Y/N + 0.0115E/Y, \qquad R^2 = 0.0754.$$
$$\quad\quad (2.27) \quad\ (0.731) \quad\quad\quad\ (0.219) \quad\quad\quad (0.403)$$

DEVELOPING

$$S_{\text{GDP}} = 0.0281 - 0.00000019Y + 0.00000305Y/N, \qquad R^2 = 0.0098;$$
$$\quad\quad (4.18) \quad\ (0.2698) \quad\quad\quad (0.221)$$

$$S_{\text{GDP}} = 0.0395 - 0.00000068Y + 0.00000962Y/N - 0.0868E/Y, \qquad R^2 = 0.1077.$$
$$\quad\quad (2.44) \quad\ (0.828) \quad\quad\quad\ (0.656) \quad\quad\quad (0.888)$$

b. Real Gross Investment

DEVELOPED

$$S_{\text{GI}} = 0.095 + 0.00000003Y - 0.00002315Y/N, \qquad R^2 = 0.2154;$$
$$\quad (4.68) \quad (0.488) \quad\quad\ (1.48)$$

$$S_{\text{GI}} = 0.0995 + 0.00000001Y - 0.00002141Y/N - 0.02348E/Y, \qquad R^2 = 0.2257.$$
$$\quad (4.0) \quad\ (0.1765) \quad\quad\ (1.247) \quad\quad\quad (0.346)$$

[6] OECD (1968). *National accounts of less developed countries 1950–1966*, Paris: Organization for Economic Cooperation and Development.

[7] The *t* ratios are given in parentheses.

DEVELOPING
$$S_{GI} = 0.1132 + 0.00000064Y + 0.0000203Y/N, \qquad R^2 = 0.0254;$$
$$\phantom{S_{GI} =} (5.3) \qquad (0.255) \qquad\quad (0.471)$$

$$S_{GI} = 0.1298 - 0.00000067Y + 0.00003567Y/N - 0.1341E/Y, \qquad R^2 = 0.0658.$$
$$\phantom{S_{GI} =} (2.33) \qquad (0.2058) \qquad\quad (0.747) \qquad\qquad (0.406)$$

c. Real Exports

DEVELOPED
$$S_E = 0.0612 + 0.00000006Y - 0.00000928Y/N, \qquad R^2 = 0.0633;$$
$$ (2.82) \quad (0.822) \qquad\qquad (0.554)$$

$$S_E = 0.0804 - 0.00000002Y - 0.0000018Y/N - 0.1008E/Y, \qquad R^2 = 0.262^{\cdot}$$
$$ (3.39) \quad (0.196) \qquad\quad (0.11) \qquad\qquad (1.56)$$

DEVELOPING
$$S_E = 0.0813 + 0.00000253Y - 0.0000179Y/N, \qquad R^2 = 0.114;$$
$$ (3.58) \quad (1.01) \qquad\quad (0.3995)$$

$$S_E = 0.1407 + 0.0000004Y - 0.0000015Y/N - 0.4093E/Y, \qquad R^2 = 0.2761.$$
$$ (2.85) \quad (0.139) \qquad\quad (0.0336) \qquad\qquad (1.339)$$

d. Real Imports

DEVELOPED
$$S_M = 0.0915 + 0.0000000638Y - 0.0000247Y/N, \qquad R^2 = 0.1836;$$
$$ (4.28) \qquad (0.939) \qquad\qquad (1.49)$$

$$S_M = 0.0987 + 0.0000000367Y - 0.0000219Y/N - 0.0379E/Y, \qquad R^2 = 0.2087.$$
$$ (3.8) \qquad (0.422) \qquad\qquad (1.22) \qquad\qquad (0.535)$$

DEVELOPING
$$S_M = 0.1184 + 0.00000354Y - 0.0000373Y/N, \qquad R^2 = 0.1448;$$
$$ (3.97) \quad (1.08) \qquad\qquad (0.634)$$

$$S_M = 0.2054 + 0.000000419Y - 0.0000132Y/N - 0.60E/Y, \qquad R^2 = 0.34.$$
$$ (3.26) \quad (0.114) \qquad\qquad (0.233) \qquad\qquad (1.54)$$

e. Real Machinery and Equipment Expenditures

DEVELOPED
$$S_{ME} = 0.1017 + 0.0000000962Y - 0.0000141Y/N, \qquad R^2 = 0.0944;$$
$$\phantom{S_{ME} =} (3.4) \qquad (1.013) \qquad\qquad (0.61)$$

$$S_{ME} = 0.101 + 0.0000000991Y - 0.0000144Y/N + 0.00408E/Y, \qquad R^2 = 0.0946.$$
$$\phantom{S_{ME} =} (2.74) \quad (0.804) \qquad\qquad (0.565) \qquad\qquad (.0405)$$

DEVELOPING
$$S_{ME} = 0.1192 - 0.0000161Y + 0.00046Y/N, \qquad R^2 = 0.5362;$$
$$\phantom{S_{ME} =} (2.06) \quad (1.87) \qquad\quad (2.56)$$

$$S_{ME} = 0.1724 - 0.0000167Y + 0.000425Y/N - 0.284E/Y, \qquad R^2 = 0.5399.$$
$$\phantom{S_{ME} =} (0.63) \quad (1.70) \qquad\quad (1.61) \qquad\qquad (0.20)$$

REFERENCES

Erb, G. F., and Schiavo-Campo, S. (1969) Export instability level of development, and economic size of less developed countries. *Bulletin Oxford Institute of Economic Statistics* **31**: 263–283.

Hoel, P. G. (1965) *Introduction to mathematical statistics*, pp. 333–335. New York: Wiley.

Leith, C. (1970) The decline of world export instability: A comment. *Bulletin Oxford Institute of Economic Statistics* **32**: 267–272.

Levin, J. V. (1960) *The export economies.* Cambridge, Massachusetts: Harvard Univ. Press.

MacBean, A. (1966) *Export instability and economic development*, pp. 1–359. Cambridge, Massachusetts: Harvard Univ. Press.

Massel, B. (1970) Export instability and economic structure. *American Economic Review* **60**: 618–630.

OECD (1968) *National accounts of less developed countries 1950–1966.* Paris: Organization for Economic Cooperation and Development.

OECD (1970) *National Account Statistics 1950–1968.* Paris: Organization for Economic Cooperation and Development.

OECD (1971) Latest information on national accounts of less developed countries. *Addition to National Accounts of Less Developed Countries 1950–1966.* Paris: Organization for Economic Cooperation and Development.

Prebisch, R. (1950) *The economic development of Latin America and its principal problems.* New York: United Nations.

Rhomberg, R. (1968) Transmission of business fluctuations from developed to developing countries. *International Monetary Fund Staff Papers* March.

Economic Indicator Analysis during 1969–1972

*GEOFFREY H. MOORE**
BUREAU OF LABOR STATISTICS
UNITED STATES DEPARTMENT OF LABOR

In 1937 the National Bureau of Economic Research, Inc., began what turned out to be a long series of studies of the cyclical behavior of selected economic indicators. Each successive study—in 1950, in 1961, and in 1966—reexamined the historical evidence, tested the performance of the indicators during a period subsequent to their selection, and investigated some of the new statistical series that had been developed in the interim. The mild business-cycle contraction of November 1969–November 1970, and the subsequent recovery, has provided another test of this type of indicator analysis. Did the previously selected leading indicators lead and the lagging indicators lag on this occasion as in the past? Was it possible to obtain from them, as in the past, early indications of the mildness or severity of the contraction? What sort of forecasting record did the leading indicators achieve?

* Present affiliation: National Bureau of Economic Research, Inc., and Hoover Institution, Stanford University.

1. Leads and Lags

Of the 12 indicators selected by the National Bureau in 1966[1] as the best representatives of the type of factors that move early in the business cycle (see Moore and Shiskin, 1967), 11 reached cyclical turning points prior to the November 1969 business cycle peak, while one (industrial materials prices) lagged behind it. A composite index of the 12 leading indicators led the peak by seven months. The reverse-trend-adjusted version of this index led by two months. At the November 1970 business-cycle trough six indicators led, three coincided with the trough, and three lagged. The composite index coincided with the trough (after reverse-trend adjustment it led by one month).[2]

Of the eight roughly coincident indicators, three did not undergo cyclical contractions corresponding to the business cycle contraction. All of these were aggregates expressed in current dollars (GNP, personal income, and retail sales) and were sustained by the continued rapid rise in prices and wage rates. Of the remaining five, four led at the peak and one lagged, while at the trough four coincided and one lagged. Of the ten turning points, seven were roughly coincident (within three months of the business cycle turn). A composite index based on five of the coincident indicators lagged by one month at the peak and coincided at the trough.

Three of the six selected lagging indicators failed to undergo cyclical contractions during 1969–1970, and these three also are series expressed in current dollar values (plant and equipment expenditures, business inventories, and unit labor costs). Of the remaining three, one led and two lagged at the peak, while all three lagged at the trough. A composite index based on the six series lagged by nine months at the peak and by six months at the trough.

Another test of the characteristic timing of the indicators can be made by examining the ratio of the composite index of the coincident to that of the lagging indicators. In earlier business cycles this ratio had been found to behave in a manner remarkably like that of the index of leading indicators— usually with somewhat earlier turning points. This pattern prevailed again in 1969–1970, with the ratio reaching its peak 12 months before the November

---

[1] In September 1969 one of the 12 selected indicators, nonagricultural placements, was replaced by initial claims for unemployment insurance. The latter is used throughout this report. For the reasons for this substitution, see United States Department of Commerce *Business Conditions Digest* (September 1969).

[2] The business cycle peak and trough dates are those designated by the National Bureau of Economic Research (Fabricant 1971). The reverse trend-adjustment of the leading index makes its long-term trend the same as that of the index of coincident indicators. In general, it tends to reduce the length of leads at peaks and increase them at troughs, as compared with the original index. The composite indexes referred to are those published in *Business Conditions Digest* (Series, 810, 820, and 830).

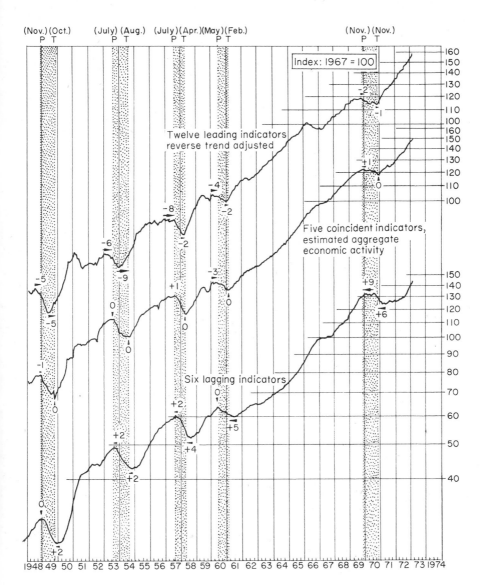

FIG. 1. Composite indexes of leading, coincident, and lagging indicators, 1948–1973. Numbers entered on the chart indicate length of leads (−) and lags (+) in months from business cycle turning dates. Shaded areas represent business cycle contractions. [Adapted from United States Department of Commerce *Business Conditions Digest* (March 1973).]

TABLE 1

LEADS AND LAGS OF 26 INDICATORS AT BUSINESS CYCLE PEAKS AND TROUGHS, 1969–1970 AND 1948–1961[a]

| | Number of business-cycle turns | | Number of timing observations | | | Percentage of timing observations in appropriate class | Average lead (−) or lag (+), in months |
	Covered (1)	Skipped (2)	Leads (3)	Rough (exact) coincidences (4)	Lags (5)	(6)	(7)
26 Individual Indicators							
At November 1969 peak and November 1970 trough							
12 Leading indicators	24	0	17	10(3)	4	71	−4.0
8 Coincident indicators	16	6	4	7(4)	2	70	−0.2
6 Lagging indicators	12	6	1	1(0)	5	83	+7.2
26 indicators	52	12	22	18(7)	11	72	−1.4
At 8 preceding peaks and troughs, 1948–1961[b]							
12 Leading indicators	96	0	83	27(10)	3	86	−7.7
8 Coincident indicators	64	4	34	47(15)	11	78	−1.4
6 Lagging indicators	48	2	3	26(5)	38	83	+3.3
26 Indicators	208	6	120	100(30)	52	83	−3.3
Composite Indexes[c]							
At November 1969 peak and November 1970 trough							
Ratio, coincident to lagging (820:830)	2	0	2	1(0)	0	100	−6.5
Leading, original trend (811)	2	0	1	1(1)	0	50	−3.5
Leading, reverse trend-adjusted (810)	2	0	2	1(0)	0	100	−1.5
Coincident (820)	2	0	0	2(1)	1	100	+0.5
Lagging (830)	2	0	0	0(0)	2	100	+7.5

At 8 preceding peaks and troughs, 1948–1961[b]

Ratio, coincident to lagging (820:830)	8	0	8	2(0)	0	100	−9.2
Leading, original trend (811)	8	0	7	2(1)	0	88	−7.6
Leading, reverse-trend adjusted (810)	8	0	8	2(0)	0	100	−5.1
Coincident (820)	8	0	2	8(5)	1	100	−0.4
Lagging (830)	8	0	0	6(2)	6	75	+2.1

[a] From U.S. Department of Commerce, *Business Conditions Digest*, February 1973, Appendix F. Three additional specific cycle turns are used here: a trough (January 1948, lead 10 months) in the unemployment rate; a peak (February 1969, lead 9 months) and a trough (November 1971, lag 12 months) in the change in manufacturing and trade inventories.

The 26 indicators are those selected in 1966 (Moore and Shiskin, 1967) with one exception: Nonagricultural placements was replaced by initial claims for unemployment insurance. This substitution was made in September 1969, at which time nonagricultural placements was dropped from the short list of leading indicators in *Business Conditions Digest* (for the reasons, see *Business Conditions Digest*, September 1969).

Rough coincidences include exact coincidences (shown in parentheses) and leads or lags of three months or less. The total number of timing comparisons is the sum of the leads, exact coincidences, and lags. This plus the number of turns skipped is the total number of business-cycle turns covered by the series. The "percentage in appropriate class" is based on the number of leads, rough coincidences, or lags, respectively, divided by the total number of timing observations for the corresponding groups of indicators.

[b] The peaks are November 1948, July 1953, July 1957, May 1960. The troughs are October 1949, August 1954, April 1958, February 1961.

[c] The leading index is based on the 12 leading incidators, the coincident index on five of the eight coincident indicators, and the lagging index on the six lagging indicators. The number in parentheses is the series number in *Business Conditions Digest*.

1969 business cycle peak and its trough one month before the November 1970 business cycle trough. Thus the ratio led the leading index by five months at the peak and by one month at the trough. This relationship can be explained by the hypothesis that a rapid rise in such lagging indicators as inventories, unit labor costs, and interest rates on mortgages and bank loans—rapid, that is, relative to the expansion in the economy as reflected in the coincident indicators—exerts a depressing effect on such leading indicators as new orders, housing starts and profits.[3]

TABLE 2

	Number of turning points		Percentage in appropriate class	Mean lead ($-$) or lag ($+$) in months
	Total	In appropriate class		
1969–1970				
12 Leading indicators	24	17 (leads)	71	-4
8 Coincident indicarors	10	7 (rough coincidences)	70	0
6 Lagging indicators	6	5 (lags)	83	$+7$
26 Indicators	40	29	72	-1
1948–1961				
12 Leading indicators	96	83 (leads)	86	-8
8 Coincident indicators	64	47 (rough coincidences)	78	-1
6 Lagging indicators	48	38 (lags)	83	$+3$
26 Indicators	208	168	83	-3

Thus the latest cyclical performance of the indicators clearly resembled the sequence suggested by their performance in previous business cycles. This is demonstrated by the summary distributions of leads and lags in Table 1, and by the composite indexes in Fig. 1. Table 1 enables us to answer the question: What percentage of the turning points in the leading indicators led at the 1969–1970 business cycle turns, and how does this compare with the percentage for earlier cycles? For the leaders as well as the other groups of indicators, the results are as shown in Table 2.

The percentages are smaller for 1969–1970 than for 1948–1961, but are

---

[3] The leads in the ratio are highly correlated with those in the leading index. The simple rank correlation for the 10 peaks and troughs, 1948–1970, is $+0.96$. For a further account of this relationship and its rationale, see the work of G. H. Moore (1969a) and K. H. Moore (1971).

still impressively large. The sequence reflected in the average leads and lags in 1969–1970 is the same as in the earlier period, but the leads are shorter and the lags longer.

2. Severity of the Contraction

In the autumn of 1969 evidence of a softening in demand pressures in the economy became clear. The composite index of leading indicators (without reverse-trend adjustment) had reached its high point in April and began a mild decline, its first since 1966. Most of the components of this index began to decline in April or May, the major exception being inventory investment. Measures of aggregate activity, such as GNP, industrial production, total employment, and retail sales continued to rise, though at a reduced pace in some instances. The price level also continued to rise sharply, but it seemed possible to conclude that its acceleration had stopped.[4]

In view of these developments, plans were worked out toward the end of 1969 and early 1970 to follow the course of the economic slowdown month-by-month along the lines used during the recessions of 1953–1954, 1957–1958, and 1960–1961 (see G. H. Moore, 1961, Chap. 5). This was a cooperative project involving the Office of Management and Budget, the Bureau of the Census, and the Bureau of Labor Statistics. An initial step was to fix upon a tentative date for a business-cycle peak (the "reference peak"). The plan then called for measurement of changes in a considerable number of economic indicators from the reference peak forward. Finally, such measures for the current period would be compared with corresponding measures for earlier recessionary periods. In 1960–1961 as well as in 1957–1958 this simple technique had been helpful in discerning the mildness or severity of those recessions at a fairly early stage, and the experiment seemed worth trying again.

In January 1970 we concluded that a reasonable choice for a tentative reference peak was November 1969. Later, in April 1970, we revised the date to December 1969. Both dates were tentative because one could not be sure at the time whether the economy would undergo a decline large enough or long enough to warrant designating the period as a business-cycle contraction comparable with earlier contractions. Furthermore, later evidence might suggest that another date would be a better choice. As it turned out, about a year later the National Bureau of Economic Research designated November

---

[4] See my testimony at the Hearing of the Subcommittee on Fiscal Policy, Joint Economic Committee, October 8, 1969. [Reprinted, with revisions; see G. H. Moore (1969b).] The composite leading index *with* reverse-trend adjustment did not reach its peak until September 1969. The adjustment generally has the effect of producing later peaks and earlier troughs.

TABLE 3

RANKING OF THE 1969–1970 CONTRACTION VERSUS FIVE EARLIER CONTRACTIONS, IN SUCCESSIVE MONTHS[a]

Months after tentative reference peak (Dec. 1969)

A. Coincident Indicators

	2nd Feb.'70	3rd Mar.'70	4th Apr.'70	5th May'70	6th June'70	7th July'70	8th Aug.'70	9th Sept.'70	10th Oct.'70	11th Nov.'70	12th Dec.'70
8 Coincident indicators											
1. Employment on nonfarm payrolls	1	1	1	2	2	2	2	2	2	2	2
2. Unemployment rate (level)	4	4	3.5	3	2	2	2	2	2	3	3
3. Unemployment rate (change)	6	5	6	4	3	2.5	3	3	3	3	3
4. Industrial production	1	1	1	1	2	2	2	2	4	3	3
5. GNP, constant dollars	3	3	2	2	2	2	2	2	4	4	4
6. GNP, current dollars	1	1	2	2	2	2	2	2	2	2	2
7. Personal income	1	1	1	1	1	1.5	1.5	1	2	2	2
8. Manufacturing and trade sales	1	1	1	1	1	1	1	1	2	2	2
9. Retail sales	1	1	1	1	1	1	1	1	1	1	2
Composite indexes, 5 coincident indicators											
10. Index, original data	2	2	2	2	2	2	2	2	2	2	2.5
11. Index, deflated data	3	2	2	2	2	2	2	2	3	3	3
Average rank											
8 Coincident indicators (lines 1, 2, 4–9)	1.6	1.6	1.6	1.6	1.6	1.7	1.7	1.6	2.1	2.4	2.5
4 Physical volume indicators (lines 1, 2, 4, 5)	2.2	2.2	1.9	2.0	2.0	2.0	2.0	2.0	2.5	3.0	3.0
4 Current value indicators (lines 6–9)	1.0	1.0	1.2	1.2	1.2	1.4	1.4	1.2	1.8	1.8	2.0
Rank of average rank											
8 Coincident indicators	1	1	1.5	2	2	2	2	2	2	2	2
4 Physical volume indicators	2	2	2.5	2	1	1	2	2	2	3	3
4 Current value indicators	1	1	1	1	1	1	1	1	2	2	2

B. Leading Indicators

12 Leading indicators

Indicator												
1. Average workweek, manufacturing	5	3	3	4	3.5	3	2	2	6	6	6	5.5
2. Initial claims, unemployment insurance	4	5	6	6	4	3	3	3	4	4	6	3
3. Index of net business formation	2	6	5	4	5	5	5	5	5	5	5	5
4. New orders, durable goods	3	4	4	3	2	2	2	2	2	2.5	3	3
5. Contracts and orders, plant and equipment	2	5	3	2	3	2.5	3	3	3	4	2	4
6. Building permits, housing	6	6	2	2	2	3	3	4	3	3	4	2
7. Change in manufacturing and trade inventories	1	3	1	1	6	2	1	1	1	3	4	4
8. Industrial materials prices	1	1	1	1	1	1	1	2	3	3	4	5
9. Stock prices, 500 common	4	4	4	4	6	6	6	6	6	6	6	5
10. Corporation profits after taxes	2	2	2	1	1	1	1	1	1	3	3	3
11. Ratio, price to unit labor cost, manufacturing	1	1	1	1	1	1	1	1	1	1	2	4
12. Change in consumer installment debt	4	6	5	5	3	3	3	3	3	6	6	6
Composite index, 12 leading indicators	2.5	3	3	3	3	2	2	3	3	3	5	5
Average rank, 12 leading indicators	2.9	3.6	2.8	3.1	2.7	2.8	2.6	2.8	3.2	3.9	4.2	4.1
Rank of average rank, 12 leading indicators	3	4	3	3	2	2	2	3	4	4	4	5

[a] A rank of 1 means that the current percentage decline in the indicator (from the tentative reference peak of December 1969 to the current month) is smaller than its decline during the corresponding interval in any of the preceding five contractions (starting from reference peaks in 1967, 1960, 1957, 1953, and 1948). The highest rank, 6, means that the current decline is larger than any of the preceding five. The reference peaks used in this table differ in three instances by one month from those used in Tables 1 and 4. In this table December 1969 is used instead of November 1969, August 1957 instead of July 1957, and October 1948 instead of November 1948. These differences do not substantially affect the results, but were believed at the time the ranking procedure was set up early in 1970 to represent slight improvements. For quarterly series the peak reference quarters are IV–1969; IV–1966; II–1960; III–1957; II–1953; and IV–1948.

1969 as the reference peak comparable with the reference peaks in its historical business-cycle chronology.[5]

Calculations using first the November 1969 and later the December 1969 date as the reference peak were carried out beginning in February 1970. As new data came in, the calculations were brought up to date. This work continued throughout 1970 and into 1971. The format of tables and charts followed that developed in studies by the National Bureau. For each indicator the level reached in December 1969 became the base, and percentage deviations from that base were calculated for each of the 12 months back to December 1968 and forward month by month as new data became available. Thus at any time, say four months after the tentative business-cycle peak, one could tell whether and by how much a particular indicator had risen or fallen from the level it had reached when the tentative business-cycle peak occurred. Similar calculations were made for periods of the same length following the four earlier business-cycle peaks (1948, 1953, 1957, and 1960), and from these one could tell whether the current change in an indicator was larger or smaller than its change over a corresponding interval on these earlier occasions. In addition, similar calculations were made for a period starting in January 1967—a period of economic slowdown that had not been recognized by the National Bureau as a business-cycle contraction because it was too brief and mild. This provided an example of a "mini-recession" against which the current period could also be compared.

Such calculations, together with charts based upon them, were made monthly for a large number of indicators. Table 3 shows the rankings of the 1969–1970 period compared with the five earlier periods in successive months from February through December 1970, for the eight coincident and 12 leading indicators, and the composite indexes. In this table a rank of 1 means that the current decline, from December 1969 (the tentative reference peak) to the current month, was smaller than the corresponding decline in the same indicator in each of the preceding periods. A rank of 6 means that the current decline was the largest among the six.

Thus in February 1970, two months after the December 1969 reference peak, the rise in the unemployment rate was larger than in any of the corresponding two-month intervals following the five earlier reference peaks (hence the rank of 6). On the other hand, the decline in nonfarm employment was smaller than in any of the five preceding periods (hence the rank of 1). Most of the coincident indicators, with the exception of the unemployment rate, had relatively low ranks throughout the 12 months following the December 1969 peak. The rank of the average rank of the eight indicators

[5] See the report by Fabricant (1971). Even at that time the November 1969 peak was still termed "tentative." The possibility that a trough was reached in November 1970 was also indicated in Fabricant's report, and subsequent data continue to support that choice.

was 2 or close to it throughout the period, and so was the rank of the composite coincident indexes. This ranking implied that the 1969–1970 contraction was larger than the mini-recession of 1966–1967, but smaller than the mildest of the four preceding contractions, that of 1960–1961. Because of the continued rapid rise in prices in 1969–1970, indicators expressed in current dollars exhibited smaller relative declines (or larger rises) than those representing the physical volume of activity.

The leading indicators, analyzed in the same way, as a group suggested a contraction more serious than that of 1966–1967 or 1960–1961, although less serious than the three preceding contractions. One of the factors that caused a deterioration in both the leading and the coincident indicators toward the end of the period covered in the table was the General Motors strike in the autumn of 1970, which had a depressing effect on the level of economic activity as well as on such leading indicators as new orders and the average workweek.

The ranking scheme produced fairly accurate indications of the relative mildness of the 1969–1970 contraction within a few months after it began. This is shown by the fact that both the average rankings and those of the composite indexes in the early months resemble those in the later months. The stability in the rankings is particularly impressive for the coincident indicators. The accuracy of the initial rankings as an indication of the relative mildness of the contraction is shown by a comparison of the rankings in Table 3 with those in Table 4. In the latter table, the changes in the coincident indicators are measured over the full periods covered by the six contractions, from reference peak to reference trough. The 1967 mini-recession is clearly the mildest, the 1969–1970 and 1960–1961 contractions are more severe, the 1953–1954 contraction is next, and the 1957–1958 and 1948–1949 contractions are the most severe. The 1969–1970 and 1960–1961 contractions are not clearly distinguishable in terms of relative severity, and neither are the 1957–1958 and 1948–1949 contractions; in both instances the rankings depend to some extent on the weight given to physical volume aggregates as compared with current dollar measures. Although there will always be some uncertainty, therefore, regarding the precise position of the 1960–1970 contraction in this scale, it is fair to say that the rankings in Table 3 came close to approximating it within a few months after it began—i.e., early in 1970.

Table 5 provides some evidence on the behavior of the ranking scheme over the entire postwar period. Within each contraction period the rankings of the two groups of indicators maintain a considerable degree of stability. Furthermore, the correlation of the rankings of the six periods with what might be termed the "ultimate" ranking (based on the peak-to-trough changes in Table 4) is fairly high. For this purpose we have ranked the 1969–1970 and 1960–1961 contractions as equal (tied ranks of 2.5) and the 1957–1958 and 1948–1949 contractions as equal (tied ranks of 5.5). The degree of correlation

TABLE 4

RANKING OF SIX PERIODS OF BUSINESS CONTRACTION ACCORDING TO SEVERITY, 1948–1970[a]

	Percentage change, reference peak to reference trough[b]					
	Nov. '69–Nov. '70	Jan. '67–May '67	May '60–Feb. '61	July '57–Apr. '58	July '53–Aug. '54	Nov. '48–Oct. '49
8 Coincident indicators						
1. Employment on nonagricultural payrolls	−1.1 (2)	0.3 (1)	−1.8 (3)	−4.0 (5)	−3.4 (4)	−5.1 (6)
2. Unemployment rate at trough	5.9 (2)	3.8 (1)	6.9 (4)	7.4 (5)	6.0 (3)	7.9 (6)
3. Unemployment rate, change from peak	2.4 (3)	0.0 (1)	1.8 (2)	3.2 (4)	3.4 (5)	4.1 (6)
4. Industrial production	−7.0 (3)	−0.9 (1)	−6.1 (2)	−12.6 (6)	−9.1 (5)	−8.9 (4)
5. GNP, constant dollars	−1.3 (2)	0.8 (1)	−1.4 (3)	−3.4 (6)	−1.6 (4.5)	−1.6 (4.5)
6. GNP, current dollars	4.3 (1)	1.3 (2)	−0.2 (3)	−1.8 (5)	−0.3 (4)	−3.4 (6)
7. Personal income	5.6 (1)	1.5 (2)	0.9 (3)	0.2 (4)	0.0 (5)	−4.7 (6)
8. Manufacturing and trade sales	−0.4 (2)	0.3 (1)	−3.2 (3)	−6.8 (4)	−7.2 (5)	−7.5 (6)
9. Retail sales	3.6 (1)	0.5 (2)	−2.4 (6)	−1.6 (5)	−0.7 (4)	0.0 (3)
Composite indexes, 5 coincident indicators						
10. Index, original data	−3.7 (2)	0.7 (1)	−4.9 (3)	−10.7 (4)	−11.2 (5)	−13.2 (6)
11. Index, deflated data	−5.9 (3)	0.6 (1)	−5.5 (2)	−12.0 (5)	−11.5 (4)	−12.2 (6)
Average rank[c]						
8 Coincident indicators	1.8 (2)	1.4 (1)	3.4 (3)	5.0 (5)	4.3 (4)	5.2 (6)
4 Physical volume indicators	2.2 (2)	1.0 (1)	3.0 (3)	5.5 (6)	4.1 (4)	5.1 (5)
4 Current dollar indicators	1.2 (1)	1.8 (2)	3.8 (3)	4.5 (4.5)	4.5 (4.5)	5.2 (6)

[a] The reference peaks and troughs are from the business-cycle chronology of the National Bureau of Economic Research, Inc., except for January 1967–May 1967, which is included as an example of a mini-recession. For the unemployment rate both the level of the rate at the reference trough (line 2) and the change in the rate (percentage points) from the peak to the trough (line 3) are shown, since both aspects indicate the severity of the contraction. The 5 coincident indicators included in the composite indexes (lines 10 and 11) are employees on nonagricultural payrolls, unemployment rate, industrial production, personal income, and manufacturing and trade sales. In the deflated version of the index the last two series are expressed in constant prices. The average ranks for the 4 physical volume series are based on the entries on lines 1, 2, 4 and 5. The average ranks for the four current-dollar series are based on the entries on lines 6–9. A rank of 1 means that the decline is the smallest (or the rise the largest) among the 6 periods; a rank of 6 means that the decline is the largest among the 6 periods. The unemployment rate is ranked invertedly.

[b] Ranks of percentage changes are given in parentheses.

[c] Ranks of average rank are given in parentheses.

TABLE 5

RANKING OF SIX PERIODS OF BUSINESS CONTRACTION IN SUCCESSIVE MONTHS, TWO GROUPS OF INDICATORS

Months after business-cycle peak	Business-cycle peak date[a]						Correlation coefficient[b]
	Dec. 1969	Jan. 1967	May 1960	Aug. 1957	July 1953	Oct. 1948	
	Rank of average rank of 12 leading (8 coincident) indicators						
2nd	3 (1)	2 (2)	1 (3)	6 (6)	5 (5)	4 (4)	0.80 (0.80)
3rd	4 (1)	2 (2)	1 (3)	6 (6)	3 (4)	5 (5)	0.80 (0.89)
4th	3 (1.5)	1.5 (1.5)[c]	1.5 (3)	6 (6)	5 (4)	4 (5)	0.86 (0.94)
5th	3 (2)	1 (1)	2 (3)	5.5 (6)	4 (5)	5.5 (4)	0.99 (0.89)
6th	2 (2)	1 (1)	3 (3)	6 (6)	4 (5)	5 (4)	0.94 (0.89)
7th	2 (2)	1 (1)	3 (3)	6 (6)	4 (4.5)	5 (4.5)	0.97 (0.94)
8th	2 (2)	1 (1)	3 (3)	6 (6)[c]	4 (5)	5 (4)	0.97 (0.89)
9th	3 (2)	1 (1)	2 (3)[c]	6 (6)	4 (4)	5 (5)	0.97 (0.97)
10th	4 (2)	1 (1)	2 (3)	3 (6)	5 (5)	6 (4)	0.71 (0.89)
11th	4 (2)[c]	1 (1)	2 (3)	5 (4)	6 (6)	3 (5)	0.63 (0.80)
12th	5 (2)	1 (1)	2 (3)	3 (4)	4 (5)	6 (6)[c]	0.63 (0.89)
	Rank of business-cycle contraction, peak to trough[d]						
	2.5	1	2.5	5.5	4	5.5	

[a] The reference peak dates are those used at the time the ranking of the 1969–1970 contraction was carried out (beginning February 1970) and differ in some instances from the standard National Bureau of Economic Research (NBER) dates. The NBER dates do not include a contraction from January 1967 to May 1967, and peaks are November 1969 instead of December 1969, July 1957 instead of August 1957, and November 1948 instead of October 1948.

[b] With rank of business-cycle contraction, peak to trough (bottom line). For six ranks the correlation coefficient should exceed 0.83 to be significant at the 0.05 level.

[c] Business-cycle trough date.

[d] Based on changes from business cycle peak to trough in eight coincident indicators.

345

is about the same for the group of 12 leading indicators as it is for the group of eight roughly coincident indicators. Within three or four months after the reference peak, the correlation of the currently available ranks with the "ultimate ranks" reached the neighborhood of 0.9. A perfect correspondence would, of course, yield a correlation of 1.0.

3. Forecasts with Leading Indicators

The method of ranking the severity of a current recession in comparison with earlier recessions, and doing so while the current recession is still in an early stage, is one method of forecasting with indicators. Its use is limited, however, to occasions of this type, i.e., when a recognizable business contraction has begun or threatens to begin. Since forecasts must be made on other occasions as well, the question arises whether leading indicators can be used in a continuing forecasting scheme. In 1968, I explored one such scheme briefly, conceiving of it more as a mechanical standard against which other forecasting methods could be compared than as a forecasting method in its own right (G. H. Moore, 1969c). It appeared to provide a better standard— i.e., tougher to beat—than the usual "naïve model," in which either the recent level of the series being forecast or its recent rate of change is simply extrapolated into the future. It is of interest now to see how the method has worked since 1968.

The method employed the composite index of leading indicators and assumed that this index led various measures of aggregate economic activity, such as GNP in current dollars or GNP in constant dollars, by a fixed interval of six months. Then forecasts of the calendar year percentage change in GNP were obtained from simple regressions based upon percentage changes in fiscal year averages of the leading index, since fiscal years predate calendar years by six months. Successive approximations to the true fiscal year changes in the leading index were obtained by using the change from one fiscal year to the first quarter of the next, then to the average of the first two quarters, then to the first three quarters, and finally to the entire fiscal year. Data for the first quarter of the fiscal year (July–September) could be obtained in October, when many forecasts for the ensuing calendar year are being made As data for later quarters became available, the initial forecast could be revised and, presumably, improved.

The 1968 study showed that regressions fitted to annual percentage changes for the period 1951–1967 produced the correlation coefficients, regression coefficients, and mean absolute errors of fcrecast (MAE) shown in Table 6.[6]

[6] See G. H. Moore, 1969c, footnote 12. These regressions use the reverse-trend-adjusted index based on 12 leading indicators.

TABLE 6

Independent variable: Leading index, percentage change from	Dependent variable: Calendar year percentage change in										
	GNP in current dollars						GNP in constant dollars					
	r	r^2	a	b	t^a	MAE	r	r^2	a	b	t^a	MAE
1. Fiscal year to III-Q	0.60	0.36	4.55	0.41	2.8	1.9	0.56	0.31	2.51	0.40	2.6	2.0
2. Fiscal year to III and IV-Q	0.74	0.55	4.34	0.40	4.1	1.6	0.71	0.50	2.27	0.40	3.8	1.6
3. Fiscal year to III, IV and I-Q	0.81	0.66	4.19	0.36	5.1	1.4	0.80	0.64	2.08	0.37	4.9	1.4
4. Fiscal year to fiscal year	0.81	0.66	4.05	0.33	5.3	1.4	0.82	0.67	1.91	0.35	5.4	1.3

[a] t-statistic for the b coefficient in preceding column.

The correlations, though modest, are statistically significant, and improve as more of the full fiscal year data become available, as would be expected. The forecasts for current and for constant dollar GNP are of about the same quality. Since the regressions for current and constant dollar GNP differ primarily with respect to the constant term (a), the implied forecast rate of change in the implicit deflator is virtually a constant, about 2% per year. This would clearly be a defect of the scheme when prices change more rapidly than by 2% a year, as they did during the Korean conflict and in recent years.

The 1968 study also showed that this simple method of using leading indicators to obtain a quantitative forecast produced results during 1952–1967 that were greatly superior—in terms of magnitude of error and degree of correlation of forecast change with actual change—to a simple extrapolation of the preceding year's change in GNP. Moreover, the leading indicator forecasts compared quite well with other forecast records for the same period, including those in the President's Economic Report, a record of private economists' forecasts, and an econometric model forecast.

The results of applying this method on a *ex-ante* basis since 1967 are set out in Table 7. They point to the following conclusions:

1. The errors in the forecasts usually diminish as more information on the leading index for the current fiscal year becomes available. Since only the forecasts using the full fiscal year data (columns 5 and 10) imply a strict six-month lead (the others imply a longer lead) and since the leading index does not lead on the average by more than six months (cf. Table 1), this is to be expected. It appeared also in the results for the period to which the regression was fitted, 1952–1967.

TABLE 7

FORECASTS OF CALENDAR YEAR CHANGES IN GNP BASED ON INDEX OF LEADING INDICATORS, 1967–1972[a]

Calendar years (1)	Forecast, using change in leading index from fiscal year to				Actual (6)	Error, using leading index to				Error, extrapolating preceding year's change (11)
	III-Q (2)	III-Q and IV-Q (3)	III-Q, IV-Q, and I-Q (4)	Fiscal year (5)		III-Q (7)	III-Q and IV-Q (8)	III-Q, IV-Q, and I-Q (9)	Fiscal year (10)	
Percentage change, GNP in current (in 1958) dollars										
1966–67					5.6 (2.5)					
1967–68	5.7 (3.7)	6.1 (4.0)	6.1 (4.1)	6.1 (4.1)	9.0 (5.0)	−3.3 (−1.3)	−2.9 (−1.0)	−2.9 (−0.9)	−2.9 (−0.9)	−3.4 (−2.5)
1968–69	6.7 (4.6)	7.2 (5.2)	7.1 (5.0)	7.0 (5.1)	7.7 (2.8)	−1.0 (1.8)	−0.5 (2.4)	−0.6 (2.2)	−0.7 (2.3)	1.3 (2.2)
1969–70	5.8 (3.7)	5.5 (3.4)	5.1 (3.0)	4.6 (2.4)	4.9 (−0.4)	0.9 (4.1)	0.6 (3.8)	0.2 (3.4)	−0.3 (2.8)	2.8 (3.2)
1970–71	3.9 (1.9)	3.9 (1.9)	4.2 (2.0)	4.7 (2.6)	7.5 (2.7)	−3.6 (−0.8)	−3.6 (−0.8)	−3.3 (−0.7)	−2.8 (−0.1)	−2.6 (−3.1)
1971–72	7.3 (5.2)	7.9 (5.8)	n.a.	n.a.	9.7 (6.4)	−2.4 (−1.2)	−1.8 (−0.6)	n.a.	n.a.	−2.2 (−3.7)
Mean absolute error										
1968–72						2.2 (1.8)	1.9 (1.7)	1.8 (1.8)	1.7 (1.5)	2.5 (2.9)
1952–67						1.9 (2.0)	1.6 (1.6)	1.4 (1.4)	1.4 (1.3)	3.7 (3.5)
Correlation coefficient, forecast and actual change										
1968–72						0.34 (0.41)	0.50 (0.53)	0.37 (0.36)	0.61 (0.58)	−0.19 (0)
1952–67						0.60 (0.56)	0.74 (0.71)	0.81 (0.80)	0.81 (0.82)	−0.17 (−0.24)

[a] The forecasts are based on the index of 12 leading indicators, reverse-trend adjusted, published by United States Department of Commerce. The regression equations used are those fitted to data for 1951–1967 and given by G. H. Moore, (1969c, p. 16, footnote 12). Data for the leading index were obtained from current issues of *Business Conditions Digest*, using the October issue for the third quarter, the January issue for the average of the third and fourth quarters, the April issue for the average of the third, fourth, and first quarters, and the July issue for the fiscal year average (except that data for the third quarter, 1968, and earlier were from the November 1968 *BCD*, which is the first issue containing the leading index). The actual percentage changes in GNP are based on the first official estimates given in the *Economic Report of the President* for the year following the year for which the forecast was made.

2. The mean errors for the period since 1967 are larger than those for the period 1952–1967, and in two years were exceptionally large. For forecasts made in the autumn of the year preceding the calendar year being forecast (columns 2 and 7), the mean errors are approximately ± 2 percentage points, which is ± 20 billion dollars at the current trillion dollar level of GNP.

3. The mean errors in forecasting percentage changes since 1967 are about the same for GNP in constant dollars as for GNP in current dollars. This was also the experience during 1952–1967.

4. As in the period 1952–1967, the mean forecast errors during 1968–1972 were smaller than those produced by extrapolating last year's change in GNP. These "naïve model" errors averaged 2.5% for current-dollar GNP and 2.9% for constant-dollar GNP.

5. As noted above, the regression equations imply approximately a 2% rate of increase in the implicit GNP price deflator. Since the actual increases in the deflator during 1968–1972 were closer to 5%, this was a substantial source of error in the forecasts, tending to produce underestimates of current-dollar GNP and overestimates of constant-dollar GNP. For forecasts made in the autumn (column 2), the average forecast increase in current dollar GNP during the five years was 5.9%, while the actual average increase was 7.8%. For constant-dollar GNP the average forecast increase was 3.8% while the actual average was 3.3%. Since some of the leading indicators included in the index are expressed in current dollars (e.g., new orders for durable goods), and two are price indexes (common stocks and industrial materials), price changes have some effect upon the index. But this does not necessarily mean that it should forecast current-dollar changes better than constant-dollar changes, and there is no evidence that it does.[7]

6. The forecast changes during 1968–1972 are poorly correlated with the actual changes, though the correlation improves as more data for the leading index become available during the year. The correlation coefficients are substantially smaller than those obtained during 1952–1967. This may reflect the usual difference between *ex-post* forecasts during the period to which the regressions were fitted (1952–1967) and *ex-ante* forecasts in the subsequent period. But it also reflects the sharp increase in the rate of inflation in the recent period (see below).

The 1968 study compared the leading indicator forecasts with those contained in the *Economic Report of the President* since 1961. Table 8 brings

[7] There is some evidence that the leading index is associated with the rate of change in prices (see G. H. Moore, 1969b). If so, it might be possible to improve the forecasts of change in current-dollar GNP by including in the regressions both the change in the leading index and the first differences of the change. This might also improve the consistency of the forecasts of current- and constant-dollar GNP.

TABLE 8

FORECASTS OF CHANGES IN GNP, LEADING INDEX METHOD AND PRESIDENT'S ECONOMIC REPORT, 1962–1972

	Percentage change in GNP in current dollars					Percentage change in GNP in constant dollars				
	Forecast		Actual[c]	Error		Forecast		Actual[c]	Error	
	Leading index[a] (1)	Economic report[b] (2)	(3)	Leading index (4)	Economic report[b] (5)	Leading index[a] (6)	Economic report (7)	(8)	Leading index (9)	Economic report (10)
1961–62	7.8	9.4	6.7	1.1	2.7	5.7	8.0[d]	5.3	0.4	2.7
1962–63	5.5	4.4	5.4	0.1	-1.0	3.5	3.5[d]	3.8	-0.3	-0.3
1963–64	6.9	6.5	6.6	0.3	-0.1	4.9	5.0	4.7	0.2	0.3
1964–65	7.0	6.1	7.5	-0.5	-1.4	4.9	4.0[d]	5.4	-0.5	-1.4
1965–66	7.1	6.9	8.6	-1.5	-1.7	5.0	5.0	5.4	-0.4	-0.4
1966–67	4.2	6.4	5.6	-1.4	0.8	2.1	4.0	2.5	-0.4	1.5
1967–68	6.1	7.8	9.0	-2.9	-1.2	4.0	4.3[d]	5.0	-1.0	-0.7
1968–69	7.2	7.0	7.7	-0.5	-0.7	5.2	3.5[d]	2.8	2.4	0.7
1969–70	5.5	5.7	4.9	0.6	0.8	3.4	1.3[d]	-0.4	3.8	1.7
1970–71	3.9	9.0	7.5	-3.6	1.5	1.9	4.5[d]	2.7	-0.8	1.8
1971–72	7.9	9.5	9.7	-1.8	-0.2	5.8	6.0	6.4	-0.6	-0.4
Mean absolute error										
1962–67				0.8	1.3				0.4	1.1
1968–72				1.9	0.9				1.7	1.1
1962–72				1.3	1.1				1.0	1.1
Correlation coefficient, forecast and actual										
1962–67	0.68	0.34				0.96	0.48			
1968–72	0.50	0.80				0.53	0.93			
1962–72	0.49	0.63				0.64	0.76			

[a] Based on data for third and fourth quarters, available in January, using regressions fitted to 1951–1967 (columns 3 and 8 of Table 7).

[b] *Economic Report of the President*, January 1962 through January 1972.

[c] Based on the first official estimate given in the *Report* following the year for which the forecast was made.

[d] Inferred from statements in the *Economic Report*. All other entries are based on figures. (dollar levels, dollar changes, or percentage changes) given in the *Report*. The inferred entries have been verified as approximately correct, though not in all cases precisely correct, by the Council of Economic Advisers.

the records up to date. In some of the years since 1968 the forecasts in the *Economic Report* were substantially better than the leading indicator forecasts, but the years in which this was true for current-dollar GNP (1968, 1971, and 1972) were not the same as those for real GNP (1969 and 1970). The *Economic Report* forecasts were clearly more realistic with regard to the increase in the price deflator. The correlation of the *Report* forecasts with actual changes improved in 1968–1972 as compared with that achieved during 1962–1967, whereas the leading indicator forecasts deteriorated.[8]

Over the entire 11-year period, however, the differences between the leading indicator forecasts and those in the *Economic Report*, with respect to either average error or correlation with actual changes, are not great. In part at least, the recent deterioration in the quality of the leading indicator forecasts is attributable to the rapid increase in the price level, which represented a sharp departure from experience during the period to which the regressions were fitted. In view of the tests made in the first two sections of this paper, however, it does not seem likely that the method has become invalid—the indicators have continued to lead, and their changes during the 1969–1970 contraction were in fact correlated with its amplitude. The method can continue to provide, therefore, a useful mechanical standard against which more sophisticated forecasts can be compared: It is an improved "naïve model."

In order to facilitate continued use of the method, the regressions have been brought up to date and have been computed using monthly rather than quarterly approximations to the current fiscal year level of the leading index. That is, changes from the preceding fiscal year are taken to the first month of the current fiscal year, then successively to the average of the first two months, the first three months, etc. This has the advantage of using all the information provided by the leading index up to the date the forecast is made.[9] In addition, the regressions have been extended to include not only changes in current-dollar and real GNP, but also changes in the unemployment rate.

The regression equations and related data bearing upon their "goodness-of-fit" are shown in Table 9. They have been fitted to two periods: 1952–1961 and 1952–1971. The first set of regressions enables us to determine how the results would have turned out during the 11-year period following that from which the regressions were derived, namely, 1962–1972. The second set uses all the data currently available, and presumably is preferable for use in the future since it is based on more observations, and more recent data.

[8] For further analysis of the *Economic Report* forecasts through 1971 and a comparison with those compiled in the American Statistical Association–National Bureau of Economic Research survey of economists' forecasts, see my note in *The American Statistician*, (G. H. Moore, 1972, pp. 52–53).

[9] Note that the same regressions can be used to forecast fiscal years, or indeed a moving 12-month period if that is desired.

Most of the results previously discussed reappear, notably the improvement in the correlation and reduction in error as additional data for the leading index in the current fiscal year become available. The correlations for current-dollar GNP continue to be about the same as for real GNP, and the implied forecast of the rate of change in the price deflator is, as before, roughly constant: about 2% when the period of fit is 1952–1961, and about 2.5% when the period of fit is 1952–1971.

The correlations for the change in the unemployment rate are somewhat higher than for GNP. For example, the adjusted r^2 based on leading index data through December are as follows:

Period of fit	Current-dollar GNP	Real GNP	Unemployment
1952–1961	0.46	0.34	0.48
1952–1971	0.41	0.39	0.54

The mean absolute error for the unemployment regressions, based on leading index data through December, is 0.7 percentage points when the period of fit is 1952–1961, and 0.5 percentage points when the period of fit is 1952–1971. In both cases the mean errors are smaller than those obtained by a naïve "no-change" model—i.e., assuming that the unemployment rate next year will be the same as last year. The mean errors of such a model are 1.0 percentage points for 1952–1961, and 0.8 percentage points for 1952–1971.[10]

When the 1952–1961 regressions are applied to data for the next 11 years, the results are as shown in Table 10. Compared with the mean errors during the period of fit, 1952–1961, the forecast errors during 1962–1972 are about the same for GNP in current dollars but smaller for real GNP and unemployment. However, simple extrapolation would have produced smaller mean errors in the second period than in the first, so that relative to the errors of simple extrapolation the forecast errors are, in each case, larger than during the period of fit, as might be expected. Furthermore, the correlations between forecasts and actual change beyond the period of fit show considerable deterioration for current-dollar GNP, but remain about the same for constant-dollar GNP and the unemployment rate.[11]

[10] In the case of the unemployment rate, unlike GNP, the "no-change" model is much more accurate than the "same-change" model. Thus the mean errors of extrapolating last year's *change* in the unemployment rate are 1.8 percentage points for 1952–1961, and 1.3 percentage points for 1952–1971.

[11] The forecasts during 1962–1972 based on regressions fitted to 1952–1961 provide a fairer comparison with the *Economic Report* forecasts in Table 8, since these regressions do not use data beyond 1961, whereas the regressions employed in Table 8 use data through 1967. On this basis the *Economic Report* forecasts show somewhat smaller MAEs and somewhat higher correlation between forecast and actual change than the leading index forecasts.

TABLE 9

REGRESSIONS BETWEEN PERCENTAGE CHANGES IN LEADING INDEX AND IN GNP IN CURRENT DOLLARS, GNP IN CONSTANT DOLLARS, AND UNEMPLOYMENT RATE[a]

Independent variable: percentage change in leading index, from fiscal year average to average of	a	t_a	b	t_b	r	r^2	MAE	RMS	DW
A. Dependent variable: Percentage change in GNP in current dollars									
Based on data for 1952–1961									
July	4.33	4.48	0.21	0.94	0.32	0	2.15	2.74	3.21
July–Aug.	4.17	4.43	0.26	1.28	0.41	0.07	2.10	2.63	3.17
July–Sept.	4.03	4.56	0.30	1.72	0.52	0.18	1.98	2.47	3.12
July–Oct.	3.89	4.75	0.33	2.18	0.61	0.30	1.83	2.29	3.06
July–Nov.	3.84	5.12	0.35	2.63	0.68	0.40	1.65	2.12	2.98
July–Dec.	3.76	5.28	0.34	2.96	0.72	0.46	1.55	2.00	2.93
July–Jan.	3.70	5.49	0.33	3.28	0.76	0.52	1.46	1.89	2.87
July–Feb.	3.63	5.64	0.33	3.57	0.78	0.57	1.39	1.79	2.77
July–Mar.	3.59	5.91	0.32	3.94	0.81	0.62	1.29	1.69	2.68
July–Apr.	3.54	5.90	0.31	4.05	0.82	0.63	1.24	1.66	2.60
July–May	3.50	5.90	0.30	4.16	0.83	0.64	1.20	1.62	2.51
Fiscal year	3.45	5.80	0.30	4.20	0.83	0.65	1.18	1.61	2.42
Based on data for 1952–1971									
July	5.19	7.55	0.30	1.83	0.40	0.11	1.80	2.36	2.44
July–Aug.	5.02	7.46	0.33	2.21	0.46	0.17	1.73	2.28	2.31
July–Sept.	4.92	7.66	0.35	2.59	0.52	0.23	1.69	2.20	2.20
July–Oct.	4.81	7.85	0.36	3.02	0.58	0.30	1.59	2.10	2.07
July–Nov.	4.74	8.23	0.36	3.44	0.63	0.36	1.49	2.00	1.95
July–Dec.	4.65	8.32	0.35	3.77	0.66	0.41	1.42	1.92	1.85
July–Jan.	4.58	8.45	0.35	4.07	0.69	0.45	1.37	1.86	1.75
July–Feb.	4.50	8.52	0.34	4.36	0.72	0.49	1.33	1.80	1.62
July–Mar.	4.42	8.70	0.34	4.73	0.74	0.53	1.28	1.72	1.51
July–Apr.	4.36	8.61	0.33	4.85	0.75	0.54	1.26	1.69	1.44
July–May	4.31	8.55	0.32	4.99	0.76	0.56	1.24	1.67	1.37
Fiscal year	4.25	8.38	0.32	5.04	0.77	0.56	1.24	1.66	1.32

TABLE 9 (*continued*)

Independent variable: percentage change in leading index, from fiscal year average to average of	a	t_a	b	t_b	r	r^2	MAE	RMS	DW
	B. Dependent variable: Percentage change in GNP in constant (1967) Dollars								
Based on data for 1952–1961									
July	2.32	2.20	0.18	0.74	0.25	0	2.32	2.99	3.12
July–Aug.	2.19	2.09	0.22	0.98	0.33	0	2.28	2.92	3.02
July–Sept.	2.03	2.04	0.27	1.37	0.43	0.09	2.19	2.78	2.92
July–Oct.	1.88	2.01	0.31	1.77	0.53	0.19	2.09	2.62	2.82
July–Nov.	1.82	2.08	0.32	2.12	0.60	0.28	1.97	2.47	2.69
July–Dec.	1.74	2.06	0.33	2.36	0.64	0.34	1.89	2.37	2.60
July–Jan.	1.67	2.08	0.32	2.67	0.69	0.40	1.79	2.25	2.54
July–Feb.	1.58	2.06	0.32	2.94	0.72	0.46	1.71	2.14	2.44
July–Mar.	1.52	2.10	0.32	3.27	0.76	0.52	1.59	2.02	2.35
July–Apr.	1.46	2.05	0.31	3.41	0.77	0.54	1.53	1.97	2.30
July–May	1.41	2.02	0.31	3.56	0.78	0.56	1.47	1.92	2.23
Fiscal year	1.35	1.94	0.31	3.66	0.79	0.58	1.43	1.89	2.16
Based on data for 1952–1971									
July	2.58	3.48	0.30	1.67	0.37	0.09	2.11	2.55	2.43
July–Aug.	2.39	3.29	0.34	2.08	0.44	0.15	2.02	2.46	2.33
July–Sept.	2.27	3.28	0.36	2.47	0.50	0.21	1.92	2.37	2.23
July–Oct.	2.13	3.24	0.37	2.92	0.57	0.28	1.84	2.26	2.14
July–Nov.	2.06	3.32	0.38	3.33	0.62	0.35	1.75	2.15	2.04
July–Dec.	1.97	3.26	0.37	3.65	0.65	0.39	1.70	2.08	1.95
July–Jan.	1.87	3.23	0.37	4.04	0.69	0.45	1.61	1.98	1.88
July–Feb.	1.77	3.17	0.37	4.39	0.72	0.49	1.55	1.90	1.78
July–Mar.	1.68	3.15	0.36	4.83	0.75	0.54	1.46	1.81	1.69
July–Apr.	1.61	3.04	0.35	5.03	0.76	0.56	1.40	1.77	1.63
July–May	1.54	2.95	0.35	5.24	0.78	0.58	1.36	1.72	1.56
Fiscal year	1.46	2.82	0.35	5.41	0.79	0.60	1.33	1.69	1.50

C. Dependent variable: Percentage point change in unemployment rate

Based on data for 1952–1961

	a	t_a	b	t_b	r	r^2	MAE	RMS	DW
July	0.57	1.20	−0.12	−1.08	−0.36	0.02	1.01	1.34	2.79
July–Aug.	0.63	1.38	−0.14	−1.37	−0.44	0.09	0.97	1.29	2.68
July–Sept.	0.70	1.63	−0.16	−1.81	−0.54	0.20	0.91	1.21	2.57
July–Oct.	0.77	1.92	−0.17	−2.28	−0.63	0.32	0.83	1.11	2.43
July–Nov.	0.79	2.16	−0.17	−2.73	−0.69	0.42	0.74	1.03	2.28
July–Dec.	0.83	2.39	−0.17	−3.06	−0.73	0.48	0.68	0.97	2.17
July–Jan.	0.86	2.61	−0.17	−3.39	−0.77	0.54	0.63	0.92	2.07
July–Feb.	0.89	2.80	−0.16	−3.64	−0.79	0.58	0.59	0.88	1.93
July–Mar.	0.91	3.00	−0.16	−3.93	−0.81	0.62	0.54	0.84	1.81
July–Apr.	0.93	3.06	−0.15	−3.96	−0.81	0.62	0.53	0.83	1.75
July–May	0.94	3.09	−0.15	−3.96	−0.81	0.62	0.53	0.83	1.69
Fiscal year	0.96	3.09	−0.14	−3.98	−0.81	0.61	0.55	0.84	1.66

Based on data for 1952–1971

	a	t_a	b	t_b	r	r^2	MAE	RMS	DW
July	0.54	1.87	−0.16	−2.22	−0.46	0.17	0.76	1.00	2.51
July–Aug.	0.63	2.23	−0.17	−2.71	−0.54	0.25	0.70	0.95	2.40
July–Sept.	0.68	2.57	−0.18	−3.22	−0.60	0.33	0.65	0.90	2.30
July–Oct.	0.74	3.01	−0.18	−3.86	−0.67	0.42	0.60	0.84	2.19
July–Nov.	0.76	3.38	−0.18	−4.44	−0.73	0.50	0.55	0.78	2.07
July–Dec.	0.80	3.70	−0.18	−4.86	−0.75	0.54	0.51	0.74	1.98
July–Jan.	0.83	4.04	−0.17	−5.30	−0.78	0.59	0.47	0.71	1.88
July–Feb.	0.86	4.30	−0.17	−5.62	−0.80	0.62	0.45	0.68	1.76
July–Mar.	0.89	4.59	−0.16	−5.99	−0.82	0.65	0.42	0.65	1.67
July–Apr.	0.91	4.67	−0.16	−6.02	−0.82	0.65	0.43	0.65	1.62
July–May	0.93	4.71	−0.15	−6.03	−0.82	0.65	0.43	0.65	1.56
Fiscal year	0.95	4.72	−0.15	−5.96	−0.81	0.65	0.44	0.66	1.55

[a] The leading index is the index of 12 leading indicators, reverse-trend adjusted, published by United States Department of Commerce. Columns a and b are the coefficients of the simple linear regression, and t_a and t_b are the corresponding values of their t statistics. Column r is the correlation coefficient; r^2 is adjusted for degrees of freedom. MAE is the mean absolute error of forecast, and RMS is the root mean square error. DW is the Durbin–Watson statistic.

TABLE 10

FORECAST CHANGES IN GNP AND UNEMPLOYMENT, LEADING INDEX METHOD, 1952–1972

Year	Percentage change in leading index[a]	Percentage change in GNP in current (constant) dollars			Change in unemployment rate		
		Forecast	Actual	Error	Forecast	Actual	Error
1951–52	−4.0	2.4 (0.4)	5.2 (3.1)	−2.8 (−2.7)	+1.5	−0.3	+1.8
1952–53	4.2	5.2 (3.1)	5.5 (4.5)	−0.3 (−1.4)	+0.1	−0.1	+0.2
1953–54	−4.0	2.4 (0.4)	0.1 (−1.4)	+2.3 (+1.8)	+1.5	+2.6	−1.1
1954–55	8.5	6.7 (4.5)	9.1 (7.6)	−2.4 (−3.1)	−0.6	−1.1	+0.5
1955–56	11.4	7.7 (5.4)	5.3 (1.8)	+2.4 (+3.6)	−1.1	−0.3	−0.8
1956–57	1.3	4.2 (2.2)	5.2 (1.4)	−1.0 (+0.8)	+0.6	+0.2	+0.4
1957–58	−2.2	3.0 (1.0)	1.4 (−1.2)	+1.6 (+2.2)	+1.2	+2.5	−1.3
1958–59	9.3	6.9 (4.8)	8.1 (6.4)	−1.2 (−1.6)	−0.8	−1.3	+0.5
1959–60	5.4	5.6 (3.5)	4.1 (2.5)	+1.5 (+1.0)	−0.1	0	−0.1
1960–61	−1.6	3.2 (1.2)	3.3 (1.9)	−0.1 (−0.7)	+1.1	+1.2	−0.1
1961–62	8.6	6.7 (4.5)	6.7 (5.3)	0 (−1.8)	−0.7	−1.2	−0.5
1962–63	3.2	4.9 (2.8)	5.4 (3.8)	−0.5 (−1.0)	+0.3	+0.2	+0.1
1963–64	7.0	6.2 (4.0)	6.6 (4.7)	−0.4 (−0.7)	−0.4	−0.5	+0.1
1964–65	7.5	6.3 (4.2)	7.5 (5.4)	−1.2 (−1.2)	−0.5	−0.7	+0.2
1965–66	7.1	6.2 (4.0)	8.6 (5.4)	−2.4 (−1.4)	−0.4	−0.7	+0.3
1966–67	0.2	3.8 (1.8)	5.6 (2.5)	−1.8 (−0.7)	+0.8	0	+0.8
1967–68	5.0	5.5 (3.4)	9.0 (5.0)	−3.5 (−1.6)	0	−0.2	+0.2
1968–69	7.2	6.2 (4.1)	7.7 (2.8)	−1.5 (+1.3)	−0.4	−0.1	−0.3
1969–70	3.0	4.8 (2.7)	4.9 (−0.4)	−0.1 (+3.1)	+0.3	+1.4	−1.1
1970–71	−1.4	3.3 (1.3)	7.5 (2.7)	−4.2 (−1.4)	+1.1	+1.0	+0.1
1971–72	8.8	6.8 (4.7)	9.7 (6.4)	−2.9 (−1.7)	−0.7	−0.3	−0.4

Mean absolute error

1952–61	1.6 (1.9)	0.7
1962–67	1.0 (1.0)	0.3
1968–72	2.4 (1.8)	0.4
1962–72	1.7 (1.4)	0.4
1952–72	1.6 (1.6)	0.5

Correlation coefficient, forecast and actual

1952–61	0.72 (0.64)	0.72
1962–67	0.69 (0.97)	0.91
1968–72	0.51 (0.55)	0.76
1962–72	0.47 (0.66)	0.75
1952–72	0.67 (0.67)	0.75

[a] Fiscal year to July–December average preceding the calendar year being forecast. *Note*: The regression equations used are based on data for 1952–1961, with the change in the leading index from fiscal year to July–December average (see Table 9).

On the whole, the regression procedure for making quantitative forecasts from the leading index holds up fairly well beyond the period to which the regressions are fitted. The forecasts are superior to those derived from a simple extrapolation procedure. Year-to-year rates of change in current-dollar and in real GNP are forecast with a mean error of about 1.5%, and year-to-year changes in the unemployment rate are forecast with a mean error of around 0.5 percentage point. The caveats noted in the previous study (1968) continue to deserve emphasis. In particular, as we have seen, forecasts of different variables generated from simple regressions on a single leading index may not be consistent with other information on the relationships among those variables. The 1968 study* concluded:

> "All that the method does is to help summarize the information contained in a group of leading indicators regarding the near-term future course of GNP or other variables that are systematically related to the business cycle. Hence it can provide the forecaster with some of the information useful in developing his actual forecast, and it can be used as a standard by which to judge his past efforts, perhaps helping him to improve upon them [p. 19]."

4. A Summing Up

Nearly 35 years have passed since Mitchell and Burns (1938) undertook, in December 1937, to compile "a list of the most trustworthy indicators of business cycle revivals." When they concluded their work, they advised the user to "be alert to changes in the making, eschew simple formulas, test his judgments by study of numerous statistical series, and stand ready to revise his list of indicators as the economic environment changes." The history of the development and use of indicators during the past 35 years attests to the soundness of this advice. The list of indicators in current use today is not the same as the Mitchell–Burns list, despite a family resemblance. Some of the series in their list have been superseded by series representing the same activity but broader in coverage or differently defined. Some series now in use—such as monthly and quarterly measures of inventory change—were not in existence at that time. The selection of indicators has been extended to cover experience during recessions as well as revivals, and attention has been given not only to turning points but also to indications of the magnitude of change. The indicators have been subjected to a continuing series of tests of performance, and this has led to changes in the lists and to new ways of summarizing their behavior and utilizing them in forecasting, as illustrated above.

* G. H. Moore (1969c).

Over the years we have learned more about the forces underlying the cyclical behavior of different types of indicators. Abramovitz' (1950) work on inventories, for example, demonstrated the importance of inventory change in the shorter swings of the business cycle, and showed how the classification of inventories by stage of process aided in the explanation of their behavior. Other studies, such as those of Zarnowitz (1973) on new orders, Hultgren (1965) on costs and profits, Bry (1959) on the average workweek, and Klein (1971) on consumer installment credit, to name but a few, have made similar contributions. Today there is scarcely an indicator in common use whose theoretical rationale has not been subject to searching examination. As a result of these investigations, together with a vigorous effort on the part of government agencies to provide relevant data in convenient analytical form, we are now far better supplied than in 1937 with current economic indicators and with empirically tested explanations of their interrelations.

Tests of the sort described in this essay have played a part in this development and should continue to do so. New cyclical episodes throw light on the validity of previous findings and raise new questions. Continued testing is especially important when the use of a particular type of analysis becomes more widespread, since new users may be unfamiliar with the limitations of the technique. Our examination of the behavior of the indicators during 1969–1972 is intended, therefore, to be simply one more step in a continuing process of evaluation of these tools for analyzing short-run economic trends.

REFERENCES

Abramovitz, M. (1950) *Inventories and business cycles.* New York: National Bureau of Economic Research.

Bry, G. (1959) *The average workweek as an economic indicator.* New York: National Bureau of Economic Research.

Economic Report of the President (Successive issues, January 1962–1972). Washington, D.C.: Government Printing Office.

Fabricant, S. (1971) Recent economic changes and the agenda of business cycle research. National Bureau of Economic Research Report 8, Supplement, May.

Hultgren, T. (1965) *Costs, prices, and profits: Their cyclical relations.* New York: National Bureau of Economic Research, Columbia Univ. Press.

Klein, P. (1971) *The cyclical timing of consumer credit.* New York: National Bureau of Economic Research, Columbia Univ. Press.

Mitchell, W. C., and Burns, A. F. (1938) Statistical indicators of cyclical revivals. National Bureau of Economic Research, Bulletin 69, May 28.

Moore, G. H. (ed.) (1961) Measuring recessions. In *Business cycle indicators.* New York: National Bureau of Economic Research, Columbia Univ. Press.

Moore, G. H. (1969a) Generating leading indicators from lagging indicators. *Western Economic Journal* 7: 137–144.

Moore, G. H. (1969b)   Hearing before Subcommittee on Fiscal Policy, Joint Economic
   Committee, October 8, 1969; reprinted with revisions as The anatomy of inflation,
   Bureau of Labor Statistics Report 373. Washington, D.C.: Government Printing
   Office.
Moore, G. H. (1969c)   Forecasting short-term economic change. *Journal of the American
   Statistical Association* **64**:1–22.
Moore, G. H. (1972)   Errors in GNP forecasts. *The American Statistician* October, 52–53.
Moore, G. H., and Shiskin, J. (1967)   *Indicators of business expansions and contractions.*
   New York: National Bureau of Economic Research, Columbia Univ. Press.
Moore, K. H. (1971)   The comparative performance of economic indicators in the United
   States, Canada and Japan. *Western Economic Journal* **9**:419–427.
United States Department of Commerce. *Business Conditions Digest.*
Zarnowitz, V. (1973)   *Orders, production and investment—A cyclical and structural analysis.*
   New York: National Bureau of Economic Research, Columbia Univ. Press.

The Dollar Standard
and the Level
of International Reserves

LORIE TARSHIS

SCARBOROUGH COLLEGE,
UNIVERSITY OF TORONTO

1. Introduction

A full-scale study of the functioning of the dollar-standard from 1946–1971, and of its breakdown, would require far more than all the pages of this volume. It would also require more perspective than analysts could hope to muster in the few months since the middle of August 1971. My excuse, then, for venturing into this field is not to be able to present a final account of the subject, but rather in order to focus attention on certain questions in respect to which views now accorded wide acceptance seem all too likely to harden into the dogmas that will mold these later judgments long before the real evidence is in.

Already, it seems obvious to many, that the system created at Bretton Woods was bound to collapse; that it confronted the world[1] with an impossible

---

[1] Obviously, I mean "the world" in an unduly provincial sense: the advanced economies of the non-Communist world. While the interests of the less-developed economies should perhaps take center stage, their concerns with this problem were essentially "indirect": Their hopes were bound to rest upon the adequacy of the system from the standpoint of the advanced Western economies.

dilemma. Either the United States balance of payments would have had to be chronically in serious deficit, with the dollar eventually becoming worthless as its convertibility into gold had to be suspended; or the West would have found its international reserves becoming more and more inadequate. Needless to say, either option was thought to be unacceptable. But the situation was even more unattractive, for not only was the system doomed to fail, but the day-by-day results of its operations came to be regarded as decidedly unwelcome. They were unfair because the system, in effect, subsidized the United States to take over the world; and unfair too because it condemned the United States to the loss of its competitive edge in the struggle for world markets and thereby threatened it with prospects of "national bankruptcy." Moreover, it raised serious problems for the control of the various national economies as the use of monetary policy for domestic goals increasingly became subject to constraints set by policy decisions abroad. While it goes without saying that most minds would find some difficulty in holding all these views simultaneously, nonetheless some "economists" who seem never to have been threatened with the loss of their amateur status apparently managed, despite all.

In my judgment, the dollar standard need not have collapsed when it did and possibly "never." The events that led to the present situation were precipated by unfortunate policies, themselves the results of faulty diagnoses of the problems. The decisive signals were often misinterpreted; many of the difficulties stemmed, in the end, from this. Yet in retrospect we can see that the system had functioned decidedly well,[2] and that it promised to do still better in furthering the economic well-being of the participating countries. Unfortunately, such a system, which rested as much on such intangibles as permit a domestic banking system to operate rather than on formal arrangements, can be brought down easily and cannot readily be put together again once the intangible elements have been destroyed. But at least, while performing this part of the autopsy, we shall perhaps become aware of what we shall miss, and of the prospects that have been, at least temporarily, lost through an overhasty response to unfamiliar developments.[3]

---

[2] In no previous period had the growth of trade been so rapid, as its liberalization extended to more and more products and countries. In no previous period had the volume of international capital flows increased so quickly, as obstacles to these movements diminished. The gains in well-being, from the extension of international specialization and from improvements in the international allocation of "finance" were surely substantial. Moreover, the occasional shocks that originated in the system—the foreign-exchange crises and the rush to gold, for instance—seemed to have had decidedly little influence upon the developments that really mattered for economic well-being, i.e., the expansion of output and the improvements in efficiency.

[3] It must be stated that had most of the economists who were concerned with these problems been willing and able to devote to them the scientific qualities that Moses Abramovitz has shown in all his work—the judgment, the objectivity, the patience, and the intelligence—the story might have been very different.

In this study, we shall consider some aspects of the buildup of international reserves which was the counterpart of the large United States balance of payments deficit that characterized most of the period 1950–1971. In particular, we shall be concerned with these questions:

(a) Should the United States deficits of the period have been interpreted as evidence of disequilibrium? Would larger deficits have implied disequilibrium?

(b) Was the collapse of the system brought about because of these United States deficits?

Unfortunately, these questions are in some ways interrelated and the answers to them therefore do not fall into separate heaps.

There can be no doubt that United States deficits, and such accompanying developments as the loss of United States gold[4] were taken, in a quite uncritical sense, to be clear indications of a disequilibrium. The bases for these beliefs will be examined first.

2. False Analogies: Faulty Signals

Although everyone, of course, knew that the world in 1946 was very different from that before 1913, their failure to recognize all the implications of the many differences appears to have been the most important reason why the situation under the dollar standard was so badly misinterpreted. New institutions came into being; the roles of some of the countries changed markedly and yet, in diagnosing the performance of the international monetary mechanism, most analysts were very strongly inclined to view it as though it were essentially the same as it had been in 1913. True, they did allow for the fact that the United States had displaced Britain as the dominant economy, and that, accordingly, the dollar served in place of sterling as the principal international money, but often, so it seems, they took their examination no further. Accordingly, they interpreted phenomena which would have signaled difficulties for sterling and the British economy in 1913, or say 1928, as though they carried the same message for the dollar and the American economy in, say, 1968. They were thus enabled to see, or at least to imagine seeing, "dollar problems" and "overextensions of the United States economy" when, as we shall try to show shortly, there were no such problems, or if they did exist, they called for very different remedies than formerly.

Let us compare the essential features of the classic gold standard, as it operated in 1913, or for a few years after 1925, with the characteristics of

---

[4] Later we shall examine the precise sense in which the loss of gold depended upon United States balance of payments deficits.

whatever we should call the system that came into being with the implementation of the Bretton Woods Agreements, beginning with December 1946.[5]

Under the classic gold standard, including such variants as the gold exchange standard which played an increasingly important role up to 1931, each nation set a buying and selling price for gold, in its own currency. Thus the dollar price for gold was set by act of Congress at $20.67 an ounce.[6] Second, each country allowed gold to be bought and sold freely, and to be imported and exported without restraint. Finally—and this reflected the economic facts of the day, not the actions of legislatures—the costs of transfer of gold from one country to another represented a very small fraction of the total value. There was no more "system" than that, and no international agreement to which participants gave their formal adherence.

Reflecting these arrangements, the whole complex of exchange rates (parities) came into being corresponding approximately to the ratios of the various prices of gold. In the operations of the mechanism, certain principles became clear:

(a) Any country could change its exchange rate—the prices of its currency expressed in each of the other currencies—simply by changing its official price of gold, always provided that it was able to act alone, or at least that its actions were not exactly matched by the actions of other countries. If it raised the price of gold as denominated in its own currency. its exchange rate would decline, and vice versa.

(b) Any country whose currency fell far enough below parity on the foreign-exchange market would lose gold; it would gain gold if the price of its currency rose far enough. Thus, the loss of gold by any country could be taken as a clear indication that its currency was weak and that it had fallen below parity; the gain of gold signaled, by contrast, an especially strong currency.[7]

(c) While balance of payments accounts were not struck in those innocent days, it seems clear that had they been prepared on a proper basis, they would have shown that a currency's weakness on the foreign-exchange market was associated with a deficit in the country's balance of payments, and vice versa.

(d) A country's loss (or gain) of gold, itself tended to bring the exchange rate back toward parity, with a loss, like any other export, strengthening the rate, and so on.

[5] And gradually extending, as more and more of the major economies ratified their commitment to the Articles of Agreement.

[6] For simplicity, we shall suppose the buying price and selling price to be identical.

[7] Gold movements were often initiated by private arbitragers who found it profitable to buy gold in the country whose exchange rate had fallen, sell it in the one whose exchange rate had risen and convert the proceeds into the weak currency.

(e) Thus, whatever was the policy proper to a balance of payments deficit—fiscal or monetary restraint, for example, or in the extreme, raising the price of gold in order to secure a currency depreciation—it should have been followed by a gold-losing country, unless it were believed that the trouble was no more than temporary.[8] The "rules of the game," which incidentally were never adopted formally and which of course could not be enforced, would lead a gold-gaining country instead toward expansion.[9]

One final point: these lessons were just as applicable to Britain, the "Banker" or "Reserve Currency Country" and its pound sterling as they were to any other country. And since her officials appreciated the importance to themselves and others of the practice of holding international reserves in the form of sterling balances, Britain was perhaps more strongly committed to these rules—for instance, interpreting the loss of gold from the Bank of England as a *certain sign* that something had to be done to strengthen sterling before confidence in it was shaken, since it was thought that a loss of confidence would lead to a withdrawal of balances from London.

These signals, and the rules which describe the responses appropriate to them were simple and clear; they had been verified by experience, they applied to all participating countries, and they were widely accepted. It is not surprising, then, that there was so general a readiness to apply them when the international monetary mechanism was rebuilt after the war.

This was the more understandable because in some ways the new system resembled the old. Gold served as the primary international reserve, with dollars, and to a lesser extent sterling, supplementing it. The system gave rise, as had the old, to a complex of relatively stable exchange rates which bore the same relation to the various national prices of gold, as had obtained under the older system.[10] With one exception—but that was, as we shall see, of vital importance—a loss of gold, or other reserves, could be understood as a signal that the currency was weak and that the balance of payments was in deficit. Nevertheless, there were very real differences which can be made clearer after we have set down the essence of the new system.

The dollar standard, as I shall call it here, rested on international agreement under the Articles of the International Monetary Fund (IMF). Each IMF member or participant apart from the United States, notified the IMF

---

[8] Even if countries held their international reserves not in gold but in sterling or, as later, in dollars, these lessons were still applicable, except that movements of foreign-exchange reserves would have to be substituted for movements of gold.

[9] The assymmetry of response: that the deficit country *had* to act, if the deficit were serious enough, and that the surplus country need not do so, was another feature which also characterized the dollar standard.

[10] However, as we shall see below the causal influence ran in the opposite direction.

of the basic par value of its currency or its basic exchange rate: that between its own currency and the American dollar.[11] It committed itself to maintaining its currency at par or within a narrow range—not more than one percentage point—of that figure. Because competitive devaluations had been so important and harmful a feature of the period of the Great Depression, the IMF members agreed not to change parities, except by small amounts, unless permission for the change had been granted by the Fund itself.

The position of the United States in this system was special, not only *de facto*, but also in respect to the rules by which it was bound. Obviously, since all other members set parities, each by notifying the IMF of the price of its own currency in terms of the dollar, there was no room for the United States to do so too.[12] In this respect, it could do nothing more than to follow along. Accordingly, the United States had no commitment, either, to maintain the price of the dollar in terms of any other currency. It had however imposed on itself another commitment; to set the price of gold in terms of the dollar. Although not required to do so, it nevertheless informed the Fund that it would freely buy and sell gold[13] at its fixed price of $35.00 an ounce. This agreement on a dollar price of gold was primarily important because it seemed to legitimize the use of gold and dollars as interchangeable reserves.[14]

It will be seen that the position of the United States with respect to exchange-rates was rather different from that of other countries. Each of the others had an active role in setting the price of its currency in terms of another (the dollar). The United States did not. Moreover, each of the others committed itself to maintaining that price within specified narrow limits. The United States did not. And each of the others could change the exchange rates involving its own currency by notifying the Fund that henceforth the dollar price of its currency would be X, rather than Y. The United States could not.

However, if the United States wanted to change all exchange rates involving the dollar it was not powerless. What gave it some power or at least the appearance of some power was that each member set the price of its currency in terms of the dollar, "of the weight and fineness in effect on July 1, 1944." While this clause, if taken literally is impossibly obscure, it is generally understood to mean that the dollar which was to be used as the measure of value refers to the dollar set by reference to the amount (and quality) of gold it would

[11] Actually, although the members were free to set par in terms of gold or the "dollar," they generally availed themselves of the latter choice.

[12] The United States however, did at least go through the motions, by notifying the IMF that 100 United States cents was to be worth one dollar (U.S.). This "price" became effective on December 18, 1946—and none too soon!

[13] Though only to official institutions abroad.

[14] Whether it gave value to the dollar, or instead to gold, is another question.

have bought in 1944. Thus, if the United States were to change the price of gold, this would mean an alteration of the measuring rod, and accordingly of exchange rates—unless its action were offset or countermanded.

To illustrate: Suppose that the British government had set the parity of the pound sterling at $4.00 (U.S.). If, subsequently, the United States had doubled the price of gold, so that two of the "new" dollars had become equivalent to one of the "measuring-rod" dollars—at least in terms of gold— the then outstanding British commitment to the Fund would be taken to mean that now £1 equaled $8.00 (new), for this would maintain the old rate at £1 equal to $4.00 (measuring rod). From then on, the British government would be obliged by reason of this commitment, to hold the pound at $8.00 rather than $4.00. And the British government would not have been obliged to notify the Fund of this change in its *actual* exchange rate for, in a legal sense, the exchange rate would not have changed. But it would nevertheless be compelled to recognize and seek to maintain what all the rest of the market would treat as a new (and greatly appreciated) exchange rate.[15] But whether the United States could in fact have forced through such a dollar depreciation without provoking retaliation is very doubtful indeed.[16] If other countries did not wish to be faced with the consequences of a cheaper dollar in foreign-exchange markets, they would have had "merely" to notify the Fund of their intention to depreciate their own currencies by 50% in terms of the measuring-rod dollar, in order to keep actual exchange rates unchanged.

Questions of retaliation apart, the United States thus had no more and no less power over exchange rates than other countries. If, say, France alone were to change the dollar price of the franc, the franc's worth in all other countries would change too, but rates that did not involve the franc would remain constant. Similarly, the United States could have (perhaps) changed all exchange rates involving the dollar on its own initiative; but rates that did not involve the dollar, would remain unaffected. One very important difference between the dollar and the rest of the currencies did, however, remain; while every country except for the United States had undertaken to hold the price of its currency constant, the United States had no such commitment toward the dollar.

The domestic price of gold in each country other than the United States would *not* be changed if the latter were to alter—say, to double—the price of gold in dollars. With the price of gold increased from, say, $35.00 an ounce to $70.00 an ounce, and the pound, as we have seen, in consequence rising from

[15] What such a move would have done to the American commitment to keep 100 cents equal to one dollar (measuring-rod), when the actual dollar had fallen in price to only one-half of the measuring-rod dollar is almost too frightening to contemplate!

[16] Unless under the special circumstances of the period August–December 1971, and with the use of unilateral bargaining weapons.

$4.00 to $8.00, the price of gold in Britain would remain unchanged.[17] Only if the British were to check, in part or fully, the rise in sterling, or the fall in the dollar, by notifying the Fund that it had established a new exchange rate (at say $5 to the pound) would the price of gold in Britain go up too—and in our example, by less than in the United States.

The price of gold, in countries other than the United States, was a *resultant*, rather than, as it had been before 1931, an *active* factor in establishing exchange rates. Once the dollar price of gold was established, its level in any other country depended simply upon that country's exchange rate against the dollar (not measuring-rod).[18]

There are other points of difference between the operations of the classic gold standard and those of the dollar standard, which merely extend from the analysis to this point.

Under the gold standard, all countries were responsible, in the same degree, for maintaining the system of exchange rates. As we have seen, this would be done through the use of their holdings of international reserves, although the moving spirits were the arbitragers, at the ready to exploit the opportunities offered by any significant departure of actual exchange rates from parities to buy gold where it was cheap and sell it where it was dear.[19] If France and Britain ran into balance of payments difficulties and the exchange rate of one of them fell, gold exports at the instance of private dealers, would keep the rate from falling too far. Then, if the country would not or could not cure the deficit by employing the conventional tools—deflation, raising trade barriers, or restricting capital exports—it would be compelled to reduce the par value of its currency by raising the price of gold.[20] In some sense then, we could say that gold losses, which were the sign of a deficit, might have to be stemmed by an increase in the price of gold. And this rule was applicable to all countries that were "on the gold standard."

With the dollar standard, the situation was rather different. Admittedly, if any country, other than the United States, had a serious deficit in its balance of payments, its exchange rate would tend to fall below the level to which the

[17] Remember, the price of gold in Britain measured in pounds sterling would have been equal to its price in the United States (in our model, $70 an ounce) times the price of the dollar, expressed in pounds (now, $\frac{1}{8}$£, rather than $\frac{1}{4}$£) or $(70 \times \frac{1}{8})$£. Earlier, it would have been, on our assumptions, $(35 \times \frac{1}{4})$£.

[18] This is the reason we choose to call the system that came into existence with the creation of the IMF, the dollar standard. While gold served, as it had before, as an international reserve, the system depended upon the nature of each currency's ties with the dollar.

[19] After taking into account actual exchange rates.

[20] It might, of course, go through a period in which, having lost the greater part of its reserves, it simply suspended the right to export gold. Its currency would then "float" (downward) until it once again permitted gold to be taken out of the country, but made it available at a higher price than before.

country had committed itself. In order to honor its commitment to prevent such a decline, it would be compelled to remove from the foreign-exchange market the *excess* supply of its own currency which was responsible for the downward pressure on its price. Its central bank would do this by using a part of its reserves of gold, dollars, or any other acceptable means of payment in order to buy up its own currency. The loss of its reserves, then, would be the price it would have to pay in order to keep its exchange rate from falling; moreover, that loss would have signaled a balance of payments deficit, for there would be no other explanation for the decline in its exchange rate. Thus, rules and signals for countries, apart from the United States, were basically the same as they had been under the gold standard.

But for the United States, *under the dollar standard* this line of analysis would have been inappropriate. The United States had no commitment to maintain the price of the dollar—to prevent any undue rise or fall in its price on the foreign-exchange market. And as we shall see, a gold loss from the United States, or an inflow of gold, would not have resulted from a weakening (or strengthening) of the dollar on foreign-exchange markets—or at least if it did, the causal chain operated quite differently. Finally, the loss, or gain, of gold, should not have been expected to strengthen, or weaken, the dollar's price in other currencies. To these matters, we now turn our attention.

3. The Role of the Banker

Deriving in part from the differences in the mechanisms under which the complex of exchange rates had been established, there were significant differences too in the roles the banker countries were expected to perform. Admittedly Britain in the earlier period and the United States after 1945 both did what banks are supposed to do: engaged in financial intermediation. Their investors bought up a disproportionate share of the long-term, relatively illiquid, and high-yield securities issued by firms and governments in other countries; in return, both, in a sense, paid for a large part of these purchases by making short-term, relatively liquid, and low-yield securities available in the form first of sterling and later of dollar balances; these were held as international reserves by official and private asset holders in other countries. The banker country, thus, "bought long and sold short," gaining or, at least hoping to gain, the margin between the high and the low yields. Other countries were compensated in two ways: first, because their securities issuers were able to sell their new issues at prices higher than would have been possible, had they been barred from access to the financial markets of the banker country; and second, because those of their asset holders who for any reason wanted financial assets in their portfolios which were relatively free of risk and which could be used for the settlement of international claims, found them readily available. On the whole, except for an enormous change in scale, these basic functions were not greatly altered.

Nevertheless, significant differences did arise to which sufficient attention has not always been paid.

In the first place, Britain as banker was under the same pressure as all other countries in respect to the obligations it had accepted indirectly to maintain the value of its currency. By contrast, after 1945 the United States as banker was exempt from the commitment that other countries had acknowledged to keep the price of their currencies from varying.

With the gold standard, as already noted, each country—including Britain—set a certain price in its own currency at which it stood ready to buy and sell gold; it undertook, too, to refrain from obstructing gold movements in either direction. Thus, while sterling enjoyed a special status by reason of its appeal as the favored international liquid asset, it was afforded no protection different from that available to other currencies; Britain had to purchase that protection by allowing its international reserves to be drawn down, just as did any other country. In a way, then, Britain as banker was simply first among equals.

With the dollar standard, the situation for the banker country—this time, the United States—was quite different. While each country, other than the United States, was required to support its own currency in terms of the dollar—not letting it fall significantly below or rise significantly above the price in dollars which it had notified the IMF, the United States had instead committed itself only to maintain the price of the dollar as 100 cents.[21] Since a decline in the price of the dollar on the foreign-exchange market implied a rise in the price of at least one other currency, the commitment to maintain stable rates rested with the country whose currency had appreciated.

It does not of course follow that the United States never lost international reserves. Her losses of gold from 1946 until August 1971 were considerable, but they did not directly reflect American efforts to set a limit on the decline of the dollar in foreign-exchange markets. Indeed, a quick check has shown that they were not even timed to coincide with periods when the dollar was notably weak. In that respect, too, the difference between the position of the United States under the dollar standard and that of Britain under the gold standard is worth noting.

The explanation for this difference deserves attention. First, with the dollar standard in effect no one could have made a profit at a time when the dollar was weak by buying gold in the United States, selling it abroad, and finally converting the proceeds back into dollars. This conclusion follows from the fact that although the dollar price of gold for purchase would have remained

---

[21] With, presumably, no margin for fluctuation!

firm at $35.00 an ounce, the price at which it could have been sold in any other country would have fallen in the same proportion as the price of the dollar in that country's currency. Hence, a would-be arbitrager who had been able to buy gold at $35.00 would have had to sell it at the same price, after converting his proceeds in the foreign currency back into dollars again; he would moreover have had to cover the expenses of the various transactions from his gross profits of zero—obviously not a prescription for a prosperous enterprise.[22] Second, with the dollar standard in effect, the United States Treasury, which recognized no commitment to maintain the dollar's value on the market, would have had no real incentive to intervene.[23] Finally, if foreign holders of dollars had, for any reason, converted their dollars into gold,[24] the operation would have left the price of the dollar on foreign-exchange markets unaffected. Although the loss or surrender of gold (or dollars) by any other country would have strengthened its currency—and indeed, it was by drawing on these reserves that a country was enabled to keep its currency from falling below the minimum allowable level—we are asserting a difference when the United States was involved. The explanation of this apparent contradiction is simply that when, say, France used gold and/or dollars to strengthen its currency, it was in effect, reducing an excess supply of francs vis-à-vis dollars; the price of the franc (in dollars) therefore rose. But when the United States paid out gold for dollars, the availability of dollars *and* gold (which were perfect substitutes) vis-à-vis other currencies was unchanged. The worth of the dollar in terms of other currencies should not then have been expected to change; for that matter we should not expect the domestic value of the dollar to be altered by a massive exchange of fifty-cent pieces for dollars, brought about by the Federal Reserve Banks. If the United States Treasury had desired, for any reason, to prevent a decline in the price of the dollar, it would have had to intervene in the foreign-exchange market with other currencies, say, marks; intervention which took the form of buying up dollars with gold, or 50-cent pieces, might have cosmetic effects, but that is all.[25] In short, the dollar, if it was to be supported at all, was supported *not with United States*

[22] It might be supposed that the arbitrager would have been motivated to buy gold, holding it until its price abroad had increased as the dollar recovered on foreign-exchange markets. But if he entertained such an anticipation he would have done as well simply to hold dollars—enjoying the yield they provided—and so saved himself the trouble and expenses of buying and holding gold.

[23] That it often did intervene, generally ineffectively, does not mean that it had to do so, or that it should have done so.

[24] Of course, only official institutions had the right to buy gold directly; others had to make indirect arrangements.

[25] The cosmetic effects of exchanging dollars for gold would have been more likely to affect the foreign-exchange value of the dollar, adversely. As the public received news of

Gold, but instead by the readiness of other countries to hold whatever amounts of dollars became available.

Why should another country be interested in supporting the dollar in this way? That it had undertaken to act on its notice to the IMF so as to limit the appreciation of its own currency could have been only a part of the explanation, and probably not the main part. At least equally important would have been its reluctance to expose its own producers to increased competition in all markets, not only from the United States but also from all other economies; for this would have been the consequence of a significant appreciation of its own currency vis-à-vis the dollar and hence vis-à-vis all other currencies too.

Just how strong was this concern—to limit the competition from outside to which domestic producers would have been exposed by an appreciation of a certain currency—can be judged from events dating from, say, August 1949. We might, first, notice how much more frequent have been the instances of depreciation than of currency appreciation or revaluation. Up to 1965, only two currencies, the German mark and the Netherlands guilder had been raised in price or revalued;[26] the IMF lists for the same period 42 instances of formal depreciation—involving either a reduction in par value or a suspension of par value which permitted the currency to float (downward) on foreign-exchange markets. Since, in this period, balance of payments surpluses were greater than deficits for countries other than the United States, and since on balance these countries were therefore gaining reserves, such a disparity in the frequency of downward and upward adjustments vis-à-vis the dollar (and other currencies, too, until they caught up) is suggestive of the widespread resistance to currency appreciation, or to a dollar depreciation. Second, through almost the whole of the period, the American balance of payments showed a large deficit which was widely believed to be very serious; yet the general direction of currency movements against the dollar was downward (Table 1). And when the situation approached "crisis," as it did in the spring and summer of 1971, the size of the revaluations actually made, despite very heavy pressures brought by the United States upon other currencies, was very modest indeed. It is evident that most countries were reluctant to revalue their currencies upward.[27] In fact, up to the summer of 1971, other countries seemed to regard a currency revaluation as even worse than a continuing inflow

---

the "gold drain," their attitude toward the dollar would have been expected to become more pessimistic; as a result, some of them would have been tempted to speculate against the dollar.

[26] In addition, the Lebanese pound "floated" upward. The net change in the dollar price of the mark and the guilder between 1948 and 1965, despite these appreciations in 1961, was downward, because of earlier depreciations.

[27] Until recently the United States actually encouraged depreciation of other currencies. It reversed itself only in 1970 or 1971.

TABLE 1

THE MAGNITUDES OF EXCHANGE DEPRECIATIONS, END OF 1948
TO END OF 1965: DISTRIBUTION OF 105 COUNTRIES
BY DEGREE OF DEPRECIATION[a]

Magnitude of depreciation[b]	Number of countries
Appreciation	1
Zero change	10 (including the United States)
Less than 30.5%	14
30.5%	29
31–65%	13
66–90%	28
More than 90%	10
	——
	105

[a] From de Vries (1969).
[b] A depreciation of 100% would have meant that the currency had become completely worthless.

of dollars. Whatever they said about how unwelcome were additions to their dollar reserves, their actions, which did nothing to stem them, revealed at least a reluctant readiness to pile up more and more dollars in their reserves.

4. Gold Losses

The United States did lose gold after 1946—more than half its beginning stock, indeed, by 1970. If gold losses were not caused, as we have argued above, by weakness of the dollar on the foreign-exchange market, and if they did not contribute to a strengthening of the dollar, why did they occur? Essentially these gold losses resulted from increasing anticipations that the dollar price of gold would be raised.

Generally speaking, official and private holders of international reserves could have held them in gold, in dollars, or for that matter in any other liquid asset that appealed to them. Dollar assets—commonly very short-term, United States Treasury Bills or interest-paying accounts in United States banks—promised a yield; and the costs of converting them into assets which were completely acceptable as means of payment were relatively low. Gold, by contrast, promised *nothing*, except the necessity of paying storage costs; while the costs of converting it into a "means of payment" were higher. Considering only these factors, it would seem that asset holders would uniformly prefer to hold dollars rather than gold. But gold also had its appeal:

from time to time asset holders came to regard the prospects of an increase in the dollar price of gold as favorable; they thus came to entertain expectations of a capital gain from holding gold.[28]

Assuming that rational economic considerations alone influenced decisions, we should then expect each (qualified) reserves holder to choose a portfolio of gold *and* dollars, whose proportions would vary with the yield to be obtained from dollars, his expectations of capital gains from an increase in the United States gold price (speculative consideration), and the special risks (akin to Keynes's precautionary motive) attaching to an all-gold portfolio—which risks before 1967 would mainly consist in the liability to additional costs from holding gold, and after 1967, when gold could often only be purchased by private asset-holders at prices higher than the official level, would consist in the danger that it would have to be sold at a lower price. Any change in any of these parameters—the yield from holding dollars, and speculative and precautionary considerations relating to gold—led to change in the preferred portfolio positions of numerous asset holders.

It is at this point that a connection *can* be drawn between a weakening of the foreign-exchange price of the dollar and United States gold losses. If, because of the dollar's decline, expectations grew that the official price of gold in the United States would have to be raised (but why?), then the demand for gold as a component of reserves would have increased and the United States would have had a gold drain. But for that matter, *any* development that strengthened these expectations would have led to an increased gold flow from the United States: The distribution of a pamphlet that forecast on the basis of the positions of the stars a doubling of gold prices, or the reminder of an eminent economist that raising the price of gold would have added to international reserves and hence deserved support, or anything else. Moreover many American officials, probably inadvertently, played an important role in encouraging these expectations, and hence the United States gold drain, by their frequent reminders to foreign central bankers that if they tried to convert too large a volume of dollars into gold, the United States would have no recourse but to withdraw from this commitment or would at least have to raise the price.[29] Remembering back to the spate of pamphlets that predicted

[28] It should be noted that *if* an increase in the official United States price of gold would have meant an equivalent depreciation of the dollar, the price of gold abroad would not have budged. But, by holding gold rather than dollars, those who expected an increase in the United States price of gold could at least have avoided a capital loss; moreover, they might have anticipated that the dollar's decline would in fact have been less, proportionately, than the rise in the United States gold price, which would have meant some increase in the price of gold in other countries and hence some capital gains too.

[29] The behavior of many American officials between 1959 and 1971 reminds one of the town's big banker who calls his friend who is the bank's largest depositer one night and

an increase, the agonized speeches of central bankers demanding action, the many muddled analyses, and the very public worrying of United States officials, one wonders why any qualified asset holder bothered to hold any dollars at all. Predictably, the system broke down in March 1967 and the private demand for gold exploded. As a result the private market for gold was allowed to operate without intervention, but separated from the market for official institutions. From then on, a United States gold drain signaled a shift in expectations by public officials, and a desire to put political and economic pressure on the United States, or perhaps nothing more than the sudden desire to beautify the vaults. This is not the place to consider whether the gold–external-dollar link was necessary or even desirable from the beginning. As of this writing, it has, of course, been broken, but so much else has been destroyed too—especially the position the dollar formerly occupied as *the* reserve currency—that experience of that single change has probably little to teach us at this stage.

5. When Is a Disequilibrium Not a Disequilibrium?

Particularly after 1955 most of the growth in international reserves, public and private, took the form of an accumulation of dollars. Until 1969, when Eurodollar operations became substantial, most of this accumulation resulted from what the United States Department of Commerce referred to as the payments deficit—on liquidity or on official settlements basis, depending upon where the added dollars were lodged. It was quickly recognized that the system generally was an unstable one, or at least that it appeared to be unstable. Without the United States deficit, international reserves would grow very slowly if at all and would quickly become inadequate as a result of which a situation of disequilibrium for all countries would develop. Balance-of-payment disequilibriums would become increasingly intractable and crises on foreign-exchange markets would grow more serious. On the other hand, if the price of avoiding these difficulties was a large United States balance of payments deficit, the dollar itself would eventually collapse; and yet without a strong dollar, the growth of dollar rseerves would be meaningless.[30] But was the situation quite so bleak?

---

pleads "the bank is in trouble—nothing serious, mind you, and we'll fix it up, but meanwhile please don't withdraw your deposit." Clearly his friend, if he were to hear such a plea, would show up first thing next morning to close out his account.

[30] This is the background first, for the arguments favoring increases in the United States official price of gold; and later for the adoption of the program of supplying special drawing rights to IMF members. The objections to the former proposal are that it is inequitable and that it would probably do more damage by causing existing dollar reserves to decline

It is pointless to argue with a name. The United States "deficit," despite the questions and doubts as to how it should be measured, seems to have a life of its own, and it is doubtful that the name can be changed even if its real essence is shown to be harmless. But at the very least, we can try to determine whether it actually denotes a disequilibrium situation.

The essence of a state of disequilibrium is that it cannot endure—that inherent forces will sooner or later cause it to change. A short-run disequilibrium situation exists, to use an example, when, in a perfectly competitive market, the amount of a product demanded at the going price differs from the amount of it supplied. Pressures from both sides of the market would lead buyers and sellers to agree on a different price, as soon as they were free to make any change—presumably with insignificant delay, A long-run disequilibrium situation would rule when, to use another example, firms, on the average, are earning significantly less than is needed to keep them in business, even when each has made the best possible adjustment of its price and output to the state of the market and its own costs; the number of firms in the industry in question is then out of equilibrium and the equilibrating process would be a shrinkage of their number. Similarly, a country with limited reserves, whose balance of payments is in a state of serious deficit, would be in long-run disequilibrium because its situation *would have to be altered* as its reserves ran out, perhaps months hence. However the country may anticipate exhaustion of its reserves and seek to modify its situation long before they have fallen to zero.

To enquire whether a United States balance of payments deficit is evidence of United States disequilibrium, then, is to look for answers to the following:

(a) Is there anything about such a deficit that would make it impossible for the United States to continue its transcations at their present levels indefinitely? Would it, that is to say, run out of "reserves" (1) either because foreign countries would sooner or later refuse to accept them (if so, they would have lost their quality of international reserves and, for all practical purposes, the U.S. would have none left), (2) or because the United States itself would become unwilling to pay out more reserves? Thus, we shall have to consider what a United States deficit does to other countries, and also what it does to the United States itself.

---

and by interfering with the later creation of new dollar reserves than it would provide in benefits by increasing the value, in dollars—but perhaps not in other currencies—of gold reserves. The objections to the latter are that it would do little to meet the growing need for international reserves of private firms and persons and that eventually it would press the United States at least partly to close its capital markets, and so would raise the costs of capital to borrowers in all countries.

A continuing United States deficit certainly meant a gradual change in the situation of other countries—most obviously that their international reserves, in the form of dollars, were gradually growing, Such a statement seems to raise in the minds of many the specter that reserve accumulation can go only so far and that a limit can be reached beyond which no additions will be accepted.

Consideration of the demand for international reserves as discussed above will suggest that such a view is too mechanical. For one thing, both the private and official demands for reserves are (or *were*, before August 1971) very likely to grow over time. With a greater volume and value of world trade year after year, and with rapid growth in the levels of international capital flows also in prospect, the *need* for reserves to settle accounts and handle prospective deficits would be almost certain to grow too.[31] But this point merely indicates the likelihood that an increasing supply of international reserves could be absorbed. However, the additional reserves we have in mind are short-term dollar assets in the hands of nonresidents. What about *their* absorption?

A limit could certainly have been reached to the amount of dollars that asset holders outside the United States would accept, *if* the dollar had lost its status as the preferred currency. They might, for example, come to prefer German marks, or Swiss francs. Such a prospect seemed decidedly improbable at the beginning of 1971 or earlier. The factors which gave the dollar its preferred status[32] were so strong that the likelihood that the mark, franc, yen, or anything else would soon supplant it seemed remote. Naturally, there could be no guarantee that its position would endure forever. After all, the pound sterling was nudged from its role, beginning after 1919, as the dollar won an increasing measure of acceptability. But in early 1971, to imagine that a similar fate would very soon confront the dollar seemed premature.

Of course there were complaints about the dollar and its management. Central bankers missed few opportunities to express their concern for the dollar, and their unreadiness to continue accumulating more and more dollars in their reserves. But their acts belied their words. The economic policies of the various countries revealed no desire to move from a position of surplus on balance of payments account, to equilibrium. In fact protectionism had probably grown stronger between 1965 and 1970; moreover, such economic aid to the less-developed countries as implied a charge upon a

[31] The analogy of the increasing demand for money in a growing domestic economy is suggestive. Just why economists should accept the one as reasonable and yet be so ready to boggle over the other is difficult to understand.

[32] The dollar had preserved its value far better than almost any other currency from 1939 to 1971; the market for short-term dollar securities was far broader than for any other potential reserve asset denominated in another currency, and finally the size and competitive strength of the United States economy were still outstanding.

country's balance of payments, instead of increasing as the income and wealth of the advanced countries grew, actually declined.

And the continued reluctance of the major surplus countries to revalue, even though most of them worried more about inflation than unemployment hints at their willingness to remain in surplus—and to accumulate more and more international reserves—even dollars.

Admittedly, Germany was ready by May 1971 to revalue the mark or at least to adopt a flexible exchange-rate policy for it. But the circumstances were unusual, and the interpretation of her actions is not at all obvious. She had adopted a policy of credit restraint to check domestic inflation. With a stable exchange rate and declining interest rates in the United States, she was on the receiving end of a flood of short-term capital imports. As a result her money supply was increased, as the German central bank bought up the dollars which were the counterpart of her capital imports; in effect, the Bundesbank engaged in massive expansionary open-market operations. And for a variety of reasons, it did not offset or sterilize these effects, restraining the increase in the money supply. Thus Germany's policy of credit restraint encountered serious obstacles. Since she refused to give up her monetary policy, she had to find some way of insulating herself from the rest of the world, and especially from the United States capital market.

Of course, the central problem here was a general one, and not one confined to the dollar and the mark. International economic integration and especially the integration of capital markets had become very significant. Any country, by 1970, would have to determine its own monetary policy with due regard to the policies adopted in other countries, failing which it might have to expect its own policy to be subverted. Its sovereignty in this field had been greatly lessened. But Germany refused to recognize this development, and her obduracy—or, if you want, that of most other countries—meant that progress toward integration would have to be reversed.

The adoption of a flexible exchange-rate policy for the mark appeared to be well designed to do just that: to check the inflow of short-term funds from the United States and to divide up the international capital market once again. But it did not prove effective for long, because by the time it was introduced, the expectations of speculators that the mark would be revalued sharply upward had established firm roots; very little—an official speech perhaps, or a minor adjustment in policy—would set off an avalanche of short-term funds toward Germany again. And, as usual, there was no hesitating on the part of European Finance Ministers, American Congressmen, experts from everywhere to participate. United States officials suddenly shifted from attempting to persuade the world that the dollar was strong to urging the view that it was overvalued and would have to be devalued. And officials from other countries agreed on the need for a dollar devaluation, though they were less ready to recommend an increase in the price of their own currencies. Only a few months later the whole system collapsed, or perhaps more accurately it was destroyed. And no small part in its destruction was taken first by the failure to recognize the folly of trying to maintain for each nation full sovereignty over its own monetary policy in a world which had advanced so far toward international economic integration, and second by the persistent efforts of the head of the bank and its major depositors to bring down the bank. Institutions which depend for their successful operations upon "confidence and trust" deserve better than this from those charged with the responsibility for them.

We are clearly not justified in concluding, on the basis of an examination of the events of 1971 that the dollar standard was doomed—inevitably doomed by the logic of its own operations. As a matter of fact, even if the United States balance of payments had been in "surplus" in 1971—whatever that really would have meant—the whole mechanism could have been brought down by such powerful, official efforts. A well-integrated capital market coupled with an active program of financial intermediation obviously create destabilizing possibilities, just as they create new opportunities for raising economic well-being. If they are to survive and contribute as much as they can to the health of the international economy, then national sovereignty over monetary policy, and the freedom of top officers to make pronouncements that are analogous to cries of "Fire!" in a crowded theater, obviously have to be restrained. In my judgment, these are the lessons that 1971 teaches—not that a continuing outflow of dollars *had* to be ended, and not even that a still larger outflow, a still more rapid buildup of dollar reserves, would have been destablizing on its own and apart from certain arbitrary and unnecessary official actions.[33]

The major danger that a large United States deficit was said to pose for the rest of the world was that it strengthened inflationary tendencies. It must be agreed that, with no counteracting change in foreign economic policies, the charge is valid.

In part, the mechanism depended upon stock effects; a succession of United States deficits would probably have led to a higher level of domestic monies in the various surplus countries. But the central banks of these

---

[33] There is a good deal to be said, indeed, on behalf of a greater outflow of dollars. Walter Salant has stressed, for one thing, that with a larger United States deficit, the likelihood and size of a deficit for any other country is lessened. In addition, with reserves very much higher, a system of irrevocably fixed exchange rates is easier (and *seen* to be easier, too) to maintain, and the potential speculator on the foreign-exchange market finds prospects less attractive. And then, coming full circle, in the absence of exchange speculation, the "need" for reserves is diminished. Thus, the more reserves there are, the less is the need for them.

countries surely could have offset these effects—say, by raising reserve requirements, through sales of securities from their portfolios to the open market, or borrowing in the market. Otherwise, the mechanism depended upon certain "flow effects": A United States deficit would have meant either a higher level of net exports in surplus countries, and thus directly a higher aggregate demand, or a higher level of capital imports (long-term, probably) and thus upward pressure on securities' prices, and so, indirectly, a higher level of aggregate demand. Again, it is hard to believe that any developed economy nowadays lacks the wisdom or the policy instruments to restore aggregate demand to the desired level—the more so since the magnitude of the effects that would have to be offset would have been relatively minor.[34]

In short, it is hard to understand the real basis for objection by any other country to a continuing inflow of dollar reserves—even to a very large one. There may be an *optimal level* of reserves for each country—and presumably, then, an *optimal rate of increase* of such reserves—but though it is easy to see that the level and rate can both be too low, it does not follow by simple extension that they can be too high.[35]

Although a large and continuing United States deficit would not injure other countries, it is possible that it would so injure the United States as to force that country to try to bring it to an end. If that were so, a United States deficit would mean a situation of disequilibrium—although not of the usual type.

The effects of such a deficit on the United States are unclear, principally because while it would raise certain problems, they appear to be unimportant when compared to the benefits it yields; moreover, the one most significant threat of injury can readily be offset by proper policy.

Clearly, the United States economy did stand to gain from its deficit. As the counterpart of the readiness of others to accumulate an ever-rising level of dollar reserves, the United States could acquire from them more goods and securities than she could have obtained had her purchases been restricted to the amount of her current exports and long-term capital imports. And she was then able to pocket the difference in yields from the high-yield securities she got and the low-yield short-term dollar securities she gave up.[36] But it

---

[34] A less-restrictive policy toward imports would have been just as effective too, and if the desire to ease the accumulation of dollars had been genuine, it could have been put into effect. That it was not, is significant.

[35] If a country's reserves were very high, it is alleged, the discipline of the balance of payments would be relaxed. And that, it is argued would have two dire consequences. It would not be under the same pressure to fight inflation, or to correct a maladjustment. This argument is unconvincing. There are strong reasons—equity, for instance—for preferring price stability to rising prices, other things being equal, which are quite apart from balance of payments pressures. And the business firms of an economy have themselves strong motives to do the kinds of things that would cure a maladjustment, without regard to the balance of payments.

would also mean that more and more of her receipts on current account would take the form of a payment for services rendered not by her existing labor force but by allowing others the use of her financial assets. Thus, many would see this as a depressive force making for greater unemployment.[37] But she could have offset this force by employing proper fiscal or monetary policies.[38]

Another deflationary force—but this time a real one, though again of very minor significance—stemmed from the open access that others had acquired to the American capital market and the uses they made of it. Their securities were available to be absorbed, and their prices were accordingly lowered. All those who sought external finance, including American firms and government bodies, therefore, would have had to pay higher interest rates *unless* the central bank adopted offsetting measures. But then the blame for deflation should have been placed where it belonged—on the Federal Reserve System.

Finally (and this issue appears to be the only substantial one), the United States role as banker, with its counter part, a large United States balance of payments deficit—opened the likelihood of a gradual *appreciation* of the dollar against most other currencies.[39] This followed because, as we have seen, any country in surplus was generally averse to raising its exchange rate, while a deficit country sometimes felt compelled to depreciate against the dollar.

United States producers who hoped to sell in foreign markets or were exposed to foreign competition at home found themselves *ceteris paribus* threatened by this gradual rise in the price of the dollar. Taking the short view, this could be made not to matter since it would not—so long as the dollar were used as the reserve currency—impair the ability of the United States to buy foreign goods and securities, and the deflationary consequences domestically could be offset. But obviously it would injure the interests of investors and workers attached to these threatened industries; and in the long run—when another currency or mechanism had stripped from the dollar its special role—the United States would be bound to face very serious problems of adjustment.

The United States could have eased this problem, as it did in August 1971, by depreciating the dollar. But this created, I believe, vast new problems for

---

[36] If domestic demand pressures had been excessive and could not have been easily brought down, she could instead have acquired goods and and services from outside, and thus ease inflationary pressures.

[37] That the economy took on these characteristics of the "idle rich" need not have condemned some of her work force to idleness. It would be more correct to regard it as allowing her to use less of her manpower in order to provide an unchanged per-capita level of income; or if she were to use all her manpower, then to enjoy higher incomes.

[38] It must be noted that, up to 1971, the yield from foreign investments represented less than 1% of all incomes, so the problem was obviously not very serious.

[39] This is the opposite of the usual fear that the dollar would lose its value.

the United States and everyone else, for it dangerously *narrowed the margin of preference of the dollar as a reserve asset over any competitor.*[40]

As an alternative, the United States could have done much more to reduce the pressures on deficit countries to depreciate by supplying them with even more ample reserves, or at least with a greatly increased access (through commitment to lend, for instance) to such reserves.[41]

6. Conclusion

The dollar standard failed, or was made to fail, by August 1971, if not earlier. I have argued here that there was nothing about its operations that was bound to lead to this situation. Under it a great deal was achieved; even more could have been achieved had its operations been more clearly understood. But the major powers, or at least some of them, misinterpreted what was happening, taking as evidence of weakness and impending collapse, developments which were perfectly normal—like the United States deficit—or which could have been handled by making minor adjustments.[42] Finally, in August 1971, the United States took the final step which has stripped from the dollar a great deal of the authority it had acquired. With nothing to take its place, I see anything but a bright future.[43]

REFERENCES

de Vries, M. G. (1969)   Exchange rate adjustments. In *The International Monetary Fund, 1945–1965; twenty years of international cooperation* (J. K. Horsefield, ed.), Vol. II, Chap. 5. Washington, D.C.: International Monetary Fund.

[40] The difficulties that this created can only be expected to surface when a system of stable rates is again created, and only gradually then as the inadequacy of international reserves begins to press. We can expect, in addition, however, large speculative swings in reserve portfolios and the resulting pressures on the various currencies, but primarily the dollar at first, that are the major components of these portfolios.

[41] Stated in this way, the proposition seems paradoxical. However it can be made familiar by considering an analog: A central bank can prevent most failures of commercial banks if it always stands ready to act as a lender of last resort to them.

[42] As the problem of United States gold losses was temporarily handled in March 1967.

[43] SDRs could take its place in official reserves, and except for the problem of getting agreement on the level of SDR creation and the threat that their creation would be too slow, I see no difficulty there. But international access to favorable financial markets would be far more difficult, since no country could export capital for long in excess of its own current account surplus and claim on newly produced SDRs unless and to the degree that its currency were acceptable as a component in private international reserves. And it is surely premature to expect any other currency yet to serve as a substitute for the dollar; and when it is ready, to expect that its investors are ready to pay more than investors elsewhere for the long-term securities that are offered from all over the world.

Long Swings and the Atlantic Economy : A Reappraisal*

BRINLEY THOMAS
UNIVERSITY COLLEGE, CARDIFF

Our understanding of long swings in the rate of growth of the American economy has been immensely enriched by the work of Abramovitz (1959, 1961, 1964). He regards them as "the outcome of interactions between the pace at which resources are developed, the generation of effective demand, and the intensity of resource use [p. 246]."† His model leads to the conclusion that "a long swing in the volume of additions, perhaps even in the rate of growth of additions, to the stock of capital, that is, in capital formation, is likely to involve a fluctuation in effective demand and thus to generate an alternation between states of relatively full and relatively slack employment. A long swing in unemployment rates in turn appears to have been among the chief causes of Kuznets cycles in the volume of additions to the labor force and perhaps in capital formation [p. 230]." According to this interpretation, swings in immigration from other countries were determined unilaterally by a "common cause" in the United States; they were "responses to the occurrences of

---

* The major portion of this chapter has been taken from the work by B. Thomas (1972).

† M. Abramovitz (1961) The nature and significance of Kuznets cycles. *Economic Development and Cultural Change* 9(3):225–248, published by the University of Chicago. Copyright 1961 by the University of Chicago.

protracted periods of abnormally high unemployment and to the recovery from such periods [p. 243]."

It is not possible here to do justice to the subtle theoretical reasoning and the sophisticated empirical testing which Abramovitz brings to bear on the problem. No one can work in this field without being profoundly influenced by his achievement. What I propose to do is to look at the American long swing in the pre-1913 period from the British viewpoint and to suggest that a more convincing explanation is to be found in the process of interaction within the Atlantic economy.[1] Then there is the solemn question whether we should say farewell to the Kuznets cycle. Abramovitz, as chief mourner, has written a moving epitaph (1968): "The Kuznets cycle in America lived, it flourished, it had its day, but its day is past. Departed, it leaves to us who survive to study its works many insights into the kinds of connections and responses which go together to make for spurts and retardations in development. We are the wiser for its life, but it is gone, *Requiescat in pace*. Gone but not forgotten [p. 367]."* My first reaction to this was to borrow Mark Twain's famous remark when he read an obituary of himself in the papers: "The news is somewhat exaggerated." However, as we shall see later, it is really a question of the identification of the deceased.

1. America's Weight in the Pre-1913 International Economy

In the course of the debate on the working of the Atlantic economy no critic has been able to refute the existence of an inverse relation between long swings in construction in Britain and the United States and in British home and foreign investment from the 1850s to 1913. There has indeed been ample confirmation [e.g., Lewis (1965), Bloomfield (1968), and Thomas (1971)]. Where disagreement enters is in interpreting the nature of the mechanism by which the economies of the two countries reacted on each other. In approaching this question one has to bear in mind that the United States for most of that period carried only a moderate weight in the international economy. In 1870 she accounted for 23% of the world's output of manufactured goods as against Britain's 32%, and over one-half her exports in the period 1861–1878 went to Britain. In 1880 Britain was responsible for 63% of world exports of capital goods and 41% of world exports of manufactured goods as compared with America's 6% and 3%, respectively; and even by the end of the century America's share of world exports of manufactured goods was still only a third of that of Britain [see Saul (1965)]. In the years 1870–1914 Britain supplied

[1] For the full analysis on which this paper is based see Thomas (1972, 1973). I am grateful to my publishers for permission to reproduce material in this article.

* M. Abramovitz (1968) The passing of the Kuznets cycle. *Economica* **35**: 349–367.

nearly 60% of the foreign investment in the United States, and from 1869 to 1893 the net inflow of capital was on the average between 10 and 16% of America's total net capital formation. London was the unchallenged financial center of the world and presided over what was virtually a sterling standard. It has been estimated that when the United States returned to the gold standard in 1879, she held only 5% of the world's monetary gold stock or about 8% of the part serving as monetary reserves and these percentages for the rest of the century were probably less than 20 (Friedman and Schwartz, 1963). "This is one rough measure of the relative importance of the U.S. economy in the gold standard world and one that almost surely overstates its importance since both the unit banking system in the U.S. and the absence of a central bank probably worked to make the ratio of the gold stock to the money stock higher than in most other important gold standard countries [p. 89]."* Given the above facts, it is hardly surprising, as Cagan recognized in his review of the pre-1913 period, that "U.S. cycles frequently stemmed from foreign influences and were not usually transmitted abroad. This country's economy during the nineteenth century could not have counted heavily with most foreign economies, while world trade clearly affected U.S. exports. Their irregular cyclical pattern ... reflected the ups and downs of foreign business activity, which often moved counter to domestic business [p. 110]."†

Any interpretation of the interaction between the British and American economies in the pre-1913 period must account for the fact that there were uniform long swings in investment throughout the overseas developing world, e.g., United States, Canada, Argentina, and Australia. Writers who have attempted a one-sided explanation of the long swing in terms of variations in American aggregate demand see supporting evidence in the fact that there were *simultaneous* swings in migration from a number of European countries to the United States: they have not asked why there were *simultaneous* immigration and investment swings in a number of countries of new settlement. This latter phenomenon, which can hardly be explained by swings in United States demand, is an important part of the problem of the causation of the inverse cycles.

The answer is to be sought in two basic features of the period. First, the opening up of new sources of food and raw materials required flows of population and capital funds to be invested in infrastructure overseas, and there was necessarily a long lag between the input phase and the output phase. As Schumpeter said, this was essentially one vast process transcending national

---

* M. Friedman and A. J. Schwartz (1963) *A monetary history of the United States*, 1867–1960, National Bureau of Economic Research, Princeton Univ. Press.

† P. Cagan (1965) *Determinants and effects of changes in the stock of money*, 1875–1960. New York: National Bureau of Economic Research, Columbia Univ. Press, 1965, p. 110.

boundaries, with the whole earth as its stage. Second, the countries were linked together by the gold standard dominated by London; and when an infrastructure boom overseas became intense, strong action by the Bank of England to protect its reserve had powerful repercussions on the supply of money in all factor-importing countries.

Space will not allow an analysis of British fluctuations in investment and trade in relation to those of countries of Europe. That the primary causal forces were within the Atlantic economy is attested by the following comparison between Germany and Britain based on the matrix of world trade in 1887 [see O'Leary and Lewis (1955)]. Germany was responsible for 11.7% of world exports, about nine-tenths going to Europe, including the United Kingdom, and under one-tenth to the United States; she took 11.5% of world exports, only 8% of which came from the United States and 88% from Europe, including the United Kingdom. The United Kingdom was responsible for 16.5% of world exports, two-thirds going overseas and one-third to Europe; she took 25% of world exports, of which 54% came from overseas (22% from the United States) and 46% from Europe. Since one-fifth of German exports went to the United Kingdom, the German export sector was geared to home construction swings in Britain and not those in the United States, and this would make the German construction cycle coincide with that of America.

2. A Model of the Atlantic Economy

We regard the Atlantic economy of the second half of the nineteenth century as comprising, on the one hand, Great Britain, highly industrialized with growing population pressure on a small land area, and on the other, a periphery of underpopulated developing countries with extensive land and natural resources. Britain practiced free trade, London was the financial center of the system, and the gold standard was virtually a sterling standard.

We make the following hypotheses about the interaction between the creditor country (C) and the factor-importing "country" (D) (representing the whole periphery).

(a) Each is divided into two sectors, home construction and export.

(b) C exports capital goods and D food and raw materials.

(c) Migration depends on the difference in real wages which can be approximated by the difference in real incomes.

(d) Export capacity is generated through population-sensitive capital formation, i.e., the building of infrastructure—railways, roads, land-clearing, ports, houses, public utilities, etc.—and this investment has a relatively long gestation period. There is an intertemporal relation between a country's infrastructure investment in one period and its export capacity in the next period.

(e) The level of activity of a country's export sector depends on the expected marginal efficiency of investment in the construction sector of the other country. The marginal efficiency of investment is the marginal physical product of capital multiplied by the ratio of the price of output to the price of capital input. Applied to exported output, this means that the marginal efficiency of investment depends on the expected future purchasing power per unit of factor input, i.e., the "single factoral terms of trade."

(f) A major fraction of total capital formation is population-sensitive, i.e., varying with the rate of change in population growth and internal migration.

(g) The population growth rate is a function of population structure (i.e., a vector showing proportions of population in various age, sex, and marital groups) and the external migration balance.

(h) The countries are linked by a gold standard with specie currency.

These assumptions imply a complicated seesaw movement in which both "real" and monetary factors are at work. The population cycle, with migration as a crucial element, determines the time-shape of capital formation in C and D, respectively. The demographic variables, through their impact on the course of investment which in turn is conditioned by the gestation lag, create a state of high sensitivity in which monetary shocks can affect the course of things. A monetary cobweb is superimposed on the instability inherent in the interplay of real magnitudes.

In this model capital formation is "population-sensitive" not just "migration-sensitive."[2] Its ability to generate long swings would seem to depend on the infrastructure lag and population structure. There are a number of different possible forms of the investment function, particularly with respect to lags, which are conceivable, and the best empirical form can be found only by experimenting. As a future development of this work it is proposed to simulate a complete model, to try out various functions with different parameters and lags so as to see what effects they have on the simulated values of the endogenous variables.

We shall now explore the nature of the interaction between the creditor country (C) and the factor-importing "country" (D) representing the whole periphery, paying particular attention to the interplay of real and monetary factors.

[2] A formal statement of the model is given in my *Migration and Urban Development* (1972, Appendix C), and the statistical justification for assumptions (d), (e), (f), and (g) is presented in the same work (pp. 81–93). See also Thomas (1973, Chapter XV).

a. The Upswing in Emigration and Lending

We can start with a movement of either labor or capital. Let us assume a large flow of young migrants from C to D, with consequent opposite impacts on the countries' population structure and internal migration. This increases population-sensitive capital formation in the receiving country and reduces it in the sending country. There will be an accompanying flow of lending from C to D attracted by the higher marginal efficiency of investment in D's construction sector. We distinguish between *ex ante* lending, i.e., the purchase of D securities by C residents, and *ex post* capital exports, i.e., the balance on current account minus gold imports. This *ex ante* lending can be considered in terms of periodic stock adjustments by C investors. The optimal portfolio of diversified home securities held by the "representative" investor in country C is necessarily subject to the risk of a change in the general level of activity. When he sees the prospect of a construction slump at home coinciding with a boom abroad, he can reduce this risk by substituting foreign securities for some of his domestic securities. In the words of Lee (1969), "given the expected rate of return, variances and covariances of return of individual securities, there is a unique optimal composition of the securities in a portfolio, and this portfolio can be considered a composite good. Likewise, an optimal portfolio is derived for foreign securities only and this portfolio forms a second composite good. In the second stage, then, the investor makes a choice concerning the allocation of his total wealth between the two composite goods [pp. 514–515]."* When the actual amount of D securities held by C residents is less than the optimum portfolio of D securities, an outflow of capital takes place, and this can occur even if the rate differential is unchanged.

The increased purchase of D securities (*ex ante* foreign lending) is followed by a rise in the demand for C exports, and the export sector in country C gets a boom at the expense of infrastructure investment. During this upswing the induced investment in C will be in export-sensitive producer durables, e.g., shipbuilding; but this is more than counterbalanced by the decline in population-sensitive construction.

Thus, in this first phase there is an infrastructure boom in D and an export sector boom in C. In country D there is an internal shift of labor and resources from the export sector to construction, and vice versa in C. The effect of the upswing on D's price structure is seen mainly in a rise in the price level of domestic goods; next come export prices, and the price level of imports rises least. An important determinant of the latter is the fact that country C in the early stage of the upswing can draw factors easily into its export sector owing

---

* C. H. Lee (1969) A stock-adjustment analysis of capital movements: The United States–Canadian case. *Journal of Political Economy* **77**:514–515, published by the University of Chicago. Copyright 1969 by the University of Chicago; all rights reserved.

to declining activity in the construction sector. A rise in productivity enables its expansion to proceed for some time without a rise in costs. During this phase the net barter terms of trade (the ratio of export prices to import prices) move against C and in favor of D.

With regard to the course of the upswing in D, it is relevant to note that in an infrastructure boom we have not only *income-induced* accelerator investment but also *investment-induced* investment. The latter is of a complementary nature and is in a fixed relation to the primary investment.[3] This introduces an additional lag into the process and helps to account for the length of the construction upswing.

There are three main determinants of the duration of the upswing in D: First, the course of the demand for additional infrastructure induced by the change in the population structure and the life-cycle spending decisions taken by the household-forming age groups; second, the interaction between the multiplier and the accelerator (with lags); and, third, the transfer problem. The financing of the lending by country C has multiplier effects on the balance of trade. When these are allowed for, the question is whether the financing and use of the transferred funds changes the demands for goods so that the improvement in C's balance of trade equals the amount lent [see Johnson (1958)]. We must note that the flow of interest payments involves wealth effects which should not be left out, since they usually are in the literature on the transfer problem. Payments of interest and dividends on foreign investment from the periphery to Britain were a very large item.

In the early part of the upswing in D there is not likely to be trouble. To simplify, let us ignore saving and postulate that the lending is entirely at the expense of home investment in C and that the borrowings are entirely spent by D; then the transfer will be effected without price or income adjustments if the marginal propensities to import add up to unity. A moderate degree of under-effected transfer will entail adjustments which will slow down the boom in D, but the infrastructure investment projects already launched are unlikely to be much curtailed.

In the later stage of the boom the situation changes. As the export up-swing gathers momentum in C, a turning point is reached. Investment induced by the growth of exports increases rapidly, and at the higher level of employment marginal costs rise, while demand is running high in construction

---

[3] For example, for a given increase in residential building, additional investment is required in public utility services, schools, hospitals, etc. For orders of magnitude see Mattila and Thompson (1956). Writing of the United States in the period 1946–1954, these authors (1956, p. 467) point out that "housing, which unassisted accounts for only 37% of all new construction activity, when bundled up with what we intend to show to be complementary construction, has constituted almost 64% of all new construction acitvity in the postwar period."

activity in D. Productivity in C's export sector has ceased to go up and may be falling, and export prices rise relatively to import prices. Meanwhile, C investors are receiving an increasing flow of interest and dividends on their foreign securities. This wealth effect is likely to promote further *ex ante* lending which now reaches a very high level. The population variable, emigration, is also at a high level but its rate of growth is already declining for demographic reasons, and after a short lag this entails an upturn in construction from the low point reached in C.

At this stage transfer becomes seriously undereffected; the growth of the current trade balance cannot keep up with the *ex ante* lending. The monetary authority in C is faced with an external drain of gold to D and an internal drain due to a combination of export-induced investment and a revival in construction. This means severe monetary instability. The central bank must take drastic action to replenish its reserves and raises the interest rate to a punitive level. This attracts a large flow of short-term balances and gold from D, and there is a fall in purchases of D securities. The representative investor in C, impressed by the increasing risk attached to D securities and attracted by the marginal efficiency of investment in home construction, will now optimize by increasing his stock of domestic securities at the expense of his foreign portfolio. The monetary cobweb thus set in motion breaks the infrastructure boom in D. The large loss of gold reduces D's money supply or sharply reduces its rate of growth and this precipitates a downturn.

b. The Downswing in Emigration and Lending

We now have the reverse process—a decline in emigration and lending, an expansion in C's construction sector and D's export sector. Given absolute confidence in the ability of the creditor country to maintain convertibility, the action taken by C, with its curb on foreign lending, quickly restores C's balance of payments equilibrium through a deflation of effective demand. The incidence of the adjustment, however, is felt mainly in the periphery, which gets the full force of the monetary contraction and the reversed accelerator–multiplier process. Prices fall in D much more sharply than in C. The vigorous upswing in construction accompanied by a downswing in the export sector in the borrowing country had made its economy much more vulnerable to monetary contraction than the economy of the creditor country, which had been through a phase of declining construction combined with expanding exports. The degree of credit restriction applied to restore monetary equilibrium in C necessarily overshoots the mark and inflicts on D a steep fall in investment and income.

Under the gold standard D's money supply is a variable dependent on outside forces. The causal sequence runs from the balance of payments and the gold flow to the money stock and then to the level of prices which is consistent with the fixed exchange rate. If the debtor country is to remain on the gold standard, the correction of undereffected transfer by the creditor necessarily entails a reduction in the debtor's money supply and a fall in its price level relatively to the creditor's.

Infrastructure investment in D responding to the population variable declines rapidly, and there is a rise in the output of the export sector geared to the expanding activity in C's construction sector. The productivity of D's export sector is directly related to the expansion which took place in infrastructure in the previous period; a substantial supply of primary produce is exported at falling prices. D's net barter terms of trade are declining; but the significant fact is that its "single factoral terms of trade" (the net barter terms corrected for the rise in physical productivity in the production of exports) are rising. This is similar to what occurred in C during the early stage of the boom in its export sector in the previous period. Each country, debtor as well as creditor, in its infrastructure boom period, lays the foundations for the performance of its export sector in the following period; and during export upswings there is a shift away from home construction to investment in producer durables the demand for which is a function of the level of activity in the export sector.

In C substantial internal migration takes the place of emigration; and population-sensitive capital formation sets the pace for the economy. *Ex ante* foreign lending falls, and the price of domestic stocks rises. With the supply schedules of labor and loanable funds facing the construction sector moving to the right, the multiplier–accelerator process draws in a growing volume of imports of primary produce. Since the export sector is in decline, the balance on current account shrinks.

It is possible for a monetary crisis to occur before the lags in the real process in C dictate a downturn. The rapidly rising current account balance of country D causes a continuing gold outflow from C and an acceleration of the rate of growth of the money supply in D. This means that sooner or later the price of D's exports will begin to rise. This will increase the strain in C where infrastructure investment has reached a high level and unemployment is at a minimum. The monetary authority in C is now facing a double strain—a continued outflow of gold together with a rapidly increasing interior demand. The representative investor in C, worried by the increasing risk attached to his domestic portfolio and attracted by the expected profitability of investment in construction abroad, will optimize by switching into D securities. This rise in *ex ante* lending adds to the instability. The reserves of the system reach the danger level, and the central bank raises its interest rate enough to replenish its reserves. Gold will then flow in from D with a consequent deceleration of the growth of the money supply in that country, and the stringent credit restriction will precipitate a downturn in C's construction sector. This down-turn brings D's export boom to an end. The stage is now set for a new upswing in infrastructure investment and a downswing in exports in D and an emigration-lending upsurge with falling infrastructure investment in C.

In this model country D stands for the periphery of countries of new settle-ment in the second half of the nineteenth century. The critical turning points in the long swings are attributable to monetary instability occurring in the lending country, the financial center of the system. The seesaw movement arises fundamentally out of the inverse demographic cycles and the alternation of infrastructure and export upsurges, but the whole thing is played according to the rules of the gold standard game, with the monetary authority in the creditor country as referee. This mechanism of interaction offers an explanation of the fact that the overseas countries of new settlement in the pre-1913 period experienced *simultaneous* long swings in capital formation which were inverse to those of the United Kingdom.

3. Historical Evidence, 1879–1901

a. The Upswing in Overseas Investment 1879–1889

The vigorous upswing in foreign investment which began in 1879 was interrupted at an early stage in 1881 when there was already undereffected transfer, with a gold outflow from London accompanied by an internal drain. By February 1882 the reserve was down to £9,175,000, a loss of £7,856,000 from a year before, intensified by the failure of the Union Générale in Paris in January 1882. The Bank of England raised its rates to 5% in October 1881 and 6% in January 1882. This had the required effect in a sharp reaction in foreign lending and a reflux of gold; by 1884 the transfer difficulty had disappeared.

The impact on the periphery can be illustrated by what happened in the United States, where the stock of gold had risen from $210 million in June 1879 to $439 million in June 1881. This increase in the money supply raised the American price level in relation to the British from 89.1 in 1879 to 96.1 in 1882. The Bank of England's intervention, through its impact on foreign lending and prices, reversed the gold flow. This was the classic gold standard mechanism in action. If the United States was to retain its fixed exchange rate, a fall in her income and price level was unavoidable. British investors, fearing that the United States would not be able to stay on the gold standard, began to sell American securities, leading to a further outflow of gold which helped to cause a panic in May 1884. Because British prices fell 12% between 1882 and 1885, the achievement of a 1% decline in American prices relative to

British necessitated an absolute fall of 13% in the American price level over these three years.[4]

The rate of growth in the United States money stock fell sharply from 1881 to 1885 from 16% a year to 3% and that of real output declined from 7% a year to 1%. Severe though the recession was, it was only an interruption in the infrastructure investment upswing which was resumed in 1885, with a further strong inflow of capital from Britain. By 1888 there was serious undereffected transfer; the flow of *ex ante* foreign lending exceeded the current balance by a large margin. The situation in Britain at the peak of portfolio investment in 1889 was as follows: There was an external and internal drain of gold; the shipbuilding cycle was at a peak; overseas emigration had begun to turn down; the upturn in home construction had already begun; and a shift in British investment away from the United States to Argentina had started. The Bank of England alarm bells were ringing loudly; the rate went up to 5% in October 1888 and to 6% at the end of December 1889, in response to which gold began to flow back. At the end of 1890 there was a further spell of dear money. The result was a huge influx of gold.

The repercussions were felt throughout the periphery. With the shock of the Baring crisis in November 1890, Argentina experienced a severe reaction.[5] In the United States there was a parallel movement of net capital imports and the purchasing power parity index; the ratio of American to British prices began falling in 1887. Looking at this from the British side, one can interpret the course of events as follows. Between 1880 and 1887, the first phase of the lending-export boom, British prices fell by 30% while money wages remained constant; this is a strong suggestion of rising productivity in the export sector which did not lead to higher money wages. There was a high elasticity of supply of factors for the export sector due to the downswing in home construction. As the boom gathered momentum, a turning point was reached; marginal costs began to rise because of bottlenecks at the higher level of employment in the export trades and export-sensitive investment, while demand was running high in oversea construction activity. The turning point came in 1887; from that year to 1890 British export prices rose by 18% and money wages by 8%; we may infer that in those years physical productivity fell. After 1887 there was a shift in the supply schedule of capital against the United States. Because of the rise in British prices, the absolute fall required in American prices was moderate.

Nevertheless, this ushered in a phase of great difficulty for the United States, with substantial gold outflows, a fall in the rate of growth of money

[4] On this episode see Friedman and Schwartz (1963, pp. 100–101).
[5] For a detailed account of the boom and collapse in Argentina see the work of Ford (1962). See also his illuminating analysis of long swings (Ford, 1971).

stock, and a banking panic in 1893. The maintenance of the gold standard once again necessitated a drastic deflation of prices and income. Meanwhile, the gold stock of the Bank of England rose to a record of £49,000,000 in February 1896. The bank rate fell to 2% and was ineffective; for much of the time the market rate of discount was under 1%.[6]

b. The Upswing in United Kingdom Home Investment, 1890–1901

The upswing in home construction in Great Britain which began in 1889 was halted in 1891–1893 and then developed into an intense boom which reached its peak in 1901. In the periphery, conditions in the early part of the decade were bordering on collapse; British portfolio investment dropped sharply from £120 million in 1889 to just over £30 million in 1893, and the current balance receded to a low trough of £22.9 million in 1898.

In the United States the reaction from the investment boom of the eighties was intensified by lack of confidence in the stability of the dollar. The Sherman Silver Purchase Act and the McKinley Tariff Act of 1890 helped to increase the uncertainty; the years 1890–1894 saw large outflows of gold, and net capital inflows declined to a trickle, foreign investors selling $300 million of American securities. The effect of the gold outflow on the money stock was strengthened by the public's tending to hold a higher ratio of currency to deposits. In the first half of the decade there was a steep decline in the rate of growth of the money supply; and, in view of falling prices abroad, America had to experience a severe price and income deflation if convertibility was to be maintained. The long crisis of confidence did not end until the triumph of the Republicans in the election of 1896: from then on there was a dramatic change in the fortunes of the American economy, aided by the powerful effect of the gold discoveries in South Africa, Colorado, and Alaska.

Similar depressive influences dominated the rest of the periphery, e.g., Argentina, Canada, and Australia, in the first half of the nineties. Whereas the export capacity of all these countries had been greatly increased by the infrastructure boom of the eighties, their export sectors did not have a real income expansion until the second half of the decade when the fall in world prices was reversed and the home construction boom in Britain really got going. Argentina is a good example of the cobweb-type instability to which the periphery was exposed because of the lag between infrastructure investment and the subsequent phase when it matured in increased exports. In the years 1885–1889 Argentina absorbed £60 million of British portfolio investment and a net total of 640,000 foreign immigrants, and by 1890 the annual servicing of the foreign debt, which had to be made in gold or sterling at a fixed rate,

---

[6] For a well-documented account of the London money market during the nineties, see Beach (1935).

took 60 million gold pesos, or 60% of the export proceeds in 1890 (Ford, 1962, pp. 140–141). According to Ford (1962, p. 142), "the slow maturing of investment projects for which the service charges were immediate was a main cause of the Baring crisis." The *volume* of exports of wheat and wool increased substantially after 1890, but export *values* did not show a marked rise until 1898. As in the United States, there was a strong export upswing in real terms in the late nineties, pivoted to a large extent on the home investment upsurge in the United Kingdom. Similarly in Canada the index of the value of exports between 1895 and 1900 rose from 114 to 192 and in Australia total exports rose from £36.5 million to £49.2 million.

Even when full allowance is made for special political and other circumstances in the oversea countries, there was undeniably a basic common factor. Their economies were seriously destabilized in the wake of the corrective measures taken by the Bank of England in 1890; when Britain caught a cold, the periphery caught pneumonia. There is no clearer demonstration of the process of interaction than the monetary series for the nineties. Gold flowing out of the United States and other countries went into the coffers of the Bank of England. Between June 1892 and June 1896 there was actually an absolute fall of 5% in the United States money stock, the first such decline since the seventies, whereas the Bank of England reserve increased spectacularly from £15 million to no less than £49 million (February 1896). When America was struggling desperately to stay on the gold standard, Britain was enjoying such a surfeit of liquidity that the market rate of discount was below 1%. In the second half of the nineties the reverse happened; the Bank of England reserve as a proportion of liabilities fell almost as rapidly as it had risen, while the money stock of the United States increased by 50%.

The demographic determinants of the inverse construction cycle have been fully demonstrated (Thomas, 1972, pp. 20–58). The upturn of the cycle in Britain preceded the downturn in the export sector. Detailed research has established the primacy of residential construction in the home boom of the nineties.[7] "This is the major single item of home investment which begins a decade's rise gradually but steadily as early as 1891–2, preceding all other types of home investment by several years (Sigsworth and Blackman, 1965, p. 78)." Its progress was accelerated by two powerful forces—abnormally cheap money and the high peak in internal migration and the natural increase component of the 20–44 population curve in the second half of the decade.

The ability to borrow money at abnormally low rates had been, according to *The Economist*, the most important cause behind the rising prices of Stock Exchange securities, having "enabled enterprising investors to carry large blocks of securities with loans obtained from the banks. While money could be obtained upon Consols at 1 per

---

[7] The subject has been admirably explored by Sigsworth and Blackman (1965).

cent and under, and while the banks were willing to lend at but little over that figure upon home railway stocks . . . it was obviously good business to enter into such transactions." . . . The favourable cost structure of the building industry in a period of cheap money and of increasing demand for new and better quality houses made housing a particularly attractive field for speculative investment; and it was this sector which dominated the expansion of the 1890s [p. 96].*

This strong investment upswing in Britain was the foundation of the export sector boom in the periphery. American exports as a proportion of imports rose from 105% early in the decade to 165% at the end, and net gold imports to the United States from mid-1896 to mid-1899 amounted to $201 million or 40% of the initial stock. With domestic mines producing at the rate of $60 million a year, the monetary gold stock had reached $859 million by the middle of 1899, a rise of 90% in three years (Friedman and Schwartz, 1963, p. 141).

In 1898 and 1899 there were signs of strain in the British economy. Construction was at a very high level, and shipbuilding was nearing a peak. The Bank of England up to 1890 had regarded a reserve of about £10 million as a sign that the rate should go up: after 1896 the critical level was held to be about £20 million. In April 1898, when the reserve had fallen to £18.3 million, the rate was raised to 4%; there was a sizable reflux and then a further loss, so that the rate was again raised to 4% in October 1898, and gold again flowed in. The internal drain was rising rapidly at the height of the boom; gold imports had to accommodate this demand and so did not strengthen the Bank's stock. The outbreak of the South African War led to the rate being raised to 6% in November 1899. For the second half of 1900 it was at 4%, and it was put up to 5% in January 1901.

The peak of the British investment boom had been reached in 1899 when unemployment was as low as 2%, interior demand for gold was running at over £10 million, and the index of share prices touched its highest point. Meanwhile in the United States the demographic cycle had already turned upward; net immigration had begun to recover in 1898 and rose from 121,000 in that year to 201,000 in 1899, accompanied by a 20% jump in real construction. This was happening at the very time when the steam had gone out of the demographic cycle in Britain. The London stock market was signaling a downturn in 1900 and unemployment rose to 2.5%; total construction reacted in 1901, unemployment rose to 3.3%, and in 1902 a vigorous upswing in portfolio foreign investment was in progress, with the index of share prices 9% down from the top. The British investment boom of the nineties was over, and the final infrastructure upswing in the periphery was under way.

* E. M. Sigsworth and J. Blackman (1965) The home boom of the 1890's. In Studies in the British Economy 1870–1914 (J. Saville, ed.). *Yorkshire Bulletin of Economic and Social Research*, Special Number 17: 75–97.

4. Long Swings in Productivity and Real Income*

With the aid of Fig. 1 (see Table 1 for summary of data) we can indicate briefly what the analysis suggests about the growth and fluctuations of productivity and real income per capita.

Both in the United Kingdom and the United States the rates of change in fixed capital formation are inverse to those in exports as a percentage of imports; in other words, export performance in any one period correlates with the movement of fixed investment in the previous period. In the United States there is a strong positive correlation between rates of change in "other" capital formation (which includes producer durables), exports as a percentage of imports, and changes in additions to the real flow of goods to consumers per capita. The course of these three variables is reflected (after a short lag) in the rate of change of real GNP per capita. In other words, in the upward phase of the long swing in population-sensitive capital formation, the economy is investing in capacity to produce more output per unit of input in the future. *Ex post*, the high rate of growth in real national income per capita is the payoff on the population-sensitive capital formation of the previous phase; *ex ante*, it is the inducement to a further round of fixed investment in the next phase. It is in the payoff phase that the balance of payments is strong, the rate of growth of the money supply is high, and the standard of living grows relatively fast; the economy is reaping the increasing returns to scale arising out of the rapid rise in immigration and investment in the previous phase. The above process is a plausible explanation of the long swings observed in productivity in the United States,[8] and it applies to the United Kingdom as well.

The inverse relation between the swings in real income per capita in the United Kingdom and the United States[9] is bound up with the seesaw movement in the population growth rate, changes in population structure (mainly

---

* This section has been taken from B. Thomas (1972). *Migration and urban development: A reappraisal of British and American long cycles*, pp. 120–123. London: Methuen, University Paperback (distributed in the United States by Harper, New York).

[8] See S. Fabricant (1959) *Basic facts on productivity change*, Occasional Paper 63, New York: National Bureau of Economic Research. The productivity estimates are based on the work of Kendrick (1961). Fabricant points out that "Kendrick's estimates, and similar data compiled earlier by Kuznets and Abramovitz for the full period following the Civil War, suggest the existence of a long cycle in productivity. High rates of increase in net national product per unit of total input came, it seems, during periods of a decade or more centered in the late 1870s, the late 1890s, the early 1920s, the late 1930s, and the late 1940s or early 1950s. Low rates of increase came during periods centered in the late 1880s, the late 1910s, the early 1930s and the 1940s [p. 17]". This confirms our analysis.

[9] This result clearly refutes the assertion by Matthews (1959) (repeated with approval by Richard A. Easterlin) that "fluctuations in *national income* in Great Britain have not generally stood in an inverse relation to those in the United States [p. 194]."

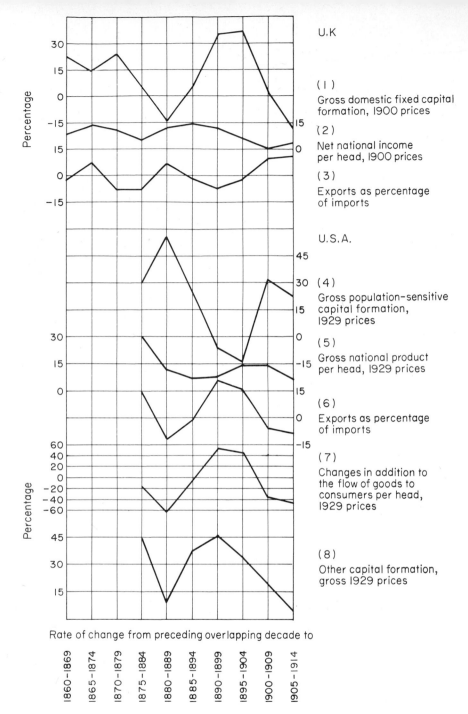

Rate of change from preceding overlapping decade to

FIG. 1. Long swings in real national product and related variables in the United Kingdom, 1855–1914, and the United States, 1870–1914. (See Table 1 for summary and sources of data.)

398

TABLE 1

DATA FOR FIG. 1

	United Kingdom			United States				
Decade	Gross domestic fixed capital formation, 1900 prices[a] (%)	Net national income per head, 1900 prices[b] (%)	Exports as percentage of imports[c] (%)	Gross population-sensitive capital formation, 1929 prices[d] (%)	GNP per head, 1929 prices[d] (%)	Exports as percentage of imports[e] (%)	Changes in additions to real flow of goods to consumers per head[d] ($)	Other capital formation, gross 1929 prices[d] (%)
1860–1869	22.4	8.1	−2.3					
1865–1874	14.0	13.6	+6.4					
1870–1879	23.4	10.3	−8.2	29.1	30.0	14.0	−17	45.5
1875–1884	4.8	4.5	−8.4	55.6	12.0	−12.7	−63	8.5
1880–1889	−14.8	11.8	6.1	24.5	6.5	−1.6	−8	36.9
1885–1894	4.8	13.5	−2.0	−6.1	7.7	20.7	53	45.6
1890–1899	34.7	11.3	−7.2	−14.1	14.3	15.4	44	33.9
1895–1904	35.9	5.3	−2.7	31.6	14.0	−5.7	−36	18.8
1900–1909	1.3	0	9.1	22.4	6.0	−8.1	−44	5.0
1905–1914	−18.2	2.4	9.8					

[a] Data from Feinstein (1961).
[b] Data from Mitchell and Deane (1962).
[c] Data from Imlah (1958).
[d] Data from Kuznets (1958).
[e] Data from Lipsey (1963).

through migration), and in population-sensitive capital formation. For the United Kingdom we have figures going back to 1856. The positive association between real income per capita and the export sector's performance holds good until the turn of the century; these variables go up together between 1860–1869 and 1865–1874 and between 1875–1884 and 1880–1889. One would have expected the same to happen between 1890–1899 and 1900–1909, but it did not. The sharp upturn in foreign investment and the export–import ratio in those years was accompanied by a relative fall in real income per capita.

Here perhaps is further evidence of the validity of the argument that important parameters had changed, to Britain's detriment, and the high propensity to invest overseas which had suited her so well in the nineteenth century had become inconsistent with a high rate of growth in the standard of living. Meanwhile, parameters affecting the United States had also changed; she had built up a large and highly productive manufacturing sector (accounting for 35% of world output in 1906–1908) and had become a net creditor country; the share of manufacturing producer durables in gross domestic capital formation increased from 31% in 1869–1878 to 57% in 1899–1908.[10] From 1834 to 1843 American income per capita was probably lower than the British. "Between 1834–43 and 1944–55 American G.N.P. increased at an exceptionally high rate of 42 per cent per decade, a rate perhaps never equalled elsewhere, for such an extended period. G.N.P. per capita also increased at a high rate, compared with British and French growth [Gallman, 1966, p. 23]."

5. Conclusions

(a) United States experience in the period 1870–1913 can best be interpreted within the ambit of the inverse long-swing relationship between the periphery and Great Britain, with an alternation of infrastructure and export upsurges. An interaction model fits the facts better than the notion of "a relatively stable rate of growth interrupted by two monetary episodes from which the system rebounded to approximately its initial path [Friedman and Schwartz, 1963, p. 187]. It also has much more explanatory power than the one-sided models based on fluctuations in the "pull" of the United States economy.[11] There is no evidence to support those scholars who have assumed

[10] See Gallman (1966). In this important paper, Gallman has shown that the movements of the real GNP series and the main components conform well to the chronology of long swings as established by Abramovitz (Gallman, 1966, pp. 21–23).

[11] Regression analysis bears this out. Williamson did a univariate test, with net expenditure on railroads in the United States as a variable to explain net capital imports in the period 1871–1914. "The best fit occurs when net capital imports ($\dot{K}$) lag Ulmer's net expenditure in the railroads (I_{us}) by one year ($\bar{R}^2 = 0.624$) where the coefficient is positive

that the United States economy was the unmoved mover in the fluctuations of the international economy between 1860 and 1913. Abramovitz did refer, in a brief section, to the inverse relation between American and British long swings. He pointed out that "the competing pressures for finance of British home investment and of demands in other areas of the world played their parts in determining whether the United States could continue to finance a large deficit," and that changes in the American stock of money "depended on the relation between the level of our current balance of international payments and that of capital imports [p. 246]."* However, these were asides: No attempt was made to quantify the competing pressures or to work out their implications. I suggest that a close study of the international interaction would have revealed that the American Kuznets cycle pursued its course within international constraints which had an important influence in determining whether American growth was slow or rapid.

(b) Home investment was dominated by population-sensitive capital formation, and inverse long swings in the latter were associated with (and probably attributable to) inverse swings in the demographic variables—population structure and migration—in Great Britain and the periphery.

(c) The fact that the United States, Canada, Argentina, and Australia had simultaneous swings cannot be fully explained without recognizing the constraints of the gold standard and the effect of the Bank of England's reserve

---

and significant:

$$(1871-1914)\, \dot{K}^t = 6.7487 + 1.0189\, I_{us}^{t-1}, \qquad \bar{R}^2 = 0.624$$
$$(0.1271)$$

When, however, we add the Cairncross series of British home investment (I_{GB}), an extraordinary thing happens. Not only does the fit improve only slightly, but also the coefficient of I_{us} becomes insignificant.

$$(1871-1914)\, \dot{K}^t = 914.45 - 0.0303\, I_{us}^t - 8.8473\, I_{GB}^t, \qquad \bar{R}^2 = 0.654$$
$$(0.2000)\ (0.1556)$$

It would seem that Ulmer's series does not add much to the explanatory power of the Cairncross series. Over the long swing, and statistically, it seems that the rate of British home investment is inversely related to the rate of net capital inflow and that conditions in the American railroad industry are somewhat unimportant. This holds true, incidentally, under all reasonable lead-lag conditions [J. Williamson (1964) *American growth and the balance of payments* 1820–1913. Univ. of North Carolina Press, pp. 147–148]." Reference should also be made to an econometric analysis by Wilkinson (1969). His conclusion refutes one-sided interpretations of American long swings. He found that "European migration to the U.S. prior to World War I was significantly influenced by both employment opportunities in the particular European country (as represented by changes in domestic output) and the gain in real income to be achieved by migration to the U.S. [p. 19]."

* M. Abramovitz (1961) The nature and significance of Kuznets cycles. *Economic Development and Cultural Change* **9**(3):225–248, published by the University of Chicago. Copyright 1961 by the University of Chicago.

policy. This is not meant to imply that the Old Lady "managed" the pre-1914 international gold standard system: On the contrary, according to her lights, she minded her own business and on critical occasions this was very much at the expense of all the borrowers.

(d) It is very difficult in the present state of knowledge to sort out the parts played by real and monetary elements in the long-swing interaction. Analysis of the available monetary data [see Thomas (1972, Chapter 4; 1973, Chap. XV)] has shown that the course of the rate of change in the growth of the American money stock (five-year moving average) traces out a long swing corresponding to that of net external gold flows (five-year moving average), with the former showing a short lag. The gold stock accounted for most of the large changes in high-powered money in the United States up to 1913. The swings in net gold flows correspond to and lag behind the swings in United States exports as a percentage of imports. There was an inverse relation between the swings in the rate of change in the growth of the American money stock and the swings in the Bank of England reserve as a percentage of liabilities. Fluctuations in net capital flows were related to those in the ratio of American to British prices (purchasing power parity, 1929 = 100).

The evidence indicates that the trade balance of the United States determined the gold flow, and the latter determined the rate of growth of the money supply. There is no basis for the suggestion that investment upswings, by generating excess demands, attracted net capital inflows which more than offset the unfavorable trade balance, thereby inducing gold inflows.[12] Gold inflow, and as a consequence the money stock, rose most rapidly in the phases of the long swing when exports were surging upward and infrastructure investment and imports were declining. Moreover, it was in these periods that upswings in additions to the labor force and to G.N.P. took place (Kuznets, 1961). In these phases Britain was having a home-investment boom, her exports as a proportion of imports were falling, and gold flowed from the Bank of England to the periphery. When the United States had its investment upswing, the trade balance deteriorated and gold tended to flow out, with the result that the rate of growth of the money stock tended to fall.

There can be no such thing as a purely monetary theory of the inverse long swing; but it seems to be equally true that no explanation will be satisfactory if it leaves out important monetary forces. First, in the words of Milton Friedman, "the major source of long-period changes in the quantity of money in the United States has been changes in high-powered money, which, until

---

[12] This is the thesis argued by Williamson (1964, p. 183), "The rate of net gold flow over United States borders . . . is predominantly caused by income movements and excess demand for real-money balances."

1914, reflected mostly changes in the amount of gold [Cagan, 1965, Foreword, p. XXV]." Second, Cagan, after a careful analysis, reached the following conclusion:

> Severe contractions are an important exception . . . to the . . . statement that fluctuations in business activity seem to produce the cycles in the money series. For severe contractions, this effect may explain the timing, but apparently a deep depression cannot account for the sharp decline in the rate of change in the money stock associated with it. . . . Panics made ordinary business contractions severe when they led to substantial decline in the rate of monetary growth, and not otherwise. . . . The variety of reasons for decline in monetary growth during severe depressions rules out any single cause and rules out, in particular, a sharp fall in business activity as the main reason for the associated decline in monetary growth. The evidence is therefore consistent with, and taken as a whole, impressively favors emphasis on the decline in the rate of monetary growth as the main reason some business contractions, regardless of what may have initiated them, became severe [p. 267].*

This conclusion is in line with our analysis of the impact of changes in the money stock when long-swing expansions came to their usually severe end. In short, our view of the pre-1913 Atlantic economy is that the inverse cycle was propelled by real determinants but that, in the crucial phases when expansion gave way to contraction, changes in the stock of money played a significant independent part in influencing the course of events.

The Kuznets Cycle: Requiescat in Pace?

Never did Abramovitz use such moving language as when he came to bury the Kuznets cycle. "We are the wiser for its life, but it is gone. *Requiescat in pace.* Gone but not forgotten." Dare one venture to murmur the famous line, "Yet each man kills the thing he loves"? There is an air of mystery about the whole thing and, maybe, even mistaken identity.

In his funeral oration Abramovitz (1968) declared that the late cycle was "a form of growth which belonged to a particular period in history and that the economic structure and institutions which imposed that form on the growth process have evolved, or been changed, into something different [p. 349]."† He was anxious "to guard the integrity and usefulness of the Kuznets-cycle hypothesis for interpreting development in the United States, Canada, and Western Europe from about the 1840s to 1914 by shielding it from an inappropriate confrontation with the different form which the growth process is taking, and is likely to take, in the contemporary world [p. 349]." He was not saying that *long swings* have had their day. This he made clear in the

---

* P. Cagan (1965) Determinants and effects of changes in the stock of money 1875–1960. New York: National Bureau of Economic Research, Columbia Univ. Press.
† M. Abramovitz (1968) The passing of the Kuznets cycle. *Economica* 35: 349–367.

following sentence. "What I do wish to argue is that the specific set of relations and response mechanisms which were characteristic of pre-1914 'long swings' in growth are unlikely to be characteristic of future long swings. These will be of a different sort and may, indeed, not have much in common with one another in, say, their durations, amplitudes or internal structure [pp. 349–350]." It would appear, then, that the deceased mourned by Abramovitz was that well-known member of the family, the American Kuznets Cycle, Born 1840: Departed this Life 1914.

One feature of the modern world weighing heavily in the elegy is the ending of mass immigration; it is held to be a matter of chance whether long swings produced merely by the echo effects of past fluctuations in births will generate the pre-1914 type of Kuznets cycle. Then there is the point that governments now know how to prevent serious depressions. Another factor is the greatly increased volume of federal, state, and local government expenditures in the United States and the prominence of government grants and loans in outflow of capital. However, Abramovitz admits that "the adaptive variation in the flows of capital funds which, before 1914, made possible regular divergent fluctuations in the growth rates of Europe and the United States, may well continue to operate in the future. But it will probably be called on to operate only sporadically; not regularly. For with the disappearance of the migration link, the chief cause of regular divergent fluctuations between the two halves of the Atlantic Community, have been removed [1968, p. 366]." This emphasis on the migration link as the basic cause of the inverse rate of growth in the pre-1914 period is in line with the main thesis of this paper; but as to the future one should keep an open mind despite the disappearance of trans-Atlantic mass migration. Much more research needs to be done on long swings in the post-1945 period. [13] It may be that a new era has started in which there could be systematic long-swing divergencies between growth rates in the United States and an enlarged European Economic Community of comparable magnitude.

Kuznets has stressed that long swings are a fundamental component of the long-term movement. Changes in population structure and their echo effects on both sides of the Atlantic must continue to be reckoned with; waves of internal or intracontinental migration can be a potent generator of long swings; and in the United States even the demographic force of immigration is by no means negligible. Between 1950 and 1970 America (other than the Southeast) received a massive influx of three million young blacks, the echo effects of which are bound to entail demographic cycles with a powerful social and economic impact. If we add the five million immigrants from

---

[13] For an instructive pioneering study see the work of Bernstein (1963). See also the work of Hickman (1963).

abroad, we get a decennial rate of over four million for 1950–1970, which is half the peak inflow in 1901–1910. Since the economic and demographic consequences are likely to conform to well-established patterns, the old American Kuznets cycle may yet show that it is not half as dead as it looks. Perhaps we should end not with a wreath but a bouquet.

REFERENCES

Abramovitz, M. (1959) Historical and comparative rates of production, productivity and prices. *Hearings before Joint Economic Committee, 86th Congress, 1st Session, Pt. 2, Washington, D. C., 1959*, pp. 411–466.

Abramovitz, M. (1961) The nature and significance of Kuznets cycles. *Economic Development and Cultural Change* **9(3)**: 225–248.

Abramovitz, M. (1964) Evidences of long swings in aggregate construction since the Civil War. Occasional Paper 90. New York: National Bureau of Economic Research, Columbia Univ. Press.

Abramovitz, M. (1968) The passing of the Kuznets cycle. *Economica* **35**: 349–367.

Beach, W. E. (1935) *British international gold movements and banking policy, 1881–1913*, pp. 122–136. Cambridge, Massachusetts: Harvard Univ. Press.

Bernstein, E. M. (1963) The post war trend cycle in the United States. In *Quarterly review* (1st quarter), pp. 1–10. New York: Model Roland and Co.

Bloomfield, A. I. (1968) *Patterns of fluctuation in international investment before 1914*, Studies in International Finance No. 21, pp. 18–24. Princeton, New Jersey: International Finance Section, Princeton Univ. Press.

Cagan, P. (1965) *Determinants and effects of changes in the stock of money 1875–1960*. New York: National Bureau of Economic Research, Columbia Univ. Press.

Fabricant, S. (1959) *Basic facts on productivity change*, Occasional Paper 63, pp. 16–17. New York: National Bureau of Economic Research.

Feinstein, C. H. (1961) Income and investment in the United Kingdom, 1856–1941. *Economic Journal* **71**: 367–385.

Ford, A. G. (1962) *The gold standard 1880–1914: Britain and Argentina*, Chapter VIII. London and New York: Oxford Univ. Press.

Ford, A. G. (1971) British investment in Argentina and long swings, 1880–1914. *The Journal of Economic History* **31**: 650–663.

Friedman, M., and Schwartz, A. J. (1963) *A monetary history of the United States, 1867–1960*. Princeton, New Jersey: National Bureau of Economic Research, Princeton Univ. Press.

Gallman, R. E. (1966) Gross national product in the United States, 1834–1909. In *Output employment and productivity in the United States after 1800*, Studies in Income and Wealth, Vol. 30, p. 15, by the Conference on Research in Income and Wealth. New York: National Bureau of Economic Research, Columbia Univ. Press.

Hickman, B. G. (1963) The post war retardation: Another long swing in the rate of growth? *American Economic Review* **53**: 490–507.

Imlah, A. H. (1958) *Economic elements in the Pax Britannica*, pp. 96–98. Cambridge, Massachusetts: Harvard Univ. Press.

Johnson, H. G. (1958) The transfer problem and exchange stability. In *International trade and economic growth*, pp. 169–195. London: Allen & Unwin.

Kendrick, J. W. (1961) *Productivity trends in the United States*. Princeton, New Jersey: National Bureau of Economic Research, Princeton Univ. Press.

Kuznets, S. (1958)   Long swings in the growth of population and in related economic variables. *Proceedings of the American Philosophical Society*, **102**: Tables 11, 13, 15.

Kuznets, S. (1961)   *Capital in the American economy*, pp. 342–346. Princeton, New Jersey: National Bureau of Economic Research, Princeton Univ. Press.

Lee, C. H. (1969)   A stock-adjustment analysis of capital movements: The United States–Canadian case. *Journal of Political Economy* **77**: 514–515.

Lewis, J. P. (1965)   *Building cycles and Britain's growth*, pp. 164–185. New York:Macmillan.

Lipsey, R. E. (1963)   *Price and quantity trends in the foreign trade of the United States*, pp. 154–155. Princeton, New Jersey: National Bureau of Economic Research, Princeton Univ. Press.

Matthews, R. C. O. (1959)   *The trade cycle*, p. 194. London and New York: Cambridge Univ. Press.

Mattila, J. M., and Thompson, W. R. (1956)   Residential-service construction: A study of induced investment. *Review of Economics and Statistics* **38**: 465–473.

Mitchell, B. R., and Deane, P. (1962)   *Abstract of British Historical Statistics*, p. 367. London and New York: Cambridge Univ. Press.

O'Leary, P. J., and Lewis, W. A. (1955)   Secular swings in production and trade, 1870–1913. *The Manchester School of Economic and Social Studies* **23(2)**: 129.

Thomas, B. (1971)   Demographic determinants of British and American building cycles, 1870–1913. In *Essays on a mature economy: Britain after 1840* (D. N. McCloskey, ed.), pp. 39–74. London: Methuen.

Thomas, B. (1972)   *Migration and urban development: A reappraisal of British and American long cycles*. London: Methuen, University Paperback (distributed in the United States by Harper, New York).

Thomas, B. (1973)   *Migration and economic growth*, 2nd edition. London and New York: Cambridge Univ. Press.

Saul, S. B. (1965)   The export economy 1870–1914. In Studies in the British Economy 1870–1914 (J. Saville, ed.). *Yorkshire Bulletin of Economic and Social Research, Special Number* **17**: 12, 16.

Sigsworth, E. M., and Blackman, J. (1965)   The home boom of the 1890's. In Studies in the British Economy 1870–1914 (J. Saville, ed.). *Yorkshire Bulletin of Economic and Social Research*, Special Number **17**: 75–97.

Wilkinson, M. (1969)   European migration to the United States: An econometric analysis of aggregate labor supply and demand (mimeographed). *European Meeting of the Econometric Society, Brussels, September 1969*.

Williamson, J. (1964)   *American growth and the balance of payments 1820–1913*, pp. 147–148. Chapel Hill: Univ. of North Carolina.

Author Index

Numbers in italics refer to the pages on which the complete references are listed.

407